Supply Chain Finance

"Dr. Cai's work stands out as a masterclass in supply chain finance, presenting a detailed exploration of its mechanisms and technological innovations. This textbook is crucial for anyone committed to deeply understanding or enhancing supply chain operations through the implementation of various supply chain finance principles. Its comprehensive analysis and practical applications position it as a foundational text in the field, making it indispensable for both professionals and scholars."

—Christian Bauwens, *Senior Vice President and Treasurer, Flex, LTD.*

"This book masterfully addresses the nuances of supply chain finance with a comprehensive and pragmatic approach. It provides a thorough overview of the current state of supply chain finance, detailing its key mechanisms, associated risks, and the innovative technologies. Dr. Cai's extensive research and clear presentation make it an indispensable resource for anyone looking to navigate the intricacies of modern supply chain finance."

—Xiuli Chao, *INFORMS Fellow, Ralph L. Disney Professor, University of Michigan, USA*

"Given the complexities of international trade, the intersection of operations and finance has captured the attention of students, practitioners, and academic scholars. Professor Gangshu Cai's authoritative text is crucial reading for those interested in this key aspect of global trade. It comprehensively covers the history, fundamentals, analytics, and technological developments in supply chain finance. The book's clear writing, compelling examples, and analytical modeling establish Professor Cai as a leading authority in this field. I am grateful to George for his significant contribution to our community."

—Maqbool Dada, *Professor, Carey Business School, Johns Hopkins University, USA*

"Dr. Cai's book is a pioneering and essential guide to supply chain finance, offering systematic insights from a leading scholar actively engaged in the field. Its thorough coverage and applied focus make it a must-read for professionals and academics seeking to master or innovate in supply chain operations."

—Jeannette Song, *INFORMS Fellow, R. David Thomas Professor, Duke University, USA*

"Dr. Cai's *Supply Chain Finance: Mechanisms, Risk Analytics, and Technology* stands out as an essential read in today's global business environment. Based on rigorous research, this book provides valuable insights into the intricate world of supply chain finance. It elucidates how strategic financial planning can enhance supply chain operations. This aspect of finance is increasingly vital given the present challenges in global supply chains. This book is indispensable for both industry professionals and scholars, offering a wealth of knowledge that is both practical and theoretical."

—Christopher S. Tang, *INFORMS Fellow, UCLA Distinguished Professor and Senior Associate Dean, University of California at Los Angeles, USA*

"As a banker deeply involved in financing small businesses, I find Dr. Cai's *Supply Chain Finance: Mechanisms, Risk Analytics, and Technology* to be an invaluable resource. It offers practical insights and detailed strategies that are crucial for understanding and implementing effective financial solutions in the context of supply chains. This book bridges the gap between academic theory and real-world financial practices, making it an essential tool for bankers looking to enhance their services to small businesses."

—Ray Wang, *President of Yillion Bank*

Gangshu Cai

Supply Chain Finance

Mechanisms, Risk Analytics, and Technology

Gangshu Cai
Santa Clara University
Santa Clara, CA, USA

ISBN 978-3-031-56124-5   ISBN 978-3-031-56125-2 (eBook)
https://doi.org/10.1007/978-3-031-56125-2

© The Editor(s) (if applicable) and The Author(s), under exclusive license to Springer Nature Switzerland AG 2024

This work is subject to copyright. All rights are solely and exclusively licensed by the Publisher, whether the whole or part of the material is concerned, specifically the rights of reprinting, reuse of illustrations, recitation, broadcasting, reproduction on microfilms or in any other physical way, and transmission or information storage and retrieval, electronic adaptation, computer software, or by similar or dissimilar methodology now known or hereafter developed.
The use of general descriptive names, registered names, trademarks, service marks, etc. in this publication does not imply, even in the absence of a specific statement, that such names are exempt from the relevant protective laws and regulations and therefore free for general use.
The publisher, the authors and the editors are safe to assume that the advice and information in this book are believed to be true and accurate at the date of publication. Neither the publisher nor the authors or the editors give a warranty, expressed or implied, with respect to the material contained herein or for any errors or omissions that may have been made. The publisher remains neutral with regard to jurisdictional claims in published maps and institutional affiliations.

Cover credit: Cheunghyo
This Palgrave Macmillan imprint is published by the registered company Springer Nature Switzerland AG
The registered company address is: Gewerbestrasse 11, 6330 Cham, Switzerland

Paper in this product is recyclable.

To my parents and my family, for their love and continuous support!

Preface

In the intricate web of global commerce, supply chains don't operate in isolation. Instead, they are a complex dance of producers, suppliers, financiers, and consumers, all moving in tandem to bring products from conception to the hands of end-users. The unprecedented economic disruption caused by the COVID-19 outbreak from 2020–2022 highlighted the critical role of supply chains in our daily lives. Worldwide, supply chains were disrupted as most countries closed their borders and imposed lockdowns, putting millions of enterprises, especially small and medium enterprises (SMEs), in dire straits. While some firms boast abundant capital, many, including most SMEs, do not. Due to insufficient capital to maintain daily operations, many of these companies, particularly SMEs, went bankrupt.

The financial underpinnings of this vast supply chain network, often referred to as "supply chain finance," play a pivotal role in ensuring its smooth operation. COVID-19 is not the first, but merely one of many crises that have significantly exposed the limitations of traditional bank financing. This highlights the value of supply chain finance, a mechanism that enhances financing for capital-constrained firms based on supply chain transactions, especially when banks are hesitant to finance such firms during turbulent times. Supply chain finance can not only improve information sharing among supply chain firms and their financiers but also mitigate financial risks due to guarantees and coordination from supply chain firms and the use of goods in transactions as collateral.

I have diligently researched supply chain finance since 2008. To date, I have published academic papers on bank financing, seller financing (e.g., trade credit and factoring), buyer financing (e.g., reverse financing), third-party financing, risk analytics in supply chain finance, the application of supply chain finance technology, and more. While these topics delve into specific aspects of supply chain finance, there's a growing need for a comprehensive overview, especially as economies expand, particularly in developing regions. People are eager to understand what is supply chain finance, why it is important, who should be involved, how specific mechanisms work, and when is the best time to implement them. Recognizing the significance of this subject for both researchers and practitioners, I began writing this book on Supply Chain Finance on May 1, 2020, amidst the COVID-19 outbreak.

Supply chain finance encompasses transaction-driven financial activities designed to mitigate risks, optimize working capital, and enhance liquidity for supply chain firms, ultimately boosting efficiency and profitability. This book, "Supply Chain Finance: Mechanisms, Risk Analytics, and Technology," delves deep into this subject, aiming to elucidate its many facets.

Supply chain finance is not just about numbers and transactions; it's about understanding the balance between risk and reward, trust and verification, and innovation and tradition. As global trade evolves, so does the need for more sophisticated, resilient, and transparent financial mechanisms. This book addresses these needs, offering a comprehensive overview of the current state of supply chain finance, its mechanisms, inherent risks, and the cutting-edge technologies shaping its future.

The first part, "Basics of Supply Chain Finance," introduces readers to the foundational concepts and structures of supply chain finance. We describe its characteristics, pros and cons, effects, and selection criteria. We then provide tools to analyze a firm's financial aspects, emphasizing working capital management to optimize cash flow.

The second part, "Mechanisms," covers everything from basic principles of trade finance to advanced structures like factoring, dynamic discounting, third-party logistics (3PL)-led inventory financing, reverse factoring, and bank payment obligations. This section offers a thorough understanding of tools and techniques used globally from the perspectives of sellers, buyers, 3PLs, and other supply chain parties.

"Risk Analytics" delves into the challenges and uncertainties of supply chain finance. In an era where disruptions can arise from geopolitical tensions, natural disasters, or pandemics, understanding and mitigating risks is paramount. This section presents a risk taxonomy for supply chain finance and offers approaches to evaluate and mitigate these risks.

Lastly, "Technology" explores the digital revolution reshaping supply chain finance. From supply chain digitalization to blockchain, and from the Internet of Things to artificial intelligence, technology is streamlining processes and introducing new paradigms of trust and efficiency. This section offers a glimpse into the future, where the dynamics of supply chain relationships, finance and technology are set to redefine trade.

Writing this book has been a journey of discovery. I hope it serves as a valuable resource for students, professionals, academics, and anyone interested in supply chain finance. For additional course materials related to this book, please visit ISCAI.net. As the global landscape shifts, it's crucial to arm ourselves with knowledge, adaptability, and foresight. This book is a step in that direction.

Thank you for embarking on this journey with me.

Silicon Valley, USA   Gangshu Cai

Acknowledgments

Writing a book is never a solitary endeavor, and "Supply Chain Finance: Mechanisms, Risk Analytics, and Technology" stands testament to this. Reflecting on the journey of bringing this work to life, I'm profoundly aware of the many hands and minds that contributed to its creation.

First and foremost, my deepest gratitude goes to my academic mentors, friends, industry peers, and students. Their insights, critiques, and unwavering support were pivotal in shaping the content and direction of this book. Their dedication to the field of supply chain finance is both inspiring and contagious.

I owe a particular debt of gratitude to Ershen Ali, whose real-world expertise in supply chain finance was invaluable, especially when crafting two case studies. Matt Johnson, a former student, brought fresh insights into the practice of blockchain technology and cryptocurrencies, which are revolutionizing the industry. I am deeply grateful to my mentors and friends, Christian Bauwens, Xiuli Chao, Maqbool Dada, Jeannette Song, Chris Tang, and Ray Wang, for their incredibly generous endorsements of this book, which hold immense significance for me. Lois Zhang's consistent support throughout this journey has been indispensable. My thanks also go to Ye Cai, Jingnong Lin, Xia Lin, Tammy Madsen, Steven Nahmias, Qiang Wei, Lei Yang, and Yanling Zheng for their encouragement and invaluable suggestions to refine the manuscript. Their collective contributions have added depth and rigor to this work.

I wish to acknowledge my numerous coauthors who have enriched my research experiences, broadened my knowledge and honing my critical thinking across various research areas. To my students and visiting scholars, Jun Chu, Xue Duan, Xueqin Hu, Zhaotong Wang, Lizhi Xing, Shuangshuang Xu, Qi Zhang, and Wubo Zhang, I deeply appreciate your invaluable contributions in proofreading the book and assisting with its presentation slides. I also extend my appreciation to my students at Santa Clara University and those from around the globe. Your enthusiasm and curiosity have been a constant source of motivation.

Special mention goes to the team at Palgrave Macmillan of Springer Nature. From the initial proposal to the final print, their professionalism, patience, and passion for the subject have been a driving force. I am especially grateful to the senior editor Marcus Ballenger, production editor Saranya Siva, production supervisor Zeenathul Raeesa, production contact Susan Westendorf, and the entire production team for their meticulous attention to detail and unwavering belief in the project.

On a personal note, my heartfelt thanks go to my parents and my family for their enduring support. Their unwavering faith in my abilities, even during moments of doubt, served as a beacon of hope, making this journey possible.

Lastly, to all the readers, practitioners, and scholars who will delve into this book, thank you. It is my sincere hope that this work enriches your understanding and advances the discourse on supply chain finance.

With heartfelt gratitude,

Gangshu Cai

Contents

Part I Basics of Supply Chain Finance

1 Introduction to Supply Chain Finance 3
   1.1   Introduction 3
   1.2   The Definition of Supply Chain Finance 5
   1.3   The History of Supply Chain Finance 8
   1.4   Financing Small Businesses 9
        1.4.1   Defining Small Businesses 10
        1.4.2   The Importance of Financing SMEs 10
        1.4.3   The Small Business Lending Gap 11
        1.4.4   Challenges in Financing Small Businesses 12
   1.5   The Importance of Supply Chain Finance 13
   1.6   Summary 15
   1.7   Exercises 16
        1.7.1   Practice Questions 16
        1.7.2   Case Study 17
   References 17

2 Supply Chain Finance Characteristics 19
   2.1   Introduction 19
   2.2   The Four Flows of Supply Chains 21
        2.2.1   Product Flow 22
        2.2.2   Information Flow 22
        2.2.3   Financial Flow 23
        2.2.4   Risk Flow 23
   2.3   Supply Chain Finance Types 25
        2.3.1   Supply Chain Finance Initiator 26
        2.3.2   Supply Chain Finance Source 26
        2.3.3   Supply Chain Finance Timing 28
   2.4   Supply Chain Finance Pros and Cons 28
   2.5   Supply Chain Finance Effects 32
        2.5.1   Supply Chain Relationship Effect 32
        2.5.2   The Seesaw Effect in Working Capital 32
        2.5.3   The Pareto Effect in Profit 32
        2.5.4   The Domino Effect in Liquidity 33

		2.5.5	The Halo Effect and Ripple Effect in Firms' Performance	34
	2.6	Principles of Measuring and Selecting Financing Schemes		34
		2.6.1	The Revised 6R Model: A Measurement Principle	34
		2.6.2	The Selection Principles	38
	2.7	Summary		40
	2.8	Exercises		41
		2.8.1	Practice Questions	41
		2.8.2	Case Study	41
	References			42
3	**Financial Analysis**			**45**
	3.1	Introduction		45
	3.2	Financial Statements		46
		3.2.1	Balance Sheet	46
		3.2.2	Income Statement	47
		3.2.3	Cash Flow Statement	50
	3.3	Profit and Asset Ratios		52
		3.3.1	Profit Margin	52
		3.3.2	Return on Equity	53
		3.3.3	Return on Capital Employed	54
		3.3.4	Return on Assets and Return on Net Assets	55
		3.3.5	Return on Invested Capital	55
		3.3.6	Economic Value Added	58
		3.3.7	Asset Turnover Ratio	59
	3.4	The DuPont Analysis		59
		3.4.1	The ROE DuPont Model	60
		3.4.2	The ROA DuPont Model	62
		3.4.3	The ROIC DuPont Model	62
	3.5	Chain Aggregated Indexes		65
		3.5.1	Performance Indexes	65
		3.5.2	Chain Equality Indexes	67
	3.6	Summary		68
	3.7	Exercises		69
		3.7.1	Practice Questions	69
		3.7.2	Case Study	69
	Appendix: Walmart Inc. Financial Statements 2018–2020			71
	References			74
4	**Working Capital Management**			**77**
	4.1	Introduction		77
	4.2	Cash and Working Capital		78
		4.2.1	Accounts Receivable and Accounts Payable	78
		4.2.2	Working Capital	79
		4.2.3	Free Cash Flow	81

4.3	Cash Conversion Cycle	81
	4.3.1	Days Inventory Outstanding	81
	4.3.2	Days Sales Outstanding	84
	4.3.3	Days Payable Outstanding	87
	4.3.4	Cash Conversion Cycle (CCC)	87
4.4	Implications of the Cash Conversion Cycle in Retailing	89
	4.4.1	CCCs of Major Retailers	90
	4.4.2	Ethic Concerns of Negative CCCs	92
4.5	Liquidity Indexes	93
	4.5.1	Current Ratio	93
	4.5.2	Quick Ratio	94
	4.5.3	Operating Cash Flow Ratio	95
	4.5.4	Leverage Ratios	95
	4.5.5	Working Capital Index	97
4.6	Summary	99
4.7	Exercises	100
	4.7.1	Practice Questions	100
	4.7.2	Case Study	100
References	101

Part II Supply Chain Finance Mechanisms

5 Trade Finance: The Early Forms of Supply Chain Finance 105

5.1	Introduction	105
5.2	Cash-in-Advance and Push Supply Chains	106
5.3	Consignment and Pull Supply Chains	107
5.4	Letter of Credit	109
	5.4.1	Process Flow	109
	5.4.2	Payment Methods	111
	5.4.3	LC Types	113
5.5	Open Account	117
	5.5.1	Seller-Oriented Trade Credit Discount	117
	5.5.2	Trade Credit vs. Bank Credit	119
	5.5.3	Buyer-Oriented Early Payment Discount	121
5.6	Documentary Collections	123
	5.6.1	Process Flow	123
	5.6.2	D/C vs. LC and Others	123
5.7	The Incoterms Rules	124
5.8	Case Study: The Enlightened Consignment Choice	127
	5.8.1	The Case	127
	5.8.2	Case Analysis	129
5.9	Summary	131
5.10	Exercises	132
	5.10.1	Practice Questions	132
	5.10.2	Case Study	132

		Appendix: Academic Perspective	133
		References	136
6	**Seller-Led Supply Chain Finance**		**139**
	6.1	Introduction	139
	6.2	Factoring	140
		6.2.1 Case Study: A Cash Flow Problem	141
		6.2.2 Process Flow	142
		6.2.3 Factoring Cost	144
		6.2.4 Factoring Amount and Cash Balance: A Simplified Analysis	145
		6.2.5 Comparison and Benefits of Factoring	147
		6.2.6 Risks and Risk Mitigation	150
		6.2.7 Variations of Factoring	150
	6.3	Forfaiting	153
		6.3.1 Process Flow	154
		6.3.2 Comparison with Factoring	155
		6.3.3 Pros, Cons, and Risk Mitigation	156
	6.4	Invoice Discounting	158
	6.5	Purchase Order Financing	161
		6.5.1 Process Flow	162
		6.5.2 Pros, Cons, and Risk Mitigation	164
	6.6	Seller-Led Accounts Receivable Securitization	166
		6.6.1 Process Flow	167
		6.6.2 Benefits	168
		6.6.3 Risks and Risk Mitigation	171
		6.6.4 Comparison to Other Financing Schemes	174
	6.7	Summary	176
	6.8	Exercises	177
		6.8.1 Practice Questions	177
		6.8.2 Case Study	178
		Appendix: Academic Perspective	179
		References	181
7	**Buyer-Led Supply Chain Finance**		**183**
	7.1	Introduction	183
	7.2	Dynamic Discounting	184
		7.2.1 Process Flow	185
		7.2.2 Pros, Cons, and Risk Mitigation	186
	7.3	Reverse Factoring	191
		7.3.1 Process Flow	192
		7.3.2 Benefits	194
		7.3.3 Risks and Risk Mitigation	199
		7.3.4 Comparisons to Other Mechanisms	204
		7.3.5 Globalization and Challenges	205
	7.4	Buyer-Led Approved Payables Reverse Securitization	207

		7.4.1	Process Flow	207
		7.4.2	Benefits and Risk Mitigation	208
	7.5	Case Study: Impact of Extended Payment Terms		209
		7.5.1	The Case	209
		7.5.2	Case Analysis	211
	7.6	Summary		215
	7.7	Exercises		216
		7.7.1	Practice Questions	216
		7.7.2	Case Study	216
	Appendix: Academic Perspective			217
	References			221
8	**Inventory and 3PL-Led Financing**			**223**
	8.1	Introduction		223
	8.2	Inventory Financing		224
		8.2.1	Process Flow	224
		8.2.2	Benefits	228
		8.2.3	Risks and Risk Mitigation	228
	8.3	3PL-Led In-Transit Inventory Financing		230
		8.3.1	Process Flow	231
		8.3.2	Benefits	234
		8.3.3	Risks and Risk Mitigation	236
	8.4	Applications of 3PL-Led Supply Chain Finance Innovation		238
		8.4.1	Case Study: UPS Capital's Custom Solution for Global Glove	239
		8.4.2	Case Study: The Role of 3PL as a Supply Chain Orchestrator	240
	8.5	Summary		242
	8.6	Exercises		243
		8.6.1	Practice Questions	243
		8.6.2	Case Study	243
	Appendix: Academic Perspective			244
	References			248
9	**Other Supply Chain Finance Mechanisms**			**249**
	9.1	Introduction		249
	9.2	Distributor Financing		250
		9.2.1	Process Flow	250
		9.2.2	Benefits	251
		9.2.3	Risks and Risk Mitigation	253
	9.3	Bank Payment Obligation		253
		9.3.1	Process Flow	254
		9.3.2	Benefits	256
		9.3.3	Supply Chain Finance in the BPO Framework	259
		9.3.4	Risk Mitigation	260

		9.3.5	Comparisons with Other Supply Chain Finance Mechanisms	262
	9.4	Structured Commodity Finance		265
		9.4.1	Variants	267
		9.4.2	Process Flow	269
		9.4.3	Benefits	270
		9.4.4	Risk Mitigation	271
	9.5	Summary		272
	9.6	Exercises		273
		9.6.1	Practice Questions	273
		9.6.2	Case Study	274
	References			275

Part III Supply Chain Finance Risk Analytics

10 Risk Taxonomy and Assessment 279
  10.1 Introduction 279
  10.2 A Conceptual SCF Risk Management System 280
  10.3 Supply Chain Finance Risk Taxonomy 281
    10.3.1 Financial Risk 282
    10.3.2 Supply Chain Risk 285
    10.3.3 Non-Commercial Risk 288
  10.4 Qualitative Risk Assessment 290
    10.4.1 Risk Severity Matrix 291
    10.4.2 5 Cs of Credit Risk Analysis 292
  10.5 Quantitative Risk Assessment 295
    10.5.1 Probability Distribution 295
    10.5.2 Standard Deviation 300
    10.5.3 Coefficient of Variation 302
    10.5.4 Altman's Z-Score 303
  10.6 Summary 305
  10.7 Exercises 306
    10.7.1 Practice Questions 306
    10.7.2 Case Studies 306
  References 308

11 Risk-Adjusted Evaluation 309
  11.1 Introduction 309
  11.2 Value-at-Risk (VaR) 310
    11.2.1 Definition of VaR 310
    11.2.2 Computation of VaR 312
    11.2.3 VaR in Risk Management 317
  11.3 Conditional VaR 318
  11.4 Stress Testing 320
    11.4.1 Stress Testing Based on Economic Insights 320
    11.4.2 Stress Testing Based on Historical Events 322

		11.4.3	Stress Testing vs. VaR	323
	11.5	Risk-Adjusted Return Ratios		323
		11.5.1	Risk-Adjusted Return on Capital	324
		11.5.2	Return on Risk-Adjusted Capital	326
		11.5.3	Sharpe Ratio	327
	11.6	Summary		327
	11.7	Exercises		328
		11.7.1	Practice Questions	328
		11.7.2	Case Study	329
	Appendix: Academic Perspective			330
	References			334
12	**Risk Mitigation and Management**			**337**
	12.1	Introduction		337
	12.2	Foundations for Supply Chain Finance Risk Mitigation		338
		12.2.1	Asymmetric Risk Theory	338
		12.2.2	Risk-Reward Pareto Frontier	339
		12.2.3	The Weakest Link Dilemma	340
		12.2.4	PPRR Risk Management Model	341
		12.2.5	PIARA Risk Management Process	342
	12.3	Traditional Risk Mitigation Strategies		344
		12.3.1	Financial Risk Mitigation	344
		12.3.2	Supply Chain Risk Mitigation	348
		12.3.3	Non-Commercial Risk Mitigation	353
	12.4	SCF-Based Insurance and Credit Guarantee		357
		12.4.1	Bank Loan Insurance	358
		12.4.2	Bank Guarantee	359
		12.4.3	Credit Guarantee Scheme	361
		12.4.4	Buyer Credit Guarantee for Export Contracts	362
		12.4.5	Trade Credit Insurance	363
	12.5	Guarantor Financing by Supply Chain Firms		365
		12.5.1	Seller Guarantor Financing	366
		12.5.2	Buyer Guarantor Financing	366
		12.5.3	3PL Guarantor Financing	367
		12.5.4	Benefits and Risk Mitigation of Guarantor Financing	367
	12.6	Financial Hedging		368
		12.6.1	Swap	369
		12.6.2	Overnight Index Swap	370
		12.6.3	Forward	371
		12.6.4	Future	373
		12.6.5	Option	377
	12.7	Operational Hedging		378
		12.7.1	Sourcing Hedging	378
		12.7.2	Inventory Hedging	378

	12.7.3	Production Hedging	380
12.8	Regulations, Ethics, and Sustainability		380
	12.8.1	Regulations	380
	12.8.2	Ethics and Sustainability	383
12.9	Summary		385
12.10	Exercises		386
	12.10.1	Practice Questions	386
	12.10.2	Case Studies	387
Appendix: Academic Perspective			389
References			391

Part IV Supply Chain Finance Technology

13 Digitalization and Technology ... 397

13.1	Introduction		397
13.2	Supply Chain Digitalization		397
	13.2.1	*5C* Advantages and *TIGER* Challenges	398
	13.2.2	A Conceptual Framework	400
	13.2.3	Goals of Supply Chain Digitalization	402
13.3	Supply Chain Finance Platforms		403
	13.3.1	Bank-Led Platform	404
	13.3.2	Buyer-Led Platform	405
	13.3.3	Manufacturer-Led Platform	406
	13.3.4	3PL-Led Platform	407
	13.3.5	Other Third-Party-Led Platforms	407
13.4	Other Supply Chain Finance Technologies		408
	13.4.1	Internet of Things	408
	13.4.2	Artificial Intelligence and Machine Learning	409
	13.4.3	Robotic Process Automation	410
	13.4.4	Cloud Computing	411
	13.4.5	Big Data Analytics	412
13.5	Summary		413
13.6	Exercises		413
	13.6.1	Practice Questions	413
	13.6.2	Case Study	414
References			415

14 Blockchain Technology ... 417

14.1	Introduction		417
14.2	Blockchain Structures		418
14.3	The Bitcoin Blockchain		420
	14.3.1	The Bitcoin Blockchain Structure	421
	14.3.2	Transactions, Cryptography, and Crypto Wallet	422
	14.3.3	Blocks	427
	14.3.4	Hash	429
	14.3.5	Why Mining?	431

	14.3.6	The Consensus Mechanism: Proof of Work	432
	14.3.7	Blockchain Forks	435
	14.3.8	Pros and Cons of Bitcoin Blockchain	437
14.4	Other Public Blockchains and Cryptocurrencies		439
	14.4.1	Altcoins	440
	14.4.2	Ether (ETH) and Ethereum	440
	14.4.3	HBAR and Hedera	443
	14.4.4	Litecoin	444
	14.4.5	Stablecoins	444
	14.4.6	Other Coins and Top Performers	446
14.5	Risks and Future of Cryptocurrencies		448
	14.5.1	CeFi vs. DeFi	448
	14.5.2	Volatility of Cryptocurrencies	450
	14.5.3	Collapses of Crypto Marketplaces in 2022	451
	14.5.4	Future of Cryptocurrencies	452
14.6	Private Blockchains		453
14.7	Consortium Blockchains		455
	14.7.1	Pros and Cons of Consortium Blockchains	455
	14.7.2	Consortium Blockchain Implementations	457
14.8	Hybrid Blockchains		459
14.9	Summary		461
14.10	Exercises		462
	14.10.1	Practice Questions	462
	14.10.2	Case Studies	463
Appendix: Consensus Mechanisms			465
References			467

15 Blockchains for Supply Chain Finance ... 471

15.1	Introduction		471
15.2	Blockchains in Supply Chain Management and Finance		472
	15.2.1	Supply Chain Visibility	473
	15.2.2	Know-Your-Customer	476
	15.2.3	Accounting and Auditing	477
	15.2.4	Smart Contract	479
15.3	Digital Tokens		483
	15.3.1	Native Token	483
	15.3.2	Asset-Backed Token	484
	15.3.3	Non-Fungible Token	487
	15.3.4	Utility Tokens	491
15.4	Initial Coin Offering		491
	15.4.1	ICO Structures and White Paper	491
	15.4.2	Pros and Cons of ICOs	493
	15.4.3	Other Variants	495
15.5	Challenges in Blockchain Supply Chains		496
	15.5.1	Management Challenges	496

		15.5.2	Technology Challenges	497
		15.5.3	Human Errors	497
		15.5.4	Implementation Costs and Scaling	497
		15.5.5	Counterfeit Prevention	498
		15.5.6	Antitrust	499
		15.5.7	Regulation Compliance	499
	15.6	Applications of Blockchain in Supply Chain Finance		499
		15.6.1	Case Studies: Application of Blockchain in Logistics	501
		15.6.2	Machine-as-a-Service	503
	15.7	Summary		504
	15.8	Exercises		505
		15.8.1	Practice Questions	505
		15.8.2	Case Studies	506
	References			508
Index				513

About the Author

Gangshu Cai is Full Professor and Chair of the Department of Information Systems and Analytics at the Leavey School of Business, Santa Clara University, USA. He is the founding director of the Institute of Supply Chain and Operations Management (ISCOM) and the founder of ISCAI, a consultancy specializing in supply chain analytics and intelligence.

As an associate editor for the *Decision Sciences* Journal and a senior editor for the *Production and Operations Management* Journal, Professor Cai's research interests span supply chain finance, competitive channel and supply chain management, the interface between operations management and marketing, e-commerce, and business analytics. He has led numerous research projects, resulting in the publication of more than 50 peer-reviewed papers in esteemed academic journals, including *Production and Operations Management, Marketing Science, Manufacturing & Service Operations Management, Management Science*, and *PNAS*.

Professor Cai has received dozens of accolades for research, teaching, and service from business schools, universities, and international associations. These accolades include the Santa Clara University Award for Recent Achievement in Scholarship, the Santa Clara University Brutocao Award for Curriculum Innovation, the Outstanding Associate Editor Award from the Decision Sciences Journal, the Wickham Skinner Award for Teaching Innovation from the Production & Operations Management Society, and more than ten Outstanding Research or Best Paper Awards from esteemed journals, conferences, and organizations. Additionally, Emerald Publishing recognized him as the #4 Prominent Retailing Author worldwide for the period 2009–2015, based on their final influence index.

List of Figures

Fig. 1.1	Percentage of companies below investment grade (*Source* National Credit Union Administration. The rating is based on the lowest published rating by S&P, Moody's, or Fitch)	4
Fig. 1.2	Ratios of SMEs in world economics in terms of business population, employment, and GDP (*Source* International Federation of Accountants (IFAC))	11
Fig. 1.3	Small business share of all commercial loans and all business loans in the U.S. (*Source* Federal Deposit Insurance Corporation, Call Report Data)	12
Fig. 2.1	Boeing's "critical operational readiness" in global supply chain management (*Source* Adapted from Boeing.com)	20
Fig. 2.2	Product, information, financial, and risk flows	22
Fig. 2.3	Supply chain product flow and SCF "trigger points" (*Source* Revised and extended from Camerinelli & Bryant, 2014, and Templar et al., 2016)	29
Fig. 2.4	Six main SCF drivers—6R model (*Source* Adapted from de Boer et al., 2015)	35
Fig. 2.5	Different performance driven representatives in 6R model	38
Fig. 2.6	Impact of an SCF scheme on a firm's 6R focuses	38
Fig. 3.1	Relationship of assets, liabilities, and equity (*Source* Adapted from Higgins et al., 2018)	47
Fig. 3.2	The ROE tree	60
Fig. 3.3	The ROE DuPont Analysis tree	61
Fig. 3.4	A ROIC tree based on Walmart data	63
Fig. 4.1	The cash flow cycle (*Source* Adapted from Higgins et al., 2018)	78
Fig. 4.2	Illustrative graph of cash conversion cycle	88
Fig. 4.3	CCC of Boeing from 2011 to 2018 (days) (*Source* Raw data is from Boeing Annual Reports from 2009 to 2019)	89
Fig. 4.4	Average CCC across S&P 1500 companies from 2011 to 2018 (days) (*Source* Raw data are from J.P. Morgan Working Capital Index 2020; JPMorgan, 2021)	89

Fig. 4.5	CCC of Walmart from January 2013 to January 2022 (days)	90
Fig. 4.6	CCC of Amazon from December 2012 to December 2021 (days)	91
Fig. 4.7	CCC of Alibaba from March 2013 to March 2021(days)	91
Fig. 4.8	CCC of JD.com from December 2012 to December 2021(days)	92
Fig. 4.9	Boeing's normalized working capital Index from 2005 to 2019	98
Fig. 5.1	Process comparison between push and pull systems	106
Fig. 5.2	Mechanism of letter of credit	110
Fig. 5.3	Sample of bill of exchange (*Source* Adapted from Swedbank)	113
Fig. 5.4	Procedure of back-to-back LC	116
Fig. 5.5	Growth of open account vs. letter of credit from 1978 to 2014 (*Source* Adapted from UniCredit, 2016, and swift.com)	118
Fig. 5.6	Illustration of trade credit 2/10 Net 30	118
Fig. 5.7	Financing equilibrium between trade credit and bank credit	120
Fig. 5.8	Firms' risks in trade finance	124
Fig. 5.9	Supply chain structure	134
Fig. 6.1	Mechanism of factoring	143
Fig. 6.2	Mechanism of forfaiting	154
Fig. 6.3	Mechanism of purchase order financing	162
Fig. 6.4	Seller-led accounts receivable securitization	167
Fig. 6.5	Sequences of events in different financing schemes	180
Fig. 7.1	Dynamic discounting	185
Fig. 7.2	Mechanism of dynamic discounting	185
Fig. 7.3	Mechanism of reverse factoring	191
Fig. 7.4	Reverse factoring through a bank	192
Fig. 7.5	Reverse factoring in a platform	193
Fig. 7.6	An illustrating case: Reverse factoring	198
Fig. 7.7	Buyer-led approved payables reverse securitization process flow	207
Fig. 7.8	Timing of events	220
Fig. 8.1	Inventory finance to a seller with materials	225
Fig. 8.2	Inventory financing for a seller with finished goods	226
Fig. 8.3	Inventory financing to a buyer	227
Fig. 8.4	Inventory financing to a buyer: A variant with trade credit	230
Fig. 8.5	Potential process flow of 3PL-led in-transit inventory financing	232
Fig. 8.6	Process flow of in-transit inventory financing with 3PL-led ILFS platform	233

List of Figures

Fig. 8.7	Impact of cargo finance on cash conversion cycle (*Source* Adapted from UPS Capital, 2018)	240
Fig. 8.8	The procurement role of eternal Asia in practice	241
Fig. 8.9	Operations and payment epochs in models T and P	246
Fig. 8.10	Manufacturer's profit as a function of payment grace period ℓg	247
Fig. 9.1	Process flow of distributor financing	251
Fig. 9.2	Process flow of BPO	254
Fig. 9.3	Process flow of structured commodity finance (pre-payment)	270
Fig. 10.1	Firms' evaluation of the importance of supply chain risk management skillsets (*Source* Adapted from Zhao & Yang, 2021)	280
Fig. 10.2	Supply chain finance risk management system	281
Fig. 10.3	Supply chain finance risk topology	282
Fig. 10.4	Credit rating distribution history, 2020 Q2	284
Fig. 10.5	Supply chain finance risk typology, sources, and events	290
Fig. 10.6	Risk severity matrix	291
Fig. 10.7	Illustration of 5 Cs of credit risk analysis	293
Fig. 10.8	Normal distributions with mean 0 and different standard deviations	301
Fig. 10.9	Comparison of two different CVs	303
Fig. 11.1	VaR description in normal distribution	311
Fig. 11.2	Histogram of historical profit data	313
Fig. 11.3	Normal distribution vs. fat-tail distribution	316
Fig. 11.4	Illustration of economic capital	325
Fig. 11.5	Timeline of supply chain events	333
Fig. 12.1	Supply chain finance risk-reward frontier	340
Fig. 12.2	Process flow of export finance with indirect guarantee	360
Fig. 12.3	Process flow of buyer credit guarantee	363
Fig. 12.4	Profits of different financing schemes under nash game with respect to the manufacturer's cost c_m	390
Fig. 13.1	Supply chain digitalization system	401
Fig. 13.2	6-able goals of supply chain digitalization	402
Fig. 14.1	Types of blockchain structures (*Source* Adapted from Wegrzyn & Wang, 2021)	420
Fig. 14.2	Comparison between blockchains and databases	420
Fig. 14.3	Centralized vs. distributed computer systems	421
Fig. 14.4	The blockchain structure	422
Fig. 14.5	Generation of public key and bitcoin address	424
Fig. 14.6	Public key encryption	425
Fig. 14.7	Digital signature	425
Fig. 14.8	Combined key encryption	426
Fig. 14.9	Blocks in a blockchain	427
Fig. 14.10	Merkle root structure	430

Fig. 14.11	Process of adding a block into the Bitcoin blockchain	433
Fig. 14.12	Procedure of finding the right nonce	434
Fig. 14.13	Bitcoin's valuation over time (*Source* sofi.com)	450
Fig. 14.14	The valuation of ETH over time (*Source* Statista, 2022)	451
Fig. 15.1	Oracles bridging blockchains with real-world scenarios	475
Fig. 15.2	The dual-accounting dilemma	478
Fig. 15.3	Tokenized asset and fractional ownership	484
Fig. 15.4	A potential ICO white paper structure	492

List of Tables

Table 2.1	Categories of SCF mechanisms	25
Table 3.1	The Boeing Company and subsidiaries 2019 consolidated statements of financial position (Balance Sheet, *Source* Boeing.com)	48
Table 3.2	The Boeing Company and subsidiaries 2019 consolidated statements of operations (Income Statement, *Source* Boeing.com)	49
Table 3.3	The Boeing Company and subsidiaries consolidated statements of cash flows (Cash Flow Statement, *Source* Boeing.com)	51
Table 3.4	Summary of select financial concepts and examples (money in millions for non-ratios, Year 2019)	57
Table 3.5	Examples of ROIC DuPont Analysis	65
Table 3.6	Computation of chain aggregated indexes for ROIC	67
Table 4.1	Inventory turnover ratio ranking by sector in 2020	83
Table 4.2	Industries ranked by best DSO in 2019	85
Table 4.3	Industries ranked by best AR turnover ratio in 2019	86
Table 4.4	Year 2021's CCCs of public companies listed in the U.S	92
Table 4.5	Examples of leverage ratios (money in millions for non-ratios, 2019)	97
Table 5.1	Comparison of red clause LC and green clause LC	115
Table 5.2	Transferrable LC vs. the back-to-back LC	116
Table 5.3	Regression analysis of bank credit (BC)	121
Table 5.4	Regression analysis of trade credit (TC)	122
Table 5.5	Incomterms® 2020 rules responsibility quick reference guide	125
Table 5.6	Financial analysis for Enlightened Inc. regarding SCANNet-21D production	130
Table 5.7	Difference between two optimal order quantities where $F \sim U[0,16]$, $r = 9$, and $c = 4$	135

Table 6.1	Effective factoring fee example	145
Table 6.2	Impact of factoring on firms' operations and risks	147
Table 6.3	Comparison between factoring and bank financing	148
Table 6.4	Risks and risk mitigation for sellers in factoring	151
Table 6.5	Risks and risk mitigation for factors in factoring	152
Table 6.6	Comparison between factoring and forfaiting	156
Table 6.7	Pros, cons, and risk mitigation for exporters	157
Table 6.8	Pros, cons, and risk mitigation for forfaiters	158
Table 6.9	Pros, cons, and risk mitigation for importers	159
Table 6.10	DO and DON'T in financing scheme selection	160
Table 6.11	Comparison between factoring and receivable securitization	175
Table 7.1	Impact of reverse factoring on firms' operations and risks	195
Table 7.2	Allocation of benefits among reverse factoring players	200
Table 7.3	Risks and risk mitigation for sellers in reverse factoring	201
Table 7.4	Risks and risk mitigation for buyers in reverse factoring	202
Table 7.5	Risks and risk mitigation for factors	203
Table 7.6	Factoring vs. reverse factoring	205
Table 7.7	Dynamic discounting vs. reverse factoring	205
Table 7.8	Quote under Net 45 with 25% ROIC	211
Table 7.9	Quote of Net 90 with 25% ROIC	212
Table 7.10	Quote of Net 90 at Net 45 price	213
Table 7.11	Quote of Net 45 with 24 inventory turns	213
Table 7.12	Quote of Net 45 with 4% profit target	214
Table 7.13	Quote of Net 90 with 4% profit target	214
Table 8.1	Risks and risk mitigation for 3PLs in in-transit inventory financing	237
Table 8.2	Risks and risk mitigation for banks in in-transit inventory financing	238
Table 9.1	Comparison between BPO and letter of credit	262
Table 9.2	Comparison between BPO and traditional open account	264
Table 10.1	Probability distribution of different risk impacts (of a $1M project)	297
Table 10.2	Comparison of SCF mechanisms with demand probability distribution	299
Table 10.3	Cash flow positions of two companies	302
Table 11.1	Worst losses data points (in $million)	319
Table 11.2	Stress categories and the number of stress shocks	321
Table 11.3	Impacts of stress envelope and stress scenario	322
Table 11.4	RAROC and RORAC for two different firms	326
Table 11.5	Sharpe ratios	327
Table 12.1	Calculation of different forward rates	373
Table 12.2	Multinational firms' offshoring tax rate difference	379
Table 13.1	Five pros and five cons of supply chain digitalization	399

List of Tables

Table 14.1	Permissionless vs. permissioned blockchains	419
Table 14.2	The block information of Block 500,000	428
Table 14.3	The first transaction information of Block 500,000	429
Table 14.4	Bitcoin vs. Ethereum	442
Table 14.5	Comparison of cryptocurrencies on January 31, 2023	444
Table 14.6	Top 30 cryptocurrencies as of November 2, 2022	447
Table 14.7	Bitcoin's valuation from (2014 to 2022)	450
Table 14.8	Major crypto marketplace collapses in 2022	452
Table 14.9	Private blockchain vs. public blockchain	453
Table 14.10	Comparison among Bitcoin, Ethereum, and XinFin	461
Table 15.1	Top NFT marketplaces on January 3, 2023 (one-day snapshot)	489
Table 15.2	All-time leading NFT marketplaces as of January 3, 2023 (one-day snapshot)	490

Part I
Basics of Supply Chain Finance

"A big business starts small."
　Richard Branson

Introduction to Supply Chain Finance 1

> **Learning Objectives:**
>
> 1. Understand the significance of supply chain finance (SCF) in optimizing financial operations and fostering business growth within supply chains.
> 2. Trace the historical evolution of SCF from traditional trade finance to modern digital solutions.
> 3. Explore how SCF supports small businesses by providing access to working capital.
> 4. Recognize the importance of SCF in enhancing operational efficiency and reducing supply chain risks for economic growth.

1.1 Introduction

Finance is an essential aspect of any successful business venture. Like blood to the human body, cash provides the life force for a company's continued operation and long-term sustainability. As supply chains expand across industries and jurisdictions, the significance and complexity of cash management within firms only continue to grow.

Traditionally, banks have been the main source of financing for capital-constrained companies. However, many of these firms have credit ratings below investment grade or lack any credit history, making it challenging for banks to provide loans.[1] According to the National Credit Union Administration (NCUA) of the U.S., as of 2019 Q2, 82.1% of US companies fell below investment

---

[1] Investment grade refers to a credit rating assigned to a debt security, indicating that the security is deemed to have a low risk of default and a high probability of timely payment of interest and repayment of principal. Typically, investment-grade ratings range from AAA (the highest rating from

© The Author(s), under exclusive license to Springer Nature Switzerland AG 2024
G. Cai, *Supply Chain Finance*, https://doi.org/10.1007/978-3-031-56125-2_1

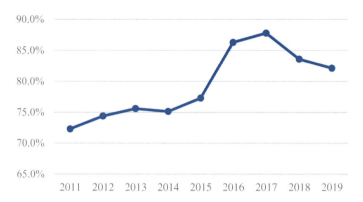

Fig. 1.1 Percentage of companies below investment grade (*Source* National Credit Union Administration. The rating is based on the lowest published rating by S&P, Moody's, or Fitch)

grade (NCUA, 2019). Figure 1.1 illustrates the increasing trend of firms below investment grade from 2011–2019.

Before the emergence of supply chain finance,[2] financial institutions often assessed firms as individual, independent applicants for loans. In this process, firms were evaluated primarily on their financial standing and loan amount request, with little attention given to their supply chain partners. As a result, lending institutions would require information such as collateral, business plans, financial statements, insurance data, loan history, and credit ratings, often overlooking or undervaluing the firm's supply chain relationships.

Despite over 80% of firms struggling to secure the necessary capital from banks, the integration of financial activities and supply chain events became increasingly important following the 2007–2009 global financial crisis and the subsequent economic downturn. This crisis led to a severe liquidity shortage, emphasizing the significance of cash flow and working capital for supply chain firms. However, subsequent bank regulations under Basel II and Basel III, aimed at mitigating financing risks and enhancing bank stability, further aggravated the liquidity challenges faced by firms.[3]

Standard & Poor's, S&P, indicating an extremely low credit risk) to BBB (the lowest investment-grade rating in S&P). Securities with investment-grade ratings are generally considered suitable for investment by conservative investors. Securities rated lower than BBB—are classified as speculative grade or "junk bonds." In Moody's credit rating system, investment-grade ratings range from Aaa to Baa3.

[2] Throughout this book, we use "supply chain finance" and "SCF" interchangeably depending on the context. In some instances, we may use "SCF" as an adjective to shorten certain expressions when necessary.

[3] Basel I, II, and III are sets of minimum capital requirements for banks proposed by the Basel Committee on Banking Supervision (BCBS) (Wikipedia, 2022).

The financial distress experienced by small businesses was further exacerbated during the colossal economic upheaval triggered by the outbreak of the Coronavirus (COVID-19) pandemic in 2020. The pandemic led to global panic and disorder. On January 23, 2020, the Chinese government enforced a 76-day lockdown in Wuhan city, which effectively brought the "world factory" to a standstill. Consequently, the backlog of container ships in Southern California ports surged to 109 in January 2020, compared to fewer than 10 in September 2021 (Ryssdal & Hollenhorst, 2022). On February 2, 2020, the U.S. government closed its borders to visitors from China and later the rest of the world, as the COVID-19 outbreak rapidly spread throughout Europe and other countries. Ultimately, the pandemic proved to be devastating for all nations, severely disrupting global supply chains.

During COVID-19, public awareness of the importance of supply chain management (SCM) and supply chain finance reached unprecedented levels. The necessity for firms to seek alternative financing sources, besides banks, has never been more urgent. Consequently, supply chain finance has emerged as a strong alternative financing source.

1.2 The Definition of Supply Chain Finance

Supply chain finance (SCF) is a concept with various definitions, and its meaning continues to evolve. One broad definition of supply chain finance includes any financial activities related to supply chain firms, encompassing financing and daily cash flow activities without a specific requirement for supply chain events. However, this broad definition may blur the boundaries between supply chain finance's unique features and traditional bank (loan) financing and other daily financial events.

Another definition views supply chain finance as the financial flow that moves in the opposite direction of product flow within the supply chain. This definition is not only broad but also somewhat passive, as it merely documents the financial flow without proactively seeking financing to facilitate supply chain transactions.

In contrast, some researchers and financial firms equate supply chain finance solely with open accounts (trade credit to buyers), arguably the most popular trade financing instrument. Many practitioners also refer to reverse factoring, buyer-oriented accounts payable financing to suppliers, as supply chain finance. Both definitions limit the entire concept of supply chain finance to only one of many popular supply chain finance mechanisms, potentially restricting its future growth and flexibility.

Financial supply chain management (FSCM) is a closely related concept that focuses on corporate management practices that facilitate transactions of goods and services, such as contracting, ordering, invoicing, cash collections, payment management, cash flow management, insurance, guarantees, and working capital management. While FSCM also uses financial instruments, techniques, and functions, its focus is more on supply chain management. In contrast, supply chain finance primarily centers on financial instruments that facilitate supply chain transactions.

According to the Global Supply Chain Finance Forum (GSCFF), the *financial supply chain* (FSC) is "the chain of financial processes, events, and activities that provide financial support" to participants in the product flow of the supply chain (Camerinelli & Bryant, 2014). While some individuals believe that supply chain finance is a subset of financial supply chain management (FSCM) or even equate the two terms, this book aligns with the GSCFF's viewpoint. It considers supply chain finance as a "service cluster supporting the FSC" (Camerinelli & Bryant, 2014). This perspective emphasizes the role of supply chain finance in facilitating and supporting the financial aspects of the supply chain rather than encompassing the entire financial management process.

The Global Supply Chain Finance Forum (GSCFF) defines supply chain finance as "the use of financing and risk mitigation practices and techniques to optimize the management of the working capital and liquidity invested in supply chain processes and transactions" (GSCFF, 2022). Likewise, the Euro Banking Association (EBA) defines supply chain finance as "the use of financial instruments, practices, and technologies to optimize the management of the working capital and liquidity tied up in supply chain processes for collaborating business partners" (Camerinelli & Bryant, 2014). Supply chain finance is primarily driven by specific events. Each financial action, whether it's financing, risk reduction, or payment, in the supply chain finance is triggered by a corresponding occurrence in the physical supply chain. The advancement of sophisticated technologies that monitor and manage events in the physical supply chain presents possibilities for automating the start of supply chain finance activities.

Both GSCFF and EBA's definitions share three key aspects:

- *Purpose (Why and Who)*: Optimizing working capital and liquidity for supply chain firms. The emphasis is on achieving sustainability and avoiding bankruptcy, rather than strictly focusing on profit maximization. In practice, firms aim to maximize profit while balancing it with working capital and liquidity management.
- *Techniques (How)*: Utilizing financing and risk mitigation instruments in supply chain finance. This allows firms and financial institutions to collaboratively address the financial burden of capital-constrained firms while mitigating risks.
- *Environment (Where and What)*: Connecting financial services and supply chain operations where supply chain events occur. In this context, capital-constrained firms can receive support from other supply chain partners and financial institutions to complete transactions and improve overall supply chain efficiency.

Theoretically, supply chain finance should align with firms' objectives of maximizing profits. Hence, supply chain finance can be considered as meeting firms' needs through a combination of financial instruments and operational expertise. It

1.2 The Definition of Supply Chain Finance

is typically event-driven, with supply chain transactions acting as the driving force behind financing activities. This is reflected in several ways:

- Completion of supply chain transactions is part of the purpose.
- Information from supply chain transactions is used to facilitate financing.
- Supply chain firms involved in the transactions are encouraged and engaged to finance capital-constrained firms.

Given that all supply chain firms aim to maximize their profits, conflicts may arise due to the interdependencies created by supply chains. Therefore, supply chain finance should have the potential to generate higher profits for all involved parties compared to situations without it. The potential benefits may be substantial, enabling partnering firms to not only benefit from completing transactions but also earn more profits than when they are not capital constrained. This potential benefit is referred to as the SCF Pareto effect.

We now formally define *supply chain finance* as follows:

> *Supply chain finance encompasses transaction-driven financial activities designed to mitigate risks, optimize working capital, and enhance liquidity for supply chain firms, ultimately boosting supply chain efficiency and profitability.*

This definition of supply chain finance emphasizes three main points:

1. ***Scope***: The scope of supply chain finance includes event-driven financial activities that involve financing and risk mitigation practices in supply chain transactions. It distinguishes supply chain finance from traditional bank financing and the broader scope of financial supply chain management.
2. ***Purpose***: The purpose of supply chain finance is to match supply with demand by satisfying the needs and desires of supply chain firms, helping them complete transactions while optimizing their working capital, liquidity, and profits.
3. ***Function***: These financial activities will mitigate risks and improve overall supply chain efficiency. Supply chain finance enables creative solutions beyond traditional financial techniques by considering alternative instruments to secure transactions.

Supply chain finance events can be led by various parties, such as suppliers, manufacturers, retailers, or logistics firms. The event can take place on a platform organized by a focal firm, a bank, or an insurance company. As a result, supply chain finance provides a way for all involved parties to creatively collaborate, even when some firms are capital constrained.

1.3 The History of Supply Chain Finance

The history of supply chain finance can be traced back to Mesopotamia (present-day Iraq, Kuwait, and Syria), where invoice factoring was used as a form of trade financing around 4000 years ago (SBC, 2022). Invoice factoring involves a factor (e.g., a bank) purchasing a firm's invoices and advancing cash or working capital against its unpaid accounts receivable. Other early forms of supply chain finance include discounted promissory notes and early payment.[4] Here is a brief history of SCF:

- Around 1754 B.C., invoice factoring rules were documented in the Babylonian law code, the Code of Hammurabi (SBC, 2022).
- In 118 B.C., during China's Han Dynasty, leather promissory notes called flying cash (Chinese: 飞钱) served as negotiable instruments for tea merchants (Wikipedia, 2020b).
- In 57 A.D., Romans sold discounted promissory notes to conscript collectors for settling trade debts (Wikipedia, 2020b).
- During the 1300s in Europe, merchant bankers started advancing early payments for the delivery and payment of grain to be shipped abroad (SBC, 2022).
- In the 1600s and 1700s, invoice factoring became a popular business practice among English colonists (SBC, 2022).
- In the 1800s, factoring gained popularity as a domestic financing instrument due to the rise of the textile industry (Cohen, 2022).
- In the 1960s and 1970s, trade financing like invoice factoring grew in popularity, as firms faced challenges obtaining traditional bank funding due to rising interest rates and bank regulations (SBC, 2022).
- In the 1980s, automobile manufacturers (e.g., Fiat) used a process similar to reverse factoring to help suppliers gain better profit margins. This approach evolved into "confirming" used by Banco Santander in Spain in 1991 (de Boer et al., 2015).
- By the 1990s, major US banks like GE Capital began formally incorporating factoring into their financial services (SBC, 2022).
- After the 2007–2009 Financial Crisis, supply chain finance emerged as a strong financing alternative to traditional bank financing.
- Following the COVID-19 outbreak in 2020, supply chain finance became a stable financial channel for supply chain firms.

---

[4] According to Wikipedia (2020a, 2020b), "A promissory note, sometimes referred to as a note payable, is a legal instrument (more particularly, a financial instrument and a debt instrument), in which one party (the maker or issuer) promises in writing to pay a determinate sum of money to the other (the payee), either at a fixed or determinable future time or on demand of the payee, under specific terms."

The market opportunity for supply chain finance is significant. The global market for receivables management of annual traded volume was estimated at $1.3 trillion in 2020. Asset-based lending and payables discounting stood at approximately $100 billion and $340 billion, respectively. The global market size for reverse factoring was estimated at $275 billion. Over half of companies planned to implement SCF mechanisms (Wikipedia, 2020c). Demand for supply chain finance tripled for some SCF-specialized companies during the COVID-19 pandemic (Eaglesham, 2020).

The potential for supply chain finance growth is enormous. Conceptually, all invoices and receipts issued by corporations that can support supply chain finance amount to $17 trillion globally, and the total assets eligible for SCF programs are estimated at $65 trillion globally as of 2018 (McKinsey, 2020). The total size of supply chain finance is projected to reach $2.5 trillion by 2025.

However, the growth of supply chain finance faces several practical challenges that need to be addressed. For instance, most SCF programs require endorsements from large corporations, such as major suppliers or buyers (e.g., Walmart), as small businesses often lack the capability to lead SCF initiatives. According to McKinsey (2020), fewer than 10% of non-investment-grade suppliers managed to obtain financing for their invoices. Additionally, technological support for SCF solutions, especially supplier-led solutions, is limited, resulting in inefficient process management and missed financing opportunities.

1.4 Financing Small Businesses

As reported by Forbes in April 2020, the COVID-19 outbreak wreaked financial havoc worldwide, leaving numerous small business owners scrambling to stay afloat. The National Federation of Independent Business (NFIB) stated that, as of March 30, 2020, 92% of small businesses experienced negative impacts due to the pandemic, while a mere 5% of owners reported no effects (Lake, 2020). The detrimental consequences of COVID-19 have persisted beyond 2020, continuing well into 2023.

The impact of COVID-19 has been more far-reaching than the 2007–2009 Financial Crisis, as it disrupted all elements of supply chains, including consumers, retailers, original equipment manufacturers, contract manufacturers, and suppliers. While the 2007–2009 Financial Crisis emphasized the crucial role of robust financial systems, COVID-19 exposed the importance and vulnerability of global supply chains. Nevertheless, a shared trait between the two events is the severe repercussions faced by small businesses in both global and local supply chains.

Forbes reported that within just two months of the COVID-19 outbreak, approximately 30 million small businesses in the United States confronted financial hardships (Lake, 2020). In response, the U.S. government unveiled a $660 billion aid program for small businesses in April 2020, supplementing nearly $350 billion in relief for small businesses as part of the $2.2 trillion economic stimulus plan passed on March 27, 2020. European countries also pledged over $1.5 trillion by March 2020, while the COVID-19 outbreak was still at its peak with no end in sight. The escalating trend of division between the U.S. and China, along with the Russo-Ukrainian War and recent conflicts between Israel and Hamas in 2023, has further intensified the turmoil in global supply chains. This underscores the urgency for governments worldwide to prioritize the financing and support of small businesses.

1.4.1 Defining Small Businesses

There is no universal definition for small businesses, as their classification varies across countries, industries, and even financial institutions. For instance, in the U.S., the maximum average revenue for a small agricultural business is $750,000 (McIntyre, 2020). In manufacturing, the maximum number of employees for a small business ranges from 500 to 1500. In retail trade, one-third of all sub-industries have a maximum average annual revenue of $7.5 million, while other sectors have a maximum employee count of 100 to 500. For small businesses in finance and insurance, the maximum number of employees is generally up to 1500, with maximum average annual revenues ranging from $32.5 million to $38.5 million (McIntyre, 2020). The Small Business Administration (sba.gov) provides a comprehensive list of standards for acceptable small business sizes by industry.

The term "small business" is often used interchangeably with small and medium enterprises (SMEs) and micro, small, and medium enterprises (MSMEs). In the European Union (EU), an MSME employs up to 250 people and has a turnover of no more than €50 million, or a total balance sheet not exceeding €43 million (Kushnir, 2010). In contrast, China's 2020 definition of an MSME encompasses businesses with 1 to 2000 employees (primarily below 300), revenues ranging from ¥10 million to ¥800 million (mainly under ¥300 million), and total assets of up to ¥1200 million, depending on the industry.

Due to the absence of a standard definition, this book will use MSMEs and SMEs interchangeably to refer to small businesses.

1.4.2 The Importance of Financing SMEs

SMEs have a significant impact on all economies. According to FinancesOnline, SMEs constituted 99% of all businesses in the U.S. and the EU in 2020 (Chang, 2021). As illustrated in Fig. 1.2, SMEs make up over 90% of the global business population, accounting for 70% of employment and approximately 44% of the world's Gross Domestic Product (GDP)—contributing up to 40% of GDP in emerging economies and 50% in developed countries.

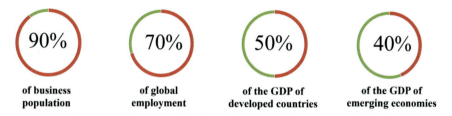

Fig. 1.2 Ratios of SMEs in world economics in terms of business population, employment, and GDP (*Source* International Federation of Accountants (IFAC))

1.4.3 The Small Business Lending Gap

Despite the significant contributions of small businesses to global economies, they often receive inadequate support from banks and other financial institutions. According to the Federal Deposit Insurance Corporation (FDIC), while the total loan amount to all businesses has increased over the years, the percentage of bank loans to small businesses in the U.S. has declined dramatically from 40% in 1995 to 21% in 2016 (see Fig. 1.3) (FDIC, 2020). Small business loans have decreased significantly over the past two decades, especially after 2008. To bridge the credit gap, small businesses have relied on internal funds, cash from friends and family, or the growing but demanding online peer-to-peer microfinancing.

> *While small businesses make a significant contribution to the global economy, they often do not receive a proportionate amount of support from banks and other financial institutions.*

Venture capital (VC) can alleviate the financial strain on small businesses. For instance, in 2018, total VC investments in the U.S. amounted to $99.5 billion, representing approximately 5% of the total financial needs of small businesses. Assuming SMEs should receive their fair share of financing, comparing SMEs' contributions to the GDP and their obtained loans plus VC reveals an approximate 20% credit gap between the percentage of GDP contributions and the percentage of all commercial loans and VC.

A similar disparity exists in China, the world's second-largest economy. As of 2016, small businesses contributed over 60% of the GDP and more than 50% of the country's total tax income. However, SMEs accounted for only about 28% of total commercial loans. Assuming a 5% VC contribution to SME funding similar to that in the U.S., there is still a credit gap of over 25% between the percentage of GDP contributions and the percentage of all commercial loans and VC.

It is evident that there is a considerable gap for small businesses seeking access to bank loans. According to the World Bank, about half of small businesses cannot

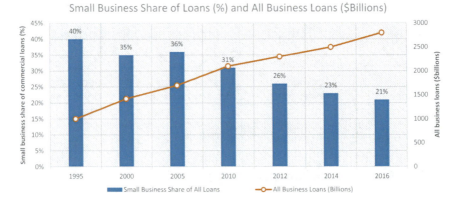

Fig. 1.3 Small business share of all commercial loans and all business loans in the U.S. (*Source* Federal Deposit Insurance Corporation, Call Report Data)

access credit from formal financial institutions (World Bank, 2020). As reported by the International Finance Corporation (IFC), approximately 65 million firms, or 40% of micro, small, and medium enterprises (MSMEs) in developing countries, have an unmet financing need of $5.2 trillion every year. This is about 1.4 times the current lending to global MSMEs. The credit gap size varies significantly across regions. East Asia and Pacific countries have the largest share (46%) of the total global credit gap, followed by Latin America and the Caribbean (23%) and Europe and Central Asia (15%) (World Bank, 2020).

The aforementioned credit gap underscores the challenges faced by small businesses. While small businesses have generated approximately 60% of the net new jobs in the U.S. since 1995, during the 2007–2009 Financial Crisis, they disproportionately accounted for over 60% of total jobs lost. This is because financial crises have a disproportionate impact on small businesses due to their limited access to credit (Mills & McCarthy, 2016). During the COVID-19 pandemic, as states worked to approve emergency funding measures for small businesses, many were unable to secure the promised loans and were forced to close their doors and lay off employees (Forbes, 2021).

1.4.4 Challenges in Financing Small Businesses

In theory, a firm may seek financial loans whenever it is capital constrained. However, compared to large firms, small businesses are much more vulnerable to cash deficiencies and bankruptcy. Given that most small businesses have credit ratings below BBB- (i.e., the lowest investment-grade rating in S&P), it is ironic that banks, while eager to expand their markets, have been reluctant to lend to small businesses in dire need of financial assistance. As a result of banks' risk control measures, according to the World Bank Group Enterprise Surveys, 79.2% of loans, on average, require collateral. On average, the value of collateral is 2.06 times the loan value, which is extremely demanding for many small businesses, especially when they lack creditworthiness (Zhou et al., 2020).

The characteristics of loans to small businesses can be described as *frequent, urgent, small,* and *short* (FUSS):

- *Frequent*: Given the larger number of small businesses in comparison to large firms, small business loans are typically more frequent.
- *Urgent*: Due to their short planning horizons and cash inefficiencies, small businesses cannot survive for long without adequate financing.
- *Small*: For small businesses, loan sizes tend to be smaller, mirroring their business sizes. The average loan size for these entities is about 5% of that for large firms. In the U.S., more than 70% of small businesses seek small-dollar loans under $250,000, with over 60% of these loans being under $100,000 (Mills & McCarthy, 2016).
- *Short*: Most small business loans are related to cash flow and are used to address short-term liquidity issues.

Small businesses are found in every layer of supply chains. They serve as suppliers, manufacturers, distributors, retailers, and service providers. However, due to their small sizes, the same uncertainties pose disproportionate risks, leading to higher bankruptcy rates than those of larger firms. From another perspective, lower bankruptcy costs associated with small sizes could make small businesses more risk-seeking, potentially leading to moral hazard in business dealings. Furthermore, their technology capabilities are more likely to be lower than those of their larger rivals, which means their communication costs could be higher and it may be more challenging to earn the same level of trust from financial institutions as larger firms. All these factors contribute to the reluctance or even unwillingness of banks and other financial institutions to lend to small businesses.

1.5 The Importance of Supply Chain Finance

The credit gap left by formal financial institutions for small businesses can be partially filled by supply chain finance. This is because supply chain finance can address two issues that persist under traditional bank financing:

- *Lack of Supply Chain Information*: Information about supply chain transactions from supply chain firms can alleviate financial institutions' concerns over risks, particularly if these institutions are risk-averse. The involvement of supply chain firms in financing makes the borrowing firm more trustworthy, which partly compensates for small businesses' lack of creditworthiness.
- *High Risks*: Risk sharing from supply chain firms (e.g., guarantees from supply chain firms) mitigates financial institutions' risks and makes lending to small businesses more profitable and attractive.

Nowadays, it is almost impossible to find a firm that operates in isolation without engaging in any supply chain activities. In the context of supply chains, the lack of financial resources in one firm can jeopardize the performance of the entire supply chain. Therefore, supply chain finance emerges as a plausible solution for capital-constrained firms, as other firms can benefit from assisting their partnering capital-constrained firms within the same supply chain.

As John Monaghan, Global Head of Supply Chain Finance at Citigroup, commented in March 2020, during the COVID-19 outbreak, "In the last couple of weeks, we are seeing companies looking at supply-chain finance to see how they can help their small suppliers and asking if this can be a tool to inject some liquidity" (Eaglesham, 2020). A spokesperson for Boeing also confirmed that Boeing offered its suppliers the option to use its supply chain finance arrangements to cope with their operating cash flow.

Supply chain firms are willing to participate in supply chain finance because it can be mutually beneficial for all parties involved. In particular, the development of supply chain finance can be attributed to the following factors:

- **Demand of Small Businesses:**
  - *Financing Need*: The urgent financing requirements of millions of capital-constrained small businesses have created a substantial market for supply chain finance.
- **Prospects for Banks:**
  - *Financing Opportunities*: Banks are regulated in all countries and face pressure to expand their markets and develop innovative financing schemes due to stricter regulations. Bank regulations serve as a double-edged sword for financing. On the one hand, these regulations improve bank liquidity and decrease bankruptcy risks. On the other hand, they shrink the traditional financial market, pushing banks to seek new business opportunities. As a result, supply chain finance quickly emerges as a new and rapidly growing market segment for most banks.
- **Appeal of Supply Chains:**
  - *Growth of Supply Chains*: As global economies have expanded significantly in recent decades; the scope and complexity of supply chains have increased tremendously. For example, Boeing procures the same component from a variety of suppliers, who in turn rely on material suppliers, distributors, and third-party logistics (3PL) firms. Consequently, there are more financial needs due to the growth of supply chains.
  - *Market Horizontal Competition*: Horizontally, firms must compete with rivals in the same market, prompting them to offer more attractive financial terms to their downstream (e.g., longer credit terms for trade credit) or upstream (e.g., buyer financing) supply chain partners.
  - *Supply Chain Relationship Management*: Vertically, supply chains become more fragile as they grow longer, making coordination among supply chain firms increasingly important. Firms are more willing to assist their partners in securing necessary financing through supply chain

finance, as the supply chain capacity is determined by the weakest link (i.e., the Barrel Principle).
- **Revenue Models**: As supply chain firms expand their businesses, they seek new revenue streams. While contract manufacturers and original equipment manufacturers (OEMs) are the primary financers of inventory due to their roles in prevailing open accounts (i.e., trade credit), other supply chain firms also participate in various supply chain financing services. For example, third-party logistics firms may provide financing services alongside their traditional logistics services, and focal firms such as large retailers may offer financial services to create new revenue sources while supporting their supply chain partners.
- **Technology Readiness**:
  - **Electronic Data Interchange (EDI) Capability**: EDI facilitates new supply chain finance instruments and transactions globally.
  - **Internet Platform**: The Internet and World Wide Web (WWW) services lay the foundation for business and financial services, enabling various supply chain finance platforms created by dominant supply chain firms, financial institutions, and third parties.
  - **Secure Data and Financial Services**: For instance, the Society for Worldwide Interbank Financial Telecommunication (SWIFT), a member-owned global cooperative platform, provides secure financial messaging for capital markets and enables the secure exchange of proprietary data while guaranteeing integrity and confidentiality. This helps reduce costs and risks associated with security transactions and financial market solutions.
  - **Blockchain Technology**: The development of blockchain technology since 2009 (i.e., the launch of Bitcoin) has provided an excellent platform for supply chain management to significantly improve efficiency (e.g., smart contracts and customer onboarding) and enhance transparency and trust (e.g., immutability) among supply chain members. Today, various blockchain structures, such as public, private, consortium, and hybrid blockchains, are widely used across industries.[5]

1.6 Summary

This chapter explores the financing challenges faced by small businesses, the lending gap in small business financing, and the importance of supply chain finance as a solution to these issues. It delves into the definitions of supply chain finance provided by various organizations and its history, highlighting its potential for growth and the practical constraints that need to be addressed.

---

[5] For a more in-depth discussion of supply chain finance technologies, please refer to Part IV: Supply chain finance technology.

Key Takeaways:

1. The Definition of Supply Chain Finance:
   - Supply chain finance is defined as event-driven financial activities that involve financing and risk mitigation techniques used in supply chain transactions, aiming to optimize working capital, liquidity, and overall supply chain efficiency.
2. The History of Supply Chain Finance:
   - The history of supply chain finance can be traced back to Mesopotamia, about 4000 years ago, with the use of invoice factoring.
   - Its evolution has been marked by the adoption of various financing instruments and techniques, such as promissory notes, early payment, and reverse factoring.
   - The growth of supply chain finance has significant potential but faces challenges, such as the need for endorsements from large corporations and limited technological support for SCF solutions.
3. Financing Small Businesses:
   - Small businesses face difficulties in obtaining financing due to a lack of credit history, collateral, and financial track records. These challenges limit their ability to grow, innovate, and compete in the market.
   - Traditional banks are often hesitant to lend to small businesses because of the perceived risks and high costs associated with small-scale lending. This creates a lending gap that hampers the growth and success of small businesses.
   - Factors such as stringent lending criteria, high-interest rates, and a lack of alternative financing options contribute to the challenges faced by small businesses in securing financing.
4. The Importance of Supply Chain Finance:
   - Supply chain finance offers a viable alternative to traditional bank financing by mitigating risks, optimizing working capital, and improving liquidity for supply chain firms.
   - This enhances supply chain efficiency and profitability, benefiting all parties involved in the supply chain.

1.7 Exercises

1.7.1 Practice Questions

1. What are some common challenges faced by small businesses when seeking financing?
2. What is the small business lending gap?
3. Why is supply chain finance important?
4. What is the SCF Pareto effect?
5. What are the three main messages delivered by the definition of supply chain finance mentioned in this chapter?

6. What were the main reasons for the growth of supply chain finance after the 2007–2009 Financial Crisis?
7. What is one major constraint in the growth of supply chain finance related to small businesses?
8. How did the rise of the textile industry contribute to the popularity of invoice factoring?
9. Why did trade financing like invoice factoring grow more popular in the 1960s and 1970s?
10. Could you detail a couple of anecdotal examples of using supply chain finance related to your work or your close friends' companies?

1.7.2 Case Study

A Small Textile Manufacturer's Supply Chain Finance Initiative

Background

ABC Textiles is a small textile manufacturer that has been operating for over two decades, supplying fabric to local and international fashion brands. They have a network of suppliers that provide raw materials, such as cotton, dyes, and threads, and a group of buyers that purchase their finished products.

Problem

ABC Textiles faces a cash flow challenge arising from slow-paying buyers. This delay in payment affects the company's capacity to settle its supplier invoices promptly. Consequently, suppliers are now demanding shorter payment terms, while buyers persist in requesting extended payment durations. This dynamic has placed a strain on the relationship between ABC Textiles, its suppliers, and its buyers, hindering the company's growth and profitability.

Question

What solutions can be proposed for ABC Textiles to overcome this challenge?

References

Camerinelli, E., & Bryant, C. (2014). *Supply chain finance—EBA European market guide version 2.0*. European Banking Association.

Chang, J. (2021). *63 Crucial Small Business Statistics for 2021/2022: Data Analysis & Projections*. FinancesOnline. https://financesonline.com/crucial-small-business-statistics/. Accessed April 2, 2022.

Cohen, P. (2022). *Invoice factoring: A history*. Factor Finders. https://www.factorfinders.com/blog/history-invoice-factoring/. Accessed October 9, 2022.

de Boer, R., Steeman, M., & van Bergen, M. (2015). *Supply chain finance, its practical relevance and strategic value: The supply chain finance essential knowledge series*. Hogeschool Windesheim.

Eaglesham, J. (2020). Supply-chain finance is new risk in crisis. *The Wall Street Journal*. https://www.wsj.com/articles/supply-chain-finance-is-new-risk-in-crisis-11585992601. Accessed July 9, 2021.

FDIC. (2020). *FDIC homepage*. https://fdic-search.app.cloud.gov/. Accessed August 11, 2021.

Forbes. (2021). *Small business relief: COVID-19 resources for startups*. https://www.forbes.com/sites/allbusiness/2020/04/07/covid-19-resources-for-small-businesses-startups/#2d7414f9169b. Accessed March 12, 2021.

GSCFF. (2022). *What is supply chain finance*. http://supplychainfinanceforum.org/. Accessed April 22, 2022.

Kushnir, K. (2010). *A universal definition of small enterprise: A procrustean bed for SMEs?* https://blogs.worldbank.org/psd/a-universal-definition-of-small-enterprise-a-procrustean-bed-for-smes. Accessed April 15, 2021.

Lake, R. (2020). *6 ways to rebuild your small business after COVID-19*. https://www.forbes.com/sites/advisor/2020/04/30/6-ways-to-rebuild-your-small-business-after-covid-19/?sh=36bb1dd16cc5. Accessed April 22, 2021.

McIntyre, G. (2020). *What is the sba's definition of small business (and why)?* https://www.fundera.com/blog/sba-definition-of-small-business. Accessed May 23, 2021.

McKinsey. (2020). *The 2020 McKinsey Global Payments Report* (Issue October). https://www.mckinsey.com/~/media/mckinsey/industries/financial%20services/our%20insights/accelerating%20winds%20of%20change%20in%20global%20payments/2020-mckinsey-global-payments-report-vf.pdf. Accessed May 16, 2021.

Mills, K., & McCarthy, B. (2016). The state of small business lending: Innovation and technology and the implications for regulation. *Harvard Business School Entrepreneurial Management Working Paper, 17–042*, 17–42.

NCUA. (2019). *Quarterly Credit Union Data Summary 2019 Q2*. https://ncua.gov/files/publications/analysis/quarterly-data-summary-2019-Q2.pdf. Accessed March 12, 2020.

Ryssdal, K., & Hollenhorst, M. (2022). *How's the container ship backlog at Southern California's ports?* https://www.marketplace.org/2022/09/29/ship-backlog-at-southern-californias-ports-eases/. Accessed May 2, 2023.

SBC. (2022). *The history and use of invoice factoring*. Mysbcapital.Com. https://www.mysbcapital.com/the-history-and-use-of-invoice-factoring/. Accessed October 12, 2022.

Wikipedia. (2020a). *Promissory note*. https://en.wikipedia.org/wiki/Promissory_note. Accessed November 2, 2020.

Wikipedia. (2020b). *Supply chain finance*. https://en.wikipedia.org/wiki/Reverse_factoring. Accessed November 12, 2020.

Wikipedia. (2020c). *Supply chain finance*. https://en.wikipedia.org/wiki/Supply_chain_finance. Accessed November 19, 2020.

Wikipedia. (2022). *Basel III*. https://en.wikipedia.org/wiki/Basel_III. Accessed November 22, 2022.

World Bank. (2020). *World Bank SME finance: Development news, research, data*. https://www.worldbank.org/en/topic/smefinance. Accessed November 16, 2020.

Zhou, W., Lin, T., & Cai, G. (2020). Guarantor financing in a four-party supply chain game with leadership influence. *Production and Operations Management, 29*(9), 2035–2056.

Supply Chain Finance Characteristics 2

Learning Objectives:

1. Identify and explain the four integral flows in supply chains: physical, financial, information, and risk.
2. Distinguish between various types of supply chain finance (SCF) solutions.
3. Assess the benefits and drawbacks of integrating SCF into business operations.
4. Utilize principles like synergy and top-down to design or evaluate SCF strategies.

2.1 Introduction

Supply chain finance revolves around financial activities driven by supply chain transactions and stands as a cornerstone of supply chain management (SCM). To further explore supply chain finance, we initiate with fundamental mechanisms of SCM.

SCM pertains to the management of goods and services transitioning from their source to the end consumer. An optimal SCM system aims to:

- Increase quality
- Improve service
- Reduce cost
- Optimize working capital
- Enhance throughput (minimize turnaround time)

To realize these goals, traditional SCM emphasizes the refinement of planning, sourcing, production (for tangible items), inventory management, delivery (logistics), and potentially, the process of return in reverse logistics. An illustrative

Fig. 2.1 Boeing's "critical operational readiness" in global supply chain management (*Source* Adapted from Boeing.com)

instance is Boeing's focus on critical operational readiness in global supply chain management (Boeing, 2023), as depicted in Fig. 2.1.

Boeing's assembly systems are intricate. Referencing Boeing's global SCM framework isn't to extol its managerial prowess but to underscore the concept. Implementation can diverge substantially from conceptual intent. Boeing's SCM excellence of yesteryears has lately seen successive setbacks, notably with the Boeing 737 Max's safety lapses in 2019 and the delay in NASA's 2022 Artemis mission due to a leakage in Boeing's rocket. Such challenges signify that a company's chase for stellar financial returns falters if its operational and quality endeavors don't align with its standards and customer commitments.

In Boeing's SCM context, given the intricacies of global supply chains, strategic planning has been paramount. Aspects like demand forecasting, production planning, and simulation stand distinguished. Boeing's vast supplier network underlines the indispensability of robust supply base management. This is evident from recurrent delays in the Boeing 787's delivery—a situation resonating with major original equipment manufacturers (OEMs) like Apple and automobile giants (Boeing, 2013).[1]

Yet, a significant portion of these suppliers grapple with capital limitations. Thus, supply chain finance avenues, especially buyer financing, have been instrumental in ensuring supply chain continuity (Deng et al., 2018). A prevalent reason for these suppliers' banking challenges is their insufficient creditworthiness or

---

[1] The Boeing 787 Dreamliner has about 2.3 million parts while the Boeing 737 has about 400 thousand parts (Boeing, 2013).

absent credit history, accentuating the significance of risk assessment in supply chain finance.

With the evolution of supply chain finance, overlooking risk dynamics when goods/services and funds interchange is untenable. Supply chain entities and banking institutions adeptly employ their expertise in product, information, and financial flows, strategizing against risks for accruing premiums in supply chain operations and aligned financial ventures.

2.2 The Four Flows of Supply Chains

Given the significance of risk in supply chain finance, we introduce the concept of *risk flow*, complementing the traditional trio of supply chain flows: product, information, and financial flows. While the product, information, and financial flows are usually measurable, either physically or digitally, the flow of risks is less frequently discussed due to its abstract nature and challenging measurability.

Risk isn't solely dependent on the three aforementioned flows but is also heavily influenced by external factors like politics, social events, and disasters, among others. Thus, evaluating risk should factor in information from the three traditional flows and various external influences.

While the extant literature hasn't yet fully delineated risks in supply chain finance, the author deems it essential to present the "risk flow" concept (Cai, 2019). This highlights its importance and aims to influence future advancements in supply chain finance. With the adoption of specific supply chain mechanisms and the evolution of the three primary flows, risks "flow" between parties. The advantages of visualizing and measuring risk flow are manifold:

- **Risk Visualization**: This facilitates and bolsters supply chain finance. A primary challenge in financing supply chain entities is determining the risks associated with these firms. Clear visualization of risk flow enhances risk control for banks, allowing them to allocate more of their reserved capital to finance firms with capital constraints.
- **Risk Mitigation**: Visualizing risk flow simplifies risk mitigation for parties in supply chain finance. This clarity enables supply chain firms to collaborate more effectively with suitable partners.
- **Risk Quantification**: This assists supply chain parties in quantifying the relevant risk premium for risk takers within supply chain finance. As a result, firms can more seamlessly partake in the implementation of supply chain finance.

To optimize a firm's profits or other objectives, it benefits the firm to seamlessly integrate product flow, information flow, financial flow, and risk flow (as depicted in Fig. 2.2).

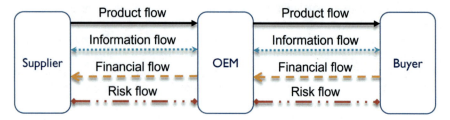

Fig. 2.2 Product, information, financial, and risk flows

2.2.1 Product Flow

Product flow, also often referred to as physical flow or material flow, is the physical movement of goods and services. Limiting the product flow to only tangible goods or material flow might not reflect the fact that intangible services can be parts of supply chains.

Products (i.e., goods and services) usually flow from upstream firms to downstream firms, although reverse logistics has also become popular in recent decades due to product returns and remanufacturing. For example, in the long supply chains of Boeing, component suppliers source from material suppliers and then produce and deliver the components to Boeing, which then assembles them into the final products to be shipped to the final customers, such as airline companies. If components do not always meet the quality standards, which could be the case in Boeing 787, components will be returned to be remanufactured or Boeing must look for alternative suppliers. The final products could also be recalled or returned due to quality issues, such as the fatal defaults of the software system in Boeing 737 Max.

2.2.2 Information Flow

Information flow encompasses the bidirectional exchange of data related to products, demand, price, cost, financial documents, and other pertinent details. The transparency and sharing of this information have been pivotal in fostering relationships and trust among supply chain firms.

> *A trustworthy information flow not only provides visibility into the product flow but also enables firms to evaluate the health of the financial and risk flows.*

A reliable information flow does more than just shed light on the product flow. It also aids firms in assessing the state of the financial and risk flows, an area gaining increased focus in the era of data analytics. For instance, information on costs and

2.2 The Four Flows of Supply Chains

demand is invaluable for production planning. Additionally, financial institutions necessitate financial documents when sanctioning loans and bonds. Over the years, advancements in technologies such as supply chain software, cloud computing, the Internet, and the recent surge in blockchain technology have continually enhanced the information flow. For instance, the adoption of blockchain technology bolsters visibility, transparency, and data immutability. The sustained enhancement of information flow will prove critical to the growth of supply chain finance, a topic set for in-depth exploration in subsequent chapters.

2.2.3 Financial Flow

Often termed cash flow, finance flow, or capital flow, *financial flow* signifies the movement of cash and working capital. Traditionally, in the absence of financial backing from banks or other supply chain entities, the financial flow traveled from buyers to suppliers, opposite to the direction of the product flow. For example, in a conventional SCM scenario, cash would move from the buyer to the seller either when an order was placed or upon product delivery.

However, with financing in the picture, the dynamics of the financial flow become more intricate. In the context of supply chain finance, a seller might need to borrow money upfront from banks for production, or a buyer might leverage their product inventory to secure financing, ensuring they can pay the seller and sustain a stable cash flow.

From an academic standpoint, supply chain literature has often sidelined the financial aspect in operational deliberations, despite long-standing assertions that finance is one of the foundational three flows of any supply chain (alongside product and information). This oversight is partly attributed to the intricacies of concurrently analyzing these three flows. On a theoretical front, it's a herculean task to incorporate financial considerations into evaluations of production, inventory, and information, especially when navigating myriad uncertainties such as market volatility, production reliability, and financial risks. From an empirical perspective, painting a holistic picture of how these three flows interplay across various firms and financial institutions presents its own set of challenges. Nonetheless, post the 2007–2009 Financial Crisis, the significance of financial flow in SCM has surged, necessitating its meticulous representation in the evolution of supply chain finance.

2.2.4 Risk Flow

Risks have been widely discussed in SCM, as uncertainties related to supply, demand, price, cost, and lead time are typically considered intrinsic features of SCM. However, most risk measurements have been isolated, and not presented in the format of risk flow. Risk flow not only quantifies the risks at each individual firm but also illustrates how risks transition from one supply chain firm to another. Properly characterizing risk flow requires measuring the risk of each involved supply chain firm and understanding how risks transfer from one firm to another, influenced by various factors.

Traditional SCM risks, excluding the consideration of financial flow, encompass the following major factors:

- *Market risks*
  - Demand risks associated with the uncertainties of consumer behaviors.
  - Price and cost risks that are heavily influenced by respective markets.
- *Operational risks*
  - Supply risks linked with disruptions caused by internal mismanagement.
  - Environmental risks such as COVID-19 and earthquakes.
  - Risks inherent in planning, production, and other processes.

These risk factors frequently appear in literature when the scope is restricted to just the physical and information flows. A shift in focus to the financial flow inevitably brings attention to the following added risks:

- Credit risks, covering risks related to all firms' credit ratings.
- Liquidity risks, inclusive of default and bankruptcy risks.
- Market risks such as interest rate risk, foreign exchange risks, and more.
- Legal and regulatory risks like significant government policy shifts and tax reforms.
- Other varied business risks.

SCF risk management and a more detailed risk taxonomy are further discussed in Chapter 10, which covers SCF risk taxonomy and assessment.

The other three flows, particularly the financial flow, are intertwined with risk flow. In fact, the success of supply chain finance is partly due to the potential for risks transitioning from one firm to another, influencing the financial health of firms and facilitating coordination between supply chain entities and financial institutions.

> *The success of supply chain finance is partly attributed to the potential for risks to flow from one firm to another.*

Other flows have been mentioned in scholarly articles. For instance, some researchers propose a value flow in exploring SCM. A *value chain* is widely defined as "a set of activities that a firm operating in a specific industry performs to deliver a valuable product (i.e., good and/or service) to the market" (Wikipedia, 2020). If we analyze the value flow of an industry, it emphasizes the value added at every stage of the supply chain. Although the value flow concept can be applied to supply chains, it centers more on the value added in delivering products to end

2.3 Supply Chain Finance Types

consumers rather than on the interaction and coordination of the four primary supply chain flows. Some scholars also introduce flows of data, demand, forecasts, etc., but many of these can be encompassed within the four foundational flows: product, information, financial, and risk.

2.3 Supply Chain Finance Types

SCF mechanisms continue to evolve. We have summarized some SCF mechanisms in Table 2.1 based on the following three dimensions: supply chain finance initiator, supply chain finance source, and supply chain finance timing. Given the plethora of definitions that can often be confusing, we have chosen to list only the most popular ones in Table 2.1. These SCF mechanisms will be further elaborated on in Part II: Supply Chain Finance Mechanisms.

Operations in Action	Order → Materials → Production → Inventory → Shipment → Invoices → Payment
SCF Types	Pre-Shipment | In-Transit | Post-Shipment

	Procurement Cycle	*Conversion Cycle (Inventory & Production)*	*Sales/Distribution Cycle*
Accounts Receivable (Seller-Centric)	Purchase order financing		Factoring, Forfaiting, Invoice discounting, Seller-led accounts receivable securitization
Inventory & Production (Seller and Buyer-Centric)	Materials financing, Work-in-progress financing	Inventory financing, Warehouse receipt financing	
Accounts Payable (Buyer-Centric)	Cash-in-advance, Early payment discount	Letter of credit, Open account	Trade credit, Payable extension, Dynamic discounting, Early payment discount, Reverse factoring, Reverse securitization
Third-Party-Centric	Contract manufacturer financing	3rd-party-logistics (3PL) financing	Guarantor financing (by bank, insurance company, focal firms)

Table 2.1 Categories of SCF mechanisms

2.3.1 Supply Chain Finance Initiator

One approach to categorize SCF mechanisms is based on the criterion of "who initiates the financing request." The categories are as follows:

- *Accounts Receivable* (*Seller-Centric*): Accounts receivable (AR) represents the money owed to a seller by buyers for goods or services that have been delivered or used but not yet paid for. AR usually takes the form of invoices and is classified as an asset on a balance sheet. In seller-centric SCF, AR is frequently used as collateral to secure a loan or is sold to receive cash at a discounted rate.
- *Inventory and Production* (*Seller and Buyer-Centric*): Inventory of goods or work-in-progress can be used by either sellers or buyers as collateral when borrowing from financial institutions.
- *Accounts Payable* (*Buyer-Centric*): Contrary to AR, accounts payable (AP) represents the money owed by a buyer to its seller for goods or services that have been ordered or delivered. AP is presented as an invoice due for payment and is considered a liability on a company's balance sheet.
- *Third-Party-Centric*: A SCF transaction might be initiated by a third-party firm, such as a third-party logistics provider, an online platform, or even an insurance company.

The above categorization (e.g., seller-centric or buyer-centric) is also linked with the type of collateral involved, such as accounts receivable, accounts payable, and inventory, utilized in supply chain financing. Unlike traditional financing, which often uses fixed assets as collateral, SCF commonly employs working capital as collateral or even sells the working capital for cash (with title rights transferred) through various mechanisms.

2.3.2 Supply Chain Finance Source

One of the key challenges in supply chain finance is determining the source of the "finance"—essentially, who will finance the supply chain transactions. There are three primary types of sources:

- **Banks**

Banks have been the most consistent traditional financing source for various business transactions from the dawn of finance and continue to play a dominant role in supply chain finance. In conventional bank financing, capital-constrained firms borrow directly from banks without involving other supply chain entities.

In contrast, when it comes to bank financing under SCF programs, banks often require supporting documents (i.e., information), guarantees, financial partnerships, and the like from firms involved in supply chain transactions. Whether it's bank-led initiatives like documentary business or seller-led and buyer-led supply chain finance, banks have consistently been the foundation of these financial transactions. For instance, banks typically act as factors in most invoice and accounts receivable financing.

- **Supply Chain Firms**

Financing sourced from supply chain firms participating in their business transactions is also termed *supply chain self-financing*. This method has seen rapid growth recently, especially when the capital-constrained supply chain firms belong to the non-investment-grade credit group. This growth might explain the rise in popularity of open accounts in trade financing and buyer-led SCF solutions, such as early payment.

Supply chain self-financing emerges when one supply chain firm has ample cash or a superior credit rating and is willing to help enhance its partnering supply chain firm's financial stability. This form of supply chain financing can also significantly foster the supply chain relationship, particularly with firms deemed strategically important.

Additionally, according to Sadlovska and Enslow (2006), financing costs account for approximately 4% of the total cost of finished goods. Hence, aiding these suppliers/buyers is crucial not only for their immediate partners but also benefits the entire supply chain due to the reduction in overall operational costs. For instance, in Walmart's supply chain finance programs, priority is given to early payments for suppliers who have a long-standing business relationship with Walmart. This supply chain self-financing model benefits the buyer, providing perks such as early payment discounts to Walmart. Conversely, suppliers can negotiate higher wholesale price margins in trade credit financing, also known as open accounts.

- **Intermediaries**

The swift evolution of supply chain finance has paved the way for third parties to launch SCF service platforms or even replace banks in some roles, such as factors. The establishment of these intermediary SCF service platforms allows other participants like governments, financial institutions, and other third parties, in addition to the primary supply chain entities and banks, to join in the SCF solutions. These intermediaries extend funding opportunities to a wide array of buyers, suppliers, and transaction types, drawing financial contributions from a diverse range of sources. This inclusivity allows all participants to share financial risks, raising the effectiveness of SCF to an unprecedented level. These SCF service platforms can be introduced by leading suppliers, buyers, banks, or third-party entities such as financial institutions, logistics firms, and even insurance companies.

2.3.3 Supply Chain Finance Timing

To categorize SCF mechanisms based on "when the financing activity occurs," we arrive at the following classifications:

- *Procurement Cycle*: This pertains to the duration post the receipt of an order by the seller and prior to the shipment of products or services to the buyer. The procurement cycle might overlap with the pre-shipment phase, which includes the production period.
- *Conversion Cycle* (*Inventory & Production*): Often termed as "in-transit," this cycle signifies the transition from materials to final products. Hence, the firm retains an inventory of materials, works-in-progress, and some finished but yet-to-be-shipped products. An enterprise's objective is to condense its cash conversion cycle. However, the objectives of supply chain entities often clash. Coordination among these entities can enhance the overall supply chain efficiency.
- *Sales/Distribution Cycle*: Also termed "post-shipment," this cycle encompasses instances where goods could be sold as backorders beforehand. The point of title transfer demarcates whether an item is "in-transit" or "post-shipment."

As highlighted in Table 2.1, SCF mechanisms might manifest at different intervals, instigated by specific supply chain incidents. We can also depict the timing of SCF mechanisms concerning the product flow of the supply chain, as illustrated in Fig. 2.3. This figure elucidates the physical progression of a standard supply chain transaction, spanning from sourcing to purchasing, invoicing, production, shipping, and payment. Financial incidents (i.e., SCF "Trigger Points" presented in textboxes atop the product flow) might be activated by a particular supply chain event. While the described transaction largely adheres to a make-to-stock model, varying supply chain transactions could stimulate financial events at alternate intervals. For instance, in a make-to-order transaction, invoice validation happens sooner. Thus, accounts receivable and payable financing might transpire in the earlier segments of the product flow.

2.4 Supply Chain Finance Pros and Cons

The value of supply chain finance is manifold. Below are some significant benefits contributing to its popularity:

- *Liquidity Enhancement*: Supply chain finance offers essential funds and working capital to capital-constrained firms, facilitating smoother operations.
- *Risk Mitigation*: Supply chain entities and financial institutions distribute risks using SCF mechanisms. For instance, in factoring, a seller transfers its accounts receivable to a bank, thereby moving the buyer's default risk to the

2.4 Supply Chain Finance Pros and Cons

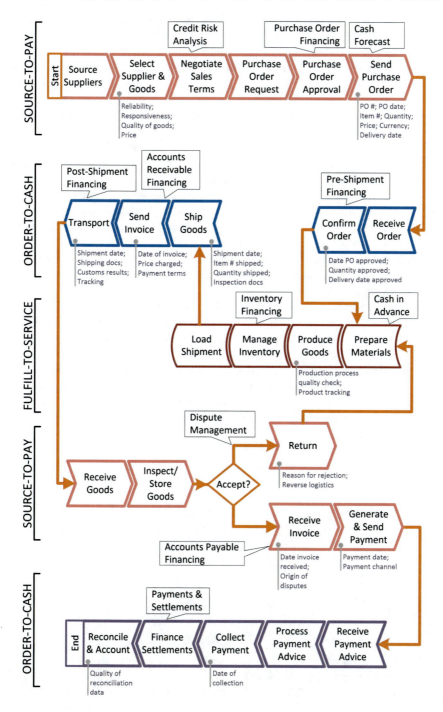

Fig. 2.3 Supply chain product flow and SCF "trigger points" (*Source* Revised and extended from Camerinelli & Bryant, 2014, and Templar et al., 2016)

bank. Risk mitigation for each SCF mechanism will be elaborated upon in subsequent chapters.
- **Credit Rating Protection**: Funds acquired from certain SCF methods, like prepayment financing to suppliers, are not recorded as loans in accounting books. Consequently, a firm's credit rating remains unaffected by the financing.
- **Cost Saving**: Supply chain finance can diminish both financial and administrative expenses for companies.
  – Firms that address capital constraints through "internal" financing methods, like open accounts, enable the entire supply chain to sidestep fees typically payable to external financial entities.
  – Even when firms engage external financial institutions, their collaborative efforts during the financing procedure (e.g., sharing information) can cut down administrative costs. This includes expenses related to credit assessments, inventory monitoring, reconciliations, and more.
- **Supply Chain Efficiency Improvement**: Most SCF strategies act as a supply chain coordination contract, enhancing performance in various ways and fostering win–win situations.
  – *Enhanced supply chain relationship*: SCF often necessitates the participation of several supply chain firms in a single financial transaction. As a result, these firms tend to collaborate more in supply chain financing compared to traditional banking.
  – *Increased information transparency*: Supply chain entities usually possess a deeper understanding of their transactions and are familiar with their partners due to historical associations. Such knowledge can curtail the risks stemming from asymmetric information, promoting trust among entities.

Nevertheless, every advantage has a corresponding drawback. Potential limitations of supply chain finance include:

- **Greater Coordination Complexity and Costs**: This drawback is inherent, arising from the need for heightened coordination and information transparency in many SCF models compared to traditional financing. This necessitates further investments in infrastructure like staffing and information technology.

Case Study

The Rise and Fall of TradeLens for Global Shipping

The TradeLens platform was a blockchain-based ecosystem jointly established by Maersk and IBM in 2016. Its remarkable success soon attracted over 170 organizations from the global shipping industry (TradeLens, 2022).

2.4 Supply Chain Finance Pros and Cons

By August 2022, TradeLens had processed an impressive 3.38 billion events, covering over 63 million containers, 13 million shipment events per week, and in excess of 120 event types. Yet, on November 29, 2022, Maersk and IBM unexpectedly announced that the TradeLens platform would be phased out by the end of the first quarter of 2023 (Maersk, 2022). As Rotem Hershko, the Head of Maersk Business Platforms at A.P. Moller, stated, "While we successfully created a functional platform, achieving full global industry collaboration proved elusive," attributing the challenge to the intricacies of coordinating numerous firms.[2]

- *Interdependence and Joint Default Risks*: Owing to risk sharing and mitigation, multiple entities could bear the brunt if one firm defaults. For instance, if an airline company goes bankrupt, it can negatively impact aircraft manufacturers like Boeing and their suppliers, especially if payments for aircraft haven't been settled.
- *Hidden Accounting Transparency Risks*: In supply chain finance, trade debts and accounts payable aren't treated as conventional loans and don't require full disclosure. However, this could heighten default risks for firms (Eaglesham, 2020).

Case Study

Hidden Accounting Transparency Risks

Fitch Ratings, a reputable credit rating agency, highlighted that "Supply-chain finance was a pivotal factor in the 2018 collapse of U.K. firm Carillion PLC." Carillion, a significant U.K. government contractor, disintegrated after its losses escalated sharply. Alarmingly, few investors were aware that Carillion had supply-chain finance obligations ranging from £400 million to £500 million ($491 million to $613 million), which it discreetly logged as "other payables." This figure vastly overshadowed its officially declared net debt of £219 million (Eaglesham, 2020).

---

[2] We delve deeper into this example in Chapter 15.6.1.

2.5 Supply Chain Finance Effects

When SCF solutions are implemented, they influence the working capital and financial performance of associated supply chain firms, as well as overall supply chain efficiency. Given the intricacies of supply chains, potential effects include the supply chain relationship effect, the seesaw effect, the Pareto effect, the domino effect, the halo effect, and the ripple effect.

2.5.1 Supply Chain Relationship Effect

Supply chain finance necessitates that involved firms share more data, such as logistics and financial information, to facilitate financial transactions. As a result, supply chain firms become more familiar with one another due to this increased information exchange. Most supply chain finance solutions are reciprocal, and some even rely on long-term credit lines, reinforcing the relationships between these supply chain entities.

The commitment to certain supply chain finance platforms can further cement these relationships, as the growing number of transactions deepens trust. In essence, firms that are onboarded can reduce opportunity costs by using the same platform for future transactions.

2.5.2 The Seesaw Effect in Working Capital

The *seesaw effect* in working capital is intuitive. Any supply chain finance solution redistributes working capital between organizations. This means when one firm's working capital increases, another's decreases. While companies can reap benefits from supply chain finance solutions, fluctuations in their working capital are common. It's crucial to ensure that all participating entities maintain a balance in their working capital to prevent financial strain or even defaults, which could impact all connected firms within the supply chain.

2.5.3 The Pareto Effect in Profit

The *Pareto effect* in profit suggests that when engaging with a specific supply chain finance solution, the involved supply chain firms stand to benefit. When a supply chain finance solution is introduced, these firms become interdependent. Theoretically, companies wouldn't engage in a given supply chain finance strategy if they weren't gaining from it. In this light, supply chain finance can synchronize the interests of supply chain firms and financial institutions, ensuring all participants benefit.

2.5 Supply Chain Finance Effects

In real-world scenarios, if a supply chain finance solution doesn't offer the Pareto effect, its sustainability is questionable. Essentially, any firm at a disadvantage will seek alternatives to boost its profitability. Hence, influential companies should prioritize long-term, mutually beneficial strategies when collaborating with less powerful supply chain partners to ensure a reliable supply chain.

> *If a supply chain finance solution lacks the Pareto effect, it isn't sustainable.*

2.5.4 The Domino Effect in Liquidity

The *domino effect* refers to the phenomenon where the failure of one firm can lead to the failure of many other firms within the same supply chain network. There are two major causes of domino effects. The first is driven by the product flow of the supply chain, in which the disruption of a key component of a key supply chain firm can negatively impact many other associated supply chain firms. This is especially true if the component is unique and strategic (Templar et al., 2016, p. 68). The COVID-19 pandemic provided numerous examples of the domino effect in supply chains. For instance, without lithium, the entire electric vehicle industry, particularly battery development, could face challenges.

Another example can be seen in the customs and port shutdowns in various countries during different periods. These disruptions led to supply shortages globally, contributing in part to the inflation experienced between 2021 and 2023. The U.S. government's decision to cease the supply of high-end chips to China, intending to hinder China's technological progress, also resulted in further supply chain disruptions, not just in China, but globally, including in the U.S. Such actions inevitably bifurcated the global market into two primary competing submarkets, reducing the market sizes for major chip companies worldwide.

The second significant cause of the domino effect arises from financial flows. As supply chain finance becomes more prevalent, firms become increasingly interdependent. One firm's financing might hinge on another firm's creditworthiness. For instance, a focal company might provide a guarantee for another firm's loan, or the payment collection from one firm might actually be settled by another.

Recent developments in major economies have seen SMEs use a dominant firm's accounts payable as "currency" to make purchases from their upstream or downstream firms. This interdependence can exacerbate the domino effect when a key or dominant firm faces financial stress, as seen in the financial crisis of the Evergrande Group in 2021.

2.5.5 The Halo Effect and Ripple Effect in Firms' Performance

The *halo effect* denotes the positive impact that a financially robust supply chain firm can have on its neighboring supply chain firms. Such influence can manifest in several ways. Firstly, a financially stable supply chain firm is more likely to place larger orders from its upstream partners. Secondly, a robust firm can offer more financial assistance, such as bank guarantees, to its supply chain counterparts. As an example, a dominant firm like Walmart might collaborate with its banking partners to extend financial services to its associates. Thus, supply chain finance can benefit not only a dominant firm but also its closely linked upstream or downstream partners.

Conversely, from a negative standpoint, a firm's financial distress can have repercussions on its surrounding firms along the supply chain. Its compromised financial status can affect both its purchasing power and product delivery capability, leading to a *ripple effect*.

2.6 Principles of Measuring and Selecting Financing Schemes

As we delve deeper into a variety of supply chain finance schemes in Part II: Supply Chain Finance Mechanisms, it's evident that these schemes each come with their set of advantages and disadvantages. To set the stage for our upcoming discussions, this subsection offers several guiding principles for measuring and selecting specific supply chain finance mechanisms.

2.6.1 The Revised 6R Model: A Measurement Principle

The original *6R model* was formulated by de Boer et al. (2015), who distilled the drivers characterizing supply chain finance into six dimensions, each beginning with the letter "R." These dimensions were: Release working capital, Return on investment, Risk management, Responsiveness & innovation, Relationship, and Responsibility & reputation. The author has made slight modifications to these 6 Rs, resulting in the following dimensions: Reviving working capital, Return on investment, Risk mitigation, Responsiveness and R&D, Reliability and relationship, and Responsibility and reputation. While these drivers echo some of the advantages mentioned in the previous subsection, they are presented within a more organized framework. The revised 6R model is depicted in Fig. 2.4 and further explained as follows:

1. **Reviving Working Capital**: Reviving working capital encompasses two facets: replenishing the cash to a desired level and transitioning net working capital

2.6 Principles of Measuring and Selecting Financing Schemes

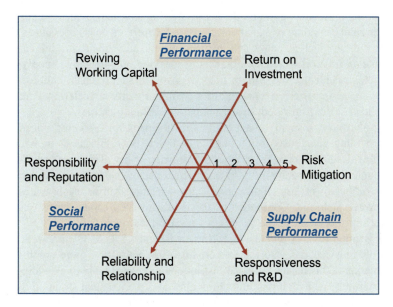

Fig. 2.4 Six main SCF drivers—6R model (*Source* Adapted from de Boer et al., 2015)

from one firm to another, and also shifting from one capital format to another (e.g., accounts receivable and inventory to cash).[3]

The primary aim of reviving working capital is not just to liberate working capital but also to use it optimally to amplify the firm's profit. For instance, while many business models aspire to diminish the cash conversion cycle (CCC), companies should recognize that reducing the CCC can lead to supply chain conflicts.[4] Especially, a negative CCC often burdens supply chain partners and can substantially undermine supply chain dependability.

A key motivator for adopting supply chain finance is to alleviate capital constraints faced by one or multiple supply chain entities, ensuring goods are aptly manufactured and delivered to satisfy end-consumer demands. These firms should maintain a robust cash position to prevent insolvency and unforeseen financial disruptions. As such, these companies should efficiently transition from inventory to accounts receivable and then to cash.

For instance, downstream entities can advance payments to upstream entities that have less capital constraints without severely hampering the supply chain. Reverse factoring is one mechanism that facilitates advance payment to the supplier while prolonging payments for the buyer with necessary backing from banks and insurers. However, since a firm's accounts receivable correlate with

---

[3] Net working capital is frequently defined as: Accounts Receivable + Inventory − Accounts Payable, see Chapter 4.1. Working capital typically includes cash plus the net working capital.
[4] We provide more discussion of CCC in Chapter 4.3.

its partner's accounts payable, the act of offering advance payment to upstream entities and extending payment durations to downstream ones necessitates third-party entities, such as banks and insurers, to rejuvenate their working capital.

2. **Return on Investment (ROI)**: Financially speaking, implementing supply chain finance can enhance the bottom lines of involved supply chain entities. Typically, under supply chain finance, order quantities increase, fostering a mutually beneficial scenario for both upstream and downstream entities.

   Furthermore, a supply chain entity's involvement (e.g., sharing information or providing guarantees) often augments the creditworthiness of transactions, thereby slashing capital costs for the borrowing entity. This cost can also dip if a large, highly creditworthy firm assists in borrowing from financial institutions on behalf of less creditworthy, capital-restricted firms, such as observed in reverse factoring. Consequently, the firm's invested capital drops (e.g., the buyer in trade credit or the supplier in reverse factoring), boosting ROI.

3. **Risk Mitigation**: As elucidated earlier in Chapter 2.4, SCF empowers firms to shift financial risks from a less creditworthy entity to a more creditworthy counterpart. This makes financial institutions more amenable to extending necessary funds. Although risk mitigation alleviates the financial strain on the less creditworthy entity, this risk is transferred to the more creditworthy one. This shift carries the potential to tarnish the credit rating of the latter, especially during financial crises. Consequently, the firm absorbing the financial risks should receive a risk premium. However, this premium should not be so substantial as to be detrimental to the other firm, ensuring mutual participation in the supply chain finance solution for mutual benefits.

   It's crucial to highlight that a supply chain finance scheme does more than just transfer risks between firms. The active participation of supply chain entities enhances supply chain transparency, subsequently bolstering the creditworthiness of the entire supply chain. This dynamic promotes a Pareto optimal outcome for all involved parties.

4. **Responsiveness and R&D**: Support from supply chain entities in supply chain finance provides firms, especially suppliers, with considerable financial resources. This allows them to invest in enhanced production capacity, enabling them to better respond to the demands of end consumers. In the same vein, an increase in working capital through supply chain finance facilitates greater investment in R&D. Consequently, firms can better cater to consumers' demand in terms of product variety, elevate product quality, and bolster service offerings, such as warranties.

5. **Reliability and Relationship**: A robust supply chain relationship greatly facilitates the implementation of supply chain finance schemes. Firms with healthier relationships are generally more inclined to extend support to each other.

   Conversely, the introduction of supply chain finance schemes can bolster these relationships. This is attributed to the enhanced transparency and payment flexibility inherent in supply chain finance, leading to heightened trust and commitment between partners (de Boer et al., 2015).

2.6 Principles of Measuring and Selecting Financing Schemes

Enhanced supply chain relationships, stemming from supply chain finance, subsequently augment supply chain reliability. For instance, retail giants like Amazon and Walmart have strategically backed their long-standing suppliers through early payment discount initiatives. This not only ensures a steady supply for these retailers but also guarantees consistent demand for the chosen suppliers.

6. **Responsibility and Reputation**: An increasing number of businesses are striving to enhance and preserve their societal reputations. Supply chain finance plays a pivotal role in this endeavor, particularly benefiting firms in developing nations by promoting greater ecological and societal responsibility (de Boer et al., 2015). Given that supply chain entities are intrinsically linked by shared products and services, prominent downstream firms in developed countries are more inclined to financially support their upstream counterparts in developing regions. This aids these firms in improving their working conditions and fostering a commitment to social responsibility.

In alignment with de Boer et al. (2015), we can further categorize the aforementioned 6 Rs into three primary areas:

- Financial performance (comprising Reviving working capital and Return on investment)
- Supply chain performance (consisting of Risk mitigation, Responsiveness and R&D, and Reliability and relationship)
- Social performance (encompassing Responsibility and reputation)

It's worth highlighting that these categories are not mutually exclusive. For instance, risk mitigation plays a crucial role in both financial and supply chain risk management. Additionally, the intersection of Reliability and relationship with Responsibility and reputation is quite significant.

By mapping a firm's values across these six dimensions (in terms of index values), we can deduce the firm's primary emphases in relation to the three performance categories. Take, for instance, in Fig. 2.5a, where the firm (perhaps a small start-up) registers an index value of 5 in both Reviving working capital and Return on investment. However, it scores 3 in Risk mitigation, 2 in Responsiveness and R&D, and 1 in both Reliability and relationship and Responsibility and reputation dimensions. As such, this firm appears predominantly driven by financial performance. Conversely, another firm (such as state-owned entities) depicted in Fig. 2.5b has a score of 5 in Responsibility and reputation and 4 in Reliability and relationship, indicating a stronger inclination towards social performance.

Furthermore, the 6R model can be employed to assess the influence of a particular supply chain scheme on a participating firm. As an illustration, consider a small startup that was primarily focused on its financial metrics. Once it reaps the advantages of supply chain finance, the company may enhance its responsiveness in supply chain delivery and channel more resources into R&D. This shift would

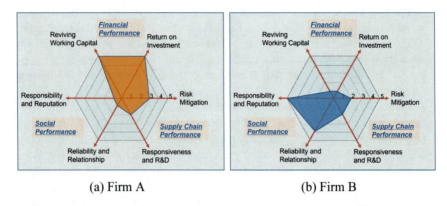

Fig. 2.5 Different performance driven representatives in 6R model

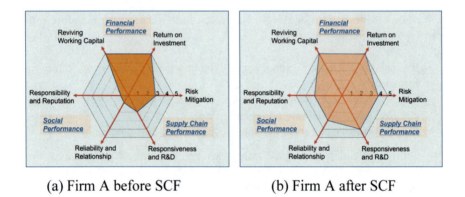

Fig. 2.6 Impact of an SCF scheme on a firm's 6R focuses

also invariably boost its Responsibility and reputation, as well as its Reliability and relationship, as depicted in Fig. 2.6.

2.6.2 The Selection Principles

According to de Boer et al. (2015), supply chain finance has evolved from purely operational and tactical to a strategic approach, emphasizing value creation and customer service. Instead of merely acting as a remedy for businesses' immediate financial challenges, supply chain finance has become increasingly pivotal in companies' long-term planning for supply chain and financial management. This shift means that executives now need to invest greater effort into enhancing both financial health and supply chain proficiency to optimize profits.

2.6 Principles of Measuring and Selecting Financing Schemes

To craft an efficient supply chain finance strategy, de Boer et al. (2015) suggest several foundational principles for the successful long-term integration of supply chain finance into a company:

- *Synergy Principle*: Rooted in the realm of supply chain relationships, this principle emphasizes mutual benefit. A viable supply chain finance strategy should benefit all stakeholders (illustrated by the Pareto effect). Otherwise, it risks being transient. Strategies founded on one-sided dominance or inequity tend to falter, especially when there's a shift in supply chain dominance or if less influential parties find superior alternatives. A strategy that is mutually advantageous paves the way for a lasting, strategic supply chain partnership.
- *Consumer Focus Principle*: A reflection of overarching supply chain performance, this principle recognizes that satisfying end consumers not only augments revenues for downstream firms but also increases order volume for upstream entities, enhancing the efficiency of the entire supply chain. If strategies lose sight of end consumers, supply chains might be optimized for only a specific subset, leading to potential profit marginalization. Often, the central or more influential entity in the supply chain may need to forgo a portion of their profit to maximize the collective supply chain performance.
- *Top-Down Principle*: An exemplary supply chain finance strategy demands unwavering commitment from senior leadership, ensuring alignment from the highest echelons of the company (e.g., the CEO) right down to operational tiers. Without such top-down orchestration, supply chain finance strategies might inadvertently prioritize fleeting financial gains over enduring supply chain relationships. This principle necessitates collaboration across executive roles in supply chain management, finance, and auxiliary departments (like IT) to achieve unified corporate objectives. Effective integration of traditional supply chain flows—physical, financial, information, and risk—is imperative. However, it's crucial that this directive approach doesn't stifle innovation at the operational levels, given that they often possess nuanced insights into supply chain finance deployment. An ideal top-down principle is rooted in transparent information-sharing and streamlined communication.
- *Measurement Principle*: Essentially operationalizing the top-down principle, the measurement principle ensures that corporate objectives are met. A robust top-down strategy needs corresponding metrics (key performance indicators, KPIs). As Goldratt and Cox (2016) contend, behavior aligns with the metrics imposed. Thus, these measurements should synthesize both supply chain and financial management perspectives to truly serve corporate goals.

> *An optimal supply chain finance strategy demands commitment from the top executive (i.e., CEO), so the strategy can be consistently implemented in line with the company's goal.*

In real-world scenarios, not every enterprise may be equipped to realize all the aforementioned principles. However, even the partial adoption of these guidelines, such as the synergy principle alone, can lay a strong foundation for supply chain finance, enabling businesses to finalize transactions and thereby optimize profits.

2.7 Summary

This chapter provides a comprehensive overview of SCF, examining its multifaceted role in modern business. It delves into the four core flows of supply chains, types of SCF, advantages and disadvantages, the effects of SCF, and the principles involved in measuring and selecting SCF. By providing insights into these key areas, the chapter emphasizes the growing strategic importance of SCF and the necessity of understanding its complexities to maximize its potential benefits.

Key Takeaways:

1. The Four Flows of Supply Chains:
   - Product Flow: Involves the movement of goods from suppliers to customers.
   - Information Flow: Includes the data exchange between different entities in the supply chain.
   - Financial Flow: Denotes the movement of cash and working capital, including transactions, payments, and credits within the supply chain.
   - Risk Flow: Refers to the management and transfer of risks within the supply chain, including financial risks.
2. Supply Chain Finance Types:
   - Characterizes supply chain finance in three dimensions: supply chain finance initiator, supply chain finance source, and supply chain finance timing.
   - Uses the dimensions of supply chain initiator and timing to categorize some SCF mechanisms.
3. Supply Chain Finance Pros and Cons:
   - Pros: Liquidity enhancement, risk mitigation, credit rating protection, cost saving, supply chain efficiency improvement.
   - Cons: Greater coordination complexity and costs, interdependence and joint default risks, hidden accounting transparency risks.
4. Supply Chain Finance Effects:

- Supply chain relationship effect, seesaw effect, Pareto effect, domino effect, halo effect, and ripple effect.
5. Principles of Measuring and Selecting SCF:
   - The revised 6R model: Reviving working capital, Return on investment, Risk mitigation, Responsiveness and R&D, Reliability and relationship, and Responsibility and reputation.
   - Selection principles: Synergy principle, consumer focus principle, top-down principle, and measurement principle.

2.8 Exercises

2.8.1 Practice Questions

1. What are the four flows essential to supply chains?
2. How does SCF potentially aid in risk mitigation within a supply chain?
3. List five benefits and three drawbacks of supply chain finance.
4. Which principle emphasizes commitment from the top executive levels for consistent SCF implementation?
5. How does a supply chain finance scheme improve supply chain transparency?
6. Why might a more dominant firm in a supply chain be inclined to sacrifice some of its profits?
7. Describe the synergy principle's emphasis on a supply chain finance strategy.
8. How does SCF potentially impact a firm's responsiveness to end consumer demand?
9. How can supply chain finance potentially improve social responsibility, especially in developing countries?
10. How does the 6R model aid in understanding a firm's main focus in performance categories?

2.8.2 Case Study

GreenTech Innovations and Supply Chain Finance

Background

GreenTech Innovations (GTI) is a small startup company located in a developing country, focused on producing eco-friendly home appliances. They have been in the market for 2 years and have shown promise with their innovative designs. However, GTI struggles with limited financial resources, which hinders its production capacity and responsiveness to surging consumer demands. GTI's ultimate goal is to expand its product range, invest in R&D to improve product quality, and offer enhanced customer services like extended warranties.

Challenge

GTI's primary challenge is managing its working capital. The company is in a strained financial position, with most of its capital tied up in inventories. GTI's suppliers, due to GTI's limited financial history and its location in a developing country, often demand immediate payments, while GTI's downstream customers, mainly big retailers, usually pay in 60–90 days. This creates a cash flow challenge. Furthermore, GTI also wishes to invest in R&D but finds itself struggling due to these financial constraints.

Supply Chain Finance Solution

Considering the strain on GTI's working capital, a large retailer from a developed country, EcoStores, proposes a supply chain finance (SCF) solution. EcoStores is known for its socially responsible initiatives and aims to support eco-friendly start-ups like GTI. They offer to collaborate with their bank, ensuring that as soon as they confirm receipt of GTI's goods, the bank pays GTI immediately. This reduces GTI's days sales outstanding (DSO) and improves their cash flow. As a return, GTI promises a 0.5% receivables discount to the bank. Meanwhile, EcoStores can delay payment to the bank for 60 days, which doesn't change its payment cycle.

Question

1. What are the benefits of this SCF solution to both GTI and EcoStores?
2. How does this solution impact GTI's focus as per the 6R model?
3. What are the potential risks associated with this SCF solution?
4. How does this case highlight the principles discussed in the chapter, such as the synergy principle or consumer focus principle?

References

Boeing. (2013). *World class supplier quality*. https://787updates.newairplane.com/787-Suppliers/World-Class-Supplier-Quality. Accessed 13 January 2023.

Boeing. (2023). *Supply chain management*. https://www.boeing.com/services/government/supply-chain-logistics.page. Accessed 13 January 2023.

Cai, G. (2019). Supply chain finance introduction. In *Beijing Behavioral Operations Management Conference*, keynote speech.

Camerinelli, E., & Bryant, C. (2014). *Supply chain finance—EBA European market guide version 2.0*. Paris (F): European Banking Association.

de Boer, R., Steeman, M., & van Bergen, M. (2015). *Supply chain finance, its practical relevance and strategic value: The supply chain finance essential knowledge series*. Hogeschool Windesheim.

Deng, S., Gu, C., Cai, G., & Li, Y. (2018). Financing multiple heterogeneous suppliers in assembly systems: Buyer finance vs. Bank finance. *Manufacturing and Service Operations Management, 20*(1), 53–69.

Eaglesham, J. (2020). Supply-chain finance is new risk in crisis. *The Wall Street Journal*. https://www.wsj.com/articles/supply-chain-finance-is-new-risk-in-crisis-11585992601. Accessed 2 April 2021.

References

Goldratt, E. M., & Cox, J. (2016). *The goal: A process of ongoing improvement*. Routledge.

Maersk. (2022). *A.P. Moller—Maersk and IBM to discontinue TradeLens, a blockchain-enabled global trade platform*. https://www.maersk.com/news/articles/2022/11/29/maersk-and-ibm-to-discontinue-tradelens. Accessed 2 April 2023.

Sadlovska, V., & Enslow, B. (2006). *Supply chain finance benchmark report: The new opportunity to improve financial metrics and create a cost-advantaged supply chain*. Aberdeen Group.

Templar, S., Hofmann, E., & Findlay, C. (2016). *Financing the end-to-end supply chain: A reference guide to supply chain finance*. Kogan Page Publishers.

TradeLens. (2022). *A smarter way to engage in trade*. https://www.tradelens.com/technology. Accessed 3 September 2022.

Wikipedia. (2020). *Value chain*. https://en.wikipedia.org/wiki/Value_chain. Accessed 8 October 2020.

Financial Analysis 3

> **Learning Objectives:**
>
> 1. Distinguish the foundational elements within financial statements to evaluate supply chain performance.
> 2. Calculate and interpret essential profit and asset ratios relevant to supply chain analysis.
> 3. Apply the DuPont Analysis to dissect and understand the components of return on invested capital (ROIC).
> 4. Utilize chain aggregated indexes to assess collective financial performance and equity within supply chain transactions.

3.1 Introduction

Is the financial flow critical in supply chain management (SCM)? At first glance, posing such a question might seem perplexing. As Goldratt and Cox (2016) elucidated, the primary objective of a firm is to generate profits. Consequently, financial flow is of paramount importance to any business. For instance, when J.C. Penney, a 118-year-old department store, sought Chapter 11 protection on May 15, 2020, amidst the COVID-19 pandemic, it lacked the necessary funds to clear its looming debts (D'innocenzio, 2020). Similarly, when Sears Holdings declared Chapter 11 bankruptcy on October 15, 2018, its assets amounted to $6.9 billion, whereas its liabilities soared to $11.3 billion (Associated Press, 2018). The company had been grappling with dwindling cash flows over the preceding years. Notably, while both Sears and J.C. Penney grappled with fierce competition from giants like Amazon and other online retailers, it's plausible that mismanagement of financial flows might have been the proverbial straw that broke the camel's back.

So, why pose the aforementioned question? It's intriguing to note that despite its significance, financial flow and cash flow topics often find themselves sidelined in

SCM literature. Many firms, when relying on a slew of KPIs, inadvertently let their internal objectives operate in silos, preventing alignment with the overarching aim of profit maximization. Consider, for instance, the incongruence of a marketing department zealously pursuing revenue augmentation, while a warehouse seeks cost minimization fervently. Such divergent goals, if left unchecked, might not immediately destabilize a firm. However, the risks festering in these disjointed financial flow stages could be grossly underestimated, potentially compromising a company's long-term fiscal health.

Though qualitative evaluation of supply chain finance events serves as a useful gauge of a firm's financial standing, its quantitative counterpart often garners more esteem and finds extensive real-world application. This chapter delves into a repertoire of widely adopted financial analysis tools tailored for dissecting supply chain finance dynamics. Our discourse commences with an exploration of financial statements, leveraging their data to calculate financial ratios and subsequently, delving into the DuPont Analysis.

3.2 Financial Statements

In the U.S., all public companies are required to adhere to the Generally Accepted Accounting Principles (GAAP) when issuing their financial statements (Crail & Main, 2022). In China, firms use the Chinese Accounting Standards (CAS), which are based on two main standards: Accounting Standards for Business Enterprises (ASBEs) and Accounting Standards for Small Business Enterprises (ASSBEs) (China Briefing, 2022). European listed companies follow the International Financial Reporting Standards (IFRS) (European Commission, 2023). However, the core principles across these standards are largely consistent.

Below, we will use financial statements from the Boeing Company as a reference to demonstrate the components of the balance sheet, income statement, and cash flow statement.[1]

3.2.1 Balance Sheet

A *balance sheet* encompasses three primary categories: Assets, liabilities, and equity. The foundational equation that represents the relationship between these categories in accounting is:

$$\text{Assets} = \text{Liabilities} + \text{Equity}$$

---

[1] The data is from the 2019 Boeing Financial Statements (Boeing, 2022). Note that financial statements from different sources may vary slightly. While accounting is not the primary focus of this book, readers seeking a more detailed description of accounting rules can refer to an accounting textbook. However, we will highlight several concepts at the intersection of operations and finance that are highly relevant to our subsequent discussions.

3.2 Financial Statements

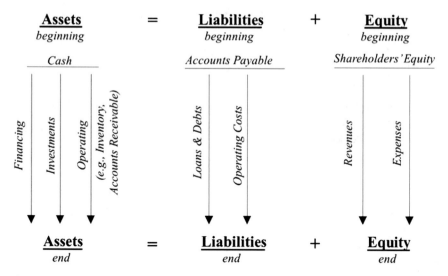

Fig. 3.1 Relationship of assets, liabilities, and equity (*Source* Adapted from Higgins et al., 2018)

This relationship between assets, liabilities, and equity, both at the start and conclusion of an accounting period, is depicted in Fig. 3.1, offering an overview of the balance sheet's structure.

As delineated in Fig. 3.1, *assets* encompass items like cash, investments, financing extended to customers or even suppliers, accounts receivable (from sales of products/services to customers), inventories, among others. As illustrated in Table 3.1, assets, from an accounting perspective, also comprise net goodwill, net acquired intangible assets, deferred income taxes, and more. Conversely, liabilities consist of debts (both short-term and long-term), accounts payable, billings, deferred income taxes, accrued retiree health care, net accrued pension plan liability, and so forth. Equity encapsulates elements such as shareholders' equity, additional paid-in capital, retained earnings, accumulated other comprehensive losses, among others.

3.2.2 Income Statement

The *income statement* provides an overview of a firm's revenue, costs, expenses, and earnings over a specific period (refer to Table 3.2). As one of the three primary financial statements, it offers valuable insights into a firm's operational efficiency by examining its revenue and costs, thus reflecting the effectiveness of its management. When contrasted with income statements from other companies, it can also indicate whether a firm is outperforming or underperforming in comparison to industry peers or those in different sectors.

Table 3.1 The Boeing Company and subsidiaries 2019 consolidated statements of financial position (Balance Sheet, *Source* Boeing.com)

(Dollars in millions, except per share data)

December 31	2019	2018
Assets		
Cash and cash equivalents	$9485	$7637
Short-term and other investments	545	927
Accounts receivable, net	3266	3879
Unbilled receivables, net	9043	10,025
Current portion of customer financing, net	162	460
Inventories	76,622	62,567
Other current assets	3106	2335
Total current assets	102,229	87,830
Customer financing, net	2136	2418
Property, plant and equipment, net	12,502	12,645
Goodwill	8060	7840
Acquired intangible assets, net	3338	3429
Deferred income taxes	683	284
Investments	1092	1087
Other assets, net of accumulated amortization of $580 and $503	3585	1826
Total assets	$133,625	$117,359
Liabilities and equity		
Accounts payable	$15,553	$12,916
Accrued liabilities	22,868	14,808
Advances and progress billings	51,551	50,676
Short-term debt and current portion of long-term debt	7340	3190
Total current liabilities	97,312	81,590
Deferred income taxes	413	1736
Accrued retiree health care	4540	4584
Accrued pension plan liability, net	16,276	15,323
Other long-term liabilities	3422	3059
Long-term debt	19,962	10,657
Shareholders' equity:		
Common stock, par value $5.00–1,200,000,000 shares authorized:		
1,012,261,159 shares issued	5061	5061
Additional paid-in capital	6745	6768
Treasury stock, at cost	−54,914	−52,348
Retained earnings	50,644	55,941

(continued)

3.2 Financial Statements

Table 3.1 (continued)

(Dollars in millions, except per share data)		
December 31	2019	2018
Accumulated other comprehensive loss	−16,153	−15,083
Total shareholders' equity	−8617	339
Noncontrolling interests	317	71
Total equity	−8300	410
Total liabilities and equity	$133,625	$117,359

Table 3.2 The Boeing Company and subsidiaries 2019 consolidated statements of operations (Income Statement, *Source* Boeing.com)

(Dollars in millions, except per share data)		
Years ended December 31	2019	2018
Sales of products	$66,094	$90,229
Sales of services	10,465	10,898
Total revenues	76,559	101,127
Cost of products	−62,877	−72,922
Cost of services	−9154	−8499
Boeing Capital interest expense	−62	−69
Total costs and expenses	−72,093	−81,490
(Total revenue + Total cost and expense)	4466	19,637
(Loss)/income from operating investments, net	−4	111
General and administrative expense	−3909	−4567
Research and development expense, net	−3219	−3269
Gain on dispositions, net	691	75
(Loss)/earnings from operations	−1975	11,987
Other income, net	438	92
Interest and debt expense	−722	−475
(Loss)/earnings before income taxes	−2259	11,604
Income tax benefit/(expense)	1623	−1144
Net (loss)/earnings	($636)	$10,460
Basic (loss)/earnings per share	($1.12)	$18.05
Diluted (loss)/earnings per share	($1.12)	$17.85

Note These data are taken directly from Boeing's Financial Statements

An income statement encompasses the sales of products and services, their associated costs, and capital interest expenses. It also presents information regarding income/loss from operating investments, general and administrative expenses, R&D expenses, other income and expenses, and taxes.

Mathematically, based on Table 3.2, in 2019:

- The (Loss)/earnings from operations is calculated as:

$$\$4466M - \$4M - \$3909M - \$3219M + \$691M = -\$1975M$$

- The (Loss)/earnings before income taxes is:

$$-\$1975M + \$438M - \$722M = -\$2259M$$

The net income, or the bottom line (which indicates the firm's profitability), is determined as follows:

$$\text{Net Income} = (\text{Revenue} + \text{Gains}) - (\text{Expenses} + \text{Losses})$$
$$= -\$2259M + \$1623M = -\$636M$$

3.2.3 Cash Flow Statement

The *cash flow statement* chronicles the movement of a firm's cash and cash equivalents (CCE). It categorizes the CCE into three main activities: operating, investing, and financing. This statement illustrates how a firm manages its cash position, generates funds to cover its operating expenses, and meets its debt obligations. Consequently, the cash flow statement can provide insights into a firm's financial stability (considering liquidity, solvency, and financial flexibility) and inform adjustments to its operations, investment, and financing strategies.

As depicted in Table 3.3:

- The net cash (used)/provided by operating activities is −$2446M, which aggregates all numbers in the preceding section, starting from net (loss)/earnings of −$636M down to "other" which amounts to $196M.
- The net cash used by investing activities stands at −$1530M, while the net cash provided/(used) by financing activities totals $5739M. Both are computed in a similar aggregation method.
- The net increase/(decrease) in cash and cash equivalents, including restricted ones, is $1758M = -\$2446M - \$1530M + \$5739M - \$5M$. This value is the cumulative result of the three aforementioned net cash activities, coupled with the effect of exchange rate changes on cash and cash equivalents, which is −$5M.

3.2 Financial Statements

Table 3.3 The Boeing Company and subsidiaries consolidated statements of cash flows (Cash Flow Statement, *Source* Boeing.com)

(Dollars in millions)		
Years ended December 31	2019	2018
Cash flows – operating activities		
Net (loss)/earnings	($636)	$10,460
Adjustments to reconcile net earnings to net cash provided by operating activities:		
Non-cash items –		
Share-based plans expense	212	202
Depreciation and amortization	2271	2114
Investment/asset impairment charges, net	443	93
Customer financing valuation adjustments	250	−3
Gain on dispositions, net	−691	−75
Other charges and credits, net	334	247
Changes in assets and liabilities –		
Accounts receivable	603	−795
Unbilled receivables	982	−1826
Advances and progress billings	737	2636
Inventories	−12,391	568
Other current assets	−682	98
Accounts payable	1600	2
Accrued liabilities	7781	1117
Income taxes receivable, payable and deferred	−2476	−180
Other long-term liabilities	−621	87
Pension and other postretirement plans	−777	−153
Customer financing, net	419	120
Other	196	610
Net cash (used)/provided by operating activities	−2446	15,322
Cash flows – investing activities:		
Property, plant and equipment additions	−1834	−1722
Property, plant and equipment reductions	334	120
Acquisitions, net of cash acquired	−455	−3230
Proceeds from dispositions	464	
Contributions to investments	−1658	−2607
Proceeds from investments	1759	2898
Purchase of distribution rights	−127	−69
Other	−13	−11
Net cash used by investing activities	−1530	−4621
Cash flows – financing activities:		
New borrowings	25,389	8548
Debt repayments	−12,171	−7183

(continued)

Table 3.3 (continued)

(Dollars in millions)		
Years ended December 31	2019	2018
Contributions from noncontrolling interests	7	35
Stock options exercised	58	81
Employee taxes on certain share-based payment arrangements	−248	−257
Common shares repurchased	−2651	−9000
Dividends paid	−4630	−3946
Other	−15	
Net cash provided/(used) by financing activities	5739	−11,722
Effect of exchange rate changes on cash and cash equivalents	−5	−53
Net increase/(decrease) in cash & cash equivalents, including restricted	1758	−1074
Cash & cash equivalents, including restricted, at beginning of year	7813	8887
Cash & cash equivalents, including restricted, at end of year	9571	7813
Less restricted cash & cash equivalents, included in Investments	86	176
Cash and cash equivalents at end of year	$9485	$7637

- The ending balance of cash and cash equivalents for the year, $9485M, is derived from adding the net increase/(decrease) in cash and cash equivalents, including restricted ones ($1758M), to the starting balance of cash and cash equivalents, which includes restricted ones ($7813M), and then subtracting restricted cash and cash equivalents that are accounted for in investments (−$86M).

3.3 Profit and Asset Ratios

While the aforementioned financial statements offer an overview of a firm's financial activities, a deeper and more comprehensive analysis is necessary to fully grasp the firm's financial health and operational efficiency. This subsection delves into commonly used financial ratios to assess a firm's performance.

3.3.1 Profit Margin

Profit margin is a fundamental indicator of profitability. It can be broadly classified into two types: gross profit margin and net profit margin. While the *gross profit margin* calculates the difference between revenues and the cost of goods sold (COGS), the *net profit margin* determines the net earnings (as seen in the income statement) after accounting for taxes, administrative expenses, and all other deductions, with both margins expressed as a percentage of revenue.

3.3 Profit and Asset Ratios

Taking 2019 as an example, Boeing reported a total revenue of $76,559M and its aggregate costs and expenses amounted to $72,093M. Hence, its gross profit can be computed as:

$$\$76,559M - \$72,093M = \$4466M$$

Subsequently, its gross profit margin can be derived as:

$$\text{Gross Profit Margin} = \frac{\text{Gross Profit}}{\text{Revenue}} = \frac{\$4466M}{\$76,559M} = 5.833\%$$

Net profit can also be interchangeably referred to as net income or net earnings. In 2019, Boeing's net earnings were -$636M, which gives its net profit margin as:

$$\text{Net Profit Margin} = \frac{\text{Net Profit}}{\text{Revenue}} = \frac{-\$636M}{\$76,559M} = -0.831\%$$

Both gross and net profit margins serve as pivotal tools in evaluating a company's fiscal health. The profit margin is quintessential for operations as it not only mirrors the company's pricing strategy but also its competence in managing operating expenses. All other things being equal, decreasing operational expenses generally contributes to an augmented net profit margin. It's imperative to recognize that while a steep selling price can boost the profit margin, it may concurrently suppress demand and revenue, thereby potentially impairing overall net profit.

It's pivotal to note that the pinnacle of revenue maximization does not typically coincide with that of profit maximization, largely owing to the significant role of costs in the profit equation. Generally, achieving a positive gross profit margin is comparatively straightforward since companies often set prices that exceed costs. However, it's feasible for a company's net profit margin to plunge into the negative territory, especially if it's grossly mismanaged (leading to escalated operational costs) and simultaneously grapples with intense competition and market anomalies like the COVID-19 pandemic or widespread product recalls. Pertaining to Boeing, its 2019 gross profit margin could not sufficiently offset its elevated administrative and other expenses, culminating in a negative net profit margin.

3.3.2 Return on Equity

For investors and executives, the *return on equity* (ROE) serves as a pivotal metric that gauges a firm's profitability in relation to its equity. Essentially, ROE evaluates a company's efficiency in leveraging its equity to generate profits.

$$\text{ROE} = \frac{\text{Net Profit}}{\text{Average Equity}}$$

Furthermore, ROE can also be interpreted as a return on assets minus liabilities. This perspective is derived from the fact that equity is the difference between total assets and total liabilities. An ROE value ranging between 15–20% is typically deemed commendable (Wikipedia, 2019). However, in a bid to bolster sustainability and pave the way for future growth, companies might sometimes curtail dividend payments to shareholders.

In most scenarios, a higher positive ROE value denotes superior profitability concerning the equity, making it more desirable. Nevertheless, there are exceptions. For instance, considering Boeing's 2019 financials, the calculation is as follows:

$$\text{ROE} = \frac{-\$636M}{-\$3945M} = 16.12\%$$

While this ROE is positive, it epitomizes a precarious situation. The equity has veered into negative terrain, as has the net profit. In such adverse scenarios, a soaring ROE underscores deteriorating company performance. Essentially, the company hemorrhages more funds, and in the unfortunate event of bankruptcy, shareholders would be left with no returns. Consequently, when equity flips negatively, the ROE metric can become misleading.

3.3.3 Return on Capital Employed

Return on capital employed (ROCE) serves as a metric to gauge both profitability and the efficiency of a firm in deploying its capital. It is mathematically expressed as (Hayes, 2023):

$$\text{ROCE} = \frac{\text{EBIT}}{\text{Capital Employed}}$$

where:

- EBIT stands for earnings before interest and taxes, also recognized as income or earnings prior to accounting for interest and taxes. This figure is typically found on the income statement.
- "Capital Employed" is computed as the difference between total assets and current liabilities.

Capital employed typically alludes to the collective capital, constituted by the sum of shareholders' equity and debt liabilities, that a firm leverages to accrue profits. The provided equation adopts a streamlined approach, representing capital employed as total assets minus current liabilities. It's worth noting that, akin to other financial indices, instead of resorting to the capital employed at a singular point in time, one could opt to compute ROCE based on the average capital employed over a period.

3.3 Profit and Asset Ratios

For Boeing in 2019, the ROCE is articulated as:

$$\text{ROCE} = \frac{-\$1913M}{\$1404M} = -136.25\%$$

To encapsulate, in 2019, Boeing's operations were not adept in efficiently generating returns on the capital employed.

3.3.4 Return on Assets and Return on Net Assets

Return on assets (ROA) and *return on net assets* (RONA) serve as indicators to determine the efficiency of a company in leveraging its assets (Yhumita, 2022).

The formula for ROA is:

$$\text{ROA} = \frac{\text{Net Profit}}{\text{Total Assets}}$$

For Boeing in 2019:

$$\text{ROA} = \frac{-\$636M}{\$133,625M} = -0.476\%$$

On the other hand, RONA is calculated using the following formula:

$$\text{RONA} = \frac{\text{Net Profit}}{\text{Net Assets}} = \frac{\text{Net Profit}}{\text{Fixed Assets} + \text{Net Working Capital}}$$

"Net profit," synonymous with net income, represents the net earnings after tax. A substantial ROA or RONA ratio is indicative of superior financial performance, reflecting the company's capability to generate significant returns from its assets.

3.3.5 Return on Invested Capital

Return on invested capital (ROIC) is a tool firms utilize to evaluate their growth potential (Damodaran, 2007).

$$\text{ROIC} = \frac{\text{NOPAT}}{\text{Invested Capital}} = \frac{\text{NOPBT} \times (1 - \text{Tax Rate})}{\text{Invested Capital}}$$

Here, NOPAT stands for *net operating profit after tax* NOPAT can also be referred to as *net operating profit less adjusted taxes* (NOPLAT). NOPBT, or *net operating profit before tax*, aligns with the earnings from operations or operating income (before taxes) as listed in the income statement. Therefore, NOPAT and NOPBT offer insights into the performance of a company's operations. Invested capital (IC) represents the capital utilized to run a business. It encompasses funds from both debtholders and shareholders, enabling business expansion and the exploration of new business avenues.

However, there isn't a standardized method for computing invested capital. Some researchers, given the ease of calculation, use capital employed (total assets minus current liabilities) as an approximation of invested capital. Some might consider the average long-term debt combined with common and preferred shares. Others might prefer the sum of average interest-bearing debt and equity. Yet another approach considers average total assets after subtracting excess cash and non-interest-bearing current liabilities (like accounts payable). In essence, while capital employed encompasses all capital minus short-term liabilities, invested capital focuses on active capital after accounting for non-active assets. Still, due to various computation methods, capital employed might sometimes be smaller than invested capital, as evidenced by companies like Boeing and Walmart in 2019 (as illustrated in Table 3.4). Given these variations, the final ROIC value might differ depending on how it's computed. It's crucial, for consistency, to maintain uniform equations throughout computations. Generally, an optimal ROIC should be at least two percent. It's worth noting that ROIC can also evaluate individual investments (refer to Chapter 7.5 Case Study: Impact of Extended Payment Terms).

For Boeing in 2019:

$$\text{ROIC} = \frac{-\$1241M}{\$35,543M} = -3.492\%$$

This negative value underscores Boeing's underwhelming performance in 2019 from an ROIC standpoint.

As per Walmart Inc.'s 2020 Annual Report (Walmart, 2022), "average invested capital" comprises the average of beginning and ending total assets, combined with average accumulated depreciation and average amortization, after subtracting average accounts payable and average accrued liabilities for that period. The following values of NOPAT and invested capital are adapted from Walmart's 2020 Annual Report (refer to the appendix in Chapter 3.8):[2]

$$\text{ROIC} = \frac{\$15,201M}{\$256,383M} = 5.929\%$$

This value suggests Walmart's commendable performance in operations, investments, and financing in that year.

---

[2] The final values and computational approaches regarding Walmart's invested capital, as presented on financial information websites like Investopedia.com, gurufocus.com, finbox.com, and stock-analysis-on.net, differ from those in Walmart's official 2020 annual report. This discrepancy suggests that ROIC values can be subject to manipulation. It also underscores the importance of maintaining consistency in the approach used for all firms and across different periods when making comparisons.

3.3 Profit and Asset Ratios

Table 3.4 Summary of select financial concepts and examples (money in millions for non-ratios, Year 2019)[3]

Financial Term	Definition	Boeing	Airbus	Walmart
Gross Profit	Revenue − cost of goods sold	$4466	€ 11,766	$129,104
Operating Income	Earnings from operations (before interest and taxes)	($1975)	€ 1036	$20,568
EBIT	Earnings before interest and taxes	($1913)	€ 1339	$20,568
EBITDA	Earnings before interest, taxes, depreciation, and amortization	$358	€ 4266	$31,555
NOPAT	Net operating profit after taxes	($1241)	€ 756	$15,201
Net Profit	Net earnings/income after interest and taxes	($636)	(€ 1362)	$14,881
Revenue	Sales of products and services	$76,559	€ 70,478	$523,964
Average Equity	Average equity of this year and the past year	($3945)	€ 5990	$80,593
Average Invested Capital	Cost of investment or cost of capital	$35,543	€ 17,392	$256,383
Capital Employed	Total assets − current liabilities	$1404	€ 52,035	$158,705
Total Assets		$133,625	€ 114,409	$236,495
Gross Profit Margin	Gross Profit/Revenue	5.83%	16.69%	24.64%
Profit Margin	Net Profit/Revenue	−0.83%	−1.93%	2.84%
ROE	Net Profit/(Average) Equity	16.12%	−22.74%	18.46%
ROCE	EBIT/Capital Employed	−136.25%	2.57%	12.96%
ROA	Net Profit/Total Assets	−0.48°%	−1.19%	6.29%
ROIC	NOPAT/Invested Capital	−3.49%	4.35%	5.93%

(continued)

---

[3] The data were collected from company annual reports and associated financial analysis websites (Airbus, 2022; Boeing, 2022; Walmart, 2022). We used "total assets" as a proxy for "average assets" when calculating the asset turnover ratio. Due to discrepancies in the financial statements obtained, these data are for demonstration purposes only.

Table 3.4 (continued)

Financial Term	Definition	Boeing	Airbus	Walmart
WACC	Weighted Average Cost of Capital	8.0%	11.6%	4.2%
EVA	(ROIC-WACC) × Invested Capital	($4084.44)	(€ 1261.17)	$4432.91
Asset Turnover Ratio	Total Revenue/Average Assets	0.57	0.62	2.22

3.3.6 Economic Value Added

The relationship between operations and finance is vital for measuring the performance of a firm's supply chain management. One method to assess this is through *economic value added* (EVA) which evaluates the firm in terms of ROIC and the cost of capital (Higgins et al., 2018).

$$EVA = NOPAT - WACC \times Invested\,Capital$$
$$= (ROIC - WACC) \times Invested\,Capital$$

Here, WACC stands for the *weighted average cost of capital*. The approach to computing invested capital is analogous to what was discussed under ROIC.

A firm creates value when its ROIC exceeds its cost of capital. The cost of capital for a firm is typically computed based on WACC, which represents the average anticipated rate that a firm expects to pay to all its security holders. These security holders may possess entities or instruments such as straight debt, convertible debt, exchangeable debt, common stock, preferred stock, executive stock options, warrants, pension liabilities, and governmental subsidies that finance the firm's assets.

In Boeing's case, the WACC in 2019 was estimated to be 8% by Finbox.com. With a ROIC of −3.49% and an average invested capital of $35,543M, its EVA for 2019 is calculated as follows:

$$EVA = (-0.03492 - 0.08) \times \$35,543M = -\$4084M$$

By contrast, Walmart's EVA for 2019 is calculated as (refer also to Table 3.4):

$$EVA = (0.05929 - 0.042) \times \$256,383M = \$4432M$$

A positive EVA is essential. Without it, a specific investment or the company as a whole is not considered profitable after accounting for its capital costs.

EVA provides insights into whether a particular investment is judicious, especially in the realm of supply chain financing. It reveals how and where a firm generates wealth, taking into account assets, expenses, and debts in the investment decision-making process. However, EVA is most apt for companies that have substantial tangible assets. Employing EVA to measure companies rich in intangible assets, such as those in the technology sector, can be challenging.

3.3.7 Asset Turnover Ratio

The *asset turnover ratio*, also known as asset turnover, indicates how efficiently a company can utilize its assets to produce revenue.

$$\text{Asset Turnover Ratio} = \frac{\text{Total Revenue}}{\text{Average Assets}}$$

For Boeing in 2019:

$$\text{Asset Turnover Ratio} = \frac{\$76,559M}{\$133,625M} = 0.573$$

It's evident that Boeing's sales saw a significant downturn in 2019 while its inventory increased, suggesting inefficiency in asset utilization. The asset turnover ratio, however, fluctuates across industries. As depicted in Table 3.4, Airbus surpassed Boeing in performance for 2019, though both substantially trailed behind Walmart.

The subsequent section uses Table 3.4 to recapitulate the financial concepts discussed in this segment, furnishing computational examples for Boeing, Airbus, and Walmart based on their 2020 Annual Reports and supplementary online resources detailing their 2019 performances. It's worth noting the primary distinction between operating income and EBIT: EBIT encompasses non-operating income, other incomes, and non-operating expenses. Furthermore, EBITDA is the sum of EBIT and depreciation and amortization. Further specifics are provided in Table 3.4.

3.4 The DuPont Analysis

The *DuPont Analysis* was first introduced by the DuPont Company in the 1920s to gauge the impact of different drivers on certain financial ratios, such as ROE and ROIC. We further delve into its mechanics through the following ROE DuPont Model, ROA DuPont Model, and ROIC DuPont Model.

3.4.1 The ROE DuPont Model

To gain a deeper insight into the various drivers of ROE, DuPont explosives salesman Donaldson Brown devised the following formula for an internal efficiency report in 1912 (Wikipedia, 2023):

$$\text{ROE} = \text{Profit Margin} \times \text{Asset Turnover} \times \text{Equity Multiplier}$$

The net profit margin gauges the firm's operating efficiency, while asset turnover reflects the efficiency with which assets are utilized. The equity multiplier, defined as assets divided by equity, is also known as financial leverage. In this context, the traditional ROE equation can be broken down as:

$$\text{ROE} = \frac{\text{Net Profit}}{\text{Average Equity}} = \frac{\text{Net Profit}}{\text{Revenue}} \times \frac{\text{Revenue}}{\text{Average Assets}} \times \frac{\text{Average Assets}}{\text{Average Equity}}$$

This equation can be visually represented in the following ROE tree (Fig. 3.2).

The decomposition of the ROE equation provides insights into the core performance factors of a firm. If the primary contribution is from the profit margin, it signals a positive aspect of the company's operations and supply chain management. A predominant contribution from the asset turnover indicates the company's proficiency in employing its assets to generate sales. However, a leading contribution from the equity multiplier suggests potential over-leverage of the company's assets, representing a riskier outlook for the company and its stock performance.

In Walmart's 2020 performance, we have:

$$\text{ROE} = \text{Profit Margin} \times \text{Asset Turnover} \times \text{Equity Multiplier}$$
$$= 2.84\% \times 2.22 \times 2.93 = 18.47\%$$

This demonstrates that Walmart's ROE was significantly influenced by both the asset turnover and equity multiplier. Although the profit margin seems low, it stands higher than many major retailers in the same industry.

As illustrated in the aforementioned ROE tree, the final ROE value can be derived from the four components on the left: net profit, sales, average assets, and

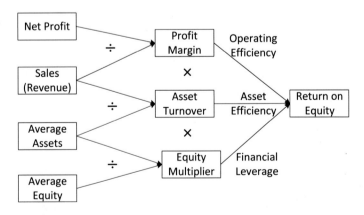

Fig. 3.2 The ROE tree

3.4 The DuPont Analysis

average equity. Considering the additional financial terms in financial statements, we can further break down the equation as:

$$\text{ROE} = \frac{\text{Net Profit}}{\text{Pretax Income}} \times \frac{\text{Pretax Income}}{\text{EBIT}} \times \frac{\text{EBIT}}{\text{Revenue}} \times \frac{\text{Revenue}}{\text{Average Assets}} \times \frac{\text{Average Assets}}{\text{Average Equity}}$$

This expanded ROE model is commonly referred to as the DuPont Analysis or DuPont Model. This can be further depicted as the DuPont Analysis tree (Fig. 3.3).

In this extended ROE tree, compared to the prior equation, the profit margin item is further broken down into the following three components:

$\frac{\text{Net Profit}}{\text{Pretax Income}}$: Represents the company's after-tax net profit, which measures the company's tax burden. A higher value indicates a lower tax burden.

$\frac{\text{Pretax Income}}{\text{EBIT}}$: Gauges the company's interest obligation. The value equals one if the company is debt-free. A higher ratio signals a significant financial obligation.

$\frac{\text{EBIT}}{\text{Revenue}}$: Represents the company's EBIT margin. A higher ratio is favored as it suggests greater business efficiency and profitablility.

The DuPont Analysis's breakdown of ROE allows us to pinpoint a company's strengths and weaknesses across essential financial performance metrics. Still, this analysis heavily leans on accounting data, which can be manipulated. To determine whether a ratio is high or low, comparisons should be made using industry data, rather than juxtaposing companies from diverse sectors. The DuPont Analysis might not be effective for industries like investment banking, where certain elements don't hold as much weight.

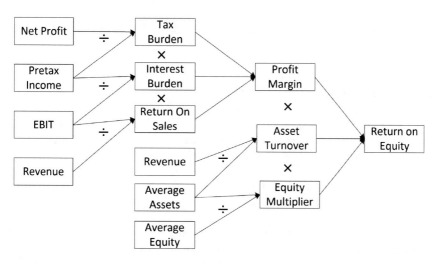

Fig. 3.3 The ROE DuPont Analysis tree

The impact of supply chain finance can be discerned in all these broken-down factors of ROE. Depending on a firm's role within a specific supply chain finance event, the impact might vary, but typically it's positive, owing to the Pareto effect:

- The profit margins can benefit from increased supply chain transactions.
- The asset turnover ratio can see considerable improvement with a higher revenue from more transactions within a specified period.
- The equity multiplier might decrease since supply chain finance can potentially replace some direct bank financing or at least mitigate a firm's loan borrowing burden, reducing financial risks.

For a company to accurately gauge the influence of supply chain finance on its performance, it should compare ROE values before and after its implementation, while being selective about the specific supply chain finance mechanisms employed.

3.4.2 The ROA DuPont Model

Using the same logic as in the DuPont Analysis for ROE, we can execute a similar decomposition analysis for other financial ratios, such as ROA and ROIC. For private companies that lack equity information, ROA can be broken down as follows:

$$ROA = \frac{\text{Net Profit}}{\text{Total Assets}} = \frac{\text{Net Profit}}{\text{Revenue}} \times \frac{\text{Revenue}}{\text{Total Assets}}$$
$$= \text{Profit Margin} \times \text{Asset Turnover}$$

Compared to the ROE decomposition, it's evident that ROA is not influenced by the equity multiplier.

3.4.3 The ROIC DuPont Model

While ROE focuses on the return on stock investment, ROIC emphasizes the return on capital investment. Following the ROIC definition, we can further decompose the equation into two primary components (Oikarainen, 2022):

$$ROIC = \frac{\text{NOPAT}}{\text{Invested Capital}} = \frac{\text{NOPAT}}{\text{Revenue}} \times \frac{\text{Revenue}}{\text{Invested Capital}}$$

All the values for the elements mentioned above can be extracted from a firm's financial statement. The first component, *NOPAT/Revenue*, indicates the after-tax profit margin per item sold. This represents operational efficiency (cost-saving) and the appeal of the products (brand recognition) the company offers to the market (optimal pricing). The second component, *Revenue/Invested Capital*, gauges the

3.4 The DuPont Analysis

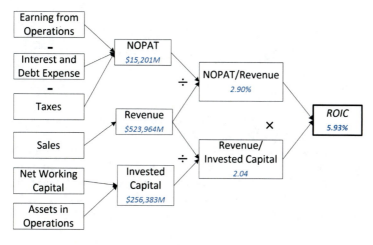

Fig. 3.4 A ROIC tree based on Walmart data

capital turnover and is closely associated with supply chain efficiency. A higher capital turnover usually corresponds to shorter lead times in production, shipping, and stocking and efficiency in every operation and supply chain process.

Based on Walmart's 2019 data (Walmart, 2022), the corresponding ROIC tree can be illustrated in Fig. 3.4 (refer to the middle and right sections). Note that this ROIC value (i.e., 5.93%) is considered highly competitive, given that Walmart's average equity in 2019 was only \$80,593M, less than a third of its invested capital.

Indeed, we can further decompose the ROIC equation by considering the effective cash tax rate:

$$\text{ROIC} = \frac{\text{NOPAT}}{\text{Invested Capital}} = \frac{\text{NOPAT}}{\text{Revenue}} \times \frac{\text{Revenue}}{\text{Invested Capital}}$$
$$= \frac{\text{NOPBT}}{\text{Revenue}} \times \text{Effective Cash Tax Rate} \times \frac{\text{Revenue}}{\text{Invested Capital}}$$

NOPAT stands for net operating profit after taxes, and NOPBT represents net operating profit before taxes. Hence,

$$\text{Effective Cash Tax Rate} = \text{NOPAT}/\text{NOPBT}$$

Because NOPAT equals revenue minus costs and tax, and since revenue can be expressed as the flow rate times price, ROIC can also be broken down as:

$$\text{ROIC} = \left(1 - \frac{\text{Fixed Costs}}{\text{Flow Rate} \times \text{Price}} - \frac{\text{Variable Costs}}{\text{Price}} - \text{Tax Rate}\right)$$
$$\times \frac{\text{Revenue}}{\text{Invested Capital}}$$

Intuitively, lower variable costs and tax rates contribute to a higher ROIC, explaining the common practices of outsourcing and seeking tax havens. If a firm's revenue increases with the help of supply chain finance, its ROIC can also rise. The advantage of supply chain finance lies in the fact that more transactions can be completed successfully with the involvement of supply chain firms in financing.

From another angle, ROIC can elucidate the operational efficiency of an individual investment. For this, we introduce an alternate method to break down invested capital:

$$\text{Invested Capital} = \text{Net Working Capital Need for Operations}$$
$$+ \text{Fixed Assets Net of Accumulated Depreciation}$$
$$+ \text{Other Assets Needed for Operations}$$

The net working capital can be computed by adding accounts receivable and inventory and then subtracting accounts payable associated with this specific investment. Typically, an individual investment contributes to the depreciation of fixed assets, which can be estimated based on this investment's proportion to all investments. Other assets needed for operations includes intangible assets (patents, trademarks, goodwill), long-term investments, and other assets that are essential for running the business but do not fall under working capital or fixed assets.

In the example provided below (refer to Table 3.5), we have, for the sake of simplicity, assumed the NOPAT, inventory, and operational assets to be consistent across three different businesses. As illustrated in Table 3.5, variations in the values of accounts receivable and accounts payable markedly influence the final ROIC. A larger accounts receivable value suggests more sales stemming from the invested capital, while a greater accounts payable value indicates the firm utilizes the capital of its upstream partners for investments. Although this approach may reduce the firm's available capital for future investments in the same business, if a dominant company can significantly delay its payments to upstream entities, its invested capital will be minimal, leading to a high ROIC. However, this comes at the cost of the upstream partners.

The application of the aforementioned ROIC decomposition for each individual business project or transaction can aid in assessing the profitability of a specific deal. It also underscores the significance of managing net working capital in supply chain finance. Computing the invested capital is less contentious at this level than at the overarching firm level because the capital considered is solely related to the specific project or transaction. This will be further illustrated in the case study titled "The Enlightened Consignment Choice" in Chapter 5.8.

3.5 Chain Aggregated Indexes

Table 3.5 Examples of ROIC DuPont Analysis

Firm A	Business 1	Business 2	Business 3
NOPAT	688	688	688
Accounts Receivable	2000	3000	4000
Inventory	2565	2565	2565
Accounts Payable	3213	3213	2356
Net Working Capital	1352	2352	4209
Assets in Operations	1321	1321	1321
Invested Capital	2673	3673	5530
ROIC	26%	19%	12%

3.5 Chain Aggregated Indexes

Thus far, we have detailed a range of financial ratios. However, they all solely gauge the performance of individual firms. When implementing a supply chain finance scheme, multiple firms, including banks, are typically involved. Thus, to gauge the total impact of supply chain finance across all these entities, we might employ the following *chain aggregated indexes* (CAIs).[4]

3.5.1 Performance Indexes

A performance index quantifies the overall efficacy of a supply chain. Consider ROIC as an example. At both the firm and individual investment levels, firms are driven to maximize their respective returns in a supply chain finance transaction. This motivation stems from their exposure to both vertical and horizontal competition within the supply chain, despite their unified goal to complete the transaction. Acknowledging the relative dominance of each firm in the supply chain, and under the assumption that no firm would engage in a deal with a negative ROIC, the optimal strategy for enhancing the overall performance of the supply chain in a given transaction is to maximize the following weighted geometric mean:

$$\text{C.ROIC}^{\text{Geometric}} = \left(\prod_{i=1}^{n} \text{ROIC}_i^{\theta_i} \right)^{1/\sum_i^n \theta_i}$$

This formula is analogous to the Nash bargaining product for two parties but extends to include all participants (e.g., buyer, seller, bank, 3PL, and insurer) involved in the supply chain finance event. The variable θ_i represents a firm's

---

[4] It's worth noting that calculating the chain aggregated indexes can be challenging for a firm, given that operational-level accounting and financial data from other firms might be inaccessible. Furthermore, even firm-level financial information isn't usually available in real-time. As a result, the determination of these chain aggregated indexes is more likely to be ex-post than ex-ante.

"negotiation power" in the transaction and denotes a "fair" proportion of a firm's stake in the supply chain finance game relative to their dominance. Given that $\sum_i^n \theta_i = n$, where n is the total number of involved firms, the specific values of θ_i can influence discussions on supply chain finance parameters such as interest rates, premiums, and loan limits. If all firms have equivalent dominance, θ_i can be set to 1; otherwise, θ_i may be either above or below 1.

Similar analyses can be applied to ROE, ROA, RONA, and EVA at the firm level, leading to the following chain aggregated indexes:

$$\text{C.ROE}^{\text{Geometric}} = \left(\prod_{i=1}^{n} \text{ROE}_i^{\theta_i} \right)^{1/\sum_i^n \theta_i}$$

$$\text{C.ROA}^{\text{Geometric}} = \left(\prod_{i=1}^{n} \text{ROA}_i^{\theta_i} \right)^{1/\sum_i^n \theta_i}$$

$$\text{C.RONA}^{\text{Geometric}} = \left(\prod_{i=1}^{n} \text{RONA}_i^{\theta_i} \right)^{1/\sum_i^n \theta_i}$$

$$\text{C.EVA}^{\text{Geometric}} = \left(\prod_{i=1}^{n} \text{EVA}_i^{\theta_i} \right)^{1/\sum_i^n \theta_i}$$

Regardless of whether supply chain entities strive to maximize these chain aggregated indexes or if the profit distribution is deemed equitable, a loftier chain aggregated index is typically indicative of both the Pareto effect and the halo effect in supply chain finance. Often, when profit distribution is viewed as "fairer" (with all else being equal), the resulting chain aggregated indexes are likely higher. This means that the relationship among the parties involved in the supply chain becomes more sustainable. Consequently, these chain aggregated indexes can also influence firms' choice of supply chain schemes.

> A higher chain aggregated index is more likely to lead to the Pareto effect and the halo effect in supply chain finance, making the relationship among the involved parties in the supply chain more sustainable.

While the aforementioned chain aggregated indexes capture the combined growth rate of all firms in a supply chain transaction, an extreme value can significantly skew the final result. For instance, the final value of C.ROIC might be substantially low if one firm's ROIC approaches zero. To mitigate the influence of

3.5 Chain Aggregated Indexes

Table 3.6 Computation of chain aggregated indexes for ROIC

Firm ID	1	2	3	4	5
Number of Firms	5				
Firm's ROIC	0.1	0.1	0.1	0.1	0.2
Firm's Power (Weight)	1	1	1	0.5	1.5
Weighted Financial Ratio	0.10	0.10	0.10	0.32	0.09
C.ROIC (Weighted Geometric Mean)	0.123				
C.ROIC (Unweighted Geometric Mean)	0.115				
C.ROIC (Unweighted Arithmetic Mean)	0.120				
C.Equality	0.196				
Coefficient of Variation (CV)	0.333				

such outliers, we could employ the weighted arithmetic mean. For instance (please also refer to Table 3.6):

$$\text{C.ROIC}^{\text{Arithmetic}} = \sum_{i=1}^{n} \theta_i \times \text{ROIC}_i / \sum_{i}^{n} \theta_i$$

$$\text{C.ROE}^{\text{Arithmetic}} = \sum_{i=1}^{n} \theta_i \times \text{ROE}_i / \sum_{i}^{n} \theta_i$$

$$\text{C.ROA}^{\text{Arithmetic}} = \sum_{i=1}^{n} \theta_i \times \text{ROA}_i / \sum_{i}^{n} \theta_i$$

3.5.2 Chain Equality Indexes

A higher θ_i suggests an anticipated superior return for firm i, usually influenced by the firm's dominance and negotiation capabilities in the event. Essentially, the core tenet of Nash bargaining allows a more dominant firm to reap greater benefits; meaning, a higher θ_i results in more favorable outcomes for firm i. If "fairness" means that all stakeholders have identical financial ratios or "equality," then θ_i should be universally set to 1.

To gauge the equity of all firms within a supply chain transaction, consider the following chain aggregated equality index:

$$\text{Chain Aggregated Equality Index} = 1 - \left(\frac{\left(\prod_{i=1}^{n} \text{ROIC}_i \right)^{1/n}}{\sum_{i}^{n} \text{ROIC}_i / n} \right)^n$$

Assuming all financial ratios are positive, the weighted geometric mean is less than the weighted arithmetic mean. For instance, if all firms possess identical ROIC values (e.g., $ROIC_1 = ROIC_2 = 0.1$ for a supply chain comprising just two firms), the final C.ROIC will match the average ROIC across firms. If there's a wider dispersion in ROIC values, then C.ROIC falls below the average ROIC. Hence, if there's a significant variance in firms' financial ratios, certain firms might benefit considerably more than others. Viewed differently, these aggregated indexes serve as a metric for the overarching equity among supply chain firms. A value of 0 for the chain aggregated equality index indicates complete equity across firms, with all boasting identical financial ratios. Conversely, a value of 1 signifies total inequality within the supply chain. Table 3.6 illustrates how these indexes are computed.

Table 3.6 presents a supply chain finance transaction involving 5 parties. From the provided data, the C.ROIC weighted geometric mean value is calculated to be 0.123. The C.Equality index stands at 0.196, which, being on the lower side, suggests that the profits across firms are relatively balanced or "fair."

An alternative measure of inequality can be derived using the coefficient of variation (CV). A higher CV denotes increased disparity among firms. In Table 3.6, the CV value is recorded as 0.333, indicating that the inequality isn't pronounced.

3.6 Summary

This chapter delves into the pivotal role financial analysis plays within the context of supply chain finance. By evaluating and breaking down various financial metrics, we gain a deeper understanding of a firm's health, efficiency, and areas of potential risk. These analyses aren't just beneficial at an individual firm level; they can also shed light on the financial symbiosis between different entities within a supply chain.

Key Takeaways:

1. Financial Statements:
   - Core of any financial analysis, these documents provide a detailed picture of a firm's financial health.
   - Comprising the balance sheet, income statement, and cash flow statement, they capture a company's financial status, performance, and liquidity respectively.
   - Essential for making informed decisions regarding investments, operations, and credit.

2. Profit and Asset Ratios:
   - These ratios, such as ROE, ROA, and ROIC, allow stakeholders to assess the profitability and efficiency of a firm relative to its equity, assets, or invested capital.
   - They play a critical role in determining a company's operational efficiency and financial structure.
   - Provide insights into how effectively a firm is using its assets or equity to generate profit.
3. The DuPont Analysis:
   - A detailed breakdown of the ROE, ROA, and ROIC ratios, reveals the factors contributing to a company's profitability.
   - Provides a more nuanced understanding of where a company's returns are coming from and helps identify strengths and potential risks.
4. Chain Aggregated Indexes:
   - These are composite metrics designed to evaluate the collective impact of supply chain finance on multiple involved firms.
   - They account for various financial ratios, considering the individual performance of each entity within a supply chain.
   - Offer insights into the overall health and sustainability of supply chain relationships and the fairness of profit allocation among participants.

3.7 Exercises

3.7.1 Practice Questions

1. What are the three primary components of financial statements?
2. What does the ROA ratio measure?
3. Using the DuPont Analysis, decompose ROA into its two primary components.
4. If a firm has a higher value of accounts receivable, what does it indicate about the sales generated from its invested capital?
5. Why might a firm with a higher value of accounts payable have a higher ROIC?
6. What are the potential implications for a dominant firm that significantly delays payments to upstream firms?
7. Define ROIC and explain its relation to operational efficiency.
8. What are the common practices that could lead to higher ROIC, according to the text?
9. What role do profit and asset ratios play in determining a company's operational efficiency?
10. Which financial metric in the DuPont Analysis reflects the company's ability to manage its assets to produce revenue?

3.7.2 Case Study

Stellar Electronics and Supply Chain Finance Dynamics

Background

Stellar Electronics is a leading manufacturer of electronic devices, including smartphones and tablets. As the company expands its operations, it has to work closely with several suppliers, vendors, and financial institutions. With the intent to optimize its finances and maintain its market position, Stellar decides to undertake a supply chain finance analysis using the principles from this chapter.

Scenario

In 2023, Stellar initiated a new project—the production of a cutting-edge tablet. To ensure the project's success, Stellar collaborated with:

1. *RawMat Co.*—Provides raw materials for tablet manufacturing.
2. *TechFin Bank*—Offers financing solutions to Stellar and its suppliers.
3. *InsureGuard*—Provides insurance coverage for the goods in-transit and production.
4. *DeliverExpress*—Ensures the timely delivery of products.

Stellar Electronics is interested in assessing the financial implications of its decisions across this supply chain.

Data Provided

From the financial statements and data available:

- Stellar Electronics has an ROIC of 15% and NOPAT of $1 million. It has accounts receivable of $2 million and accounts payable of $1 million. Please refer to Chapter 4.1 for an understanding of the concepts of accounts receivable and accounts payable.
- RawMat Co. has an ROIC of 10%. The company has recently increased its accounts receivable owing to increased demand but has been consistent with its accounts payable.
- TechFin Bank, owing to its diversified interests, has an ROIC of 12%.
- InsureGuard, given its industry nature, works on a smaller margin with an ROIC of 8%.
- DeliverExpress, given its efficiency, has maintained an ROIC of 11%.

Questions

1. Which firm in the supply chain has the highest ROIC? What could be the implications for Stellar Electronics?
2. Given the increase in accounts receivable for RawMat Co., how could it affect their ROIC, and what should Stellar take into account for future collaborations?
3. Compute the C.ROIC for this supply chain, assuming $\theta_i = 1$ for all firms.

4. Discuss the implications of the computed C.ROIC for Stellar Electronics and its partners.
5. Compute the Aggregated Equality Index value for this transaction.

Appendix: Walmart Inc. Financial Statements 2018–2020

Consolidated Balance Sheets	Fiscal Years Ended January 31		
(Amounts in millions)	2020	2019	2018[5]
ASSETS			
Current assets			
Cash and cash equivalents	$9465	$7722	
Receivables, net	6284	6283	
Inventories	44,435	44,269	
Prepaid expenses and other	1622	3623	
Total current assets	61,806	61,897	
Property and equipment, net	105,208	104,317	
Operating lease right-of-use assets	17,424	–	
Finance lease right-of-use assets, net	4417	–	
Property under capital lease and financing obligations, net	–	7078	
Goodwill	31,073	31,181	
Other long-term assets	16,567	14,822	
Total assets	$236,495	$219,295	
LIABILITIES AND EQUITY			
Current liabilities			
Short-term borrowings	$575	$5225	
Accounts payable	46,973	47,060	
Accrued liabilities	22,296	22,159	
Accrued income taxes	280	428	
Long-term debt due within one year	5362	1876	
Operating lease obligations due within one year	1793	–	
Finance lease obligations due within one year	511	–	
Capital lease and financing obligations due within one year	–	729	
Total current liabilities	77,790	77,477	
Long-term debt	43,714	43,520	
Long-term operating lease obligations	16,171	–	

---

[5] Data from 2018 was missing in Walmart's 2020 Annual Report. Those interested in obtaining the missing data can refer to Walmart's 2019 Annual Report or explore other sources.

Consolidated Balance Sheets	Fiscal Years Ended January 31		
(Amounts in millions)	2020	2019	2018
Long-term finance lease obligations	4307	–	
Long-term capital lease and financing obligations	–	6683	
Deferred income taxes and other	12,961	11,981	
Commitments and contingencies			
Equity			
Common stock	284	288	
Capital in excess of par value	3247	2965	
Retained earnings	83,943	80,785	
Accumulated other comprehensive loss	(12,805)	(11,542)	
Total Walmart shareholders' equity	74,669	72,496	
Noncontrolling interest	6883	7138	
Total equity	81,552	79,634	
Total liabilities and equity	$236,495	$219,295	
Consolidated Statements of Income	Fiscal Years Ended January 31		
(Amounts in millions, except per share data)	2020	2019	2018
Revenues			
Net sales	$519,926	$510,329	$495,761
Membership and other income	4038	4076	4582
Total revenues	523,964	514,405	500,343
Costs and expenses			
Cost of sales	394,605	385,301	373,396
Operating, selling, general and administrative expenses	108,791	107,147	106,510
Operating income	20,568	21,957	20,437
Interest			
Debt	2262	1975	1978
Finance, capital lease and financing obligations	337	371	352
Interest income	−189	−217	−152
Interest, net	2410	2129	2178
Loss on extinguishment of debt	–	–	3136
Other (gains) and losses	−1958	8368	–
Income before income taxes	20,116	11,460	15,123
Provision for income taxes	4915	4281	4600
Consolidated net income	15,201	7179	10,523
Consolidated net income attributable to noncontrolling interest	−320	−509	−661
Consolidated net income attributable to Walmart	$14,881	$6670	$9862

Appendix: Walmart Inc. Financial Statements 2018–2020

Consolidated Statements of Cash Flows	Fiscal Years Ended January 31		
	2020	2019	2018
Cash flows from operating activities			
Consolidated net income	15,201	7179	10,523
Adjustments to reconcile consolidated net income to net cash provided by operating activities:			
Depreciation and amortization	10,987	10,678	10,529
Unrealized (gains) and losses	(1886)	3516	–
(Gains) and losses for disposal of business operations	15	4850	–
Asda pension contribution	(1036)	–	–
Deferred income taxes	320	(499)	(304)
Loss on extinguishment of debt	–	–	3136
Other operating activities	1981	1734	1210
Changes in certain assets and liabilities, net of effects of acquisitions:			
Receivables, net	154	(368)	(1074)
Inventories	(300)	(1311)	(140)
Accounts payable	(274)	1831	4086
Accrued liabilities	186	183	928
Accrued income taxes	(93)	(40)	(557)
Net cash provided by operating activities	25,255	27,753	28,337
Cash flows from investing activities			
Payments for property and equipment	(10,705)	(10,344)	(10,051)
Proceeds from the disposal of property and equipment	321	519	378
Proceeds from the disposal of certain operations	833	876	1046
Payments for business acquisitions, net of cash acquired	(56)	(14,656)	(375)
Other investing activities	479	(431)	(77)
Net cash used in investing activities	(9128)	(24,036)	(9079)
Cash flows from financing activities			
Net change in short-term borrowings	(4656)	(53)	4148
Proceeds from issuance of long-term debt	5492	15,872	7476
Repayments of long-term debt	(1907)	(3784)	(13,061)
Premiums paid to extinguish debt	–	–	(3059)
Dividends paid	(6048)	(6102)	(6124)
Purchase of Company stock	(5717)	(7410)	(8296)
Dividends paid to noncontrolling interest	(555)	(431)	(690)
Purchase of noncontrolling interest	–	–	(8)
Other financing activities	(908)	(629)	(261)
Net cash used in financing activities	(14,299)	(2537)	(19,875)

(continued)

(continued)

Consolidated Statements of Cash Flows	Fiscal Years Ended January 31		
	2020	2019	2018
Effect of exchange rates on cash, cash equivalents and restricted cash	(69)	(438)	487
Net increase (decrease) in cash, cash equivalents and restricted cash	1759	742	(130)
Cash, cash equivalents and restricted cash at beginning of year	7756	7014	7144
Cash, cash equivalents, and restricted cash at end of year	$9515	$7756	$7014

References

Airbus. (2022). *Financial results.* https://www.airbus.com/en/investors/financial-results-annual-reports. Accessed 5 September 2022.

Associated Press. (2018). *Sears files for Chapter 11 bankruptcy protection amid plunging sales, massive debt.* https://www.nbcnews.com/business/business-news/sears-files-chapter-11-amid-plunging-sales-massive-debt-n920011. Accessed 1 April 2020.

Boeing. (2022). *Quarterly reports.* https://investors.boeing.com/investors/reports/. Accessed 5 September 2022.

China Briefing. (2022). *China's accounting standards.* https://www.china-briefing.com/doing-business-guide/china/accounting-and-operations/accounting-standards. Accessed 2 December 2022.

Crail, C., & Main, K. (2022). *Generally Accepted Accounting Principles (GAAP) Guide.* https://www.forbes.com/advisor/business/generally-accepted-accounting-principles-gaap-guide/. Accessed 11 December 2022.

Damodaran, A. (2007). *Damodaran, Aswath, Return on Capital (ROC), Return on Invested Capital (ROIC) and Return on Equity (ROE): Measurement and Implications.* Available at SSRN: https://ssrn.com/abstract=1105499/. Accessed December 21, 2022.

D'innocenzio, A. (2020). *Pandemic claims another retailer: 118-year-old J.C. Penney.* https://apnews.com/article/virus-outbreak-tx-state-wire-business-wy-state-wire-ap-top-news-c1c81cf36150f0586993e8bd15410b10. Accessed 9 January 2024.

European Commission. (2023). *What the EU is doing and why.* (2023). https://finance.ec.europa.eu/capital-markets-union-and-financial-markets/company-reporting-and-auditing/company-reporting/financial-reporting_en. Accessed 2 December 2023.

Goldratt, E. M., & Cox, J. (2016). *The goal: A process of ongoing improvement.* Routledge.

Hayes, A. (2023). *Return on Capital Employed (ROCE): Ratio, interpretation, and example.* https://www.investopedia.com/terms/r/roce.asp. Accessed 3 November 2023.

Higgins, R. C., Koski, J. L., & Mitton, T. (2018). *Analysis for financial management* (12th ed.). McGraw Hill Education.

Oikarainen, E. (2022). *The DuPont formula helps understand the dynamics of value creation.* https://www.inderes.dk/en/articles/the-dupont-formula-helps-understand-the-dynamics-of-value-creation. Accessed 5 May 2022.

Walmart. (2022). *Quarterly Reports.* https://stock.walmart.com/financials/quarterly-results/default.aspx. Accessed 23 November 2023.

Wikipedia. (2019). *Return on equity.* https://en.wikipedia.org/wiki/Return_on_equity. Accessed 7 July 2019.

References

Wikipedia. (2023). *DuPont analysis.* https://en.wikipedia.org/wiki/DuPont_analysis. Accessed 6 June 2023.

Yhumita, S. R. (2022). The effect of return on assets, return on equity, current ratio, and debt to equity ratio on stock return on coal sub-sector companies listed on the Indonesia Stock Exchange, 2017–2021. *Journal of World Conference (JWC), 4*(6), 300–305.

Working Capital Management 4

Learning Objectives:

1. Understand working capital's role in daily operations and the balance between current assets and liabilities.
2. Explore the cash conversion cycle, from resource investment to cash collection.
3. Assess the cash conversion cycle's impact on retail liquidity, financial health, and ethics.
4. Identify and evaluate liquidity indexes, gauging a company's short-term debt capacity and industry variations.

4.1 Introduction

In traditional supply chain management (SCM), the emphasis has typically been placed on a firm's production, inventory, and sales, as illustrated in the lower section of Fig. 4.1. Nonetheless, financial and cash flow management have been pivotal in SCM, particularly when considering supply chain finance (SCF).

As illustrated in Fig. 4.1, a firm's cash level diminishes when it settles payments with its suppliers for material orders. Investments in fixed assets are used to create merchandise that flows into inventory. Over time, these investments are recorded as depreciation in the accounting books, with the expectation of generating returns. The cash levels surge after products are sold in the market. While profits do not equate directly to cash flow, cash flow remains the vital lifeline for any firm. Thus, ensuring a robust cash flow is essential for firms to mitigate default risks. A firm, even if profitable, can face insolvency if it lacks sufficient cash to cover maturing debts and other responsibilities, such as disbursing salaries. Therefore, preserving a healthy cash flow should be a paramount consideration alongside

Fig. 4.1 The cash flow cycle (*Source* Adapted from Higgins et al., 2018)

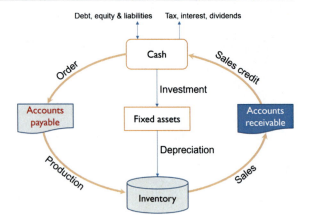

profit maximization. This was glaringly evident during the 2007–2009 Financial Crisis and the onset of COVID-19 in 2020.

4.2 Cash and Working Capital

Cash is essential for operating any business. While working capital is not synonymous with cash, it can often be converted into cash within a short term, though conversion is not always guaranteed. For instance, a firm might require years to sell off its inventory or, in the worst scenario, may even need to write off its inventory.[1]

4.2.1 Accounts Receivable and Accounts Payable

In addition to inventory, *accounts receivable* (AR) constitutes another significant portion of current assets. Accounts receivable arises when a company allows its customers to purchase products on credit. It represents the legally enforceable amount owed to a company for products or services it has provided to its customers. Typically, this obligation is in the form of an invoice, which the customer is expected to settle based on mutually agreed-upon payment terms.

An invoice usually outlines details of the sale, the amount received for the products, and the outstanding amount due based on the stipulated payment terms. An accounts receivable age analysis, often known as the debtors book, can be broken down based on AR maturity periods: current, 30 days, 60 days, 90 days, or longer.

---

[1] For instance, in April 2001, Cisco Systems wrote off $2.5 billion in inventory because they overestimated demand forecasting (Narayanan & Raman, 2004).

4.2 Cash and Working Capital

> *"Of the three elements of supply chain working capital—payables, receivables, and inventory—executives tend to focus on inventory. However, to minimize working capital requirements during challenging times, it's important to apply a coordinated approach that addresses all three areas."*
>
> The Wall Street Journal, Apr 14, 2020

Conversely, *accounts payable* (AP) is a significant component of current liabilities. While accounts receivable represents amounts customers owe to the company, accounts payable is the legally enforceable amount the company owes for products or services it has procured from suppliers. A seller's accounts receivable aligns with a buyer's accounts payable in terms of value, and both are recognized simultaneously.

An accounts payable entry is documented once the invoice receives approval for payment and is recorded in the AP subledger as an outstanding obligation. To optimize cash flow, companies often aim to settle these outstanding payables as close to their due dates as feasible. Fluctuations in AR and AP can be observed in a firm's cash flow statement (e.g., refer to Table 3.3).

4.2.2 Working Capital

Working capital (WC) is a financial metric used to gauge operating liquidity. Generally, working capital management encompasses inventory management, the management of accounts receivable and payable, and cash management. The computation of working capital derives from an entity's gross current assets and current liabilities (Higgins et al., 2018):

$$\text{Working Capital} = \text{Current Assets} - \text{Current Liabilities}$$

Net working capital, another closely related and frequently utilized concept, is defined by:

$$\text{Net Working Capital} = \text{AR} + \text{Inventory} - \text{AP}$$

which excludes cash and other short-term assets and liabilities when compared to standard working capital.

Simply put, a firm possesses more net working capital when it can swiftly collect payments from its buyers while prolonging its own payments (i.e., AP) to its sellers. Given their significance, the payment terms of accounts receivable and accounts payable become central negotiation points between buyers and sellers in supply chain finance. Dominant supply chain entities may occasionally exploit payment terms to their benefit when transacting with weaker partners.

Although a greater inventory contributes to a higher net working capital value, consistently maintaining elevated inventory levels isn't always advantageous for a firm. Using inventory to artificially inflate net working capital should be approached with caution. A firm risks liquidity issues if it cannot expedite the sale of its inventory to meet short-term debt obligations.

Taking Boeing as an example, its working capital for 2019 is:[2]

$$\$102,229M - \$97,312M = \$4917M$$

This isn't exorbitant for a behemoth like Boeing. Its working capital experienced a dip from $6240M in 2018. Although Boeing's cash saw an uptick from $7637M in 2018 to $9485M in 2019, both its inventory and accounts payable also swelled considerably.

From a comprehensive perspective, the aggregate of accounts payable across all firms equals the combined accounts receivable of all companies; thus, the total net working capital remains positive, given that the cumulative inventory of all firms is also positive. In this light, it's standard for a firm to boast a positive net working capital. For the majority of enterprises, positive working capital is indispensable to ensuring sustainability in operations and profitability within the supply chain.

Regular occurrences of negative working capital suggest that the firm is adept at quickly accumulating cash from accounts receivable, yet significantly defers cash outflows for accounts payable to an extent where the inventory is entirely neutralized. Subscription service providers, for instance, usually gather subscription fees in advance of content delivery, often with minimal or no inventory on hand. On platforms like Alibaba's Taobao, consumers remit payment upon purchase, but Taobao, which holds no inventory, delays remitting these payments to the vendors. Thus, whether a firm's working capital is in the black or red could hinge on its business strategy.

Unless a company's business model is overwhelmingly dominant, maintaining negative working capital can spell trouble. When a firm's working capital dives into the negatives—termed a working capital deficiency or deficit—it signals a liquidity crunch, often because inventory levels are critically low in comparison to historical averages, or because accounts receivable are dwindling due to reduced sales. Such a deficiency can endanger future credit and should raise red flags for most entities. From another perspective, in the case of Taobao, stalling payments to online vendors escalates operating costs for these primarily smaller enterprises, potentially undermining their service quality or even product standards, ultimately backfiring on Taobao itself. In essence, a business model driven by negative net working capital comes at the expense of other stakeholders, possibly jeopardizing the entire supply chain's efficiency.

---

[2] Please refer to Chapter 3 for more detailed information on the data of Airbus, Boeing, and Walmart.

> A business model operating on negative net working capital may disadvantage other business partners, potentially compromising the performance of the entire supply chain.

4.2.3 Free Cash Flow

Free cash flow (FCF), often referred to as free cash flow to the firm (FCFF), gauges a company's profitability. It takes into account non-cash expenses such as depreciation and amortization, but deducts changes in working capital and expenses for capital goods, such as fixed assets. While there are multiple methods for computing FCF (Wikipedia, 2019), a commonly adopted formula is:

$$FCF = EBIT \times (1 - \text{Tax Rate}) + \text{Depreciation \& Amortization}$$
$$- \text{Change in Working Capital} - \text{Capital Expenditure (CapEx)}$$

Distinct from net earnings, FCF incorporates the expense to purchase capital goods (CapEx) and the alteration in working capital, in addition to EBIT and depreciation & amortization. FCF represents the segment of cash flow that can be extracted from a firm and allocated to security holders and creditors without adversely impacting the company's ongoing operations. Consequently, if the sum of FCF and CapEx demonstrates an upward trajectory, it can enhance the stock's value.

4.3 Cash Conversion Cycle

The cash conversion cycle is a concept that integrates inventory, accounts receivable, and accounts payable.

4.3.1 Days Inventory Outstanding

As illustrated in Table 3.1, inventory stands as one of the significant assets of a business. Inventory encompasses the raw materials used for product creation, the work-in-progress or partially finished goods, and the completed goods ready for sale.

4.3.1.1 Inventory Measurement
Inventory can be evaluated using three primary methods: first-in, first-out; last-in, first-out; and the weighted average method (Khan et al., 2018).

First-In, First-Out (FIFO)

With the FIFO approach, the earliest acquired inventory items are recorded as sold first, regardless of the actual items being sold. Consequently, the inventory's carrying cost is calculated based on the most recently purchased or acquired items. Once this inventory is sold, the inventory's carrying cost is designated as the cost of goods sold (COGS, as presented in the income statement).

Consider Company A's inventory as illustrated below, sequenced by acquisition time with the earliest items on the left:

Number of units	50	100	150
Unit cost	$10	$11	$12

The total inventory cost sums up to: $50 \times \$10 + 100 \times \$11 + 150 \times \$12 = \$3400$. If Company A sold 80 units in May, then using the FIFO method, the COGS after the sale would be $50 \times \$10 + 30 \times \$11 = \$830$. The residual carrying cost of the inventory stands at: $\$3400 - \$830 = \$2570$.

For perishable items, FIFO might be substituted with the first expired, first out (FEFO) approach, given that expired goods must be eliminated from inventory due to consumption safety concerns post their expiration dates.

Last-In, First-Out (LIFO)

In the LIFO approach, the most recently acquired inventory items are recorded as sold first. This means the carrying cost of the inventory is determined by the earliest purchased or acquired items. Using the aforementioned example, if Company A sold 80 units in May under the LIFO method, the COGS post sale would be $80 \times \$12 = \$960$. The subsequent carrying cost of the inventory would be $\$3400 - \$960 = \$2440$.

It's notable that LIFO is predominantly a US-centric method. Some American companies adopted LIFO in the 1970s as a strategy to reduce income taxes during inflationary periods. The difference in residual inventory between FIFO and LIFO is termed the LIFO reserve, amounting to $\$2570 - \$2440 = \$130$. This reserve represents the taxable income Company A can defer through the LIFO method. However, the International Financial Reporting Standards (IFRS) prohibits LIFO, so FIFO remains prevalent among most firms.

Weighted Average Method

Another viable technique involves determining the inventory cost and COGS based on the average costs of all goods and materials during a given accounting period.

4.3.1.2 Inventory Turnover Ratio

One of the fundamental indicators reflecting the efficiency of inventory management is the *inventory turnover ratio* within a specified accounting period. It's defined as:

$$\text{Inventory Turnover Ratio} = \frac{\text{COGS}}{\text{Average Inventory Cost}}$$

4.3 Cash Conversion Cycle

Table 4.1 Inventory turnover ratio ranking by sector in 2020

Ranking	Sector	Ratio
1	Utilities	451.74
2	Financial	209.36
3	Services	32.85
4	Transportation	16.27
5	Technology	10.02
6	Retail	8.95
7	Energy	8.19
8	Consumer discretionary	7.44
9	Consumer non-cyclical	7.16
10	Basic materials	5.39

Source csimarket.com

The COGS is determined using the FIFO method or other relevant approaches. The average inventory cost can either be based on the average ending inventory or the mean of both the beginning and ending inventory costs.

Using Company A's scenario, let's assume the COGS for a particular year is $198,495 and the average inventory cost is $20,050. This results in:

$$\text{Inventory Turnover} = \frac{\$198,495}{\$20,050} = 9.9$$

This implies that Company A turned over its inventory 9.9 times that year.

The inventory turnover ratio offers insights into how swiftly a company can sell its inventory and gauges the efficacy of its inventory management. A higher inventory turnover ratio is typically favored as it suggests robust sales. Faster-selling inventory translates to a reduced average inventory cost per item. However, it's essential to note that a higher turnover necessitates timely restocking to avoid inventory shortages (i.e., running out of stock).

When making comparisons of inventory turnover ratios across similar businesses, it's crucial to recognize that enhancing inventory turnover shouldn't compromise return on investment and profitability. For further insights, one can consult the inventory turnover ratio ranking for various industry sectors presented in Table 4.1 (CSIMarket, 2022).

4.3.1.3 Days Inventory Outstanding

The *days inventory outstanding* (DIO) offers a counter perspective to inventory turnover. It is defined as:

$$\text{DIO} = \frac{365 \text{ days}}{\text{Inventory Turnover}} = \frac{\text{Average Inventory Cost}}{\text{COGS}} \times 365 \text{ days}$$

DIO is alternatively known as days sales of inventory (DSI), days in inventory (DII), or average age of inventory. This metric denotes the number of days a company's current inventory would last under continuous sales without any replenishment.

For companies in the S&P 1500 index, the average DIO hovered around 63 days between 2011 and 2018 (Shah et al., 2019). Intriguingly, smaller companies exhibited an average DIO that was approximately 6 days longer than their larger counterparts. This disparity implies that smaller companies, on average, tend to have lower operational efficiency than larger firms.

Consider Company A, for which:

$$DIO = \frac{365 \text{ days}}{9.9} = 36.9 \text{ days}$$

This suggests that Company A's average inventory can sustain 36.9 days of sales without needing replenishment.

For Boeing in 2019, the combined cost of goods sold (encompassing both products and services) amounted to:

$$COGS = \$62,877M + \$9154M = \$72,031M$$

Given that the inventory stood at $76,622M, its inventory turnover and DIO are calculated, respectively, as:

$$\text{Inventory Turnover Ratio} = \frac{\$72,031M}{\$76,622M} = 0.94$$

$$DIO = \frac{\$76,622M}{\$72,031M} \times 365 \text{ days} = 388.3 \text{ days}$$

While a DIO of 388.3 days seems substantial, it is explicable given the extended duration typically required to assemble an aircraft.

4.3.2 Days Sales Outstanding

The efficiency with which a company manages its accounts receivable is reflected in its collection period, which is the average number of days taken between the dates of credit sales and the receipt of payment from customers.

4.3.2.1 Days Sales Outstanding
The collection period is also known as the days sales in accounts receivable or days sales outstanding (DSO). It can be calculated as:

$$DSO = \frac{\text{Average Accounts Receivable}}{\text{Credit Sales per Day}}$$

4.3 Cash Conversion Cycle

Table 4.2 Industries ranked by best DSO in 2019

Ranking	Industry	DSO
1	Department & discount retail	1.1
2	Cruise and vacation	6.7
3	Grocery stores	9.3
4	Wholesale	12.4
5	Tobacco	13.6
6	Oil refineries	15.1
7	Airline	15.9
8	Technology retail	16.0
9	Restaurants	17.7
10	Specialty retail	20.1

Source Computation is based on csimarket.com data

In this formula, average accounts receivable can sometimes be replaced with end accounts receivable, and credit sales per day can be replaced with average net sales per day (Wikipedia, 2023).

A company's DSO can be compared to that of its competitors to assess the efficiency of its receivable collection. A lower DSO is preferable as it indicates quicker collection, providing the company with more available cash. On the other hand, a high DSO implies a prolonged collection period from customers, potentially affecting cash flow negatively. Although a fluctuating DSO may raise concerns, a predictable, seasonal DSO can be less alarming.

Considering Boeing, the total accounts receivable on its balance sheet (refer to Table 3.1) stands at $12,309M, encompassing net accounts receivable and net unbilled receivables. Assuming that the proportion of cash in the net sales is insignificant, the credit sales per day can be approximated by net sales ($76,559M) per day. Therefore, Boeing's DSO for 2019 is:

$$DSO = \frac{\$12{,}309M}{\$76{,}559M/365 \text{ days}} = 58.7 \text{ days}$$

This indicates that, in 2019, Boeing experienced an average delay of 58.7 days between making a sale and receiving the corresponding payment. Notably, this DSO is significantly higher than the company's average over the past decade.[3] Furthermore, it is considerably more than the 15.9-day average DSO of Boeing's primary clients, airline companies (as detailed in Table 4.2, showcasing the DSO industry rankings for 2019).

It's essential to note that the typical DSO length can vary significantly across industries and is influenced by business type and structure. This variability is illustrated in Table 4.2 (CSIMarket, 2022).

---

[3] Additional analysis reveals that Boeing's DSO had been steadily increasing from 2012 to 2019.

For companies in the S&P 1500, the average DSO was around 50 days between 2011 and 2018, showing a slight deterioration over this period (Shah et al., 2019). Among these companies, the DSO for smaller firms exceeded that of larger companies by just over 2 days. Consequently, Boeing's DSO lagged behind the average of other S&P 1500 companies.

4.3.2.2 Accounts Receivable Turnover Ratio

We can define the *accounts receivable turnover ratio* as follows:

$$\text{AR Turnover Ratio} = \frac{\text{Credit Sales}}{\text{AR}}$$

The AR turnover ratio measures how effective a company is at collecting accounts receivable owed by its customers. A higher AR turnover ratio indicates better cash flow and is thus preferred.

In the case of Boeing in 2019, the calculation is:

$$\text{AR Turnover Ratio} = \frac{\$76{,}559\text{M}}{\$12{,}309\text{M}} = 6.22$$

The average AR turnover ratio in the airline industry was about 22.99 in 2019 (as shown in Table 4.3). Therefore, Boeing's AR turnover ratio is significantly below those of airline companies.

Given the definitions of DSO and AR turnover ratio, the relation between them is:

$$\text{DSO} = \frac{365 \text{ days}}{\text{AR Turnover Ratio}} = \frac{365 \text{ days}}{6.22} = 58.7 \text{ days}$$

Table 4.3 Industries ranked by best AR turnover ratio in 2019

Ranking	Industry	Ratio
1	Department and discount retail	325.86
2	Cruise and vacation	54.24
3	Grocery stores	39.19
4	Wholesale	29.52
5	Tobacco	26.76
6	Oil refineries	24.18
7	Airline	22.99
8	Technology retail	22.79
9	Restaurants	20.59
10	Specialty retail	18.14

Source https://csimarket.com/screening/index.php?s=rt

4.3.3 Days Payable Outstanding

Days payable outstanding (DPO), also referred to as the payables period, represents the average time a company takes to settle its outstanding accounts payable with its creditors. The formula is:

$$\text{DPO} = \frac{\text{Accounts Payable}}{\text{Credit Purchases per Day}}$$

DPO serves as an indicator of a company's liabilities. Companies with high DPOs can leverage this by utilizing their cash for short-term investments prior to settling their accounts payable. However, elevated DPOs can disadvantage upstream firms, potentially leading to supply chain disruptions as a result of these firms' capital constraints. Therefore, a company with a high DPO might earn the tag of a "bad client."

For external observers of a company, the exact value of credit purchases isn't readily accessible. An approximation can be made using the cost of goods sold from the income statement (Higgins et al., 2018). In the case of Boeing for 2019, the accounts payable amounting to \$15,553M is available in its balance sheet, while the combined cost of goods sold (encompassing both products and services) is represented by \$62,877M + \$9154M = \$72,031M. From this, we derive the DPO (Boeing, 2022):

$$\text{DPO} = \frac{\$15{,}553\text{M}}{\$72{,}031\text{M}/365\,\text{days}} = 78.8\,\text{days}$$

Comparing this with Boeing's DSO of 58.7 days in 2019, it's evident that Boeing holds a dominant position in the airplane industry. This is because Boeing, on average, deferred cash payments to its suppliers for 78.8 days post procuring products from them, yet managed to collect its accounts receivable within a shorter time frame of 58.7 days.

According to a study, the average DPO of S&P 1500 companies between 2011 and 2018 was around 47 days and showed a slight deterioration over this period (Shah et al., 2019). Interestingly, larger companies had a DPO approximately 13 days longer than their smaller counterparts, likely attributed to the market dominance of the larger entities.

4.3.4 Cash Conversion Cycle (CCC)

DIO, DSO, and DPO individually illuminate specific facets of working capital management. However, an amalgamation of these offers a comprehensive perspective on a firm's cash management.

The operating cycle of a firm can be defined as the sum of DIO and DSO:

$$\text{Operating Cycle} = \text{DIO} + \text{DSO}$$

Given the preference for both shorter DIO and DSO, a shorter operating cycle is desirable. For Boeing in 2019, its operating cycle stands at 388.3 days + 58.7 days = 447 days. This implies that, on average, Boeing's cash would be engaged for 447 days in 2019. As established earlier, Boeing can prolong cash payments to its suppliers up to 78.8 days (DPO). However, the lengthiness of its DIO only allows the benefits of a long DPO to minimally alleviate its cash constraints.

By integrating DIO, DSO, and DPO, we can outline the firm's *cash conversion cycle* (CCC):

$$CCC = \text{Days Inventory Outstanding (DIO)} \\ + \text{Days Sales Outstanding (DSO)} \\ - \text{Days Payable Outstanding (DPO)}$$

The CCC, alternatively known as cash-to-cash (C2C) cycle, net operating cycle, working capital cycle, or simply the cash cycle, signifies the duration taken by a company to transform its inventory investments into cash (de Boer et al., 2015). It evaluates a company's prowess in operations, inventory management, and cash handling.

An illustrative relationship between DIO, DSO, DPO, and CCC is depicted in Fig. 4.2.

An elevated CCC indicates that a company requires a more extended period to transition from inventory acquisition to sales, and eventually to cash receipts. This might be a sign that the company's capital is extensively tied up across inventory, production, and sales stages. In order to curtail the CCC, companies should work towards reducing both DIO and DSO while ethically extending their DPO.

For Boeing in 2019 (Boeing, 2022):

- DIO is 388.3 days
- DSO is 58.7 days
- DPO is 78.8 days

Fig. 4.2 Illustrative graph of cash conversion cycle

Fig. 4.3 CCC of Boeing from 2011 to 2018 (days) (*Source* Raw data is from Boeing Annual Reports from 2009 to 2019)

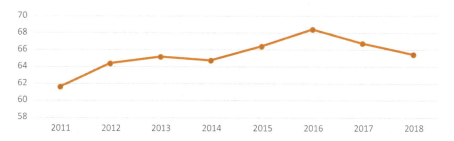

Fig. 4.4 Average CCC across S&P 1500 companies from 2011 to 2018 (days) (*Source* Raw data are from J.P. Morgan Working Capital Index 2020; JPMorgan, 2021)

Consequently, Boeing's CCC for 2019 calculates to:

$$CCC = (388.3 + 58.7 - 78.8) \text{ days} = 368.2 \text{ days}$$

As highlighted in Fig. 4.3, Boeing's CCC displayed an increasing but worsening trend between 2009 and 2019.

The average CCC for S&P 1500 companies spanning 2011–2018 is showcased in Fig. 4.4. The graph reveals a rising trend in the CCC during this interval. When juxtaposed with the S&P 1500's average CCC, Boeing's 2019 CCC is considerably elevated.

4.4 Implications of the Cash Conversion Cycle in Retailing

It's beneficial to assess the CCC across various time frames and juxtapose them with benchmark companies. At an intuitive level, for a business model to be deemed sustainable, a lower CCC value is preferable. However, if a company's low CCC is predicated on extracting maximum profits from its supply chain partners, such a low CCC is unlikely to be sustainable over the long run. Consequently, it might be advantageous for firms within the supply chain to harmonize their CCCs, ensuring mutual benefits for all involved parties.

4.4.1 CCCs of Major Retailers

This section details and contrasts the CCC values of major retailers, namely Amazon, Walmart, Alibaba, and JD.com. Amazon and Walmart stand as the largest retailers in the U.S. Alibaba operates China's most expansive retailing platforms, which include Taobao.com and Tmall.com. In contrast, JD.com is China's premier online retailer, maintaining its own inventories and logistics, akin to Amazon. Unless stated otherwise, all data in this subsection is sourced from the finbox.com website (Finbox, 2022).

Between January 2013 and January 2022, Walmart's CCC trended downwards, moving from over 10 days to under 3 in the latter 5 years, indicating an improvement in Walmart's CCC over this duration (Fig. 4.5). Walmart's average CCC was a mere 6.5 days during this span. Given Walmart's dependence on global supply chains and the extended time it takes to ship products from overseas to local markets (e.g., 30–40 days considering ocean freight, local transportation, and shelf time), it suggests that Walmart might leverage its market dominance to significantly delay payments to suppliers. As an illustration, in the fiscal year 2021, Walmart reported accounts receivable of $8280M, inventories of $56,511M, and accounts payable of $55,261M. This implies that Walmart possibly postponed supplier payments almost until the products reached the end consumers, all at the suppliers' expense.

Amazon's retail dominance is even more pronounced. During December 2012 to December 2021, Amazon's average CCC was −33.8 days. Delving into Amazon's balance sheet for 2021, accounts receivable stood at $26,500M, inventories at $31,758M, and accounts payable at $78,664M (see Fig. 4.6) (Fidelity, 2022).

Comparing Amazon to Walmart: Despite Amazon registering a smaller COGS than Walmart ($249,435M vs. $418,342M), it had a more significant accounts payable ($78,664M vs. $55,261M). This implies that Amazon even more considerably delayed payments to suppliers than Walmart did, potentially leading to greater imbalances in supplier relationships. When juxtaposing Walmart's COGS ($418,342M) and net sales ($569,962M) with Amazon's figures ($249,435M in

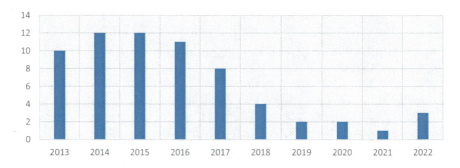

Fig. 4.5 CCC of Walmart from January 2013 to January 2022 (days)

4.4 Implications of the Cash Conversion Cycle in Retailing

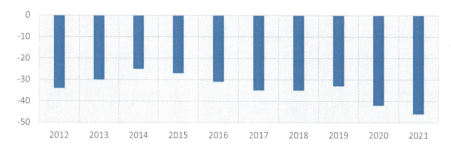

Fig. 4.6 CCC of Amazon from December 2012 to December 2021 (days)

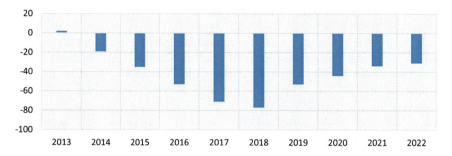

Fig. 4.7 CCC of Alibaba from March 2013 to March 2021 (days)

COGS and $469,822M in net sales), it becomes evident that Amazon enjoys a higher profit margin than Walmart.

A negative CCC suggests that the retailer effectively utilizes funds from its suppliers or customers to operate, negating the need for any of its own cash. To offer another perspective: if Amazon's 2021 COGS was $272 billion and, hypothetically, it could loan the surplus cash at an APR of 10% to suppliers or customers, Amazon could garner an additional profit of approximately $33.8/365 \times 0.1 \times \$272 = \$2.52$ billion in just one year.[4]

The advantages of being dominant online shopping platforms are evident in Alibaba and JD.com, China's foremost online retailers. Their online business models have significantly influenced their CCCs. Alibaba's CCC initially declined and then surged from 2013 to 2022, bottoming out at an impressive −77 days in 2018. The subsequent increase in CCC coincided with the anti-monopoly actions against Alibaba. Nevertheless, Alibaba's average CCC remained substantially lower than JD.com's (see Figs. 4.7 and 4.8). This difference can be partly ascribed to JD.com's inventory model, while Alibaba operates as a pure online platform without managing its own inventory.

---

[4] The APR for Amazon loans ranges from 6 to 16%, as reported by McIntyre (2020).

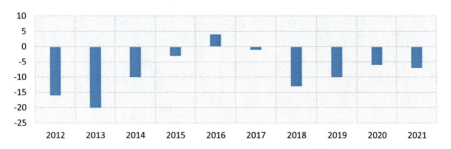

Fig. 4.8 CCC of JD.com from December 2012 to December 2021(days)

4.4.2 Ethic Concerns of Negative CCCs

Table 4.4 lists representative retailing companies listed in the U.S. but serving two major global markets. As discussed earlier, a company more dominant in the supply chain is likely to have a lower CCC. The CCCs of −671 days for Pinduoduo and −116 days for Sohu.com in 2021 are extremely perplexing and merit further investigation (Finbox, 2022). Conversely, high CCC values might also indicate opportunities for those firms to utilize inventories and accounts receivable in supply chain financing.

There's a pressing ethical concern regarding severe payment delays. It's clear that a buyer's dominance, particularly that of online retailing platforms, grants unfair advantages in terms of significant payment delays. But the act of a retailer

Table 4.4 Year 2021's CCCs of public companies listed in the U.S

China Market		USA Market	
Company Name	CCC	Company Name	CCC
Pinduoduo Inc.	−671 days	Amazon.com, Inc.	−31 days
Sohu.com Limited	−116 days	eBay Inc.	−12 days
Vipshop Holdings Limited	−28 days	Target Corporation	−2 days
Alibaba Health IT Limited	−27 days	Walgreens Boots Alliance, Inc.	1 days
JD.com, Inc.	−21 days	Costco Wholesale Corporation	1 days
LightInTheBox Holding Co., Ltd.	−5 days	PriceSmart, Inc.	5 days
Alibaba Group Holding Limited	0 days	Walmart Inc.	6 days
Jowell Global Ltd.	43 days	Macy's, Inc.	8 days
Consumer Discretionary	50 days	Dollar General Corporation	34 days
Leju Holdings Limited	73 days	Consumer Staples	45 days
Baozun Inc.	94 days	Dollar Tree, Inc.	54 days
Shengda Network Technology, Inc.	264 days	Kohl's Corporation	61 days

Source Finbox.com

benefiting from lending money to its supplier (e.g., via an early payment discount) while concurrently delaying payments is arguably unethical.

> *It's arguably unethical for a retailer to benefit from lending money to its supplier while concurrently delaying significant payments to them.*

This unjust practice not only undermines the profitability of sellers, predominantly small businesses, but also jeopardizes supply chain sustainability (e.g., small businesses facing bankruptcy due to limited liquidity) and societal welfare (e.g., higher bankruptcy rates of small businesses contributing to increased unemployment). Hence, governments have the responsibility to enact relevant legislation to curb these excessive payment delays, safeguarding small businesses and bolstering the economy.

One potential solution to address late payments is enforcing a penalty or instituting automatic payment transfers from the buyer to the seller upon crossing predetermined delay thresholds. In a bid to combat late payments, several countries have enacted relevant legislation. For instance, the European Union introduced the Late Payment Directive in 2000 and revised it in 2013. This directive mandates that buyers pay interest and reasonable recovery costs to suppliers if they don't remit payment for goods or services timely. As stated by Whittaker et al. (2019), if a payment date agreed upon is later than 60 days after delivery, invoicing, or acceptance (whichever occurs last) and this significantly disadvantages the supplier, then interest begins to accumulate after those 60 days. The Act implicitly incorporates specific terms into contracts, which grants creditors the right to automatic interest accumulation from the scheduled payment date until the payment is fully made, at an interest rate of 8% above the base rate. This stipulation is more stringent for customers who are public authorities.

4.5 Liquidity Indexes

Studies have shown that optimizing working capital can enhance a firm's value (de Boer et al., 2015) and has increasingly become a priority for many firms. This practice becomes even more vital during economic downturns, such as the 2007–2009 Financial Crisis and the 2020–2023 COVID-19 pandemic, to mitigate liquidity risks and maintain the firm's strategic priorities. The following ratios are commonly used to assess a firm's liquidity and risk levels.

4.5.1 Current Ratio

Liquidity ratios gauge a firm's ability to repay short-term debts within one year. The *current ratio*, which is a widely used metric, measures a company's liquidity level as follows (Olmo, 2022):

$$\text{Current Ratio} = \frac{\text{Current Assets}}{\text{Current Liabilities}}$$

The current ratio is also known as the liquidity ratio or the working capital ratio. While working capital quantifies the absolute value of a company's liquidity, the liquidity ratio provides a relative measure of this liquidity, making it simpler to compare across firms regardless of their size. Sustainable current ratios differ across industries but typically range from 1.5 to 3 for solvent companies (Olmo, 2022).

In 2019, Boeing had a liquidity ratio of

$$\text{Current Ratio} = \frac{\$102{,}229M}{\$97{,}312M} = 1.05$$

This figure is relatively low (i.e., < 1.5). Nevertheless, a current ratio under 1.5 is not always a cause for concern for a company, especially if the firm possesses promising long-term prospects. These prospects allow the company to borrow against them to repay short-term liabilities or if the inventories can be liquidated much faster than accounts payable come due. In the case of Boeing, its long-term outlook is generally favorable, especially given its expertise in military products and its role as a vital national security asset. However, its inventory turnover was a cause for concern in 2019 (i.e., 0.94 < 1), a result of order and production disruptions stemming from the Boeing 737 Max crashes.

4.5.2 Quick Ratio

Given that there's no guarantee an inventory can be converted into accounts receivable or cash within one year, a more stringent measurement, the quick ratio, is utilized.

$$\text{Quick Ratio} = \frac{\text{Current Assets} - \text{Inventory}}{\text{Current Liabilities}}$$

The *quick ratio* is often referred to as the acid test ratio. Generally, a higher value is better. During liquidation, the company may only receive 40% or even less of the inventory's book values, considering the inventory might not be sold immediately (Higgins et al., 2018). As such, the acid test ratio provides a more accurate gauge of a firm's capability to cover current liabilities without hastily liquidating inventory. While a satisfactory acid test ratio can differ by industry, a ratio above 1 is generally preferable.

For 2019, Boeing's quick ratio was:

$$\text{Quick Ratio} = \frac{\$102{,}229M - \$76{,}622M}{\$97{,}312M} = 0.26$$

This result represents a concerning acid test value. As we know, 2019 was a challenging year for Boeing due to the halt in production of the Boeing 737 Max following two fatal crashes. This situation led to an inventory buildup, which resulted from decreased sales.

4.5.3 Operating Cash Flow Ratio

A reliable method for a firm to address its liabilities is by utilizing only its cash flows, without resorting to selling assets. This strategy is represented by the *operating cash flow ratio* (Tuovila, 2023):

$$\text{Operating Cash Flow Ratio} = \frac{\text{Cash \& Cash Equivalents}}{\text{Current Liabilities}}$$

Evidently, the operating cash flow ratio is typically lower than the acid test ratio. During economic downturns, employing a more stringent liquidity ratio can better equip a firm to navigate heightened uncertainties.

4.5.4 Leverage Ratios

Leverage ratios measure a firm's debt level in relation to its other financial metrics. These ratios highlight the proportion of a firm's debt within its capital and the firm's ability to fulfill its financial obligations. Here, we introduce some frequently used leverage ratios (CFI, 2022).

4.5.4.1 Debt-to-Equity Ratio

$$\text{Debt-to-Equity Ratio} = \frac{\text{Total Debt}}{\text{Total Equity}}$$

The *debt-to-equity ratio* quantifies a firm's total debt relative to its total shareholders' equity. A high debt-to-equity ratio indicates that the firm is aggressively financing its growth through debt, which can result in increased pressure to repay interest and principal and a higher risk of default. An investment in a firm is typically perceived as risky if the debt-to-equity ratio exceeds 2.0, though acceptable levels can vary by industry. For a comprehensive understanding of a firm's leverage, one should compare its ratios both with other companies and with its historical performance.

4.5.4.2 Debt-to-Assets Ratio

$$\text{Debt-to-Assets Ratio} = \frac{\text{Total Debt}}{\text{Total Assets}}$$

The *debt-to-assets ratio* represents the proportion of a firm's debt to its assets. A ratio exceeding one means the firm's debts surpass its assets. As with the debt-to-equity ratio, a lower debt-to-assets ratio generally indicates a more favorable debt position.

4.5.4.3 Debt-to-Capital Ratio

$$\text{Debt-to-Capital Ratio} = \frac{\text{Total Debt}}{\text{Total Debt} + \text{Total Equity}}$$

The *debt-to-capital ratio* illustrates the proportion of a firm's debt relative to its total capital base (where total capital equates to the sum of debt and equity). This metric provides insight into how a firm finances its operations.

4.5.4.4 Asset-to-Equity Ratio and Equity-to-Asset Ratio

$$\text{Asset-to-Equity Ratio} = \frac{\text{Total Assets}}{\text{Total Equity}}$$

$$\text{Equity-to-Asset Ratio} = \frac{\text{Total Equity}}{\text{Total Assets}}$$

The *asset-to-equity ratio* signifies how much of a firm's assets are financed by shareholders. Conversely, the *equity-to-asset ratio* reveals the proportion of total assets funded by shareholders.

4.5.4.5 Debt-to-EBITDA Ratio

$$\text{Debt-to-EBITDA Ratio} = \frac{\text{Total Debt}}{\text{EBITDA}}$$

where EBITDA stands for earnings before interest, taxes, depreciation, and amortization, this ratio indicates a firm's efficiency at paying off its debt. A high value suggests limited capability to clear its obligations.

4.5.4.6 Net-Debt-to-EBITDA Ratio

$$\text{Net-Debt-to-EBITDA Ratio} = \frac{\text{Total Debt} - \text{Cash \& Cash Equivalents}}{\text{EBITDA}}$$

This metric refines the debt-to-EBITDA ratio by subtracting cash & cash equivalents from the total debt. It indicates the duration (in years) the firm would need to repay its debt. If this ratio exceeds 4 or 5, it signals a concerning ability to manage debt.

We employ data from Boeing, Airbus, and Walmart to exemplify these leverage ratios in Table 4.5 (Airbus, 2022; Boeing, 2022; Walmart, 2022).

Upon examination, we observe several of Boeing's ratios are negative, an atypical outcome attributed to Boeing's negative equity in 2019. Meanwhile, both Airbus and Walmart's ratios appear within healthy ranges.

4.5 Liquidity Indexes

Table 4.5 Examples of leverage ratios (money in millions for non-ratios, 2019)

Financial Term	Definition	Boeing	Airbus	Walmart
EBITDA	Earnings before Interest, taxes, depreciation, and amortization	$358	€4266	$31,555
Total Debt	Short-term debt + long-term debt	$27,302	€10,148	$50,621
Cash & Equivalents		$9485	€9371	$7722
Total (Average) Equity	Average equity of this and the past year	($3945)	€5990	$80,593
Total Assets		$133,625	€114,409	$236,495
Debt-to-Equity Ratio	Total Debt/Total Equity	−6.92	1.69	0.63
Debt-to-Assets Ratio	Total Debt/Total Assets	0.20	0.089	0.21
Asset-to-Equity Ratio	Total Assets/Total Equity	−33.87	19.10	2.93
Equity-to-Asset Ratio	Total Equity/Total Assets	−0.030	0.052	0.34
Debt-to-EBITDA Ratio	Total Debt/EBITDA	76.26	2.38	1.60
Net-Debt-to-EBITDA Ratio	(Total Debt-Cash & Equivalents)/EBITDA	49.77	0.18	1.36

4.5.5 Working Capital Index

In 2019, J.P. Morgan introduced an average net working capital index to capture the working capital metrics of the S&P 1500 companies (JPMorgan, 2021).[5]

$$\text{Average Net Working Capital Index} = \frac{\sum_{i=1}^{n} \text{NWC}_i/\text{Sales}_i}{n}$$

where NWC stands for *net working capital*, defined as NWC = AR + Inventory − AP. Here, n is the total number of firms in the index, and "Sales" represents the net sales of the company during the period.

J.P. Morgan also introduced an average cash index (JPMorgan, 2021):

$$\text{Average Cash Index} = \frac{\sum_{i=1}^{n} \text{Cash}_i/\text{Sales}_i}{n}$$

Likewise, we can define an *average working capital index*:

$$\text{Average Working Capital Index} = \frac{\sum_{i=1}^{n} \text{WC}_i/\text{Sales}_i}{n}$$

---

[5] Companies may use different working capital index formulas. For instance, using data from Markit's Purchasing Managers' Index (PMI) surveys, the Lloyds Bank Working Capital Index calculates the momentum change in operational working capital as follows: Working Capital Index = Δ Accounts Receivable + Δ Inventories − Δ Accounts Payable. The index is then multiplied by 10 and increased by 100 for simpler interpretation.

If we apply the same concepts for a single company with $n = 1$, then the above-average indices become an individual firm's indices. For instance, in 2019, Boeing had the following index values (Boeing, 2022):

$$\text{Net Working Cash Index} = \frac{\$(12{,}471M + 76{,}622M - 15{,}553M)}{\$76{,}559M} = 0.9606$$

$$\text{Cash Index} = \frac{\$10{,}030M}{\$76{,}559M} = 0.1310$$

For convenient tracking, one can designate a certain year as the base year and compute relative values for these two indices. For instance, J.P. Morgan set the base level to 100 using 2011 as the benchmark (JPMorgan, 2021). However, this benchmarking method might pose a challenge when the benchmark year records a negative or zero index value.

To simplify the computation of the working capital index, this author suggests multiplying the aforementioned indices by 100 (where one point is interpreted as a one percent change against the total net sales/revenue) and then adding 100 as the benchmark. This is called the *normalized working capital index*. Thus, the formula becomes:

$$\text{Normalized Working Capital Index} = \frac{\sum_{i=1}^{n} WC_i/\text{Sales}_i}{n} \times 100 + 100$$

Using Boeing's data from 2005 to 2019 as an example for the normalized working capital index (Boeing, 2022), the outcomes are depicted in Fig. 4.9:

> A firm's operations cannot sustain if its normalized working capital index is continuously below 100 for multiple periods.

If the normalized working capital index exceeds 100, it suggests that Boeing's current assets surpass its current liabilities (i.e., the working capital, equivalent to current assets minus current liabilities, is positive). Otherwise, the opposite holds true.

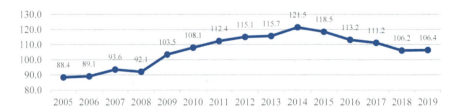

Fig. 4.9 Boeing's normalized working capital Index from 2005 to 2019

The working capital index typically rises during robust economic periods because firms might accumulate more inventory in anticipation of increased demand. Concurrently, accounts receivable might also rise due to heightened sales. A firm's operations become unsustainable if its normalized working capital index consistently falls below 100 over multiple periods.

4.6 Summary

The chapter focuses on the intricate dynamics of working capital management, including cash handling, the cash conversion cycle, its implications in the retail sector, and the utilization of liquidity indexes. It illustrates the necessity of maintaining sufficient liquidity and efficient working capital management, delves into the time required to turn inventory into cash, examines retail practices, and introduces various tools for assessing a company's liquidity and risk levels.

Key Takeaways:

1. Cash and Working Capital:
    - Working capital represents the difference between a company's current assets and current liabilities.
    - Adequate working capital is indispensable for the day-to-day operations of a firm, ensuring it can meet short-term debts and invest in growth.
2. Cash Conversion Cycle:
    - Measures the time span from when a company invests in resources (like inventory) until it receives cash from sales of products/services made from those resources.
    - A shorter cycle usually indicates better management of cash flow and efficient operations, which is especially crucial for sectors like retailing.
3. Implications of the Cash Conversion Cycle in Retailing:
    - The way retailers manage their cash conversion cycle can greatly influence their liquidity and financial health.
    - While delaying payments to suppliers can provide short-term liquidity benefits to retailers, it can be viewed as unethical and potentially harm supplier relationships.
4. Liquidity Indexes:
    - These ratios gauge a company's liquidity levels, offering insights into its ability to repay short-term debts.
    - The chapter presents the current ratio and quick ratio among others, explaining their significance and computation.
    - Acceptable levels for these ratios can vary by industry, and they serve as comparative tools across businesses of varying sizes.

4.7 Exercises

4.7.1 Practice Questions

1. What is the primary difference between current assets and working capital?
2. If Company A's current assets are $500M and its current liabilities are $400M, what is its current ratio?
3. Explain how the quick ratio differs from the current ratio. Why is the quick ratio considered a stricter measure of liquidity than the current ratio?
4. Given that Company B has current assets of $450M, inventory of $150M, and current liabilities of $300M, what is its quick ratio?
5. What does a high debt-to-equity ratio indicate about a company's financial strategy?
6. If a firm's total debt is $1B and its total equity is $500M, what is its debt-to-equity ratio?
7. How does the Lloyds Bank working capital index measure changes in operational working capital?
8. Why might a company, especially in retail, choose to delay payments to its suppliers?
9. If the normalized working capital index of a firm is 110, what does this suggest about the firm's current assets and current liabilities?
10. What does a continuous normalized working capital index below 100 indicate for a firm's operations?

4.7.2 Case Study

Working Capital Management at TechTonic Innovations Inc.

Background

TechTonic Innovations Inc., a budding tech startup, has been making waves in the smart home devices industry. Founded in 2018, the company has grown significantly over the last two years. With a robust sales record, the company plans to expand its product line and enter new markets.

However, as with many growing businesses, managing working capital has proven to be a challenge. TechTonic's CFO, Ms. Janet Hayes, recently noticed several anomalies in the company's working capital ratios and wants to address these concerns to ensure the financial health of the company.

Data

1. **2019 Financial Data:**
   - Current assets: $350,000 (of which inventory is $80,000)
   - Current liabilities: $230,000
   - Net sales: $1,500,000

- Cash: $45,000
- Accounts receivable (AR): $100,000
- Accounts payable (AP): $60,000

2. **2019 Industry Averages:**
   - Quick ratio: 1.2
   - Net working capital index: 0.12
   - Cash index: 0.1

Tasks

1. Calculate TechTonic's quick ratio, net working capital index, and cash index for 2019.
2. Compare the company's ratios with industry averages and identify potential red flags.
3. Suggest potential solutions or strategies to address these concerns.

References

Airbus. (2022). *Financial results.* https://www.airbus.com/en/investors/financial-results-annual-reports. Accessed 5 September 2022.
Boeing. (2022). *Quarterly reports.* https://investors.boeing.com/investors/reports/. Accessed 5 September 2022.
CFI. (2022). *Leverage ratios.* https://corporatefinanceinstitute.com/resources/accounting/leverage-ratios/. Accessed 21 December 2022.
CSIMarket. (2022). *Year to date stock performance by sector and industry.* https://csimarket.com/markets/markets_glance.php?days=ytd. Accessed 26 October 2022.
de Boer, R., Steeman, M., & van Bergen, M. (2015). *Supply chain finance, its practical relevance and strategic value: The supply chain finance essential knowledge series.*
Fidelity. (2022). *Financial reports.* Fidelity.com. Accessed 28 October 2022.
Finbox. (2022). *Summaries of related companies via searching on* https://finbox.com/. Accessed 26 October 2022.
Higgins, R. C., Koski, J. L., & Mitton, T. (2018). *Analysis for financial management* (12th ed.). McGraw Hill Education.
JPMorgan. (2021). *Working capital index 2020.* https://www.jpmorgan.com/content/dam/jpm/treasury-services/documents/jpmc-working-capital-index-2020.pdf. Accessed 1 October 2021.
Khan, A. K., Faisal, S. M., & Aboud, O. A. A. (2018). An analysis of optimal inventory accounting models-pros and cons. *European Journal of Accounting, Auditing and Finance Research, 6*(3), 65–77.

McIntyre, G. (2020). *Amazon lending: Is an amazon loan the best choice for you?* https://www.fundera.com/business-loans/guides/amazon-lending. Accessed 16 October 2020.

Narayanan, V. G., & Raman, A. (2004). Aligning incentives in supply chains. *Harvard Business Review, 82*(11), 94–103.

Olmo, M. Del. (2022). *Current ratio: Calculation, formula & examples.* https://blog.golayer.io/finance/current-ratio-calculation#:~:text=Acurrentratiobetween1.5,bemismanagingorunderutilizingassets. Accessed 19 October 2022.

Shah, G., Mandhana, V., & Vikrant, V. (2019). *J.P. Morgan working capital index* (Issue July). https://www.jpmorgan.com/global/treasury-services/benchmarking-working-capital. Accessed 11 November 2019.

Tuovila, A. (2023). *Operating Cash Flow (OCF): Definition, cash flow statements.* https://www.investopedia.com/terms/o/operatingcashflow.asp. Accessed 3 December 2023.

Walmart. (2022). *Quarterly reports.* https://stock.walmart.com/financials/quarterly-results/default.aspx. Accessed 23 November 2023.

Whittaker, B., Frisby, M., & Flynn, B. (2019). *Late payment of commercial debts.* https://www.stevens-bolton.com/cms/document/late_payments_of_commercial_debts__2019_.pdf. Accessed 19 December 2019.

Wikipedia. (2019). *Free cash flow.* https://en.wikipedia.org/wiki/Free_cash_flow. Accessed 16 December 2019.

Wikipedia. (2023). *Days sales outstanding.* https://en.wikipedia.org/wiki/Days_sales_outstanding. Accessed 6 December 2023.

Part II
Supply Chain Finance Mechanisms

"You can't connect the dots looking forward; you can only connect them looking backwards. So you have to trust that the dots will somehow connect in your future. You have to trust in something—your gut, destiny, life, karma, whatever. This approach has never let me down, and it has made all the difference in my life."
   Steve Jobs

Trade Finance: The Early Forms of Supply Chain Finance

5

Learning Objectives:

1. Understand the dynamics of cash-in-advance, consignment, and their implications in supply chain management.
2. Gain insights into the role and significance of letters of credit in facilitating international trade.
3. Delve into the concept of open accounts, their benefits, and associated risks in trade transactions.
4. Grasp the essentials of documentary collections and their role in guaranteeing payment and delivery in trade.
5. Familiarize with the Incoterms rules, outlining responsibilities between buyers and sellers in international shipping.

5.1 Introduction

Supply chain finance originates from transactions between supply chain firms, which typically occur in business-to-business trades. In this regard, trade finance can be viewed as the precursor to supply chain finance.

Trade finance takes place both domestically and internationally. While international trade opens up overseas markets for sellers, it also introduces a range of risks. These arise from factors like the vast distances involved, cultural differences, variations in currency and court systems, and the less stable nature of international supply chain relationships.

A frequent point of contention in trade finance is the timing of payment. Sellers (exporters) usually prefer to receive payments as swiftly as possible, ideally in cash, either when an order is placed, shipped, or upon receipt. Conversely, buyers (importers) are inclined to delay payments, preferring to settle long after the delivery of goods or even after they've sold all the goods. As such, the finalized payment terms are often determined by the relative market dominance of the sellers and buyers.

In a market where supply is scarce, sellers tend to have the upper hand and can demand prompt payments. On the other hand, when faced with intense global competition, sellers might need to offer more favorable credit terms to remain competitive, resulting in delayed payments.

Depending on firms' relative market dominance and negotiation prowess, there are five primary types of trade finance: cash-in-advance, consignment, documentary collections, letters of credit, and open accounts. These will be explored in greater depth in this chapter.

5.2 Cash-in-Advance and Push Supply Chains

In trade finance, *cash-in-advance* means that sellers receive payment in cash before dispatching the goods. This method is becoming less popular as buyers gain more dominance and horizontal competition among sellers intensifies. Typically, wire transfers, credit cards, and escrow services are the chosen payment methods for cash-in-advance.

In supply chain management, cash-in-advance payment terms align with push supply chain models. In a *push supply chain*, buyers reserve inventory from the seller before the sales season and assume all inventory risk by paying the seller in advance. The push supply chain is illustrated on the left side of Fig. 5.1, while the right side showcases a pull model. Contrary to the push model, in a *pull model*, the seller maintains inventory control at the buyer's location, and the buyer (usually a reseller) compensates the seller once the item is sold (further details in the following section).

In a single-period push model, the seller sets a one-time wholesale price and doesn't entertain instant orders during the sales season. Push supply chains, often seen in practices like channel stuffing or supplier sales to a newsvendor-type

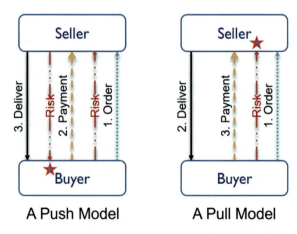

Fig. 5.1 Process comparison between push and pull systems

buyer, operate such that when a buyer places recurring orders, the seller mandates cash payments before each dispatch to maintain its production. Typically, upon receiving payment, the seller promptly delivers goods to the buyer, passing on the inventory title.

Ownership of the final product's inventory determines the associated inventory costs. However, transferring inventory ownership doesn't just modify the inventory costs but also the timelines for accounts receivable/payable. This, in turn, influences the working capital level and cash conversion cycle.

While sellers can sidestep credit risk in cash-in-advance (given payment is ensured prior to goods ownership transfer), paying the complete order in cash upfront is usually the least appealing choice for buyers. Specifically, the push model offers several disadvantages to buyers:

- Cash payments in advance strain the buyer's cash flow.
- Particularly for international importers, there may be concerns about the actual shipment of goods to the intended destination.
- If the product quality doesn't match the predetermined standard, the buyer has limited leverage against the seller.

Consequently, persisting with cash-in-advance terms might drive a seller's clientele towards competitors. Viewing it from a different angle, inventory ownership serves as the backbone for inventory financing in supply chain finance.[1] Notably, transferring inventory ownership might either be a tangible product transfer or simply an accounting procedure (with inventory moving to a consignment account instead of accounts receivable/payable).

5.3 Consignment and Pull Supply Chains

Cash-in-advance and *consignment* represent two polar opposites in the trade finance spectrum. In this domain, consignment is a unique case of open account, which we will delve into later in this chapter. Within supply chain management, consignment aligns with the pull supply chain model. Here, the buyer makes immediate orders during the selling season, while the seller manages inventory and assumes all related risks, as depicted in the right portion of Fig. 5.1.

Pull supply chains are characterized by practices such as retailers purchasing from a newsvendor, vendor-managed inventory, consignment inventory, and drop shipping. These methods have become more prevalent in big-ticket retail inventory items, like furniture or sporting goods. This approach enables buyers to defer payment until products sell, with the added benefit of returning unsold items.

---

[1] Inventory financing is introduced in more detail in Chapter 8.2.

In practice, pull systems manifest in various ways:

1. The first scenario mirrors what was previously described: the buyer pays upon the sale of the product.
2. In the second scenario, ownership transitions after or within a set period.
3. The third scenario, order-to-order consignment, involves billing the previous order when the next consignment order is made.

The pull model presents both advantages and disadvantages when compared to the push model. From the buyer's perspective, consignment allows them to remain competitive by considerably delaying payments, which enhances their cash flow, albeit at the seller's expense. However, this means relinquishing inventory control to the seller, potentially impacting customer satisfaction.

For sellers, the pull model offers key benefits:

- *Demand and Inventory Visibility*: This model often necessitates buyers sharing point of sale (POS) data, facilitating better inventory planning. Owing to inventory ownership, the seller gains enhanced demand and inventory insights, leading to superior production planning, inventory management, and faster goods delivery.
- *Inventory Cost Reduction*: Since inventory primarily resides with the buyer, consignment can curtail warehousing and inventory expenses, burdening the buyer further.

However, sellers also face challenges:

- *Cash Flow Reduction*: Transferring inventory costs to the seller increases its inventory responsibility, elevating their net working capital but diminishing cash flow.
- *Extended Cash Conversion Cycle (CCC)*: Retaining product inventory ownership means a reduced inventory turnover ratio, leading to a protracted cash conversion cycle. If the selling season is lengthy, liquidity can become a pressing concern.
- *No-Payment Risk*: Consignment exports present considerable risk, as sellers have no payment assurances while their goods are with independent distributors or buyers. While sellers can purchase insurance to offset non-payment risks, it augments their costs. Thus, engaging a reliable distributor or third-party logistics (3PL) provider is essential.

Inventory ownership distribution can influence supply chain efficiency. Theoretically, when both seller and buyer are risk-neutral, pull supply chains will have a higher optimal order quantity than push systems due to consignment's payment delays, making pull supply chains more efficient. In a pull-centric scenario, pull contracts can withstand challenges from push models since buyers lack the incentive to stock inventory before the sales season (Cachon, 2004). Yet, this dynamic can invert if both parties are risk-averse, especially if the supplier's risk aversion is greater than the retailer's (Yang et al., 2018). Consequently, company risk attitudes can sway supply chain structure decisions and performance. For a deeper exploration of this topic, refer to Appendix: Academic Perspective.

> *The optimal order quantity may be higher in push than in pull if the supplier is significantly more risk-averse than the retailer.*

5.4 Letter of Credit

A *letter of credit* (commonly abbreviated as LC, L/C, or LOC) is a long-standing form of supply chain finance. Predominantly used in long-distance and international trades, it doesn't necessitate financing by supply chain firms. Instead, it involves significant participation from multiple banks. Other names for it include bankers' commercial credit, documentary credit, or letter of undertaking. Simply put, a letter of credit is a document provided by a reputable bank, guaranteeing a seller that they will receive payment on time from the buyer. This guarantee becomes crucial, particularly when sellers and buyers are unfamiliar with each other or when buyers are situated in developing regions with limited credit histories.

5.4.1 Process Flow

Letters of credit (LCs) have been utilized since ancient times. Initially documented on paper, they evolved and were supplemented by travelers' checks, credit cards, and automated teller machines (Wikipedia, 2020). With the advent of the internet, the majority of LCs are now electronic. As of 2015, LCs constituted 41% of export trade finance. However, with the rise of other supply chain finance instruments, this percentage has been on a decline in recent years (PYMNTS, 2015).

The LC process, depicted in Fig. 5.2, can be illustrated using the following hypothetical scenario:

1. A buyer in Silicon Valley, California, intends to buy steel materials from a seller in Xiamen, a southern city in China. Both parties finalize the terms of price, quantity, shipping, handling, customs, and insurance.

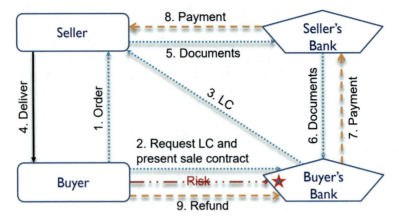

Fig. 5.2 Mechanism of letter of credit

2. However, as they haven't previously transacted, and due to the low trust level, the seller requests an LC for the transaction. In response, the buyer, using the sales contract, applies for an LC from its trusted bank in Silicon Valley.
3. After verifying the contract, the buyer's bank, known as the issuing bank, issues the LC to the seller and sends it to the seller's bank, referred to as the advising bank, which is usually located near the seller.
4. Once the seller reviews and approves the LC, they begin the product shipment.
   The LC typically includes:
   a. The payment amount.
   b. Beneficiary details and contact information.
   c. Shipping terms: initiation and arrival times, methods, etc.
   d. Additional financial particulars.
5. When the LC matures or upon product delivery, the seller presents the LC and associated documents to its bank.
6. The seller's bank then shares the documents with the buyer's bank. Note that the LC's maturity might extend beyond the shipment date, perhaps 60 days post-delivery, as mutually agreed.
7. The buyer's bank, after document verification and ensuring the seller's adherence to LC conditions (like product shipment), processes the payment to the seller's bank.

8. The seller's bank pays the seller.
9. The buyer then settles the amount with its issuing bank.

As illustrated, LCs are prevalent when trading companies lack familiarity. Hence, globally recognized banks, such as Citibank, often offer LCs in developing countries, mitigating challenges associated with obtaining international credit and dealing with less creditworthy buyers. In these contexts, LCs shield sellers from the geographical and credit risks of buyers.

Given their significance, LC issuance generally incurs a fee, ranging between 0.75% and 1.5% of the agreed payment amount (Miller, 2021). This fee is influenced by factors such as the buyer's creditworthiness, the relationship between firms and banks, payment size, and more.

While LCs significantly reduce risks for stakeholders, even minor errors, like typos, can lead to severe issues, possibly invalidating the LC. Hence, sellers must meticulously review the LC, ensuring all required documents align with the LC's terms and are submitted promptly.

Predominantly, LCs are perceived as safeguards for sellers. This perception holds weight, as, upon receiving an LC, a seller is assured payment, even if the buyer goes bankrupt—unless both involved banks default. Conversely, LCs can also secure buyers, especially against less trustworthy sellers. Such sellers might compromise on product quality or attempt premature credit extraction using fraudulent documents. The predetermined payment maturity period of an LC can counteract such scenarios.

> *A letter of credit can protect both the seller and the buyer.*

5.4.2 Payment Methods

According to the Uniform Customs & Practice for Documentary Credits (UCP 600),[2] an LC must specify whether it is available by deferred payment, sight payment, acceptance, or negotiation. The following are the most common payment methods:

---

[2] The UCP 600 is a set of rules established by the International Chamber of Commerce (ICC) that applies to financial institutions issuing LCs. It consists of 39 articles governing the issuance and use of LCs and is recognized in 175 countries worldwide, facilitating approximately $1 trillion USD in trade annually.

1. ***Payment at Sight***: Payment is made immediately, typically within five to ten days, after the documents are presented to the issuing bank or the nominated bank (a bank designated by the issuing bank to make payment either immediately or upon maturity). Once the seller meets the LC's requirements, the nominated bank can make the payment instantly upon request but with a recourse condition. This means the nominated bank can reclaim the payment if the documents are non-compliant. It's worth noting that the payment obligation of the nominated bank isn't as binding as that of the issuing or confirming bank, and the nominated bank usually deducts a portion of the payment as a discount.

> ***Case Study***: *The issuing bank receives the LC documents on August 24 and forwards them to the nominated bank on the same day. By doing this, the issuing bank entrusts the nominated bank to verify the documents, facilitate the payment, and possess the capability to reclaim funds in the event of seller non-compliance. On August 26, the nominated bank verifies the documents and processes the payment by August 28.*

2. ***Deferred/Usance Payment***: In a deferred LC, the seller and buyer agree that credit will only be available after a stipulated period post-delivery or after the products have been sold. A typical method to determine the due date is by adding the agreed-upon duration to the shipment or document presentation date.

> ***Case Study***: *The LC stipulates payment 30 days post-shipment. The issuing bank gets the documents on August 24. Upon verification and ensuring compliance with the LC's terms, the bank confirms the shipment date as August 11. Thus, by adding 30 days to the shipment date, the LC's due date falls on September 10.*

3. ***Acceptance***: This method mirrors the deferred payment. However, the seller/beneficiary must also present a bill of exchange (refer to Fig. 5.3) alongside other documents. The due date aligns with the LC's stipulations. If either the issuing or nominated bank accepts the bill of exchange, it commits to pay the bill's amount on the given due date. In some cases, sellers might opt for an early payment by selling the bill of exchange, albeit at a reduced price.

5.4 Letter of Credit

Fig. 5.3 Sample of bill of exchange (*Source* Adapted from Swedbank)

4. *Negotiation*: The seller can negotiate with the issuing bank upon presenting the documents for an advance payment based on the LC. In such negotiations, the nominated bank might pay the seller before the LC's original due date. This payment is usually the LC's value minus the interest between the real payment date and the original due date. If the presented documents align with the LC's terms and another bank confirms the LC, the negotiation typically does not involve any recourse to the seller. However, if the LC lacks confirmation, the nominated bank might reserve a recourse right, allowing it to reclaim funds if the issuing bank defaults on payment.

> **Case Study**: The LC is payable 60 days after the date of shipment. The issuing bank receives the documents on August 24. The original due date of the LC is October 23. On August 27, the seller negotiates with the nominated bank and receives payment on the same day. The payment amount is the value of the LC minus one month's interest. The nominated bank receives the payment from the issuing bank on October 23.

5.4.3 LC Types

In the LC process, the issuing bank may arrange for another bank, referred to as the nominated bank, to make the payment. The issuing bank might also involve a confirming bank, which commits to pay the beneficiary for a compliant presentation if the nominated bank fails to deliver the credit. Based on the needs and situations of firms, there are various LC categories as follows:

1. **Confirmed LC**: To mitigate the risk of non-payment or significant delays from the issuing bank, the seller/beneficiary can request confirmation of the LC.

Adding a confirming bank, often the seller's bank, provides additional security to the beneficiary but typically comes at an extra cost. This bank guarantees the LC if the issuing and the nominated banks default, as long as the seller meets the terms of the LC. If the buyer and the issuing bank are in politically unstable regions or if the issuing bank lacks strong creditworthiness, a confirmed LC becomes particularly crucial. Given that both the confirming and the issuing banks are obligated to pay for compliant documents, the sellers need not concern themselves with disputes between these banks.

2. **Standby LC**: This LC acts as an additional payment guarantee. It is not intended as the primary payment mechanism under the contract, as long as the issuing or nominated bank fulfills the payment. It serves as a backup should there be any breach of contract.
3. **Revocable/Irrevocable LC**: A revocable LC allows the buyer and the issuing bank to alter its content without notifying or obtaining permission from the seller. The issuing bank might revoke such an LC due to political uncertainties, worsening market conditions, or liquidity issues. For instance, during the 2007–2009 Financial Crisis, banks like Merrill Lynch might have revoked their revocable LCs. While a revocable LC can be secured by the buyer/applicant's assets, it's generally risky and rare nowadays. Most LCs are irrevocable, necessitating seller approval for any changes. Sellers should typically insist on an irrevocable LC when initiating the process.
4. **Unrestricted LC**: Here, the seller can receive payment from any bank by presenting the LC. Unless otherwise specified, an LC defaults to being restricted, meaning it must be presented directly to the issuing bank.
5. **Revolving LC**: Suitable for ongoing business relationships, this LC facilitates multiple payments over a period, eliminating the need for a new LC for each transaction. These LCs are typically valid for multiple transactions up to a year.
6. **Transferable LC**: An intermediary seller or first beneficiary can use a transferable LC to benefit its suppliers (the second beneficiaries). If goods are shipped directly from suppliers to the buyer and the intermediary wishes to pay suppliers directly via the LC, they can request the nominated bank to transfer parts of the LC to each supplier. This LC necessitates direct shipping terms from the suppliers to the buyer, with the second beneficiary obliged to submit documents complying with the LC terms.
7. **Advance LC**: These comprise two main types: red clause LC and green clause LC. Both facilitate early-stage payments, aiding the seller's production, logistics, and cash management.
    a. **Red Clause LC**: Allows the seller to access part of the LC value upfront to procure materials, facilitate production, and ship goods. This type of LC is essentially an unsecured loan within the LC framework. To obtain it, specific documents outlining the purpose of the advance payment (e.g., goods ready for shipping) are required.
    b. **Green Clause LC**: Extending the red clause LC's scope, it covers not only raw material procurement, production, processing, and packaging but

5.4 Letter of Credit

Table 5.1 Comparison of red clause LC and green clause LC

	Red Clause LC	**Green Clause LC**
Ink Color	The clause is in red ink	The clause is in green ink
Purpose	Advance payment for the raw material procurement, production, processing, and packaging of goods	Advance payment for the raw material procurement, production, processing, packaging of goods, and pre-shipment warehousing
LC Value Percentage	Around 20–25% (Trade Finance Global, 2023)	Can be as high as 75–80% (Trade Finance Global, 2023)

also pre-shipment warehousing and insurance (Hoffman, 2022). Thus, a green clause LC demands all red clause LC documents plus warehousing evidence. They're prevalent in the commodities sector.

Both red and green clause LCs permit early-stage advance payments from buyers, aiding sellers in production, logistics, and cash management. Such LCs seem to transition supply chain management from push to pull. Sellers typically sign a letter of indemnity ensuring the buyer doesn't incur financial losses if the seller fails to meet obligations. Given that the LC boosts the seller's working capital via an unsecured loan, sellers might offer buyers a discount in exchange for the advance payment. However, the risk remains with the buyer if the seller misuses the advance payment and fails to meet the LC's terms. Consequently, advance LCs often entail extra fees from buyers (Table 5.1).

8. *Discounting LC*: If the seller requires funds, they can sell the LC to the issuing bank at a discount, provided they have complying documents. LC discounting functions similarly to advance payments in red and green clause LCs. However, since it's not pre-specified in the LC, there's no assurance the seller will receive early payment or won't lose too much through discounting.
9. *Differed/Mixed Payment LC*: A mixed payment LC can consist of an advance payment, payment against shipping documents, and post-shipment payment. The LC dictates the payment dates, methods, and respective amounts.

> *Case Study*: After sealing a deal to buy 1,000 laptops from an overseas firm, Firm O, Company A secures a mixed LC from Bank B. The LC stipulates:
> 1. *To aid Firm O's production planning, 40% of the total LC value is immediately payable upon presentation of an invoice.*

> 2. Another 40% of the LC value becomes due once the shipment documents are presented.
> 3. The remaining 20% is payable 60 days post-shipment.

10. **Back-to-Back LC**: At the behest of an intermediary seller (like a trader), the bank initiates a secondary back-to-back (import) LC in the seller's favor, utilizing the pre-existing primary (export) LC as collateral. Here, the intermediary can use the sequential transactions to compensate its supplier without deploying its own capital. This process is depicted in Fig. 5.4.

The initial and the back-to-back LCs might also be termed primary/secondary LCs, mother/child LCs, or master/subsidiary LCs. While there's a link between the two LCs, the back-to-back LC is typically viewed as standalone and non-transferable.

A comparison between transferable LC and back-to-back LC is presented in Table 5.2.

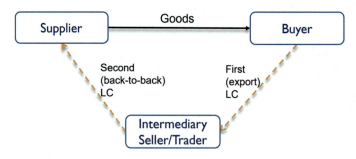

Fig. 5.4 Procedure of back-to-back LC

Table 5.2 Transferrable LC vs. the back-to-back LC

	Similarities	Differences (Advantages of Back-to-Back LC)
Payment Mechanism	Both allow traders to use the end buyer's payment to settle with the supplier	In a back-to-back LC, there's no need for buyer's consent to shift the credit to a new beneficiary (e.g., the supplier), unlike in a transferable LC
Financing	Both allow traders to finance transactions without their own capital, enabling them to operate beyond their financial reach	In a back-to-back LC setup, the supplier and end buyer may remain unaware of each other's identities

5.5 Open Account

Contrary to a letter of credit which involves multiple banks, an open account facilitates a direct transaction between the seller and the buyer without any bank's involvement in financing. However, banks may facilitate transferring the payment from the buyer's bank to the seller's bank upon request. An open account transaction occurs when a seller dispatches goods or services and all corresponding documents directly to a buyer. The buyer, in turn, commits to paying the invoice on a later date. In international trades, payments are typically due 7, 30, 60, 90, or 120 days post the delivery of goods. While LCs are often leveraged by new business partners, open account is typically chosen between established and trusted trade partners.

Open account is often viewed as a trade credit extended to the buyer (Jiménez, 2013). According to the Federal Reserve Board, trade credit in 1987 comprised roughly 15% of non-farm nonfinancial businesses' liabilities and about 20% of liabilities of small American firms (Cai et al., 2014). Rajan and Zingales (1995) determined that trade credit made up 17.8% of all assets for American companies in 1991 and over a quarter of total corporate assets in European nations, including Germany, France, and Italy. Based on data from 674 companies listed on the Shanghai and Shenzhen Stock Exchanges from 2001 to 2007, Cai et al. (2014) deduced that trade credit equaled about 9.1% of these companies' total assets. The 2019 Small Business Credit Survey reported that 13% of small businesses leveraged trade credit finance, ranking it the third most sought-after financing tool. Kagan (2022) pointed out that trade credit is a pivotal capital source for numerous enterprises, and it dominates the capital utilization for a majority of B2B sellers in the U.S. As per the U.S. Flow of Funds Accounts, by September 2012, trade credits were approximately three times the value of bank loans and 15 times that of commercial paper on aggregate financial statements for nonfinancial U.S. enterprises (Barrot, 2016). As depicted in Fig. 5.5, the growth of open account has surpassed that of the letter of credit over recent decades. A 2021 report approximated that open account trade represented 80% of global trade transactions, translating to $28.5 trillion in 2021 (Jdsupra, 2021).

Recognizing the prominence of open accounts, several banks have launched open account platforms to streamline buyer–seller transactions. Within these platforms, banks don't assume the roles they do in LCs but function as third-party platform providers. For instance, both buyers and sellers can exploit the open account platform offered by J.P. Morgan to streamline their document exchanges and payment transfers.

5.5.1 Seller-Oriented Trade Credit Discount

For buyers, trade credit (reflected as accounts payable) operates much like a 0% loan on their balance sheet. Sellers might offer various types of trade credit discounts to encourage earlier repayments by buyers. For instance, with terms like "2/

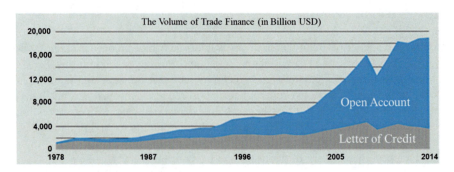

Fig. 5.5 Growth of open account vs. letter of credit from 1978 to 2014 (*Source* Adapted from UniCredit, 2016, and swift.com)

10 Net 30" or "2%/10 Net 30," a buyer is entitled to a 2% discount if they make the payment within the initial 10 days of a 30-day credit period (refer to Fig. 5.6). Likewise, in "2/30/90," the buyer can avail a 2% discount if they complete the payment within the first 30 days of a 90-day credit term.

The 2% discount may seem inconsequential at first glance. However, for large transaction volumes, this discount can be substantial. To illustrate using the "2/10 Net 30" as an example, the *annual percentage rate* (APR) can be calculated as:

$$\text{APR} = 2\% \times \frac{365 \text{ days}}{30 \text{ days - 10 days}} = 36.5\%$$

Indeed, this translates to an interest of 36.5% APR, which can be substantial if the buyer pays early. To provide context, consider Walmart's fiscal data from 2020 (ending January 31, refer to the appendix in Chapter 3). The net profit over the cost of sales can be expressed as:

$$\frac{\text{Net income}}{\text{Cost of Sales}} = \frac{\$14,881M}{\$523,964M} = 2.84\%$$

Fig. 5.6 Illustration of trade credit 2/10 Net 30

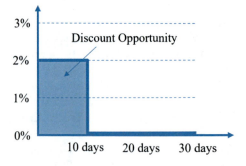

Therefore, if Walmart could effectively earn an "interest income" of 36.5% APR based on the cost of sales, it would undoubtedly bolster its profit margins. However, from a seller's viewpoint, offering such trade credit discounts can be expensive.

It's crucial to acknowledge that dominant companies might exploit trade credit terms, even delaying payments beyond the stipulated period in the contract. Fearing potential loss of business to these major buyers, smaller businesses often hesitate to publicly call out the unfair practices or legally challenge them for violating the agreed-upon contractual terms. Consequently, large buyers may leverage the capital of numerous small suppliers to boost their profits, thereby consuming the latter's working capital.

However, every situation has its pros and cons. Although buyers might benefit from short-term cost reductions by delaying payments, they risk compromising product quality, post-sale service standards, and overall supply chain relations in the long term. In these scenarios, even if suppliers don't proactively offer trade credit discounts, it might still be advantageous for buyers to initiate early payments, particularly to support capital-constrained sellers. This approach is explored further in Chapter 5.5.3.

5.5.2 Trade Credit vs. Bank Credit

Trade credit has become increasingly popular over the years, largely because open account eliminates the bank fees and complex documentation processes associated with letters of credit. In seller-driven trade credit, the seller primarily dictates payment terms and wholesale pricing. Though delayed payments typically incline the seller to levy higher invoice prices, dominant sellers may find it difficult to do so. To offset the risk of non-payment, sellers might consider insurance or even offer a trade credit discount to incentivize early payment.

However, if the buyer holds significant leverage, the seller assumes more risk by extending payment to a much later date—a preference of the buyer but not necessarily of the seller. Extended payment terms mean the seller must maintain ample liquidity or have external financing options. In fiercely competitive markets, sellers may feel cornered into accepting longer payment delays, especially when dealing with dominant buyers. Notably, many global retailers utilize trade credit far more than they do bank borrowings. As a case in point, Walmart's trade credit is eightfold the capital contributed by its shareholders (Wikipedia, 2021). In some cases, buyers might even postpone payments beyond the agreed-upon date without incurring penalties, especially if sellers are dependent on them for future orders.

Compared to bank credit, *trade credit* offers payment deferments for capital-constrained buyers, making them more likely to order in larger volumes. However, this means the seller assumes the risk of potential buyer default if demand falls short of order quantity. Therefore, sellers might set a higher wholesale price with trade credit than with bank credit. A balance is struck based on the unit production cost of goods (Jing et al., 2012). Lower production costs reduce the potential losses

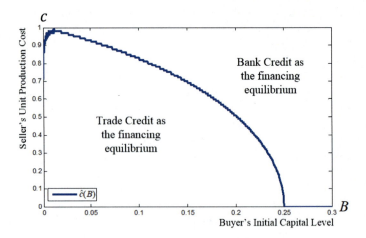

Fig. 5.7 Financing equilibrium between trade credit and bank credit

from buyer default, making it more appealing for sellers to offer trade credit to boost demand. Conversely, when production costs are high, potential losses from trade credit might outweigh the benefits from increased order volumes, making sellers more hesitant to extend such credit.

Jing et al. (2012) further posit that, given a buyer's initial capital level, trade credit is the more likely financing equilibrium when internal capital levels are low. Conversely, when internal capital levels are higher, bank credit tends to be the preferred choice (refer to Fig. 5.7). This is corroborated by empirical studies. For instance, Deloof and Jegers (1999) found a negative correlation between the amount of trade credit and internally generated cash when studying Belgian firms. Similarly, Petersen and Rajan (1997) observed that a company's ability to generate cash internally reduces its demand for trade credit.

When firms employ both trade and bank credits, complementary and substitute effects emerge based on the firm's initial capital level (Cai et al., 2014). Using data from Chinese firms listed on the Shanghai and Shenzhen Stock Exchanges from 2001 to 2007, Cai et al. (2014) adopted a simultaneous equations framework to model the dependencies between bank and trade credits. They defined bank credit using short-term debt and trade credit through accounts payable. They considered various firm characteristics:

- *Solvency*: Ratio of shareholders' equity to total assets, indicating risk.
- *Assets*: Total real assets, indicating firm size.
- *Inventory*: Ratio of inventory to total assets, reflecting short-term assets.
- *Sales*: Total real sales, indicative of activity level.
- *Cash*: Real cash holdings, gauging the funds substituting for both credit types. Classified as Type L (low cash) if below or equal to ¥40 million, and Type H (high cash) otherwise.

5.5 Open Account

Table 5.3 Regression analysis of bank credit (BC)

Dependent Variable = BC, Type L Firms			Dependent Variable = log(BC), Type H Firms		
Y	Coef.	Std. Err.	Y	Coef.	Std. Err.
TC	0.997***	0.317	log(TC)	−0.200***	0.046
log(Assets)	0.154***	0.022	log(Assets)	1.021***	0.053
Inventory	−0.021	0.02	Inventory	6.15×10^{-5}	2.73×10^{-4}
MS	−0.529	0.757	MS	−2.582	1.768
log(Sales)	−0.003	0.007	log(Sales)	0.011	0.012
Solvency	−0.055***	0.012	Solvency	−2.728***	0.128
Year	0.007	0.018	Year	0.058	0.042
d	0.017	0.055	d	0.279	0.131
Constant	−17.446	30.115	Constant	−113.713	83.943
R^2	0.46		R^2	0.55	
No. obs.	576		No. obs.	3468	

Source The Wind Financial Database of China
*Significance at 10%
**Significance at 5%
***Significance at 1%

Cai et al.'s findings, detailed in Tables 5.3 and 5.4, reveal that firms with higher solvency ratios tend to borrow less, irrespective of cash holdings. Firm size consistently favors credit acquisition, while riskiness acts as a deterrent. For firms with low internal capital (Type L), trade credit complements bank credit. However, when internal capital is substantial, the two credit types become substitutes as firms look to both for addressing capital constraints.

5.5.3 Buyer-Oriented Early Payment Discount

To alleviate the financial strain on sellers, especially from open accounts, major retailers like Costco, Amazon, Macy's, and Walgreens have facilitated early payments for their capital-constrained suppliers via the C2FO financing platform (Chen et al., 2020). In 2009, Walmart introduced its "Supplier Alliance Program," vowing to pay qualifying suppliers approximately 60 days in advance (O'Connell, 2009). By 2015, Walmart extended early payment terms to nearly 10,000 trusted suppliers, allowing them access to funds in just 10 days through the "early real-time payment software" (Green, 2015). Since 2015, Home Depot has also accelerated payments to its sellers using Taulia's supply chain finance systems, as noted by Marks (2015). In China, JingDong, the largest online business-to-consumer retailer (with a net revenue of $67.2 billion in 2018, as per jd.com), has extended early credit to its suppliers. JingDong Finance has, since 2013, disbursed more than ¥30 billion annually in advance buyer credit to its suppliers (Chen et al., 2020).

Table 5.4 Regression analysis of trade credit (TC)

Dependent Variable = TC, Type L Firms			Dependent Variable = log(TC), Type H Firms		
Y	Coef.	Std. Err.	Y	Coef.	Std. Err.
BC	0.085***	0.026	log(BC)	−0.164***	0.032
log(Assets)	0.025***	0.007	log(Assets)	1.145***	0.035
Inventory	0.021***	0.005	Inventory	−0.003	0.002
MS	−0.136	0.182	MS	−2.287**	1.136
log(Sales)	0.005***	0.0016	log(Sales)	0.005	0.008
Solvency	−0.0066**	0.003	Solvency	−1.628***	0.111
Year	−0.001	0.004	Year	0.056**	0.027
d	−0.012	0.013	d	−0.021	0.085
Constant	2.17	8.44	Constant	−113.409**	54.28
R^2	0.43		R^2	0.7	
No. obs.	576		No. obs.	3468	

Source The Wind Financial Database of China
*Significance at 10%
**Significance at 5%
***Significance at 1%

Bank financing accounts for approximately 35–40% ($5.5–6.4 trillion) of trade financing. However, the World Bank estimated that cash-in-advance comprised about 19–22% ($3–3.5 trillion) of all trade finance deals in 2008 (Chauffour & Malouche, 2011). Yet, to secure early payments, sellers often have limited options and must typically concede a portion of the payment as a discount, determined by the retailer. For instance, Walmart demands a 2% discount for its early payment provision (Green, 2015).

Typical discount rates for early payments hover between 1% and 2%, with terms spanning 30 to 60 days. A fairly lenient deal, offering a 1% discount for payment 60 days in advance, translates to a reasonable interest rate of 6.08% (calculated as 1% × 365 days/60 days = 6.08%). Yet, these major retailers aren't as charitable in their early payment schemes as they might seem. It's somewhat paradoxical that these dominant buyers first enforce an extended credit term (e.g., 90 days) in open accounts and then "benevolently" propose to "assist" their sellers by prepaying 30 days ahead, but for a 2% discount. While a dominant seller may be in a position to negotiate shorter credit terms or raise the wholesale price, many smaller businesses find themselves at the mercy of these retail giants.

> *It's ironic that dominant buyers initially request an extended credit term (e.g., 90 days) and then propose to "assist" their sellers by prepaying 30 days ahead, but only in exchange for a 2% discount.*

5.6 Documentary Collections

In *documentary collection* (D/C), the seller entrusts its bank (remitting bank) to collect payment from the buyer's bank (collecting bank) using documents provided and agreed upon by the buyer.

5.6.1 Process Flow

A typical procedure is as follows:

1. Upon finalizing the contract, the seller ships the goods to the buyer.
2. At the time of shipment, the seller submits a collection order, accompanied by the shipping documents and any other required documents, to its bank (remitting bank).
3. The remitting bank forwards these documents to the buyer's bank (collecting bank).
4. The collecting bank retrieves the payment from the buyer and transfers it to the remitting bank.
5. The remitting bank then disburses the payment to the seller.

There are two main types of payment collections in D/C: document against payment (D/P) and document against acceptance (D/A). In D/P, the buyer settles the face amount upon receipt of the documents. In D/A, the buyer makes the payment on a specified date, as outlined and agreed upon in the document.

5.6.2 D/C vs. LC and Others

D/C, like LC, involves banks, but their role is more limited, focusing primarily on document collection and payment transfer. Neither the remitting nor collecting banks supply funds or guarantee the payments.

Regarding payment timing, D/C adheres to the terms laid out in the documents, mutually agreed upon by both seller and buyer—akin to the procedure in LC. However, in D/C, banks neither verify the documents nor offer recourse in case of non-payment. Consequently, D/Cs typically cost less than LCs.

Fig. 5.8 Firms' risks in trade finance

In comparison with LC, D/C is more cost-effective for both seller and buyer. It offers reduced risk to the buyer, is simpler to execute, and allows for better cash flow management than cash-in-advance. Conversely, D/C presents a heightened risk to sellers due to the absence of bank guarantees and document verification.

Given the distinct advantages and disadvantages of these trade finance instruments for sellers and buyers—often contrasting in nature—we have summarized the risks to each party in Fig. 5.8. This is based on the timing of cash acquisition/retention. From a seller's perspective, consignment is the least secure since payment isn't received until the goods are sold, while cash-in-advance is the most secure. For buyers, the situation is reversed.

5.7 The Incoterms Rules

Payment obligations and inventory ownership can be nuanced in global trades. The International Chamber of Commerce has been publishing Incoterms since 1936, updating the rules every 10 years since 1980 to reflect changes in the global trade environment (ICC, 2020). The most recent version is Incoterms® 2020, preceded by Incoterms® 2010.

Incoterms® 2020 comprises 11 terms, ranging from EXW to DDP, as presented in Table 5.5. Of these, 4 terms are specific to waterway transport, while the remaining 7 are applicable to all modes of transport (ICC, 2020). The EXW term imposes the least obligation on the seller, and the buyer's obligation gradually diminishes across the subsequent terms, as detailed in Table 5.5. Given the potential for extended lead times during transport, especially via waterways, the precise moment of inventory ownership transfer significantly influences both the seller and buyer's inventory costs in financial statements.

For the convenience of readers, the subsequent 11 terms provide descriptions of the rules for sea and inland waterway transport, as sourced from the International Chamber of Commerce (ICC) Incoterms® 2020 (ICC, 2020):

EXW—*Ex-Works* or *Ex-Warehouse* indicates that the seller has fulfilled their delivery obligation once the goods are made available for the buyer at the seller's

5.7 The Incoterms Rules

Table 5.5 Incoterms® 2020 rules responsibility quick reference guide

	Any Transport Mode		Sea/Inland Waterway Transport				Any Transport Mode				
	EXW Ex Works	**FCA** Free Carrier	**FAS** Free Alongside Ship	**FOB** Free on Board	**CFR** Cost and Freight	**CIF** Cost Insurance & Freight	**CPT** Carriage Paid To	**CIP** Carriage & Insurance Paid to	**DAP** Delivered at Place	**DPU** Delivered at Place Unloaded	**DDP** Delivered Duty Paid
Invoicing & Export Packaging	Seller	Seller	Seller	Seller	Seller	Seller	Seller	Seller	Seller	Seller	Seller
Loading, Delivery, Taxes, & Export Duty	Buyer	Seller	Seller	Seller	Seller	Seller	Seller	Seller	Seller	Seller	Seller
Origin Terminal Charges	Buyer	Buyer	Seller	Seller	Seller	Seller	Seller	Seller	Seller	Seller	Seller
Loading on Carriage	Buyer	Buyer	Buyer	Seller	Seller	Seller	Seller	Seller	Seller	Seller	Seller
Carriage Charges	Buyer	Buyer	Buyer	Buyer	Seller	Seller	Seller	Seller	Seller	Seller	Seller
Insurance	Negotiable	Negotiable	Negotiable	Negotiable	Negotiable	Seller	Negotiable	Seller	Negotiable	Negotiable	Negotiable
Destination Terminal Charges	Buyer	Buyer	Buyer	Buyer	Buyer	Buyer	Seller	Seller	Seller	Seller	Seller
Delivery to Destination	Buyer	Buyer	Buyer	Buyer	Buyer	Buyer	Buyer	Buyer	Seller	Seller	Seller
Unloading at Destination	Buyer	Buyer	Buyer	Buyer	Buyer	Buyer	Buyer	Buyer	Buyer	Seller	Buyer
Import Duty, Taxes & Customs Clearance	Buyer	Buyer	Buyer	Buyer	Buyer	Buyer	Buyer	Buyer	Buyer	Buyer	Seller

Source Adapted from Global Trade Guide, IncoSolutions Pty Ltd. (ICC, 2020)

specified location (such as a factory, warehouse, etc.). The seller is not responsible for loading the goods onto a collection vehicle or for handling any export clearances if they are required.

FCA—Free Carrier implies that the seller hands over the goods to the buyer's designated carrier or another specified individual either at the seller's location or another predetermined site. It's prudent for both parties to distinctly pinpoint the exact spot within the designated delivery location since the buyer assumes the risk from that juncture.

CPT—Carriage Paid To indicates that the seller provides the goods to the carrier or another designated individual chosen by the seller at a mutually agreed-upon location (if such a location has been established between the parties). The seller is responsible for arranging and covering the carriage expenses to transport the goods to the specified destination.

CIP—Carriage and Insurance Paid To signifies that the seller hands over the goods to the carrier or a designated individual chosen by the seller at a mutually agreed location (if one has been established between the parties). The seller undertakes to arrange and cover the transport expenses required to take the goods to the specified end location. Additionally, the seller ensures coverage against any potential loss or damage to the goods during transportation. It's important for the buyer to be aware that under CIP, the insurance procured by the seller offers only the basic coverage.

DAP—Delivered At Place indicates that the seller completes delivery when the goods are made available to the buyer, ready for unloading, on the arriving transport method at the specified destination. The seller assumes all risks associated with transporting the goods to this designated location.

DPU—Delivered At Place Unloaded signifies that the seller completes delivery when the goods are unloaded and made available to the buyer at the specified destination. The seller takes on all risks associated with transporting and unloading the goods at the designated location.

DDP—Delivered Duty Paid indicates that the seller completes the delivery when the goods, cleared for import, are made ready for unloading and available to the buyer at the specified destination. The seller assumes all expenses and risks associated with transporting the goods to the destination and is responsible for all export and import customs clearances, paying any relevant duties, and handling all customs procedures.

FAS—Free Alongside Ship indicates that the seller has fulfilled their delivery obligation once the goods are positioned next to the vessel (for example, on a dock or barge) specified by the buyer at the designated port of shipment. The liability for potential loss or damage to the goods transfers to the buyer as soon as the goods are situated next to the ship, with the buyer responsible for all subsequent expenses.

FOB—Free On Board stipulates that the seller's responsibility ends once the goods are loaded onto the vessel chosen by the buyer at the specified port of shipment, or if the goods have already been delivered in this manner. The responsibility for any potential loss or damage to the goods transfers to the buyer once they are aboard the vessel, and any subsequent expenses fall on the buyer.

CFR—Cost and Freight dictates that the seller is responsible for getting the goods onboard the vessel or ensuring they have been delivered in that manner. Once the goods are on the vessel, any risk of damage or loss transitions to the buyer. Additionally, the seller is obligated to arrange and cover the expenses and freight to transport the goods to the designated port of destination.

CIF—Cost, Insurance and Freight stipulates that the seller ensures the goods are either onboard the vessel or confirms they've been delivered in such a manner. Once the goods are on the vessel, the responsibility for any potential damage or loss shifts to the buyer. The seller is tasked with arranging and covering the expenses, freight, and insurance to safeguard against any potential damage or loss to the goods during transit to the specified port of destination (ICC, 2020).

5.8 Case Study: The Enlightened Consignment Choice

5.8.1 The Case[3]

Case Study

The Enlightened Consignment Choice

Background

Liana served as the Vice President of Operations at Enlightened Inc., a leading original equipment manufacturer (OEM) in the technology equipment sector based in Silicon Valley, California. The firm recently introduced a new 3-D printer, the SCANNet-21D, priced at $19,995.

Following extensive research, Liana opted to collaborate with Lucastronics Ltd., a prospective contract manufacturer (CM) situated in Malaysia, to produce 35,000 units of SCANNet-21D. These finished products would then be imported to Enlightened's San Francisco distribution center. The shipping duration from Malaysia to San Francisco typically spanned 45 days, with the days of inventory (DOI) averaging at 30 days.

The Laser Component

Liana noted that from the bill of material ($10,800), the priciest component was the high-end laser, essential for the printer's cutting function. This component alone was priced at $4500. Enlightened co-developed this part

---

[3] This case and the following case analysis were developed based on a real practice of a company in Silicon Valley, California during the writing of this book. All company names are pseudonymous. Data are revised for confidentiality.

with LNET Inc. and subsequently sold it to Lucastronics at its cost, $4500, plus a 5% markup (covering acquisition costs, capital costs, and shipment to Lucastronics' manufacturing site) as per their agreement. Lucastronics also took charge of procuring the remaining components. The total production cost amounted to $12,725, exclusive of shipping expenses.

Liana was contemplating two choices for this particular laser component:

- **Option 1**: As stated above, permit Lucastronics to purchase and possess the laser inventory. The company would then ship the complete product DDP (delivery duty paid as per Incomterms® 2020, refer to Table 5.5 and Chapter 5.7) to Enlightened Inc.'s San Francisco hub. Under the DDP mode, Lucastronics would initially shoulder the shipment and importation costs of each printer unit, which Enlightened would later cover, adding $1000 per unit.
- **Option 2**: Enlightened could use a consignment model for the component, with Lucastronics only taking ownership before the product's completion. Enlightened would assume ownership once the final product was assembled at Malaysia's Port of Penang. The shipment to San Francisco would then be FCA (free carrier, with $950 per unit borne by Enlightened). This model would spare Enlightened the 5% markup.

Other Financial Information

After discussions with the R&D team and the CFO, Liana discovered that the total R&D expense for SCANNet-21D was projected at $70,000,000. This cost was anticipated to be equally spread across the 35,000 SCANNet-21D units ($2000 for each unit). The average SG&A expense was projected at $1300 per unit. All other costs were nominal and could be overlooked. Enlightened extended a 53-day payment term to its clientele (days sales outstanding, DSO) and a 45-day term to Lucastronics (days payable outstanding, DPO). If Enlightened needed to secure funds to cover its inventory, the interest rate could soar to 20%, given its subpar credit score. The CFO also indicated that Enlightened aspired to sustain an operating profit margin of over 15% and ensure that *Inventory/Total Sales* remained below 15% to guarantee smooth cash flow.

Liana was now at a crossroads, deciding between the two options.

Questions

1. Which option should Liana select: Option 1 or Option 2?
2. From this scenario, what managerial insights can you deduce?

5.8.2 Case Analysis

From the provided case, it's evident that under Option 2, where Enlightened consigns the laser component to Lucastronics, the procurement cost is lower compared to Option 1. Specifically, in Option 1, Enlightened's total procurement cost per unit amounts to $12,725 + $1000 = $13,725$. In contrast, Option 2 comes to $12,500 + $950 = $13,450$. This means Option 1 is pricier by $275 per unit than Option 2. The added R&D and SG&A costs for both alternatives sum up to $2000 + $1300 = 3300. Ignoring potential inventory financing costs, the unit operating profit for Option 1 stands at $19,995 - $13,725 - $3300 = 2970, translating to a $2970 / $19,995 = 14.85\%$ pre-tax operating profit margin. On the other hand, Option 2 offers a profit margin of $19,995 - $13,450 - $3,300 = 3245 and a $3245 / $19,995 = 16.23\%$ pre-tax operating profit margin. Detailed computations can be found in Table 5.6.

For Option 1 (DDP without consignment), the entire inventory duration for Enlightened is strictly the time spent in the distribution center (DC): 30 days. Conversely, Option 2 (FCA with consignment) leads to an inventory period of 30 days + 45 days = 75 days. By assessing the total value of inventory during these periods against total sales, we get *Inventory/Total Sales* ratios of 5.64% and 13.82% for Options 1 and 2 respectively, which is computed as follows:

$$Option\ 1: \frac{Inventory}{Total\ Sales} = \frac{\$13,725 \times 35,000 \times \frac{30\ days}{365\ days}}{\$19,995 \times 35,000} = \frac{\$39,482,877}{\$699,825,000} = 5.64\%$$

$$Option\ 2: \frac{Inventory}{Total\ Sales} = \frac{\$13,450 \times 35,000 \times \frac{30\ days + 45\ days}{365\ days}}{\$19,995 \times 35,000} = \frac{\$96,729,452}{\$699,825,000} = 13.82\%$$

To conclude, if Enlightened Inc. aims to sustain an operating profit margin above 15% and ensure *Inventory/Total Sales* stays under 15% for healthy cash turnover, Option 2 emerges as the more suitable choice.

However, when accounting for potential additional inventory costs due to cash flow deficits, it becomes necessary to adjust the operating profit by deducting the potential opportunity costs (calculated as = interest rate × cost of goods sold [COGS] × inventory days/365 days). Consequently, when evaluating operational profit minus inventory costs, we find margins of 13.73% and 13.46% for Options 1 and 2 respectively, which is computed as follows:

$$Option\ 1:\ Profit\ Margin = \frac{\$2970 - 0.2 \times \$13,725 \times \frac{30\ days}{365\ days}}{\$19,995} = 13.73\%$$

$$Option\ 2:\ Profit\ Margin = \frac{\$3245 - 0.2 \times \$13,450 \times \frac{30\ days + 45\ days}{365\ days}}{\$19,995} = 13.46\%$$

In this context, neither option satisfies the financial benchmarks set by Enlightened's CFO. Yet, Option 1 offers superior performance in both profit (i.e.,

Table 5.6 Financial analysis for Enlightened Inc. regarding SCANNet-21D production

SCANNet-21D	Option 1 (DDP)	Option 2 (FCA)
Sales Price	$19,995	$19,995
Production Cost w/o Laser	$8000	$8000
Laser Cost	$4500	$4500
Laser Markup Cost	$225	
Cost Paid to CM	$12,725	$12,500
DDP Cost	$1000	
FCA Cost		$950
Cost of Goods Sold	$13,725	$13,450
Gross Profit	$6270	$6545
Gross Margin	31.36%	32.73%
Total R&D	$70,000,000	$70,000,000
Average R&D	$2000	$2000
SG&A	$1300	$1300
Financing Cost Interest Rate	20%	20%
Inventory Financing Cost (if charged) per Unit	$226	$553
Operating Profit (Before Tax)	$2970	$3245
Operating Profit Margin (Before Tax)	14.85%	16.23%
Operating Profit Margin (Before Tax) and Minus Inventory Financing Cost	13.73%	13.46%
Volume	35,000	35,000
Total Sales	$699,825,000	$699,825,000
Total COGS	$480,375,000	$470,750,000
Total Gross Profit	$219,450,000	$229,075,000
Total Operating Profit	$103,950,000	$113,575,000
Days of Inventory DC	30	30
Days of Inventory Shipping	45	45
Value of Inventory DC	$39,482,877	$38,691,781
Value of Inventory Shipping		$58,037,671
Total Inventory	$39,482,877	$96,729,452
Inventory/Total Sales (%)	5.64%	13.82%

higher) and the *Inventory/Total Sales* percentage (i.e., lower), rendering it the more favorable choice.

Considering the cash conversion cycle (CCC), given DSO = 53, DPO = 45, and DIO values of 30 for Option 1 and 75 for Option 2, we obtain CCC values of 38 and 83 for Options 1 and 2 respectively. Thus, even excluding inventory financing costs, Option 1 can reduce the CCC by 83 days − 38 days = 45 days.

Should Enlightened be facing a significant cash flow challenge, Option 1 would again be more advantageous.

5.9 Summary

Trade finance tools are critical for successful international commerce, providing a framework that protects the interests of both buyers and sellers. From securing payments in advance to using letters of credit that ensure sellers get paid even if the buyer defaults, these instruments offer both parties security and peace of mind. Meanwhile, supply chain strategies, whether push or pull, align production with market demand, optimizing inventory levels and sales. Finally, Incoterms provide standardized contractual terms, clarifying roles and responsibilities in cross-border transactions.

Key Takeaways:

1. Cash-in-Advance and Push Supply Chains:
   - Cash-in-Advance: This method minimizes the risk for the seller, where the buyer pays before the goods or services are delivered. Particularly beneficial when the buyer's creditworthiness is questionable.
   - Push Supply Chains: Here, goods are produced based on forecasts or planned demand. Once manufactured, these products are "pushed" into the market, often using aggressive sales techniques and promotions.
2. Consignment and Pull Supply Chains:
   - Consignment: Goods are dispatched to the buyer or distributor who only pays for them when they are sold. Until then, the goods remain the property of the seller. This method elevates the risk for the seller, as payment is not guaranteed upon delivery.
   - Pull Supply Chains: Contrary to the push model, this is based on actual demand. Goods are "pulled" into production based on real-time sales data, reducing the risk of overproduction and stockouts.
3. Letter of Credit:
   - A letter of credit is a document issued by a bank that guarantees payment to the seller on behalf of the buyer. It's a trusted method in international trade to eliminate credit risk. If the buyer fails to pay, the bank will cover the amount.
4. Open Account:
   - An open account transaction allows the buyer to make payments at a future agreed date. Given that the seller ships the goods before payment is due, this method is more favorable for buyers but poses more risk to sellers.

5. Documentary Collections:
   - This process involves a bank (or several banks) acting as intermediaries without providing any guarantee of payment. The bank handles documents (like bills of lading or invoices) that the buyer needs, but only releases them once payment is made or a commitment to pay is given.
6. The Incoterms Rules:
   - Published by the International Chamber of Commerce, Incoterms define the responsibilities of buyers and sellers in international trade, including who pays for what, risks, responsibilities, and the point at which the risk transfers from seller to buyer.

5.10 Exercises

5.10.1 Practice Questions

1. What does the term "Trade Finance" refer to?
2. What is the primary advantage of using the cash-in-advance method for sellers in international trade?
3. In the cash-in-advance payment method, which party bears the risk?
4. How does a pull supply chain determine production levels?
5. Under consignment, when does the buyer or distributor pay for the goods?
6. What document issued by a bank guarantees payment to the seller on behalf of the buyer?
7. Which payment method is more favorable for buyers as they can pay at a future agreed date?
8. In documentary collections, what role does the bank play?
9. What is the role of a bank in a letter of credit transaction in international trade?
10. In which Incoterm does the seller deliver goods and cover all costs, including import duties and taxes, until the goods are received by the buyer?

5.10.2 Case Study

Stellar Fashions' Trade Financing Decision

Background

Stellar Fashions, a fast-growing fashion brand based in London, specializes in designing and selling sustainable fashion to European markets. Given the growing demand for eco-friendly products, they have seen a substantial increase in orders. To cope with this demand, they decided to source organic cotton fabric from FabTex Co., a manufacturer in India.

Details

1. FabTex Co. offers high-quality organic cotton and has the capacity to fulfill large orders that Stellar Fashions requires. The cost of each unit of fabric is $10, and Stellar Fashions plans to order 100,000 units for the upcoming fashion season.
2. FabTex Co., having had issues with previous clients not paying on time, is wary and asks Stellar Fashions for a "cash-in-advance" payment method.
3. Stellar Fashions, while having a good credit rating, is tight on cash flow due to other operational expenses. They are more comfortable with an "open account" payment method where they could pay a few weeks after receiving the fabric.
4. Both parties consider the "letter of credit" and "documentary collections" as potential middle-ground solutions. The shipment duration from FabTex Co. to Stellar Fashions is approximately 3 weeks.
5. Stellar Fashions' bank charges a 1% fee on the amount for opening a letter of credit. On the other hand, the documentary collections fee from FabTex Co.'s bank is 1.5%.

Problem Statement

How should Stellar Fashions and FabTex Co. proceed to ensure a smooth trade transaction ensuring both parties' comfort and financial security?

Appendix: Academic Perspective

Push, Pull, and Supply Chain Risk-Averse Attitude
   Lei Yang, Gangshu (George) Cai, and Jian Chen[4]

Introduction

In the real world, suppliers and retailers often deviate from risk neutrality. Koller et al. (2012) conducted a survey involving 1500 executives across 90 countries and

---

[4] This section presents research findings from one of my publications, Yang et al. (2018). For a more comprehensive understanding, readers are encouraged to consult the full article: Yang, L., Cai, G., and Chen, J., 2018. Push, pull, and supply chain risk-averse attitude. *Production and Operations Management, 27*(8), pp.1534–1552. We've omitted most references for brevity; for further details, please refer to Yang et al. (2018).

found that these executives displayed significant levels of risk aversion, irrespective of the investment size. This was the case even when the projected expected value of a venture was notably positive. As noted by the Wall Street Journal, companies tended to retain more cash, reflecting heightened risk aversion among management, often influenced by past bankruptcies. Some economists argued that a heightened sense of risk aversion was evident just as there was an observable shift in the economy. This shift occurred precisely when business investment spending was substantially lower than expected. Gurnani et al. (2014) further substantiated these findings, noting through their experimental research that firms exhibit behavioral inclinations towards risk aversion, especially when placing orders.

Given the inherent inventory risks in supply chains, a firm's stance on risk becomes crucial in the decision-making process. This raises some pivotal questions: Would the prevailing belief that "pull" strategies are superior to "push" strategies still hold in a context where firms are risk-averse? If so, how might the Pareto sets evolve, and what impact would this have on supply chain coordination? Is it possible to devise a specific contract that aligns with the risk aversion tendencies within the supply chain?

The Model

To delve into the effects of a risk-averse attitude, we adapted the classic push and pull newsvendor models to allow for both the supplier and the retailer to exhibit risk aversion. Our model is a nuanced extension of the archetypal newsvendor model, where a supplier transacts through a retailer to reach end customers. Here, the retailer procures a quantity, Q, from the supplier at a wholesale price w (refer to Fig. 5.9). The unit production cost stands at c, while the unit retail price is pegged at r. Both of these factors are exogenous, adhering to conventional literature standards. Demand, represented as D, is probabilistic and follows a distribution F, with a related density function, f. We designate the failure rate function as $h(x) \triangleq f(x)/(1-F(x))$. Our model assumes an increasing failure rate (IFR), symbolized by $h'(x) \geq 0$. This assumption aligns with various distribution functions, including but not limited to Normal, Log-Normal, Uniform, Exponential, Gamma, and Weibull distributions. For the sake of simplicity, we account for lost sales and disregard any salvage costs.

What differentiates our model from traditional push and pull newsvendor models is the incorporation of firms' risk attitudes which may not strictly align with

Fig. 5.9 Supply chain structure

Table 5.7 Difference between two optimal order quantities where F ~ U[0,16], r = 9, and c = 4

$Q_r - \hat{Q}_s$		ρ_r						
		0.7	0.75	0.8	0.85	0.9	0.95	1.0
ρ_s	0.7	0.2111	0.0333	-0.1244	-0.2922	-0.4600	-0.6378	-0.8056
	0.75	0.3911	0.2233	0.0556	-0.1122	-0.2800	-0.4478	-0.6156
	0.8	0.5611	0.4033	0.2356	0.0678	-0.1000	-0.2678	-0.4256
	0.85	0.7311	0.5733	0.4156	0.2478	0.0800	-0.0878	-0.2556
	0.9	0.9111	0.7533	0.5856	0.4278	0.2600	0.1022	-0.0656
	0.95	1.0711	0.9233	0.7656	0.6078	0.4400	0.2822	0.1144
	1.0	1.2411	1.0933	0.9356	0.7778	0.6200	0.4622	0.2944

risk neutrality. In order to gauge the risk quotient inherent to a supply chain decision, and consistent with established literature, we employ the Conditional Value-at-Risk (CVaR) as a metric representing a firm's objectives. CVaR is defined as[5]:

$$CVaR_\rho(\pi(Q)) = max_{v \in R}\{v + (1/\rho)\mathbb{E}[min(\pi(Q) - v, 0)]\}$$

Here, $\pi(Q)$ symbolizes the firm's profit, Q represents the order quantity, and v serves as a benchmark profit value. $\rho \in (0, 1]$ is a percentile indicative of a firm's risk aversion stance. When $\rho = 1$, the equation $CVaR\_\{\rho\}(\pi(Q)) = \mathbb{E}[\pi(Q)]$ holds true, thereby rendering the CVaR model equivalent to the traditional risk-neutral newsvendor model.

Within our framework, the supplier's risk disposition is represented by ρ_s, while the retailer's is denoted by ρ_r. Our study ascertains that in both push and pull supply chains, the supplier and retailer determine their optimal order quantities by maximizing their individual CVaRs. Both the push and the pull supply chain models yield a singular optimal order quantity.

Theoretical Findings

Our analysis indicates that the pull system can consistently outperform the push system when both the supplier and retailer possess the same risk attitude (i.e., they are on the same risk aversion level). However, the optimal order quantity for push ($\hat{Q}_s$) may be greater than that of pull (Q_r), provided the supplier is substantially more risk averse than the retailer (refer to Table 5.7).

Consequently, the efficiency of the supply chain under push contracts can surpass that of pull contracts. This discrepancy primarily stems from the difference

---

[5] There are various forms of CVaR tailored to firms' objectives and preferences. We introduce another version of CVaR in Chapter 11.3."

in risk attitudes between the supplier and the retailer. In a push system, the supply chain is only sensitive to the retailer's risk attitude since the retailer bears all inventory risks and would be affected if the demand is lower than the order quantity. In this scenario, the supplier's risk attitude doesn't influence the retailer's order quantity and, by extension, the wholesale price. Conversely, in a pull system, the inventory risk is borne by the supplier, making both the supplier's and the retailer's decisions vulnerable to demand uncertainty. Hence, the pull supply chain is influenced by the risk attitudes of both firms. Since risk-averse firms typically order less, a more risk-averse supplier would likely stock less inventory to mitigate risk in a pull supply chain.

To discern the optimal supply chain order quantity under risk for both push and pull contracts, we employ the concept of Pareto optimality, which maximizes the aggregate objectives of all stakeholders. The unified supply chain also exhibits risk aversion when both the supplier and retailer are risk averse. If the retailer is less risk averse, the risk attitude of a push supply chain is less pronounced than that of a pull supply chain. Consequently, the maximum supply chain CVaR for push surpasses that for pull. This differentiation also extends to the push Pareto set and pull Pareto set. If the supplier is considerably more risk averse than the retailer, certain aspects of the pull contract might become vulnerable to the push system (i.e., the retailer might benefit more from pre-ordering some inventory).

Furthermore, our study demonstrates that three-part tariff revenue sharing and buy-back contracts can both effectively elevate the supply chain's CVaR to its peak value. However, these contracts cannot elevate supply chain profits to their maximal point, as seen when the supply chain risk is neutral. The supply chain risk is contingent on the revenue sharing rate or buy-back rate, implying that modifying these rates can influence overall supply chain profits.

Our research yields several managerial insights. Firstly, it offers an augmented perspective on risk-averse suppliers and retailers within the conventional push and pull newsvendor model, highlighting that a push strategy can eclipse a pull strategy in the context of risk aversion. Secondly, it underscores the importance for managers to be cognizant of firms' risk attitudes since these can skew efficient ordering and allow push to surpass pull, regardless of supply chain coordination. Lastly, the introduction of either a three-part tariff revenue sharing contract or a three-part tariff buy-back contract to push or pull agreements can lead to the maximization of the cumulative supplier-retailer CVaR. The resultant supply chain risk attitude can then be modified by these coordinating contracts.

References

Barrot, J. N. (2016). Trade credit and industry dynamics: Evidence from trucking firms. *The Journal of Finance, 71*(5), 1975–2016.

Cachon, G. P. (2004). The allocation of inventory risk in a supply chain: Push, pull, and advance-purchase discount contracts. *Management Science, 50*(2), 222–238.

Cai, G., Chen, X., & Xiao, Z. (2014). The roles of bank and trade credits: Theoretical analysis and empirical evidence. *Production and Operations Management, 23*(4), 583–598.

References

Chauffour, J. P., & Malouche, M. (2011). *Trade finance during the 2008–9 trade collapse: Key take aways* (Report, The World Bank, NW Washington, DC, U.S.A.).

Chen, X., Lu, Q., & Cai, G. (2020). Buyer financing in pull supply chains: Zero-interest early payment or in-house factoring? *Production and Operations Management, 29*(10), 2307–2325.

Deloof, M., & Jegers, M. (1999). Trade credit, corporate groups, and the financing of Belgian firms. *Journal of Business Finance & Accounting, 26*(7), 945–966.

Green, L. (2015). *Wal-Mart extends supplier payment terms, but it's not necessarily a bad thing.*

Gurnani, H., Ramachandran, K., Ray, S., & Xia, Y. (2014). Ordering behavior under supply risk: An experimental investigation. *Manufacturing & Service Operations Management, 16*(1), 61–75.

Hoffman, C. (2022). *Red clause vs green clause letters of credit – A 2022 letter of credit guide.* https://www.tradefinanceglobal.com/posts/red-letters-credit-green-letters-credit/#:~:text=WhilearedclauseLC,originandinsuranceintoaccount. Accessed 2 January 2023.

ICC. (2020). *Incoterms® 2020.* https://iccwbo.org/resources-for-business/incoterms-rules/incoterms-2020/. Accessed 22 January 2022.

Jdsupra. (2021). *Shift to open account trade highlights evolving risks in the maritime sector | k2 Integrity.* https://www.jdsupra.com/legalnews/shift-to-open-account-trade-highlights-9822805/. Accessed 12 January 2022.

Jiménez, G. (2013). *ICC guide to export-import: Global standards for international trade.* International Chamber of Commerce.

Jing, B., Chen, X., & Cai, G. G. (2012). Equilibrium financing in a distribution channel with capital constraint. *Production and Operations Management, 21*(6), 1090–1101.

Kagan, J. (2022). *Trade credit.* https://www.investopedia.com/terms/t/trade-credit.asp. Accessed 12 November 2022.

Koller, T., Lovallo, D., & Williams, Z. (2012). *Overcoming a bias against risk.* https://www.mckinsey.com/~/media/mckinsey/businessfunctions/strategyandcorporatefinance/ourinsights/overcomingabiasagainstrisk/overcomingabiasagainstrisk.pdf?shouldIndex=false. Accessed 6 July 2021.

Marks, G. (2015, March 23). How to get paid faster from Home Depot. *Forbes.*

Miller, D. (2021). *What is a letter of credit?* https://www.lendio.com/blog/what-is-letter-of-credit/#:~:text=Thestandardcostofa,couldfallcloseto1.5%25. Accessed 16 July 2021.

O'Connell, V. (2009). Wal-Mart looks to Bolster suppliers. *The Wall Street Journal.*

Petersen, M. A., & Rajan, R. G. (1997). Trade credit: Theories and evidence. *Review of Financial Studies, 10*, 661–692.

PYMNTS. (2015). *The downfall of the letter of credit.* https://www.pymnts.com/in-depth/2015/the-downfall-of-the-letter-of-credit/. Accessed 21 December 2022.

Rajan, R. G., & Zingales, L. (1995). What do we know about capital structure? Some evidence from international data. *The Journal of Finance, 50*(5), 1421–1460.

Trade Finance Global. (2023). *Letters of credit.* https://www.tradefinanceglobal.com/letters-of-credit/. Accessed 26 July 2021.

UniCredit. (2016). *Bank Payment Obligation—BPO. Case studies of UniCredit as of Febuary 2016.*

Wikipedia. (2020). *Letter of credit.* https://en.wikipedia.org/wiki/Letter_of_credit. Accessed 6 October 2020.

Wikipedia. (2021). *Trade credit.* https://en.wikipedia.org/wiki/Trade_credit. Accessed 11 October 2021.

Yang, L., Cai, G., & Chen, J. (2018). Push, pull, and supply chain risk-averse attitude. *Production and Operations Management, 27*(8), 1534–1552.

Seller-Led Supply Chain Finance

Learning Objectives:

1. Differentiate factoring from traditional debt and assess its impact on company finances.
2. Identify forfaiting's role in medium to long-term trade finance and risk mitigation.
3. Contrast invoice discounting with factoring and understand purchase order financing's impact on liquidity and business expansion.
4. Explore seller-led accounts receivable securitization and its role in optimizing credit quality.

6.1 Introduction

Many manufacturers are small, capital-constrained, and lack the creditworthiness to borrow enough cash to fund their production. According to Chen et al. (2020), millions of small businesses account for 60–80% of all U.S. jobs. However, 43% of small business owners have faced capital constraints at least once in the past four years and could not secure any financing. As reported by the World Bank Group Enterprise Surveys, 27% of 130,000 firms across 135 countries identify "access to finance" as a major business constraint.

This financial distress can further burden capital-constrained manufacturers, particularly if the production lead time is long. In such situations, the manufacturer must produce and stockpile products before the retailer places an order, especially when demand peaks in short selling seasons (e.g., seasonal and holiday sales). The situations can deteriorate when dominant buyers like Amazon, Walmart, Alibaba, and JingDong wield significant power and demand longer payment terms in open accounts (e.g., extending from net 30 days to net 90 days).

Supply chain finance designed to assist upstream firms can be driven by the seller, the buyer, or a third party, such as a third-party logistics (3PL) firm, a bank, an internet platform, or even an insurance company. In *seller-led supply chain finance* mechanisms, the seller initiates financing requests to banks or other financial institutions based on supply chain transactions. These transactions might be rooted in accounts receivable, note receivables, purchase orders, or inventory.

Seller-led supply chain finance has become a predominant financial instrument in business transactions. For instance, in 2018, seller-led supply chain finance accounted for about 41% of the total supply chain finance turnover (McKinsey, 2020). The overall volume of seller-led finance amounted to approximately $3 trillion, compared to the total supply chain finance turnover of $7.3 trillion.

In this chapter, we will explore various seller-led supply chain finance mechanisms, with an emphasis on accounts receivable financing as well as purchase order financing. In *accounts receivable financing*, a supplier sells its accounts receivable, note receivable, or other receivables to a bank, a factor, or even another company to obtain advanced funds to support its operations and repay debts. Popular receivable financing methods include factoring, forfaiting, and invoice discounting, among others. The financing company facilitating the purchase of accounts receivable might assume the risk of non-payment from the buyer in exchange for a significant profit margin. Depending on the financing mechanism, the seller might obtain 70–90% or even up to 100% of the face value of the accounts receivable.

While seller-led supply chain finance continues to expand, many financing terminologies used by the industry often overlap, are imprecisely defined, or can be confusing. Therefore, this chapter will not enumerate all terminologies utilized by financing companies and websites but will concentrate on the most commonly used terms. A similar approach has been adopted in other chapters.

6.2 Factoring

Factoring is a principal financing mechanism within the broader category of accounts receivable financing.[1] As one of the oldest forms of financial mechanisms, factoring allows companies to leverage their outstanding invoices or accounts receivable to quickly secure cash. The allure of factoring lies in its capacity to grant companies immediate access to cash based on their accounts receivable, thus enabling them to pursue further business activities, such as production and R&D.

---

[1] Factoring is also referred to as invoice factoring, accounts receivable factoring, and accounts receivable financing. However, these alternative names are also used for invoice discounting and other receivable-based financing. To avoid confusion, we mostly use only "factoring" in our discussion.

6.2 Factoring

In *seller-led factoring*, often termed supplier-led factoring, the seller approaches its affiliated banks to purchase all or a portion of its accounts receivable at a discounted rate. In many instances, sellers also opt to outsource other back-office tasks to the financing company involved in the factoring process.

6.2.1 Case Study: A Cash Flow Problem

Case Study

The Cash Flow Problem of Harbor Tree Manufacturing Inc.

The Challenge

Harbor Tree Manufacturing Inc. (HTM) is a burgeoning startup that assembles high-quality electronic products for its clientele. Recently, HTM locked in a long-term contract, set to commence in a month, promising them a payment of $250,000 monthly. Every month, at the outset, the client issues an invoice. It then takes precisely one month for HTM to assemble and dispatch the product, satisfying the stipulations of the invoice. Payment for this invoice is made 60 days post-issue.

Currently, HTM's cash reserves stand at $100,000. However, they grapple with a monthly payroll demand of $120,000, coupled with other miscellaneous expenses totaling $90,000. HTM's present monthly financial standing is depicted below:

Cash	A/R (Net 60)	Payroll	Expenses
$100,000	$250,000	$120,000	$90,000

After a month, their cash position will be at a deficit of $110,000 (i.e., $100,000 − $120,000 − $90,000 = −$110,000). Even though HTM has been performing relatively well, they'll confront this shortfall since the accounts receivable can't be converted to cash within that time frame. HTM's constricted cash flow implies a scarcity in working capital, hampering their ability to cover routine operational costs or seize growth opportunities, such as product diversification or penetrating new markets.

In theory, HTM could approach a bank for a loan to bridge this gap. However, banks often hesitate to back small-scale entities lacking an extensive credit history, especially if they don't showcase consistent profitability or substantial collateral. Regrettably, HTM doesn't fit the bill for conventional bank (loan) financing, and given the time-consuming nature of such processes, this route won't timely address HTM's immediate cash crunch.

The Solution

A feasible remedy for HTM is to resort to factoring, a financing mechanism that can swiftly convert its accounts receivable into cash. Through factoring, HTM can obtain up to 90% of its outstanding invoices' value upfront, while the remaining 10% is held in reserve until full payment of the invoices is realized. Post factoring, HTM's monthly financial position evolves as:

Cash	Reserve	Payroll	Expenses
$325,000	$25,000	$120,000	$90,000

With a month's progression, and after transforming 90% of the accounts receivable into cash, HTM's cash status surges to a positive $325,000 − $120,000 − $90,000 = $115,000.

The Trade-off

Factoring's primary caveat is that its cost might surpass that of traditional bank loans. Nonetheless, the advantages are clear-cut. Post factoring, HTM not only elevates its cash flow but can also amplify its market footprint by clinching more contracts. Additionally, HTM mitigates its credit risk, as the factoring entity assumes the role of collecting dues from clients. With sustained profitability, HTM's credit standing can only improve, paving the way for more economical commercial loans directly from banks in the future.

Questions

1. Why is factoring beneficial for HTM?
2. Can you provide another anecdotal example illustrating the use of factoring?

6.2.2 Process Flow

A typical factoring process is depicted in Fig. 6.1 and can be elucidated using the following hypothetical case:

1. **Order Placement**: LoisYZ Electronics (LYZ) Inc., a buyer, places monthly orders with Harbor Tree Manufacturing Inc. (HTM, the seller) after entering a long-term contract.
2. **Invoice Issuance**: Once HTM delivers the product, they issue an invoice to LYZ. As per their agreement, the invoice could be issued earlier—potentially when the order is placed but before product delivery. To be eligible for factoring, these invoices typically need to have payment terms of 90 days or shorter (i.e., net 90 or less).

6.2 Factoring

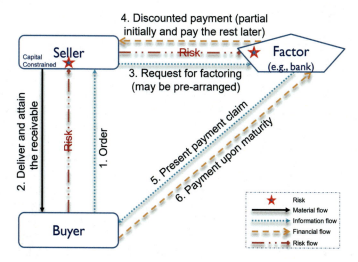

Fig. 6.1 Mechanism of factoring

3. **Factoring Request**: HTM seeks factoring services from a factor (like a bank or a financial institution). If HTM hasn't done so already, they'll establish a factoring account with the factor. Once this relationship is in place, HTM can continue to submit any subsequent factoring requests to the same institution. Within the factoring contract, terms such as factoring fees and the percentage of accounts receivable to be factored are specified. Given that payment terms can vary based on which buyers will be settling the accounts receivable, it's the factor's duty to conduct due diligence, assessing the specific credit risks associated with each buyer.
4. **Initial Payment**: In accordance with the factoring contract, the factor transfers the discounted initial advance payment to HTM, with the discount rate commonly referred to as the "advance rate."
5. **Claim Presentation**: As the accounts receivable's due date approaches, the factor presents a payment claim to LYZ.
6. **Final Settlement**: LYZ settles the invoice with the factor at the agreed price. The factor then disburses the outstanding accounts receivable balance to HTM, deducting the factoring fees.

As illustrated in Fig. 6.1, upon product delivery, should the buyer fail to make payment due to unforeseen circumstances, the financial risk migrates from the buyer to the seller. Once the factor forwards the advance rate to the seller, this risk then transitions from the seller to the factor. To buffer against this financial risk, terms are usually negotiated in the factoring contract between the firms and the factor.

6.2.3 Factoring Cost

The cost associated with factoring is termed as either a factoring fee or discount rate. Since sellers of accounts receivable are often capital-constrained, the *factoring fee* typically manifests as a discount from the face value of the accounts receivable. This discount rate may comprise a fixed fee set by the factor and an interest expense for the fund advance. For instance, a factor might charge a 5% fee for an invoice due in 60 days. If the discount rate is applied monthly, a 2.5% discount rate would compound to slightly more than 5% (specifically, 5.0625%). If an invoice is settled early, the factor reimburses the interest difference to the firm as a factoring rebate.

On average, factoring fees usually range between 1% and 5% of the value of corresponding accounts receivable (Truckstop, 2023). Factoring companies often employ a variable fee structure. Should an invoice remain unpaid, these companies typically discount an additional small percentage (1–3%) for payment delays (FactorFinders, 2020). Consequently, the factoring fee increases if the firm's client postpones payment. For instance, a factor might charge 2% for the initial 30 days and an additional 0.5% for every subsequent 10 days.

Banks typically refrain from covering 100% of the accounts receivable because of potential payment uncertainties from buyers. Banks often remit between 70% and 90% of the value of accounts receivable, influenced by the size of the receivable, the industry, and their risk assessment, especially concerning buyers (Sillay, 2012). The remaining portion of the accounts receivable is retained as a reserve, safeguarding against payment failures from buyers, which might arise due to reasons like product failures or subsequent returns.

To mitigate risks, factors usually account for some expected bad debt expense, which pertains to the share of accounts receivable that may remain unpaid and non-collectable. One common risk management strategy is capping the factoring percentage. For example, a bank might stipulate that the financing ratio shouldn't surpass 80%.

Given that the discount rate is typically determined based on the invoice's total face value, the factoring client can only advance a portion of the invoice value. Even if the factoring fee remains constant, the effective factoring fee alters with the advance percentage. The formula for the effective factoring fee is:

$$\text{Effective Factoring Fee} = \frac{\text{Quoted Factoring Fee}}{\text{Advance Percentage (of the Invoice Value)}}$$

For instance, with a quoted factoring fee of 2% and an advance percentage of 70%, the calculation is:

$$\text{Effective Factoring Fee} = \frac{2\%}{70\%} = 2.86\%$$

A sample Table 6.1 illustrating effective fees at various advance percentages.

6.2 Factoring

Table 6.1 Effective factoring fee example

Quoted Factoring Fee	Advance Percentage (%)	Effective Factoring Fee (%)
2%	70	2.86
	80	2.50
	85	2.35
	90	2.22

Because the *effective factoring fee* represents the actual discount rate that the factoring client incurs for what they receive, comparing these fees becomes essential before finalizing a factoring company.

In practice, effective factoring fees vary considerably due to elements like the total invoice amount, buyer creditworthiness, duration of factoring, advance percentages, and other stipulations. To ensure profitability, a factor might also set a minimum for monthly invoice submissions. Such a stipulation allows the factor to reduce client onboarding costs, consequently offering lower factoring fees and fostering a long-term relationship. In a "whole ledger" scenario, clients consistently submit all their invoices to one particular factor over an extended duration.

6.2.4 Factoring Amount and Cash Balance: A Simplified Analysis

Factoring has been a strategy for businesses, notably SMEs and burgeoning enterprises, to secure liquidity. Nonetheless, a company must decide whether to forward all its accounts receivable to a factoring company or be discerning to maintain a robust cash balance. On one side, having an ample cash reserve bolsters a company's liquidity. Conversely, factoring all accounts receivable brings about elevated opportunity costs due to having idle cash in the bank, especially after bearing significant factoring fees. This situation places the firm in a predicament concerning factoring: liquidating excessive accounts receivable prematurely could be overly expensive even if deemed essential.

> The firm faces a dilemma in factoring: liquidating too many accounts receivable in advance could prove too expensive, even if necessary.

For a company's sustainability, revenues should surpass expenditures. In this context, the cumulative value of its accounts receivable should outweigh the total costs in each cycle. Moreover, while a company might be compelled to forgo some marginal profit when factoring its accounts receivable, its ultimate objective remains maximizing profits. Accordingly, the company needs to strategize on optimizing the proportion of accounts receivable allocated for factoring.

For this analysis, we'll presume that a company requires a fixed budget, represented by B, to cover its administrative, staffing, debt payments, and other obligatory expenditures over a given period, t. The company aims to maintain a minimum safety cash threshold, C_0, to ward off financial instability during unforeseen swift cash depletions. Let's use β to signify the unpredictability of all these uncertainties. Thus, for operational continuity, the company should uphold an average cash reserve as:

$$\overline{C} = \beta(C_0 + \frac{B}{t})$$

It's crucial to understand that the required safety cash balances diverge across companies. Generally, companies with greater asset volatility (β) should maintain a heftier cash cushion. When establishing this reserve, numerous factors should be considered, including the volume and nature of disbursements, banking relationships, risk profile, branch locations, customer distribution, political climate, fund management, and more.

A consistent correlation between cash and sales improves predictions for minimal cash requirements. For emerging, fast-paced businesses, historical financial data can guide in determining this safety cash threshold. As an approximation, one might set aside cash equivalent to one or two weeks of disbursements, computed from the sum of cost of goods sold and overheads (Accountleaning, 2023). However, such a reserve might prove inadequate for many SMEs during significant disruptions, as witnessed during the COVID-19 outbreak in 2020. Hence, determining an appropriate safety cash reserve necessitates expertise and an assessment of a firm's risk appetite. A conservative risk stance would advocate for a higher β.

Assuming a company engages in a long-term agreement with a factoring firm and commits to forwarding all its invoices, and anticipating certain invoices, represented by a_i, to mature at diverse intervals within the period t, the cumulative value of all accounts receivable at their respective maturity is $\sum_i a_i$. The factoring charge for a_i is specified as f_i, with an advance rate of ρ_i. The firm will receive a cash advance proportionate to $\rho_i a_i$, and the remaining balance minus the factoring fee is $(1 - \rho_i - f_i)a_i$ upon the receivables' maturity. Consequently, the aggregate value of all accounts receivable post-factoring is:

$$A = \sum_i [\rho_i a_i + (1 - \rho_i - f_i)a_i] = \sum_i (1 - f_i)a_i$$

Assuming cash inflow from these accounts receivable is the sole revenue stream, the projected average cash reserve post-factoring is $A/2$. Logically, $A/2$ should exceed $\overline{C}$ to ensure business continuity. Otherwise, alternative financing avenues might be necessary.

6.2 Factoring

Table 6.2 Impact of factoring on firms' operations and risks

	Seller	Buyer	Factor
Cash	↑		↓
AR	↓		↑
Inventory	Potentially ↑		
AP		Potentially ↑	
NWC	↓		↓
Risks	↓		↑

Note The arrows (↑) indicate an increase, while (↓) indicate a decrease

If $A/2$ surpasses $\overline{C}$, a firm might also deliberate on whether to liquidate all accounts receivable immediately, given the substantial costs associated with factoring. To merely break even, a company might adopt a more selective stance on the number of accounts receivable to convert into cash upfront. The cashout ratio is then expressed by:

$$\text{Cashout Ratio} = \frac{\overline{C}}{A/2} = \frac{2\beta(C_0 + B/t)}{\sum_i (1 - f_i) a_i}$$

6.2.5 Comparison and Benefits of Factoring

In this section, we compare factoring to traditional bank financing and discuss the benefits of factoring for both sellers and the factors.

6.2.5.1 Impact of Factoring on Firms' Operations and Risks

Table 6.2 provides an illustrative overview of the effects of factoring on companies' operations and risks. Clearly, factoring enhances the seller's liquidity, decreases its accounts receivable (AR) and net working capital (NWC), while transferring the risks to the factor. The opposite applies to the factor. Notably, the seller's inventory may rise due to the additional cash, which can be used to tap into new markets. This could also prompt the seller to encourage buyers to place larger orders, potentially inflating the buyer's inventory as well.

6.2.5.2 Factoring vs. Bank Financing

Bank loan financing stands as a common reference when contrasting with factoring. Below, we highlight the key differences between factoring and bank financing (refer to Table 6.3).

Table 6.3 Comparison between factoring and bank financing

	Factoring	Bank Financing
Type	Not a loan; no assumption of debt	Loan with principal and interest repayments
Qualification	Based on valid invoices and creditworthiness of the client's customers (i.e., the buyer)	Creditworthiness, financial health, assets, and liabilities are considered
Time	A few days to establish a factoring account; post-setup, funds can be accessed within 24 hours	Usually takes months to secure a loan; funds are instantly accessible once approved
Process	Minimal paperwork	Detailed documentation and extensive information are required
Costs	Generally higher fees, but they're flexible and based on the factoring amount and advance timing	Typically, lower costs with a fixed annual percentage rate (APR)
Amount	Up to the face value of invoices	Loan limit set based on creditworthiness, assets, and other financial criteria
Other Services	Factors may offer credit insights about a client's customers, AR maintenance and reports, collection services, and back-office services	Typically, no auxiliary services provided

6.2.5.3 Benefits of Factoring for Sellers

Compared to bank financing and other traditional financing methods, factoring offers several distinct advantages to sellers:

- *Liquidity Improvement*: Sellers turn to factoring when they require immediate cash to sustain daily operations and fuel business growth. By facilitating this, factoring enhances the seller's liquidity. This ensures that sellers can maintain a healthy cash balance to fulfill their immediate financial obligations and accommodate other business needs. It's worth noting that certain industries, such as textiles and apparel, utilize factoring more frequently due to its historical role in their financing.
- *Credibility Enhancement*: Sellers with limited creditworthiness or no credit history often struggle to obtain traditional bank loans. However, accounts receivables are grounded on completed transactions, and the likelihood of payment hinges on the buyer's creditworthiness. As such, even a seller with less favorable credit can easily access factoring if the buyer has a robust credit rating. The advanced amounts from factoring, being limited to the invoices, facilitate establishing a long-term relationship between the seller and the factoring company. Over time, this also contributes to enhancing the

seller's credibility, paving the way for more favorable financing options in the future.
- *Financial Statement Benefit*: Factoring isn't categorized as debt because it represents an advance on funds for goods and services already sold. To put it differently, factoring is essentially the sale of accounts receivable rather than borrowing against them as collateral. This distinction can improve the appearance of a seller's financial statement and boost its credit rating—a significant advantage, especially if the seller is navigating a tight liquidity situation with elevated debt levels.

> Factoring is not considered debt, which benefits the seller.

- *Process Expedition*: Factoring often necessitates less paperwork and yields quicker access to funds compared to conventional bank financing. In numerous cases, sellers can receive the cash they need in as short a timeframe as 24 hours, particularly with whole ledger factoring. This expedited process alleviates challenges for smaller businesses when converting their accounts receivable into cash.
- *Effective Payment Collection*: Some emerging companies, especially if the factor has a robust payment collection mechanism, leverage factoring as a means of outsourcing their accounts receivable collection operations.

6.2.5.4 Benefits of Factoring for Factors

While the benefits of factoring to the seller are significant, factors also derive substantial advantages from offering this service.

- *Increased Revenue*: Through factoring, the factoring company can charge a relatively high interest rate when financing the seller, enhancing the company's profit margins.
- *Market Expansion*: By purchasing accounts receivable, a factoring company (e.g., a bank) can diversify beyond traditional loan financing. This expansion allows the factor to capture new business opportunities.
- *Improved Collections*: Factoring companies often possess a broader network and a higher level of expertise in collecting payments on outstanding invoices. This not only results in more efficient collections but also presents more business opportunities as they can assist sellers in faster and hassle-free payment collections. In the unfortunate event of the buyer declaring bankruptcy, purchasing the seller's accounts receivable offers an advantage for the factor over other creditors.

In summary, factoring provides companies with opportunities to leverage their collection expertise, expand their market, and increase profitability, leading to new business avenues.

6.2.6 Risks and Risk Mitigation

In this section, we delve into the risk mitigation strategies for both sellers and factors in the realm of factoring.

6.2.6.1 Risk Mitigation for Sellers

While companies may choose factoring when the benefit of immediate cash outweighs the factoring costs, it's essential to recognize that a company's cash flow fluctuates. As a result, they might not always opt for factoring, especially when the factoring discount rate is steep. Although factors might prefer consistent invoice inflow through extended factoring agreements, it's imperative for firms to evaluate their cash advance needs and decide judiciously about using factoring.

Additionally, the seller might grapple with operational risk, reputation risk, and discount rate risk. Below, we encapsulate these risks and their respective mitigation strategies in Table 6.4.

6.2.6.2 Risk Mitigation for Factors

Once accounts receivable transition to factoring companies, they inherit the financial risks previously shouldered by the sellers. Factoring companies may encounter a spectrum of risks, including credit, operational, market, and reputation risks. Table 6.5 presents these risks alongside their respective mitigation strategies.

In conclusion, adept risk mitigation in factoring demands a blend of meticulous planning, due diligence, continuous monitoring, and dynamic management. Adhering to these strategies, factoring companies can navigate the risk landscape, securing their financial objectives.

6.2.7 Variations of Factoring

Factoring, as established, permits sellers to obtain cash earlier and simultaneously transfers financial risks to the factor. The specific type of factoring chosen can be instrumental in risk mitigation. The various types of factoring, based on the nuanced involvement of the parties, are elaborated below.

6.2.7.1 Notification Factoring vs. Non-Notification Factoring

Traditionally, given that the buyer is integral to an invoice, sellers typically inform the buyer when accounts receivable or an invoice is sold. Such transactions are termed as *notification* or *disclosed factoring*. Within this paradigm, the factor typically interacts directly with the buyer to authenticate the invoice and secure approvals. Consequently, instead of reimbursing the seller, the buyer pays the factor.

In contrast, contemporary practices have witnessed a surge in transactions wherein sellers do not inform buyers about this sale. This method is dubbed non-notification, non-disclosed, or confidential factoring. Here, the buyer remains unaware of the factoring agreement. During payment collection, the buyer sends

6.2 Factoring

Table 6.4 Risks and risk mitigation for sellers in factoring

Risks	• **High Financing Cost Risk**: Factoring can come at a higher cost than standard bank loans. For instance, a 3% monthly factoring fee equates to an 36% APR, substantially higher than most bank loans. With prolonged engagements, companies can often negotiate reduced factoring fees • **Operational Risk**: Successful factoring can be disrupted by factors like shipment delays, product quality issues, returns, or a defaulting buyer • **Reputation Risk**: Stakeholders might perceive factoring as an indication of a company's financial instability, which could harm its reputation and relationships • **Discount Rate Risk**: A primary concern is the high discount rate in factoring, which could escalate unpredictably • **Interdependence Risk**: The discount rate hinges on the buyer's creditworthiness. While a good credit rating from the buyer is beneficial, a low rating can lead to higher rates. In whole ledger factoring, where all buyers are pooled, the rate becomes an average. Factors, however, are vulnerable to defaults from the buyer
Risk Mitigation	• **High Financing Cost Risk**: Firms can alleviate this risk by ensuring positive cash flow and trimming expenses, which reduces their dependency on external funding. Exploring other financial avenues, like reverse factoring, is also advisable • **Operational Risk**: To foster a lasting relationship with the factor, sellers must ensure prompt product deliveries and maintain transparency about product details, buyer information, and their own operations • **Reputation Risk**: Proper communication management and partnering with reputable factors can help mitigate this risk • **Discount Rate Risk**: Understanding the factoring contract's terms, especially concerning the discount rate and repayment, is vital. Regularly monitoring the discount rate and adjusting financing strategies are also crucial. Furthermore, incorporating highly risky buyers into the accounts receivable pool without the factor's consent should be avoided to prevent future rate hikes • **Interdependence Risk**: Addressing this risk necessitates a multifaceted strategy, such as diversifying relationships, building ties with multiple key stakeholders, contingency planning, proactive risk management, resilience investments, and collaborating with peers

payment for the invoice to a factor-managed lock-box or electronic deposit account—details of which are provided by the seller upon invoice generation (CorsaFinance, 2023).

6.2.7.2 Recourse Factoring vs. Non-Recourse Factoring

Standard factoring is without recourse, implying that if a buyer defaults on a payment, the consequent loss falls upon the factor. Often, financial entities may eschew offering factoring services if a preliminary risk assessment highlights substantial financial risks.

If a factor is tentative about rendering the service, the seller can offer a guarantee to facilitate the factoring, converting factoring without recourse (*non-recourse factoring*) to factoring with recourse (*recourse factoring*). In the latter scenario, the factor reserves the right to recover the unpaid invoice amount from the seller

Table 6.5 Risks and risk mitigation for factors in factoring

Risks	• **Credit Risk**: If buyers default on their commitments, factoring companies stand to suffer. Risks can further escalate if the creditworthiness of buyers isn't meticulously assessed or if the collection process is ineffectively managed
	• **Operational Risk**:
	  – **Product Delivery**: Even as invoices are submitted for factoring, products/services might still be in the process of delivery (Bryant & Camerinelli, 2014)
	  – **Process Error and Miscommunication**: Given that factoring often involves multiple entities and the possibility of outsourcing accounts receivable management to third-party factors, risks such as processing errors or miscommunications can arise
	• **Market Risk**:
	  – **Product Quality**: Due to uncertainty regarding product quality, buyers often demand policies that allow for hassle-free returns in the event of defects. Yet, these return policies are typically not reflected on the invoices, meaning factoring companies might not recover the full invoice value in case of product returns
	  – **Demand Volatility**: Sellers might offer lenient return policies to incentivize bulk orders. However, if actual demand undershoots expectations, a surge in product returns can ensue, jeopardizing the factoring company's accounts receivable value
	• **Reputation Risk**:
	  – **Misreporting of Invoices**: Companies might erroneously record invoice values within the factoring system. In scenarios involving whole ledgers, firms might bundle spurious invoices with genuine ones. An audit system is essential to weed out these false invoices and rectify the accurate invoice value
	  – **Hidden Information**: Credit notes might accompany invoices, referencing concerns like overpayments, errors, product damages, or other related credits. However, these might not be transparently reported to the factoring company. Concurrently, undisclosed commercial disputes between sellers and buyers could remain hidden from factors, potentially impacting the realization of accounts receivable

Risk Mitigation	• **Credit Risk**: Evaluating a buyer's creditworthiness is paramount. This necessitates an in-depth review of their financial trajectory and an assessment of their repayment capability • **Operational Risk**: Engaging a credible auditor to verify logistics can address product delivery risks. To tackle processing and communication errors, well-defined, documented processes are indispensable • **Market Risk**: Typically, factoring companies hold back a percentage of the invoice value as a reserve to offset this risk. This approach can also buffer against other risks • **Reputation Risk**: Proper communication management, combined with partnering with a respected auditor, is essential. Instituting punitive measures can act as deterrents against misconduct by sellers or buyers

if the buyer defaults on payment. This shifts the onus of assessing the buyer's creditworthiness from the factor. Therefore, depending on whether the agreement is with or without recourse, the risk assessment strategy of a bank will vary.

When operating without recourse, the factor concentrates solely on the buyer's credibility. But with recourse, the focus is on both the buyer and the seller since the seller assumes greater liability. However, by sharing the financial risk in case of the buyer's default, the seller can often negotiate a reduced factoring fee.

6.2.7.3 Whole Ledger Factoring vs. Spot Factoring

Whole ledger factoring sees firms forwarding all invoices from a designated set of clients to the factor, symbolizing a long-term relationship underpinned by enduring contracts and monthly minimums. By consolidating invoices from a single client, the factor can more reliably forecast invoice volume and credibility. This creates a risk pooling effect typical in factoring. Moreover, by merging invoices from various factoring clients, the overall factoring risk diminishes when compared to the anticipated risk for individual invoices.

> *Whole ledger factoring creates a risk pooling effect, thereby reducing the factoring risks associated with any individual accounts receivable.*

Conversely, *spot factoring*, also known as selective factoring, permits firms to present individual or selected invoices to the factor. This provides greater flexibility for the firms. However, it introduces unpredictability for the factor concerning the volume and quality of factoring (like the creditworthiness of the firm's buyers) and there's no commitment to monthly minimums. Typically, the factor has to assess the creditworthiness of every individual debtor to accept any "eligible" receivable. Often, this credit underwriting service is delegated to a third-party trade credit insurance company, which then assumes the majority of the default risk for the insured portfolio. Consequently, the fees for spot factoring tend to be steeper than those of whole ledger factoring.

6.3 Forfaiting

Forfaiting is often seen as equivalent to factoring within the realm of international trade finance in terms of its procedural mechanism. However, there are several fundamental differences. Specifically, in forfaiting, a third-party financing institution, known as a forfaiter, advances funds at a discount to a supplier based on its receivables. These receivables encompass accounts receivable (typically in the form of invoices) and note receivables (such as promissory notes, documentary credit, bills of exchange, and letters of credit). In French, "forfeit" translates to "relinquish the right." In this financial context, *forfaiting* implies that the exporter gives up the right to receive payment for goods or services provided to the importer by transferring the receivables to the forfaiter in return for an advance payment. Consequently, the forfaiter takes on all the risks from the exporter and certain risks associated with the importer, aiming to make a profit margin. Notably, forfaiting is executed without any recourse to the exporter, setting it apart from factoring, which offers both with and without recourse options (Brainkart, 2020).

> *Forfaiting provides funds to the exporter based on receivables, without recourse.*

The costs associated with forfaiting are twofold. The first component is the interest charged to the importer (i.e., the buyer, not the exporter or seller—a distinction that further differentiates it from factoring). The second component is the commitment fee, which is levied once the forfaiter agrees to provide the financing.

6.3.1 Process Flow

The standard forfaiting process is depicted in Fig. 6.2 and proceeds as follows:

1. The importer and the exporter establish their commercial relationship and sign an international export trade contract, which includes payment terms.
2. The exporter approaches a forfaiter to inquire if they are willing to offer forfaiting services. In many instances, the exporter might already have a

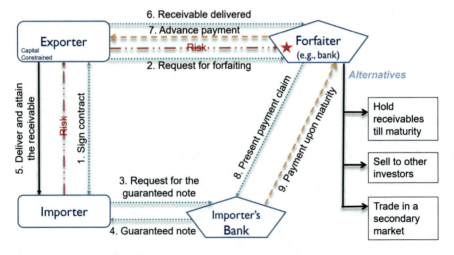

Fig. 6.2 Mechanism of forfaiting

long-standing relationship with a bank that acts as a forfaiter. At this stage, the forfaiter typically requests the following information:
a. The name of the importer and its country of origin.
b. The type and value of the goods/services.
c. Delivery details, such as the shipment date.
d. Payment terms specified by the importer.
e. The nature of the instruments, for instance, whether the note receivable is bank-guaranteed and, if so, by which bank.

If the forfaiter agrees to advance funds to the exporter, the commitment usually contains the following details (Brainkart, 2020):
a. Information on the transaction between the importer and the exporter.
b. The nature of the receivables.
c. The interest rate charged to the importer and any other related costs.
d. Documentation required to validate and enforce the receivable.
e. Delivery dates and payment terms.

3. The importer asks their bank to issue a guaranteed note, such as a deferred-payment letter of credit (commonly used to reduce credit risk) or a promissory note. If the importer and exporter have a long-standing business relationship, the exporter might issue an invoice without requiring a guaranteed note from the importer.
4. The importer receives the guaranteed note from their bank.
5. The exporter delivers the goods or services to the importer and collects the receivable from them.
6. The exporter presents the receivable to the forfaiter in exchange for advance funding.
7. The forfaiter advances funds to the exporter. Unlike factoring, where factors usually advance 70–90% of the invoice value, in forfaiting, the forfaiter might provide up to 100% of the receivable's value because the importer bears the interest.
8. The forfaiter seeks payment from the bank associated with the importer.
9. Upon maturity, the importer's bank settles the amount with the forfaiter. The forfaiter bears all non-payment risks.

It's important to highlight that, traditionally, receivables in forfaiting could be traded on a secondary market, unlike factoring (Surbhi, 2020). However, as explored in Chapter 6.6, factors have begun to sell receivables on secondary markets through securitization, aiming for faster profit realization.

6.3.2 Comparison with Factoring

Forfaiting can best be compared to factoring. When juxtaposed with factoring, forfaiting tends to offer a higher percentage of the receivable's face value to the seller/exporter (Surbhi, 2020). This distinction arises because, in factoring, the seller bears the fees, whereas in forfaiting, the buyer (i.e., importer) covers them. Given

Table 6.6 Comparison between factoring and forfaiting

	Factoring	Forfaiting
Financing Limit	70–90% of the face value of accounts receivable	100% of the face value of receivables
Seller/Exporter Guarantee	Recourse or non-recourse	Non-recourse only
Costs	Borne by the seller (i.e., factoring client)	Borne by the overseas buyer (i.e., importer)
Maturity of Receivables	Short-term accounts receivable (e.g., 60–90 days)	Medium to long-term maturities (e.g., 180 days or more)
Nature of Instruments	Accounts receivable in invoice form, non-negotiable payment terms	Accounts and note receivables, such as bills of exchange and promissory notes
Relationship	Preference for long-term factoring relationships	Transaction-based relationships

that the importer is responsible for the interest in forfaiting, they are more inclined to actively negotiate payment terms with both the forfaiter and the exporter. Meanwhile, factoring tends to be more discerning regarding the types of receivables it accepts, while forfaiting is amenable to both accounts receivable and note receivables (Surbhi, 2020). A comparison between factoring and forfaiting is tabulated in Table 6.6.

6.3.3 Pros, Cons, and Risk Mitigation

Like factoring, forfaiting enhances the exporter's (i.e., the seller's) cash flow and promotes international trade. As forfaiting doesn't require recourse from the exporter, the exporter benefits from reduced risks and costs associated with payment collection. In comparison with traditional financing mechanisms, the exporter gains various advantages and disadvantages. It's worth noting that the benefits accruing to the exporter might come at the expense of the forfaiter and the importer.

6.3.3.1 Pros, Cons, and Risk Mitigation for Exporters

To offer a holistic perspective on the influence of forfaiting on the exporter, we delve into the advantages, disadvantages, and risk management strategies pertinent to exporters as outlined below (refer to Table 6.7).

6.3.3.2 Pros, Cons, and Risk Mitigation for Forfaiters

For forfaiters to delve into the financing process, the venture must be lucrative, yet they are not devoid of risks. We present a detailed exposition on the advantages, disadvantages, and risk management strategies for forfaiters as shown in Table 6.8.

Table 6.7 Pros, cons, and risk mitigation for exporters

Advantages	• *Improved Cash Flow*: By liquidating trade receivables, the exporter obtains immediate cash, bolstering its cash flow. The acquired funds can be channeled towards working capital needs, debt repayment, or business expansion • *Risk Reduction*: Forfaiting alleviates the risk of non-payment for the seller as the forfaiter shoulders the credit risk tied to the trade receivables. The assurance from the buyer's relationship bank (that payment will be fulfilled upon maturity) further diminishes default risk. This allows the exporter to navigate financial and exchange rate uncertainties and sidestep credit and political risks tied to geographical and political dynamics • *100% Financing of Receivables*: This proposition is immensely attractive as it significantly enhances the financial position and liquidity of the exporter upon fund advancement • *Minimum Financing and Administration Costs*: As the importer (buyer) settles the forfaiting fees, exempting the exporter from recourse, the latter doesn't bear any administrative costs linked to managing these receivables • *Earlier Tax Refund*: Within international trade finance, forfaiting also empowers the exporter to expedite tax refunds since verification of export can be procured in advance
Disadvantages	• *Loss of Control*: Liquidating its trade receivables causes the exporter to relinquish control over the collection process, possibly limiting visibility into the status of its receivables • *High Financing Cost*: Forfaiting can be pricier than alternative financing avenues such as factoring or trade financing due to the associated transaction fees and charges. Although these costs primarily fall upon the importer, the exporter often has to offer a reduced wholesale price to set the forfaiting process in motion • *Reduced Flexibility*: Forfaiting, typically being a one-time transaction, might not proffer the flexibility intrinsic to other financing strategies like lines of credit or whole ledger factoring
Risk Mitigation	• *Due Diligence*: Prior to entering a forfaiting deal, rigorous due diligence concerning the forfaiter and the receivables on sale is crucial • *Contractual Safeguards*: The forfaiting contract should embed clauses safeguarding both parties' interests, encompassing covenants, warranties, and default-associated remedies • *Credit Insurance*: To pare down default risk, companies might mull over securing credit insurance to hedge against potential buyer non-payment. Even if forfaiting imposes no recourse on the exporter, such insurance can bolster the exporter's reputation and foster future forfaiting prospects • *Credit Surveillance*: Periodically monitoring the buyer's fiscal performance can flag impending credit risks, enabling companies to institute relevant measures

6.3.3.3 Pros, Cons, and Risk Mitigation for Importers

When juxtaposed with the buyer's role in factoring, the importer (i.e., the buyer) in forfaiting assumes a more hands-on role, particularly given their responsibility for the interest payment. Consequently, the importer is compelled to actively broker deals with both the exporter and the forfaiter concerning payment terms and interest rates. As a quid pro quo for covering the interest, the importer typically

Table 6.8 Pros, cons, and risk mitigation for forfaiters

Advantages	• *Market and Revenue Expansion*: By offering financing to businesses against their trade receivables, the forfaiter can accrue revenue from the transaction-related fees and interest. Moreover, it serves as an auxiliary financing tool to entice a broader clientele • *Risk and Portfolio Diversification*: Forfaiting grants the forfaiter access to a vast and varied collection of trade receivables, facilitating risk distribution and portfolio diversification. The versatility of the receivables, in turn, widens the forfaiter's financing horizon • *Higher Profit Margin*: Since forfaiting operates without recourse, it enables the forfaiter to seek a more substantial profit margin
Disadvantages	• *Complexity*: The forfaiting process can be intricate and time-intensive, necessitating profound expertise and specialized acumen • *Credit Risk*: Even with diligent credit evaluations, there lurks the default risk by businesses offloading the trade receivables, which could lead to considerable fiscal setbacks for the forfaiter • *Limited Liquidity*: Forfaiting might emerge as a relatively illiquid financing modality, given that the forfaiter might encounter challenges offloading the trade receivables in secondary markets
Risk Mitigation	• *Credit Assessment*: To diminish default risk, the forfaiter ought to conduct exhaustive credit assessments of businesses vending the trade receivables. This risk wanes if the forfaiter selectively procures receivables that align with their credit benchmarks • *Contractual Safeguards*: The forfaiting contract should encapsulate robust protective clauses to curtail default risks and guarantee the forfaiter receives fair compensation in loss events. For instance, risk alleviation is feasible if the receivable comes with a guarantee from the importer's primary bank • *Monitoring*: Periodic surveillance of the trade receivables and their vending companies can spotlight impending risks, empowering the forfaiter to enact suitable countermeasures • *Credit Insurance*: To fortify against default risks, the forfaiter might contemplate investing in credit insurance, thus minimizing potential transaction-related losses

possesses the leverage to negotiate a more favorable payment package. We delve into the advantages, disadvantages, and risk management strategies for importers, as outlined in Table 6.9.

6.4 Invoice Discounting

Factoring and forfaiting are prominent mechanisms within the realm of trade/supply chain finance. However, there exist other receivable-based financial instruments. A prime example of this is *invoice discounting*.

In the US, invoice discounting is akin to factoring in many ways, yet distinct in several key areas. Often referred to as the assignment of accounts receivable in American accounting, invoice discounting allows a seller to use an invoice, which stands as evidence of a receivable, as collateral to obtain a loan from a bank or

6.4 Invoice Discounting

Table 6.9 Pros, cons, and risk mitigation for importers

Advantages	• *Payment Flexibility*: Forfaiting accords the importer with augmented flexibility in payment timelines. This allows the importer to procure goods ahead of payment, a boon especially for those requiring swift merchandise deliveries • *Accounting Advantage*: From the importer's perspective, the deferred payment manifests as an accounts payable rather than an explicit financial debt or bank liability • *Improved Cash Flow*: Beyond the aforementioned payment latitude, by bearing the forfaiting charges, the importer can secure extended payment durations. Additionally, the importer may be granted a grace period upon maturity to account for delays inherent in international fund transfers • *Fixed Interest Rate*: Throughout the deferred payment's tenure, the interest rate remains static, eliminating interest rate volatility
Disadvantages	• *Higher Cost*: In comparison to conventional trade finance avenues, forfaiting might come at a premium, given the fee typically levied on the importer by the forfaiting entity • *Reduced Negotiating Power*: By entering the forfaiting arena, the importer's bargaining clout vis-à-vis the exporter might wane, particularly as they also have to hash out terms with the potentially dominant forfaiter
Risk Mitigation	• *Due Diligence*: Prior to committing to a forfaiting accord, the importer should rigorously assess both the forfaiter and the exporter's fiscal health and credit stature • *Insurance*: To safeguard against potential defaults, the importer might contemplate subscribing to trade insurance • *Structured Forfaiting*: To ensure their interests are protected, the importer can meticulously craft the forfaiting contract to embed specific stipulations and covenants • *Professional Counsel*: It's prudent for the importer to solicit guidance from financial consultants or experts in supply chain finance. Such advice not only elucidates the intricacies of forfaiting but also equips the importer to make judicious decisions

factor. From this standpoint, invoice discounting is perceived as a loan, contrasting with factoring which isn't (Wikipedia, 2021). This distinction perhaps represents the most significant divergence between the two.

> In the US, unlike factoring, invoice discounting is considered debt financing, with the invoices serving as collateral.

Under the banner of invoice discounting, the loan's quantum typically ranges from 75% to 90% of the invoice's face value (Peterdy, 2022). The seller retains control over the accounts receivable and amasses the proceeds upon maturity.

Table 6.10 DO and DON'T in financing scheme selection

Concern	DO	DON'T
Commercial Disputes	Ensure that commercial disputes are broadly defined to circumvent pitfalls	Avoid restricting the definition to solely litigation. It's advisable to encompass all potential disagreements
UCC Filing[2]	Engage in UCC filing to determine if the lender already has an interest or lien against the involved receivables	Refrain from presuming that the seller won't leverage the same receivables for diverse financing avenues or procrastinate the UCC filing request
True Sales in Accounting	Grasp the essence of a true sale as delineated by the financier in the context of receivables	Avoid assuming that the interpretation of a true sale remains consistent across jurisdictions
Representations and Warranties[3]	Explicitly define the representations and warranties for each purchase date, request, and execution date	Avoid confining this definition solely to the execution date, as it's beneficial to preempt any potential intervening events
Local Law	Assess the seller and their client in terms of the regulations governing filings, notifications, enforceability, etc.	Avoid the presumption that all jurisdictions mirror your legal system. Rules and procedures for receivables purchase agreements might vary widely across territories
Notification	Ascertain if a mandate exists to notify the account debtor (the seller's client) about the purchase agreement	Avoid generalizing notification policies across nations. Some countries might necessitate notification to streamline the financing trajectory

Although the title of the accounts receivable is transferred to the bank or factor, this transaction remains undisclosed to the buyer. Notably, both factoring and invoice discounting can be orchestrated by the same financial institutions.

---

[2] According to Tucker (2020), "A UCC filing is a legal notice a lender files with the secretary of state when they have a security interest against one of your assets. It gives notice that the lender has an interest, or lien, against the asset being used by you to secure the financing. The term 'UCC filing' comes from the uniform commercial code."

[3] According to Westlaw (2023), "A representation is an assertion as to a fact, true on the date the representation is made, that is given to induce another party to enter into a contract or take some other action. A warranty is a promise of indemnity if the assertion is false. The terms 'representation' and 'warranty' are often used together in practice. If a representation is not true it is 'inaccurate.' If a warranty is not true it is 'breached.'"

In other nations, such as the UK, invoice discounting isn't interpreted as a loan but rather a specialized form of factoring (Wikipedia, 2021). Similar to factoring in the US, this arrangement remains undisclosed to the buyer. Consequently, a cardinal difference between factoring and invoice discounting revolves around the confidentiality of the financial arrangement. However, the discretion to disclose remains with the firms.

For all mechanisms pertaining to receivable financing, encompassing factoring, forfaiting, and invoice discounting, there exist considerations that both sellers and purchasers of receivables (e.g., banks or other financial entities) must mull over prior to committing to a particular financial tool. Specifically, Haynesboone (2016) has posited certain "DO" and "DON'T" guidelines as illustrated in Table 6.10.

6.5 Purchase Order Financing

Receivable-based financing typically kicks in after orders have already been shipped, often termed post-shipment financing. However, sellers can frequently encounter capital constraints prior to shipping the products, sometimes lacking the working capital to even commence production. For many small firms, particularly startups, pre-shipment financing may prove even more vital.

Purchase order (PO) financing has emerged as an essential financial tool to aid such capital-constrained sellers. This form of financing allows these sellers to secure contracts from buyers ahead of the actual product shipments.

Consider this scenario: Supplier A gets an order from a customer, but the invoice from this customer won't be settled until 60 days after receiving the shipment. Without the necessary funds, Supplier A can't produce the required products, risking the potential loss of future orders. If Supplier A lacks the creditworthiness to obtain traditional bank financing, purchase order financing can step in to provide the necessary working capital for production.

Under PO financing, suppliers leverage their purchase orders as collateral to solicit advanced payment from a funder (e.g., a bank or another financial intermediary), facilitated by the buyer. This mode of financing is also known by names such as pre-shipment financing, packing credit/finance, and contract monetization financing.

Like factoring, PO financing isn't viewed as a loan. Since purchase orders haven't yet materialized into products, the non-payment risk is significantly higher. Defaults can result from the supplier's operational failures or market risks on the buyer's end. Hence, PO financing is typically available only to suppliers with a solid operational track record (Klapper, 2006). Due to the greater risks linked to purchase orders compared to receivables, suppliers usually face higher interest rates with PO financing.

In assessing the risks of PO financing, the buyer's commitment to the purchase order is pivotal for the financier's decision. Understandably, if the buyer is more likely to honor the order, the supplier's chance to repay the financier increases. Therefore, the buyer's commitment level is crucial in risk assessment. Absent a robust commitment from the buyer, the financing interest rate could become prohibitively high, rendering PO financing unattractive to suppliers.

Yet, a capital shortage can compromise a supplier's product quality and service levels, jeopardizing long-term supply chain relationships. Consequently, it's in the buyer's interest to facilitate PO financing for the supplier. Doing so enhances the supplier's operational performance, which ultimately benefits the buyer.

Should the buyer choose a more proactive role in PO financing, they can spearhead the initiative. This variant is termed *buyer-backed PO finance* (BPOF) and falls under buyer-led supply chain finance. In BPOF, the buyer often offers a guarantee or firm commitment to the purchase. Such an assurance reduces the financier's risk and improves liquidity for the supplier. Consequently, the supplier's financial costs decrease, and the buyer benefits from reduced wholesale prices. Since the procedures for both PO financing and BPOF are akin, we address both in this chapter, although their emphasis on the buyer's role varies. For clarity, our primary focus is on PO financing.

6.5.1 Process Flow

The processes of PO financing and BPOF are outlined as follows (see Fig. 6.3).

1. The supplier enters into a purchase contract with the buyer.
2. Leveraging the PO, the supplier approaches its relationship funder (e.g., a bank or a third-party financing company). Typically, the supplier must

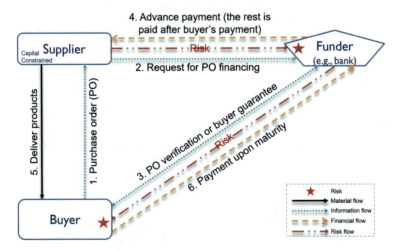

Fig. 6.3 Mechanism of purchase order financing

present the PO along with its financial data, business details, legal credentials (for assessing creditworthiness), and possibly purchase orders for materials.
3. The funder reaches out to the buyer to authenticate the PO. Concurrently, the funder assesses the creditworthiness of both the supplier and the buyer. In the case of BPOF, the buyer may offer a degree of purchase commitment or even an outright guarantee to the funder. When such a commitment or guarantee is provided, a portion of the financial risk transfers from the funder to the buyer.
4. Backed by the buyer's PO validation or purchase commitment/guarantee, the funder supplies the requisite working capital to the supplier. Here, the funder might either offer cash or place direct orders for materials required by the supplier, thereby aiding production.
5. Subsequently, the supplier finishes the production and dispatches the goods to the buyer.
6. Upon the invoice's maturity, the buyer remits payment directly to the funder. After deducting the initial advance and financing charges, the funder then transfers the residual amount to the supplier.

It's pertinent to mention that the funder might also garner payments directly from the buyer's clientele. Incorporating these clients into the PO financing transaction can expedite collections and deter the buyer from diverting payments elsewhere. In such scenarios, suppliers might directly ship products to the buyer's clients.

Although stipulations vary across funders, there are some prevalent traits concerning PO financing (Fundbox, 2020). For example,

- The supplier ought to be financially stable and must have earned a commendable reputation with a consistent history of fulfilling orders.
- The supplier should possess a robust operational history. A gross margin exceeding 20% on the transaction is anticipated (Fundbox, 2020).
- It's imperative that the buyer is creditworthy. Credit assessments of the buyer are routine. Funders commonly delve into the buyer's payment background and scrutinize any bankruptcy or litigation histories.
- The PO's value should be substantial (e.g., exceeding $20,000 or $50,000, contingent on the funder), ensuring a decent profit margin for the funder.
- To curtail risks during manufacturing, minimal final product production is preferred. For instance, the supplier might be reselling items from another vendor and only needs to affix its branding and packaging (Shirshikov, 2019). This strategy diminishes risks tied to product quality and manufacturing. Partly for this reason, purchase order financing is prevalently utilized by wholesalers, resellers, distributors, government contractors, outsourced manufacturers, and trading entities dealing in finished goods. For these enterprises, PO financing can be instrumental in broadening their customer base.

6.5.2 Pros, Cons, and Risk Mitigation

As highlighted earlier, factoring typically takes place after the supplier has delivered the finished goods to the buyer. Conversely, PO financing provides funds to the seller for production prior to product delivery. Thus, relative to factoring, PO financing supports the seller at an earlier phase of the business cycle. Specifically, PO financing is most effective when the seller faces consistent cash flow shortages, significant growth, or seasonal fluctuations (Shirshikov, 2019).

- *Consistent or Cyclical Cash Flow Shortage*: For suppliers encountering regular cash flow challenges, PO financing stabilizes their cash flow and furnishes funds to reinvest in their ventures.
- *Substantial Growth*: For rapidly expanding startups that outpace their existing credit lines, PO financing can bolster working capital, facilitating market expansion.
- *Seasonal or Peak Sales*: When seasonal sales surge, the cost of fulfilling peak purchase orders may exceed available working capital. PO financing can remedy cash shortfalls and fulfill customer demands.

From the discussion above, the benefits of using PO financing for suppliers/sellers include:

- *Access to Working Capital*: It enables suppliers to secure funds not available through conventional financing, ensuring business continuity.
  - *Improved cash flow*: It helps businesses navigate cash flow issues stemming from pre-payment for inventory before getting paid by customers.
  - *Ability to take on larger orders*: Businesses can undertake larger orders, potentially leading to increased sales and growth.
- *Accounting Benefit*: As PO financing isn't a loan, there's no monthly repayment. The funder directly collects payments from the buyer, simplifying the supplier's collection process.
- *Future Financing Opportunities*: Establishing a good rapport with the funder eases future funding processes, especially beneficial for startups with limited credit history.
- *Faster Turnaround Times*: It aids suppliers in fulfilling orders swiftly, thereby improving customer satisfaction.

While PO financing offers numerous advantages, businesses must consider its associated costs and conditions before diving in. Potential drawbacks include:

- *High Cost*: PO financing, while beneficial, is costly and can surpass credit card borrowing rates. Fees usually range from 1.5% to 6% of the advance amount per month (Schneider, 2017). The actual cost can exceed the nominal interest rate because suppliers might reduce the wholesale price in exchange for the buyer's commitment, diluting profitability.

- *Restrictive Terms*: PO financing agreements may include strict terms and conditions that can limit a business's flexibility, such as restrictions on the suppliers or customers that can be used, or penalties for late delivery.
- *Limited Availability*: PO financing might not be accessible to all suppliers, particularly smaller or newer ones lacking a history of successful PO fulfillment or with limited credit backgrounds.
- *Order Size Limitation*: Such financing also often excludes smaller purchase orders, either because of an inadequate profit margin or heightened financing risk. Generally, securing PO financing is more straightforward when the product has broad market appeal. In the case of small purchase orders, suppliers sometimes find it more cost-effective to use credit cards for short-term funding compared to the costs of PO financing.
- *Scope Limitations*: Due to the associated risks, funders usually impose constraints on how the advanced payment can be used, primarily directing it towards materials and production expenses. Consequently, PO financing is typically more suited for tangible goods than services.
- *Reputation Damage*: It might indicate to customers that the business is grappling with liquidity issues.

Given the aforementioned pros and cons, suppliers must meticulously assess both the advantages and disadvantages and determine if PO financing is the most suitable financing option for them. Several risk mitigation strategies for suppliers include:

- *Reduce Funding Ratio*: Suppliers have the option to seek funding for only a fraction of the purchase order, even if 100% financing is attainable. This action can potentially lower the interest rate.
- *Obtain the Buyer's Purchase Commitment*: PO financing often relies on the buyer's commitment to purchase or a full guarantee provided to the funder. Largely due to this arrangement, PO financing is typically non-recourse in nature. While this arrangement transfers financial risk to the buyer, the buyer, in turn, can benefit from reduced wholesale prices and prompt delivery.
- *Negotiate Favorable Terms*: It's prudent for suppliers to negotiate favorable conditions with funders, which might encompass lower interest rates, extended repayment durations, and adaptable repayment plans.
- *Maintain Adequate Inventory Levels*: To prevent potential delays in order fulfillment, suppliers should ensure they have sufficient inventory of materials on hand and also have contingency plans in place.

Adhering to these risk mitigation measures allows suppliers to reduce potential risks linked with PO financing and enhances the probability of successful dealings. The approaches for risk mitigation for both buyers and funders closely resemble those in factoring and forfaiting, and are therefore not elaborated upon in this section.

6.6 Seller-Led Accounts Receivable Securitization

Owing to financial risk regulations, such as Basel I–IV, financial institutions occasionally encounter capital shortages. As a result, they may be unable to accommodate some financing requests, even when the associated risks align with their acceptable thresholds. This has led financial institutions to seek solvency-efficient products, particularly in light of the heightened solvency mandates set out by Basel III and Basel IV (Kerle & Gullifer, 2013).

To tap into more sources of capital support for supply chain finance, *asset securitization* has emerged as a viable alternative to traditional financial institutions. This approach introduces new investment avenues for institutional and private investors, who often remain on the fringes of conventional supply chain finance methods. Within the realm of asset securitization, proprietors of income-generating assets offload these assets at a reduced rate to a special purpose vehicle (SPV) company, which can also be designated as a *special purpose entity* (SPE). This SPV then converts these assets into *asset-backed securities* (ABS) and markets them to a pool of institutional and private investors within the capital market (Hofmann et al., 2017). A distinguishing feature of securitization is its emphasis on the performance of the securitized assets over the seller's performance (Kilgour, 2005).

Though many SPVs are under the ownership umbrella of the financing company, it's crucial for an SPV to operate autonomously from its parent firm, maintaining distinct assets, liabilities, and responsibilities. Importantly, the SPV remains shielded even if its parent entity declares bankruptcy. This insulation from bankruptcy is tailored to safeguard both entities against insolvency and can notably enhance the creditworthiness of SPVs. Moreover, the establishment of SPVs carves out a unique conduit for the parent company to amass capital, often with a reduced regulatory burden compared to the parent firm itself.

> *An SPV creates a special channel for its parent company to raise capital while potentially facing fewer regulations than its parent company.*

Ever since Sperry Lease Finance pioneered a novel securitization model, underpinned by computer equipment leases in the mid-1980s, asset securitization has steadily grown into a vital liquidity source for global corporations and financial institutions (Gimple, 2018). Notably, in 2005, it was approximated that the value of outstanding ABS (inclusive of asset-backed commercial paper) surpassed $4 trillion in the U.S. alone (Kilgour, 2005).

In the realm of seller-led supply chain finance securitization, ABS can be derived from various instruments including purchase orders, inventory, accounts receivable, credit card receivables, and (sanctioned) accounts payable. A notable

6.6 Seller-Led Accounts Receivable Securitization

subset of this domain is trade receivable securitization, which revolves around trade receivables.

Conventionally, receivables have been securitized in two primary formats. Historically, the majority of accounts receivable have been channeled through asset-backed commercial paper conduits (CP conduits). These conduits, often backed by major banks, necessitate an impressive credit rating, typically at least A1 (Moody's long-term)/P1 (Moody's short-term) and traditionally involve sizable purchases, often exceeding $100 million (Katz, 2011). The alternate model is the multi-year standalone term securitization, which similarly mandates a substantial size to offset fixed expenses.

6.6.1 Process Flow

In *seller-led accounts receivable securitization*, the seller offloads its accounts receivable to its own SPV. Subsequently, the SPV markets the transformed ABS at a discount to institutional and private investors. The "seller-led" nature of this process signifies that the seller usually shoulders the responsibility of underwriting the receivables, endorsing them for securitization, and overseeing the collection of cash flows stemming from these receivables. As delineated in Fig. 6.4, a standard seller-led accounts receivable securitization unfolds in the following sequence:

1. A seller finalizes contracts with its buyers and subsequently delivers products/services. Accounts receivable materialize since buyers typically defer payments to the seller for a few months.

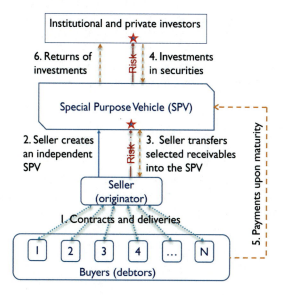

Fig. 6.4 Seller-led accounts receivable securitization

2. To harness receivable securitization as a financing mechanism, the seller establishes an autonomous, bankruptcy-remote SPV within the company's framework. Alternatively, a third-party bank can instantiate the SPV, with the seller retaining a stake in the SPV. Importantly, the SPV's inception does not warrant alterations to the seller's extant payment collection protocols. The buyers (i.e., the seller's clientele) maintain their standard payment regimen, oblivious to the securitization of the receivables (PNC, 2018).
3. The seller earmarks a cohort of qualifying accounts receivable and transitions them to the SPV. Once shifted, these receivables are legally sequestered from the seller's broader asset pool. Consequently, the cash flows generated from this select set of receivables are shielded from other creditors, safeguarding against potential defaults or insolvencies.
4. The SPV amalgamates these accounts receivable and markets them as ABS at a discount to the capital market, targeting institutional and private investors.
5. Upon maturity, the SPV assimilates payments from the buyers.
6. The SPV disburses returns to investors and garners its profit.

In the general schema, the invoices are offloaded to the SPV sans any recourse. This arrangement absolves the seller from any financial onus arising from potential defaults by the buyers. However, owing to the established supply chain rapport with buyers, sellers often retain the reins of the payment collection apparatus.

6.6.2 Benefits

Receivable securitization not only addresses capital deficiencies left by conventional financing means like bank financing but also furnishes additional advantages for both the seller and financial institutions.

6.6.2.1 Benefits for Sellers and SPVs

Seller-led accounts receivable securitization extends multiple benefits for sellers and their SPVs:

- *Low Interest Cost*:
  – Receivable securitization is based on the debtor's risk profile rather than the creditor's (i.e., the seller's) rating, often resulting in decreased risks and more affordable financing (Kerle & Gullifer, 2013).
  – Although receivable securitization operates without recourse, using an SPV segregates the chosen receivables from potential risks (like bankruptcy) linked to the seller (PNC, 2018). Credit rating agencies, when assigning ratings, consider various factors like the historical performance of chosen receivables, the prudence of the seller's credit, collection

6.6 Seller-Led Accounts Receivable Securitization

strategies, and debtor composition (Accountingtools, 2020). Sellers can't reassert control over receivables once transferred to the SPV. Due to the selectiveness of these receivables and the SPV's relative autonomy, it often boasts a high credit rating, ranging from A to AAA. Thus, sellers can secure a more favorable interest rate compared to conventional debt financing when pledging the same receivables as collateral.
  - Anecdotal evidence from banker interviews suggests that the interest cost for receivable securitization can be 25% more affordable than relationship lending (Kerle & Gullifer, 2013). This advantage is particularly pronounced for sub-investment-grade firms, unrated entities, and highly leveraged corporations, which typically grapple with accessing capital markets.
- *Diversification*:
  - Receivable securitization lets sellers broaden their financing avenues, which can mitigate financial risks if other sources become inaccessible.
  - Seller-led accounts receivable securitization enables sellers to consolidate a vast array of receivables from diverse customers, sectors, and regions. This can minimize the overall risk profile of the receivables and boost the securities' appeal to investors. As a result, the spreads on securitization initiatives tend to remain consistent. For instance, spreads for single-B or double-B companies may vary by 100–150 basis points annually, but spreads on securitization programs might sway by just a few basis points (Kilgour, 2005).
- *Liquidity*:
  - Much like other financial instruments, receivable securitization offers sellers an alternative to procure early payments. By securitizing its accounts receivable, sellers can liquidate these receivables, bolstering their liquidity and furnishing the working capital essential for their operations.
- *Capital Efficiency and Opportunities*:
  - Securitization can heighten a seller's enterprise value due to its enhanced financing capabilities. As banks typically allocate more funds to a securitization than a traditional loan, sellers can reap the benefits of interacting with fewer financial institutions (PNC, 2018).
  - Owing to its autonomy and bankruptcy-remote attributes, receivable securitization can continuously offer vital capital, even if the seller defaults. Sellers might also boost their capital efficiency by tapping into growth opportunities earlier, even if it means accepting a minor discount for the securitization.
- *Improvement in Financial Metrics*:
  - The proceeds from receivable securitization can be allocated to settle existing debt, thereby lowering debt ratios such as the debt-to-equity

ratio (Katz, 2011). It can also positively impact other financial metrics, including days sales outstanding (DSO), quick ratio, and return on assets (ROA).
- *Supply Chain Relationship Improvement*:
  – Given its potent support to sellers, receivable securitization can alleviate their financial strains and indirectly aid buyers, fostering a harmonious supply chain relationship.

6.6.2.2 Benefits for Banks

In seller-led accounts receivable securitization, banks have the option to either establish an independent SPV or collaborate with the seller in doing so. Banks might also play the role of investors in this type of securitization. Therefore, this model offers numerous advantages to banks:

- *Additional Capital*:
  – Banks, often in the form of investment or commercial entities, can enjoy supplementary capital sourced from other institutional and private investors. As a result, securitization helps retain banks' financing capabilities, allowing them to extend other types of financing to various debtors through revolving bank facilities (PNC, 2018).
- *New Financing Opportunity*:
  – Securitization can present banks with a more viable financing solution for sellers due to the relatively lower risks associated with SPVs. Without this, banks might not be willing to offer sellers the same extent of commitment. Consequently, banks can broaden their operational scope without proportionately elevating their risk exposure.
  – Additionally, securitization allows banks to cater to a fresh clientele, especially those within the sub-investment-grade bracket or sectors less frequented by orthodox banking products. This can pave the way for enlarging the bank's customer spectrum, fostering prospects for expansion and heightened profitability.
- *Credit Risk Reduction*:
  – By channeling the accounts receivable into its SPV, which are then made available to investors, a bank can delegate the credit risk associated with these receivables to the buyers of these securities. This act reduces the bank's vulnerability to credit risk, liberating its balance sheet capacity, which can then be redirected towards other lending ventures.
- *Diversification of Assets*:
  – Engaging in securities backed by a conglomerate of accounts receivable allows a bank to diversify its asset collection. This step cuts down its susceptibility to concentration risk and bolsters its risk-adjusted returns.
- *Improved Regulatory Capital Ratios*:
  – The mandates under Basel III and IV necessitate banks to reserve a more substantial regulatory capital against their assets, especially those deemed high risk. Investing in securities underpinned by receivables, which are

generally perceived as less risky compared to other assets, enables a bank to refine its regulatory capital ratios. This ensures easier adherence to regulatory stipulations.

In conclusion, seller-led accounts receivable securitization bestows benefits upon both sellers and banks. It emerges as a crucial instrument for managing credit risks and refining access to capital markets.

6.6.3 Risks and Risk Mitigation

This section discusses the risks and risk mitigation approaches in seller-led accounts receivable securitization.

6.6.3.1 Risks

Despite its manifold benefits, establishing an independent SPV within a company is more intricate than traditional bank financing. Consequently, seller-led accounts receivable securitization has generally been an avenue for larger entities possessing substantial accounts receivable, often amounting to millions (Merritt, 2020). However, the recent trend indicates a shift with smaller firms also exploring this mode of securitization. Previously, the requisite portfolio size often surpassed $100 million, but now we witness portfolios even as modest as $20 million (Kilgour, 2005). Historically, only firms with an investment-grade credit rating could embark on securitization. In contrast, the present scenario allows non-investment grade or even unrated companies to harness securitization funding.

Additional risks include:

- *Credit Risk*: The securitization's creditworthiness is intrinsically linked to the credit quality of the underlying accounts receivable. A downward spiral in the credit quality of these receivables can potentially depreciate the securities' value, leading to possible investor losses.
- *Liquidity Risk*: Economic or market dynamics might sway the cash flows from the primary receivables, thereby influencing the securities' liquidity. Any hindrance for investors in selling their securities or securing financing against them could spell liquidity challenges for the issuer.
- *Operational Risk*: The securitization procedure encompasses several intricate operational facets, from underwriting and servicing to accounting. Operational glitches or setbacks might culminate in financial losses or tarnish the issuer's reputation.
- *Legal and Regulatory Risk*: Securitization navigates through a multifaceted regulatory landscape, susceptible to evolution. Non-compliance by the issuer with the pertinent legal and regulatory mandates could invite penalties or legal repercussions.

In essence, while the seller-led accounts receivable securitization offers numerous advantages, both issuers and investors should meticulously weigh the inherent risks. It is paramount to adopt appropriate risk management strategies to navigate these challenges.

6.6.3.2 Risk Mitigation

In the realm of receivable securitization, the inherent financial risks linked to the chosen receivables transition from the seller to the SPV due to the non-recourse nature of the transactions. This transition aids in counteracting the risk of default or non-payment, thereby augmenting the seller's balance sheet capacity to bolster other business endeavors.

Subsequently, as the SPV offloads the ABS to a consortium of investors, these risks are then apportioned and diluted among them. The financial vulnerabilities facing the SPV and its investors in the context of receivable securitization are mitigated through the following mechanisms:

- **Risk Isolation**: Segregating specific receivables into the SPV from the larger pool boosts its credit rating. The SPV's exposure to the financial risks of those chosen receivables diminishes since other creditors can't lay claim to those singled-out, transferred receivables. Furthermore, the original seller is prohibited from retrieving any relocated receivables, which remain uncharted on its balance sheet. Essentially, the migration of receivables to the SPV should be a genuine transaction or a "true sale." While the SPV might lean on the seller for debtor payments, adherence to the true sale prerequisite is pivotal in receivable securitization; any deviation jeopardizes the insolvency/bankruptcy protection. Backed by the true sale stipulation, most receivable securitizations are structured to secure high credit ratings, predominantly A or even AAA (Kerle & Gullifer, 2013; Leonard, 2015). These impressive ratings lure institutional investors, including pension funds and insurance corporations, that primarily opt for top-tier investment-grade assets.

Case Study

Finacity Corporation

Illustratively, Finacity orchestrated a securitization in 2009 for the prominent global cement manufacturer, Cemex, which had a single-B minus rating. Yet, the transaction's structuring to a triple-A local rating piqued the interest of Mexican pension funds and insurance entities, who would have otherwise sidestepped the company's unenhanced corporate debt (Leonard, 2015).

6.6 Seller-Led Accounts Receivable Securitization

- **Risk Pooling**: Introducing a multitude of sellers into the securitization augments the risk dilution effect by accumulating a vast collection of receivables. Such an expansive pool equips the SPV to undertake a more informed risk analysis for the entirety of the consolidated receivables. The zenith of the risk pooling effect is realized when the SPV integrates a diverse array of account debtors, catalyzing an elevated advance rate for the whole portfolio to the advantage of all sellers. Consequently, this type of pooled receivable securitization beckons even medium or smaller enterprises to explore this funding mechanism.
- **Continuous Risk Assessment**: In operational terms, an SPV is duty-bound to perpetually evaluate the risk profile of the transferred receivables. Given that an SPV generally acquires receivables from a vast spectrum of sellers, a portfolio-centric statistical method is employed to monitor the real-time performance of the entire receivable pool (Leonard, 2015). Furthermore, there's an imperative to constantly and uniformly appraise credit risks across various sectors and regions to ensure meticulous credit rating intelligence. To curb the risks tied to receivables fraud and buyer defaults, rigorous verification of transferred receivables is essential. This is complemented by enhanced collection services and heightened transparency and accuracy in reporting. For firms with limited or shaky credit, in-depth diligence and unwavering discipline in these domains are indispensable for a successful securitization endeavor.
- **Dynamic Advance Rate Adjustment**: One method of risk management in receivable securitization is the use of dynamic advance rates, typically recalculated monthly based on the previous month's portfolio performance. If, for instance, payment collection lags, there are defaults, or dilution rises in a particular month, the advance rate for the subsequent month would decrease. Conversely, an improving portfolio performance would result in an increase in the advance rate. Such dynamic adjustments enable the SPV to continually self-regulate, thereby stabilizing the credit quality of the securitization. The fluctuating monthly advance rates can be further stabilized by employing a moving average across several key performance indicators from preceding months (Leonard, 2015).

> *Dynamic advance rates enable the SPV to continually self-adjust, ensuring the maintenance and stabilization of the securitization's credit quality.*

- **Legal Framework Assessment**: Beyond the aforementioned risk mitigation strategies, the establishment of a securitization program necessitates addressing legal concerns, fixed setup costs, standardized credit underwriting, credit

enhancement, and globalization (Katz, 2011). The legal framework supporting receivable securitization must be resilient enough to bolster its own expansion, while governmental regulations should not significantly diminish its inherent appeal (Kerle & Gullifer, 2013).
- *Communication and Transparency*: Transparency in reporting is paramount in the regulatory process. A lack of sufficient transparency and diligent reporting could obscure the underlying risks of the securitization program from investors. This opacity can jeopardize the program's credit rating and might set off a cascading effect in the financial markets due to a misunderstanding of the risk profiles of these financial instruments (Kerle & Gullifer, 2013). Prospective investors ought to have immediate and complete access to all essential information regarding the creditworthiness and performance of each individual exposure underlying the securitization, as well as the cash flows and the collateral backing it. Additionally, they should have access to vital data necessary for carrying out comprehensive and informed stress tests on the cash flows and the value of the collateral underpinning these exposures.
- *Credit Enhancement*: There are two primary forms of credit enhancement: internal and external.
  - *Internal Credit Enhancement*: This typically involves overcollateralization, where the securitizing entity uses an excess of assets or collateral to mitigate credit risks for the investors. This maneuver thus augments the credit rating of the securitization. The securitizing entity might also subordinate the commercial notes across diverse risk tranches (Hofmann et al., 2017).
  - *External Credit Enhancement*: Here, the acquisition of receivables insurance and securing financial guarantees can temper credit risks, enhancing the securitization's credit rating. For instance, the European Investment Fund (EIF) offers triple-A-rated credit enhancements for securitizations (Nassr & Wehinger, 2015). In a practical sense, firms might also collaborate with specialized entities, such as banks, to streamline the securitization process.

6.6.4 Comparison to Other Financing Schemes

We compare seller-led accounts receivable securitization with two other popular financing schemes: traditional bank debt financing and factoring.

6.6.4.1 Comparison to Debt Financing

Receivable securitization shares some similarities with debt (Kilgour, 2005). Firstly, much like debt, receivable securitization is priced as a spread over a benchmark, for example, the London Interbank Offered Rate (LIBOR). Secondly, receivable securitization is often arranged by the same financial institutions that also provide debt financing. Lastly, capital raised from both receivable securitization and debt does not dilute shareholders (Kilgour, 2005).

However, receivable securitization is not the same as traditional loans. Firstly, in receivable securitization, sellers transfer their accounts receivable to the SPV in true sales without recourse, ensuring that these receivables do not reappear on the balance sheet (Kilgour, 2005). Secondly, the structure of securitization doesn't consist of principal plus interest like debt does. Instead, the investor's payment hinges on the collection of payments and any predefined reserve. Thirdly, while securitization is insulated from the seller's bankruptcy, debt may default in the event of bankruptcy.

Given these distinctions, receivable securitization can offer sellers more advantages than debt in terms of lower financing costs, increased capital efficiency, and so on.

6.6.4.2 Comparison to Factoring

In receivable securitization, the SPV functions similarly to a "factor" in factoring. However, the SPV also transforms accounts receivable into ABS and then markets these ABS to institutional and private investors.

While both factoring and receivable securitization are seller-led financing mechanisms based on accounts receivable, there are numerous distinctions between them. Some of these differences are summarized in Table 6.11.

Table 6.11 Comparison between factoring and receivable securitization

	Factoring	**Receivable Securitization**
Advance Rate	70–90% (100% minus discounts and reserves)	Higher (100% minus interests/discounts)
Seller/Exporter Guarantee	Recourse or non-recourse	Non-recourse only (true sales of accounts receivable to the SPV)
Interest Rate	Higher	Lower
Type of Seller	Any type	Larger firms
Nature of Instruments	Accounts receivable in the form of invoices	Asset-backed securities (ABS)
Independent SPV	None	Yes. SPVs are typically independent with superior credit ratings
Capital Sources	Factor (e.g., bank)	A group of institutional and private investors via SPV
Accounts Receivable	All receivables can be accepted into the pool	Selected receivables are transferred to the SPV
Credit Enhancement	No	Yes

Two particular distinctions warrant further mention. Firstly, while factoring has traditionally been a domestic practice, receivable securitization spans multiple countries and currencies (Leonard, 2015). As an illustration, in 2015, the US-based Finacity Corporation assisted a prominent international trading company in managing a $700 million receivable securitization. These receivables originated from ten selling subsidiaries across eight different countries, comprising invoices in "four different currencies due from over 4,000 obligors in more than 30 different countries" (Leonard, 2015). In fact, approximately 75% of the obligors in securitization programs managed by Finacity are located outside the U.S. (Katz, 2011).

Secondly, while the advance rate and discounts in factoring depend on the credit ratings of both the seller and its buyers, receivable securitization offers a unique credit arbitrage opportunity. This means that a meticulously structured securitization program can achieve an investment-grade credit rating of A or higher, even if the seller's credit rating isn't investment-grade or unrated. Achieving such a high rating requires proper structuring, standardized underwriting, credit enhancement, and robust servicing (Katz, 2011).

6.7 Summary

This chapter delves into the various financing mechanisms within the realm of seller-led supply chain finance, focusing on methods that leverage receivables or future income as a means of obtaining current funds. Such methods provide sellers with the liquidity necessary for operations, while also transferring some of the risks associated with future payments.

Key Takeaways:

1. Factoring:
   - Factoring is a financial transaction in which a business sells its accounts receivable to a third party (called a factor) at a discount.
   - This method is an efficient way for businesses to quickly raise funds.
   - It can be either recourse (the business is liable for any unpaid debts) or non-recourse (the factor bears the risk of unpaid debts).
2. Forfaiting:
   - Forfaiting is the sale of a company's future receivables at a discount to a "forfaiter," which takes on the risks of those receivables.
   - This technique is usually used for international transactions and typically deals with medium to long-term receivables.
3. Invoice Discounting:
   - Here, a business borrows a percentage of the value of its outstanding invoices from a financial institution.
   - The business retains control over the sales ledger and is responsible for collecting the payments.

- It offers confidentiality since customers are unaware of the financing arrangement.
4. Purchase Order Financing:
   - This method allows businesses to obtain financing based on confirmed purchase orders from their customers.
   - The finance provider may pay the supplier directly, ensuring the completion of the order. When the customer pays, the business repays the finance provider with a fee.
   - Ideal for businesses that lack funds to fulfill large orders.
5. Seller-led Accounts Receivable Securitization:
   - This involves a seller transferring their accounts receivable to an SPV which then packages these receivables and sells them as securities in the financial market.
   - Receivable securitization provides liquidity to the seller, transfers the risk to the SPV, and can be an attractive option for investors looking for asset-backed securities.
   - It is distinct from traditional debt and offers several advantages including potential lower financing costs and better capital efficiency.

6.8 Exercises

6.8.1 Practice Questions

1. Describe factoring in the context of seller-led financing.
2. How does forfaiting differ from factoring?
3. Why might a business prefer invoice discounting over other financing methods from a customer relations perspective?
4. What is the primary advantage of purchase order financing for businesses?
5. In seller-led accounts receivable securitization, to whom does the seller transfer their accounts receivable?
6. Why might receivable securitization offer more benefits than traditional debt financing for the seller?
7. What is the role of an SPV in receivable securitization?
8. How does the advance rate in factoring generally compare to that in receivable securitization?
9. Which financing method primarily involves domestic transactions, factoring or receivable securitization?
10. What is the credit arbitrage opportunity offered by receivable securitization?

6.8.2 Case Study

Stellar Exports Inc.'s Financing Scheme Selection

Background

Stellar Exports Inc., based in London, specializes in manufacturing high-end electronics, exporting them to various countries, including emerging markets. Over the past year, Stellar has faced significant cash flow issues due to extended payment terms given to its overseas buyers, which typically range between 60 and 120 days. The company is considering various seller-led financing options to alleviate its cash flow pressures and to support its growth ambitions.

Details

1. Stellar's annual revenue is £10 million.
2. Outstanding invoices amount to £2 million, spread across multiple buyers.
3. The company received a new purchase order worth £1.5 million from a reputable company in Brazil, which is expected to increase the cash flow strain.
4. Stellar has a long-standing relationship with a local bank that has previously provided them with traditional debt financing.
5. The company's credit rating is "BB," indicating a non-investment grade but with a stable outlook.
6. Stellar has never previously used any seller-led financing methods.

Financing Options

1. **Factoring:** A financial institution offers to buy Stellar's outstanding invoices for 85% of their value upfront. They will collect the payments directly from the buyers and take a fee of 2% of the total invoice value. Once they collect the payment, they will give Stellar the remaining 13%.
2. **Invoice Discounting:** Stellar's bank offers an invoice discounting service where they will provide Stellar with a loan up to 90% of its outstanding invoice value. Stellar will still be responsible for collecting payments from its buyers. The interest rate for this service is 4% annually.
3. **Purchase Order Financing:** Considering the new purchase order from Brazil, a financier is willing to provide Stellar with financing based on the purchase order. They offer to cover 80% of the purchase order upfront at an interest rate of 5% annually.

Task

Evaluate the three seller-led financing options available to Stellar Exports Inc. Consider the immediate cash inflow, costs associated with each method, the relationship with buyers, and potential impacts on the company's balance sheet and reputation. Recommend the best option or combination of options for Stellar.

Appendix: Academic Perspective

Buyer Financing in Pull Supply Chains: Zero-Interest Early Payment or In-House Factoring?
Xiangfeng Chen, Qihui Lu, Gangshu (George) Cai[4]

Introduction

Dynamic discounting allows for early payment to sellers, which buyers would typically pay upon maturity. Generally, these early payments are not viewed as loans. However, in practice, some buyers opt to impose interest on these early payments to sellers, treating them as loans via a specialized financing arm. For instance, JingDong leverages its financing subsidiary, JingDong Finance, to present the JingBaoBei financing service to its suppliers as loans with a fixed interest rate. Similarly, Amazon extends loans to its small business suppliers through its Amazon Lending program. Unlike traditional factoring financing, JingDong Finance and Amazon Lending act as the internal "third-party" financiers for their respective parent firms. This kind of advance payment will be referred to as in-house factoring financing for the rest of this section.

From an accounting perspective, early payment is recorded as a pre-payment for the retailer's procurement from the manufacturer, while in-house factoring financing is classified as a loan. Procedure-wise, early payment is integrated into the order payment process and bypasses the formal loaning procedure. In contrast, in-house factoring necessitates adherence to the loaning protocol. Consequently, in-house factoring financing is typically practiced when the retailer has a financing division equipped with the appropriate licenses. Meanwhile, early payment is feasible as long as the retailer possesses enough capital to cover its order in advance. Regarding interest rates, early payment as pre-payment does not have an associated interest rate but might offer a discount on the invoice amount. In comparison, in-house factoring financing usually stipulates a clear, positive interest rate.

Model

To determine whether early payment and in-house factoring consistently outperform bank financing (or the other way around), we examine a simplified pull supply chain model. In this model, a capital-constrained manufacturer (i.e., seller)

---

[4] This section summarizes research findings from one of my publications, Chen et al. (2020). For those interested in a detailed exploration, please refer to the complete article: Chen, X., Lu, Q., and Cai, G., (2020). Buyer financing in pull supply chains: Zero-interest early payment or in-house factoring? *Production and Operations Management, 29*(10), 2307–2325. We've omitted most references for brevity, so please consult the paper for further details.

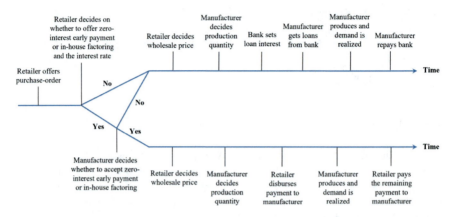

Fig. 6.5 Sequences of events in different financing schemes

sells a product to a capital-abundant retailer. The manufacturer has the option to borrow either from a bank through bank financing or from the retailer via no-interest early payment or through positive-interest in-house factoring (as illustrated in Fig. 6.5).

Main Findings

When compared to bank financing, early payment financing offers a superior risk-sharing mechanism for coordinating the supply chain. This is because both the retailer and the manufacturer share a portion of the uncertainty risk. When the manufacturer's production cost is reasonably low, the retailer will lean towards early payment financing over bank financing.

However, under early payment financing, the retailer may be tempted to set a very low wholesale price. This could make both the manufacturer and the entire supply chain less profitable compared to using bank financing. Using the viability of bank financing as a counterweight, the retailer must offer a more attractive wholesale price when employing early payment financing to entice the manufacturer. A win–win wholesale price range exists wherein both parties benefit from early payment financing, provided the manufacturer's production cost remains low. Despite the retailer potentially earning less due to competition from bank financing, the manufacturer's increased production, resulting from a higher profit margin, can increase overall supply chain profits. This highlights how competition from bank financing can push the retailer in early payment financing to yield some of its profits to the manufacturer, leading to better supply chain coordination.

In comparison to bank financing, in-house factoring maintains the advantage of merging finance and operational decisions by the retailer. When juxtaposing early payment with in-house factoring, neither can consistently overshadow the other. Interestingly, the firm commitment of no interest in early payment can sometimes outperform in-house factoring that comes with interest. Specifically, early payment takes precedence over in-house factoring when production costs are low (this advantage amplifies if the latter incurs setup costs). However, as production costs rise, in-house factoring becomes more appealing and can eventually surpass early payment financing.

While both early payment and in-house factoring are perceived as superior risk-sharing mechanisms compared to bank financing, the advantages of interest in in-house factoring (interest benefit), a more competitive wholesale price (wholesale-price benefit), and a larger production volume (production-quantity benefit) fluctuate depending on the manufacturer's production cost. As a result, retailers should tailor their interest strategies appropriately. Typically, the retailer's ideal interest rate grows as the manufacturer's production cost increases until it reaches a peak. After this point, it decreases with the production cost to guarantee a baseline profit for the manufacturer when borrowing via bank financing.

From a mathematical standpoint, early payment resembles a specific instance of in-house factoring when we consider the interest rate of in-house factoring to be zero. Given the aforementioned observations, the optimal interest rate for in-house factoring is zero when production costs are on the lower end. Yet, this conclusion assumes that the procedures for the two financing options are identical and that there are no setup costs for in-house factoring. This isn't feasible in reality, considering the retailer would need to employ additional staff to manage the factoring and secure the necessary licenses. This discrepancy might be the reason why zero-interest in-house factoring isn't observed in real-world scenarios.

References

Accountingtools. (2020). *Accounts receivable securitization.* Accountingtools.Com. https://doi.org/10.3905/jsf.2011.2011.1.011. Accessed 29 July 2020.

Accountleaning. (2023). *How to establish minimum cash balance?* https://accountlearning.com/how-to-establish-minimum-cash-balance/. Accessed 23 May 2023.

Brainkart. (2020). *Forfeiting.* https://www.brainkart.com/article/Forfeiting_6235/. Accessed 10 October 2020.

Bryant, C., & Camerinelli, E. (2014). Supply chain finance—EBA European market guide (Version 2.0). *Report, June* (pp. 1–152).

Chen, X., Lu, Q., & Cai, G. (2020). Buyer financing in pull supply chains: Zero-interest early payment or in-house factoring? *Production and Operations Management, 29*(10), 2307–2325.

CorsaFinance. (2023). *Non-notification invoice factoring.* https://corsafinance.com/non-notification-factoring-receivables-financing. Accessed 27 March 2023.

FactorFinders. (2020). *Factoring fees: What to expect.* https://www.factorfinders.com/resources/factoring-faq/cost-of-factoring/. Accessed 3 July 2020.

Fundbox. (2020). *Purchase order funding and financing guide.* https://fundbox.com/resources/guides/purchase-order-financing/. Accessed 23 June 2020.

Gimple, D. (2018). The evolution of the asset-backed securities market. *Fixed Income Perspectives* (Issue November).

Haynesboone. (2016). *Receivables purchase agreements.* www.haynesboone.com. Accessed 23 February 2020.

Hofmann, E., Strewe, U. M., & Bosia, N. (2017). *Supply chain finance and blockchain technology: The case of reverse securitisation.* Springer.

Nassr, I., & Wehinger, G. (2015). Unlocking SME finance through market-based debt. *OECD Journal: Financial Market Trends, 2014*(2), 89–190.

Katz, A. (2011). Accounts receivable securitization. *The Journal of Structured Finance, 17*(2), 23–27.

Kerle, P., & Gullifer, L. (2013). The future of trade receivables securitization in Europe. *The Journal of Structured Finance, 19*(1), 71–76.

Kilgour, C. L. (2005). *Receivables securitization and capital structure.* The Global Treasurer. https://www.theglobaltreasurer.com/2005/12/15/receivables-securitization-and-capital-structure/. Accessed 19 February 2020.

Klapper, L. (2006). The role of factoring for financing small and medium enterprises. *Journal of Banking and Finance, 30*(11), 3111–3130.

Leonard, J. (2015, June). Introduction to receivable securitization. *The Secured Lender*, 16–19

McKinsey. (2020). *The 2020 McKinsey global payments report* (Issue October). https://www.mckinsey.com/~/media/mckinsey/industries/financialservices/ourinsights/acceleratingwindsofchangeinglobalpayments/2020-mckinsey-global-payments-report-vf.pdf. Accessed 16 February 2021.

Merritt, C. (2020). *The securitization of accounts receivable.* https://smallbusiness.chron.com/securitization-accounts-receivable-56095.html. Accessed 13 May 2021.

Peterdy, K. (2022). *Accounts receivable factoring.* https://corporatefinanceinstitute.com/resources/accounting/accounts-receivable-factoring/. Accessed 13 April 2023.

PNC. (2018). *Trade receivables securitization.* http://pnc.com/cib. Accessed 13 February 2020.

Schneider, D. (2017). *What is purchase order financing?* https://www.rtsinc.com/articles/what-purchase-order-financing. Accessed 13 March 2020.

Shirshikov, D. (2019). *Purchase order financing: What po financing is & how it works.* https://fitsmallbusiness.com/purchase-order-financing/. Accessed 23 February 2020.

Sillay, J. (2012). *Factoring costs: The 10 most misunderstood cost drivers advance* (Federal National Commercial Credit Report).

Surbhi, S. (2020). *Difference between factoring and forfaiting.* https://keydifferences.com/difference-between-factoring-and-forfaiting.html. Accessed 13 February 2020.

Truckstop. (2023). *What is the cost of factoring? 3 ways to lower costs.* https://truckstop.com/blog/cost-of-factoring. Accessed 23 February 2023.

Tucker, J. (2020). *How UCC filings can affect your business credit scores.* nav.com. https://www.nav.com/blog/ucc-filings-and-business-credit-scores-8189/. Accessed 8 December 2020.

Westlaw. (2023). *Representations and warranties.* https://content.next.westlaw.com/practical-law/document/I1559f7a3eef211e28578f7ccc38dcbee/Representations-and-Warranties. Accessed 5 September 2023.

Wikipedia. (2021). *Factoring (finance).* https://en.wikipedia.org/wiki/Factoring_(finance). Accessed 8 August 2021.

Buyer-Led Supply Chain Finance

7

> **Learning Objectives:**
>
> 1. Analyze the benefits and challenges of dynamic discounting in supply chain finance.
> 2. Explore reverse factoring's role and its effect on liquidity and supplier relations.
> 3. Understand the liquidity implications of buyer-led approved payables reverse securitization.
> 4. Evaluate the impact of extended payment terms through real-world case studies.

7.1 Introduction

Many suppliers are small and capital-constrained. Indeed, a majority of these suppliers lack the creditworthiness to borrow the necessary funds to support their production. Owing to their limited size and creditworthiness, supply chain finance initiatives started by these suppliers often cannot secure low interest rates. Consequently, these suppliers become financially vulnerable, and their associated supply chains might be jeopardized. Compounding the problem, corporate buyers have often reduced prices to such an extent that suppliers' margins are whittled down to the bare minimum, leaving scant room for these suppliers to further decrease wholesale prices or enhance production efficiency (Miller, 2007).

An alternative financing solution is *buyer-led supply chain finance*. This approach capitalizes on the potentially superior creditworthiness of larger buyers, such as Amazon and Walmart. Assurances from these buyers, whether in the form of guarantees or payment commitments, offer financiers the required independent payment obligation, thereby diminishing the risk of invoice value dilution. As a result, sellers can secure more favorable financing terms based on the improved credit profiles of their buyers. Coupled with the rapid advancement of technology platforms, buyer-led supply chain finance has established its presence and witnessed swift growth in recent years.

7.2 Dynamic Discounting

Dynamic discounting is a nuanced form of early payment discount financing, previously discussed in Chapter 5.5.3. A limitation of the early payment discount is its lack of continuity, often termed static (early payment) discounting. For instance, in a 2/10 Net 30 arrangement, if the buyer remits payment on the 11th day, the discount is forfeited. This means the incentive for the discount only holds if payment is made within 10 days. Beyond that, there's no incentive for the buyer to expedite payment.

Dynamic discounting, a continuous version of the early payment discount, was introduced as a solution. This mechanism encourages faster payment by the buyer to the seller while also reciprocating benefits. Unlike its static counterpart, dynamic discounting offers a variable, continuous discount rate for early payment. It establishes a more adaptable framework between the seller and buyer, enabling the former to receive funds ahead of the predetermined due date, following invoice approval. The sooner the seller receives the payment, the more substantial the discount for the buyer.

> *Dynamic discounting provides an incentive for the buyer to make early payments before the due date.*

There are two primary forms of dynamic discounting: fully dynamic discounting and semi-dynamic discounting. In *fully dynamic discounting*, illustrated in Fig. 7.1a, a linear discounting mechanism is employed. For comparative purposes, Fig. 7.1 references the 2/10 Net 30 format of static early payment discounting. Here, since the buyer has a 2% early payment discount available for 30 days − 10 days = 20 days, the incremental discount rate is 2% ÷ 20 days = 0.1% daily. If the buyer decides to pay 15 days early, the accrued discount is 0.1% × 15 days = 1.5%. This translates to an annual percentage rate (APR) of 0.1% × 365 = 36.5%, a substantial payment reduction for the buyer. This incremental rate is consistent throughout the period between the invoice issuance and its due date.

Conversely, in *semi-dynamic discounting*, portrayed in Fig. 7.1b, no added discount is allotted if payment is made within the initial 10 days. This duration serves as a grace period for the seller and might be extended if the buyer is cash-rich and the supply chain relationship is thriving. Alternatively, the buyer can stipulate in the contract that the supplier cannot request payment within these 10 days.

7.2 Dynamic Discounting

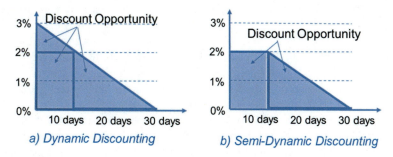

Fig. 7.1 Dynamic discounting

Considering discounts are determined daily, robust IT infrastructure is imperative for executing dynamic discounting. Such systems generally encompass ERP and e-invoicing systems for all participating firms. Essentially, these IT systems should ensure both parties have access to pertinent information and facilitate prompt payment from buyer to seller.

7.2.1 Process Flow

The dynamic discounting process flow varies depending on the initiator: the buyer, the seller, or a third-party. However, the majority of dynamic discounting solutions typically involve the steps depicted in Fig. 7.2:

Fig. 7.2 Mechanism of dynamic discounting

1. After making a purchase of goods or services, the buyer issues an invoice to the seller.
2. Opting to leverage dynamic discounting, the seller uploads the invoice to a dedicated platform. This platform could be overseen by the buyer, a bank, or a third-party financial service firm. Notably, initializing a dynamic discounting program on a third-party platform is often free for both parties, but the seller might incur fees when submitting invoices.
3. Upon receiving the early payment request, the buyer reviews, then either verifies or approves the invoice for such payment. The applicable discount rate might be determined at this juncture or may have been pre-established in the purchase contract.
4. The seller assesses the dynamic discounting payment alternatives and designates their preferred payment date. By formally submitting this early payment request, the seller confirms acceptance of the chosen discount terms.
5. On the selected date, the seller is remunerated, with the discount amount already deducted.

7.2.2 Pros, Cons, and Risk Mitigation

Dynamic discounting does not necessitate advance negotiation, granting the buyer increased flexibility to determine the early payment limit and the discount rate. Subsequently, the seller elects whether to accept the early payment offer. Apart from this flexibility, dynamic discounting can be advantageous for both buyers and sellers in multiple ways (Taulia, 2021a).

7.2.2.1 Pros, Cons, and Risk Mitigation for Buyers
The buyer realizes several benefits when utilizing dynamic discounting:

- *Financial Returns*: As discussed earlier, a 2/10 Net 30 early payment discount can equate to a 36.5% interest APR for the buyer. Even less enticing dynamic discounting agreements often yield double-digit APR returns for the buyer. Thus, dynamic discounting can substantially cut purchasing expenses, serving as a rapid, profitable, and adaptable investment tool. Additionally, reduced costs can enhance buyers' KPIs, like profit margins and cost of goods sold (COGS).
- *No-Risk Investment*: In most scenarios, sellers have already provided goods or services to the buyers prior to receiving early payments. This makes dynamic discounting an attractive proposition; the buyer essentially repays an amount they would've disbursed to the seller sooner. As a result, many early payment discounts, including those under dynamic discounting, present virtually no investment risks for buyers.

- **Supply Chain Reliability**: By facilitating quicker and more straightforward cash access for sellers, dynamic discounting markedly diminishes the likelihood of seller defaults and subsequent supply chain interruptions.
- **Supplier Relationship**: Assisting suppliers fosters stronger ties between them and the buyers. This could be a reason why buyers often prioritize early payment discounts for loyal suppliers with whom they have enduring relationships.
- **Information Transparency**: Implementing dynamic discounting necessitates fully integrated IT systems shared by both the seller and the buyer. This arrangement ensures that all parties in the supply chain benefit from the transparency upheld by these IT systems.

There are potential risks associated with some of the above benefits though.

- **Worsened Cash Conversion Cycle (CCC)**: When buyers pay their sellers earlier, their cash position, and consequently their working capital level, reduces. Buyers are essentially trading off the working capital level for the aforementioned benefits. By settling accounts payable sooner, the days payable outstanding (DPO) is reduced, which adversely affects the CCC, leading to a larger CCC for buyers. However, for buyers flush with capital, this trade-off can be justified.
- **Seller Default**: If a seller fails to meet its obligations to deliver quality products, the buyer could lose the discount and might be left with an outstanding invoice due in its entirety. This could also arise if the quality of goods or services doesn't meet stipulated standards.
- **Operational Risks**: Efficient and precise invoice processing is essential for dynamic discounting. Any discrepancies or delays can lead to missed discounts, belated payments, or even stress the buyer–supplier relationship. While dynamic discounting promises several benefits to sellers—with about 80% aiming to tap into them—only 27% manage to fully harness all available discounts (WNS, 2014). Some potential causes include:
  - Delays in invoice processing lead to overdue invoices.
  - IT systems supporting dynamic discounting aren't top-tier, resulting in early payment request delays.
  - The absence of an effective spend analysis means firms don't fully grasp dynamic discounting's benefits.
- **Reputation Risk**: A buyer perceived as exploiting suppliers by demanding large discounts could tarnish its reputation and strain supplier relationships.
- **Legal Risks**: Improper structuring of a dynamic discounting program might breach antitrust laws or pose legal liabilities due to high discount rates.
- **Financial Risks**: It's vital for buyers to have adequate cash flow to capitalize on dynamic discounting, ensuring they don't jeopardize their liquidity for short-term gains.

Buyers need to meticulously evaluate the pros and cons of dynamic discounting prior to its adoption, endeavoring to offset potential risks through comprehensive due diligence and risk management tactics. Here are some risk mitigation methods:

- *Cash Flow Management*: By forecasting their cash requirements and maintaining sufficient liquidity, buyers can deftly manage their cash flow. They can also broker extended payment terms with sellers, ensuring they have ample time to pay without forfeiting discounts. Notably, not all buyers, even big players like Amazon and Walmart, have the liquidity to pre-pay all invoices. This explains their selectiveness regarding suppliers included in early payment programs.
- *Seller Due Diligence*: Buyers should conduct thorough checks on sellers to ascertain their financial robustness and their history of delivering quality goods/services. This can involve examining financial statements, credit scores, and seeking references from other buyers.
- *Supplier Diversification*: Diversifying their supplier pool allows buyers to hedge supplier risks. By allocating their spending across multiple suppliers, they can curtail the ramifications of supply chain disruptions and lessen their reliance on any individual supplier.
- *Operational Controls*: Instituting controls and protocols ensures effective management of the dynamic discounting process. This entails laying down clear policies, training relevant personnel, and consistently tracking performance metrics for potential refinements.

Adopting these risk mitigation techniques allows buyers to diminish potential dynamic discounting risks and enhances the probability of the financing strategy's success.

7.2.2.2 Pros, Cons, and Risk Mitigation for Sellers

Dynamic discounting offers several advantages to sellers:

- *Improved Cash Flow and Liquidity*: One of the primary benefits for sellers is an enhancement in their working capital and optimized cash flow. Without such early payments, some sellers might struggle with day-to-day operations. With dynamic discounting, sellers can finance up to 100% of selected invoices (after deducting the discount), typically a higher percentage than in traditional factoring. By receiving payments sooner, the days sales outstanding (DSO) decreases, improving the CCC.
- *Financing Opportunity*: While most early payment discounts may seem costly in terms of APR for sellers, other financing options could be even more expensive or unavailable. Sellers constrained by capital might have limited creditworthiness or a sparse credit history. Hence, dynamic discounting offers a dependable financing avenue for such sellers, bringing more predictability to their cash flows and enabling better future planning.

- **Collection Costs**: Dynamic discounting reduces the costs associated with payment collection for sellers. As an illustration, in the UK, small and medium-sized enterprises (SMEs) had an average outstanding payment of £12,000 each in 2016, amounting to £55bn nationwide (Sheppard, 2016). Collecting overdue payments, especially from influential buyers, could jeopardize essential sales channels for smaller sellers. Employing dynamic discounting can alleviate these collection challenges.
- **Supply Chain Reliability**: By extending early payment discounts, sellers can motivate buyers to settle invoices promptly, fostering better relationships and increasing the chances of ongoing business collaborations. Given these advantages, a seller is better positioned to deliver products or services to honor new agreements, meeting new customer demands efficiently. This reliability strengthens trust with buyers, ensuring steady demand for sustainable growth.
- **Competitive Advantage**: Offering dynamic discounting can serve as a unique selling proposition for sellers. It showcases their readiness to collaborate with buyers and provides a distinctive service that differentiates them from rivals.
- **Financing Flexibility**: Sellers benefit from the flexibility dynamic discounting offers, allowing them to select which invoices to discount and when. Whether financing a single invoice or multiple ones, this flexibility enables sellers to better control and optimize their cash flows.

Despite the benefits, dynamic discounting also introduces challenges and risks for sellers:

- **High Financing Cost**: Dynamic discounting can be costly for sellers. When offering early payment discounts, sellers might see reduced profit margins, as they are essentially forgoing a part of their revenue to ensure quicker payments. Paradoxically, sellers incur a significant cost for payments they rightly should have received earlier, especially once goods and services have already been rendered.
- **Buyer Dependency**: Sellers leaning heavily on dynamic discounting for cash flow improvement might find themselves overly reliant on their buyers' promptness in payment. This could pose a risk if those buyers decide to postpone payments.
- **Consequence of Buyer Dominance**: Discounts for early payment might inadvertently motivate buyers to procrastinate until the discount period, possibly affecting the seller's cash flow negatively. Historically, payment delays in business transactions have been a standard practice across many industries. Upstream competition often encourages buyers to use extended accounts payable as a negotiation tool, conserving their working capital and shortening their CCC.

    This trend has been exacerbated in recent times, with dominant buyers like Walmart and Amazon demanding lengthier payment terms. In China, powerhouse retailers such as Alibaba and JD.com exert such dominance that they often require exclusivity from suppliers, further diminishing these suppliers' negotiating leverage regarding payment terms.

To aid smaller businesses, there's a growing call for regulatory measures to limit such buyer dominance in payment terms. This would inherently alleviate financial pressures on sellers. A case in point is the European Union's Late Payment Directive. It mandates debtors to pay both interest and any reasonable recovery costs if they don't make timely payments for goods or services. The stipulated payment windows are 60 days for businesses and 30 days for public authorities (Wikipedia, 2022).

> *Government regulations are needed to curtail buyers' dominance in payment terms.*

To mitigate the aforementioned risks, sellers can adopt the following potential strategies:

- ***Spend Analysis***: Effective dynamic discounting requires both buyers and sellers to conduct spend analytics to optimize their cash flow. When their cash flow is healthy, sellers ideally should not cash out every invoice to reduce financing costs. During their spend analysis, firms ought to review their ideal cash position, monthly spend, invoice values, and more.
- ***Diversify Buyer Base***: Sellers should strive to diversify their buyer base. This reduces dependence on a single buyer and minimizes the dominance of any one buyer in determining payment terms.
- ***Establish Clear Payment Terms***: Sellers must define clear payment terms with buyers. This includes penalties for late payments and incentives for early ones.
- ***Set Discount Rates Based on Risk***: Sellers should adjust discount rates according to the risk level associated with each buyer. Higher discount rates should apply to riskier buyers and lower rates for more creditworthy ones. This approach enables sellers to collect payments from riskier buyers earlier, reducing the potential for future default.
- ***Monitor Buyer Creditworthiness***: Regular monitoring of a buyer's creditworthiness is crucial for sellers. Establishing credit limits can minimize the risk of default. Additionally, sellers can opt for insurance coverages, such as credit insurance, to shield against potential losses from buyer default.

By employing these risk mitigation strategies, sellers can reduce potential threats and amplify the advantages of dynamic discounting.

7.3 Reverse Factoring

Owing to its widespread use, *reverse factoring* is also commonly termed as approved payables finance, supplier finance, payable finance, trade payable management, confirmed payables finance, vendor pre-pay, or buyer-led supply chain finance. Some financial providers even label it "supply chain finance" to market this distinct financing approach. However, it isn't entirely accurate to use reverse factoring as a synonym for the broad field of supply chain finance, but such nomenclature possibly highlights the mechanism's significance and potential. Introduced first in the automobile industry during the 1980s, reverse factoring has found its footing in numerous other sectors. To maintain clarity, this book will consistently use the term "reverse factoring" when discussing this financing method.

As depicted in Fig. 7.3, in reverse factoring, a seller forwards its invoice to a factor (like a bank) for an early discounted payment, contingent on the buyer's binding commitment to settle the amount with the factor upon maturity without any recourse to the seller. Much like factoring, reverse factoring introduces prompt payments into the sellers' cash flow, bolstering their working capital. However, unlike conventional factoring, reverse factoring is initiated by the buyer and boasts its unique merits.

Financing in reverse factoring leans on the superior credit ratings of buyers, ensuring that sellers typically incur lower financing costs than those prevailing in the open market based on their individual credit standings. This cost differential becomes even more pronounced when there's a significant disparity between the credit ratings of the buyer and the seller. The resulting financial terms might be so favorable for sellers that they find it hard to refuse, especially when juxtaposed with seller-initiated factoring and buyer-driven dynamic discounting.

Buyers too stand to gain, reaping the advantages of enhanced working capital stemming from potentially extended payment timelines, as re-negotiated under the reverse factoring scheme. A study from 2007 disclosed that over 70% of sizable

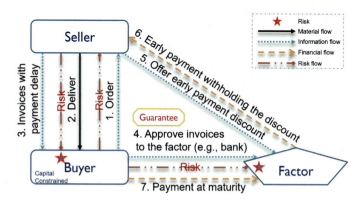

Fig. 7.3 Mechanism of reverse factoring

European enterprises actively sought to protract their payment terms while bargaining with suppliers, aiming to ease their working capital strains (Miller, 2007). Thus, reverse factoring admirably bridges the gap, catering not only to suppliers' working capital requisites but also addressing buyers' aspirations for elongated payment periods.

Given its distinct advantages for all participating entities, reverse factoring has registered a brisk growth rate, charting double-digit expansion in recent years. Data from the UK's Association of Chartered Certified Accountants (ACCA) suggests that reverse factoring could account for a substantial 20 to 25 percent of a buyer's accounts payable across all trade financing (Camerinelli, 2014). Citing Wikipedia (2020), the global market cap for supply chain finance was pegged at a hefty $275 billion in yearly traded volume back in 2013, escalating to $447.8 billion by 2016. While the reverse factoring market has matured notably in the US and Western Europe, emerging markets like India and China are perceived to be teeming with untapped potential.

7.3.1 Process Flow

The reverse factoring mechanism, as depicted in Figs. 7.3, 7.4, and 7.5, operates as follows:

1. A buyer enters into a contract with a seller for the acquisition of goods and/or services. Both parties mutually agree on a reverse factoring financing program. This program could have prior approval from a relationship bank or a

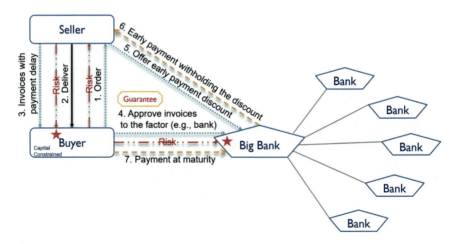

Fig. 7.4 Reverse factoring through a bank

7.3 Reverse Factoring

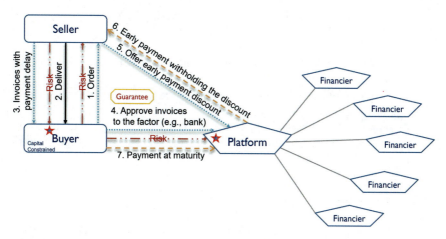

Fig. 7.5 Reverse factoring in a platform

financial institution that offers a comprehensive program for the buyer. Alternatively, they can join a third-party reverse factoring platform post invoice generation, as shown in Fig. 7.5.
2. The seller delivers the goods and/or services to the buyer.
3. The seller forwards the invoice to the buyer.
4. The buyer verifies and relays the invoice to a factor (e.g., a bank or a platform). On certain platforms, the seller may directly submit the invoices. As depicted in Fig. 7.4, the factor might be a major bank. This bank can subsequently offload the accounts receivable to smaller banks or collaborate with these banks to fund corresponding reverse factoring requests. Alternatively, the factor could be a financial service platform backed by a consortium of financiers, as shown in Fig. 7.5. The participation of multiple banks or financiers becomes indispensable, especially for large corporations with extensive capital requirements.
5. The seller reviews the reverse factoring proposal from the factor. By default, the seller will receive the complete payment upon maturity. However, if the seller opts for reverse factoring, they initiate the process by transferring the accounts receivable to the factor, agreeing to the early payment discount rate.
6. The factor can then remit the early payment (less the agreed-upon discount) to the seller by the subsequent business day. Since the buyer's commitment to the payment is absolute and non-recourse, the financing ratio in reverse factoring usually surpasses that of traditional factoring. Following the payment to the seller, the factor and buyer may renegotiate the payment conditions (e.g., extending the payment term by 30 days from the original agreement).
7. When the invoice matures, the buyer settles the full amount with the factor. Due to potential extensions in the payment period solicited by the buyer, payments to the factor typically occur later than originally stipulated.

As depicted in Fig. 7.5, platforms for reverse factoring have been prevailing in recent years. These platforms can be managed by:

1. **Bank proprietary platforms**: Here, prominent commercial banks act as the factor.
2. **Third-party platforms**: Fintech companies can establish these platforms, supported by a group of financiers.
3. **Buyer-owned platforms**: Large buyers, such as JD.com, create their proprietary platforms, sometimes leveraging their subsidiary capital firms to finance their sellers.

7.3.2 Benefits

Reverse factoring is increasingly being recognized as a valuable financing mechanism for firms, offering a fresh marketing opportunity for banks and other financial institutions. According to estimates by the Swiss bank Credit Suisse Group AG, reverse factoring is evolving "rapidly," with the potential to tap into $2 trillion of financeable payables worldwide (Eaglesham, 2020). Similarly, Bank of America has witnessed robust support from both suppliers and buyers in their reverse factoring offerings.

Reverse factoring is a unique and intricate mechanism that actively involves the seller, the buyer, and the factor. Table 7.1 delves deeper into the influence of reverse factoring on companies' operations and risks. At its core, reverse factoring bolsters the seller's cash flow, curtails its accounts receivable (AR) and net working capital (NWC), and transfers associated risks to the factor and the buyer. The buyer, in turn, enjoys the dual advantages of a more reliable seller and extended payment timelines. The factor realizes additional profits from financing the seller, fortified by the buyer's guarantee. As with traditional factoring, the supplementary cash equips the seller to broaden their market reach, and the buyer might consequently increase their orders, potentially benefiting the entire supply chain.

While the benefits that reverse factoring confers upon sellers are comparable to other financial mechanisms, such as dynamic discounting, nuances do exist. What follows is a breakdown of the benefits for sellers, buyers, and factors, respectively.

7.3.2.1 Benefits for Sellers

Reverse factoring provides several advantages to sellers, including:

- *Improved Cash Flow*: Through reverse factoring, sellers obtain payments ahead of the original due dates. This bolsters their working capital and contracts their CCC, allowing sellers to strategize their operations and fine-tune their cash flow. Such a financial boon can be pivotal for sellers—particularly smaller firms—enabling them to grow their business, channel funds into research and development, and even sustain daily operations seamlessly.

7.3 Reverse Factoring

Table 7.1 Impact of reverse factoring on firms' operations and risks

	Seller	Buyer	Factor
Cash	↑	↑	↓
AR	↓		↑
Inventory	Potentially ↑		
AP		↓	
NWC	↓	↑	↓
Risks	↓	↑	↑

Note The arrows (↑) indicate an increase, while (↓) indicate a decrease

- **Lower Financing Costs**: In contrast to traditional factoring or dynamic discounting, the early payment discount rates in reverse factoring hinge on the buyer's credit rating. Typically, dominant buyers boast a more solid credit standing than their sellers, resulting in discount rates that are generally lower than those associated with factoring and dynamic discounting.
- **Accounting Benefits**: Analogous to factoring, an early payment in reverse factoring doesn't qualify as debt for sellers, thereby remaining absent from the balance sheet.
- **Reduced Collection Costs**: In line with dynamic discounting, reverse factoring trims the collection costs for invoices that buyers have greenlit for the program.
- **Supply Chain Reliability**: By leveraging reverse factoring, sellers can entice buyers to expedite payments, fostering stronger business relationships and enhancing the probability of continued partnerships. When pitted against dynamic discounting, reverse factoring strengthens supply chain relationships due to the full payment guarantees offered by buyers. Possessing commendable credit ratings, buyers assist sellers in securing more affordable financing. This mutual benefit can subsequently translate to reduced wholesale prices and a more streamlined, reliable supply chain.
- **Financing Flexibility**: Sellers retain the discretion to accept or decline the early payment discount, possessing the option to await the invoice's maturity to retrieve the complete payment.
- **Diminished Credit Risk**: Reverse factoring reallocates the credit risk from the seller to the buyer since the buyer shoulders the responsibility of settling the invoice. This risk transfer proves advantageous for sellers with less robust credit backgrounds or those operating within high risk sectors.

7.3.2.2 Benefits for Buyers

Reverse factoring offers multiple advantages to buyers:

- *Improved Working Capital*: Contrary to initial expectations of buyer-led supply chain finance, reverse factoring can amplify the working capital for buyers. In providing a non-recourse commitment to payment upon maturity, buyers frequently negotiate extended payment terms with their sellers or the factor, often at reduced costs. This financial advantage results in a decreased CCC and bolstered liquidity. This benefit is even more attractive for buyers with superior credit ratings. Therefore, reverse factoring stands out as a unique financing mechanism that optimizes cash conversion rates for both buyers and sellers while simultaneously presenting financing opportunities for factors. This creates a win–win–win situation.

> **Case Study**
>
> ***The Impact of Reverse Factoring***
>
> Keurig Dr Pepper Inc., a major player in the coffee and soda industry, collaborated with various banks to delay supplier payments amounting to $2.1 billion by the close of the previous year, an increase from $1.4 billion the prior year, as indicated in a securities document. The company mentioned in the same filing that their payment terms can extend to as long as 360 days, a practice they noted as being standard in the coffee sector (Eaglesham, 2020).

- *Accounting Benefit*: Mirroring factoring, early payments in reverse factoring aren't classified as debt for buyers either, so they remain off the balance sheet. Unlike dynamic discounting, where sellers have leeway in deciding which invoices to discount and when, in reverse factoring, it's the buyers who determine which invoices qualify for early payment.
- *Reduced Procurement Costs*: Beyond the advantage of extended payment terms, buyers can potentially procure goods at a reduced wholesale price when incorporating reverse factoring into contract discussions. This savings can subsequently reduce the costs for downstream firms, triggering an uptick in demand and overall efficiency in the supply chain.
- *Improved Supplier Relationship*: By championing reverse factoring, buyers can assist their sellers in enhancing cash flow, curbing financing expenses, and effectively managing credit risk. Early payments via reverse factoring substantially diminish the chances of seller defaults and disruptions in the supply chain, fostering stronger, more resilient relationships with sellers and bolstering overall supply chain efficiency. As a result, buyers can attract and retain more dedicated suppliers.

- **Competitive Advantage**: Proposing reverse factoring can give buyers a competitive edge. It signals a readiness to collaborate closely with sellers and provides an invaluable service that distinguishes them from rivals.
- **Information Transparency**: Successful reverse factoring necessitates robust IT systems integration between the buyer and the seller. The transparency afforded by these IT systems is paramount for the success of reverse factoring, as buyers must have comprehensive knowledge of their sellers prior to committing to full payment without recourse. In the absence of sophisticated IT infrastructure, reverse factoring might only cater to a limited cohort of suppliers (e.g., 20–50 suppliers). Yet, cutting-edge IT solutions enable buyers to accommodate thousands of suppliers (Taulia, 2021b), magnifying the benefits for both parties on a grander scale.
- **Lower Administration Cost**: Leveraging sophisticated IT support, buyers can alleviate administrative overhead by liaising directly with the factor, bypassing the need to engage with thousands of individual suppliers or sellers for payments.

The forthcoming illustrative case will further elucidate the myriad benefits of reverse factoring for both sellers and buyers.

Case Study

Reverse Factoring

Supplier ABC sells products priced at $2 million to Buyer XYZ. If they follow the industry standard without reverse factoring (RF), Supplier ABC would extend a 2-month credit line to Buyer XYZ (as shown in the upper portion of Fig. 7.6).

Assuming Supplier ABC borrows from banks to finance its operations at an interest rate of 8%, its capital cost, using a 365-day fiscal year, would be:

$$\text{Capital Cost without RF} = \$2,000,000 \times 8\% \times 60/365 = \$26,301.37$$

Given the strong credit rating of Buyer XYZ, both Supplier ABC and Buyer XYZ decide to utilize RF to finance Supplier ABC. This is done at an interest rate of 1.75%, starting from the 15th day. In exchange, Supplier ABC offers a 90-day credit term, as illustrated in the lower portion of Fig. 7.6.

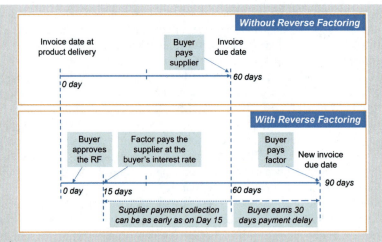

Fig. 7.6 An illustrating case: Reverse factoring

With RF, Supplier ABC incurs a capital cost at the 8% interest rate for the first 15 days and then 1.75% for the subsequent 75 days (90 days minus 15 days). Its total capital cost would be:

$$\text{Capital Cost with RF} = \$2{,}000{,}000 \times 8\% \times 15/365 + \$2{,}000{,}000 \times 1.75\% \times 75/365 = \$13{,}767.12$$

The capital cost saved by Supplier ABC by using RF compared to not using RF is:

Saved Capital Cost with RF for Supplier ABC = $26,301.37 − $13,767.12 = $12,534.25

For Buyer XYZ, the benefit is the ability to manage the working capital of $2 million for an additional 30 days, which is equivalent to:

$$\text{Saved Capital Cost with RF for Buyer XYZ} = \$2{,}000{,}000 \times 1.75\% \times (90-60)/365 = \$2{,}876.71$$

This case underscores that both the supplier and buyer can reap advantages from reverse factoring. It's worth noting that in the real world, suppliers are often SMEs with less favorable credit ratings or possibly no credit history, meaning they could be faced with even higher interest rates than 8% without RF.

7.3.2.3 Benefits for Factors

The benefits of reverse factoring to factors include:

- **Lower Investment Risk**: Since the buyer is typically more creditworthy than the seller in reverse factoring, funding the seller with a non-recourse commitment from the buyer is financially less risky than directly funding the buyer, as seen in dynamic discounting. This helps shield factors from potential defaults or insolvencies. As stipulated by Basel III, a decrease in investment risks also diminishes the capital requirement.
- **More Financing Opportunities**: Reverse factoring allows factors to enhance their business volume by introducing a novel financing product to both buyers and suppliers. This can lead to an expanded customer base and an increase in revenue. Specifically, reverse factoring can considerably enlarge the financial market for a factor in two distinct manners:
  - Landing a reverse factoring deal with a sizeable, high-credit-rating buyer essentially grants access to its plethora of suppliers. This action also trims the factor's administrative costs, which would otherwise be incurred from separately dealing with numerous suppliers.
  - The structure of reverse factoring also unveils financing opportunities for thousands of smaller businesses that might not be creditworthy or those that hold credit ratings below the investment grade. Typically, these smaller enterprises possess limited financial channels, even if their financial needs may surpass those of larger entities.
- **Risk Pooling Effect**: Merging thousands of suppliers/sellers into a singular program leads to a risk pooling effect, where the risks associated with each supplier compensate for one another. This effect enhances the predictability of both risks and financial demand for the factor.
- **Improved Supply Chain Relationship**: Proposing reverse factoring can serve as a competitive edge for factors. It provides a distinctive financing product that differentiates them from rivals and has the potential to lure new clients. Moreover, reverse factoring can fortify a long-lasting bond between the factor, the seller, and the buyer. This means that the relationship the factor shares with supply chain firms might be more robust in reverse factoring compared to traditional factoring which might only involve the seller.

The distribution of benefits among sellers, buyers, and factors can also be influenced by industry practices and the negotiating power of firms. A 2014 study from the UK's ACCA indicated that sellers, buyers, and factors all reap substantial benefits from reverse factoring (Camerinelli, 2014). As depicted in Table 7.2, buyers may seize the most significant portion, ranging from 35% to 50%. Sellers come next with a share ranging from 25% to 45%, and then factors with 15% to 18%.

7.3.3 Risks and Risk Mitigation

While all financing is subject to common risks such as market, financial, policy, product quality issues, and others, reverse factoring presents unique nuances. Post the signing of the ordering contract by the buyer, the seller confronts the risk

Table 7.2 Allocation of benefits among reverse factoring players

	Share of Reverse Factoring Savings Captured	
	Min	Max
Buyers	35%	50%
Sellers	25%	45%
Factors	15%	18%
Platform Providers	2%	5%

Source Adapted from Camerinelli (2014) based on expert interviews

of the buyer's default, such as canceling the order after the seller has procured materials and commenced production. Once the product/service and the invoice are delivered, some risk shifts to the buyer, primarily due to the obligation to pay the seller and possible product quality concerns. Upon the buyer's approval of invoices submitted to the factor, the latter assumes certain risks, even if the buyer has vouched for payment upon maturity, given potential buyer defaults due to weak demand or product issues. However, the buyer's guarantee minimizes risks for the seller, a relief not seen in dynamic discounting or factoring.

Below, we detail potential risks tied to reverse factoring for sellers, buyers, and factors.

7.3.3.1 Risk Mitigation for Sellers

Potential risks and their corresponding mitigation strategies for sellers are enumerated in Table 7.3.

In summary, while reverse factoring can amplify a seller's cash flow and curtail financing expenses, inherent risks mandate prudent consideration. Employing the aforementioned risk mitigation tactics can help sellers curtail potential hazards, ensuring they reap the rewards of reverse factoring offers.

7.3.3.2 Risk Mitigation for Buyers

In reverse factoring, the brunt of financial risks migrates from the seller to the buyer, saddling the latter with greater risks compared to traditional factoring. Table 7.4 elucidates the risks and relevant risk mitigation approaches for buyers.

By integrating these risk mitigation blueprints, buyers can pare down the risks inherent in reverse factoring, thereby fortifying their liquidity and market competitiveness.

7.3.3.3 Risk Mitigation for Factors

Even with payment guarantees from buyers, factors still face potential hazards arising from credit, operational, and market risks. Table 7.5 delineates these risks along with corresponding mitigation strategies.

Table 7.3 Risks and risk mitigation for sellers in reverse factoring

Risks	• *Dependence on the Buyer*: The buyer typically orchestrates reverse factoring, tethering the seller to the buyer's financial health to procure financing at favorable rates. If the buyer faces fiscal challenges or defaults, the seller might experience payment delays • *Less Control on Payment Process*: Dominance by the buyer and factor can limit the seller's control over payments. They might also have to acquiesce to the payment terms set by the buyer or factor, potentially at odds with their preferred terms • *Potential Legal and Reputational Risks*: A defaulting buyer could lead financial entities to seek legal redress against the seller, which might attract legal fees, mar the seller's reputation, and jeopardize future business ventures • *Operational Risk*: The intricate nature of reverse factoring, demanding synchrony between the seller, buyer, and factor, is pivotal. Its success could be compromised by product quality, returns, shipment delays, unforeseen fees, and buyer default • *Potential Damage to the Relationship*: Though reverse factoring bridges supply chain entities and factors, it might strain relations if the seller perceives coercive, unfavorable terms
Risk Mitigation	• *Diversify Their Customer Base*: Sellers can mitigate risks by diversifying clientele, diluting dependency on any singular buyer • *Maintain Control over Receivables*: Sellers can hold sway over their receivables by cementing terms with financial institutions, ensuring they retain collection rights if buyers default • *Coordinate Financing Processes*: Impeccable coordination, auditing, reporting, and monitoring can pare down operational risks. Ambiguous contracts and rules could render reverse factoring exorbitant for sellers if not deployed astutely • *Negotiate Favorable Terms*: Engaging with financial institutions to clinch terms ensuring reasonable fees and satisfactory profit margins is vital for sellers • *Consider Other Financing Options*: Should the financial institution's fees be steep, sellers might evaluate alternatives like traditional bank credit lines or factoring • *Monitor Buyer Creditworthiness*: A continual assessment of the buyer's fiscal health helps sellers sidestep potential payment defaults • *Manage Relationships*: A symbiotic relationship between sellers, financial institutions, and buyers thrives on transparency, prompt issue resolution, and meticulous documentation

By rigorously vetting buyers, suppliers, and market conditions, diversifying their portfolios, and cementing strong client relationships, factors can adeptly navigate these challenges. Additionally, it's imperative for factors to embed robust risk management and compliance mechanisms to pinpoint and adeptly tackle potential threats.

Table 7.4 Risks and risk mitigation for buyers in reverse factoring

Risks	• *Hidden Invoice Issues*: Reverse factoring hinges on accounts payable. The credibility of invoices could be compromised by potential credit notes issued by the seller to the buyer, especially concerning product returns. Additionally, challenges might arise from invoice inaccuracies, such as miscalculations, typographical errors, or fraudulent activities • *Supplier's Default*: The buyer is contingent on the seller's timely delivery and adherence to quality standards. Should the seller face insolvency or fail to uphold their delivery commitments, the buyer, having guaranteed an advanced payment, stands vulnerable • *Reputation Risks*: While extended payment terms in reverse factoring often incentivize buyer participation, any perception of the buyer willfully stalling payments can tarnish their reputation and strain relations with the seller • *Credit Risks*: Rooted in the buyer's creditworthiness and their assurance of final payment to the factor, reverse factoring might sway the buyer's credit score and fiscal stability, especially if there are operational snags like delivery lags or disagreements with the factor
Risk Mitigation	• *Perform Due Diligence*: To navigate the quagmire of hidden invoice issues, buyers should meticulously scrutinize each invoice prior to greenlighting payments and conduct thorough due diligence on both the factor and the seller • *Diversify Suppliers*: Engaging with an array of suppliers dilutes the risk of supplier default or insolvency • *Monitor Continuously*: Given the multiple stakeholders in reverse factoring, unwavering vigilance allows the buyer to spot potential pitfalls promptly, ensuring protocol adherence • *Negotiate Favorable Terms*: Buyers should haggle for optimal terms with the factor, perhaps in the form of amenable interest rates and fees, potentially in return for cut-rate wholesale prices. Concurrently, hashing out payment stipulations with sellers to align with their cash flow imperatives is essential • *Maintain Supply Chain Relationship*: Sustaining transparent communications and data transparency with sellers, particularly around payment protocols, is paramount. This fosters trust and diminishes the threat of reputational degradation

7.3.3.4 The Debate of Accounts Payable as "Debt"

As previously mentioned, reverse factoring financing operates as an off-balance sheet mechanism for both buyers and sellers. While it's straightforward to understand why sellers don't view reverse factoring as a loan (they're simply receiving their payments earlier), the same clarity is elusive for buyers.

It's important to note that factors have settled the buyers' accounts payable to sellers in advance. These buyers then settle their accounts with the factors when the invoices mature. This brings up the intricate question: should such arrangements be classified as accounts payable or as debt? Financial institutions like Citigroup Inc., Greensill Capital, and HSBC Holdings PLC, as well as companies utilizing reverse factoring such as Coca-Cola Co., Boeing Co., and other prominent firms, dispute the labeling of this as "debt" (Steinberg, 2020).

The inherent ambiguity in this financing method for buyers has led to concerns about concealed financial risks, which might become "latent hazards" in crises, as observed during the COVID-19 pandemic. Because reverse factoring remains off

7.3 Reverse Factoring

Table 7.5 Risks and risk mitigation for factors

Risks	• **Demand Forecasting Mistakes**: A primary reason a buyer pledges full payment to the factor is their confidence in demand forecasts. However, unexpected significant demand shortfalls can impede timely repayments by buyers. In instances of buyer defaults, the factor stands to incur losses, even with full payment guarantees in place • **Double Financing Risks**: Buyers and sellers may recycle the same accounts receivable and accounts payable to secure additional financing • **Buyer Default Risk**: Should a buyer fail to fulfill repayment obligations, the factor becomes saddled with the resultant bad debt • **Credit Risk**: If the seller falters in delivering products punctually or maintaining requisite quality standards, unpaid invoices can plague the factor, complicating fund recovery efforts • **Reputational Risk**: Factors risk reputational damage when associating with buyers or suppliers of dubious repute or those known for unethical practices • **Market Risk**: Substantial dips in demand expose the factor to market risks, potentially jeopardizing both buyer and seller in fulfilling their obligations
Risk Mitigation	• **Conduct Due Intelligence**: Considering that buyers often introduce sellers into reverse factoring arrangements, factors should diligently vet the reputation and creditworthiness of both during onboarding and in subsequent evaluations, as recommended by the Globe SCF Forum (2016). Emerging technologies like blockchain can be pivotal in curtailing double financing • **Establish Credit Limits**: Instituting credit ceilings for buyers based on their accounts payable is pivotal in managing default risks. Ensuring that buyer commitments align with their repayment capacities is paramount • **Monitor Market and Firms' Performance**: Regularly surveilling market dynamics (e.g., through forecasting) and closely tracking buyer and supplier performances can diminish market and credit risks • **Strengthen Supply Chain Relationship**: Fostering robust supply chain relationships with buyers and sellers, characterized by transparency and open communication, helps allay misunderstandings and bolster trust, thus countering reputational risks • **Diversify Portfolio**: By collaborating with a diverse clientele spanning different sectors and geographies, factors can insulate themselves against risks stemming from problematic clients

the balance sheet, a company's financial strain may go undetected until it encounters significant difficulties. For instance, after employing reverse factoring with various banks, Keurig Dr Pepper Inc., an espresso and soda company, was able to delay supplier payments, increasing the amount from $1.4 billion to $2.1 billion within a year (Eaglesham, 2020).

In October 2019, the Big Four accounting firms addressed the Financial Accounting Standards Board (FASB)—a private, non-profit organization that sets US accounting standards—proposing that "investors would benefit if companies disclosed the terms, size of the deals, and related cash flows" (Scaggs, 2020). On October 22, 2020, the Wall Street Journal reported that the FASB was considering more extensive disclosures regarding reverse factoring arrangements.

Designating reverse factoring as "debt" could likely deter buyer participation. Yet, keeping such information off the balance sheet might amplify financial risks for companies and banks, potentially undermining supply chain stability. There are instances where companies have postponed payments for up to 360 days through reverse factoring without reporting them in their financial statements (Scaggs, 2020), potentially jeopardizing supply chain stability if these companies default and their risk ratings plummet.

In conclusion, while excluding reverse factoring from debt considerations can enhance supply chain financial metrics for buyers, greater transparency and disclosure to the public could reinforce supply chain dependability.

7.3.4 Comparisons to Other Mechanisms

No single financing mechanism can consistently meet all of a firm's financial needs. As the business environment and economic climate evolve, so do a firm's requirements. Consequently, what may be an effective financial solution today might not be suitable a year from now. For this reason, it's advisable for companies to adjust their financing strategies as needed.

7.3.4.1 Reverse Factoring vs. Factoring

While reverse factoring has similarities with factoring, especially regarding the discounted early payment, there are key distinctions between the two:

- *Initiator*: In factoring, the buyer is not a participant in the financing process. In contrast, with reverse factoring, the buyer often initiates the process and fully guarantees payment to the factor upon maturity. This makes the buyer a pivotal player in reverse factoring.
- *Eligibility of Invoices*: With factoring, factors often prefer a long-term contract with the seller to enhance the predictability and volume of invoices, allowing the seller to factor all invoices. In reverse factoring, as the buyer takes on more risk, they exercise more caution in fully guaranteeing all invoices. Concerns about product quality and the seller's credibility make buyers more selective about which invoices to include in reverse factoring.
- *Creditworthiness and Discount Rate*: Factoring places emphasis on both the seller's and the buyer's creditworthiness when the seller has recourse. In reverse factoring, however, it is the buyer's creditworthiness that is paramount because the seller offers an unconditional guarantee for the final payment to the factor. Given that the buyer is usually more creditworthy in reverse factoring, the risk transfer from the seller to the more creditworthy buyer considerably diminishes the financial risk for the factor. This risk mitigation increases the likelihood of financing from the factor and results in a reduced discount rate for the seller.
- *Payment Terms*: In both mechanisms, the buyer settles the full amount with the factor upon the invoice's maturity. However, in reverse factoring, the buyer might defer the invoice payment by an additional 30 days or even

7.3 Reverse Factoring

Table 7.6 Factoring vs. reverse factoring

	Factoring	Reverse Factoring
Initiator	Seller	Buyer
Invoice Eligibility	All invoices	Invoices validated by the buyer
Creditworthiness and Discount Rate	Relies on both the seller's and buyer's creditworthiness when the seller has recourse	Predominantly depends on the buyer's creditworthiness and is generally lower than in factoring
Payment Terms	Due date as per standard terms	Due date is typically extended beyond standard factoring terms

Table 7.7 Dynamic discounting vs. reverse factoring

	Dynamic Discounting	Reverse Factoring
Involved parties	Seller and buyer	Seller, buyer, and factor
Funder	Buyer	Factor
Invoice Eligibility	All invoices	Invoices validated by the buyer
Creditworthiness	Financing is based on the seller's creditworthiness	Financing is based on the buyer's creditworthiness
Interest/Discount	Higher	Lower
Wholesale Price	Might be higher to compensate for the increased discount rate	Might be lower if the payment term isn't negotiated, given the buyer's payment commitment/guarantee
Payment Terms	Due date as stated in the original payment terms	Due date is typically extended, negotiated along with the wholesale price
Working Capital	Seller↑ Buyer↓	Seller↑ Buyer↑

longer. This delay increases costs for the seller and can be viewed as compensation for the buyer's unwavering commitment to the final payment to the factor.

For ease of reference, the primary distinctions between the two are further detailed in Table 7.6.

7.3.4.2 Reverse Factoring vs. Dynamic Discounting

Reverse factoring and dynamic discounting are two primary types of buyer-led supply chain finance mechanisms. Below are their key distinctions, as presented in Table 7.7.

7.3.5 Globalization and Challenges

Owing to the globalization of business, supply chains have extended and can now span multiple continents. The pursuit of offshoring to find cheaper manufacturing costs has resulted in many manufacturers and suppliers being situated in developing countries, which often lack robust financial support systems. These firms find it challenging to secure financing for stages such as material purchasing, production, research and development, and warehousing. Elevated financing costs not only destabilize these firms financially but also escalate procurement costs for buyers. Consequently, buyer-led reverse factoring has gained traction among both sellers and buyers in more developed countries, offering advantages like supply chain stabilization and enhanced efficiency.

Crises like the 2007–2009 Financial Crisis and the COVID-19 pandemic have highlighted the vulnerabilities of supply chains, both logistically and financially. Both buyers and sellers are motivated to fortify their supply chains by infusing more capital to assist capital-constrained entities. The globalization of the supply chain presents opportunities for buyers, sellers, and financial institutions across three main dimensions:

1. ***Need of Sellers***: Numerous manufacturers and suppliers in developing nations are keen on tapping into the buyers' financial markets to secure early payments, especially when an increasing number of buyers demand open accounts in international trades.
2. ***Need of Buyers***: Buyers gravitate towards a more stable supply chain to ensure the consistent delivery of quality products. Concurrently, the ability to delay inventory ownership through reverse factoring appeals to buyers aiming to refine their balance sheets.
3. ***Need of Financial Institutions***: The shift towards offshoring has reduced domestic capital demand for manufacturing, which in turn shrinks the financial market for affluent financial institutions scouting for investment opportunities. With the gradual replacement of letters of credit by open accounts in international trades, reverse factoring aptly addresses the needs of these financial entities.

However, even as reverse factoring finds favor in global supply chains, it faces several challenges:

- ***Know-Your-Customer (KYC)***: While reverse factoring allows buyers the discretion to choose specific sellers for the program, the global landscape necessitates stringent KYC checks on these sellers. This is crucial to mitigate any latent risks, though it does add to the program's overall cost.
- ***Seller Onboarding***: Upon approving a seller for the program, the onboarding process can become more complex and costly due to the lack of adequate IT infrastructure in developing regions (issues might include system compatibility and other technical challenges).
- ***Capital Availability and Liquidity***: Regardless of the appeal of reverse factoring for all stakeholders, regulatory constraints like Basel I–IV mean that financial institutions can't accommodate every seller. To manage risks,

reverse factoring typically extends only to sellers transacting with large, creditworthy buyers.
- **Standardization**: Varied regulations across countries, disparate legal requirements, and even differences in terminologies and definitions related to reverse factoring can lead to confusion among supply chain participants. Embracing standardization can alleviate such misunderstandings.

7.4 Buyer-Led Approved Payables Reverse Securitization

In *buyer-led approved payables reverse securitization*, buyers sell their accounts payable to a special purpose vehicle (SPV) at a discount. The SPV then converts these assets into asset-backed securities (ABS) and sells them in the capital market to institutional and private investors.

7.4.1 Process Flow

As depicted in Fig. 7.7, the typical reverse securitization process flow encompasses the following steps:

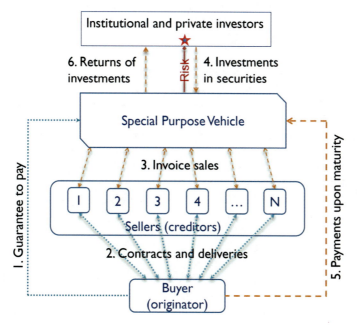

Fig. 7.7 Buyer-led approved payables reverse securitization process flow

1. The buyer establishes an SPV, possibly in partnership with a bank.
2. The buyer enters into contracts with its sellers and provides them with the invoices.
3. Sellers convey the invoices to the SPV through genuine sales.
4. The SPV sells the securitized ABS to a range of investors.
5. Upon reaching the due date, the buyer remits payment to the SPV.
6. The SPV disburses returns to investors and earns profits.

7.4.2 Benefits and Risk Mitigation

Reverse securitization bears resemblance to reverse factoring in the sense that in both financing mechanisms, the buyer guarantees payment. In essence, reverse securitization appears as an amalgamation of reverse factoring and accounts payable securitization. Consequently, reverse securitization inherits many of the benefits associated with reverse factoring and securitization.

Similar to reverse factoring, reverse securitization empowers sellers, particularly those with weaker credit ratings, to secure more affordable financing based on the superior credit rating of the buyer. Furthermore, reverse securitization curtails capital exposure typically demanded of a funding bank by distributing the payables among multiple investors in the capital markets. This provision grants the funding bank greater latitude in managing its capital. Simultaneously, since the buyer persists in assuring full payments without any recourse, it can negotiate the same or potentially even more favorable prices for identical goods or services (Miller, 2007).

While the securitization processes of accounts receivable and accounts payable reverse securitization share similarities, a key distinction exists between them. The credit rating for receivable securitization hinges on a diversified pool of buyers, while the credit rating for payable reverse securitization is predicated exclusively on the creditworthiness of the securitizing buyer in a single-buyer reverse securitization structure (Hofmann et al., 2017). Stemming from this unique characteristic, the securitizing buyer is usually a sizable enterprise boasting a commendable investment-grade credit rating.

To harness the pooling benefits attributed to multiple buyers, a viable strategy involves establishing a financing framework composed of a varied assortment of buyers (Miller, 2007). To truly realize the dividends of such diversity, a multi-buyer setup would necessitate the inclusion of at least 20 buyers to constitute an efficient pool (Hofmann et al., 2017). To amplify the credit rating of the securitization, further credit enhancements may be essential, such as internal overcollateralization, external credit insurance, or endorsements from public support programs like the European Investment Fund (Nassr & Wehinger, 2015).

7.5 Case Study: Impact of Extended Payment Terms

7.5.1 The Case[1]

Case Study

Impact of Extended Payment Terms

Background

DatacenterWare Inc. specialized in the data center industry, designing data storage and server racks for installation in their data centers. Customers availed of their storage capacity through a subscription model, charged based on gigabyte usage. With a demand growth rate of 30% annually, DatacenterWare recognized the need to source a fresh supply of data center hardware. To this end, they invited several contract manufacturers (CMs) to quote for material procurement (servers and racks), assembly, testing, and shipping for an annual total of 1,000 racks. The material cost of system (MCOS) for each rack was estimated at $250,000, largely attributed to memory, central processing units (CPUs), and solid state drives (SSDs).

The Buyer's Demand

For DatacenterWare Inc., maintaining robust cash flow was imperative to sustain their growth. Simultaneously, they aimed to achieve the lowest possible cost per unit. They approached the CMs with quote requests for both Net 45 and Net 90 payment terms. Additionally, CMs were informed to base their quotes on a vendor managed inventory (VMI) system, which would necessitate holding approximately two weeks of inventory at any given time (roughly 26 turns annually). This includes both finished goods and materials in transit. The component material vendors typically extended Net 45 payment terms to the CMs.

The Seller's Dilemma

Jonastronics, one of the approached CMs, undertook a detailed analysis of the quote request. Their calculations indicated that manufacturing and assembling each rack at the requested volume would cost $10,000, inclusive of labor, overhead, freight, and SGA (i.e., transformation cost). To handle this volume, an investment of $10M in additional capital equipment and facilities was necessary. For Jonastronics to secure the contract, a highly competitive pricing strategy was crucial, even if it meant compromising on their standard

---

[1] This case study is developed based on the real practices of a company in California during the writing of this book. All company names are pseudonymous. Data have been revised for confidentiality.

profit margin of 4%. The anticipated $250M+ revenue would account for more than 10% of their existing revenue, so any adjustment in profit margin would significantly influence their overall profitability. They were hesitant to lower their current aggregate profit margin of 4%. Equally concerning was the working capital this venture would demand. Merely two weeks of inventory would necessitate a $10M capital, and Jonastronics perceived a potential risk with the 26-turn rate quoted, especially if the growth projections were overly ambitious. The Net 90 payment term would also mean an additional $62M in Accounts Receivable consistently reflected in their books. Jonastronics' board was acutely attuned to profitability and their ROIC, which stood at 25%. If these metrics were adversely impacted, even the promise of additional revenue might not save their stock price.

Yet, the potential to augment their revenue in this sector was too tempting to dismiss. Consequently, Jonastronics resolved to competitively price their Net 45 quote in a bid to secure the contract and maintain a 25% ROIC (as illustrated in Table 7.8 based exclusively on this transaction). They were now tasked with determining their strategy for the Net 90 terms and devising a plan to offset the risk associated with additional inventory holdings.

Questions

In an effort to gauge the likelihood of their proposal being accepted, Jonastronics sought answers to the following queries:

1. To sustain a 25% ROIC for this transaction, what should be the unit price per rack charged by Jonastronics in Net 90 terms? How does this differ between Net 45 and Net 90 terms?
2. If the unit price under Net 90 matched that under Net 45, what would be the projected new ROIC?
3. How would the ROIC be affected if inventory turns reduced from 26 to 24, with the unit price remaining the same as in Net 45?
4. In Table 7.8, we've presupposed no opportunity cost for the "invested capital" and no inventory storage charges. Now, assuming Jonastronics factors in a 4% capital opportunity cost through financing (i.e., a 4% interest rate on the invested capital) and a 2% inventory storage cost, and they are willing to compromise on ROIC while ensuring a 4% profit margin under both Net 45 and Net 90 (with a 26-turn inventory), what should be the new unit prices for Net 45 and Net 90? How do these prices compare between the two terms?

7.5 Case Study: Impact of Extended Payment Terms

Table 7.8 Quote under Net 45 with 25% ROIC

Units		1000		
Quote under Net 45 with 25% ROIC				
Line Item	$ Amount		% of Total	Per Unit
Annual Revenue	$ 26,61,46,000			$ 2,66,146
Annual Material Cost of System	$ 25,00,00,000		93.9%	$ 2,50,000
Annual Transformation Cost	$ 1,00,00,000		3.76%	$ 10,000
Annual Profit	$	61,46,000	2.31%	$ 6146
Customer Payment Terms (Net Days)		45		
Component Payment Terms (Net Days)		45		
Inventory Turns		26		
Accounts Receivable	$	3,32,68,250		
Accounts Payable	$	3,12,50,000		
Inventory on Hand	$	96,15,385		
Capital Equipment and Facilites	$	1,00,00,000		
Invested Capital	$	2,16,33,635		
Tax Rate		12.0%		
ROIC		25.0%		

7.5.2 Case Analysis

Given that we lack a complete set of accounting details, our analysis will strictly rely on the transaction information provided. The computations in Table 7.8 are anchored on the subsequent formulas:

$$\text{Profit} = \text{Revenue} - \text{MCOS} - \text{Transformation Cost}$$

$$\text{Invested Capital} = \text{Accounts Receivable} - \text{Accounts Payable} + \text{Inventory on Hand} + \text{Capital Equipment and Facilities}$$

$$\text{Margin Profit Ratio} = \text{Profit/Revenue}$$

$$\text{ROIC} = \text{Profit} \times (1 - \text{Tax Rate})/\text{Invested Capital}$$

Here are the answers to the aforementioned questions:

Question 1:
As outlined in Table 7.8, to sustain a 25% ROIC, Jonastronics should charge a unit price per rack of $266,146. In this scenario, achieving a 4% profit margin for Jonastronics isn't feasible.

However, under Net 90 with a 25% ROIC, the necessary unit price per rack rises to $276,320 (refer to Table 7.9). Here, the profit margin escalates to 5.91%.

Table 7.9 Quote of Net 90 with 25% ROIC

Units		1000		
Quote of Net 90 with 25% ROIC				
Line Item		$ Amount	% of Total	Per Unit
Annual Revenue		$ 27,63,20,000		$ 2,76,320
Annual Material Cost of System		$ 25,00,00,000	90.5%	$ 2,50,000
Annual Transformation Cost		$ 1,00,00,000	3.62%	$ 10,000
Annual Profit		$ 1,63,20,000	5.91%	$ 16,320
Customer Payment Terms (Net Days)		90		
Component Payment Terms (Net Days)		45		
Inventory Turns		26		
Accounts Receivable		$ 6,90,80,000		
Accounts Payable		$ 3,12,50,000		
Inventory on Hand		$ 96,15,385		
Capital Equipment and Facilites		$ 1,00,00,000		
Invested Capital		$ 5,74,45,385		
Tax Rate		12.0%		
ROIC		25.0%		

Hence, if DatacenterWare consents to a unit price of $276,320, Jonastronics could realize both a 4% profit margin and a 25% ROIC.

The price differential between the two payment terms amounts to: $276,320 – $266,146 = $10,174.

Question 2:
Under Net 90 terms, if the unit price remains at $266,146, the resultant ROIC dwindles to 9.85%. In both cases, the profit margin stands at 2.31%, given the absence of supplementary capital costs (refer to Table 7.10).

Question 3:
With the Net 45 terms, if inventory turns are scaled down from 26 to 24, inventory holding duration extends, accruing more costs. This drives the ROIC down to 24.1% (refer to Table 7.11).

Question 4:
Let's assume Jonastronics incorporates a 4% capital opportunity cost through financing (i.e., a 4% interest rate on the invested capital) and a 2% inventory storage cost. This modifies the profit calculation to:

$$\text{Profit} = \text{Revenue} - \text{MCOS} - \text{Transformation Cost} - \text{Financing Cost} - \text{Inventory Storage Cost}$$

In the context of Net 45, to retain a 4% profit margin, Jonastronics would need to set a unit price of $271,960, which results in an ROIC of 42.8%.

For Net 90 terms, ensuring a 4% profit margin necessitates a unit price of $273,400. The consequent ROIC is 17%.

7.5 Case Study: Impact of Extended Payment Terms

Table 7.10 Quote of Net 90 at Net 45 price

Units		1000		
Quote of Net 90 at Net 45 Price				
Line Item	$ Amount		% of Total	Per Unit
Annual Revenue	$ 26,61,46,000			$ 2,66,146
Annual Material Cost of System	$ 25,00,00,000		93.9%	$ 2,50,000
Annual Transformation Cost	$ 1,00,00,000		3.76%	$ 10,000
Annual Profit	$ 61,46,000		2.31%	$ 6146
Customer Payment Terms (Net Days)		90		
Component Payment Terms (Net Days)		45		
Inventory Turns		26		
Accounts Receivable	$ 6,65,36,500			
Accounts Payable	$ 3,12,50,000			
Inventory on Hand	$ 96,15,385			
Capital Equipment and Facilites	$ 1,00,00,000			
Invested Capital	$ 5,49,01,885			
Tax Rate		12.0%		
ROIC		9.85%		

Table 7.11 Quote of Net 45 with 24 inventory turns

Units		1000		
Quote of Net 45 with 24 Inventory Turns				
Line Item	$ Amount		% of Total	Per Unit
Annual Revenue	$ 26,61,46,000			$ 2,66,146
Annual Material Cost of System	$ 25,00,00,000		93.9%	$ 2,50,000
Annual Transformation Cost	$ 1,00,00,000		3.76%	$ 10,000
Annual Profit	$ 61,46,000		2.31%	$ 6146
Customer Payment Terms (Net Days)		45		
Component Payment Terms (Net Days)		45		
Inventory Turns		24		
Accounts Receivable	$ 3,32,68,250			
Accounts Payable	$ 3,12,50,000			
Inventory on Hand	$ 1,04,16,667			
Capital Equipment and Facilites	$ 1,00,00,000			
Invested Capital	$ 2,24,34,917			
Tax Rate		12.0%		
ROIC		24.1%		

The price difference between these terms is: $273,400 − $271,960 = $1440 (refer to Tables 7.12 and 7.13).

Conclusion:

All factors held constant, an extended payment term amplifies a company's accounts receivable, thereby augmenting net working capital and invested capital. This invariably depresses the ROIC. If capital isn't freely accessible, both the

Table 7.12 Quote of Net 45 with 4% profit target

Units		1000		
Quote of Net 45 with 4% Profit Target				
Line Item		**$ Amount**	**% of Total**	**Per Unit**
Annual Revenue	$	27,19,60,000		$ 2,71,960
Annual Material Cost of System	$	25,00,00,000	91.9%	$ 2,50,000
Annual Transformation Cost	$	1,00,00,000	3.68%	$ 10,000
Financing Interest	$	8,94,415		
Inventory Storage Cost	$	1,92,308		
Annual Profit	$	1,08,73,277	4.00%	$ 10,873
Customer Payment Terms (Net Days)		45		
Component Payment Terms (Net Days)		45		
Inventory Turns		26		
Accounts Receivable	$	3,39,95,000		
Accounts Payable	$	3,12,50,000		
Inventory on Hand	$	96,15,385		
Capital Equipment and Facilites	$	1,00,00,000		
Invested Capital	$	2,23,60,385		
Tax Rate		12.0%		
ROIC		42.8%		

Table 7.13 Quote of Net 90 with 4% profit target

Units		1000		
Quote of Net 90 with 4% Profit Target				
Line Item		**$ Amount**	**% of Total**	**Per Unit**
Annual Revenue	$	27,34,00,000		$ 2,73,400
Annual Material Cost of System	$	25,00,00,000	91.4%	$ 2,50,000
Annual Transformation Cost	$	1,00,00,000	3.66%	$ 10,000
Financing Interest	$	22,68,615		
Inventory Storage Cost	$	1,92,308		
Annual Profit	$	1,09,39,077	4.00%	$ 10,939
Customer Payment Terms (Net Days)		90		
Component Payment Terms (Net Days)		45		
Inventory Turns		26		
Accounts Receivable	$	6,83,50,000		
Accounts Payable	$	3,12,50,000		
Inventory on Hand	$	96,15,385		
Capital Equipment and Facilites	$	1,00,00,000		
Invested Capital	$	5,67,15,385		
Tax Rate		12.0%		
ROIC		17.0%		

ROIC and profit margin are adversely impacted. A reduction in inventory turns (i.e., longer inventory hold times) similarly erodes the bottom line.

7.6 Summary

This chapter delves deep into the realm of buyer-led supply chain finance, emphasizing the essential role of the buyer in driving innovative financial solutions within the supply chain. As global supply chains evolve and expand, there's a mounting need for dynamic financing mechanisms that can adapt to varying economic climates. This chapter primarily focuses on three major buyer-led financing mechanisms: dynamic discounting, reverse factoring, and buyer-led approved payables reverse securitization. Through these mechanisms, the chapter elucidates the intricate interplay between buyers, sellers, and financial institutions, highlighting the benefits, challenges, and underlying processes of each method.

Key Takeaways:

1. Dynamic Discounting:
    - It's a financing mechanism where sellers offer discounts to buyers in exchange for early payment of invoices.
    - The arrangement benefits both parties: sellers obtain quicker access to cash, while buyers benefit from reduced invoice amounts.
    - The main parties involved are the seller and the buyer, with the financing relying predominantly on the seller's creditworthiness.
2. Reverse Factoring:
    - Reverse factoring, unlike traditional factoring, involves the buyer initiating the financing process and partnering with a financial institution (the factor) to facilitate early payments to the seller.
    - This mechanism shifts the focus from the seller's creditworthiness to that of the buyer, making it an attractive option for sellers, especially in developing countries with limited access to financing.
    - Crucial challenges include the KYC process, seller onboarding, capital availability and liquidity, and the need for standardization.
3. Buyer-Led Approved Payables Reverse Securitization:
    - Here, buyers sell their accounts payable at a discounted rate to an SPV company. The SPV then converts these payables into ABS, which are sold to investors.
    - This method combines the benefits of reverse factoring and securitization, allowing sellers with weaker credit ratings to leverage the better credit rating of the buyer.
    - Given its complexity, it's often large companies with good credit ratings that partake in this form of financing. Diversity in the pool of buyers and additional credit enhancements can further improve the process's efficacy.

7.7 Exercises

7.7.1 Practice Questions

1. What is the primary difference between reverse factoring and traditional factoring in terms of initiator?
2. In the context of reverse factoring, who typically has a better credit rating: the buyer or the seller?
3. Which financing mechanism allows buyers to sell their accounts payable to an SPV?
4. In dynamic discounting, on whose creditworthiness does the financing primarily rely?
5. What is one challenge associated with reverse factoring in a global context?
6. Why might a buyer prefer reverse factoring in terms of balance sheet optimization?
7. In buyer-led approved payables reverse securitization, what does the SPV do with the accounts payable it acquires?
8. What challenge might arise due to differences in regulations and definitions concerning reverse factoring across countries?
9. How does reverse securitization potentially benefit sellers with weaker credit ratings?
10. Which financing mechanism looks like a combination of reverse factoring and securitization of accounts payable?

7.7.2 Case Study

Supply Chain Finance Solutions for ElectronTech

Background

ElectronTech, a prominent electronics manufacturer, faced numerous challenges concerning supply chain payments. Like DatacenterWare Inc., ElectronTech depended on contract manufacturers (CMs) for their component needs. Recently, ElectronTech's CFO, Ms. Clara Jensen, observed a rise in procurement costs. The financial instability of their suppliers, coupled with their constrained access to financing, led to increased risks and disruptions. Clara surmised that addressing this could stabilize ElectronTech's supply chain, enhance efficiency, and potentially reduce costs.

ElectronTech's recent orders necessitated components totaling $1,000,000 from Supplier A, subject to a standard 60-day payment term (Net 60). ElectronTech sought to determine the most beneficial method without jeopardizing supplier relationships. To fine-tune their supply chain finance, they considered various financing options: dynamic discounting, reverse factoring, and buyer-led approved payables reverse securitization (BLAPRS).

Options

- **Dynamic Discounting**: ElectronTech could receive a 2% discount by paying Supplier A within 10 days.
- **Reverse Factoring**: A financial intermediary agrees to pay Supplier A $1,000,000 on ElectronTech's behalf within 10 days. The intermediary levies a 1% fee, and ElectronTech repays the full amount to the bank at Net 90, considering an annual risk-free rate of 3%.
- **BLAPRS**: ElectronTech transforms its approved payables into tradeable securities. An institution proposes purchasing these at 98% of their face value.

Questions

1. Which financing method is the most cost-effective for ElectronTech?
2. How does each option influence ElectronTech and Supplier A's relationship?
3. What are the enduring financial health implications of each strategy for ElectronTech?

Appendix: Academic Perspective

Financing Multiple Heterogeneous Suppliers in Assembly Systems: Buyer vs. Bank Finance
Shiming Deng, Chaocheng Gu, Gangshu (George) Cai, and Yanhai Li.[2]

Introduction

Many manufacturers globally source components from suppliers of varying sizes. Smaller suppliers often grapple with limited working capital and cannot readily access fairly priced capital markets. These financial challenges can lead to component price hikes or even halt production, particularly impacting large manufacturers/assemblers with intricate Bill of Materials (BOM) configurations.

To combat these financial hardships, numerous big manufacturers/assemblers have aided their suppliers in obtaining bank loans (subsequently termed as bank finance). For instance, since 2012, Boeing Company has participated in a Supply Chain Financing Program endorsed by the Export–Import (Ex-Im) Bank of the US. This program enables numerous small suppliers to procure reasonable loans from

---

[2] This section presents research findings from one of my publications, Deng et al. (2018). For a more comprehensive understanding, readers are encouraged to consult the full article: Deng, S., Gu, C., Cai, G., & Li, Y. (2018). Financing multiple heterogeneous suppliers in assembly systems: Buyer finance vs. bank finance. Manufacturing & service operations management, 20(1), 53–69. We've omitted most references for brevity; for further details, please refer to Deng et al. (2018).

associated banks. Additionally, automakers such as PSA and VW have assisted suppliers in securing finances post the 2007–2009 Financial Crisis.

Contrary to bank finance, certain companies have directly extended financial support to their suppliers (henceforth labeled as buyer finance). This support manifests in diverse manners including upfront payment for orders, instituting a general finance scheme for suppliers, or even purchasing supplier stocks to mitigate their financial strains. Within the automobile sector, to counter the economic challenges post-2008, BMW and PSA have advanced payments for parts, Ford has extended loans, and Porsche has funded supplier production tooling. Notably, in 2011, Airbus acquired a 51% stake in PFW Aerospace to guarantee an uninterrupted supply of pivotal aircraft components. Similarly, Boeing disbursed $590 million to its fuselage supplier, Vought Aircraft Industries, in 2009, ensuring the steady supply of components for the Boeing 787. As per World Bank estimates, in 2008, buyer advance payments constituted approximately 19%–22% (equivalent to $3–$3.5 trillion) of all trade finance modalities.

While both buyer and bank finance aim to bolster suppliers' financial robustness and fortify supply chain dependability, they exhibit distinct characteristics. Through bank finance, assemblers can harness bank resources, thereby alleviating their capital burdens and administrative overheads. Conversely, with buyer finance, downstream manufacturers/assemblers can potentially reap additional profits by financing their suppliers and integrating their financial and operational supply chain decisions.

This divergence in financing strategies prompts several pivotal research inquiries: Under what circumstances would manufacturers/assemblers opt for buyer finance over bank loans for their suppliers? How do suppliers respond to downstream firms' financial choices? How do these financial determinations influence operational decisions under each financing approach? Lastly, how does the intricacy of the supply chain structure, such as the diversity and variance of suppliers' working capitals and costs, affect these financing verdicts?

Supply Chain Finance Game Model

We examine a stylized assembly supply chain that includes one dominant assembler and N capital-constrained component suppliers. The demand, represented by D, is uncertain and follows a cumulative distribution function $F(.)$ and a probability distribution function $f(.)$. We operate under the assumption that the demand distribution possesses an increasing failure rate (IFR), a standard assumption in supply chain literature, met by various typical distributions. All firms are privy to this common knowledge of the demand distribution. The end product is priced at p, and the unit production cost for component supplier i is c^i, where $i = 1, ..., N$.

To simplify, we presuppose that the assembler requires exactly one unit from each component supplier to construct a single product. The assembler determines the purchasing price w^i for each component $i, i = 1, ..., N$. Thereafter, component suppliers select their stock levels q^i in unison. These levels are bounded by their initial capital levels k^i and are chosen before the uncertainty of demand is settled. Consequently, the minimum system stock level becomes $q = min\{q^i, i = 1, ..., N\}$. When the demand manifests at x, the assembler procures a quantity of $min(x, q)$ from every component supplier and disburses $w^i \cdot min(x, q)$. We've assumed that any components left unsold by the suppliers hold no salvage value.

Our analysis encompasses two financing strategies:

1. Suppliers secure loans from banks at a competitively determined interest rate (referred to as "bank finance").
2. The assembler offers direct financing to its suppliers, over and above bank finance, levying an interest rate at its discretion (termed "buyer finance").

Given capital limitations, suppliers might opt for loans either from a bank (bank finance) or the assembler (buyer finance), should both options be feasible. Companies ideally utilize internal funds before turning to pricier external debt. The subscripts bk and br are used to signify bank finance and buyer finance, respectively.

In each financing scenario, every component supplier i must settle on a loan amount $B^i \geq 0$, alongside deciding the production quantity. We presume that any surplus capital supplier i possesses can be invested in risk-free ventures with an expected return rate, denoted as r_s^i. Once demand is ascertained, the supplier garners its wholesale revenue, represented by $w^i \cdot min(q^i, D)$, in addition to interest earnings from surplus capital investments.

Unlike the bank finance where the bank interest rate r_f is predetermined, in buyer finance, the assembler sets the target expected rate of return r_b for financing suppliers at will. The assembler also jointly determines r_b with the component purchasing prices w^i, $i = 1, 2, ..., N$ to optimize its projected profits from both buyer finance and product sales. Let's define the real interest rate levied on component supplier i in buyer finance as r_{br}^i. It's evident that for any supplier i, with other variables constant, r_{br}^i is directly proportional to r_b. In a manner similar to bank finance, r_{br}^i may vary among suppliers for a stipulated target r_b, attributed to supplier heterogeneity. If the assembler extends a loan B^i to supplier i via buyer finance, it incurs a financial charge of $r_a B^i$, where r_a represents the assembler's unit capital cost.

The event progression is delineated in Fig. 7.8 and unfolds in four decision-making phases:

1. As the period commences and in the face of demand ambiguity, the assembler contemplates offering buyer finance to its suppliers. This juncture is pivotal as it directs the trajectory of the finance strategies in play.
2. Should the assembler opt for buyer finance, in its role as the Stackelberg leader, it finalizes r_b and the purchase price w^i for each component i. In the absence of this decision, only the purchasing prices are set.
3. In light of the assembler's determinations, suppliers (acting as Stackelberg followers) collectively decide on their production quantities q^i and the

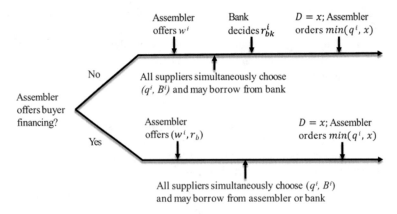

Fig. 7.8 Timing of events

required loan sizes B^i through a Nash game. Suppliers can opt to borrow from either the bank or the assembler, contingent on the availability of buyer finance. The time period culminates with the realization of demand.

4. The assembler procures components from its suppliers, assembles them into final products, and caters to the demand.

Main Findings

Our analysis reveals that the financial cost to the assembler of offering buyer finance plays a pivotal role in the decision to adopt this financing strategy. The assembler's decision adheres to a threshold policy concerning its unit capital cost. Specifically, the assembler should opt for buyer finance if, and only if, its unit capital cost falls below a certain threshold. We demonstrate that this threshold exceeds the risk-free interest rate. Within the range spanning the risk-free interest rate to this threshold, buyer finance proves superior to bank finance. This holds true even if the assembler is a less efficient lender than banks—that is, if the assembler's unit capital cost surpasses the bank's risk-free interest rate. These benefits underscore the value of harmonizing finance and operational decisions.

The relative financial efficiency of the assembler and the suppliers, especially in terms of unit capital (opportunity) costs, as well as the aggregate and diversity of the suppliers' starting capitals and production costs, significantly influence the assembler's inclination towards buyer finance. Our findings suggest that if the assembler's unit capital cost exceeds the highest unit capital opportunity costs among the suppliers, the assembler will face losses with buyer finance. Buyer finance's edge over bank finance grows with an increase in the suppliers' collective initial capital or a decrease in their cumulative costs. This is because an elevated initial capital or diminished cost alleviates the financial pressure on the assembler, who bears the default risks in buyer finance. Conversely, if suppliers exhibit substantial disparities in capital or cost, buyer finance loses its appeal to the assembler, as variations can make certain suppliers more prone to bankruptcy, thereby demanding increased financial support. However, if the assembler's unit capital cost is beneath the highest unit capital opportunity costs of all suppliers, the proposition of financing suppliers becomes lucrative, leading the assembler to invariably favor buyer finance.

Interestingly, the suppliers' preferences don't always echo those of the assembler. The direction of a supplier's preference hinges on the assembler's unit capital cost and its borrowing status. When the assembler's capital cost is sufficiently modest, all entities, including every supplier, fare better under buyer finance, thanks to the surge in production quantity. Yet, as the assembler's capital cost rises, a divergence in preference emerges between the assembler and its suppliers. Suppliers that borrow might find themselves at a disadvantage in buyer finance because the assembler, aiming to offset the financing load, might reduce the component purchasing price due to the enticingly low interest rate in buyer finance. This dynamic diminishes the allure of buyer finance for borrowing suppliers, potentially impacting non-borrowing suppliers as the equilibrium production quantity dwindles. Once the assembler's unit capital cost escalates beyond the threshold, all firms show a collective preference for bank finance.

This study augments existing literature in multiple ways. To begin with, it pioneers the comparison of buyer and bank finance within an assembly supply chain comprising a dominant assembler and several diverse suppliers. We've elucidated the equilibrium responses of firms under both financing conditions. Additionally, we pinpoint the threshold beyond which the assembler should pivot towards buyer finance and delve into how variables such as the assembler's capital cost, the cumulative initial capital/production cost of suppliers, and supplier heterogeneity influence the selection of the optimal financing scheme. Lastly, our research delineates both the Pareto zones, where all stakeholders favor the same financing mechanism, and areas of preference discord, wherein the assembler and suppliers (whether borrowing or non-borrowing) might lean towards different financing strategies.

References

Camerinelli, E. (2014). *A study of the business case for supply chain finance.* Accountants For Business by the Association of Chartered Certified Accountants.

Deng, S., Gu, C., Cai, G., & Li, Y. (2018). Financing multiple heterogeneous suppliers in assembly systems: Buyer finance vs. Bank finance. *Manufacturing and Service Operations Management, 20*(1), 53–69.

Eaglesham, J. (2020). Supply-chain finance is new risk in crisis. *The Wall Street Journal.* https://www.wsj.com/articles/supply-chain-finance-is-new-risk-in-crisis-11585992601. Accessed August 8, 2020.

Globe SCF Forum. (2016). *Standard definitions for techniques of supply chain finance.* Report.

Hofmann, E., Strewe, U. M., & Bosia, N. (2017). *Supply chain finance and blockchain technology: The case of reverse securitisation.* Springer.

Nassr, E., & Wehinger, G. (2015). Unlocking SME finance through market-based debt. *OECD Journal: Financial Market Trends, 2014*(2), 89–190.

Miller, A. (2007). Trade services—Pooled payables securitisation. *Global Trade Review*. https://www.gtreview.com/news/global/trade-services-pooled-payables-securitisation/. Accessed August 16, 2020.

Scaggs, A. (2020). *What is reverse factoring? A report highlights a problematic, fast-growing financing technique*. https://www.barrons.com/articles/what-is-reverse-factoring-a-growing-concern-in-finance-51576891841. Accessed August 18, 2021.

Sheppard, E. (2016). Australian model for payment disputes could help small UK suppliers. *The Guardian*. https://www.theguardian.com/small-business-network/2016/apr/28/australian-model-for-payment-disputes-could-help-small-uk-suppliers. Accessed October 9, 2021.

Steinberg, J. (2020). FASB to explore greater disclosure of supply-chain financing. *The Wall Street Journal*. https://www.wsj.com/articles/fasb-to-explore-greater-disclosure-of-supply-chain-financing-11603361147. Accessed August 28, 2020.

Taulia. (2021a). *What is dynamic discounting?* https://primerevenue.com/what-is-dynamic-discounting/. Accessed August 18, 2021.

Taulia. (2021b). *What is reverse factoring?* https://taulia.com/glossary/what-is-reverse-factoring/. Accessed August 28, 2021.

Wikipedia. (2020). *Supply chain finance*. https://en.wikipedia.org/wiki/Reverse_factoring. Accessed August 29, 2020.

Wikipedia. (2022). *Late payment directive*. https://en.wikipedia.org/wiki/Late_Payment_Directive. Accessed October 29, 2022.

WNS. (2014). *Reduce COGS with dynamic discoutning*. https://www.wns.com/insights/articles/articledetail/17/reduce-cogs-with-dynamic-discounting-combining-spend-analytics-p2p-processing-and-accounts-payable-automation. Accessed August 23, 2020.

Inventory and 3PL-Led Financing 8

Learning Objectives:

1. Grasp the principles of inventory financing and its impact on cash flow.
2. Delve into 3PL-led in-transit inventory financing and its supply chain benefits.
3. Differentiate between traditional and 3PL-led inventory financing in cost and efficiency.

8.1 Introduction

Both accounts receivable and accounts payable are generated only after invoices have been issued from the seller to the buyer. In practice, however, capital-constrained suppliers (i.e., sellers) often need to purchase materials and other items to prepare for production before they can issue invoices and ship products. In certain scenarios, such as seasonal sales, the preparation and production periods can be lengthy. This extended duration can significantly strain the limited capital of suppliers. In these cases, inventory or in-transit financing becomes a valuable financing mechanism for both suppliers and buyers.

Inventory can exist in various stages: raw materials, finished components, unsold or pre-sold finished products in a warehouse, inventory in transit, and inventory on shelves. Within the context of supply chain transactions, inventory can play a pivotal role in inventory financing and inventory in-transit financing, especially when third-party logistics (3PL) firms are involved.

8.2 Inventory Financing

Inventory financing is a mechanism where a company uses its inventory as collateral to secure a loan from a bank in anticipation of potential supply chain transactions. Inventory financing can be seller-led, buyer-led, third-party-led, or platform-led. In essence, both sellers and buyers can utilize inventory financing, depending on who owns the inventory throughout the production and transaction cycles.

In practice, certain companies, such as suppliers, may need to obtain a loan to prepare and produce products that have been contracted by buyers. However, these products might not be sold or delivered immediately. Consequently, entities like retailers and wholesalers might amass a substantial inventory. To exacerbate the situation, for many of these businesses, inventory represents their most significant capital. In these challenging circumstances, the inventory serves as collateral to secure a loan from the bank, ensuring timely product delivery as stipulated in the supply chain agreement.

Typically, companies resorting to inventory financing are small and possess limited assets, making it challenging to obtain substantial loans through traditional debt financing methods. Moreover, these firms often lack access to alternative financing options. For sellers, inventory financing injects the necessary working capital to support the production and eventual delivery of finished goods to buyers. On the buyer's side, inventory financing can be leveraged to acquire loans to settle payments with suppliers in advance. This approach proves especially beneficial when products need to be warehoused for an extended period before being sold to the final consumers. Hence, inventory financing becomes particularly indispensable in seasonal sales scenarios, where both the production ahead of the season and storage durations can be protracted.

Inventory financing mainly manifests in two forms:

1. **Inventory Loan**: This refers to a one-time debt financing option where inventory is used as collateral.
2. **Inventory Line of Credit**: A more long-term financing approach, an inventory line of credit is contingent upon ongoing business and is accessed as needed. Companies tend to favor the inventory line of credit due to its continuity, ensuring a steadier cash flow and equipping them to better manage any forthcoming financial uncertainties.

8.2.1 Process Flow

Typically, the value of raw materials and finished goods can be better assessed, making them suitable candidates for inventory financing. In contrast, work-in-progress inventory is less ideal due to its limited marketability (Camerinelli & Bryant, 2014). Given the distinct flow of materials and finished goods in inventory

8.2 Inventory Financing

financing, it's pertinent to further categorize the financing process flow into three distinct types.

8.2.1.1 Inventory Financing to Seller with Materials

We begin with inventory financing for a capital-constrained seller possessing materials to manufacture contracted goods for a buyer. The process flow is as follows (refer to Fig. 8.1):

1. The buyer signs a contract with the seller to order specific finished goods. However, the seller only has raw materials on hand. While there's a lead time to produce and deliver the contracted items, the seller faces a working capital shortage before receiving the final payment from the buyer.
2. Recognizing the viable sale of products to the buyer, the seller opts to use the raw materials as collateral and procures a loan from the bank. Concurrently, a three-way contract is drawn up with the bank, allowing it to monitor the transformation of materials (stored in a certified warehouse) into finished goods.
3. The bank then disburses the loaned amount to the seller.
4. Leveraging the loan, the seller processes the raw materials to produce the finished goods. The bank, upon the seller's request to access the materials, might mandate monthly repayments.
5. Once the production is complete, the seller ensures timely delivery of the goods as stipulated in the initial agreement.
6. Upon maturity of the payment, the buyer has two options:

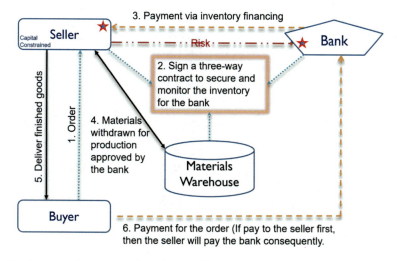

Fig. 8.1 Inventory finance to a seller with materials

a. Transfer the payment directly to the bank: In this scenario, the bank will deduct the loan principal and interest and then forward the residual amount to the seller.
b. Make the payment directly to the seller: Following this, the seller is obliged to settle the loan principal and interest with the bank on the predetermined loan repayment date.

8.2.1.2 Inventory Financing to Seller with Finished Goods

Next, we outline a potential process flow for inventory financing catered to a seller possessing finished goods (refer to Fig. 8.2).

1. The buyer enters into a contract with the seller to order specific finished goods, with delivery scheduled for a later date.
2. The seller dispatches the completed goods to a warehouse.
3. A tripartite agreement is executed involving the seller, buyer, and bank. In this contract, the bank takes the responsibility of securing and overseeing the finished goods.
4. Following the agreement's terms, the bank disburses the loan to the seller.
5. In accordance with the stipulated timeline, the seller ensures the delivery of the finished goods to the buyer.
6. Upon the payment due date, the buyer remits the requisite amount directly to the bank.
7. Finally, the bank deducts the loan principal and interest and then forwards the residual amount to the seller.

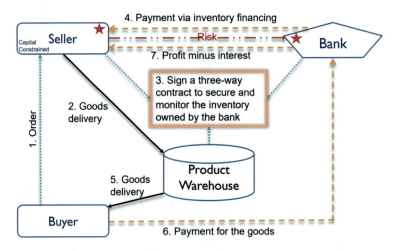

Fig. 8.2 Inventory financing for a seller with finished goods

8.2 Inventory Financing

8.2.1.3 Inventory Financing to Buyer

Inventory financing can also be leveraged by capital-constrained buyers. The procedure outlined below depicts how such a buyer can utilize inventory financing to mitigate its working capital deficit (refer to Fig. 8.3).

1. A tripartite agreement is forged between the buyer, seller, and bank concerning the order and inventory. In this setup, the bank assumes ownership of the goods until they are sold to the end market.
2. To mitigate potential risks, the bank requires a cash deposit from the buyer. However, at this juncture, the buyer does not settle the payment to the seller for the intended goods.
3. The seller transports the finished goods to the specified warehouse. Here, the bank takes on the roles of owner, custodian, and overseer of the delivered goods.
4. The end market (i.e., final customers) places orders with the buyer.
5. Payments for the ordered goods are made directly to the bank by the end market.
6. Upon receipt of payment, the bank instructs the warehouse to release the corresponding goods for delivery to the end market.
7. The goods are then dispatched and received by the end market.
8. After ensuring delivery, the bank settles the payment with the seller for the supplied goods.
9. Finally, the bank forwards the residual amount to the buyer.

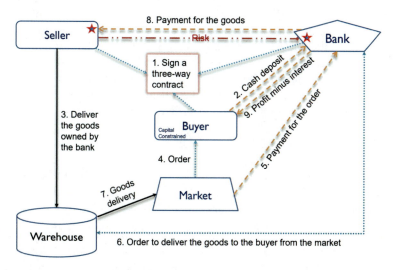

Fig. 8.3 Inventory financing to a buyer

8.2.2 Benefits

According to the World Bank Group Enterprise Surveys, in traditional debt financing, the value of collateral averages 2.06 times the loan value. This ratio poses a considerable challenge for many small businesses, especially those with limited assets and lacking established creditworthiness (Zhou et al., 2020). Given these circumstances, inventory finance emerges as an invaluable solution for such businesses that might otherwise lack financing alternatives.

Both sellers and buyers who opt for inventory finance can benefit from improved working capital availability, even before the products are delivered. The backing of a supply chain contract ensures that the loan size might closely align with the value of the inventory.

From a lender's perspective, this model presents a fresh avenue for offering financial services. However, it's worth noting that the associated risks tend to be elevated compared to accounts receivable financing. Factors such as potential contract breaches by the buyer or possible damage or loss of inventory prior to shipment to the buyer amplify these risks. However, if the borrowing entity can consistently uphold a robust stream of supply chain transactions, inventory finance can serve as a sustainable revolving financing mechanism for the firm.

8.2.3 Risks and Risk Mitigation

Inventory financing inherently carries certain risks due to the often unsecured nature of the inventory. Generally speaking, using raw materials as collateral is seen as less secure than finished goods, which in turn are deemed less secure than accounts receivable. The possibility exists that the inventory may not be converted into finished goods or sold. In such scenarios, the bank might find itself burdened with the inventory and could be forced to liquidate it at a substantially reduced price. Consequently, inventories that can be quickly sold in the market are more valuable in inventory financing in case of defaults.

> *Using raw materials as collateral is less secure than using finished goods, which are less secure than accounts receivable.*

Inventory is also prone to deterioration, theft, and depreciation over time. Banks typically regard inventory financing as akin to an unsecured loan (Investopedia, 2021). Consequently, inventory financing tends to be more costly than factoring based on accounts receivable. Heightened risks, especially in the aftermath of the 2007–2009 Financial Crisis, have made banks more reticent about inventory financing.

Borrowing companies, through their subsidiaries or affiliated entities, might also produce multiple duplicate inventory receipts based on identical inventory. Regrettably, such frauds have been committed frequently. For instance, in the 1930s, the American drug and chemical manufacturer McKesson & Robbins was revealed to have inflated their inventory (Investopedia, 2020). Other corporations, such as Salad Oil Swindle, Equity Funding, ZZZZ Best, and Phar-Mor, were also implicated in inventory data manipulation (Wells, 2001). Notably, in 2011, owing to insufficient risk controls by banks, Shanghai-based steel companies fabricated fictitious inventory receipts for financing purposes. By the end of June 2011, the inventory reported as collateral amounted to 1034.5 K tons, a staggering 2.79 times the actual steel inventory. Such inventory frauds further exacerbate the already unsecured nature of inventory (The Paper, 2016).

For effective risk mitigation when using inventory as collateral, lending institutions must have the capability or resources to oversee, assess, and manage the storage and physical movement of the inventory. Due diligence efforts, such as facility inspections, inventory system evaluations, accounting system reviews, and inventory appraisals can bolster inventory security (Commercial Capital, 2021). Lenders might also request documentation of sales histories, sales forecasts, and business strategies to mitigate potential inventory unmarketability risks. The associated due diligence costs and logistical intricacies typically confine inventory financing to a select few financial institutions that possess reliable partners to execute the necessary management and monitoring tasks (Camerinelli & Bryant, 2014). To enhance their proficiency in inventory financing, these institutions can collaborate with third-party entities skilled in storage, warehouse monitoring, and management. Typically, the closer the warehouse's location, the simpler it becomes to authenticate and manage the inventory.

To further alleviate financial risks, as illustrated in Fig. 8.3 regarding inventory financing for a buyer, banks might require a cash deposit from the purchaser. While a more substantial deposit undoubtedly favors banks, an excessive deposit requirement can strain an already capital-limited buyer, which contradicts the primary objective of inventory financing—supporting the buyer's funding needs.

As practiced by Sichuan Yuanyao Supply Chain Management Co., Ltd., a supply chain finance company in China, the seller is required to provide trade credit to the financial institution. This arrangement allows the financial institution to delay payment to the seller, further mitigating financial risks, as depicted in Fig. 8.4. The application of trade credit here is a variant of trade credit extended to the buyer. Since the buyer is obtaining funds from the bank in a revolving inventory financing arrangement, the trade credit serves as collateral to the bank.

To ensure the buyer can sell the inventory as scheduled, prudent credit analytics can assist the financing institution in better understanding the buyer's marketing capabilities, thus minimizing the risk of repayment delays. Banks can also either purchase or mandate borrowers to acquire third-party insurance, safeguarding against potential losses in inventory finance due to inventory damage, mismanagement, or fraud.

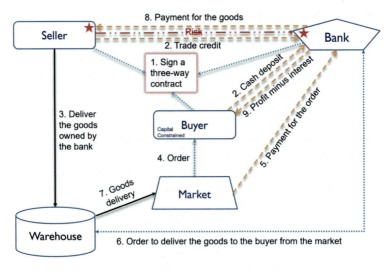

Fig. 8.4 Inventory financing to a buyer: A variant with trade credit

In inventory financing directed at a seller, banks typically advance only a portion of the inventory's value to the seller to establish a reasonable risk margin (Globe SCF Forum, 2016). As adopted by Commercial Capital LLC, the lender might advance funds equivalent to 75% of the appraised value or 50% of the inventory's cost—whichever is lower (Commercial Capital, 2021). Since the inventory is evaluated to determine its net orderly liquidation value (NOLV), which might be significantly lower than the market value, the borrowing capacity of the borrower can be adversely impacted. To bolster their borrowing capacity, companies can amalgamate inventory with accounts receivable and other assets to augment the loan amount.

8.3 3PL-Led In-Transit Inventory Financing

Companies are increasingly relying on third-party logistics providers (3PLs) for logistics tasks to better concentrate on their core competencies. Such tasks may encompass packaging, transportation, and warehousing (Lambert et al., 1999). Notably, the U.S. 3PL market reported a $142 billion revenue in 2012, and globally, the 3PL market garnered over $550 billion. As per Inbound Logistics (2014), "92 percent of [3PL] service providers surveyed said they grew their client base by at least five percent over the past year." This was an increase from 90% in 2013, 88% in 2012, and 73% in 2010. Furthermore, "93 percent of 3PLs report they increased sales by at least five percent during the past year" (Inbound Logistics, 2014). Clearly, the significant and growing contributions of 3PLs to supply chain operations are undeniable.

8.3 3PL-Led In-Transit Inventory Financing

In many theoretical supply chain models, the role of a 3PL firm tends to be minimal or entirely overlooked. This oversight mainly stems from the traditional view that a 3PL firm is but an auxiliary part of the supply chain, primarily responsible for transporting purchased products from the vendor to the buyer. In this model, the buyer pays the manufacturer upon ordering and subsequently compensates the 3PL once the products are dispatched. Yet, real-world dynamics are shifting. With escalating competition in the 3PL sector, mere shipping services no longer guarantee substantial revenue. Consequently, 3PLs are exploring avenues beyond their conventional offerings.

Asset-based bank financing, encompassing inventory financing, has been pivotal for cash-strapped firms (Barnett, 1997). But the inherent challenge for banks lies in the real-time monitoring of product transactions. Without this critical information, there's a hesitancy to extend financial services due to potential misappropriation of funds by retailers into riskier ventures (Burkart & Ellingsen, 2004). UPS Capital (2018) elaborates, "Products like accounts receivable financing (factoring), purchase order financing, and inventory financing are accessible when traditional bank loans fall short, but often at a high cost: substantial collateral prerequisites, steep interest rates, and occasionally restrictive contractual terms." A solution emerges in the form of integrating logistics and financial services (ILFS) via 3PL firms. By partnering with financial institutions, these firms offer combined logistics and financial solutions to cash-constrained buyers. Noteworthy examples include UPS, which owns UPS Capital; AIMS Logistics, LLC, acquired by US Bank National Association in 2007; and the collaboration between US Bank and Schneider Logistics, Inc. in 2007. These entities have pioneered in-transit inventory financing (Chen & Cai, 2011; Chen et al., 2019).

In-transit inventory financing, often termed cargo financing, is predicated on in-transit inventory overseen by a logistics firm offering ILFS. Given the usually prolonged holding period of in-transit inventory, it is aptly treated as collateral. The unique supply chain relationship between the logistics firm and the in-transit inventory owner ensures that the advance rate for in-transit inventory financing typically surpasses that of traditional inventory finance.

8.3.1 Process Flow

The in-transit inventory financing process flow is typically dictated by the financing terms set forth by the 3PL firm, which usually holds a dominant position in the arrangement. Often, the 3PL provides financing to the seller. However, there are instances where the 3PL finances the buyer, especially if the buyer makes payments upon placing an order with the seller. Figure 8.5 elucidates a potential process flow for in-transit inventory financing tailored to a capital-constrained seller.

1. The buyer places an order with the seller.
2. The seller, basing the request on the invoice value, seeks cargo/in-transit inventory financing from the 3PL firm. Subsequently, a tripartite contract is signed among the buyer, seller, and the 3PL.
3. The 3PL firm collects the goods from the seller.

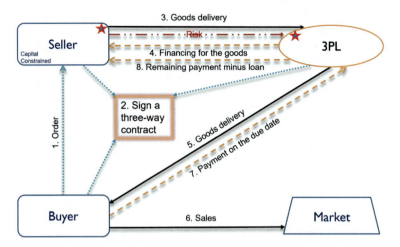

Fig. 8.5 Potential process flow of 3PL-led in-transit inventory financing

4. Concurrently, the capital unit associated with the 3PL (e.g., UPS Capital) offers financing based on the inventory's invoice value. Depending on the credibility of the involved firms and the nature of their supply chain relationship, the 3PL might finance the seller up to 100% of the invoice value.
5. The 3PL firm delivers the goods to the buyer.
6. The buyer, in turn, sells these goods to its customers.
7. On the mutually agreed-upon due date, the buyer remits payment directly to the 3PL.
8. If the initial financing from the 3PL did not cover 100% of the invoice value, the 3PL then settles the remaining amount with the seller.

It's important to highlight that the borrower can be the buyer rather than the seller if the buyer settles payment to the seller upon ordering and holds ownership of the in-transit inventory. In such situations, the buyer is the one financed by the 3PL's capital unit. If the 3PL provides financing to either the seller or buyer that is significantly below the invoice value, the borrower might seek an additional credit line from either the 3PL or a traditional bank. The presence of in-transit inventory sends a positive message to the bank regarding the reliability of the supply chain transaction. Consequently, banks are generally more inclined to approve additional funding, especially when the 3PL has already financed the in-transit inventory.

Engaging firms can further leverage the vast expertise of 3PLs in supply chain management. Large-scale 3PL entities, such as UPS, often operate ILFS platforms that facilitate seamless communication between all parties involved. ILFS enhances supply chain operations in two principal ways: first, by assisting financially restricted firms in acquiring funds, and second, by aiding companies in synchronizing both the material and financial flows within the supply chain. Given

8.3 3PL-Led In-Transit Inventory Financing

these benefits, leading 3PL organizations like UPS and FedEx offer ILFS to their clientele, which consequently sharpens their competitive edge (Chen & Cai, 2011).

For example, UPS markets its UPS Capital financing service alongside its traditional logistics offerings (Chen & Cai, 2011). It extends global asset-based lending (GABL) and inventory financing to its clients, allowing them to capitalize on offshore or in-transit inventory, thereby boosting their liquidity. The ILFS model has also gained traction in emerging markets. For instance, since 2006, China's renowned logistics company, China National Foreign Trade Transportation Group Corporation (SINOTRANS), embarked on a collaboration with the Industrial and Commercial Bank of China (ICBC) in logistics finance. By 2007, SINOTRANS had partnered with over ten banks to deliver ILFS to its clients. Additionally, several other prominent logistics service providers, including DHL, Exel, Kuehne and Nagel, Schenker, Panalpina, C. H. Robinson, TNT Logistics, Schneider, and NYK Logistics, have integrated financial services into their conventional logistics portfolios (Chen & Cai, 2011).

The process flow for firms borrowing through a more complex ILFS is depicted in Fig. 8.6.

1. The buyer places an order with the seller for goods.
2. Using the ILFS platform, the seller submits the invoice and requests in-transit inventory financing from the 3PL firm.
3. Once the buyer and its customers agree on making direct payments to the 3PL, the 3PL approves the combined logistics and financing service request.

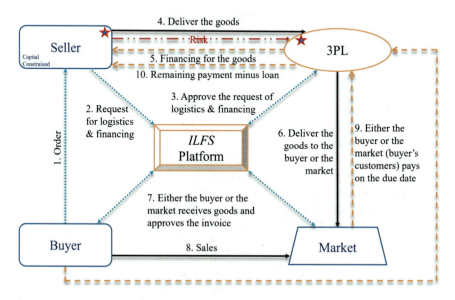

Fig. 8.6 Process flow of in-transit inventory financing with 3PL-led ILFS platform

4. The 3PL begins shipping goods directly to the buyer's customers, as outlined in the ILFS platform.
5. The 3PL capital unit makes an early payment to the seller. In a different scenario, where the buyer holds the in-transit inventory, the 3PL would finance the buyer.
6. Goods are dispatched to the intended destination, which could either be the buyer or the market.
7. The buyer or the buyer's customers confirm the delivery using the ILFS platform.
8. The buyer completes the sale to its customers.
9. The buyer or its customers remit payment to the 3PL upon reaching the payment due date.
10. After deducting the amount lent for in-transit inventory financing, the 3PL transfers the remaining sum to the seller.

8.3.2 Benefits

In-transit inventory financing builds upon the typical advantages of inventory financing (as explored in Chapter 8.2.2), offering a fresh financing alternative for capital-constrained sellers and buyers centered on inventory. Owing to the 3PL's ability to manage and monitor in-transit inventory, the benefits can extend beyond traditional inventory financing.

8.3.2.1 Benefits for Borrowers
In-transit inventory financing offers several advantages to borrowers, whether they are buyers or sellers. Here are the potential benefits:

- *Improved Cash Flow*: By securing financing for inventory while it's still in transit, borrowers can access cash sooner, helping to optimize their cash flow. This means they aren't tying up funds in inventory and can redirect resources to other facets of their business, such as marketing, sales, or research and development.
- *Higher Loan Limit*: Typically, the amount financed for in-transit inventory surpasses that of conventional inventory financing. To illustrate, UPS Capital might finance up to 100% of the invoice value, a considerably more generous offer than the advance rates of standard inventory financing.
- *Additional Line of Credit*: The borrower, whether a buyer or seller, might also procure an extra credit line from the 3PL capital unit or an affiliated bank, enhancing the working capital of the borrowing entity. As per UPS Capital (2016), "funds can be accessed in as little as one day" post the UPS shipment. The amalgamation of logistics and financial services enables the 3PL firm to present appealing financing conditions.
- *ILFS Benefits*: Borrowers can tap into the 3PL's wealth of knowledge in supply chain management through the adoption of the 3PL's ILFS platform.

- *Improved Credit Rating*: Leveraging in-transit inventory financing curtails the borrower's reliance on standard debt financing. This reduction in debt can bolster their credit rating, paving the way for easier future financing.
- *Strengthened Supplier Relationships*: Ensuring suppliers are paid on time, made possible through this mode of financing, can foster and uphold robust supplier relations. This might translate to advantageous pricing, priority during stock shortages, or other favorable terms.

In essence, in-transit inventory financing can furnish borrowers with a slew of benefits, from enhancing cash flow and boosting purchasing power to solidifying supplier relationships, culminating in a more nimble and adaptive operation.

8.3.2.2 Benefits for Non-Borrowing Firms

In-transit inventory financing isn't solely beneficial for borrowing firms; the non-borrowing firms stand to gain as well. Here are the potential benefits:

- *Improved Working Capital*: Having more working capital for borrowers means the non-borrowing firm can negotiate better payment terms. When financing is extended to the buyer, the non-borrowing firm (i.e., the supplier) may receive payments for the goods more promptly than through conventional payment terms. This accelerates the supplier's cash flow and refines working capital management.
- *Increased Order Quantity*: The order quantity might see an uptick due to enhanced financial positions of both supply chain firms, augmenting overall supply chain efficiency for all participating entities.
- *Reduced Credit Risk*: Should the lender shoulder the credit risk linked to the transaction, the non-borrowing firm can minimize its risk against potential payment defaults or delays from the buyer.
- *Improved Competitive Position*: By offering financing alternatives to buyers, the non-borrowing firm (i.e., the supplier) can set itself apart from rivals. This can allure new customers or fortify relationships with existing ones.

Even though the non-borrowing firm doesn't directly partake in the financing, these secondary benefits can foster a robust cash flow, cultivate business relationships, and bolster the overall growth and resilience of its operations. These perks become more pronounced if the 3PL firm's creditworthiness surpasses that of other supply chain entities, making the financing cost more attractive for the borrower compared to alternate financing avenues.

8.3.2.3 Benefits for 3PLs

The 3PLs, given their pivotal roles in in-transit inventory financing, reap several benefits, as outlined below:

- *Increased Business Volume*: In-transit inventory financing facilitates trade by enabling borrowers to have more funds at their disposal to either buy or sell goods. The resulting increase in transactions can boost business for

3PLs, who manage the transport, storage, and overarching logistics of the financed merchandise.
- **Expanded Business Opportunities**: The integration of ILFS allows 3PL firms to transition from solely providing logistics services to offering combined logistics and financial services. This diversification means that 3PLs can harness a new revenue stream by accruing interest from their financial offerings. This proves especially profitable if the 3PL boasts a stellar credit rating.
- **Honed Competitive Edge**: By extending in-transit inventory financing options to clientele, 3PLs can carve out a unique niche for themselves in the market. This distinct positioning can attract budding clients while ensuring the retention of existing ones.
- **Strengthened Supply Chain Ties**: Collaborations with financial entities that proffer in-transit inventory financing allow 3PLs to deliver a comprehensive suite of services to clients. Such a holistic approach simplifies supply chain and fiscal management for clients, cementing their trust and allegiance to the 3PL. Furthermore, the ILFS framework guarantees an influx of logistics requests from partnering sellers and buyers, resulting in a mutually beneficial scenario for all stakeholders.
- **Accelerated Inventory Turnover**: In-transit inventory financing equips clients to hasten the procurement or disposition of goods, catalyzing a swifter inventory turnover. This surge in activity can culminate in a greater influx of consignments and bolstered business for the 3PL.
- **Bolstered Reputation**: By forming alliances with esteemed financial institutions for in-transit inventory financing, 3PLs can elevate their standing and trustworthiness in the industry, making them a prime choice for enterprises in search of logistics solutions.

In summary, while 3PLs might not directly profit from in-transit inventory financing, the ripple effect of this service amplifies their business prospects, fortifies client rapport, and augments their competitive stature in the marketplace.

8.3.3 Risks and Risk Mitigation

Upon completion of in-transit inventory financing, the majority of the payment default risk transitions from the borrower to the 3PL and the bank. Even though 3PLs possess and monitor the in-transit inventory, they still have vested interests in mitigating financial risks (refer to Table 8.1).

By implementing these risk mitigation strategies, 3PLs can minimize the risks associated with in-transit inventory financing or cargo financing, ensuring a successful and profitable operation.

Assuming that the bank takes on the responsibility of lending to the borrower, the table outlines the risks that the bank would want to mitigate, particularly in in-transit inventory financing (refer to Table 8.2).

8.3 3PL-Led In-Transit Inventory Financing

Table 8.1 Risks and risk mitigation for 3PLs in in-transit inventory financing

Risks	• **Logistics Risk**: Products could be damaged during transportation, and lead times might be prolonged, as seen in incidents like the 2021 Suez Canal Crisis, where the canal was obstructed by the 400-meter-long Ever Given container ship. Additionally, theft or pilferage of goods is a potential hazard. Such risks are inherent for the 3PL firm, whether in-transit inventory financing is involved or not • **Market Risk**: Regardless of whether the seller or buyer is the borrower in in-transit inventory financing, repayment to the 3PL is contingent upon the buyer's financial health. A default from the buyer or its customers could compromise repayment liquidity • **Credit and Moral Risks**: The creditworthiness of the seller can be gauged by its assurance of product quality, while that of the buyer may be linked to its efficacy in marketing those products. With the 3PL retaining possession of the goods, concocting a sham transaction between the seller and buyer is highly unlikely. However, these entities might falsify financial records to facilitate financing • **Legal Risk**: Given that in-transit inventory financing frequently entails international shipping, 3PL firms may confront legal challenges in foreign jurisdictions with disparate legal systems. Additionally, if the ownership of in-transit inventory is ambiguous, disputes might arise (de Boer et al., 2015)
Risk Mitigation	• **Logistics Risk**: To counter logistics risks, 3PLs must establish rigorous handling guidelines and capacitate staff with proper handling skills. Optimal packaging materials and secure cargo mechanisms are crucial to minimize damage risks. Enhanced security protocols, including access management, CCTV systems, and security personnel, are vital. Constantly tracking cargo movement and ensuring a transparent chain of custody are also recommended. Furthermore, refining risk estimations and advancing shipping technology can alleviate capital strain for the 3PL • **Market Risk**: The 3PL should stay abreast of market inclinations and demand variations to recalibrate capacity as needed. Crafting adaptable contracts with carriers and suppliers can facilitate adjustments based on demand shifts. To buffer against market default risks, the 3PL can diminish the advance rate of financing or procure insurance, either from supply chain entities or external insurance providers • **Credit and Moral Risks**: Addressing credit and moral risks necessitates meticulous due diligence on supply chain firms to appraise their financial robustness and reputation. Diversifying the network of suppliers and carriers can mitigate the repercussions of any single entity defaulting • **Legal Risk**: To temper legal risks, the 3PL firm should assiduously plug any legal or documentation gaps within its ILFS platform

Table 8.2 Risks and risk mitigation for banks in in-transit inventory financing

Risks	• *Borrower Default Risk*: This pertains to the possibility of the borrower failing to fulfill their repayment obligations, leading to financial setbacks for the bank • *Collateral Risk*: This concerns the possibility that the collateral offered by the borrower either falls short in value, is not readily convertible to cash, or depreciates, thereby complicating the bank's efforts to recoup its loan in the event of default • *Logistics Risk*: This revolves around the potential for goods to get damaged, misplaced, or pilfered during transit. Such incidents could devalue the collateral and impede the borrower's capacity to settle the loan with the bank. Delays or interruptions in the transportation process could also strain the borrower's cash flow and repayment capabilities
Risk Mitigation	• *Borrower Default Risk*: The bank should conduct meticulous credit evaluations of borrowers. This would encompass scrutinizing their credit track record, financial declarations, and past repayment practices. Furthermore, routinely observing the borrower's fiscal health and ensuring transparent communication can help in identifying early indicators of potential defaults • *Collateral Risk*: The bank must stipulate substantial collateral or assurances from borrowers, which can be sold off if a default occurs. Periodic reevaluation and adjustment of collateral valuations are pivotal to ensure they stay commensurate with the loan value • *Logistics Risk*: The bank needs to ascertain that borrowers maintain appropriate insurance policies for the merchandise in transit. This could incorporate cargo insurance, safeguarding the worth of the commodities, and shielding the bank's stake in case of mishaps. The bank should also keep tabs on the transportation chain and foster transparent communication channels with both borrowers and logistics entities. If notable delays transpire, the bank ought to gauge its implications on the borrower's fiscal stability and ability to repay

By deploying these risk mitigation tactics, banks can adeptly navigate the challenges tied to in-transit inventory financing, guaranteeing a triumphant, and rewarding lending venture.

8.4 Applications of 3PL-Led Supply Chain Finance Innovation

The involvement of 3PLs in supply chain financing for both sellers and buyers has marked a significant evolution in complementing traditional financing mechanisms. Below are several financing innovations initiated by 3PLs.

8.4.1 Case Study: UPS Capital's Custom Solution for Global Glove

Case Study

UPS Capital's Custom Solution for Global Glove[1]

UPS Capital, a financial services division of UPS based in Atlanta, Georgia, offers financial services and insurance products like cash on delivery (COD) and early payment services primarily to UPS's vendors, including small businesses (UPS Capital, 2023).

Global Glove and Safety Manufacturing, Inc., headquartered in Ramsey, Minnesota, US, has been a manufacturer of personal protection equipment since 2003 (Global Glove, 2023). Beginning in that year, Global Glove started importing and distributing high-quality safety gloves and personal protection equipment (PPE) to a diverse range of industries and consumers. With a prolonged lead time in shipping and a significant portion of its working capital tied up in offshore and in-transit inventory, Global Glove sought additional financing to remain competitive and explore new markets.

To address this, Global Glove approached UPS Capital. Although not a bank, UPS Capital functions as a financial subsidiary of UPS. Matt Lissner, a business development officer at UPS Capital, explains that UPS Capital addresses needs traditional banks might overlook: Given that UPS oversees and transports a customer's inventory, UPS can offer loans based on its worth (UPS Capital, 2016). Essentially, holding in-transit inventory and possessing comprehensive logistics data adds value for 3PL firms.

With the UPS Capital Cargo Finance program, businesses can access a credit line between $300,000 and $1 million, usually with terms spanning 45 to 75 days (UPS Capital, 2018). They can also finance up to 70% of the commercial invoice's value. In 2018, UPS Capital enhanced this program, enabling companies to cover rates of up to 100% of their supplier's commercial invoice, obtain an unsecured credit line of up to $1.5 million with repayment terms of up to 90 days, and receive funds as quickly as one day after the products are dispatched (UPS Capital, 2018).

As depicted in Fig. 8.7, UPS Capital Cargo Finance can expedite the cash conversion cycle for associated companies (e.g., Company C or specifically,

---

[1] This case is based on published stories and case studies from UPS Capital and Global Glove and Safety Manufacturing, Inc. For more detailed information, please refer to the cited sources.

Global Glove). This enables borrowers to access cash sooner, approximately 15 days earlier in this example, to fund various operations.

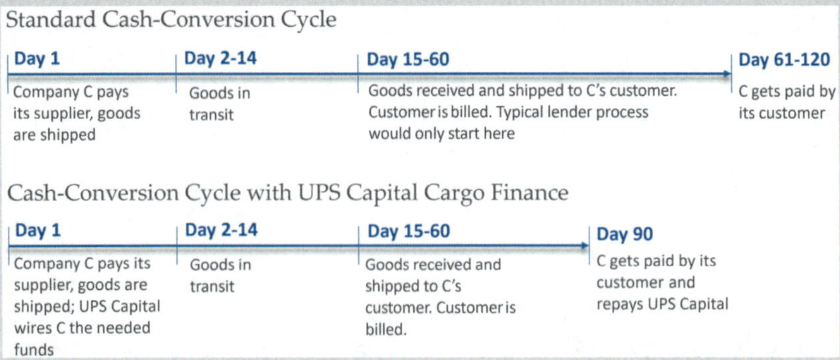

Standard Cash-Conversion Cycle

Day 1	Day 2-14	Day 15-60	Day 61-120
Company C pays its supplier, goods are shipped	Goods in transit	Goods received and shipped to C's customer. Customer is billed. Typical lender process would only start here	C gets paid by its customer

Cash-Conversion Cycle with UPS Capital Cargo Finance

Day 1	Day 2-14	Day 15-60	Day 90
Company C pays its supplier, goods are shipped; UPS Capital wires C the needed funds	Goods in transit	Goods received and shipped to C's customer. Customer is billed.	C gets paid by its customer and repays UPS Capital

Fig. 8.7 Impact of cargo finance on cash conversion cycle (*Source* Adapted from UPS Capital, 2018)

However, for this system to benefit Global Glove, the company had to entrust its freight to UPS in exchange for the financial service. Initially, Global Glove was reluctant to hand over all its freight to UPS. Yet, they soon recognized the dual advantage of comparable shipping rates and substantial financing based on in-transit inventory. With this arrangement, Global Glove swiftly secured a $4 million cargo finance loan. Consequently, in 2016, Global Glove introduced a new range of safety glasses, 40 fresh glove designs, and a novel line of hearing protection products. Their profit margin notably improved by 5% during the same period (UPS Capital, 2016).

8.4.2 Case Study: The Role of 3PL as a Supply Chain Orchestrator

Case Study

The Role of 3PL as a Supply Chain Orchestrator

In the intersection of joint logistics and financing services, Eternal Asia, a prominent Asian 3PL firm, offers a notable innovative procurement service (Chen et al., 2019). Under this business model, Eternal Asia acts on behalf of buyers to place orders with a manufacturer. Rather than demanding payment from each buyer when the order is placed, the manufacturer permits Eternal Asia to pay later, using special trade credit terms (usually between 30 and 60

8.4 Applications of 3PL-Led Supply Chain Finance Innovation

days) or a letter of credit (typically 30 days). Once the products are delivered to a buyer, Eternal Asia receives both the payment for the purchase and the logistics fee from that buyer. This structure means that buyers no longer need direct communication with the manufacturer; Eternal Asia effectively becomes the go-between for both orders and payments (Eternal Asia, 2007a).

Furthermore, Eternal Asia can share some of the benefits of the favorable credit terms with its buyers, often extending payment terms to 20 days after product delivery (refer to Fig. 8.8). This is particularly valuable to its many clients who are small and medium-sized enterprises (SMEs). Such integrated procurement and logistics services effectively provide financing for these SMEs, a crucial service in emerging economies where these firms might struggle to secure bank loans (Eternal Asia, 2007b). Since 1998, the company has been extending this procurement service to Chinese SMEs, procuring components and parts from well-regarded manufacturers like Cisco, GE, Acer, Lenovo, Haier, and various smaller suppliers (for further details, visit http://eternal-asia.com/). Sina Finance reported that in 2016, Eternal Asia generated revenue of 57.91 billion RMB (with an estimated market value of $2.7 billion as of June 2017), enjoying a profit growth rate of 14.12%—notably higher than the industry average of 8.12% (Chen et al., 2019).

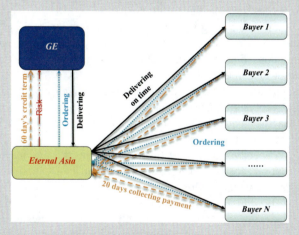

Fig. 8.8 The procurement role of eternal Asia in practice

Through this novel business model, the 3PL firm essentially positions itself as a supply chain orchestrator, delivering added value for SMEs. Other 3PL firms have also ventured into similar integrated services. For instance, C&D Logistics assists small to medium-sized buyers in purchasing raw materials from global corporations (Zhou & Wang, 2009). Here, C&D Logistics manages payments to upstream firms using letters of credit, subsequently collecting payments from the buyers within the letter of credit's time frame.

8.5 Summary

In this chapter, we delve into the nuanced relationship between inventory management and financing, with a special focus on the role of third-party logistics (3PL) providers. As supply chains have grown in complexity and scale, traditional financing mechanisms have often fallen short of addressing the needs of businesses, particularly when it comes to in-transit inventory. 3PL providers have emerged as key players in this space, offering innovative financial solutions that are intertwined with their logistics expertise.

Key Takeaways:

1. Inventory Financing:
   - Inventory financing refers to a line of credit or short-term loan obtained by businesses to purchase products for sale. These products or the inventory act as collateral for the loan.
   - This form of financing is crucial for businesses that need to stock up on inventory before they can make sales and generate revenue. It ensures a continuous flow of goods, thereby preventing stockouts and meeting customer demand.
   - Risks include fluctuating market demands which could lead to unsold inventory, potential depreciation of inventory value, and the complexities of managing goods spread across various geographical locations.
2. 3PL-Led In-Transit Inventory Financing:
   - This is a specialized form of financing where 3PL providers offer financial solutions for in-transit inventory. Given their expertise in logistics, 3PL providers are well-positioned to understand the value and risks associated with goods that are still in transit.
   - Such financing mechanisms are highly valuable for businesses that have significant capital tied up in goods that are in transit. It provides them with much-needed liquidity, enabling them to meet other operational costs and invest in growth opportunities.
   - The main risks are associated with the potential damage, loss, or theft of goods in transit, delays or disruptions in transportation, and any other factors that could impact the borrower's ability to repay the loan.
3. Applications of 3PL-Led Supply Chain Finance Innovation:
   - Companies like UPS Capital have leveraged their logistical prowess to offer unique financing solutions that banks and traditional financial

institutions can't. Their deep understanding of the entire supply chain, from manufacturer to end consumer, allows them to mitigate risks more effectively and extend credit based on the value of in-transit inventory.

8.6 Exercises

8.6.1 Practice Questions

1. Define inventory financing.
2. Name one benefit of inventory financing.
3. What are some challenges or risks associated with inventory financing?
4. What role do 3PL providers play in in-transit inventory financing?
5. How has the involvement of 3PLs in supply chain financing been beneficial to both sellers and buyers?
6. Why is the integrated procurement and logistics service important for SMEs in emerging economies?
7. How can 3PL firms, through their new business models, create additional value for SMEs?
8. Please explain why inventory financing and 3PL-led in-transit inventory financing can shorten the cash conversion cycle.
9. Please compare inventory financing to 3PL-led in-transit inventory financing.
10. Please find an anecdotal example for both inventory financing and 3PL-led in-transit inventory financing.

8.6.2 Case Study

Stellar Fashions—Financing and Logistics Challenges for a Trendy Retailer

Background

Stellar Fashions is a burgeoning apparel retailer based in a metropolitan area. With the summer season approaching, the retailer is gearing up to introduce a fresh clothing line from its overseas manufacturer, TrendyTextiles Ltd. Facing a tight cash flow situation, Stellar Fashions is mulling over three distinct financing schemes to back its inventory requirements:

1. Inventory financing (offered from a bank)
2. 3PL-led in-transit inventory financing (via 3PL)
3. Traditional bank financing (based on Stellar's credit rating)

To add to the complexity, Stellar Fashions must also consider the logistics cost linked with transporting the inventory. Stellar Fashions pays back at the end of the selling season.

Scenario Details

- Order requirement: 10,000 units of apparel
- Unit cost from TrendyTextiles Ltd.: $20
- Total procurement cost: $200,000
- Anticipated sale price per unit: $60
- Transportation time (from manufacturer to Stellar Fashions): 30 days
- Anticipated selling time: 60 days post-arrival
- Traditional bank financing interest rate: 15% percent per annum (p.a.) due to a low credit rating
- Inventory financing fee: 8% p.a.
- 3PL service and financing fee: 10% p.a. with 60 days Payment Grace Period offered by 3PL (conditional on using the 3PL's joint financing and logistics services)
- Transportation/Logistics cost: $2 per unit or $20,000 in total.

Questions

1. Given the three financing schemes, how do the logistics costs and interest rates impact Stellar Fashions' overall cash flow and profitability?
2. Which scheme offers the best balance between cost and cash flow benefits for the company?
3. How does the 3PL-led in-transit inventory financing scheme strategically position Stellar Fashions in terms of inventory management and response to market demand, compared to the traditional Inventory Financing without 3PL?

Appendix: Academic Perspective

The Cash Flow Advantages of 3PLs as Supply Chain Orchestrators

Xiangfeng Chen, Gangshu (George) Cai, Jing-Sheng Song[2]

Introduction

The rising trend of in-transit inventory financing has spotlighted the pivotal role 3PLs play in ILFS. Even in the absence of in-transit inventory financing, a 3PL can significantly influence supply chain management. As Chen et al. (2019)

---

[2] This section presents research findings from one of my publications, Chen et al. (2019). For a comprehensive understanding, readers are encouraged to consult the complete article: Chen, X., Cai, G., & Song, J.S. (2019). The cash flow advantages of 3PLs as supply chain orchestrators. Manufacturing & Service Operations Management, 21(2), 435–451. To maintain brevity, we have omitted most references from the original paper. Hence, please refer to the article for further details. For clarity in this section, we use both Chen et al. (2019) and "we" interchangeably.

highlighted, a 3PL firm can augment supply chain efficiency by acting as an orchestrator and modifying the cash flow patterns within supply chain entities.

There are numerous benefits tied to the integrated services of supply chain orchestrators. However, our primary interest lies in their unique cash flow dynamics, exemplified by firms like Eternal Asia and C&D Logistics. Our concentration is on the operational improvements derived from payment scheduling with SMEs during the 3PL's procurement process. By zeroing in on this aspect, we aim to evaluate the operational value of advanced financing, which holds paramount importance for the efficient distribution of products and services catering to local needs in developing nations. This raises the pressing question: under what circumstances can such innovations be advantageous for all stakeholders in the supply chain? It's crucial to understand that this novel method can only thrive if it brings mutual benefits to all involved parties.

The Model and the Cash Flow Dynamics

To investigate the cash flow dynamics of the 3PL's procurement service, we established a game-theoretic model featuring a three-player supply chain: one manufacturer, one 3PL, and one buyer. The buyer has a single selling season marked by uncertain demand and a fixed market price. The supply chain operates under wholesale price-only contracts for both procurement and shipping. We delve into two situations. In the traditional scenario (Model T), the 3PL merely transports products from the manufacturer to the buyer. The buyer settles the payment upon ordering with the manufacturer and upon delivery with the 3PL. In the alternative procurement service scenario (Model P), the 3PL accepts orders from the buyer and sources the goods from the manufacturer. This setup allows the buyer to settle the purchase and logistics service fees upon product delivery. Subsequently, the 3PL remits the order payment to the manufacturer following an agreed grace period.

Notably, the minimum transport time from the manufacturer to the buyer is $\ell_s > 0$, determined to be the ideal Nash bargaining solution between the buyer and the 3PL. Thus, in the baseline model, we set the transportation time at ℓ_s. As depicted in Fig. 8.9, production starts at time epoch O, shipping at time S, and demand arises at time R. The 3PL settles the order cost with the manufacturer on the buyer's behalf at time G. The interval from production epoch O to the 3PL payment point G is ℓ_g, while the period from production epoch O to the demand point R is $\ell_o \geq \ell_s$. Within each model, given the transportation duration and payment grace period, the participants determine the wholesale price, shipping fee, and order quantity to maximize their individual expected profits. We then juxtapose the outcomes of both models.

Model T expands on the two-player model from (Lariviere & Porteus, 2001) in two distinct ways. Firstly, it incorporates a third tier—the 3PL—into the supply chain, leading to triple-marginalization. Secondly, it infuses payment timing into the classic newsvendor model, considering the time value of money. Model P

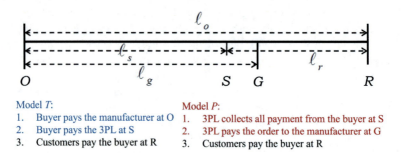

Fig. 8.9 Operations and payment epochs in models T and P

builds on this by modifying the order flow and introducing varied payment timings to represent the 3PL's revamped procurement and financing roles.

Main Findings and Contributions

With equivalent unit cash opportunity costs, we demonstrated that under the 3PL's Stackelberg leadership in model P, all firms benefit provided the manufacturer agrees to a payment grace period longer than the shipping duration (or the physical order lead time). However, this grace period should not exceed a specific threshold. A longer payment grace period than the shipping time allows the 3PL to retain cash for an extended period, subsequently decreasing the logistics cost for the buyer. As a result, the buyer places larger orders, enhancing the supply chain's revenue.

Nevertheless, for the manufacturer, the situation presents complexities. The benefit of increased order size is offset by the 3PL's payment delay. If the grace period is overly short, the advantages of the additional order volume don't compensate for the loss due to the payment postponement. On the contrary, if the grace period is too prolonged, the costs associated with the payment delay rise considerably. Consequently, a Pareto zone emerges, where the payment grace period is optimal, making all firms in model P more profitable than in model T (refer to Fig. 8.10).

Model P emphasizes the 3PL's paramount role in leadership and finance in two distinct ways. Firstly, model P's advantage under 3PL leadership diminishes if the manufacturer takes the lead. In such cases, the manufacturer increases the wholesale price in model P to account for the delayed payment. While the 3PL might reduce the shipping fee, the combined cost of wholesale price and shipping fee in model P surpasses that in model T, eradicating the Pareto zone. Secondly, if all factors remain consistent in model P but the manufacturer offers the buyer a direct payment grace period (bypassing the 3PL), the profits for all players remain identical to those in model T. This signifies the irreplaceability of the 3PL in model P.

Appendix: Academic Perspective

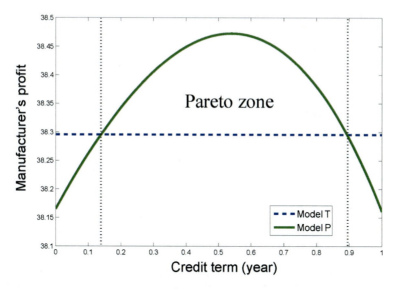

Fig. 8.10 Manufacturer's profit as a function of payment grace period ℓg

In scenarios with varied cash opportunity costs among firms, model P's Pareto zone appears regardless of the Stackelberg leader. Especially, model P's advantage over model T becomes more pronounced when the buyer's cash opportunity cost exceeds the manufacturer's. Additionally, a manufacturer with a lower cash opportunity cost is more inclined to offer an extended payment delay, resulting in even larger orders from the buyer. Model P remains superior if the 3PL's cash opportunity cost is considerably lower than that of other firms. In such cases, the 3PL might even settle with the manufacturer in advance and only collect payment upon product delivery to the buyers. While model P's Pareto zone can be broader under manufacturer leadership than with 3PL leadership, the entire supply chain's profit is greater with the 3PL at the helm, provided the payment delay grace period is adequately extended.

Further findings indicate a more pronounced risk pooling effect in model P compared to model T with an increased number of buyers (keeping market size constant). This expansion leads to a broader Pareto zone and a significant rise in profits in model P. Conversely, if the buyer faces capital constraints, firm profits decrease as financial market interest rates climb. We also discovered that under Nash bargaining negotiation, both the buyer and the 3PL prefer the shortest possible transportation time. Even if the manufacturer and the 3PL determine an optimal payment delay grace period through Nash bargaining, the results from prior scenarios remain valid.

References

Barnett, W. (1997). What's in a name? A brief overview of asset-based lending. *Secured Lender, 53,* 80–83.

Burkart, M., & Ellingsen, T. (2004). In-kind finance: A theory of trade credit. *American Economic Review, 94*(3), 569–590.

Camerinelli, E., & Bryant, C. (2014). *Supply chain finance—EBA European market guide version 2.0.* European Banking Association.

Chen, X., & Cai, G. G. (2011). Joint logistics and financial services by a 3PL firm. *European Journal of Operational Research, 214*(3), 579–587.

Chen, X., Cai, G., & Song, J. S. (2019). The cash flow advantages of 3PLs as supply chain orchestrators. *Manufacturing & Service Operations Management, 21*(2), 435–451.

Commercial Capital. (2021). *How does inventory financing work?* https://www.comcapfactoring.com/blog/how-does-inventory-financing-work/. Accessed May 16, 2023.

de Boer, R., Steeman, M., & van Bergen, M. (2015). *Supply chain finance, its practical relevance and strategic value: the supply chain finance essential knowledge series.* Hogeschool Windesheim.

Eternal Asia. (2007a). *Eternal Asia's 2007 IPO prospectus.* http://www.p5w.net/stock/ssgsyj/zqgg/200709/P020070910663946257459.pdf. Accessed August 1, 2016.

Eternal Asia (2007b) *Eternal Asia's O2O supply chain business ecosystem.* http://www.flandersinvestmentandtrade.com/export/sites/trade/files/trade_proposals/Eternal%20Asia%20Introduction.pdf. Accessed August 1, 2016.

Global Glove. (2023). *About Global Glove and safety manufacturing inc.* https://www.globalglove.com/about-us. Accessed May 19, 2023.

Globe SCF Forum. (2016). *Standard definitions for techniques of supply chain finance.* Report.

Inbound Logistics. (2014). *Market research: 3PL perspectives 2014.* https://www.inboundlogistics.com/articles/market-research-3pl-perspectives-2014/. Accessed May 11, 2023.

Investopedia. (2020). *4 famous inventory frauds you've never heard of.* https://www.investopedia.com/articles/economics/12/four-unknown-massive-frauds.asp. Accessed May 3, 2023.

Investopedia. (2021). *Inventory financing: Definition, how it works, pros, and cons.* https://www.investopedia.com/terms/i/inventory-financing.asp. Accessed March 22, 2023.

Lambert, D. M., Emmelhainz, M. A., & Gardner, J. T. (1999). Building successful logistics partnerships. *Journal of Business Logistics, 20*(1), 165.

Lariviere, M. A., & Porteus, E. L. (2001). Selling to the newsvendor: An analysis of price-only contracts. *Manufacturing & Service Operations Management, 3*(4), 293–305.

The Paper. (2016). *The full record of the steel trade industry reshuffle: Many people committed suicide, 300 people were imprisoned, and tens of billions of bad debts were made.* https://www.thepaper.cn/newsDetail_forward_1472922. Accessed September 10, 2021.

UPS Capital. (2016). *An unexpected lender that fit like a glove.* https://upscapital.com/wp-content/themes/upscapital/assets/uploads/Global-Glove-Case-Study.pdf. Accessed March 6, 2023.

UPS Capital. (2018). *Turn in-transit inventory into working capital without a magic wand.* https://upscapital.com/assets/media/cargo-finance-landing-download.pdf. Accessed March 3, 2023

UPS Capital. (2023). *Homepage of UPS capital.* https://upscapital.com/. Accessed March 3, 2023.

Wells, J. T. (2001). Ghost goods: How to spot phantom inventory. *Journal of Accountancy, 191*(6), 33.

Zhou, W., Lin, T., & Cai, G. (2020). Guarantor financing in a four-party supply chain game with leadership influence. *Production and Operations Management, 29*(9), 2035–2056.

Zhou, Y. W., & Wang, S. D. (2009). Manufacturer-buyer coordination for newsvendor-type-products with two ordering opportunities and partial backorders. *European Journal of Operational Research, 198*(3), 958–974.

Other Supply Chain Finance Mechanisms

9

Learning Objectives:

1. Examine distributor financing as a means to optimize cash flow in supply chains with extended payment terms.
2. Identify the application of bank payment obligation (BPO) to secure and streamline international trade payments.
3. Evaluate the use of structured commodity finance in managing risks and financing assets with fluctuating values.

9.1 Introduction

So far, we have discussed seller-led, buyer-led, and 3PL-led supply chain finance (SCF). Owing to the intricacies of supply chains and their interconnected relationships with financial institutions, certain SCF mechanisms do not neatly fit into any of the aforementioned three categories. In fact, some SCF mechanisms might be considered hybrids of these categories, or they may be led by other supply chain firms, financial institutions, or even insurance companies. This chapter delves into several other major financing mechanisms, such as distributor financing, and introduces the bank payment obligation (BPO) as a banking framework. Moreover, structured commodity finance stands out as a unique category of supply chain finance tailored for commodities.

© The Author(s), under exclusive license to Springer Nature Switzerland AG 2024
G. Cai, *Supply Chain Finance*, https://doi.org/10.1007/978-3-031-56125-2_9

9.2 Distributor Financing

Distributor financing, sometimes referred to as channel finance, dealer finance, or floor plan finance,[1] is a type of distribution channel-based finance (Globe SCF Forum, 2016). Within this framework, a financier offers funds to a distributor (e.g., an exporter or a dealer) to settle payments with its seller, who is typically a larger manufacturer. Given that distributor financing can be initiated by either the seller or the buyer, it can potentially fall into the categories of either buyer-led or seller-led supply chain finance. Nonetheless, distributors might also leverage other SCF mechanisms such as factoring, invoice discounting, and inventory financing to broaden their funding avenues.

Often, distributor financing takes the form of a long-term loan commitment from a financial institution (like a bank) to the distributor, made available through a line of credit and subject to yearly reviews. Such financing is prevalent when there's a stable relationship between the distributor and the seller, and the distributor's operations are robust. In many cases, the distributor might be a third-party company or one that is partially owned by the seller. Given the pivotal role of the seller in distributor financing, they are sometimes referred to as the "anchor party" (Globe SCF Forum, 2016).

9.2.1 Process Flow

The distributor financing process flow unfolds as follows (refer to Fig. 9.1):

1. The financier enters into an agreement with the distributor. The manufacturer (or seller) typically plays a pivotal role in distributor financing, ensuring successful transaction flow. There may also be a separate agreement between the financier and the manufacturer. In this tri-party agreement, the manufacturer might even offer risk-sharing with the financier, bolstering the financing security for the distributor.
2. Within the confines of this agreement, the manufacturer dispatches goods to the distributor. The distributor typically requires time to resell these goods to its end customers.
3. After receiving the goods, the distributor verifies and approves the invoice sent by the manufacturer. Subsequently, the distributor sends a notice of invoice acceptance along with the pertinent transaction documents back to the manufacturer.
4. The manufacturer then forwards the invoice acceptance and the related transaction paperwork to the financier.

---

[1] Floor plan financing is a specialized form of distributor finance tailored for dealers of vehicles and machinery displayed for sale on dealership floors (Hayes, 2020). It is also viewed as a type of inventory financing since the loan is grounded in the value of the large-ticket-item inventory, with repayment due once the inventory is sold.

9.2 Distributor Financing

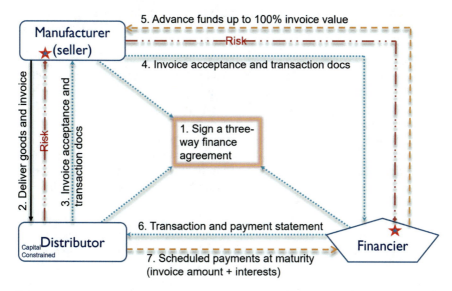

Fig. 9.1 Process flow of distributor financing

5. The financier releases funds equivalent to the value of the invoice to the manufacturer.
6. The financier dispatches a statement detailing the transactions and the associated payment to the distributor.
7. On the predetermined due dates, the distributor settles the account with the financier. This repayment encompasses both the initial payment made to the manufacturer and the accruing interest.

In a variant of distributor financing, to enhance the distributor's liquidity, the manufacturer might offer extended credit terms (Globe SCF Forum, 2016). In this setup, the manufacturer and the financier can strike a deal to furnish the distributor with this elongated credit time frame.

9.2.2 Benefits

Distributor financing emerges from the combined endeavors of the distributor and the seller. Given the distributor's vital role within the supply chain, its financing can usher in advantages for every chain participant. Hence, distributor financing offers tangible benefits to both the manufacturer and the distributor as outlined below.

Benefits for the Distributor

- ***Working Capital Enhancement:*** The financier's upfront payment to the manufacturer alleviates the distributor's immediate payment obligations,

augmenting its working capital. This proves especially advantageous when there's a significant gap between the sales of goods and their delivery by the manufacturer.
- *Financing Cost Reduction:* The distributor's collaboration with the seller (i.e., manufacturer)—often a substantial entity—elevates its credit standing during the financing. This generally results in reduced financing costs for the distributor compared to conventional bank loans.
- *Greater Financial Flexibility:* Certain distributor finance schemes permit the distributor to cover just the interest and use product sales revenue to pare down the credit line. Some financiers don't even mandate the distributor to pledge other assets as security. This absence of collateral requisites further magnifies the distributor's financial flexibility, enabling it to undertake new projects and fulfill more orders.
- *More Business Growth:* Strengthened supply chain bonds with the manufacturer lead to a more predictable and lasting product supply for the distributor. Consequently, the distributor can fine-tune its ideal product inventory levels across various brands and amplify business growth.

Benefits for the Manufacturer

- *Stabler Revenue:* Distributor financing allows the distributor to maintain regular purchases from the manufacturer, reinforcing the production cycle and demand. A financially well-equipped distributor is less inclined to seek extended payment terms from the manufacturer, which lightens the financial load on the latter. This can trim down the manufacturer's days sales outstanding (DSO).

> The manufacturer's anchoring role is pivotal in distributor financing.

- *Strengthened Relationship:* Assisting the distributor also cements the manufacturer's supply chain relationship with them, paving the way for potential sales ventures. This is particularly advantageous when the manufacturer is venturing into fresh markets.

Benefits for the Financier

- *New Business Opportunities:* Distributor financing carves out a fresh revenue stream for the financier. The manufacturer's active participation in the financing process also gifts the financier a clearer view of transactions. To alleviate the financier's financial vulnerabilities, the manufacturer might even offer risk-sharing measures, such as guarantees.

9.2.3 Risks and Risk Mitigation

The paramount risk in distributor financing lies in the distributor's potential default. Such defaults can stem from various factors including market risks, credit risks, and political risks, especially when the distributor operates in an international market. As a preventive measure, the financier should undertake comprehensive due diligence, examining the distributor's creditworthiness, historical business performance, and overall business stability.

To further minimize risks, it's essential for the financier to seek open communication and enhanced involvement from the manufacturer, fostering supply chain stability. When the manufacturer actively participates and shares risks with the financier, the information relayed can notably enhance transaction transparency.

Both the financier and manufacturer should also press for heightened financial transparency from the distributor to avert moral hazards (for instance, the distributor redirecting funds to unrelated ventures). This can be achieved through greater automation in information systems (such as cloud computing), software enhancements, rigorous auditing, and consistent monitoring of the distributor's inventory.

9.3 Bank Payment Obligation

In June 2013, the International Chamber of Commerce (ICC) Banking Commission in collaboration with the Society for Worldwide Interbank Financial Telecommunication (SWIFT) introduced the Uniform Rules for Bank Payment Obligations (URBPO) under Publication 750 (Wynne & Fearn, 2014). Technically, the *bank payment obligation* (BPO) doesn't serve as a distinct method of supply chain finance. Instead, it's a contemporary payment framework rooted in electronic data matching (SWIFT, 2016). BPO is seen as a conditional "interbank instrument," securing payments through the successful matching of trade data within trade and supply chain finance. Additionally, it functions as an "enabling framework," facilitating flexible payment and risk mitigation services in both trade finance and supply chain finance realms (Globe SCF Forum, 2016). As per the International Chamber of Commerce (ICC), "The BPO stands as an alternative instrument for trade settlement, devised to augment rather than supplant existing solutions" (ICC QATAR, 2018).

According to URBPO, a BPO represents "an irrevocable and independent commitment from an obligor bank to either pay upfront or undertake a deferred payment obligation, fulfilling the specified sum to a recipient bank after presenting all necessary data sets required by an Established Baseline. This commitment is contingent upon achieving a Data Match or the acceptance of a Data Mismatch" (URBPO, ICC Publ. No. 750E) (ICC, 2013). Additionally, BPO can be interpreted as a unique form of bank guarantee, extended by the obligor bank (usually the buyer's bank) to the recipient bank (seller's bank). This guarantee is contingent on the successful electronic data match in accordance with ICC regulations (Eker, 2018).

All banks involved in BPO are mandated to adhere to the stipulations laid out in the URBPO guidelines. As such, there's no obligation for banks to deliberate on the specifics of BPO. However, if companies seek supplementary supply chain financing within the BPO structure, all participating entities must concur on those incremental financing provisions.

9.3.1 Process Flow

The BPO procedure is typically segmented into three phases: establishing the baseline, the shipment of goods followed by data matching, and finally, delivery and payment settlement. The initial baseline establishment lays the groundwork for the subsequent electronic data matching and the eventual payment resolution. Fig. 9.2 illustrates the BPO mechanism as detailed below.

Baseline Establishment

1. The buyer expresses an interest in procuring goods from the seller. Once a consensus is reached regarding the order, both parties agree to utilize BPO for their transactions and payment settlements. Subsequently, the buyer forwards the sales contract, which encompasses details of the purchase order (PO) and BPO, to the seller.

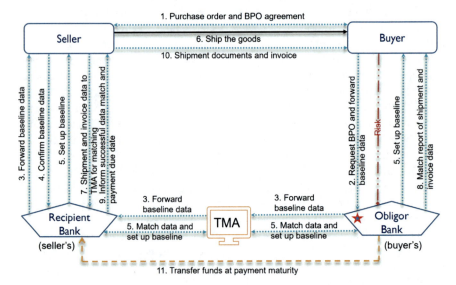

Fig. 9.2 Process flow of BPO

2. The buyer then solicits a BPO service from its obligor bank, providing the requisite baseline data derived from the PO and BPO. This baseline data, deemed sufficient for assessing credit risk, is ratified by all stakeholders involved. By mandating only the minimum necessary information for this baseline, the likelihood of discrepancies during subsequent data matching is reduced, thereby streamlining the transaction and settlement phases.
3. The obligor bank transmits this baseline data to the Transaction Matching Application (TMA). In turn, TMA conveys this information to both the recipient bank and the seller. It's worth noting that TMA employs the ISO20022 Trade Services Management (TSMT) format—an XML standard curated specifically for data exchanges between the TMA and the respective banks (Globe SCF Forum, 2016).
4. Once the recipient bank receives the baseline data, it is shared with the seller for validation, based on the previously signed sales contract with the buyer.
5. Post validation, both the recipient bank and the obligor bank finalize the baseline within the TMA system. Following this, TMA produces a report that it dispatches to both banks. The ratification of this baseline is an indication that both banks have mutually agreed to employ BPO for any subsequent transactions.

Shipment of Goods and Data Matching

6. The seller dispatches the goods as outlined in the sales contract to the buyer. The seller may either handle the transportation directly or employ a third-party logistics firm for the task. The terms concerning shipment responsibility and ownership of the goods are detailed in the sales contract.
7. The seller forwards the trade data (such as shipment details, invoice, insurance documentation, and certificates) to its recipient bank. This data is then relayed to the TMA for comparison.
8. If the electronic trade data provided by the seller aligns with the baseline data, the obligor bank conveys this match report to the buyer, prompting an automatic payment to the recipient bank. In cases of discrepancies, the buyer is given an opportunity to review and, if acceptable, endorse the variances. Following the buyer's validation, the obligor bank communicates with the TMA, which then forwards a successful data match report to the recipient bank. If the BPO is activated, the payment obligation becomes unalterable, compelling the obligor bank to process the payment to the recipient bank on the stipulated date.

> Once activated, the BPO creates an irrevocable payment obligation, requiring the obligor bank to pay the recipient bank on the due date.

9. The recipient bank notifies the seller of the successful trade data match and advises on the expected payment maturity date.

Delivery and Payment Settlement

10. Upon receipt, the buyer sends the trade documentation (like shipment details, invoice, insurance, and certificates) to the seller and cross-checks the shipment's data. It's important to note the emerging shift in the industry toward electronic documentation, such as the electronic bill of lading (eB/L), to supersede traditional paper-based trade documents.[2] For instance, sellers can transmit the eB/L to buyers through platforms like essDOCS Paperless Trade Solutions.
11. On the designated day, the obligor bank remits the owed funds to the seller's account held with the recipient bank. The buyer settles its dues with the obligor bank as per their mutual agreement. This could either be a regular payment commitment (prior to the BPO's maturity date) or a deferred-payment obligation (post the BPO's maturity date).

In launching BPO, SWIFT introduced the Trade Services Utility (TSU) as the TMA for data matching, and it was adopted by major commercial banks. However, due to the relatively slow uptake of BPO and competition from other TMAs, the growth in volume for TSU did not meet SWIFT's expectations. Consequently, SWIFT decided to discontinue the TSU in December 2020 (Morton, 2019). Banks have since shifted their focus to blockchain initiatives for TMAs, such as Marco Polo. For instance, in July 2019, Commerzbank completed its first live commercial pilot BPO transaction on the Marco Polo blockchain platform. This transaction involved the export of special hydraulic couplings from Germany to China (Wragg, 2019).

9.3.2 Benefits

Employing BPO in payment transactions offers a plethora of advantages to the involved parties. Foremost, electronic data matching enhances the traceability and visibility of product and payment transactions considerably. This improvement allows parties to conserve substantial time and effort in scrutinizing documents and verifying data. The automated electronic data matching process can minimize discrepancies typically introduced by manual methods. As a result, this streamlined process curtails the need for intensive investigations, dispute resolutions, and undue payment delays. Such efficiency translates to significant cost savings in verification time, investigation expenses, and other resources allocated for the financing process.

Additionally, the automated nature of BPO facilitates faster payment transfers compared to the traditional letter of credit. For instance, while a conventional

---

[2] The bill of lading (B/L), is a document commonly used in maritime logistics. It serves to verify the delivery of goods, establish the contract of carriage, and transfer the rights of the goods to another party (Raunek, 2023).

letter of credit might take up to 6 working days for document verification between advising and issuing banks, BPO can accomplish electronic data matching within a day (SWIFT, 2016).

Furthermore, the irrevocable payment commitment made by the obligor bank serves as a bank guarantee against a buyer's payment default. This assurance alleviates payment uncertainties and strengthens risk mitigation, benefiting all parties involved in the BPO.

Below, we itemize the specific benefits for each involved party.

Benefits for the Seller

- *Enhanced Security*: BPO provides a more secure payment method compared to both letters of credit and open accounts. This is largely due to BPO's guarantee of irrevocable payment. In comparison, payments under a letter of credit can be altered, and those in an open account can be delayed beyond the due date. With BPO, once trade data aligns with the baseline data, the seller can rely on the agreed payment terms. This electronic data matching ensures that transaction and payment terms are executed as initially agreed upon by the parties involved.
- *Prompt Payment*: Owing to the electronic data matching process, sellers can access funds immediately upon the payment due date. In contrast, payments through letters of credit or open accounts, which depend on manual document verification, can experience delays.
- *Reduced Transaction Costs*: The electronic data matching in BPO typically incurs lower total costs than a letter of credit.
- *Decreased Cancellations*: The initiation of the BPO process reduces the likelihood of buyers canceling orders.
- *Greater Financing Flexibility*: Within the BPO framework, sellers have the option to obtain pre-shipment (based on purchase orders) or post-shipment (based on approved payables) financing from the recipient bank, backed by the obligor bank's irrevocable payment commitment.
- *Strengthened Supply Chain Relationships*: Commitments from the obligor bank, coupled with transaction transparency and visibility, enhance supply chain relationships.

Benefits for the Buyer

- *Enhanced Security*: BPO offers greater security to buyers compared to advance payments. With BPO, the obligor bank remits payment to the recipient bank only after the goods have been shipped by the seller, not beforehand. This mechanism helps prevent issues like non-shipments or late shipments. The electronic data matching ensures that the transaction and payment terms are executed as initially agreed upon by the buyer.
- *Increased Creditworthiness*: Adopting BPO can serve as an indicator that the buyer is reliable and in good financial standing. This can enhance the buyer's ability to secure orders. The irrevocable payment commitment under BPO

makes it a more appealing option than instruments such as open accounts or document collections.
- **Flexible Payment Options**: Within the BPO framework, buyers have the opportunity to request payment extensions from the obligor bank, with terms like "60 days after match" or "90 days after match." If approved, such deferred-payment arrangements can further bolster the buyer's working capital.
- **Strengthened Supply Chain**: Payment automation under BPO can fortify the financial stability of the seller, leading to enhanced efficiency and reliability across the entire supply chain, which in turn benefits the buyer.

Benefits for the Bank

- **Streamlined Financing Processes**: The use of electronic data matching can substantially reduce the manual workload faced by banks, leading to more streamlined financing processes.
- **Enhanced Revenue Opportunities**: The increased efficiency brought about by BPO paves the way for augmented financing opportunities for both the obligor and recipient banks.

To truly harness the aforementioned benefits and the risk mitigation inherent to BPO, it's crucial for all stakeholders—sellers, buyers, and banks—to invest in the necessary technological infrastructure for BPO. Yet, a swift BPO implementation has not been universally embraced, in part due to the intricate nature of the process, particularly concerning the setup and utilization of TMA software. A case in point: As per Euromoney's 2018 Trade Finance Survey, a mere 23% of corporations had incorporated BPO into their operations (Doyle, 2021).

Several factors contribute to this hesitancy:

- **Restructuring Challenges:** Embedded processes within participating entities and a steep learning curve can deter rapid adoption. For instance, banks accustomed to relying on tangible shipping documents via letters of credit may find the transition to BPO daunting. This shift does not merely represent a significant financial outlay but also challenges bank personnel to master novel technologies.
- **Diverse Technological Capabilities:** There exists a wide disparity in technological aptitude across companies and banks. Some firms still lean on physical documents, which can be a roadblock to BPO adoption. The absence of a unified technological standard renders BPO implementation problematic. Exemplifying the challenges, SWIFT's TSU application, which was central to many BPO processes, was discontinued in December 2020 (Wragg, 2019).
- **Inconsistency Across TMA Platforms:** Some banks have developed proprietary TMA platforms. The resultant fragmentation creates inconsistencies, leading to compatibility issues. To effectively navigate these challenges,

heightened coordination efforts are required to ensure seamless interbank operations.

In conclusion, championing BPO usage on a broader scale necessitates the collective commitment of businesses and banks toward a universally recognized and compatible TMA platform for efficient BPO services.

9.3.3 Supply Chain Finance in the BPO Framework

BPO, as previously highlighted, can serve as a foundational structure for supply chain finance, facilitating seller-led pre-shipment financing, seller-led post-shipment financing, and buyer-led payment extension financing. However, since these additional financing terms are not part of the standard BPO procedure, it's crucial for the involved parties to mutually agree on these provisions beforehand. Beyond these specific SCF mechanisms, both the recipient bank and the obligor bank have the option to negotiate interbank financing agreements. Such agreements could encompass early bank-to-bank payments at a discounted rate to the recipient bank or delayed bank-to-bank payments favoring the obligor bank.

Seller-Led Pre-Shipment Financing

- *Initiation by the Seller to the Recipient Bank*: Upon establishing a BPO baseline by the companies and banks, there's an inherent assurance regarding the eventual shipment of goods, which further solidifies the foundation for repayment related to pre-shipment financing (Globe SCF Forum, 2016). However, the final rollout of this mechanism is contingent upon the seller fulfilling its contractual duties.

    Given the arrangement where the obligor bank commits to settling the payment with the recipient bank upon reaching the maturity date, the seller is empowered to seek pre-shipment financing from the recipient bank. In this scenario, the seller can procure an upfront payment, reduced by the corresponding interest. This framework essentially enhances the traditional purchase order financing model. With the added payment assurance from the obligor bank, the seller can potentially secure an advance payment at a higher rate than what's typically available in conventional purchase order financing.

Seller-Led Post-Shipment Financing

- *Request by the Seller to the Recipient Bank*: After the data is matched post-shipment, the seller can seek financing from the recipient bank, similar to approved payables financing. The seller can then access the full BPO payment amount, reduced by the discount attributed to the advanced payment.

    An added advantage of this post-shipment financing mechanism is that it doesn't tap into the seller's credit line. This is due to the advance payment being a portion of the ultimate payment set to be transferred from the obligor bank to the recipient bank.

Notably, the recipient bank may proactively pre-match the trade data against the previously established baseline (even pre-shipment) as a modification to possibly incorporate a BPO later, supporting the approved payables financing (ICC QATAR, 2018). With this adjustment, the recipient bank is positioned to submit the data for a complete match (even post-delivery), being assured that the BPO will be forthcoming.

- ***Request by the Buyer to the Recipient Bank***: Following the shipment and data match, the obligor bank, representing the buyer, petitions the recipient bank to expedite the BPO payment to the seller (Globe SCF Forum, 2016). Here, the financing taps into the obligor bank's credit line, leading the obligor bank to remit the BPO amount, augmented by interest, to the recipient bank. This financial setup mirrors an early payment scenario from the buyer to the seller. Consequently, it's essential to have a pre-agreed consensus among all stakeholders, separate from the BPO.

Buyer-Led Deferred-Payment Financing

- ***Petition by the Buyer to the Obligor Bank***: The buyer prompts its obligor bank to delay the BPO payment due date, enabling it to settle the amount with the obligor bank post the BPO maturity. Subsequently, the buyer repays the BPO sum increased by the interest for the extended tenure. This arrangement stands as an independent agreement between the buyer and its obligor bank.

To illustrate, in 2015, ZF, a German technological exporter, entered into a contractual agreement to supply spare parts to TEMSA, a Turkish automotive industry importer, and they consented to a BPO (SWIFT, 2016). The recipient bank, UniCredit, along with the obligor bank, TEB, facilitated the BPO. TEMSA, the buyer, additionally sought deferred-payment financing (extended by 180 days) from the obligor bank.

9.3.4 Risk Mitigation

For the successful implementation of BPO, both the buyer and seller must initially align on the payment terms, payment obligation amount, and other pertinent details of the sales contract. Upon reaching a consensus on the BPO conditions, two pivotal matching procedures safeguard the final transaction: (1) baseline data matching and (2) trading data matching against the baseline (Globe SCF Forum, 2016). This safeguarding mechanism furnished by BPO offers a payment guarantee from the obligor bank to the seller upon maturity. In the BPO framework, the risk of non-payment default transitions from the buyer to the buyer's obligor bank.

> In BPO, the risk of non-payment default transitions from the buyer to the buyer's obligor bank.

Following the obligor bank's BPO proposal to the recipient bank, and its subsequent acceptance, the obligor bank is mandated to fulfill the payment on the stipulated due date once an electronic match is achieved between the baseline and trade data. Given that the payment obligation becomes binding once activated, it is crucial for the obligor bank to gauge the associated risk, practice due diligence (e.g., know-your-customer, KYC) on the buyer, and appropriately price the BPO. The obligor bank's risk is then mitigated based on the buyer's credit reliability and other relevant credit and insurance tools.

Conversely, the onus falls on the recipient bank to ensure internal compliance with the seller and to validate the data forwarded by the seller to the TMA (SWIFT, 2016). If a mutually agreed baseline exists and payment remains pending (in the case of deferred-payment BPO), the recipient bank may opt to fulfill the seller's payment beyond the scope of the URBPO if it had previously accepted the obligor bank's default risk (ICC, 2018).

As per URBPO guidelines, the recipient bank isn't obligated to settle the seller's payment. A distinct legal contract must articulate the inherent agreement between the recipient bank and the seller. Thus, BPO empowers a bank to provide risk mitigation within open account frameworks and other SCF mechanisms. In supplementary supply chain finance pursuits anchored in BPO, if the obligor bank defaults, the recipient bank must craft an essential credit line for the obligor bank (Globe SCF Forum, 2016). Since BPO is exclusively a bank-to-bank transaction, it can't be "confirmed" in the traditional sense like in letters of credit. However, a separate agreement between the seller and its recipient bank for an additional commitment (i.e., "silent confirmation") may be in place (ICC, 2018).

Should the recipient bank grant an advanced payment for pre-shipment financing to the seller, it becomes vital for the bank to conduct rigorous due diligence on the seller's production capability and ensure final product delivery to the buyer. The recipient bank must also meticulously assess the seller's creditworthiness based on supply chain efficiency, product standards, and delivery success. Additionally, the discount rate should factor in the credit stability of the obligor bank to safeguard against defaults. As a result, the recipient bank's fees to the seller would encompass BPO processing charges and a risk premium, considering the seller's supply chain efficiency and the obligor bank's credit standing.

If the buyer initiates an advanced payment request, urging the obligor bank to settle the seller's payment prematurely, the buyer's creditworthiness must also be integrated into the recipient bank's risk evaluation. The fees the obligor bank charges the buyer would then incorporate BPO-related costs and a risk premium rooted in the buyer's credit profile.

9.3.5 Comparisons with Other Supply Chain Finance Mechanisms

Given its role as a payment framework, BPO operates in ways that resemble a letter of credit, open account, and other SCF mechanisms. It's especially noteworthy to compare BPO with a letter of credit and an open account.

9.3.5.1 BPO vs. Letter of Credit

BPO bears similarities to a letter of credit, especially regarding the four-corner process flow (refer to Fig. 5.2 and Fig. 9.2). With a letter of credit, both the confirming bank and the issuing bank are obligated to pay, but this is contingent upon the physical presentation of compliant documents. For BPO, the obligor bank's obligation to pay hinges on the matching of trade data with the baseline data. This has led some to view BPO as an electronic version of a letter of credit. However, significant distinctions separate the two.

Table 9.1 contrasts BPO with a letter of credit. Table 9.1 suggests that in many aspects, BPO offers advantages over a letter of credit. In some respects, BPO incorporates the best elements of a letter of credit, furnishing banks with a comprehensive overview and full automation for transactions. Nevertheless, it's anticipated that BPO and letters of credit will coexist for a significant period. This is because many businesses and banks are accustomed to transacting using letters of credit. Additionally, the technological compliance and intricacies involved in employing BPO might further postpone its widespread adoption in trade and supply chain finance.

Table 9.1 Comparison between BPO and letter of credit

	BPO	Letter of Credit
Payment Obligation	The obligation of the obligor bank is irrevocable	Irrevocable from issuing bank, nominated bank, and/or confirmed bank
Obligation Parties	Bank-to-bank	Bank-to-seller
Documentation Process	Electronic baseline data matching; banks don't require physical trade documents	Physical trade documents required; manual checking
Data Discrepancy	Fewer discrepancies due to electronic data matching	Risks of errors from human mistakes in documentation and data verification
Financing Costs	Reduced costs due to automated electronic data matching	Higher costs due to manual paperwork and potential human errors
Financing Speed	Quicker due to electronic data matching	Slower, given the manual verification process

(continued)

9.3 Bank Payment Obligation

(continued)

	BPO	**Letter of Credit**
ICC Rules	URBPO 750 (Uniform Rules for Bank Payment Obligations Publication 750)	UCPDC 600 (Uniform Customs and Practice for Documentary Credits Publication 600)
Capital Sources	Obligor bank	Issuing bank
Shipment Documents	Directly from seller to buyer	From seller to banks
Financing Flexibility	Provides an enabling framework for SCF opportunities, such as seller-led pre-shipment or post-shipment financing from the recipient bank and buyer-led deferred-payment financing from the obligor bank	The issuing bank can alter the payment during document verification; it can also be used as collateral for additional financing

> BPO integrates the best practices of the letter of credit, providing banks with complete visibility and automated transactions.

Case Study

BPO vs. Letter of Credit

Polytrade, a marketing and logistics service provider for polymers, polyester, and related additives and raw materials, entered into a contract with PTT Polymer, a marketing company in Thailand, in 2014 (UniCredit, 2016). Historically, both companies utilized letters of credit for their international transactions. However, Polytrade's slim profit margins made it sensitive to the high transaction costs associated with letters of credit. Furthermore, the company wanted to streamline its trade processes due to tight delivery timelines. Seeking a financing method that could expedite operations, minimize data discrepancy risks, and cut financing costs, Polytrade opted for BPO with guidance from UniCredit. PTT Polymer, with assistance from its recipient bank, Bangkok Bank, also agreed to the BPO arrangement. Polytrade selected UniCredit as its obligor bank and secured an additional 60-day payment extension from them (UniCredit, 2016).

9.3.5.2 BPO vs. Traditional Open Account

BPO, as a payment framework, expands the service portfolio for banks. Moreover, it offers risk mitigation for a range of trade and SCF mechanisms, including open account transactions (ICC, 2018). Essentially, BPO can be adapted as a platform to carry out tasks associated with traditional open account transactions. However, the involvement of both the recipient bank and obligor bank introduces a variation from the conventional open account mechanism. A clear advantage of incorporating BPO into open account transactions is the assurance it provides to the seller regarding payment receipt from the buyer (via the obligor bank) to its designated recipient bank.

> **Case Study**
>
> *Using BPO for Open Account*
>
> The distinction of being the "first open account BPO" goes to a transaction between Mitsui & Co. Plant Systems. Ltd., a Japanese energy infrastructure importer, and RVT Systeme, a German machine-building exporter, in 2014 (SWIFT, 2016). The designated obligor bank was MUFG in Tokyo, while the recipient bank was UniCredit in Germany. According to their contract, Mitsui & Co. placed an order for gearboxes and couplings from RVT Systeme. Both parties agreed to a "BPO at 7 days after TSU data match," facilitated by the implementation of the SWIFT TSU system (SWIFT, 2016).

Table 9.2 Comparison between BPO and traditional open account

	BPO	Traditional Open Account
Payment Obligation	Irrevocable	Riskier; the buyer might further delay or even default on payments
Obligation Parties	Bank-to-bank	Buyer-to-seller
Financing Type	From obligor bank to buyer	From seller to buyer
Risk Taker	Obligor bank	Seller
Capital Sources	Obligor bank	Seller
Financing Costs	Reasonable for the buyer due to automated electronic data matching	The seller often must offer a significantly high discount rate for advance payment
Financing Speed	Faster due to electronic data matching	Slower because of manual verification processes
Documentation Process	Electronic data matching	Physical documents are sent directly from the seller to the buyer
ICC Rules	URBPO 750	N/A
Transparency	Enhanced supply chain transparency due to electronic data matching	Limited

(continued)

(continued)

	BPO	**Traditional Open Account**
Financing Flexibility	Greater financing options, such as seller-led pre-shipment or post-shipment financing from the recipient bank, and buyer-led deferred-payment financing from the obligor bank	The dominant buyer might delay payment, jeopardizing the seller and supply chain stability

Comparison of BPO to traditional open account is further summarized in Table 9.2.

As Tables 9.1 and 9.2 demonstrate, BPO integrates the best practices of both letter of credit and open account transactions. The inherent financing flexibility in BPO also enables, such as pre-shipment and post-shipment financing, within the BPO framework. This versatility enhances the appeal of BPO, especially for businesses that are capital-constrained. With the advent of enabling technologies like blockchain, we anticipate an increase in the adoption of BPO in trade finance and supply chain finance.

> BPO integrates the best practices from both documentary credit (such as letters of credit) and open account.

9.4 Structured Commodity Finance

Structured commodity finance is viewed as a specialized form of supply chain finance centered on commodities like oil, agricultural commodities, energy, metals, and mining products. This finance method is prevalent in cross-border trade, especially in emerging markets where traditional bank loans are scarce. It's particularly handy when financing commodity suppliers is crucial to ensure a consistent commodity supply.

Structured commodity finance is a bespoke supply chain financing tailored to commodity trade. The structure revolves around the commercial terms set by the seller (or exporter) and the buyer (or importer). Advanced funds cater to costs such as raw materials, production, storage, and transportation, as well as investments in plants, machinery, and infrastructure (Lexis PSL, 2021). For instance, suppliers (like farmers or oil producers) might receive an advance on a portion of the anticipated purchase price or production cost. This advance enables them to commence production, be it crop cultivation or oil extraction. As collateral, supply chain entities often resort to purchase orders, export/sales contracts, accounts receivable, and collection accounts (Mizuho, 2021).

Structured commodity finance is especially indispensable for industries dealing with high-volume commodities but typically operating on slender margins (Global

Trade Funding, 2020). Depending on the production cycle of the commodity, the finance can be short term or extend to a medium-long term (e.g., 3–5 years). To remain competitive, financiers have crafted their facilities to cater to specific industry sectors and particular professional procedures (Suták, 2012).

Beyond profit-oriented financial institutions, the International Finance Corporation of the World Bank Group has also launched initiatives like the structured trade and commodity finance, Critical Commodities Finance Program, and Global Warehouse Finance Program to aid developing countries in commodity trades. By 2021, the STCF initiative had facilitated over $3 billion in global trade spanning energy and agricultural commodities (IFC, 2021).

Most commodities are deemed excellent collateral, owing to attributes (Suták, 2012) such as:

- Verifiability,
- Assessability,
- Enforceability—even in liquidation or bankruptcy scenarios,
- Value stability,
- Legal clarity,
- Marketability.

Given the ease of reselling commodities at prevailing market rates, structured commodity finance often leans less on the borrower's financial health and more on the collateral value of commodities. Such a dynamic somewhat lightens the financier's task of discerning the genuine value of the borrower's balance sheet (de Boer et al., 2015). Thus, financiers might only need the commodities in trade as collateral. Depending on the financial framework's structure, financiers might also employ hedging against future commodity prices to further cut down financial risks (Agiboo, 2018).

> Structured commodity finance may rely less on the financial status of the borrowing firm and more on the collateral value of the commodities.

Another noteworthy aspect of structured commodity finance is the potential for buyers to guarantee procurement of commodities from sellers (de Boer et al., 2015). To assist sellers in production planning, buyers might also disclose their demand forecasts. If a buyer is deemed more creditworthy and enjoys a higher credit rating, then the borrowing cost can be slashed, thereby streamlining the supply chain.

9.4.1 Variants

Structured commodity finance has various forms depending on the structured terms. In practice, similar SCF mechanisms can be found within the structured commodity finance framework. While we can't prevent financiers from using traditional SCF mechanisms for commodity transactions by treating commodities as regular collaterals, structured commodity finance remains particularly attractive in the commodity sector due to its often high capital needs and lengthy trade cycles. To avoid confusion with traditional SCF mechanisms, we will briefly introduce a few representative structured commodity finance mechanisms below.

9.4.1.1 Pre-Export Finance

Pre-export finance parallels purchase order finance, as discussed in Chapter 6.5, but within the context of the commodity supply chain. It empowers capital-constrained commodity sellers to optimize production to meet the buyer's demand (Trade Finance, 2021). Unsurprisingly, commodity firms are among the primary users of pre-export financing, especially in supporting extensive, capital-intensive production operations.

With pre-export finance, the seller (or borrower) employs export contracts/purchase orders as collateral to ensure pre-payment before export. The funds procured are then used to produce and ship the agreed goods. Given the prolonged production cycles common with many commodities, pre-export finance tends to be long term. The financier retains ownership of the commodity—whether in storage, transit, or the ground—until repayment is completed. In most cases, the seller will direct the buyer to pay the financier directly (e.g., the special purpose vehicle (SPV) as shown in Fig. 9.3).

A typical pre-export finance agreement incorporates numerous provisions centered on the commodity firm's performance and its ability to deliver the contracted goods. These provisions might pertain to the offtake contract between seller and buyer, goods rights, production standards, regulatory compliance, performance reporting, insurance coverage, debt servicing, and the designated collection accounts (Lexis PSL, 2021). These collection accounts serve to gather payments from the commodity buyers.

To assist companies in preparing their documentation, the International Loan Market Association has released two standard forms: the Single Currency Term Facility Agreement for Pre-Export Finance Transactions and the Pre-Export Finance Term Sheet (Porteous, 2018). In practice, companies can either use their internal facility documents or these standard forms to streamline a pre-export finance transaction.

9.4.1.2 Pre-Payment Finance

Pre-payment finance closely resembles pre-export finance. However, in this arrangement, it's the buyer who acts as the borrower, using the loan to prepay the seller. Consequently, the seller secures funds upfront, which might not be accessible through conventional banking channels. According to the offtake agreement binding all involved parties, the delivery of goods by the seller will offset the principal and the accompanying interest of the pre-payment. The procedural flow of pre-payment finance is depicted in Fig. 9.3.

Usually, pre-payment finance is long term, spanning between one to five years (Porteous, 2018). It has found favor among international traders tasked with sourcing goods for their end consumers. As of recent data, it's more prevalently employed in the oil sector compared to other commodity industries (Payne, 2020). Providing an advance payment to the seller empowers the buyer to negotiate a long-term commodity supply agreement. Generally, the commodity seller is contractually bound to supply the buyer under pre-payment financing.

9.4.1.3 Tolling Finance

Tolling finance entails the borrower soliciting a financier for funds to purchase raw materials. These materials are then transported to a production facility (i.e., toller) where they undergo transformation into finished products before being dispatched to the final buyer. The financier retains ownership rights over the raw materials and might also cover additional production (or tolling) fees to ensure the completion of the goods (Trade Finance Guide, 2021). The financing for these raw materials can be facilitated through both pre-export and pre-payment financing mechanisms. The final transaction is settled when the end buyer compensates for the financing.

9.4.1.4 Borrowing Base Facilities

Assets securing the *borrowing base facility* typically comprise commodity goods, sales proceeds from these goods, stored or in-transit goods, and rights to payment for the commodities. Given the continuous trading and replenishment of these assets, it's imperative that a borrowing base report is updated regularly to maintain risk control (LexisNexis, 2021).

The loan limit is usually a certain percentage of the overall value of the collateral pool. This percentage or financing ratio can vary depending on the type of collateral, reflecting the inherent risks associated with each. For instance, grains might have a financing ratio of 90–95%; other commodities could range between 60–80%; while goods that are less liquid in the secondary market may only be financed at 50–60% (Suták, 2012).

Revolving credit facilities stand out as a distinct kind of borrowing base facility, prominently utilized by major oil and commodity trading entities. These facilities function similarly to letters of credit but offer enhanced flexibility to borrowers. Borrowers can continually draw from and repay the credit as long as the borrowing remains below the set limit (Payne, 2020). These borrowers are typically substantial commodity trading houses, enabling them to draw and reimburse the financier as per their requirements, thereby enjoying greater flexibility (Global Trade Review, 2020). While revolving credit facilities lack the bank guarantee inherent to letters of credit, the presence of an SPV and the buyer's guarantee serves to offset some of the financier's financial risks.

9.4.1.5 Warehouse Financing for Commodity
Warehouse financing for commodities operates similarly to inventory financing, as discussed in Chapter 8.2. The seller deposits commodities in a warehouse, where they serve as collateral for the financier. A prominent commodity trader might act as the borrower, prepaying the commodity supplier to ensure a consistent supply to a warehouse controlled by a collateral manager.

9.4.2 Process Flow

Apart from the usual commercial agreements among supply chain entities, structured commodity financing encompasses purchase commitment contracts and financial accords. To facilitate these transactions and leverage the risk isolation attributes of a SPV, a bankruptcy-remote SPV is often established (de Boer et al., 2015). Although structured commodity finance has various forms, some, like pre-export finance and pre-payment finance, have analogous process flows. Other variants mirror the traditional SCF methodologies examined in preceding chapters and are thus omitted here for brevity. Fig. 9.3 depicts a representative process flow for pre-payment finance within the framework of structured commodity finance:

1. Stakeholders, which include the seller, buyer, bank, and the bank's SPV, finalize a financing framework agreement. Once this is in place, both the seller and buyer adhere to the agreement's directives during its tenure without the need to reapply for financing. In the absence of an SPV, the bank assumes the SPV's role throughout the process.
2. The bank channel funds to the SPV, initiating the financing phase.
3. When ordering commodities from the seller, the buyer notifies the SPV. In some instances, the buyer might relay the purchase orders to the seller via the SPV. The order schedule could also be predefined in the offtake agreement.
4. In the context of pre-payment finance, the SPV offers an advance payment to the seller before exportation. The exact timing of this pre-payment could vary based on different financing contexts and is typically outlined in the framework agreement.
5. The seller dispatches the commodities to the buyer. Often, the seller first sends the goods to a designated warehouse and then, under the SPV's guidance, distributes them to the buyer or the buyer's clients.
6. According to a predetermined payment scheme, the buyer settles the dues with the SPV for the acquired commodities.
7. In line with the schedule, the SPV reimburses the bank.

As the structured commodity finance framework is tailored to the commodities' unique features and the demands of supply chain entities, the process flow can differ based on the terms mutually agreed upon by all participants.

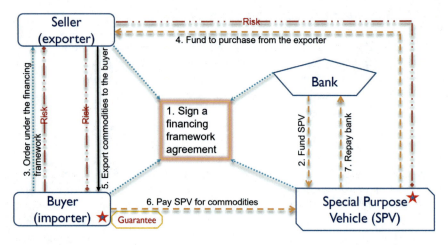

Fig. 9.3 Process flow of structured commodity finance (pre-payment)

9.4.3 Benefits

Structured commodity finance is often favored as a best practice solution for financing commodity assets subject to frequent value and ownership shifts, compared to other SCF mechanisms (Agiboo, 2018). The asset-based financing structure aptly supports the variations in commodity value and location. Moreover, it facilitates seamless ownership transitions between financiers and supply chain entities.

Benefits for the Seller

Many commodities, especially those in agriculture, demand a significant duration for production and preparation. Hence, structured commodity finance serves as a crucial bridge connecting the production phase with the buyer's payment. The intrinsic marketability of these commodities diminishes the need for other collaterals, which could be otherwise cumbersome. This scenario paves the way for sellers to attain financing more effortlessly, leading to reduced capital costs. The protection offered by the bankruptcy-remote SPV and the buyer's guarantee bring additional advantages to the seller.

However, establishing the complete financing framework and the SPV can be resource-intensive, both in terms of cost and time. As a result, structured commodity financing is typically more efficient for large-scale transactions (de Boer et al., 2015). Its efficiency wanes when commodities are less liquid in secondary markets.

Benefits for the Buyer

Structured commodity finance fortifies sellers financially, resulting in a robust supply chain marked by consistent and abundant commodity availability for buyers.

9.4 Structured Commodity Finance   271

By backing the financing, buyers can wield their influence to broker better transaction terms with both sellers (like reduced cost of goods sold) and banks (like improved payment conditions). In scenarios involving pre-payment finance, buyers can also expect sellers to commit to long term, reliable goods deliveries in exchange for upfront payments.

Benefits for the Bank

Incorporating an SPV within structured commodity finance strategies effectively shields the bank's other holdings from potential financial risks tied to the financing agreement. The inherent liquidity of the commodities under finance and the buyer's purchase commitment further alleviate the bank's financial exposure. Additionally, the bank can enjoy the perks of high transaction volumes and a lasting, reciprocal business relationship between sellers and buyers.

9.4.4 Risk Mitigation

In pre-export finance and pre-payment finance models, there exists a distinct possibility that the seller might receive an advance payment several years ahead of the actual goods delivery. Given this, it becomes paramount to rigorously assess performance risks linked to the seller. The seller should demonstrate the capability to produce and deliver the agreed-upon commodities, even amidst volatile political and financial scenarios (Global Trade Funding, 2020). To offset such uncertainties, the seller is often advised to obtain insurances like political risk insurance, ensuring unpredictable events do not impede the structured commodity finance process.

> The performance risks associated with the seller can be substantial and, as such, necessitate thorough examination.

To address inherent risks like quality degradation throughout a product's lifecycle—especially prevalent in agricultural products prone to issues like insect infestation or perishability—regular quality surveillance of the goods is essential. Additionally, swift transportation and timely sales strategies for the commodities are recommended to curtail issues like value depreciation, quality deterioration, and stock damage. Implementing such measures effectively minimizes potential losses, ensuring the commodities' optimal condition throughout their supply chain journey (Suták, 2012).

Given that the financier's ultimate repayment hinges on the market's final sales, a buyer's purchase commitment significantly diminishes market unpredictability risks. The integration of an SPV also serves to dampen the financier's risks during substantial financing losses, credited to the SPV's bankruptcy-remote feature.

However, thorough vetting of the buyer's reliability is vital to circumvent possible payment delays or default risks. A third-party evaluation of both qualitative and quantitative risks tied to the buyer is recommended, with the additional suggestion of acquiring buyer insurance when deemed essential.

Owing to the volatile nature of commodity values, financiers often mandate periodic reports detailing commodity production and sales as per the contract's stipulations. If collateral value dips beneath the specified leverage benchmark, the financier might necessitate supplementary commodities to bridge the deficit. In such instances, several solutions might be weighed, including amplifying the buyer's order volume, early loan repayment to the financier, entering new sales agreements, or tendering extra cash to enhance the debt service cover ratios (Porteous, 2018).

When managing commodity marketability risks, the financier might lean toward assigning a reduced financing rate grounded on collateral value. Given the myriad of choices available, expect substantial amendments and negotiations regarding the financing document and available alternatives.

As the financier will intermittently take on the commodity ownership as a collateral measure, efficient tracking, supervision, and handling of the commodity—whether in transit or warehoused—becomes indispensable within structured commodity finance. Establishing robust information exchange mechanisms between supply chain entities and financiers is vital for complete transparency. Employing cutting-edge information systems can be instrumental in realizing this objective.

Additionally, a financier should be proficient in discerning the nuances in international jurisdictions and laws to adeptly handle potential global disagreements. Nonetheless, the financier has the option to secure insurance against probable losses, or insist that the borrower obtain insurance, mitigating both credit and political risks (Trade Finance, 2021).

9.5 Summary

This chapter delves into a variety of non-traditional supply chain finance mechanisms. These mechanisms provide tailored solutions to complex financing challenges within the supply chain, encompassing the areas of distributor financing, bank payment obligation, and structured commodity finance. With the primary aim of enhancing liquidity and optimizing cash flow, these mechanisms are adaptable to various industry demands and can mitigate potential risks through strategic arrangements.

Key Takeaways:

1. Distributor Financing:
    - This mechanism aids distributors in purchasing goods without immediate payment, facilitating increased sales and smoother operations. By relying

on the creditworthiness of the distributor, suppliers can receive payment upfront from financiers while allowing distributors extended payment terms.
2. Bank Payment Obligation (BPO):
   - BPO is a digital and legally binding alternative to the traditional letter of credit. Leveraging electronic data matching, it provides security in international trade transactions. Both sellers and buyers benefit from enhanced transaction speed and reduced paperwork, while banks see reduced risks with BPO's automation and precise matching processes.
3. Structured Commodity Finance:
   - A tailored finance technique specifically for commodities that often have frequent fluctuations in value and ownership. This method emphasizes assets, primarily commodities, to secure financing. Key variants include pre-export finance, pre-payment finance, tolling finance, borrowing base facilities, and warehouse financing for commodity.
   - Benefits span across all involved parties:
     - Sellers receive advanced payments, ensuring a steady cash flow.
     - Buyers can ensure a consistent and ample supply of commodities.
     - Banks experience reduced financial risks, facilitated by the use of special purpose vehicles and buyer guarantees.
   - Risks, such as performance risks of the seller, quality degradation of commodities, and fluctuations in commodity values, can be mitigated through insurance, regular monitoring, and contractual stipulations.

9.6 Exercises

9.6.1 Practice Questions

1. What differentiates pre-payment finance from pre-export finance?
2. Describe the purpose of a borrowing base report in borrowing base facilities.
3. What is a unique feature of revolving credit facilities as compared to traditional letters of credit?
4. What purpose does the SPV serve in structured commodity finance?
5. List one benefit each for the seller, buyer, and bank in the context of structured commodity finance.
6. Why is it vital to examine the performance risks associated with the seller in pre-export and pre-payment finance?
7. Why is regular quality monitoring of goods especially essential for agricultural products in structured commodity finance?
8. How can the financier mitigate risks when the value of the collateral falls below the required leverage level?
9. What purpose does a framework agreement serve in structured commodity finance?

10. What is the relationship between structured commodity finance and warehouse financing for commodity?

9.6.2 Case Study

Sunrise Agro Limited and Structured Commodity Finance

Background

Sunrise Agro Limited (SAL) is a medium-sized agricultural company located in Brazil, specializing in the production of soybeans. The company has been experiencing growth in the local and international markets due to the increasing demand for soy-based products.

In recent years, SAL entered into a contract with GreenFood Corp (GFC), a significant food distributor based in Europe. The agreement entails SAL supplying large volumes of soybeans to GFC over five years.

The Problem

Despite its growth and lucrative contracts, SAL faces cash flow challenges. The time between cultivating, processing, and shipping soybeans to Europe, and the eventual payment from GFC, can extend to several months. This delay puts considerable strain on SAL's liquidity, making it challenging to invest in the next planting season, pay local suppliers, or cover its daily operational expenses.

Moreover, SAL is aware of the fluctuating nature of commodity prices and the risks associated with ensuring the quality of soybeans during storage and transit.

Options

1. **Distributor Financing**: SAL could approach a financial institution to provide distributor financing based on the strength and reliability of its contract with GFC. This would bridge the cash flow gap and ensure SAL has enough working capital.
2. **Structured Commodity Finance**: Given the nature of SAL's operations and the high value of its soybean contracts, structured commodity finance could be a good fit. By using soybeans as collateral, SAL could secure financing, ensuring liquidity during the entire cultivation and sales cycle.
3. **Bank Payment Obligation (BPO)**: SAL and GFC could agree on a BPO, where a bank ensures payment under specified conditions, providing SAL with the assurance that they will receive funds once those conditions, such as delivery of goods, are met.

What Sunrise Agro Limited Did

SAL opted for a combination of distributor financing and structured commodity finance.

1. SAL and GFC agreed to involve their respective banks. These banks arranged a bank payment obligation, ensuring SAL would receive payment promptly upon soybean delivery.
2. SAL approached its local bank, explaining its contract with GFC and the need for structured commodity finance. The bank agreed to finance SAL's operations using the soybeans as collateral. An SPV was created, making the arrangement bankruptcy-remote and protecting both SAL and the bank.

Outcome

Thanks to the financial arrangements, SAL maintained a healthy cash flow, ensuring smooth operations and honoring its contract with GFC. The quality of soybeans remained high as SAL could invest in storage facilities and expedite shipments.

Discussion Questions

1. What were the primary challenges faced by SAL?
2. How can structured commodity finance support businesses like SAL?
3. How does a BPO differ from traditional letters of credit?

References

Agiboo. (2018). *Structured commodity financing: What you need to know?* http://www.agiboo.com/structured-commodity-financing/. Accessed 1 December 2023.

de Boer, R., Steeman, M., & van Bergen, M. (2015). *Supply chain finance, its practical relevance and strategic value: The supply chain finance essential knowledge series.* Hogeschool Windesheim.

Doyle, M. (2021). *Slow adoption of SWIFT's bank payment obligation for digital trade finance.* https://www.americanexpress.com/us/foreign-exchange/articles/swift-bpo-digital-trade-finance/. Accessed 11 November 2020.

Eker, O. (2018). *Bank payment obligation—BPO.* https://www.letterofcredit.biz/index.php/2018/10/29/bank-payment-obligation-bpo/. Accessed 11 November 2020.

Wynne, G. L., & Fearn, H. (2014). The bank payment obligation: Will it replace the traditional letter of credit now, or ever? *Butterworths Journal of International Banking and Financial Law*, 102–104.

Global Trade Funding. (2020). *What is structured commodity finance?* https://tradefinanceanalytics.com/what-is-structured-commodity-finance. Accessed 13 Febuary 2021.

Global Trade Review. (2020). *Structured trade and commodity finance.* Exporta Publishing & Events Ltd. https://www.gtreview.com/structured-trade-and-commodity-finance/. Accessed 19 November 2020.

Globe SCF Forum. (2016). *Standard definitions for techniques of supply chain finance.* A joint report by BAFT, Euro Banking Association (EBA), Factors Chain International (FCI), International Chamber of Commerce (ICC), International Trade and Forfaiting Association (ITFA).

Hayes, A. (2020). *Floor planning: Definition, in auto sales.* Investopedia. https://www.investopedia.com/terms/f/floor-planning.asp. Accessed 11 January 2021.

ICC. (2013). *Uniform rules for bank payment obligations.* https://2go.iccwbo.org/uniform-rules-for-bank-payment-obligations-config+book_version-Book/. Accessed 29 November 2020.

ICC. (2018). *Bank payment obligation (BPO)* (Issue Document No. 010613).

ICC QATAR. (2018). *The ICC bank payment obligation—A digital instrument for a digital age*. https://iccqatar.org/wp-content/uploads/2018/05/ICCQATARBPO.pdf. Accessed 13 October 2020.

IFC. (2021). *Structured trade commodity finance*. International Finance Corporation. https://www.ifc.org/en/what-we-do/sector-expertise/financial-institutions/global-trade/structured-trade-commodity-finance. Accessed 13 January 2024.

Lexis PSL. (2021). *Pre-export finance and prepayment finance—Overview*. Lexisnexis.Com. https://www.lexisnexis.com/uk/lexispsl/bankingandfinance/document/391289/5617-JTC1-F185-X3X6-00000-00/. Accessed 5 January 2022.

LexisNexis. (2021). *Trade finance: Borrowing base facilities and warehouse financing—Overview*. https://www.lexisnexis.com/uk/lexispsl/bankingandfinance/document/391289/5F9Y-37H1-F185-X2WH-00000-00/. Accessed 6 March 2022.

Mizuho. (2021). *Structured trade finance-Mizuho Bank 2021*. https://www.mizuhogroup.com/bank/what-we-do/structured_finance/. Accessed 16 March 2022.

Morton, K. (2019). *Pulling the plug on TSU and the wiring of trade finance: What next for BPO?* https://www.txfnews.com/articles/6733. Accessed January 13, 2024.

Payne, J. (2020). *Explainer how commodity trade finance works*. Reuters. https://www.reuters.com/article/us-trade-financing-banks-explainer/explainer-how-commodity-trade-finance-works-idUSKCN2582EX. Accessed 6 May 2022.

Porteous, J. (2018). *Pre-export finance and prepayment finance—Overview*. Stevens & Bolton LLP. https://www.stevens-bolton.com/site/insights/articles/preexport-finance-and-prepayment-finance-overview. Accessed 9 June 2024.

Raunek. (2023). *Bill of lading in shipping: Importance, purpose, and types*. https://www.marineinsight.com/maritime-law/what-is-bill-of-lading-in-shipping/. Accessed 13 January 2024.

Suták, P. (2012). Structured commodity finance. *Applied Studies in Agribusiness and Commerce*, 6(5), 77–83. https://doi.org/10.19041/apstract/2012/5/13. Accessed 16 August 2022.

SWIFT. (2016). *Bank payment obligation—A new payment method* (Issue July). https://www.swift.com/sites/default/files/documents/swift_corporates_presentations_bankpaymentobligation.pdf. Accessed 3 October 2022.

Trade Finance. (2021). *What is pre-export finance*. Euromoney Institutional Investor PLC. https://tradefinanceanalytics.com/what-is-pre-export-finance. Accessed 19 July 2022.

Trade Finance Guide. (2021). *Structured funded trade finance*. Trade Finance Global. https://issuu.com/tradefinanceglobal/docs/trade_finance_guide_final/s/10947009. Accessed 22 March 2022.

UniCredit. (2016). *Bank payment obligation (BPO)* (Issue February). https://www.swift.com. Accessed 23 January 2022.

Wragg, E. (2019). *Exclusive: Swift calls time on TSU*. https://www.gtreview.com/news/global/exclusive-swift-calls-time-on-tsu/. Accessed 10 October 2022.

Part III
Supply Chain Finance Risk Analytics

"Let us never negotiate out of fear. But let us never fear to negotiate."
  John F. Kennedy

Risk Taxonomy and Assessment 10

> **Learning Objectives:**
>
> 1. Understand the core components and importance of a conceptual supply chain finance (SCF) risk management system in financial decision-making.
> 2. Distinguish between different categories of risks using the SCF risk taxonomy framework.
> 3. Evaluate potential risks using qualitative risk assessment methodologies, considering both internal and external factors.
> 4. Apply quantitative risk assessment techniques, such as the coefficient of variation and Altman's Z-Score, to determine the financial stability and risk of an entity.

10.1 Introduction

Change is a constant factor in the universe, leading to an inevitable presence of uncertainty and risks in social events, including supply chain finance (SCF). While the definition of risk has been broadened to include the "effect of uncertainty on objectives" (Wikipedia, 2021), negative and undesirable risks remain the primary concern for individuals. Risks are generally associated with unwanted events that have the potential to occur.

> *Given the constant changes in the universe, uncertainty is a constant factor in all social events.*

Fig. 10.1 Firms' evaluation of the importance of supply chain risk management skillsets (*Source* Adapted from Zhao & Yang, 2021)

In previous discussions, we have addressed risk mitigation in SCF schemes, but we have yet to provide a comprehensive qualitative and quantitative analysis framework. To effectively manage risk in supply chain finance, it is necessary to identify, track, mitigate, manage, and resolve potential problems for all involved parties. A 2021 survey conducted by Shanghai Jiaotong University and the Dun & Bradstreet Corporation revealed that firms highly value their ability to identify, monitor, control, and manage various supply chain risks, including those related to supply chain finance (Zhao & Yang, 2021) (refer to Fig. 10.1).

In the following sections, we will first introduce a conceptual framework for supply chain risk management and then delve into discussing the SCF risk taxonomy and various risk measurement approaches.

10.2 A Conceptual SCF Risk Management System

Supply chain finance involves both supply chain events and financing activities, thus SCF risks encompass both financial and supply chain risks, which overlap in some areas. SCF risks are considered unique financial risks that are utilized in the realm of supply chain management, and their management requires a holistic approach that incorporates both financial and supply chain risk elements. Given the significant impact of supply chain risks, it is crucial to integrate both financial and supply chain risks into the SCF risk management system.

The risks in supply chain finance are on the rise; however only 5% of B2B trading is credit insured, leaving the majority of global transactions exposed to risk (Nordea, 2018). Unlike traditional bank financing, SCF involves the shift of financing risk to another party, meaning that traditional risk management methods focused solely on the borrowing firm are no longer sufficient to address the concerns of lending financial institutions.

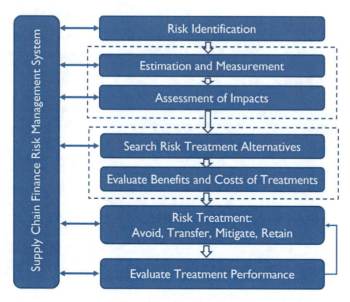

Fig. 10.2 Supply chain finance risk management system

A common approach for SCF risk management begins with identifying risks, estimating and measuring them, and assessing their potential impact, as shown in Fig. 10.2. Next, the business will search for available risk treatments and select the most suitable option based on the risk assessment. The firm can choose to avoid, transfer, mitigate, or retain the risks. After implementing the risk treatment, the company can evaluate its performance and decide whether to renegotiate with business partners or seek alternative risk treatments.

> *A firm can choose to avoid, transfer, mitigate, or retain the risks.*

10.3 Supply Chain Finance Risk Taxonomy

We begin by examining the typical risk types categorized in the finance industry, but then reclassify them specifically for the context of supply chain finance. Figure 10.3 illustrates a risk typology that has been adapted for SCF risks.

Using a single risk measure is not recommended for firms as it can lead to the industry focusing solely on one type of risk, neglecting others, and increasing market volatility. Employing a range of risk measurement methods can help firms diversify their risk management strategies and lead to unexpected risk pooling effects.

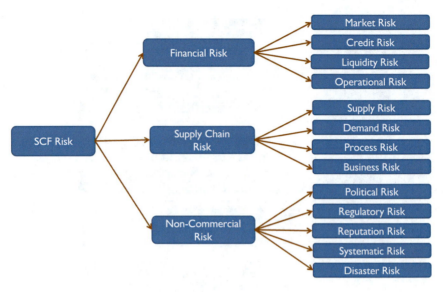

Fig. 10.3 Supply chain finance risk topology

10.3.1 Financial Risk

The finance literature has extensively discussed and explained financial risks. While different sources may draw varying conclusions, the following risk categories have been thoroughly studied.

10.3.1.1 Market Risk

Market risk in its broadest sense, refers to the potential hazards arising from fluctuations within the marketplace. For instance, in the consumer goods sector, traditional retail stores may face increased market risk due to the growing preference among consumers for online shopping (Maverick, 2019). Companies can also encounter unexpected shifts in market prices as a result of competitive forces and various other factors. To better understand and manage market risk, it is helpful to break it down into distinct components, which may be linked to the overall market or even specific transactions, and could lead to declines in value (Crouhy et al., 2013, Chapter 1).

In the financial market, risks often stem from fluctuations in prices and rates. Typically, these risks are classified into four main categories: equity price risk, interest rate risk, foreign exchange risk, and commodity price risk. Depending on the nature of the transaction and the financing structure employed, these four risk types can play a significant role in supply chain finance.

1. *Equity Price Risk*: Equity or stock prices in the market are often volatile and difficult to predict. When equity serves as collateral for a loan, a significant

drop in its value can negatively impact the lending financial institution's bottom line.
2. **Interest Rate Risk**: Interest rate risk is a major concern for nearly all financing arrangements, as fluctuations in interest rates can affect both borrowers and lenders.
3. **Foreign Exchange Risk**: This risk is particularly pronounced in global supply chain transactions, especially when there is a lengthy lead time involved (e.g., payment delays spanning months following a sea shipment).
4. **Commodity Price Risk**: In inventory financing, commodity price risk can be crucial if the commodity in question is part of the collateral and the supply chain transaction. Price fluctuations can affect the overall value of the collateral, posing risks for both parties involved.

10.3.1.2 Credit Risk

Credit risk originates from a borrower's inability to meet their contractual obligations to a financial institution, potentially leading to delayed, missed, or defaulted payments. Depending on the severity of the consequences, credit risk can be broken down into settlement risk, downgrade risk, default risk, and bankruptcy risk.

1. **Settlement Risk**: Settlement risk occurs when a firm is unable to settle a trade according to the contract terms by the specified deadline. This risk may be linked to the firm's default risk but can also arise from other factors, even if all involved parties act in good faith. Settlement risk can be mitigated by employing a clearinghouse, establishing a special purpose vehicle (SPV), or opting for payment upon delivery.
2. **Downgrade Risk**: A firm's financing capabilities can be significantly impaired if its credit rating is downgraded.
3. **Default Risk**: Default risk arises when a firm fails to make the required payments on schedule. This risk is typically higher when a firm's cash position is weaker. Payment defaults can lead to credit rating downgrades.
4. **Bankruptcy Risk**: Also known as insolvency risk, bankruptcy risk refers to the possibility that a firm cannot meet its debt obligations and must undergo a bankruptcy process.

It is important to emphasize the distinction between default and bankruptcy. A default occurs when a firm fails to make a payment on interest and/or principal. In contrast, bankruptcy entails the liquidation of a firm's assets, with the proceeds from the asset sale being distributed to claim holders according to a predefined priority rule (Crouhy et al., 2013).

When credit risk materializes, borrowers may lose a portion or the entirety of their assets, making it impossible to fully recover the asset's value and subsequently hindering their ability to fulfill obligations. As a result, managing credit risk has become a crucial aspect of risk management within financial institutions, which often rely on credit ratings from agencies such as Standard & Poor's (S&P),

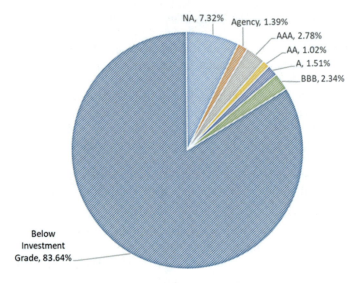

Fig. 10.4 Credit rating distribution history, 2020 Q2

Moody's, or Fitch. Borrowers with lower credit ratings must pay higher interest rates, resulting in increased risk premiums for the lending institutions.

It is important to note that, as of the second quarter of 2020, a mere 2.78% of businesses were rated AAA, 1.02% AA, and 1.51% A, while the majority (over 80%) of businesses held credit ratings below the investment grade (BBB), as illustrated in Fig. 10.4 (NCUA, 2021).

10.3.1.3 Liquidity Risk

Liquidity risk pertains to a company's inability to carry out transactions due to insufficient liquidity. There are two primary forms of liquidity risk: funding liquidity risk and trading liquidity risk (also known as asset liquidity risk).

1. **Funding Liquidity Risk**: Funding liquidity risk arises when a company is unable to raise the necessary cash to fulfill its debt obligations. To mitigate this risk, a company should maintain a robust cash balance, cash equivalents, or readily accessible credit lines for cash withdrawals.
2. **Trading Liquidity Risk**: Trading liquidity risk occurs when a company is unable to execute transactions due to a lack of willing buyers or sellers. The inability to complete transactions can exacerbate funding liquidity risk if the cash position is jeopardized by insufficient buyers.

10.3.1.4 Operational Risk

Operational risk stems from operational failures that can be attributed to management shortcomings, technological breakdowns, fraudulent activities, or human errors. Common operational risks encompass fraud risk, human factor risk, technology risk, and model risk.

1. ***Fraud Risk***: Fraud risk arises when employees misrepresent information or deliberately conceal potential risks in transactions, leading to fraudulent activities.
2. ***Human Factor Risk***: Human factor risk pertains to the potential for errors, misconduct, or unethical behavior by individuals within an organization that can lead to financial losses or damage to the company's reputation.
3. ***Technology Risk***: As companies increasingly depend on technologies like cloud computing and software for their operations, technology-related incidents have become more frequent in day-to-day activities.
4. ***Model Risk***: Model risk stems from inaccuracies in financial and risk management modeling.

10.3.2 Supply Chain Risk

Supply chain risks are crucial in SCF mechanisms that are applied to facilitate supply chain transactions. The success of a transaction often depends on the supplier's ability to deliver goods and the buyer's capacity to sell those goods and make timely payments to the supplier and/or the lending financial institution. Consequently, all risks within the supply chain influence the ultimate SCF decisions. Common risks include supply risk (originating from upstream), demand risk (stemming from downstream), process risk (associated with internal operations), and business risk (related to business relationships).

10.3.2.1 Supply Risk

Supply risk, also known as sourcing risk or supply disruption risk, encompasses various types of risks related to the procurement of goods or services. Typical supply risks include supplier risk, supply quality risk, supply quantity risk, supply price risk, miscommunication risk, and supply delivery risk.

1. ***Supplier Risk***: The supplier relationship may deteriorate to the point where new or additional suppliers must be found. The risk of a supplier's reputation impacting the buyer's product brand reputation also exists. Moreover, a supplier may discontinue a product line or go out of business.
2. ***Sourcing and Procurement Risk***: Reliance on a limited number of suppliers or ineffective procurement practices can expose the supply chain to disruptions, price fluctuations, and reduced bargaining power.
3. ***Supply Quality Risk***: Supplies may be damaged upon arrival or even before shipment. Components or parts may appear to be in good condition but fail to meet required standards or specifications.
4. ***Supply Quantity/Shortage Risk***: Shortages of raw materials (e.g., high-demand materials such as adiponitrile used in car parts and lithium used in electric cars), components, and parts have often occurred, as seen during the COVID-19 pandemic.

5. **Supply Price Risk**: Prices of components and parts can fluctuate significantly due to low supply, high demand, sudden changes in costs, or tariffs.
6. **Miscommunication Risk**: Miscommunication with suppliers can lead to various issues, such as unplaced orders, incorrect order quantities, or products with wrong specifications.
7. **Supply Delivery Risk**: Delivery may be delayed, items may be lost, or components may be damaged during transit from the supplier to the buyer, especially in long-distance shipments.

10.3.2.2 Demand Risk

Demand is often volatile, and *demand risk* arises when actual demand falls short of expectations, which may result from inaccurate demand forecasting or misunderstandings of consumer behavior. Common types of demand risks include:

1. **Demand Volatility Risk**: Fluctuations in customer demand, often driven by seasonality, economic cycles, or sudden market changes, can create challenges in accurately forecasting demand and managing inventory levels.
2. **Forecasting Risk**: Since no forecast is perfect, forecasting errors are expected. However, some forecasting models can yield better accuracy, significantly assisting buyers in planning and ordering. Inaccurate predictions can result in actual demand being too high or too low.
3. **Consumer Preference Risk**: Forecasting accuracy may be within an acceptable range based on historical data. However, rapid shifts in consumer preferences due to new fashion trends or disruptive shopping channels can cause demand to deviate significantly from expectations.
4. **Product Lifecycle Change Risk**: Changes in product life cycles, such as shorter life spans or the introduction of new products, can create uncertainties in demand, making it challenging to plan and manage the supply chain effectively.
5. **Receivable Risk**: The business might be running well, and all goods sold, but customers may be unable to pay as scheduled, leading to delays in accounts receivable.
6. **Price Sensitivity Risk**: Changes in the pricing of products or services, either due to competition or market conditions, can impact demand, affecting the profitability and efficiency of the supply chain.
7. **Regulatory and Legal Change Risk**: Changes in regulations, policies, or legal requirements can impact demand by affecting product specifications, production processes, or market access.

10.3.2.3 Process Risk

Process risks, also known as operational risks, pertain to the internal operations of the focal firm involved in supply chain finance. These risks differ from the operational risks in Chapter 10.3.1 Financial Risk, which focus on other operational risks in financing. Smooth internal operations are crucial for a firm to deliver satisfactory products to its end consumers.

10.3 Supply Chain Finance Risk Taxonomy

1. ***Design/Innovation Risk***: An incorrect design may necessitate adjustments to the entire production plan, causing shortages in specific components or parts.
2. ***Planning Risk***: This risk occurs when a firm lacks a proper procedure or a well-designed plan to execute production, which could be due to inaccurate demand forecasting or issues in ordering from suppliers.
3. ***Information, Cybersecurity, and Coordination Risk***: This risk can arise from information systems failure, human errors, or other internal communication issues. In Allianz's annual Risk Barometer survey in 2020, cybersecurity risk was ranked as the most critical risk to businesses for the first time (Nordea, 2020).
4. ***Production/Manufacturing Risk***: Disruptions to personnel, management, unplanned downtime, equipment malfunctions, component flaws, or inefficiencies in the manufacturing process can affect production schedules and overall supply chain performance.
5. ***Capacity Risk***: A firm may lack sufficient capacity to produce goods in line with demand.
6. ***Inventory Risk***: Overstocking or understocking inventory can lead to higher carrying costs, stockouts, or obsolescence, which can negatively impact the efficiency and profitability of the supply chain. Goods can be damaged or lost during storage, transit within the firm's facilities, or delivery to end consumers.[1]
7. ***Transportation and Logistics Risk***: Delays or disruptions in transportation, customs clearance, or warehousing can impact the timely and cost-effective delivery of goods, affecting the overall efficiency of the supply chain.
8. ***Service Risk***: Inadequate after-sales service may fail to address product warranties, returns, and other service inquiries properly.
9. ***Quality Control Risk***: Insufficient quality control processes can lead to defective products or inconsistent quality levels, resulting in customer dissatisfaction, returns, or recalls.
10. ***Labor Risk***: Labor shortages, strikes, or high employee turnover can disrupt operations and negatively impact the supply chain's performance.
11. ***Social, Environmental, and Sustainability Risk***: Firms must adapt to new social and environmental regulations or changes. Banks and investors increasingly scrutinize a firm's sustainability and its efforts to fulfill its social and environmental responsibilities. Firms may face fines or regulations for causing negative impacts on water, air, and soil, leading to potential operational disruptions.

---

[1] According to Trade Finance Global, approximately 80% of major global goods transportation occurs by sea (see https://issuu.com/tradefinanceglobal). Consequently, transit risks can arise from various factors, such as cargo theft, piracy, fire, collisions, leakage, spoilage, storms, and other transportation issues. One notable example is the 2021 Suez Canal Crisis, in which the 400-meter-long Ever Given container ship became stranded, blocking the Suez Canal and causing significant disruptions to global shipping.

10.3.2.4 Business Risk
Business risk refers to the potential for contract breaches or failures to fulfill contractual obligations due to mismanagement or disagreements between business partners.

1. *Legal Risk*: Legal risk arises when one business partner changes their stance on the contract, fails to meet contractual obligations in a timely manner, or disputes occur due to differing interpretations of contractual terms. Legal risk can also stem from violations of intellectual property protection or other civil laws.
2. *Strategic Risk*: A firm may make a strategic mistake by investing heavily in the wrong business, resulting in substantial losses that hinder the firm's ability to fulfill specific contractual obligations.
3. *Competition Risk*: The competitive landscape is constantly evolving, and some firms might become complacent, failing to adapt to new customer preferences or make necessary adjustments to product design. This lack of adaptability can result in a loss of competitive advantage to rival businesses.
4. *Contractual Risk*: Poorly drafted or ambiguous contracts can lead to disputes that disrupt the smooth functioning of the supply chain and impact the ability of parties to fulfill their contractual obligations. It is essential to have clear and well-defined contracts to minimize the potential for misunderstandings and disagreements.

10.3.3 Non-Commercial Risk

While financial risk reflects the risks related to financing operations and supply chain risk represents the risks embedded in supply chain firms and relationships, there are risks that do not directly stem from commercial practices of financial institutions and supply chain firms but from the nature and surrounding environments. These non-commercial risks are typically beyond the control of the involved supply chain firms.

10.3.3.1 Political Risk
Economic globalization generates significant business opportunities for supply chain firms, but it also unavoidably creates conflicts among countries and different economies. *Political risk* materializes when governments intervene in the market for political reasons. For instance, the tariff war between the U.S. and China is just one of many political risks affecting numerous businesses in these two countries and beyond. Geopolitical risks have unexpectedly surged since 2020 due to the

rivalry between the U.S., China, Russia, and the EU and will likely remain elevated for some time. To protect domestic businesses, countries often erect barriers for foreign companies and enforce import/export quotas on a range of goods and services. Nations might even prohibit certain "illegal" or "harmful" goods in the name of national security.

10.3.3.2 Regulatory Risk
Regulatory risk, also known as compliance risk, arises when companies must adapt to new or changing regulations and laws that might be introduced with little notice. For example, social media websites had to cope with regulations related to data privacy and account security policies during the U.S. Election in 2020. Firms must also comply with regulations enforced by local, state, federal, and international agencies, such as the Environmental Protection Agency.

10.3.3.3 Reputation Risk
Reputation risk takes various forms. The first is associated with individual firms' scandals, such as the Enron accounting scandal, which could be preventable to some extent through the firm's efforts. Due to the threat of reputation risk, it is in a firm's interest to demonstrate its social, ethical, and environmental responsibility to the public. The second type of reputation risk relates to the reputation of an entire industry. For example, the reputation of the entire banking industry suffered during the 2007–2009 Financial Crisis after the collapse of Lehman Brothers (Crouhy et al., 2013). The third reputation risk stems from the rapid development of social media. A firm could easily suffer from reputation risk due to unfounded rumors.

10.3.3.4 Systematic Risk
Systematic risk is tied to the chain reaction or domino effect of one firm's failure. The case of Lehman Brothers is also considered a systematic risk. Panic selling in the stock market is another example of systematic risk posed to a firm's equity value. Typically, the failure of a larger firm can cause a greater systematic risk to the system. To minimize the impact of systematic risks, the Dodd-Frank Act in the U.S. established the Financial Stability Oversight Council to identify systemic risks and recommend corresponding regulations (Crouhy et al., 2013).

10.3.3.5 Disaster Risk
Although occurrences are generally rare, natural and man-made catastrophes, such as terrorism and earthquakes, can cause widespread negative impacts on many businesses. Climate change, including extreme weather events, also poses unwanted risks to supply chain operations.

The above discussion on SCF risk typology is summarized in Fig. 10.5.

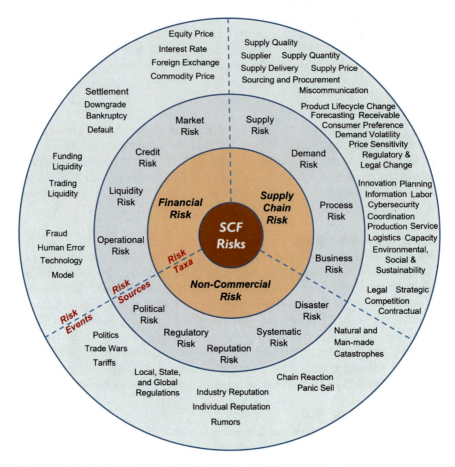

Fig. 10.5 Supply chain finance risk typology, sources, and events

10.4 Qualitative Risk Assessment

Risk assessment is a fundamental step in effectively managing risks. It is essential to emphasize the importance of using multiple risk measurement tools, as no single tool can cover all aspects of every risk. Employing a diverse range of risk measures helps to partially address specific limitations of certain approaches, considering that each method has its unique strengths and weaknesses.

There are two primary methodologies: qualitative analysis and quantitative analysis. *Qualitative analysis* is particularly useful when there is little or no historical data available regarding risk events. It also offers an intuitive means of evaluating risk probability and severity when prioritizing risks. Qualitative analysis can be applied to various risk assessments. When data is available, *quantitative analysis* can deliver more accurate risk estimations and enhance our understanding of

10.4.1 Risk Severity Matrix

Risk severity matrix is one qualitative analysis approach that is subjective but often provides a clear depiction of risk likelihood and severity. As risk severity matrix generally results in numerical levels of risk severity, it is sometimes referred to as a semi-quantitative analysis. As illustrated in Fig. 10.6, a typical risk severity matrix comprises two dimensions: risk probability (i.e., frequency) and risk impact. While these two dimensions may be expressed using different terms and scales in the literature, it is easy to comprehend that higher risk probability and impact levels indicate more significant risks.

In Fig. 10.6, the risk probability features five distinct levels: (1) Unlikely, (2) Seldom, (3) Occasional, (4) Likely, and (5) Frequent. The risk impact also comprises five categories: (1) Negligible, (2) Minor, (3) Moderate, (4) Hazardous, and (5) Catastrophic. Although the numeric values are approximate, we can use this matrix to estimate risk severity as follows:

$$\text{Risk Severity} = \text{Risk Probability} \times \text{Risk Impact}$$

Using this equation, we can partially quantify the risk severity based on specific values of risk probability and risk impact. For instance, if the risk probability is 3 (Occasional) and the risk impact is 4 (Hazardous), the value of risk severity can be calculated as $3 \times 4 = 12$. This value can then be referenced in Fig. 10.6.

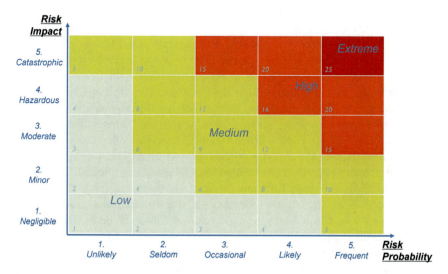

Fig. 10.6 Risk severity matrix

Based on the risk severity scores and a specific company's risk tolerance, we can further categorize the risk severity into the following four groups, as highlighted in Fig. 10.6:

Risk Severity Segment	Low Risk	Medium Risk	High Risk	Extreme Risk
Risk severity score	1–4	5–14	15–24	25

Although these four-group categories are commonly adopted (Templar et al., 2016), the classification also depends on a given firm's risk tolerance. A more risk-averse firm might define 1–3 as low risk and 4–7 as medium risk, as illustrated below:

Risk Severity Segment	Low Risk	Medium Risk	High Risk	Extreme Risk
Risk severity score	1–3	4–7	8–14	15–25

Nonetheless, once a firm establishes its risk tolerance level, the risk severity levels should remain relatively stable to ensure consistent communication about risk severity to stakeholders.

10.4.2 5 Cs of Credit Risk Analysis

The *5 Cs of credit* is a widely used framework that lenders use to evaluate a borrower's creditworthiness. This framework provides a standardized method of assessing a borrower's financial position and credit risk. The 5 Cs include Character, Capacity, Capital, Collateral, and Conditions, and each of these factors plays a critical role in determining the borrower's creditworthiness. We illustrate the 5 Cs in Fig. 10.7 and will explain them further below.

1. ***Character***: This refers to the borrower's reputation and history of meeting financial obligations. Lenders look at factors such as credit history, employment history, and references to assess the borrower's character. Regarding credit history, credit reports from the three major credit bureaus, Equifax, Experian, and TransUnion, have been widely used to evaluate a borrower's creditworthiness. Scoring systems such as the FICO Score and the VantageScore have been used to predict the likelihood that a borrower will repay their loan. However, for a startup firm without credit history, the character of the founder and other information such as references may play a critical role for them to borrow from any financial institution.
2. ***Capacity***: This refers to the borrower's ability to repay the loan. Lenders evaluate the borrower's income, expenses, and debt-to-income (DTI) ratio to assess their capacity to repay the loan. The DTI ratio is calculated by dividing a borrower's total monthly debt payment by the borrower's total monthly income. Even though lenders vary, many lenders might not approve a new loan if the borrower's DTI is too high. For example, Consumer Financial

10.4 Qualitative Risk Assessment

Fig. 10.7 Illustration of 5 Cs of credit risk analysis

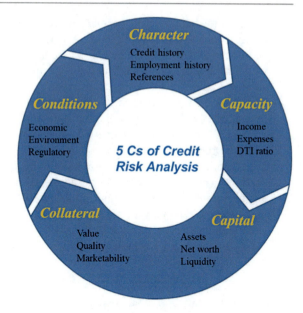

Protection Bureau recommends not to provide a new mortgage to a borrower with a DTI higher than 43% (Segal, 2023).

3. **Capital**: This refers to the borrower's assets and net worth. Lenders evaluate the borrower's financial resources to determine whether they have sufficient capital to repay the loan. Lenders will evaluate a borrower's assets, which include things like real estate, vehicles, investments, and cash reserves. Net worth is another important consideration when evaluating a borrower's capital. Net worth represents the difference between a borrower's total assets and their total liabilities. A borrower with a higher net worth is generally seen as a lower credit risk, as they have more resources to draw on in case of financial difficulties. Finally, lenders will also consider the borrower's liquidity when evaluating their capital. Liquidity refers to the borrower's ability to convert assets into cash quickly, which can be important in the event of a financial emergency. Lenders may look at factors such as the borrower's cash reserves, credit lines, or other sources of liquidity to assess their ability to contribute to the loan if necessary.

4. **Collateral**: This refers to assets that the borrower pledges as security for the loan. Lenders evaluate the value and quality of the collateral to determine its ability to cover the loan in case of default. Collateral can take many forms, including real estate, vehicles, equipment, inventory, or accounts receivable. When evaluating collateral, lenders will consider factors such as the value, quality, and liquidity of the assets being pledged. Lenders prefer collateral that is easily marketable, meaning that it can be sold quickly and at a fair price in the event of default. Collateral that is difficult to sell or that has a limited market may be less desirable to lenders. In general, the amount

of collateral required will depend on the amount of the loan and the perceived credit risk of the borrower. A borrower with a strong credit history and financial position may be able to secure a loan with minimal collateral, while a borrower with a higher credit risk may be required to provide more collateral to secure the loan.
5. **Conditions**: This refers to factors outside of the borrower's control that may impact their ability to repay the loan, such as economic conditions, industry trends, or regulatory changes. Lenders consider the overall conditions of the borrower's business or financial situation to assess their creditworthiness. Lenders use conditions to assess the overall risk of the loan and the borrower's ability to repay it. For example, if economic conditions are weak and unemployment rates are high, lenders may view the borrower as a higher credit risk, as they may be more likely to experience financial difficulties in such an environment. Similarly, if there are regulatory or legal challenges facing the borrower's industry, lenders may view the borrower as a higher credit risk due to potential compliance costs or legal liabilities.

The 5 Cs of credit is an important framework for lenders because it provides a standardized method for evaluating a borrower's creditworthiness. By assessing the borrower across these five key areas, lenders can gain a more holistic understanding of the borrower's financial position and assess their overall credit risk. This, in turn, can help lenders make more informed decisions about whether to approve a loan, and at what interest rate and terms.

The 5 Cs of credit are also important for borrowers because they provide a clear set of criteria that they can use to assess their own creditworthiness and identify areas where they may need to improve. By understanding how lenders evaluate credit risk, borrowers can take steps to improve their credit score, build their net worth, or improve their cash flow, all of which can increase their chances of being approved for credit on favorable terms.

Finally, the 5 Cs of credit are important for the broader economy because they help ensure that credit is allocated efficiently and effectively. By using a standardized method for evaluating creditworthiness, lenders can more accurately assess the risk associated with different borrowers, which can help prevent over-investment in risky ventures or markets. This can ultimately contribute to greater financial stability and sustainable economic growth.

10.5 Quantitative Risk Assessment

Firms, including financial institutions, are often risk averse. In a survey conducted by McKinsey & Company involving 1500 executives from 90 countries in 2012, the executives displayed high levels of risk aversion, irrespective of their investment size—even when the projected value of their proposed projects was overwhelmingly positive (Yang et al., 2018). As the Wall Street Journal reported, companies were holding onto more cash because management's risk aversion remained above average, stemming from the impact of bankruptcies in previous years (Zuckerman, 2005). Economists suggested that an increase in risk aversion and the economic reversal were happening precisely when business investment spending had been much lower than anticipated (Lp & Whitehouse, 2007).

To mitigate financing risks, banks exhibit risk aversion and typically implement loan limits to keep the probability of the principal loss ratio below a certain level, similar to the Value-at-Risk (VaR) approach (Yang et al., 2018). Banks' risk control is driven not only by self-protection but also by government regulations, such as Basel Accords I, II, and III, which are supported by the Federal Reserve Board (Wang & Cai, 2023). To enforce risk control mechanisms, banks also use loan recovery rates and individual loan potential losses to evaluate the performance of loan officers.

To manage risk severity based on their risk tolerance levels, firms employ *quantitative risk analysis* to generate probabilistic estimates of risks and the associated costs of addressing them. Quantitative analysis typically necessitates high-quality data and specialized modeling expertise to assess and prioritize a range of risks. Various methodologies are used for measuring and controlling risk, including descriptive probability distribution, standard deviation, coefficient of variation, and different VaR approaches. We discuss these methodologies sequentially as follows.

10.5.1 Probability Distribution

In qualitative risk assessment, we categorize risk probability into five different levels: (1) Unlikely, (2) Seldom, (3) Occasional, (4) Likely, and (5) Frequent. However, these estimates are approximate. To enable more accurate decision-making, it is desirable to have more comprehensive information to further quantify the precise likelihood of these different risk levels. Fortunately, in the era of big data, we can collect more data to facilitate this task.

Probability distribution is one of the most fundamental statistical tools used to measure the precise likelihood of events in decimal fractions from 0 to 1, or in percentages from 0 to 100%, as shown in Table 10.1. Table 10.1 provides a more accurate estimation of the different risk impacts described in the previous qualitative risk assessment. This table is hypothetically based on a project valued at $1 million. The average loss percentage is derived from the average percentage of the lower and upper bounds of each risk impact category. The loss value for each category is then calculated by multiplying $1 million by the percentage of the risk category, and the net value is determined by subtracting the corresponding loss value from the total value.

Using the probability distribution, we can estimate the expected value (EV) from this project. This is calculated by multiplying the net value of each risk category by the probability of each risk category, as follows:

$$\text{EV} = \sum_{i=1}^{n} x_i \times p_i \qquad (10.1)$$

where x_i = value of event i and p_i = probability of event i.

Applying data of Table 10.1 into Eq. (10.1), we have

$$\text{EV} = 995K \times 0.829 + \ldots + 150K \times 0.001 = \$969,505$$

From a risk prevention perspective, we can calculate the expected loss (EL) value as follows:

$$\text{EL} = \sum_{i=1}^{n} L_i \times p_i \qquad (10.2)$$

where L_i = loss of event i and p_i = probability of event i.

Similarly, applying data of Table 10.1 into Eq. (10.1) gives us:

$$\text{EL} = 5K \times 0.829 + \ldots + 850K \times 0.001 = \$30,495$$

10.5 Quantitative Risk Assessment

Table 10.1 Probability distribution of different risk impacts (of a $1M project)

Risk Impact	1. Negligible (Lose <1%)	2. Minor (1%–10%)	3. Moderate (10%–30%)	4. Hazardous (30%–70%)	5. Catastrophic (>70%)
Average Loss Percentage	0.50	5.5	20	50	85
Loss Value	$5000	$55,000	$200,000	$500,000	$850,000
Net Value	$995,000	$945,000	$800,000	$500,000	$150,000
Probability (%)	82.90	10	5	2	0.10

Both expected value and expected loss can be used in decision-making, such as the selection of a better SCF mechanism as discussed in the following case.

Case Study

Which SCF Mechanism is More Profitable?

When making supply chain financing decisions, firms often have to choose from multiple SCF mechanisms. In this hypothetical example, we compare three simplified versions of SCF mechanisms: factoring, reverse factoring, and traditional bank financing, respectively.

Let's assume that a capital-constrained seller needs to borrow from external financiers to produce a product that a buyer wants to purchase. To showcase the use of probability distribution in decision-making, let's assume that the seller finances its entire production cost through an external financial institution. Due to its low credit rating, the seller would have to pay an 18% interest rate to a bank. However, the interest rate from a factor via factoring would be lower, at 12%. If the buyer guarantees the transaction, the interest rate would be even lower at 3% (based on the buyer's credit rating) in reverse factoring. We can estimate the unit selling price of the product at $1300 and the unit production cost at $500. Additionally, we can assume that if the buyer orders more products than the final demand during the selling season, the unit salvage value of each overstocked product is $400. Let's assume that all items will be sold on day 90.

Selling Price	Production Cost	Salvage Price	Factoring Interest Rate	Buyer's Capital Cost	Bank Interest Rate	Demand Realized on Day
$1300	$500	$400	12%	3%	18%	90

In this supply chain transaction, the buyer plans to purchase 10,000 units of the same product at $900/unit (i.e., the wholesale price). The seller is willing to offer a 1% discount for the buyer's assistance in reverse factoring and a 90-day credit term, while typically allowing only a 30-day credit term in factoring and bank financing. The buyer incurs an interest cost for paying for the items before demand realization, while the seller incurs a financing cost for borrowing capital to produce all necessary products.

The demand for the product is uncertain. Based on historical data, firms estimate that there is a 30% chance that the demand will be high at 12,000 units, a 50% chance that the demand will be average at 10,000 units, and a 20% chance that the demand will be low at 8000 units. The related information and computation results are summarized in Table 10.2.

10.5 Quantitative Risk Assessment

Table 10.2 Comparison of SCF mechanisms with demand probability distribution

		Factoring	Reverse Factoring	Bank Financing	Probability
	Order quantity	10,000	10,000	10,000	
	Wholesale price	900	891	900	
	Payment delay term (days)	30	90	30	
Demand & Distribution	High demand	12,000	12,000	12,000	30%
	Middle demand	10,000	10,000	10,000	50%
	Low demand	8000	8000	8000	20%
Buyer's Profit Calculation	Interest rate (%)	3	3	3	
	Revenue	$12,480,000	$12,480,000	$12,480,000	
	Salvage value	$160,000	$160,000	$160,000	
	Purchase cost	$9,000,000	$8,910,000	$9,000,000	
	Financial cost	$61,545.21	–	$61,545.21	
	EV	$3,578,454.79	$3,730,000	$3,578,454.79	
Seller's Profit Calculation	Interest rate (%)	12	3	18	
	Revenue	$9,000,000	$8,910,000	$9,000,000	
	Financial cost	$49,315.07	$36,986.30	$73,972.60	
	EV	$8,950,684.93	$8,873,013.70	$8,926,027.40	
Supply Chain Welfare	Total EV	$12,529,139.73	$12,603,013.70	$12,504,482.19	

We use the expected value approach to compute the revenue and salvage value for the buyer. For example, in factoring, the buyer's revenue is given by:

$$\text{Expected Revenue} = \$1300 \times \begin{pmatrix} 30\% \times \min(10,000, 12,000) \\ +50\% \times \min(10,000, 10,000) \\ +20\% \times \min(10,000, 8,000) \end{pmatrix}$$

$$= \$12,480,000$$

The cost of the buyer's purchase is equivalent to the wholesale price multiplied by the order quantity, which is the same as the revenue earned by the seller. Meanwhile, the buyer's potential salvage value can be determined by:

$$\text{Expected Salvage Value} = \$400 \times \begin{pmatrix} 30\% \times \max(10,000 - \min(10,000, 12,000), 0) \\ +50\% \times \max(10,000 - \min(10,000, 10,000), 0) \\ +20\% \times \max(10,000 - \min(10,000, 8,000), 0) \end{pmatrix}$$

$$= \$160,000$$

Assuming demand realization at the present time, we can calculate the financial costs for both the buyer and the seller in factoring as follows:

$$\text{Buyer's Financial Cost} = 3\% \times \text{Revenue} \times (90-30)/365 = \$61,545.21$$
$$\text{Seller's Financial Cost} = 12\% \times \text{Production Cost} \times 30/365 = \$49,315.07$$

The EV can be calculated by subtracting the costs for each supply chain firm from the revenue (and salvage value, if applicable). By applying this approach to reverse factoring and bank financing, we obtain the results in Table 10.2. We then compare the EVs of each SCF mechanism from the perspective of each supply chain firm. Based on the given parameter values, reverse factoring has the highest EV for the buyer ($3,730,000), while factoring has the higher EV for the seller ($8,950,684.93).

Therefore, the seller may not choose reverse factoring unless the final financing choice is dominated by the buyer. However, the highest joint supply chain profit is achieved in reverse factoring. If the buyer offers additional benefits, such as purchasing credit insurance or increasing the order quantity in reverse factoring, it can be a win–win scenario for both firms. For instance, if the wholesale price increases from the negotiated $891 to $898 and the payment term is reduced to 30 days, reverse factoring yields the highest EVs for both the seller and the buyer. This observation highlights the importance of precise quantitative analysis based on probability distribution to make a well-informed choice among SCF mechanisms, which can lead to significant benefits for a firm.

So far, we have shown how probability distributions can be used to estimate the EV of discrete events based on available data. It's important to note that probability distributions can also be applied to continuous variables and used to calculate the EV based on continuous payoff functions.

10.5.2 Standard Deviation

The aforementioned probability distribution describes how events are distributed and offers an approach to make informed decisions under risk. However, the probability distribution alone does not convey the level of risk to its audience. To measure risk level, one approach is to calculate the standard deviation, a commonly used statistic that gauges the dispersion of the distribution. The standard deviation based on the preceding probability distribution, can be calculated as

10.5 Quantitative Risk Assessment

follows:

$$\text{Standard Deviation } (\sigma) = \sqrt{\sum_{i=1}^{n} (x_i - \bar{x})^2 \times p_i} \quad (10.3)$$

where

x_i = The value of event i
$\bar{x}$ = The mean of the expected value of event i
p_i = Probability of event i.

Statistically, the variance of event i is given by σ^2. The following table lists the mean and variance of popular probability distributions, both discrete and continuous, that can be used to describe uncertainty and risk distributions.

Name of Distribution	Probability Distribution Function	Mean	Variance
Geometric Distribution	$\Pr(X = k) = (1-p)^{k-1} p$	$\frac{1}{p}$	$\frac{(1-p)}{p^2}$
Binomial Distribution	$\Pr(X = k) = \binom{n}{k} p^k (1-p)^{n-k}$	np	$np(1-p)$
Normal Distribution	$f(x\|\mu, \sigma^2) = \frac{1}{\sqrt{2\pi\sigma^2}} e^{-\frac{(x-\mu)^2}{2\sigma^2}}$	μ	σ^2
Uniform Distribution	$f(x\|a, b) = \frac{1}{b-a}$ for $a \leq x \leq b$	$\frac{a+b}{2}$	$\frac{(b-a)^2}{12}$
Poisson Distribution	$f(x\|\lambda) = \frac{e^{-\lambda} \lambda^x}{x!}$	λ	λ
Exponential Distribution	$f(x\|\lambda) = \lambda e^{-\lambda x}$	$\frac{1}{\lambda}$	$\frac{1}{\lambda^2}$
Gamma Distribution	$f(x\|k, \theta) = \frac{1}{\Gamma(k)\theta^k} x^{k-1} e^{-\frac{x}{\theta}}$	$k\theta$	$k\theta^2$

We use the normal distribution to demonstrate the shapes of the distribution with different standard deviations. As illustrated in Fig. 10.8, a larger standard deviation results in a wider spread of the distribution. Consequently, an event with a higher standard deviation is perceived as more risky.

We will now use an example with discrete distributions to demonstrate how to compare the risk profiles of two companies. In this scenario, two companies are

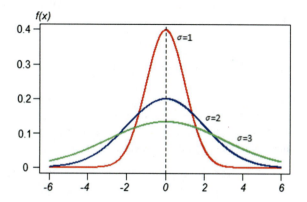

Fig. 10.8 Normal distributions with mean 0 and different standard deviations

Table 10.3 Cash flow positions of two companies

	Company A		Company B	
	Cash Flow	Probability	Cash Flow	Probability
	6000	0.1	6000	0.1
	6500	0.2	6500	0.1
	7000	0.35	7000	0.2
	7500	0.2	7500	0.35
	8000	0.1	8000	0.2
	8500	0.05	8500	0.05

forecasting their cash flow positions for the upcoming fiscal years. Using historical data and projected projects, the companies estimate that their cash flow positions will follow the distributions described in Table 10.3.

Using the expected value approach, we can obtain the expected cash flow in both companies as follows:

$$\overline{x_A} = 6000 \times 0.1 + 6500 \times 0.2 + \ldots 8500 \times 0.05 = 7075$$

$$\overline{x_B} = 6000 \times 0.1 + 6500 \times 0.1 + \ldots 8500 \times 0.05 = 7300$$

Following Eq. (10.3), we can obtain the standard deviations of Companies A and B as follows:

$$\sigma_A = 637.87 < \sigma_B = 659.55$$

The standard deviation of Company A is smaller than the standard deviation of Company B, suggesting that Company B's cash flow situation is riskier than Company A's.

However, using standard deviation alone to measure risk level can be misleading. For instance, in Table 10.3, the expected cash flow position of Company B is higher than Company A's. In other words, solely focusing on standard deviation may overlook the positive impact of a higher expected value of Company B. This concern can be addressed by using the coefficient of variation approach, which is discussed below.

10.5.3 Coefficient of Variation

The *coefficient of variation* (CV) is a measure of relative variability that takes into account both the expected value and the standard deviation of a probability distribution. It is calculated as the ratio of the standard deviation to the expected value, expressed as a percentage. The formula for CV is:

$$CV = \frac{\text{Standard Deviation}}{\text{Expected Value}} = \frac{\sigma}{EV}$$

10.5 Quantitative Risk Assessment

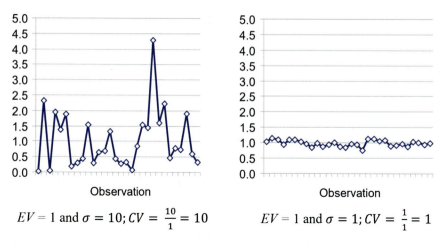

Fig. 10.9 Comparison of two different CVs

The CV provides a way to compare the riskiness of different probability distributions. A lower CV indicates that a distribution is less risky, as the standard deviation is relatively small compared to the expected value. Conversely, a higher CV indicates that a distribution is more risky, as the standard deviation is relatively large compared to the expected value.

The values in Fig. 10.9 illustrate that events with the same expected values can vary greatly in terms of standard deviations, resulting in significant differences in the final CV values. This observation suggests that the standard deviation has a greater impact on the variability reflected in the CV.

It is worth noting that events with similar coefficient of variations (CVs) can differ in expected values (EVs). To illustrate, we refer to the example in Table 10.3, where the calculated CVs suggest that the risk of Company B is slightly higher than that of Company A, despite their EVs being similar as shown below:

$$CV_A = \frac{637.87}{7075} = 0.09016 < CV_B = \frac{659.55}{7300} = 0.09035$$

10.5.4 Altman's Z-Score

The *Altman Z-score* model is a multivariate classification model based on the observation that financial ratios and trends are significantly different between financially healthy firms and those that default. This model uses multiple discriminant analysis to distinguish between firms that succeed and those that fail. The basic Z-score model is as follows[2]:

$$Z = 1.2W + 1.4R + 3.3E + 0.6M + 0.999S$$

where

$$W = \frac{\text{Working Capital}}{\text{Total Assets}} = \frac{\text{WC}}{\text{TA}}$$

$$R = \frac{\text{Retained Earnings}}{\text{Total Assets}} = \frac{\text{RE}}{\text{TA}}$$

$$E = \frac{\text{Earnings Before Interest and Taxes (EBIT)}}{\text{Total Assets}} = \frac{\text{EBIT}}{\text{TA}}$$

$$M = \frac{\text{Market Value of Equity}}{\text{Book Value of Total Liabilities}} = \frac{\text{MVE}}{\text{TL}}$$

$$S = \frac{\text{Sales}}{\text{Total Assets}} = \frac{\text{SA}}{\text{TA}}$$

The WC/TA ratio is commonly used in corporate financing to indicate a firm's liquidity level, while the RE/TA ratio is less popular as it reflects the total amount of reinvested earnings of a firm's entire life, making it biased towards younger firms that are more likely to fail. The EBIT/TA ratio represents a firm's earning power, while the MVE/TL ratio adds a market value dimension by indicating how much a firm's assets can decline in value before becoming insolvent. The SA/TA ratio is a capital turnover ratio that shows a firm's sales generating ability.

The Z-score model suggests that a score below 1.81 (i.e., lower bound) is considered a "failed" score,[3] while a score above 2.99 (i.e., upper bound) is deemed "nonfail." Any score between 1.81 and 2.99 is treated as falling within the "zone of ignorance," where the difference between "failed" and "nonfail" credits is insignificant. In Altman's samples, the model's overall classification accuracy was 95% one year before a firm's bankruptcy and 72% two years before a firm's bankruptcy (Altman, 1968; Caouette et al., 2011).

Initially based on a group of 66 firms, 33 of which were bankrupt and 33 were not, the Z-score model has since been widely applied in the industry. However, due to the different characteristics of industries, Altman has provided several variants

---

[2] The first four ratios are measured in decimals rather than percentages, while the fifth ratio is measured in terms of the number of times (Caouette et al., 2011). In Altman's 1968's paper (Altman, 1968), the original model is:

$$Z = 0.012W + 0.014R + 0.033E + 0.006M + 0.999S$$

[3] A lecture presented by Professor Altman himself in 2019 suggested that recent data supported a failed score of 0 (see https://www.investopedia.com/terms/a/altman.asp for more information).

for different types of firms. For instance, the Z-score model is revised for private firms as follows:

$$Z = 0.717W + 0.847R + 3.107E + 0.420M + 0.998S$$

In this revised Z-score model, Altman advocated to replace the market value in M with the book values of equity (Altman, 2013).

For nonmanufacturers, the Z-score model is given by Altman (2013):

$$Z = 6.56W + 3.26R + 6.72E + 1.05M$$

To account for changes over time, Altman et al. (1977) also introduced the ZETA model, which includes seven additional variables. They claimed that the ZETA model outperforms the Z-score model, particularly for recent predictions. However, they kept the model confidential due to proprietary concerns. Readers can refer to Altman et al. (1977) for more information. Despite the effectiveness of these models over the years, their evolution demonstrates the continuous changes and improvements in the field of risk management.

10.6 Summary

This chapter delves into the complexities of supply chain finance (SCF) risk by laying out a comprehensive taxonomy. Through a systematic breakdown, it offers readers a detailed understanding of both qualitative and quantitative assessment techniques. By harnessing mathematical tools like the Coefficient of Variation and Altman's Z-Score, the chapter underscores the interplay between theoretical constructs and practical applications in evaluating financial stability and risks associated with different firms.

Key Takeaways:

1. A Conceptual SCF Risk Management System:
   - The foundation for SCF risk management lies in understanding the intricacies of supply chain finance dynamics.
   - It emphasizes the importance of a structured framework that aids in identifying, evaluating, and mitigating risks.
2. SCF Risk Taxonomy:
   - A classification system that categorizes risks associated with supply chain finance.
   - Provides clarity on different risk types and helps in pinpointing potential threats and vulnerabilities.
3. Qualitative Risk Assessment:

- This method utilizes descriptive, non-numerical data to assess risks.
- While it might lack the precision of numbers, it brings forward insights that are often overlooked in purely quantitative approaches, such as organizational culture or human factors.

4. Quantitative Risk Assessment:
   - Anchored in numerical data, this approach employs mathematical models and statistical tools.
   - The chapter elucidates the Coefficient of Variation and Altman's Z-Score as pivotal tools. The former allows for a standardized comparison of the riskiness of different probability distributions, while the latter, a multivariate classification tool, differentiates between financially stable companies and those nearing default.

10.7 Exercises

10.7.1 Practice Questions

1. What is the SCF risk taxonomy and why is it important for SCF risk management?
2. Explain the difference between qualitative and quantitative risk assessment.
3. What are the four steps involved in the risk management process?
4. How can probability distributions be used in decision-making for SCF?
5. What is the Altman Z-score model and how is it used in risk assessment for firms?
6. What is the coefficient of variation and how does it help in measuring risk level?
7. What are some popular probability distributions used to describe uncertainty and risk distributions?
8. What is the expected value approach and how is it used in computing for revenue and salvage value in SCF?
9. How can the standard deviation be used to measure the risk level of a probability distribution?
10. What is the ZETA model and how does it differ from the Z-score model in risk assessment?

10.7.2 Case Studies

Case Study 1: The Financial Health of XYZ Corporation

Background

XYZ Corporation is a mid-sized manufacturing company that has been operating for 10 years. Recently, due to increasing competition and changing market dynamics, its financial health has come into question. Stakeholders, including shareholders and creditors, have raised concerns regarding the company's ability to continue its operations in the long run.

Given Financial Data for XYZ Corporation

1. Working capital (WC) = $2,000,000
2. Total assets (TA) = $10,000,000
3. Retained earnings (RE) = $1,500,000
4. Earnings before interest and taxes (EBIT) = $1,000,000
5. Market value of equity (MVE) = $5,500,000
6. Book value of total liabilities (TL) = $4,500,000
7. Sales (S) = $8,000,000

Task

Using the Altman Z-score model and the provided data, evaluate the financial health of XYZ Corporation. Determine if the company is at risk of failure in the near future based on the calculated Z-score.

Case Study 2: Evaluating Risk Through CV Analysis of Two Startup Ventures

Background

TechTown is a budding city known for its startup culture. Among its new startups, two tech firms, AlphaTech and BetaTech, have shown promising results in their early phases. Both companies operate in the software domain but cater to different markets. AlphaTech is developing a groundbreaking virtual reality (VR) platform, while BetaTech is centered around advanced cloud storage solutions.

As an investment analyst at Pioneer Investments, you're considering adding one of these firms to the firm's tech portfolio. However, given the inherent risks of startups, you wish to delve deeper into the variability of their potential returns.

Given Financial Data

AlphaTech:

1. Expected value (EV) of returns: $500,000
2. Standard deviation (σ): $50,000

BetaTech:

1. Expected value (EV) of returns: $480,000
2. Standard deviation (σ): $40,000

Task

Utilize the coefficient of variation (CV) to evaluate the relative risk of both startups and recommend which might be a safer investment option for Pioneer Investments based on the calculated CV.

References

Altman, E. I. (1968). Financial ratios, discriminant analysis and the prediction of corporate bankruptcy. *The Journal of Finance, 23*(4), 589–609.

Altman, E. I., Haldeman Robert, G., & Narayanan, P. (1977). Zeta analysis: A new model to identify bankruptcy risk of corporations. *Journal of Banking and Finance, 10*, 29–54.

Altman, E. I. (2013). Predicting financial distress of companies: Revisiting the Z-Score and ZETA® models. *Handbook of research methods and applications in empirical finance*, 428.

Caouette, J. B., Altman, E. I., Narayanan, P., & Nimmo, R. (2011). *Managing credit risk: The great challenge for global financial markets* (vol. 401). John Wiley & Sons.

Crouhy, M., Galai, D., & Mark, R. (2013). *The essentials of risk management* (vol. 1). McGraw-Hill New York.

Lp, G., & Whitehouse, M. (2007). Market's fall may augur a waning appetite for risk: Change in attitude could raise cost of capital globally. *Wall Street Journal (Eastern Edition), 1*.

Maverick, J. B. (2019). *Financial risk: The major kinds that companies face*. https://www.investopedia.com/ask/answers/062415/what-are-major-categories-financial-risk-company.asp. Accessed March 1, 2022.

NCUA (National Credit Union Administration). (2021). Ratings distribution history. https://www.ncua.gov/support-services/guaranteed-notes-program/ratings-distribution-history. Assessed May 31, 2021.

Nordea. (2018). *Trade finance is going open account*. https://test.insights.nordea.com.nrd.fkly.dk/en/business/trade-finance-is-going-open-account/. Assessed May 3, 2021.

Nordea. (2020). *Risk management: The top 12 risks every business owner should know*. https://test.insights.nordea.com.nrd.fkly.dk/en/business/risk-management-the-top-12-risks-every-business-owner-should-know/. Accessed March 3, 2022.

Segal, T. (2023). *5 cs of credit: What they are, how they're used, and which is most important*. Investopedia. https://www.investopedia.com/terms/f/five-c-credit.asp. Accessed March 23, 2022.

Templar, S., Hofmann, E., & Findlay, C. (2016). *Financing the end-to-end supply chain: A reference guide to supply chain finance*. Kogan Page Publishers.

Wang, W., & Cai, G. (2023). Curtailing bank loan and loan insurance under risk regulations in supply chain finance. *Management Science*. https://doi.org/10.1287/mnsc.2023.4827

Wikipedia. (2021). *Risk*. https://en.wikipedia.org/wiki/Risk. Accessed March 18, 2022.

Yang, L., Cai, G., & Chen, J. (2018). Push, pull, and supply chain risk-averse attitude. *Production and Operations Management, 27*(8), 1534–1552.

Zhao, W., & Yang, H. (2021). *The resilient supply chain—What procurement leaders are prioritizing in 2021*. https://www.dnb.com/ca-en/perspectives/supply-chain/resilient-supply-chain-infographic.html. Accessed December 1, 2024.

Zuckerman, G. (2005). Cash-rich firms feel pressure to spend. *The Wall Street Journal C*.

Risk-Adjusted Evaluation

11

Learning Objectives:

1. Apply Value-at-Risk (VaR) to gauge maximum potential loss over a set period for a given confidence level.
2. Explore Conditional Value-at-Risk (CVaR), understanding its distinction from VaR and its role in identifying tail risks.
3. Conduct stress testing to assess investment strategy vulnerabilities under extreme scenarios.
4. Calculate risk-adjusted returns to compare investment performances against their respective risks.

11.1 Introduction

In practice, supply chain firms often exhibit risk-averse behavior when confronted with potential threats. A survey of 1500 executives from 90 countries conducted by Koller et al. (2012) found that these executives displayed significant risk aversion, regardless of the investment size, even when the expected value of a proposed project was overwhelmingly positive. The Wall Street Journal reported that companies retained higher cash reserves as a result of above-average risk aversion among management, stemming from the lingering effects of previous years' bankruptcies (Zuckerman, 2005).

Economists have posited that an increase in risk aversion contributed to the economic downturn, occurring precisely when business investment spending had fallen significantly below expectations. Gurnani et al. (2014) further substantiated these observations through an experimental study, which revealed that firms exhibit risk-averse tendencies in their ordering behavior. In order to address risk aversion concerns, it is crucial for firms to utilize risk-adjusted performance evaluation tools to support and enhance their decision-making processes.

11.2 Value-at-Risk (VaR)

Value-at-Risk (VaR) is a widely used risk metric and an effective summary statistical tool for measuring and managing risk exposure. It quantifies aggregate risks across all factors within a security, portfolio, or firm over a specified time frame and can be employed to evaluate risk exposure at each level of a company's operations. In practice, VaR serves as a valuable guideline for firms and regulators in estimating the capital needed to cover potential losses in risk management.

> *A risk-taking institution that does not compute VaR might escape disaster, but an institution that cannot compute VaR will not.*—Brown (2007)

11.2.1 Definition of VaR

VaR is typically defined as the worst expected loss for a security, portfolio, or firm over a specific time horizon (e.g., one day or one month) at a given confidence level (i.e., probability), relative to the expected value, under normal market conditions. For instance, a daily VaR of $1 million at the 99% confidence level indicates a 1% chance of incurring a loss of more than $1 million below the expected profit over a one-day period. In other words, we expect at least a loss of more than $1 million relative to the expected value on 1 day out of 100 days (i.e., 1%).

Three primary components make up VaR: *maximum loss, confidence level* (usually 95% or 99%), and *time period*. VaR_p is the VaR at the confidence level p of X, where p represents the confidence level and X represents the distribution of the random profit of the security, portfolio, or firm. We further define $L := -X$ as the corresponding random loss, and α denotes the significance level, where $p = 1 - \alpha$. Hence, $\text{VaR}_p(X)$ also means the value of VaR is the smallest number of x such that the probability of X not exceeding x is at least p. In other words, VaR_p is the worst-case loss of l such that the probability of L exceeding l is at most α. Therefore, mathematically, we have the following (Acerbi & Tasche, 2002; Wikipedia, 2024):

$$\text{VaR}_p = -\inf\{x \in \mathbb{R} : Pr(X \leq x) \geq p\} \text{ for } p \in [0, 1]$$

Or, equivalently,

$$\text{VaR}_p = \inf\{l \in \mathbb{R} : Pr(L > l) \leq \alpha\} \text{ for } \alpha \in [0, 1]$$

where inf (abbreviation of infimum) is the greatest lower bound of a set, $\mathbb{R}$ signifies the domain of x and l, and Pr represents the probability. $\text{VaR}_p(X)$ is a non-sub-additive, non-convex, and discontinuous function of confidence level p. A *VaR breach* occurs if the loss surpasses the VaR threshold (Wikipedia, 2024).

11.2 Value-at-Risk (VaR)

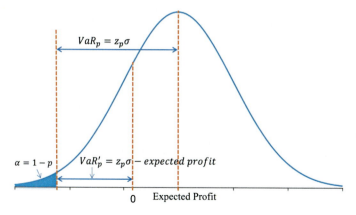

Fig. 11.1 VaR description in normal distribution

VaR_p can also be expressed as pVaR. For example, the daily VaR of $1 million at the 99% confidence level can be referred to as the 99% VaR of $1 million, meaning there is a maximum 1% probability that the specified portfolio or firm will lose more than $1 million within a one-day time frame.

Graphically, VaR can be illustrated in a profit and loss distribution. In Fig. 11.1, we assume that the specified events adhere to a normal distribution. The mean corresponds to the expected profit, which is positive in this graph but can also be any positive or negative value in other examples, and is located at the center of the distribution. The significance level (i.e., $\alpha = 1 - p$) is depicted in the bottom-left corner of the distribution.

In this normal distribution, the VaR value is determined as the distance between the upper boundary of the α value and the expected profit (Crouhy et al., 2013):

$$\begin{aligned} VaR_p &= z_p \sigma \\ &= \text{expected profit} \\ &\quad + \text{worst-case loss at the confidence level } p \end{aligned}$$

Here, z_p is the z-score corresponding to a standard normal distribution at the confidence level p, and σ represents the standard deviation.

The distance between the upper boundary of the α value and zero is defined as VaR′, also referred to as *absolute VaR* (Crouhy et al., 2013):

$$\begin{aligned} VaR'_p &= z_p \sigma - \text{expected profit} \\ &= \text{worst-case loss at the confidence level } p \end{aligned}$$

It is important to note that VaR is typically larger than the absolute VaR, which is necessary in practice since risk management requires firms to prepare for the worst unexpected loss (i.e., a value below the expected profit) while maintaining a positive expected profit. Economically, the VaR$_p$ represents the amount of capital a firm should allocate to mitigate the probability of default at a given confidence level p. From a regulatory standpoint, VaR is the minimum amount of capital required to prevent a firm's default at a confidence level, typically 95% or 99%. A cautious firm, such as a financial institution, may also set a very high confidence level to minimize its default risks.

The above explanation is based on a single-day time period. However, regulators often establish a 10-day time horizon for regulatory capital requirements. In this case, banks generally approximate the 10-day VaR from daily VaR data by multiplying the daily VaR by the square root of time (i.e., $\sqrt{10}$ times the daily VaR for the specified 10 days in this scenario), an approach widely accepted by regulators (Crouhy et al., 2013).

Case Study

Computing VaR and VaR′ in Multiple Time Periods

Question: Calculate VaR and VaR′ for an investment portfolio with an expected return of 5%, a standard deviation of 8%, a holding period of 10 days, and a confidence level of 99%. Use the above parametric method.

Solution: Referring to the (one-sided) z-table based on a standardized normal distribution, we find $z_{99\%} = 2.33$. The expected return (i.e., expected profit margin) is given by 5%. The standard deviation $\sigma = 8\%$, and the time t = 10. We then calculate VaR$_p$ and VaR′$_p$ as follows:

$$\text{VaR}_{99\%} = z_{99\%} \sigma \sqrt{t} = 2.33 \times 8\% \times \sqrt{10} = 58.9\%$$

$$\text{VaR}'_{99\%} = (z_{99\%} \sigma - \text{expected return})\sqrt{t}$$
$$= (2.33 \times 8\% - 5\%) \times \sqrt{10} = 43.1\%$$

11.2.2 Computation of VaR

In practice, there are three primary methods for calculating VaR: the historical simulation method, the variance–covariance method, and the Monte Carlo simulation method. While the Monte Carlo simulation and variance–covariance methods are parametric approaches that rely on parameter assumptions, the historical simulation method is non-parametric. A 2012 McKinsey report estimated that 85% of large banks used historical simulation, while the remaining 15% employed Monte Carlo methods (Neukirchen, 2012).

11.2.2.1 Historical Method

The *historical method* is considered the simplest among the three. It utilizes historical data to directly construct the profit and loss distribution, assuming that future behavior will mirror the past. However, to construct the distribution, a sufficient amount of data (e.g., one to three years or more than a few hundred data points) is needed to produce meaningful results.

The most straightforward approach within the historical method is to create a histogram using historical data, which can be called the *historical histogram method*. The histogram-based distribution can then be used to estimate the worst α (e.g., 1% or 5%) of all data. For example, as shown in Fig. 11.2, if the left tail of the histogram contains 5% of the data, ranging from a $1 million to $4 million loss (away from the expected profit), we can assert with 95% confidence that the worst daily loss will not surpass $1 million. Given that the average value of the data (i.e., mean) is approximately $2.5 million, the VaR at the 95% confidence level is $3.5 million (i.e., the distance from the 5% percentile point to the mean). Note that the $1 million loss is not the worst among all available data ($4 million is the worst in this hypothetical example). If a higher confidence level is desired, we may move further left on the tail by setting a higher confidence level, say 99%, at which the worst loss could range, for instance, from $3 million to $4 million. In this latter case, we can state with 99% confidence that the worst daily loss is not expected to exceed $3 million, or a VaR of $5.5 million ($= \$2.5 - (-\$3)$) at the 99% confidence level.

If we lack the data for the objective in question, the histogram can also be constructed based on all relevant risk factors used to estimate the target objective (e.g., profit); this approach is called the *historical simulation method* (Allen, 2012; Crouhy et al., 2013). To do this, we gather historical data for all risk factors over a period of time. Then, we use a model to transform the values of risk factors into the value of the target in question. For example, in each simulation scenario j,

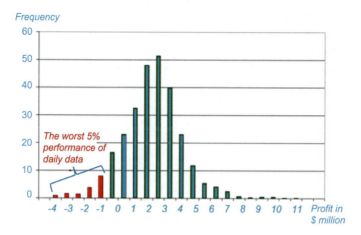

Fig. 11.2 Histogram of historical profit data

the value of the target can be given by $\sum_i s_i m_{i,j}$, where s_i represents the firm's risk exposure to each market variable, $m_{i,j}$. Note that the estimation model can be more complex to better estimate the final target value. Finally, by using the histogram of the final values of the objective, we can estimate the VaR value.

The historical method offers the advantage of simplicity, as it does not rely on any mathematical models or parameters. For example, this method does not necessitate the assumption of a normal distribution or any other specific distribution, whether the distribution exhibits fat tails or whether there is a correlation among market variables. Additionally, it still provides the convenience of calculating confidence intervals for VaR. It aggregates all influencing factors without delving into the details, such as historical volatilities and correlations, because they are reflected in the data.

However, the historical method requires a sufficient pool of data, which could be challenging for many firms, especially in supply chain finance transactions. Even if we have sufficient data, we risk the idiosyncrasies of the data, as the past data may not accurately represent the future. For instance, before 2020, we could not foresee the catastrophic impact of COVID-19, and the three-year data prior to that does not reflect this impact. On the other hand, the event of COVID-19 might not be repeated in the next three years right after the end of the pandemic. The historical data cannot account for changes brought about by the utilization of new technology (e.g., blockchain technology) in the future. Moreover, the final VaR value seems to be determined by only a few specific historical periods, which might not be representative.

11.2.2.2 Variance–Covariance Method

The central limit theorem suggests that the mean of a large enough number of samples of independent random variables from a well-behaved distribution will converge to a normal distribution. As we know, a normal distribution can be nicely characterized by its two moments: the mean (μ) and the variance (σ^2). If all risk factors and the return value follow a log-normal distribution, we can estimate the VaR from the distribution of relevant market variables. Let r_i be the firm's risk exposure (e.g., the weight of investment) to risk factor i, σ_i be the standard deviation (i.e., volatility) of risk factor i, and $\rho_{i,j}$ represent the correlation coefficient of the two risk factors, i and j. The standard deviation of the total investment can be expressed as follows (Allen, 2012):

$$\sigma_T = \sqrt{\sum_{i,j} r_i r_j \sigma_i \sigma_j \rho_{i,j}}$$

11.2 Value-at-Risk (VaR)

Case Study

Computing VaR Using the Variance–Covariance Method

Let's consider the following two examples.

Example 1 (Only One Risk Factor):
A firm has allocated $10 million to one investment. It is assumed that the return of the investment follows a normal distribution with a standard deviation of 50% of the mean value. The VaR at a 95% confidence level ($z_{95\%} = 1.645$) is given by:

$$\text{VaR}_{95\%} = 1.645 \times 10 \times 0.5 = \$8.225 \text{ million}$$

Example 2 (Two Risk Factors):
A firm has two different investments, and the total investment is $10 million. The return of the first investment follows a normal distribution with a standard deviation of 50% of the mean value. The return of the second investment follows a normal distribution with a standard deviation of 80% of the mean value. The weight of the first investment is 40% of the total investment (i.e., $4 million), while the second one is at 60% (i.e., $6 million). The correlation coefficient between the two investments is 25%. The standard deviation of the joint investments is given by:

$$\sigma_T = \sqrt{0.4^2 \times 0.5^2 + 0.6^2 \times 0.8^2 + 2 \times 0.4 \times 0.6 \times 0.5 \times 0.8 \times 0.25} \times \text{mean} = 56.43\% \times \text{mean}$$

The VaR at a 95% confidence level ($z_{95\%} = 1.645$) for the firm is given by:

$$\text{VaR}_{95\%} = 1.645 \times 10 \times 0.5643 = \$9.28 \text{ million}$$

The VaR of these two investments is higher than that of Example 1 because the second investment is riskier. Now suppose the standard deviation of the second investment is reduced to the same level as the first investment (i.e., 50%); then, the new joint standard deviation is given by:

$$\sigma_T = \sqrt{0.4^2 \times 0.5^2 + 0.6^2 \times 0.5^2 + 2 \times 0.4 \times 0.6 \times 0.5 \times 0.5 \times 0.25} \times \text{mean} = 40\% \times \text{mean}$$

> The VaR at a 95% confidence level for the firm is given by:
>
> $$\text{VaR}_{95\%} = 1.645 \times 10 \times 0.40 = \$6.58 \text{ million}$$
>
> This new VaR is lower than that of the single investment, suggesting that diversification reduces the risk of the total investment

The parameters above can be estimated using historical data; however, the assumption of a normal distribution for all risk factors can be problematic. It is well-known that events do not always follow normal distributions or multivariate normal distributions, which are often unverified in estimation. Even if they do follow bell-shaped distributions, there is evidence that many return distributions exhibit a feature called *"fat tails,"* which indicates that more observations are distributed further from the mean than in a normal distribution (see Fig. 11.3). If the actual data follow fat-tail distributions, the worst loss could occur more frequently than the VaR suggested under a normal distribution assumption. Thus, the variance–covariance method could underestimate the VaR and the severity of potential loss. To mitigate the impact of fat tails, one approach is to diversify investments to take advantage of the central limit theorem; however, this makes computing the VaR more challenging.

The variance–covariance method also has other disadvantages, such as its inability to describe the clustering phenomenon, where risk factors are highly correlated and often cluster together to a greater degree than can be expressed in correlation coefficients (i.e., the joint normal distribution is no longer bivariate) (Allen, 2012). Furthermore, compared to other simulation approaches, the variance–covariance method lacks flexibility to cope with complex scenarios.

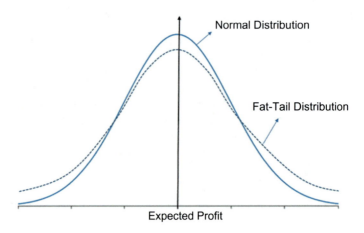

Fig. 11.3 Normal distribution vs. fat-tail distribution

11.2.2.3 Monte Carlo Simulation Method

Monte Carlo simulation is a method that employs numerous simulations of the random processes that govern the objective in question. If enough simulations are run, the simulated distribution will presumably converge to the true, unknown distribution, from which we can infer the VaR.

Monte Carlo simulation typically involves the following three steps:

1. *Identify all relevant risk factors*: We need to specify all the relevant risk factors that will influence the return (dependent variable).
2. *Construct the simulation model*: We need to describe the dynamic relationship of these risk factors (e.g., the distribution of each risk factor, their correlations, and stochastic processes) to the dependent variable. When some risk factors are highly correlated, we cannot treat them as independent variables using individual randomization but must simulate multivariate distributions for these affected risk factors.
3. *Run the simulation*: We generate a set of values for each of those risk factors that are used as input into the model. We repeat the process many times, say 20,000 times, to generate the necessary distribution of the return.

Based on the final distribution, we can then infer the value of VaR. Compared to the historical simulation method, which is limited by data availability, Monte Carlo simulation can generate many more data points as needed. Monte Carlo simulation also offers more flexibility in handling missing data. Additionally, it has the advantage of combining experiences learned from historical data (i.e., not limited to recent data) and selecting the most relevant dataset to estimate each parameter of the simulation model.

One obvious disadvantage of Monte Carlo simulation is its dependence on the specification of risk factors and model assumptions (e.g., parameters of distribution). To avoid subjectivity in the specification process, we can use historical simulation to describe the correlations between variables (Allen, 2012).

Our discussion above has implicitly assumed equal weighting for any given data points. However, one can assign different weights to focal data points to emphasize the negative impact of some significant losses. For any model used to estimate VaR, it is helpful to test the prediction against real results, which is referred to as back-testing or validation in prediction.

11.2.3 VaR in Risk Management

Despite its many limitations and imperfections, VaR has proven useful, particularly for short time horizons within a relatively static framework. It can also be employed to compare the risk levels of various portfolios or assets.

> *Risk managers should not be overly risk-averse; otherwise, the firm may miss numerous profitable opportunities.*

In practice, risk managers may categorize risk into two groups: inside the VaR limit and outside the VaR limit. Within the VaR limit, all events are considered normal and may occur frequently. Risk managers should not be overly risk-averse; otherwise, the firm may miss numerous profitable opportunities. Beyond the VaR limit, data points may be rare, making statements inferred from probability less meaningful. Consequently, risk managers should also utilize other risk management tools, such as stress testing, based on long-term and broader data to prevent the worst scenarios from occurring.

In a specific system, Brown (2007) suggests a three-regime method for applying VaR when the worst scenarios are anticipated in the following regimes:

1. **Within 1–3 times VaR**: Periodic VaR breaks are expected, especially if the VaR is obtained at a lower confidence level. A firm cannot survive for long if it cannot withstand losses of three times VaR occasionally.
2. **Within 3–10 times VaR**: Stress testing should be implemented to examine all foreseeable events in this range, and firms should be prepared to endure these worst-case scenarios.
3. **More than 10 times VaR**: These events may not be foreseeable. Therefore, firms should typically purchase insurance or hedge against these worst-case scenarios.

11.3 Conditional VaR

Although VaR is widely used in risk management, its limitations should not be ignored. For instance, it struggles to capture the volatility, correlations, disruptions in liquidity, and strong nonlinearities in complex structured financial products. In practice, there is often limited data on defaults, making it challenging to accurately estimate the potential correlation between historical defaults and future ones. Due to its importance, firms may also be inclined to modify this metric to achieve the "right" numbers, which could amplify risks due to unintended "improvements" in the VaR model.

Another issue with VaR is that its value is simply derived from a threshold point, or the value of the percentile at the confidence level, without considering larger losses. Consequently, losses beyond the percentile are ignored, even if they could be significantly worse than the VaR value, a phenomenon referred to as "tail risk." For example, the VaR value is likely to fail in capturing the disastrous impact of the 2007–2009 Financial Crisis or the COVID-19 pandemic that began in 2020. As a result, VaR may underestimate the severe impacts of those losses below the VaR threshold value. This might also encourage risk managers to hide

11.3 Conditional VaR

risk in the tail (Allen, 2012). A simple remedy is to apply another effective risk measure known as conditional VaR.

Conditional VaR (CVaR), also known as expected shortfall (ES), shortfall VaR, average VaR (AVaR), and expected tail loss (ETL), measures the average loss at a given confidence level. In terms of expected shortfall, CVaR measures the expected value of all losses that exceed the VaR. In this sense, CVaR gauges the downward risk greater than the VaR at a given confidence level.

Mathematically, assuming that the data distribution is continuous, we can describe CVaR as follows (Acerbi & Tasche, 2002; Wikipedia, 2024):

$$\text{CVaR}_p(X) = \frac{1}{\alpha} \int_0^\alpha \text{VaR}_{1-\theta}(X) d\theta$$

Instead of a single threshold value at the confidence level, CVaR calculates the weighted average of all losses greater than the VaR at the given confidence level p. Therefore, CVaR is larger than VaR and more representative of all worst losses at the same confidence level. Because the main difference between VaR and CVaR lies in whether using a single percentile point or the average of all points included and beyond the percentile point, the computation procedure of CVaR is similar to that of VaR.

In Table 11.1, we illustrate the difference between VaR and CVaR. In this example, the 95% confidence level includes the worst three cases of each investment plan, which are part of the listed six data points (among many other points that are not listed here). For Plan A, the $\text{VaR}_{95\%}$ is $30 million, while the $\text{VaR}_{95\%}$ for Plan B is $36 million. The corresponding $\text{CVaR}_{95\%}$ values for Plans A and B are $39.33 million and $41.67 million, respectively, which are evidently larger than the $\text{VaR}_{95\%}$ values.

In this hypothetical example, the $\text{CVaR}_{95\%}$ happens to represent the expected loss of the three worst cases. This is akin to the 3W statistic, which refers to the average of the worst three losses within a year.

Table 11.1 Worst losses data points (in $ million)

	Investment Plan A	Investment Plan B	Joint Plans A&B
Data Point 1	56	23	79
Data Point 2	32	36	68
Data Point 3	30	43	73
Data Point 4	25	46	71
Data Point 5	22	13	35
Data Point 6	21	23	44
VaR$_{95\%}$ (the value of the third worst case)	30	36	71
CVaR$_{95\%}$ (expected loss of the three worst cases)	39.33	41.67	74.33

As previously discussed, VaR is non-sub-additive, meaning the VaR value of a combined investment portfolio can be larger than the sum of the VaRs of each individual investment. Due to this characteristic, VaR is not considered a coherent risk measure, which requires sub-additivity. For example, as illustrated in Table 11.1, the sum of VaRs of Plan A and Plan B is $30 + 36 = 66$, which is smaller than 71, the VaR of the joint portfolio, demonstrating an undesirable negative diversification effect. In contrast, CVaR is a coherent risk measure. As shown in Table 11.1, the sum of the CVaRs of Plan A and Plan B is $39.33 + 41.67 = 81$, which is larger than 74.33, the CVaR of the joint portfolio, indicating a positive diversification effect.

11.4 Stress Testing

Stress testing also known as torture testing, is a formal requirement of Basel III and has become an essential tool in risk management. The 2007–2009 Financial Crisis and COVID-19 pandemic exposed the limitations of most VaR models, which struggle to account for risks related to multi-year trending markets, credit downgrades, operational risk events (e.g., fraud), nonlinear price movements, and more (Crouhy et al., 2013). The inadequacy of other quantitative approaches in understanding systemic interconnections during global financial crises further highlights the importance of stress testing.

The purpose of stress testing is to develop a comprehensive understanding of risk by evaluating an institution's ability to withstand crisis situations. Stress testing can be considered a specialized form of sensitivity analysis in risk management, but with a more extreme focus. In simple terms, stress testing answers intuitive questions such as, "What if 30% of our current customers were to switch to our biggest competitor?" In this regard, stress testing is designed to assess the impact of extreme events on a firm's financial performance, such as earnings and liquidity. Although historical data may not always support certain hypothetical crisis scenarios, a qualitative thought process in stress testing can effectively complement quantitative risk metrics like VaR and aid in the strategic planning of the institution.

There are two approaches to conducting stress testing. One is based on historical events, while the other relies on economic insights. Since historical events may not always be available, economic insights can often be more useful. However, probability judgments of scenarios based on economic insights are inherently subjective. As such, both historical events and economic insights can complement each other well in selecting testing scenarios.

11.4.1 Stress Testing Based on Economic Insights

As stress testing becomes more prevalent, one challenge lies in rigorously and consistently defining a portfolio of scenarios. Crouhy et al. (2013), propose a

11.4 Stress Testing

methodology called the "stress envelope," which consolidates the worst possible stress shocks across all situations. After assessing the most severe stress shocks, it becomes easier to select a combination of ad hoc scenarios at lower stress levels.

The stress envelope methodology consists of two steps. In the first step, a number of relevant stress categories are developed, such as interest rates, credit spreads, commodity prices, political environment, international regulations, foreign exchange rates, equity prices, market volatility, and more. In the second step, for each stress category, the worst possible stress shocks that could realistically occur are identified. The number of stress shocks within each category can be further specified.

For instance, in Table 11.2, an envelope of stress categories with their respective numbers of stress shocks is developed. Hypothetically, these six stress categories are the most relevant for a given SCF transaction. The number of stress shocks allows for the comparison of different levels of stress across a broader range.

Based on the developed stress envelop in Table 11.2, we have the following specific "envelope" scenario with three extreme (worst) stress shocks:

1. A 40% fall in the U.S. equity indices.
2. A 40% fall in the Asian equity indices.
3. A 30% increase in foreign exchange rates.

A less impactful focal scenario corresponding to the above specific scenario with three moderate stress shocks:

1. A 15% fall in the U.S. equity indices.
2. A 20% fall in the Asian equity indices.
3. A 10% increase in foreign exchange rates.

If we construct the impact (i.e., loss) of the stress envelope (the corresponding impact is shown on the left-hand side of Table 11.3), then we can calculate the potential loss of a focal scenario as illustrated in Table 11.3. Note that Table 11.3 is

Table 11.2 Stress categories and the number of stress shocks

#	Stress Category	Stress Shocks
1	Interest rates	4
2	International regulations	4
3	Foreign exchange rates	2
4	Credit spreads	2
5	Equity	4
6	Environmental impacts	2

Table 11.3 Impacts of stress envelope and stress scenario

#	Stress Envelope Shocks (%)	Stress Envelope Impact	Focal Scenario Shocks (%)	Focal Scenario Shock Weights (%)	Focal Scenario Impact
1	40	($5000)	15	15/40 = 37.5	($1875)
2	40	($3000)	20	20/40 = 50	($1500)
3	30	($1000)	10	10/30 = 33.33	($333.33)
				Total	($3708.33)

a simplified illustration of the potential impact of stress on a firm's profit. A comprehensive review of stress testing should cover all concerned areas of the firm, such as profit performance, liquidity, assets, and equity. The linear interpolation in the calculation of the "focal scenario shock weights" is also a simplified estimation, which could underestimate or overestimate the actual loss due to nonlinear relationships in those stress categories.

Factor-Push Stress Tests: Table 11.3 illustrates only a specific scenario. To gain a comprehensive understanding of potential stress impacts, it is important to explore all plausible combinations based on the potential stress shocks identified earlier, using an approach known as factor-push stress tests. This necessitates the examination of numerous potential scenarios. A notable criticism of the factor-push methodology is that it can produce implausible combinations. For instance, a two-year treasury rate might move in the opposite direction of a three-year treasury rate in the simulation, which is deemed unrealistic (Allen, 2012).

Monte Carlo Stress Tests: To address the correlation issue inherent in the factor-push methodology, one can assume a probability measure for the stress shocks. While it can be argued that correlation relationships may be disrupted during financial crises (Kim & Finger, 2000), incorporating a specified correlation (e.g., based on historical data) in the Monte Carlo model helps to exclude infeasible combinations. This approach is akin to the one used for VaR; however, the probability assumed here is not supported by historical data but instead relies on a plausible economic scenario.

11.4.2 Stress Testing Based on Historical Events

Though rare historical events, such as the 2007–2009 Financial Crisis, may not be present in most recent data, utilizing these plausible real-world occurrences can help mitigate concerns of subjectivity when generating scenarios solely based on economic insights. For instance, the following historical scenarios can be employed in stress testing:

- 1997 Asian Financial Crisis
- 2000 Dot-com Bubble
- 2001 9/11 Terrorist Attacks in the U.S

- 2007 Great Recession
- 2010 European Sovereign Debt Crisis
- 2020 COVID-19 Pandemic

To assess stress impacts based on a historical event, it is necessary to research the historical values of relevant market variables and generate values for any missing data. Afterward, we must determine the start and end dates of the stress.

11.4.3 Stress Testing vs. VaR

To make stress tests credible and useful, a well-planned process should encompass a clear outline of risk tolerance and capital objectives, strong internal controls, and the integration of stress testing and its outcomes into the decision-making framework (Crouhy et al., 2013). Additionally, it should ensure effective governance involving senior management and the board of directors, along with clearly defined policies for capital allocation that detail decision-making processes in line with projected future scenarios. Litterman (1996) also emphasizes the importance of reporting in stress tests and suggests that reporting must allow for various types of decomposition for business lines, highlight critical risks, accommodate organizational structure, and offer the drill-down capability.

While VaR is more suited for measuring earnings volatility, the impact of extreme market movements can be better assessed using stress tests. Nevertheless, both VaR and stress testing aim to provide guidelines for maintaining adequate capital cushion to prevent bankruptcy. This capital cushion is necessary to protect against earnings volatility and market shifts.

Compared to VaR, stress testing offers a unique perspective on potential outcomes if extreme events occur. It complements the VaR methodology by preparing management for certain types of financial disasters (Allen, 2012). Since scenarios used in stress testing are typically not included in a firm's historical data, stress testing generally relies on human judgment and is more subjective, making it prone to manipulation. In contrast, VaR is a statistically based, more objective methodology. As a result, VaR has been more widely adopted by regulators to mandate sufficient capital cushion. However, it has been shown that firms using stress testing are better equipped to perform well during crises (Allen, 2012).

11.5 Risk-Adjusted Return Ratios

This subsection introduces several risk-adjusted ratios to compare the relative performance of firms or business units with different risk levels.

11.5.1 Risk-Adjusted Return on Capital

Risk-adjusted return on capital (RAROC) is a metric used to measure return on capital, taking into account various risk factors. Bankers Trust introduced this concept in the late 1970s to evaluate whether an investment yielded a higher return than the bank's minimum expected rate of return on equity (Crouhy et al., 2013, p588). The RAROC equation is written as:[1]

$$\text{RAROC} = \frac{\text{Risk-Adjust} - \text{Expected Net Income}}{\text{Economic Capital}}$$

$$= \frac{\text{Revenue} - \text{Expenses} - \text{Expected Loss} - \text{Taxes} + \text{Return on Risk Capital}}{\text{Economic Capital}}$$

Here, *revenue* represents the institution's income (e.g., interest income, non-interest income, and potential transferred funds) for the specific activity. Expenses include all related direct and allocated costs and other expenses (e.g., funds-transfer-pricing used to incorporate risks into the costs). *Expected losses* can be computed as:

$$\text{Expected Loss} = \text{Probability of Default} \times \text{Loss Given Default} \times \text{Exposure at Default}$$

where the *probability of default* is the likelihood of non-repayment; *loss given default* is the fraction of loss due to default; and *exposure at default* is the total amount of exposure to risks at default. *Taxes* represent the expected amount of taxes paid at the institution's effective tax rate. *Return on risk capital* is typically calculated as the risk-free return on the risk capital.

Economic capital comprises risk capital and strategic capital. *Risk capital*, also known as *capital at risk*, is the capital set aside to cover unexpected losses due to credit risk, market risk, operational risk, and other risks. *Strategic capital* includes capital allocated for burn-out costs (e.g., strategic failure of recent acquisitions) and goodwill (e.g., amount paid above the net asset value during acquisition), which can be estimated at zero if no acquisition is involved. Generally, riskier investments require larger economic capital to cover unexpected losses.

In the literature, the economic capital value has often been approximated by VaR. However, more precisely, we have (Kenton, 2020):

$$\text{Economic Capital} = \text{VaR} - \text{Expected Loss}$$

In this sense, if the expected loss is minimal, the economic capital value is close to the VaR value (see Fig. 11.4).

---

[1] The equation may differ across various sources, but the central message remains consistent.

11.5 Risk-Adjusted Return Ratios

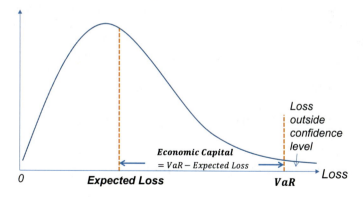

Fig. 11.4 Illustration of economic capital

Here we use expected values on an *ex-ante* basis. However, when employing RAROC *ex-post* to evaluate the performance of a loan or investment, the calculation incorporates the realized revenue and expenses.

RAROC takes risk into account when comparing the profitability of different investments. Unlike return on capital, RAROC adjusts the expected net income (i.e., a proxy for reward) in the numerator by subtracting the expected loss due to risks and replacing accounting capital with economic capital (i.e., a proxy for risk) in the denominator. As a result, RAROC can be viewed as a measure of the trade-off between reward and risk for a unit of capital (Crouhy et al., 2013, p. 588). Generally, the RAROC value is lower when the risk level is higher.

Case Study

Computation of RAROC

To further illustrate the RAROC calculation, let's consider the following example. Suppose a loan to Firm A is valued at $10 million with an interest rate of 7%. The lender will incur a direct related cost of 0.9% of the loan value for managing the loan per year. The loan will be funded by retail deposits at a rate of 4.5% of the loan value. The expected loss is assumed to be 1% of the loan value. The tax rate is 25% for the lender. The economic capital is estimated at 6% of the loan amount with zero strategic capital, and the risk-free interest rate is 4%. The RAROC is calculated as follows:

$$\text{RAROC} = \frac{(1 - 0.25)\begin{pmatrix} 10 \times 0.07 - 10 \times 0.009 - 10 \\ \times 0.045 - 10 \times 0.01 + 10 \times 0.06 \times 0.04 \end{pmatrix}}{10 \times 0.06}$$

$$= 10.5\%$$

Whether the aforementioned 10.5% performance is satisfactory depends on the lender's expectations. If the lender expects a return of 15%, then the performance is considered poor; however, if the expectation is only 10%, then the performance exceeds the expectation. For a firm, you may also compare the RAROC value to the firm's hurdle rate, which is calculated as the after-tax weighted average cost of equity capital (Crouhy et al., 2013, p. 598). If the RAROC is higher than the firm's hurdle rate, it is considered that the investment adds value to the firm; otherwise, the investment may not be as favorable.

11.5.2 Return on Risk-Adjusted Capital

The *Return on Risk-Adjusted Capital* (RORAC) is another financial measure used to assess the profitability of a firm while considering the risks taken to achieve that profitability. RORAC is given by:

$$\text{RORAC} = \frac{\text{Net Income}}{\text{Economic Capital}} = \frac{\text{Revenue} - \text{Expenses}}{\text{Economic Capital}}$$

Compared to the RAROC equation, RORAC does not include three components in the numerator: expected losses taxes, and return on risk capital. Using the same data from the RAROC illustration, we have:

$$\text{RORAC} = \frac{10 \times 0.07 - 10 \times 0.009 - 10 \times 0.045}{10 \times 0.06} = 26.67\%$$

In this example, the RORAC value is higher than the RAROC value, primarily because the tax rate has a significant impact on the final outcome.

To demonstrate the influence of risk level on the final values of RAROC and RORAC, let's assume another loan to Firm B, which has a lower credit rating than Firm A, so Firm B's economic capital is estimated at 10% of the loan amount (i.e., requiring a larger capital to cover unexpected losses due to risks). We also assume all other factors are identical between the two firms. We can then calculate the corresponding values for RAROC and RORAC, as shown in Table 11.4.

Given that Firm B is less creditworthy, it requires a larger economic capital to cover potential unexpected losses due to risks. Consequently, its RAROC and RORAC values are lower than those of Firm A's due to the risk impact.

Table 11.4 RAROC and RORAC for two different firms

	Risk Level	Economic Capital	RAROC	RORAC
Firm A	Low (6% exposure)	0.60	10.50%	26.67%
Firm B	High (10% exposure)	1.00	7.50%	16.00%

11.6 Summary

Table 11.5 Sharpe ratios

	Return	Risk-Free Rate	Volatility	Sharpe Ratio
Investment 1	10.50%	1.50%	10%	90.0%
Investment 2	10.50%	1.50%	15%	60.0%

11.5.3 Sharpe Ratio

The *Sharpe ratio* measures how much a return, either expected or actual, outperforms a risk-free security.[2]

$$\text{Sharpe Ratio} = \frac{\text{Return} - \text{Risk-Free Rate}}{\text{Volatility}}$$

We now compare two investments' Sharpe ratios in Table 11.5. As shown in Table 11.5, the two investments have the same return and risk-free rate, but their volatility rates differ. As a result, their Sharpe ratios vary: the less risky investment has a higher Sharpe ratio.

11.6 Summary

This chapter provided an in-depth overview of various risk management tools and techniques, focusing on VaR, CVaR, stress testing, and risk-adjusted return ratios. These tools play a crucial role in the decision-making process, allowing firms and investors to assess and manage risk levels effectively.

Key Takeaways:

1. Value-at-Risk (VaR):
   - VaR is a widely used risk measurement tool that estimates the potential loss of an investment portfolio over a given time horizon at a specific confidence level.
   - VaR can be calculated using various methods, including historical simulation, variance–covariance method, and Monte Carlo simulation.
   - Limitations of VaR include its inability to capture tail risk and its sensitivity to the choice of the confidence level and holding period.
2. Conditional VaR (CVaR):

---

[2] Sharpe Ratio was developed and named after William Sharpe, a Nobel laureate.

- CVaR addresses some of the limitations of VaR by estimating the expected loss in the tail of the loss distribution.
- CVaR is a more coherent risk measure that accounts for the size and likelihood of extreme losses.
3. Stress Testing:
    - Stress testing assesses the resilience of financial institutions and investment portfolios under extreme and plausible adverse scenarios.
    - Various stress testing methods include economic insight-based stress tests and historical event-based stress tests.
    - Despite its subjective nature, stress testing helps firms prepare for financial disasters, making them better equipped to perform well during crises.
4. Risk-Adjusted Returns:
    - Risk-adjusted return measures, such as risk-adjusted return on capital (RAROC), return on risk-adjusted capital (RORAC), and Sharpe ratio, are used to compare the relative performance of firms or business units with different risk levels.
    - RAROC and RORAC take into account the economic capital and risk-adjusted expected net income, while the Sharpe ratio compares the excess return over the risk-free rate to the investment's volatility.
    - These measures help investors make more informed decisions by accounting for the trade-off between reward and risk.

11.7 Exercises

11.7.1 Practice Questions

1. What is VaR and what are the three main methods used to calculate VaR?
2. Calculate the VaR and VaR' for a portfolio with an expected return of 5%, a standard deviation of 8%, and a confidence level of 95%. Assume a one-day holding period.
3. Explain the differences between VaR and CVaR. What advantages does CVaR offer compared to VaR?
4. What are factor-push stress tests and how do they differ from stress testing based on historical events?
5. Calculate the RAROC for a loan valued at $5 million with an interest rate of 6%, direct related cost of 1.2% of the loan value, funding cost of 3.5% of the loan value, expected loss of 0.8% of the loan value, tax rate of 30%, economic capital of 4% of the loan value, and a risk-free interest rate of 3%.
6. Briefly explain the purpose of stress testing and the best practices to ensure its credibility and usefulness.
7. Calculate the Sharpe ratio for an investment with an expected return of 12%, a risk-free rate of 2%, and a standard deviation of 10%.
8. Explain the difference between RAROC and RORAC.

11.7 Exercises

9. What is the main limitation of the historical simulation method when calculating VaR?
10. Explain the concept of economic capital and its role in risk management.

11.7.2 Case Study

The Loan Insurance Dilemma at PreciseMech Global

Background

PreciseMech Global, an offshoot of the renowned German precision mechanical engineering company Heidelberger, is a significant supplier in the niche market of advanced industrial machinery. They provide equipment to firms worldwide, many of which are small to medium enterprises (SMEs). Amidst global economic uncertainties and tightening financial regulations, PreciseMech is revisiting its financial strategies to optimize risk management and ensure sustainability.

Challenges

1. **SME Reliance on Loan Insurance**: Many of PreciseMech's clients depend on loan insurance to enhance their purchasing capabilities. The terms of these insurances vary significantly and influence SMEs' purchasing decisions.
2. **Market Dynamics**: The continuously changing dynamics in finance and insurance markets affect the buying power of PreciseMech's clientele.
3. **Balancing Stakeholder Interests**: Striking a balance between assuring robust sales numbers and not pressuring SMEs into unfavorable financial arrangements.
4. **Regulatory Impacts**: Evolving financial and insurance regulations can sway SME purchasing patterns, impacting PreciseMech's bottom line.

Discussion Questions

1. How can PreciseMech ensure that its clientele of SMEs is adequately insured without exerting undue influence over their financial decisions?
2. Discuss how PreciseMech's CVaR assessment results could shape its strategic approach to client engagement.
3. What insights can PreciseMech derive from its stress tests concerning its resilience in the face of economic downturns or severe regulatory changes?
4. How can risk-adjusted returns help PreciseMech in prioritizing its investments and partnerships, considering its unique market position?

Appendix: Academic Perspective

Curtailing Bank Loan and Loan Insurance Under Risk Regulations in Supply Chain Finance
Wenli Wang and Gangshu (George) Cai[3]

Introduction

Banks, in their bid to manage financing risks, often set loan limits to ensure that the risk of principal loss remains within controlled boundaries, a process echoing Value-at-Risk (VaR) mechanisms. For instance, certain banks assess loan officers' performance based on the loan recovery rate and potential individual loan losses. Such risk management by banks is rooted not only in self-preservation but is also enforced by governmental regulations like Basel Accords I, II, and III (Basel Committee on Banking Supervision, 2010), endorsed by the Federal Reserve Board. These conservative practices further curtail the financing potential for numerous businesses.

In scenarios where borrowing firms lack ample collateral to secure bank loans, third-party insurers offer loan insurance as a viable alternative. This approach allows borrowing firms to transfer financing risk from banks to insurers, garnering increasing attention over time. Through loan insurance, insurers guarantee creditors (i.e., banks), facilitating larger loans for debtors (i.e., borrowers such as buyers). The borrower pays for the loan insurance, and should they default, the lender is the beneficiary.

Loan insurance finds favor in both developing and developed nations, primarily because insured businesses become more appealing to banks. Illustratively, Megal S.A., a Uruguayan SME, secured a substantial loan insured by the Norwegian Guarantee Institute for Export Credits (GIEK) to procure gas cylinders from Hexagon Ragasco, a leading global producer based in Norway. Conversely, in a domestic scenario, Ping An Property & Casualty Insurance covered bank loans taken by distributors to source food products from COFCO Group, China's premier food processor. In some cases, to foster a loan-through-insurance ecosystem, governments might offset part of the loan insurance premiums. An instance of this is Singapore's Loan Insurance Scheme, wherein the government subsidizes up to 55% of the loan insurance premium. However, akin to banking, the insurance sector is stringently regulated, necessitating insurers to maintain their insured loan limits to manage their risks effectively.

---

[3] This section presents research findings from one of my publications, Wang and Cai (2023). For a more comprehensive understanding, readers are encouraged to consult the full article: Wang, W., & Cai, G. (2023). Curtailing Bank Loan and Loan Insurance Under Risk Regulations in Supply Chain Finance. *Management Science*. https://doi.org/10.1287/mnsc.2023.4827. We've omitted most references for brevity; for further details, please refer to Wang and Cai (2023).

Appendix: Academic Perspective

The primary intent behind bank loans and loan insurance is to assist firms limited by capital. Within a supplier–buyer supply chain, it is often assumed that both parties would prefer minimized bank fees and insurance premiums, stemming from the belief that elevated costs might reduce order volumes, affecting both businesses and the supply chain at large. It then seems reasonable to argue that both parties would be inclined toward higher loan and insured loan limits, wishing for banks and insurers to be less risk-averse. Yet, there's a conspicuous absence of studies that delve into the intricate dynamics between stakeholders in a capital-restricted supply chain intersecting with risk-averse banks and insurers, and the mutual influence of bank loans and loan insurance on actual supply chain outcomes.

This leads us to a few pertinent research queries:

- How do the risk aversion levels and the terms of bank loans and loan insurance impact the equilibrium and strategic interplay among supply chain entities?
- Is it always in the supplier's best interest to advocate loan insurance for the buyer?
- How do government insurance subsidies to buyers influence the profits of supply chain entities and overall societal welfare?

Supply Chain Finance Model with Intermediate Product

In this model, a supply chain consists of a supplier vending an intermediate product—be it materials, commodities, or component products—to a buyer who subsequently manufactures an end product.

Ordering Process

At the season's onset, the buyer procures Q units of the intermediate product from the supplier, priced at w per unit. The supplier incurs a production cost of c for each unit. Simplifying the process, we deduce that crafting a single unit of the end product requires one unit of the intermediate product, and this manufacturing cost is normalized to zero. By the season's end, the end product retails to consumers at a price of p, standardized to 1 for manageability. The customer demand is symbolized by ξ and remains unpredictable.

Financial Dynamics

The buyer, constrained by capital with an initial amount of l, must resort to a bank loan amounting to $wQ - l + \tau$ to fulfill the order. This loan, featuring an interest rate $r(Q)$ based on Q, culminates in a repayment sum of $z(Q) = [(wQ - l + \tau)(1 + r(Q))]$. The buyer is obligated to settle the full loan amount if their revenue meets or exceeds $z(Q)$. Inability to do so results in bankruptcy, with the bank securing the remaining value, ξ. Hence, the bank's future cash flow stands at $Y(Q) = min(\xi, z(Q))$, with an expected value of $EY(Q) = S(z(Q))$.

To mitigate financing risks, banks stipulate a loan limit, ensuring that the principal's loss ratio doesn't exceed α (where $0 < \alpha < 1$), remaining within a risk tolerance threshold of β ($0 < \beta < 1$). This is articulated as: $Pr\{Y(Q) < (1-\alpha)(wQ - l + \tau)\} \leq \beta$. This risk regulation, mirroring the VaR approach, aligns with global banking guidelines, notably the Basel Accords I, II, and III.

To determine the order amount in alignment with this risk management strategy, wQ should not exceed $u + l - \tau$. Here, $u = \left[(1/(1-\alpha))F^{-1}(\beta)\right]$ defines the initial loan limit—the maximum permissible loan without insurance, provided $u > \tau$. Naturally, the initial loan limit escalates with α and β and can be proportionally increased with market growth.

Banks fix interest rates based on the actual loan amount and anticipated profit margins. Consistent with established literature, this rate ensures that the expected return mirrors the risk-free return, accounting for market risk and buyer insurance status. For the sake of simplicity, we've set the risk-free interest rate to zero, but note that a positive risk-free interest rate would only augment computational intricacy without altering our core insights.

Insurance Dynamics

The capital-limited buyer deliberates on acquiring third-party loan insurance. Such insurance reduces lending risk for banks, potentially elevating the loan and order limits. In scenarios featuring a deductible insurance policy, the buyer determines the coverage level, b, and pledges this to the bank. If the post-bankruptcy residual value (ξ) is below b, the insurer compensates the bank for the difference; else, no payment is made.

Practical implementation often sees insurers charging a fixed premium alongside a variable one. The fixed premium, in essence, safeguards the insurance company's continuity. Our model assumes the insurance premium encompasses both the variable component, calculated as the expected compensation payment $\mathbb{E}max(b - \xi, 0)$, and a fixed premium, t. Hence, the total premium is represented by $m(b) = \int_0^b (b - x)f(x)dx + t$, which grows with b.

Like banks, insurers also operate within stringent regulations. To manage risks, they adhere to the VaR principle. Consequently, the insurer's coverage limit is determined by $b = S^{-1}(F^{-1}(\delta))$. Additionally, $v \equiv (1/(1-\alpha))b - \int_0^b F(x)dx$ represents the insured loan limit. Given this insured limit, a buyer's order shouldn't exceed $((v + l - \tau - t)/w)$.

Supply Chain Game Dynamics

In this Stackelberg game of the supply chain, the supplier, post the announcements of loan limits by the bank and insurer, determines the wholesale price. The buyer then chooses whether to procure insurance, the level of coverage, the loan amount, and the order quantity. The bank, upon reviewing the buyer's loan application, sets the interest rate. Following these decisions, the buyer places the order, the demand gets actualized, and the product is sold to consumers. This entire process flow is graphically illustrated in Fig. 11.5. The game's solution is deduced by retracing the steps.

Appendix: Academic Perspective   333

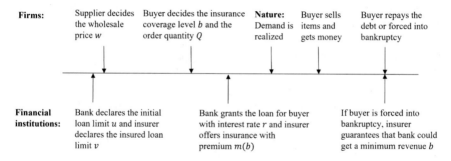

Fig. 11.5 Timeline of supply chain events

Main Findings

From the buyer's perspective, purchasing loan insurance with a suboptimal policy (i.e., a higher fixed insurance premium and a lower insured loan limit) isn't necessarily a disadvantage. The buyer can strategically leverage the less favorable insurance policy to negotiate a lower wholesale price from the supplier, resulting in a mutually beneficial outcome for both parties.

From the supplier's standpoint, selling to a buyer who confronts a higher bank fee and a lower initial loan limit isn't necessarily a negative, especially if the buyer is willing to acquire loan insurance to enhance its order capacity. To prevent buyers from strategically exploiting subpar insurance conditions to the supplier's detriment, it's advantageous for suppliers to assist their buyers in securing better insurance deals. Large suppliers, like Heidelberger, a renowned German precision mechanical engineering firm, often follow this approach in reality. Additionally, when the fixed insurance premium is relatively low, the supplier stands to benefit more from loan insurance in a dual-buyer scenario than in a single-buyer situation.

From the vantage point of supply chain companies concerning risk regulations, buyers are more inclined to benefit from stringent insurance regulations, while suppliers often benefit from tighter financial regulations. Consequently, a buyer might advocate against stringent banking regulations, while a supplier could oppose stricter insurance guidelines. Nonetheless, thanks to the judicious restrictions on both bank loans and loan insurance, the entire supply chain can profit from reasonably regulated financial and insurance sectors. Properly balanced regulations in finance and insurance can bolster both the financial and insurance sectors and amplify overall supply chain efficiency.

Our analysis also reveals a Stackelberg prisoner's dilemma when either the insurance policy is too strict (as evidenced by excessively high fixed premiums or low insured loan limits) or the banking regulations are too lax (represented by minor fixed bank fees or high initial loan limits). In such cases, buyers refrain from buying insurance due to exorbitant costs. Aye Min Thein, the Managing Director of Myanmar Insurance, observed a similar pattern with few SMEs opting for credit guarantee insurance when banking loans are restrictive. Policymakers should, therefore, ease constraints on insurance limits and reduce premiums while simultaneously tightening banking regulations. This balance can deter the Stackelberg prisoner's dilemma and augment supply chain efficacy.

In practical terms, governments can mitigate the Stackelberg prisoner's dilemma by offering insurance subsidies to loan seekers, thereby boosting societal welfare. This approach often provides a cost-effective solution for governments aiming to support SMEs, as subsidizing loan insurance is generally cheaper than direct loan provision. This strategy aligns with the policies of numerous governments regarding credit guarantees. By 2003, almost 100 countries had instituted over 2250 credit guarantee programs in various formats. Many governments subsidize insurers to enhance coverage and decrease premiums for SMEs. In 2020 alone, in the wake of the COVID-19 crisis, 41 countries introduced 57 new credit guarantee schemes targeting SMEs.

Additionally, officials might promote insurance premium co-funding to alleviate the Stackelberg prisoner's dilemma, driving supply chain efficiency. Analogous cost-sharing models have been adopted by supply chain entities. For instance, when Megal S.A. sought a loan from Export Credit Norway to buy gas cylinders from Hexagon Ragasco, the supplier covered 10% of the guarantee in conjunction with the insurance firm GIEK, offering an alternative mode of sharing insurance premiums with the buyer.

Regarding supply chain finance mechanisms, suppliers should exercise caution when extending trade credit to capital-limited buyers, especially if their production costs are elevated. Conversely, to attain a more substantial order limit, buyers might find it advantageous to borrow from fewer banks.

References

Acerbi, C., & Tasche, D. (2002). On the coherence of expected shortfall. *Journal of Banking & Finance, 26*(7), 1487–1503.

Allen, S. L. (2012). *Financial risk management: A practitioner's guide to managing market and credit risk* (vol. 721). John Wiley & Sons.

Brown, A. (2007). On stressing the right size. *GARP Risk Review*.

Crouhy, M., Galai, D., & Mark, R. (2013). *The essentials of risk management* (vol. 1). McGraw-Hill New York.

Gurnani, H., Ramachandran, K., Ray, S., & Xia, Y. (2014). Ordering behavior under supply risk: An experimental investigation. *Manufacturing & Service Operations Management, 16*(1), 61–75.

Kenton, W. (2020). What is Economic Capital (EC)? How to calculate and example. *Investopedia.com*. https://www.investopedia.com/terms/e. Accessed March 23, 2020.

Kim, J., & Finger, C. C. (2000). A stress test to incorporate correlation breakdown. *Journal of Risk, 2*, 5–20.

Koller, T., Lovallo, D., & Williams, Z. (2012). *Overcoming a bias against risk*. https://www.mckinsey.com/capabilities/strategy-and-corporate-finance/our-insights/overcoming-a-bias-against-risk. Accessed May 3, 2020.

Litterman, R. (1996). Hot spots and hedges. *Journal of Portfolio Management, 52*.

Neukirchen, M. (2012). Managing market risk: Today and tomorrow. *Mckinsey & Company, 32*, 3.

Wang, W., & Cai, G. (2023). Curtailing bank loan and loan insurance under risk regulations in supply chain finance. *Management Science*. https://doi.org/10.1287/mnsc.2023.4827

Wikipedia. (2024). Value at risk. https://en.wikipedia.org/wiki/Value_at_risk. Accessed January 8, 2024.

Zuckerman, G. (2005). Cash-rich firms feel pressure to spend. *The Wall Street Journal C, 1*.

Risk Mitigation and Management 12

Learning Objectives:

1. Evaluate traditional and modern risk mitigation techniques in supply chain finance (SCF).
2. Understand SCF-based insurance, credit guarantees, and guarantor financing mechanisms and benefits.
3. Compare financial versus operational hedging in stabilizing supply chains.
4. Study the regulatory framework affecting SCF practices and supply chain operations.
5. Discuss the ethical and sustainability aspects in SCF and their roles in responsible business decisions.

12.1 Introduction

In supply chain management, there are four primary flows: product, information, financial, and risk. While the product, information, and financial flows are tangible and relatively easier to quantify, the risk flow is more abstract and challenging to measure. Risk is intrinsically interconnected with the other flows, continuously evolving based on changes in these flows or the external environment, even when other factors remain constant. Consequently, risk flow depends not only on the internal dynamics of product, information, and financial flows, but also on external factors such as jurisdictional laws and regulations, political crises, social events, and natural phenomena (e.g., earthquakes, climate change, and pandemics).

A widely accepted risk management framework entails "Stopping, Reducing, Transferring, or Accepting" risks in various situations. As risks do not vanish automatically, stopping them often means ceasing business with a specific firm associated with those risks. In practice, supply chain finance primarily involves a combination of reducing, transferring, and accepting risks by different parties engaged in supply chain transactions.

12.2 Foundations for Supply Chain Finance Risk Mitigation

12.2.1 Asymmetric Risk Theory

Organizations, with their diverse physical and financial characteristics, are inherently unique. It is therefore intuitive that no single risk will be identical for all organizations. In essence, each risk is distinct and must be approached and managed individually by each organization. This concept can be encapsulated in the *Asymmetric Risk Theory*.

> **Axiom 1 (Asymmetric Risk Value):** *Different organizations assign unique values to the same risk.*
> **Axiom 2 (Asymmetric Risk Mitigation Capability):** *Risk mitigation capabilities differ among organizations.*
> **Axiom 3 (Asymmetric Risk Control):** *Various organizations approach and manage the same risk differently.*
> **Theorem (Value of Asymmetric Risk Mitigation):** *Optimally mitigating, exchanging, and managing asymmetric risks can enhance the overall supply chain value.*

Axiom 1, *Asymmetric Risk Value*, asserts that the same risk (e.g., a pandemic's negative impact or an identical debt amount) is perceived differently by organizations due to their varied financial statuses (e.g., cash flow), risk attitudes, and positions in the environment. For instance, a $1 million loan is insignificant for a large company like Apple but could be a considerable burden for a small family-run startup. Moreover, it is easier for a creditworthy firm to secure a loan than a firm without a credit history.

Axiom 2, *Asymmetric Risk Mitigation Capability*, posits that organizations possess diverse risk mitigation capabilities stemming from their unique credit scores, credit histories, and financial statuses. Consequently, creditworthy companies can obtain loans using their credit scores, while others may need to provide substantial collateral for the same loan amount. This variation also leads to differing interest rates among organizations.

Axiom 3, *Asymmetric Risk Control*, states that organizations address the same risk in distinct ways, which is logical considering their differing perspectives and approaches to risk.

Drawing from Axioms 1–3, it is evident that organizations have incentives to collaborate on supply chain risk mitigation. A more creditworthy supply chain firm assuming greater risks can generate added value for a less creditworthy firm,

12.2 Foundations for Supply Chain Finance Risk Mitigation

fostering cooperation in supply chain financing, such as in reverse factoring. This risk mitigation philosophy can also be applied to other SCF mechanisms.

12.2.2 Risk-Reward Pareto Frontier

Building on the Asymmetric Risk Theory, we can deduce that a fundamental aspect of supply chain finance is the risk-reward exchange. For supply chain firms to benefit from supply chain finance, there must be a trade-off between risks and rewards. For example, in trade credit financing, a seller gains from a larger order by extending the credit line (i.e., assuming more risks). In factoring, a bank takes on risks when purchasing accounts receivable, with the benefit of earning a discount on those receivables. In reverse factoring, the buyer assumes more risks by providing guarantees for the bank loan in exchange for a longer credit term.

> *The underlying foundation for supply chain finance is the risk-reward exchange.*

Another foundational aspect making supply chain finance more appealing is its ability to create mutually beneficial risk-reward scenarios for all parties involved in supply chain transactions. A single firm can find a balance between risk and reward, generally choosing not to assume excessive risks, although greater risks could lead to higher rewards (Chopra & Sodhi, 2004). The firm can benefit from improving efficiency in reducing risks and simultaneously increasing rewards. Supply chain finance can be such an efficiency improvement, enhancing all parties' profits in risk-reward exchanges due to their varying risk situations and attitudes implied in the Asymmetric Risk Theory.

As illustrated in Fig. 12.1, the total reward for all parties can increase after implementing a supply chain finance mechanism. For instance, in reverse factoring, the less creditworthy seller benefits from early payment from the bank endorsed by the more dominant buyer, the bank gains from the buyer's guarantee and better credit rating, and the buyer benefits from a longer credit payment term and a more reliable seller. Due to the buyer's superior credit rating, the total risk posed to the entire system, particularly the bank, is reduced. The entire system benefits from not only higher rewards but also lower risks, thanks to the implementation of reverse factoring.

This phenomenon is not exclusive to reverse factoring but applies to many supply chain finance mechanisms. For example, in factoring, collecting payment from a more creditworthy buyer using the accounts receivable may be easier than collecting payment directly from the capital-constrained seller. Since financial institutions typically have higher creditworthiness than borrowing firms, all involved parties benefit from supply chain transactions supported by supply chain finance when risks shift from lower creditworthy firms to financial institutions.

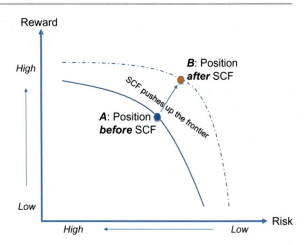

Fig. 12.1 Supply chain finance risk-reward frontier

These risks to financial institutions are generally mitigated because the goods in supply chain transactions can serve as collateral, as well as guarantees from related supply chain firms.

12.2.3 The Weakest Link Dilemma

The *Barrel Principle* states that the maximum capacity of a container is determined by its shortest board. Analogously, some argue that a supply chain's strength relies on its weakest link, which could be due to poor management, insufficient raw materials, or financial distress. For example, during the COVID-19 pandemic, logistics emerged as a weak link due to disrupted international port operations stemming from certain countries' pandemic policies. In high-tech industries, China's supply chains have faced challenges with chips as a weak link.

> *A supply chain's strength relies on its weakest link.*

From a financial flow perspective, a particular supply chain member—either a buyer or supplier—may be more susceptible to financial distress, becoming the weakest link due to their high default risk. Supply chain finance programs can mitigate a firm's default risk; for instance, the most creditworthy supply chain firm can help secure a loan for the weakest link firm.

However, the most creditworthy supply chain firm faces a dilemma: when assisting the weakest firm, they also risk losing money by financing the weaker entity. Should they help the weakest firm or replace it with a stronger one? There is no straightforward solution to this dilemma. Firms should exercise caution when adopting any drastic measures, such as replacing the weakest link. It is critical to

12.2 Foundations for Supply Chain Finance Risk Mitigation

recognize that cooperation in supply chain financing can generally enhance overall supply chain efficiency.

Due to geopolitical competition, the weakest link scenarios in supply chains are more complex than ever. There are three types of weakest links:

1. ***Individual Supply Chain Weakest Link***: Assuming there are no geopolitical barriers, a firm can optimize its supply chain as best as possible. In this case, the weakest link for each firm's supply chain will differ and may change dynamically over time.
2. ***Global Supply Chain Weakest Link***: This perspective offers a holistic view of global supply chains across various industries, such as food, computer, and automotive industries. Economic globalization allows the world to cooperate on addressing the weakest link issues in most cases.
3. ***National Supply Chain Weakest Link***: This perspective takes a holistic view of a country's overall supply chains across various industries. As intense competition between countries like the U.S. and China continues, access to raw materials, products, and financial resources may become restricted. Firms in one country might be unable to obtain resources from another rivaling country (e.g., the U.S. ban on selling high-tech products to China and prohibiting firms from purchasing 5G products from China). Consequently, weakest links may be politically created due to competition under the guise of national security. As globalization recedes and weaknesses become more prevalent, countries may face increased isolation when reallocating resources to strengthen their weakest links. Although national capital will be utilized to address these issues, the global market will likely become further segregated and divided, harming all countries in various ways.

It is important to note that simply replacing a weaker firm with a stronger one is not always feasible, as building supply chain relationships can be costly, particularly when the link is strategically important or challenging to replace quickly. Supply chain finance mechanisms will continue to be effective in addressing the weakest link dilemma; however, it is never a panacea. The focal firm can either provide financial relief to the weakest link directly or offer guarantees to partnered financial institutions to assist the weakest link.

12.2.4 PPRR Risk Management Model

Break of the weakest link usually leads to disruption of the entire supply chain, as we have seen so many cases during the COVID-19 pandemic. To reduce the impact of the negative impact of potential supply chain disruptions caused by the weakest link, the following *PPRR risk management* model can be used (Marotta, 2022):

- ***Prevention***: Be proactive and precautionary against any supply chain risks, such as the break of the weakest link.

- ***Preparedness***: Construct a contingency plan to cope with potential supply chain disruptions.
- ***Response***: Implement the contingency plan to reduce the negative impact of a disruption.
- ***Recovery***: Recover to the normal capacity as fast as possible.

12.2.5 PIARA Risk Management Process

The *PIARA risk management* process, which stands for Prioritize, Identify, Assess, Respond, and Audit, is an approach that can be used to assess and manage supply chain finance risks. This method helps organizations identify and manage potential risks within their supply chains while considering the context of supply chain finance (Witte, 2023). Here's an overview of the PIARA process:

1. ***Prioritize***: The first step in the PIARA process involves prioritizing risks by identifying the most critical aspects of the supply chain and determining which risks could significantly impact the organization's overall performance. Prioritizing risks enables organizations to focus their resources and efforts on addressing the most critical risks first, including those related to supply chain finance, such as credit risks and liquidity risks.
2. ***Identify***: After prioritizing the risks, the next step is to identify potential sources of risk in the supply chain. This may include suppliers, logistics providers, financial institutions, or any other third party involved in the supply chain finance process. The identification process may involve gathering information, conducting surveys, or using tools like risk registers or supplier questionnaires to collect data on potential risk factors.
3. ***Assess***: Once the risks have been identified, the next step is to assess their likelihood and potential impact. This can be done using qualitative and quantitative risk assessment techniques, such as risk severity matrices or Monte Carlo simulations. The goal of this step is to understand the potential consequences of each risk, including financial impacts, and determine the organization's level of exposure.
4. ***Respond***: After assessing the risks, the organization must develop and implement appropriate risk mitigation strategies. These may include risk avoidance, risk reduction, risk transfer (e.g., through insurance or supply chain finance mechanisms), or risk acceptance. The response should be tailored to the specific risk factors and the organization's risk tolerance.
5. ***Audit***: The final step in the PIARA process is to audit and review the effectiveness of the risk management strategies in place. This involves monitoring and measuring the performance of the risk mitigation efforts, including the effectiveness of supply chain finance solutions, and making adjustments as needed to ensure the organization remains protected against supply chain risks.

In summary, the PIARA process is an approach to supply chain risk assessment and management that incorporates considerations of supply chain finance, helping organizations prioritize, identify, assess, respond to, and audit risks in their supply chains to ensure their resilience and success.

Case Study

Implementing PIARA

Here's a simplified example of the PIARA process in the context of supply chain finance for a manufacturing company:

1. ***Prioritize***: The manufacturing company identifies credit risk, liquidity risk, and operational risk as the most critical risks affecting its supply chain finance.
2. ***Identify***: The company gathers data on the following risk factors:
   - Supplier payment terms and credit ratings
   - Customer payment terms and credit ratings
   - Inventory turnover ratio
   - Access to financing options and interest rates
   - Historical payment delays and disputes
   - Economic and political factors affecting the industry
3. ***Assess***: The company uses a risk severity matrix to assess the identified risks based on their likelihood and potential impact. The following values are assigned to each risk:
   - Credit risk: Likelihood (3 out of 5), Impact (4 out of 5)
   - Liquidity risk: Likelihood (2 out of 5), Impact (5 out of 5)
   - Operational risk: Likelihood (4 out of 5), Impact (3 out of 5)
4. ***Respond***: The company develops risk mitigation strategies for each risk:
   - Credit risk: Implement a reverse factoring program to reduce credit risk for suppliers, where the company's bank provides financing to suppliers at a lower interest rate based on the company's credit rating.
   - Liquidity risk: Set up a dynamic discounting program that allows customers to receive a discount for early payment, thus improving the company's cash flow.
   - Operational risk: Invest in supply chain management software to improve visibility and control over inventory levels, reducing the risk of stockouts or excess inventory.
5. ***Audit***: The company monitors the performance of its risk mitigation strategies by tracking the following key performance indicators (KPIs):
   - Credit risk: Reduction in supplier payment delays and improved supplier credit ratings.
   - Liquidity risk: Increase in early payment discounts taken by customers and improvement in the company's cash conversion cycle.

- Operational risk: Reduction in inventory carrying costs and stockout occurrences.

By following the PIARA process, the manufacturing company can effectively manage and mitigate risks related to supply chain finance, ensuring the resilience and success of its supply chain.

12.3 Traditional Risk Mitigation Strategies

Mitigating risks is crucial for managing projects or businesses. Traditional risk mitigation strategies, which have been utilized for years, focus on identifying, assessing, and addressing potential risks. Despite the emergence of newer techniques, traditional strategies remain relevant and effective. By employing these proven methods, individuals and organizations can better navigate the uncertainties of today's business environment. The following discussion presents risk mitigation suggestions for risks outlined in Chapter 10.3.

12.3.1 Financial Risk Mitigation

Successful financial risk mitigation involves implementing policies, procedures, and practices that decrease the likelihood or impact of risks. Strategies include diversifying investments, maintaining adequate cash reserves, and using risk management tools like hedging or insurance. Proactively identifying and addressing potential financial risks enables businesses to safeguard their bottom line, enhance financial stability, and make well-informed decisions.

12.3.1.1 Market Risk Mitigation
To mitigate market risks, organizations can employ a variety of strategies. Some of the most common approaches include:

- *Equity Price Risk Mitigation*:
  - To mitigate this risk, lenders may set a cap on the amount of financing that can be secured by equity collateral.
  - Spreading investments across different assets, industries, or geographic regions can help minimize the impact of market risks on the overall portfolio.
- *Interest Rate Risk Mitigation*:
  - To manage interest rate risk, organizations can use financial instruments such as interest rate swaps, caps, and floors to stabilize cash flows and protect against adverse movements in interest rates.

– Borrowers can also negotiate a fixed interest rate for the loan rather than a variable rate and consider refinancing their loans if interest rates drop significantly.
- **Foreign Exchange Risk Mitigation**:
  – For businesses with international exposure, implementing currency risk management strategies such as currency hedging, natural hedging, or diversification of currency exposure can help mitigate foreign exchange risks.
  – One potential strategy to mitigate foreign exchange risk is to negotiate contracts and payments in the local currency of each party involved in the transaction.
- **Commodity Price Risk Mitigation**:
  – Companies can use tools like commodity futures, options, and swaps to hedge against fluctuations in commodity prices, ensuring more predictable costs and revenues.
  – Organizations can also enter into fixed-price contracts that lock in the price of a commodity for a specific period, thus minimizing the impact of price fluctuations.

In addition, continuously monitoring market conditions and adjusting the organization's risk exposure accordingly can help reduce the impact of market risks. Evaluating the potential impact of adverse market events on the organization's performance can help identify vulnerabilities and take preventive actions.

12.3.1.2 Credit Risk Mitigation
Some key credit risk mitigation techniques include:

- **Settlement Risk Mitigation**:
  – To mitigate settlement risk, firms can consider using a clearinghouse, which serves as an intermediary between the parties involved and ensures that settlement takes place on time.
  – Alternatively, firms can establish a special purpose vehicle (SPV) to manage the transaction and ensure timely settlement.
  – Another option is to use payment upon delivery, which eliminates the risk of settlement failure.
- **Downgrade Risk Mitigation**:
  – Firms can mitigate downgrade risk by maintaining a strong credit profile and financial position. This can include improving financial ratios, diversifying funding sources, and maintaining adequate liquidity.
  – Firms can also consider seeking credit insurance to hedge against the risk of rating downgrades.
  – Another option is to transfer credit risk to third parties through instruments such as credit default swaps, credit-linked notes, or securitization.

- *Default Risk Mitigation*:
  - To mitigate default risk, lenders can perform thorough credit assessments before extending credit to borrowers. This can include reviewing credit scores, financial statements, and other relevant information. Lenders can also consider securing collateral or obtaining guarantees from third parties.
  - Lenders may develop internal credit scoring and rating systems to evaluate the credit risk of borrowers and monitor their creditworthiness over time.
  - Lenders can establish credit exposure limits for individual borrowers, industries, or sectors to manage concentration risk and reduce potential losses.
  - Diversifying the loan portfolio across different industries, sectors, and geographies can also help reduce the impact of a default by any single borrower or sector. Including financial covenants in loan agreements to establish performance criteria for borrowers, such as maintaining specific financial ratios, can provide early warning signs of potential default.
- *Bankruptcy Risk Mitigation*:
  - To mitigate bankruptcy risk, lenders can limit their exposure to individual borrowers by diversifying their loan portfolios.
  - Lenders can also obtain security interests in the borrower's assets or obtain guarantees from third parties.
  - Additionally, lenders can monitor borrowers' financial performance regularly to detect signs of financial distress early and take corrective action.

In addition to the above measures, firms should regularly monitor borrowers' financial performance and credit risk profiles to identify signs of potential distress or default and take corrective actions as needed. They should also conduct thorough credit analysis and underwriting processes to assess borrowers' creditworthiness and determine appropriate lending terms.

12.3.1.3 Liquidity Risk Mitigation

Some key liquidity risk mitigation techniques are:

- *Funding Liquidity Risk Mitigation*:
  - Regularly forecast cash inflows and outflows to anticipate liquidity needs, identify potential shortfalls, and take timely corrective actions.
  - A company can maintain a cash reserve to meet its debt obligations in case of a cash shortfall.
  - Companies can establish a line of credit with financial institutions to provide access to additional cash in times of need.
  - Diversifying funding sources, such as borrowing from multiple financial institutions or issuing bonds, can help mitigate the risk of relying on a single source of funding.

12.3 Traditional Risk Mitigation Strategies

- *Trading Liquidity Risk Mitigation*:
  - Developing relationships with a network of counterparties can help ensure there is always a willing buyer or seller.
  - Maintaining a diversified portfolio of assets can reduce the impact of trading liquidity risk on the overall portfolio.
  - Monitoring market conditions and being aware of potential liquidity shocks can help companies prepare and respond to any potential trading liquidity risk.
  - Develop and regularly update contingency funding plans that outline actions to be taken during liquidity crises, including identifying alternative funding sources.
  - Streamline operations and optimize working capital management to reduce cash conversion cycles and improve overall liquidity.

By employing these risk mitigation strategies, companies can better manage liquidity risk and maintain financial stability even amidst market turmoil or unforeseen occurrences.

12.3.1.4 Operational Risk Mitigation

To mitigate operational risks in financial risk management, organizations can implement various techniques, including:

- *Fraud Risk Mitigation*:
  - Implement robust anti-fraud policies and procedures.
  - Provide regular fraud awareness training to employees.
  - Conduct background checks on new hires.
  - Use fraud detection tools and systems to identify and prevent fraudulent activities.
- *Human Factor Risk Mitigation*:
  - Provide comprehensive training to employees on risk management, ensure adequate supervision and oversight, establish clear guidelines and protocols for operations, and conduct regular performance reviews and assessments.
  - Organizations can also implement strong internal controls to prevent and detect operational risks. This includes segregation of duties, dual approvals, and regular audits.
- *Technology Risk Mitigation*:
  - Implement and maintain robust cybersecurity measures, such as firewalls, intrusion detection systems, and encryption, regularly update and patch software.
  - Perform regular backups and disaster recovery tests, and monitor technology systems for anomalies and suspicious activities. Having a comprehensive disaster recovery plan in place may help minimize the impact of any potential technological breakdowns or natural disasters.

- *Model Risk Mitigation*:
  - Ensure that all models are regularly reviewed, validated, and tested, and that they comply with regulatory requirements and industry standards.
  - Establish clear documentation and governance frameworks for model development, deployment, and maintenance, and provide regular training and support to employees involved in model development and usage.
  - Models should be subject to independent validation and reviewed regularly to ensure their accuracy and relevance.

Overall, effective risk management involves a combination of these techniques and requires ongoing monitoring and assessment of potential risks. Organizations should have a business continuity plan in place to ensure that critical operations can continue in the event of an operational failure.

12.3.2 Supply Chain Risk Mitigation

12.3.2.1 Supply Risk Mitigation

Some key risk mitigation strategies for supply risks include:

- *Supplier Risk Mitigation*:
  - Diversify supplier relationships and maintain good communication and collaboration with them to stay aware of any potential issues. Having multiple suppliers can help mitigate the risk of relying on a single supplier. If one supplier fails to deliver, the buyer can turn to another supplier to fulfill their needs.
  - Regularly assessing suppliers' financial stability, quality control processes, and delivery capabilities can help identify potential issues before they become major risks.
  - Develop contingency plans and identify alternative suppliers in advance to minimize any potential disruptions.
- *Sourcing and Procurement Risk Mitigation*:
  - Implement a robust procurement process that includes identifying and vetting suppliers, establishing clear contracts and service level agreements, and continuously monitoring suppliers' performance to identify potential risks.
  - Effective procurement practices, such as competitive bidding and supply chain visibility, can help reduce supply risk.
- *Supply Quality Risk Mitigation*:
  - Conduct regular quality checks and inspections on incoming supplies to ensure they meet the required standards and specifications.
  - Establish a clear quality control process and enforce compliance with standards and regulations.
- *Supply Quantity Shortage Risk Mitigation*:
  - Maintain good inventory management practices and monitor supply levels to identify potential shortages or disruptions.

12.3 Traditional Risk Mitigation Strategies

- Identify alternative sources and establish backup plans to minimize the impact of supply shortages.
- Maintaining safety stock can help mitigate the risk of supply shortages and ensure that production can continue even in the event of supply chain disruptions.
- Planning for potential supply disruptions and having contingency plans in place can help minimize the impact of supply chain disruptions.
- **Supply Price Risk Mitigation**:
  - Monitor market trends and pricing fluctuations to stay aware of any potential changes that could impact the supply chain.
  - Consider negotiating long-term contracts with suppliers to lock in prices and reduce uncertainty.
- **Miscommunication Risk Mitigation**:
  - Develop clear communication channels with suppliers and establish a system for verifying orders and specifications to minimize any potential miscommunications.
  - The use of supply chain technology, such as real-time monitoring and predictive analytics, can help improve supply chain visibility and identify potential issues before they become major risks.
- **Supply Delivery Risk Mitigation**:
  - Establish clear delivery schedules and monitor shipments closely to ensure on-time delivery.
  - Identify potential risks and develop contingency plans to minimize any potential disruptions.

Regularly monitoring supply chain performance can help identify potential issues and provide insights for improving the supply chain's overall performance.

12.3.2.2 Demand Risk Mitigation

To mitigate demand risk, businesses can take various measures, such as:

- **Demand Volatility Risk Mitigation**:
  - Implement demand sensing and advanced analytics to improve forecasting accuracy.
  - Diversify the customer base and product portfolio to reduce the reliance on a single customer or product.
  - Adopt flexible inventory management practices and have a flexible supply chain that can quickly adjust to changing demand.
  - Closely monitor market trends to anticipate changes in demand.
- **Forecasting Risk Mitigation**:
  - Implement multiple forecasting methods and models, and continuously evaluate and update them based on actual demand data and market trends.
  - Use advanced forecasting models, continuously improve and update forecasting methods, and leverage machine learning algorithms to refine predictions.

- Collaborate with supply chain partners for better data sharing and planning.
- **Consumer Preference Risk Mitigation**:
  - Conduct market research and track consumer trends to identify potential shifts in demand, and adjust the product design, marketing strategy, and pricing accordingly.
  - Establish strong relationships with customers, especially those key customers, to better understand their preferences and needs.
  - Adopt agile supply chain strategies to quickly respond to shifts in preferences.
- **Product Lifecycle Change Risk Mitigation**:
  - Regularly evaluate the product life cycle and monitor industry trends and competitor actions.
  - Invest in new product development and innovation and introduce new products or product variations to meet changing customer needs and preferences.
  - Adopt flexible supply chain strategies to manage changing product life cycles effectively and ensure that the supply chain is flexible and can quickly adapt to changes in product demand.
- **Receivable Risk Mitigation**:
  - Implement a stringent credit risk management policy and monitor the creditworthiness of customers regularly.
  - Consider implementing trade credit insurance to protect against non-payment or default by customers.
- **Price Sensitivity Risk Mitigation**:
  - Develop pricing strategies based on value, cost, and competition.
  - Optimize supply chain efficiency to minimize costs.
  - Monitor market trends and competitors' pricing strategies to adjust pricing proactively.
  - Consider implementing price incentives, such as discounts and promotions, to stimulate demand during slow periods.
- **Regulatory and Legal Change Risk Mitigation**:
  - Maintain strong compliance management systems.
  - Monitor regulatory changes and adapt product specifications and production processes accordingly.
  - Establish contingency plans for potential regulatory impacts on the supply chain and quickly respond to changes in regulations or legal requirements.

In summary, in order to mitigate demand risks in supply chain risk management, it is crucial to focus on employing advanced analytics, diversification, agile strategies, and continuous improvement in forecasting and planning. Additionally, they should maintain strong relationships with customers, invest in innovation, implement credit risk management policies, develop value-based pricing strategies, and closely monitor regulatory changes.

12.3.2.3 Process Risk Mitigation

Risk mitigation strategies for process risks in supply chain risk management include the following:

- *Design/Innovation Risk Mitigation*:
  - Ensure that firms have a well-structured product design and development process that includes feedback loops to identify and correct design errors early.
  - Implement a rigorous design review process, incorporate customer feedback, and use prototyping and simulations to validate designs before full-scale production.
- *Planning Risk Mitigation*:
  - Establish a formal production planning process that involves regular forecasting and monitoring of inventory levels.
  - Maintain strong communication channels with suppliers to ensure timely, adequate capacity to meet demand, and accurate planning.
- *Information, Cybersecurity, and Coordination Risk Mitigation*:
  - Implement comprehensive cybersecurity measures, invest in employee training on cybersecurity practices, and establish protocols for information sharing and coordination among departments.
  - Invest in information systems security and establish protocols to safeguard against cyberattacks.
  - Regular coordination and communication with suppliers and customers can also mitigate this risk.
- *Production/Manufacturing Risk Mitigation*:
  - Regular maintenance of equipment and quality control processes can mitigate this risk.
  - Invest in workforce training and adopt continuous improvement methodologies to minimize disruptions and enhance manufacturing efficiency.
  - Have a contingency plan in place to address any potential manufacturing disruptions.
- *Capacity Risk Mitigation*:
  - Monitor capacity levels and invest in additional capacity when necessary to avoid production bottlenecks.
  - Monitor demand trends, utilize flexible production strategies, and consider outsourcing or partnering with third parties to ensure adequate capacity.
- *Inventory Risk Mitigation*:
  - Establish appropriate inventory management policies and procedures to optimize inventory levels and avoid stockouts or overstocking.
  - Implement real-time tracking systems and employ robust warehouse management practices to minimize inventory-related risks.
- *Transportation and Logistics Risk Mitigation*:
  - Diversify transportation modes and logistics partners and leverage real-time tracking technologies to mitigate transportation-related disruptions.

- Establish relationships with reliable transportation providers and establish contingency plans for unexpected disruptions.
- **Service Risk Mitigation**:
  - Have robust customer service policies and procedures in place to ensure timely and effective resolution of customer inquiries and issues.
  - Implement comprehensive after-sales service policies, invest in customer support infrastructure, and closely monitor service performance to ensure customer satisfaction.
- **Quality Control Risk Mitigation**:
  - Enforce stringent quality control procedures to ensure that products meet or exceed customer expectations.
  - Invest in employee training on quality assurance and establish systems for monitoring and correcting quality issues.
- **Labor Risk Mitigation**:
  - Establish a robust human resources policy and procedure to minimize employee turnover, monitor labor shortages, and address potential labor disputes.
  - Offer competitive compensation and benefits, invest in employee engagement and retention programs, and establish contingency plans for labor disruptions.
- **Social, Environmental, and Sustainability Risk Mitigation**:
  - Adopt sustainable practices and regularly monitor and assess their social and environmental impact.
  - Develop and implement comprehensive sustainability policies, engage with stakeholders, and monitor compliance with social and environmental regulations to minimize operational disruptions.

Overall, to mitigate supply chain risks, organizations should focus on rigorous design and planning processes, cybersecurity measures, manufacturing efficiency, and robust inventory management. Additionally, investing in employee training, diversifying transportation and logistics partners, and ensuring sustainability and compliance can help reduce potential disruptions and enhance overall supply chain performance.

12.3.2.4 Business Risk Mitigation

Risk mitigation strategies for business risks in supply chain risk management can include:

- **Legal Risk Mitigation**:
  - Legal counsel can draft, review, and negotiate contracts, establish clear communication channels with partners, and implement robust compliance and intellectual property protection measures to minimize the potential for misunderstandings and disputes.
  - Ensure that contracts are well-written and clearly define obligations and expectations.

12.3 Traditional Risk Mitigation Strategies

- Regularly monitor legal developments that could impact their operations, such as changes in intellectual property laws.
- **Strategic Risk Mitigation**:
  - Conduct thorough market research, competitor analysis, and risk assessments before making significant investments, and involve cross-functional teams in strategic decision-making processes.
  - Perform regular strategic reviews to ensure that investments align with business objectives and minimize the potential for significant losses.
  - Continuously monitor the competitive landscape and adapt quickly to changing market conditions and customer preferences.
- **Competition Risk Mitigation**:
  - Regularly assess the competitive position and adapt strategies as needed to maintain a competitive advantage. This can include investing in research and development, improving product design, and providing excellent customer service.
  - Continuously monitor market trends, invest in innovation and product development, and stay agile to adapt to changing customer preferences and evolving competitive landscape.
- **Contractual Risk Mitigation**:
  - Collaborate with legal experts to draft clear and well-defined contracts, outline dispute resolution mechanisms, and ensure all parties have a mutual understanding of contractual terms and obligations.
  - Contractual agreements should be regularly reviewed to ensure they are up-to-date and reflect current business conditions.
  - Disputes should be resolved through open communication and negotiation to minimize the potential for legal action.

In summary, to mitigate various business risks, organizations should engage legal counsel for contract drafting and compliance, conduct market research and competitor analysis, continuously monitor market trends and adapt to customer preferences, and collaborate with legal experts to create clear contracts with dispute resolution mechanisms.

12.3.3 Non-Commercial Risk Mitigation

Non-commercial risk mitigation strategies play a crucial role in managing the unpredictable and complex challenges businesses face beyond the realm of purely financial and supply chain concerns. These risks, which include political, regulatory, reputation, systematic, and disaster risks, can significantly impact a company's performance and long-term viability. An effective non-commercial risk mitigation strategy involves a comprehensive understanding of the potential risks, leveraging expert counsel, and developing agile and adaptable processes to minimize their impact on the organization's success. By proactively addressing these risks, businesses can maintain a competitive edge and ensure a more resilient supply chain in an ever-changing global landscape.

- *Political Risk Mitigation*:
    - Reducing reliance on a single country or region for sourcing materials, production, or sales can help minimize the impact of political risks. Diversifying supply chains helps businesses become more resilient to sudden changes in political landscapes.
    - Stay informed about political developments in countries where the business operates or sources materials. Regularly assess the potential impact of these developments on the business and be prepared to adapt operations accordingly.
    - Forming strategic partnerships with local businesses can help navigate complex political environments and regulatory landscapes. Local partners can provide valuable insights and support in dealing with changing regulations and political risks.
    - Consider obtaining political risk insurance to protect against the financial impact of political risks, such as expropriation, currency inconvertibility, or political violence.
    - Engage in lobbying and advocacy efforts to influence government policies that impact the business positively. Building relationships with key policymakers can help ensure the company's interests are considered during policy development.
    - Develop contingency plans for potential political risks that could disrupt operations. These plans should outline alternative sourcing strategies, backup suppliers, and potential production adjustments to minimize disruptions in the supply chain.
    - Ensure strict compliance with local laws and regulations to reduce the risk of fines, penalties, or negative publicity. Understanding and adhering to the legal framework of the countries in which the business operates can help maintain a favorable reputation and mitigate potential political risks.
- *Regulatory Risk Mitigation*
    - Develop and maintain a comprehensive compliance program that includes policies, procedures, and training to ensure adherence to all applicable laws and regulations.
    - Regularly monitor regulatory changes and updates at local, state, federal, and international levels. Establish processes to identify, analyze, and communicate the potential impact of new regulations on the business.
    - Collaborate with legal and regulatory experts to ensure a thorough understanding of the regulatory landscape and to develop strategies for compliance.
    - Involve all relevant departments in the compliance process to ensure that everyone is aware of and adhering to the regulations that apply to their specific areas of responsibility.

12.3 Traditional Risk Mitigation Strategies

- Perform periodic internal and external audits to assess the effectiveness of the compliance program and identify areas for improvement.
- Encourage a culture of compliance within the organization by promoting ethical behavior and clear communication about the importance of adhering to regulations.
- Create contingency plans to address potential non-compliance situations or regulatory changes. These plans should outline corrective actions, resources needed, and communication strategies to minimize the impact on the business.
- Encourage employees to report any potential compliance concerns or violations through confidential reporting mechanisms, such as hotlines or anonymous reporting tools.
- Participate in industry associations and engage in advocacy efforts to influence the development of regulations and stay informed about emerging trends and best practices in regulatory compliance.
- Regularly review and update the compliance program to address changes in the regulatory landscape and improve the effectiveness of the organization's compliance efforts.

- *Reputation Risk Mitigation*:
  - Foster a culture of integrity, ethics, and transparency within the organization to minimize the risk of scandals and unethical behavior.
  - Establish strict governance and compliance mechanisms to detect and prevent potential misconduct, including regular audits and employee training programs.
  - Regularly monitor social media and online platforms for mentions of the company and respond proactively to any negative sentiment, rumors, or misinformation.
  - Develop a comprehensive crisis management plan to address potential reputation risks and ensure a timely, coordinated, and effective response to minimize damage to the company's reputation.
  - Actively participate in corporate social responsibility (CSR) initiatives that demonstrate the company's commitment to social, ethical, and environmental responsibility.
  - Maintain open and transparent communication with stakeholders, including customers, employees, investors, and the public, to build trust and credibility.
  - Engage in industry associations and collaborate with peers to address common reputation risks and improve the overall reputation of the industry.
  - Invest in marketing and public relations efforts to create and maintain a strong, positive brand image that can withstand potential reputation risks.
  - Keep track of competitor activities and industry trends to identify potential reputation risks and develop strategies to address them proactively.

- Regularly review and update risk management processes to identify and address emerging reputation risks and maintain a strong, resilient reputation in the market.
- **Systematic Risk Mitigation**:
  - Diversify investments, suppliers, and customers to reduce reliance on a single firm or market segment, minimizing the impact of any single failure on the entire system.
  - Ensure sufficient capital reserves to withstand unexpected market shocks and maintain business operations during periods of uncertainty or crisis.
  - Conduct regular stress tests to identify potential vulnerabilities and assess the firm's ability to cope with various scenarios, including economic downturns, market crashes, or the failure of a significant counterparty.
  - Establish comprehensive risk management processes to identify, assess, and mitigate systematic risks, including regular monitoring and reporting of risk exposures and potential contagion effects.
  - Keep a close watch on macroeconomic indicators and global financial markets to anticipate potential systematic risks and adjust business strategies accordingly.
  - Engage with industry associations, peers, and regulatory bodies to share information, best practices, and develop collaborative approaches to managing and mitigating systematic risks.
  - Develop contingency plans to address the potential impacts of systematic risks on operations, including alternative supply chain arrangements, liquidity management strategies, and communication plans.
  - Maintain conservative leverage levels, manage liquidity risk, and avoid excessive risk-taking in investment and business operations to reduce the firm's vulnerability to systematic risks.
  - Leverage technology and innovation to improve operational efficiency, enhance resilience, and create a more agile organization capable of responding to systematic risks more effectively.
- **Disaster Risk Mitigation**:
  - Establish a thorough plan that addresses various disaster scenarios, including evacuation, communication, resource allocation, and recovery efforts.
  - Obtain appropriate insurance policies to cover potential losses resulting from natural disasters, terrorist attacks, or other catastrophic events.
  - Invest in resilient infrastructure and facilities to minimize the impact of disasters on supply chain operations, including building facilities to withstand extreme weather conditions and implementing redundant power and communication systems.
  - Diversify suppliers, production facilities, and distribution centers across different geographic locations to minimize the impact of a disaster in a specific region.
  - Identify and develop alternative supply routes to ensure the continuous flow of goods and materials during a disaster or disruption.

- Ensure proper data backup and recovery mechanisms are in place to safeguard essential business information and facilitate quick recovery after a disaster.
- Train employees on disaster preparedness and response procedures and conduct regular drills to ensure readiness in the event of an emergency.
- Regularly assess potential disaster risks, including changes in climate patterns and geopolitical tensions, to identify emerging threats and adjust disaster preparedness plans accordingly.
- Establish strong relationships with local authorities, industry partners, and emergency response organizations to facilitate effective disaster response and recovery efforts.
- Develop and implement a communication strategy to keep employees, customers, suppliers, and other stakeholders informed during and after a disaster, including updates on the status of operations and recovery efforts.

In sum, to mitigate non-commercial risks, businesses should diversify their supply chains and establish local partnerships to minimize political risks, maintain robust compliance programs and stay informed about regulatory changes to address regulatory risks, foster a culture of integrity and transparency to protect against reputation risks, diversify investments and maintain adequate capital reserves to manage systematic risks, and develop comprehensive disaster preparedness plans while strengthening infrastructure resilience to reduce disaster risks.

12.4 SCF-Based Insurance and Credit Guarantee

A major obstacle for many startups and small firms, particularly in the retail industry, is securing financing due to their limited fixed assets. A recent survey of 131,000 firms across 139 countries found that 26.5% face significant challenges in obtaining financing (Zhou et al., 2020). In developing regions such as Sub-Saharan Africa, this figure can rise to 38.3%. Bank loans are a common solution, but the survey reveals that 79.2% of loans require collateral worth 2.06 times the loan value on average. This is a significant barrier for small or startup firms with few assets. High collateral requirements stem from banks seeking to manage financing risks and the potential for borrowers to default on loans or face bankruptcy.

To manage financing risks, banks typically impose loan limits and charge fixed fees to cover administration and transaction costs. This approach, similar to Value-at-Risk (VaR), ensures the probability of loss remains below a specific threshold (Mudge & Wee, 1993). Banks' risk management practices are not only for self-protection but also comply with government regulations like Basel Accords I, II, and III, supported by the Federal Reserve Board (Wang & Cai, 2023). Banks also evaluate loan officers' performance based on loan recovery rates and potential individual loan losses (Jorion, 2007). These risk-averse practices inadvertently further limit firms' financing capabilities.

Loan guarantee insurance provided by third-party insurers has emerged as an effective tool for businesses lacking sufficient collateral to secure the necessary funds from banks. This approach transfers financing risk from banks to insurers and has increasingly gained attention (Caillaud et al., 2000). In loan insurance, the insurer guarantees the creditor (e.g., the bank), allowing the debtor (e.g., the borrower, such as a buyer) to obtain a larger loan. The borrower purchases the loan insurance, and either the borrower or the lender becomes the beneficiary in case of default.

Loan insurance premiums typically consist of two components: a variable premium and a fixed insurance premium (Dong & Tomlin, 2012). The variable premium, equivalent to the expected reimbursement payment, depends on the coverage level and follows the principle of fair pricing. The fixed insurance premium covers administrative costs associated with the insurance contract, such as credit evaluation, risk monitoring, and claim administration. These fees vary depending on the insurance scheme.

Like the banking industry, the insurance sector is highly regulated, and insurers must impose insured loan limits to control risk and maintain a certain level of stability.

12.4.1 Bank Loan Insurance

Banks often require insurance protection when providing loans, particularly for personal loans such as mortgages, car loans, and other personal financing. These insurance policies compensate lenders in the event of borrower default. A similar mechanism is applicable in commercial settings, including supply chains.

In the context of supply chains, loan insurance is prevalent in both developing and developed countries. Banks are more inclined to lend to businesses that have insured their payment obligations. For instance, in a global supply chain scenario, Megal S.A., a small Uruguayan business with 135 employees, secured a loan of over $1 million from Export Credit Norway, insured by the Norwegian Guarantee Institute for Export Credits (GIEK), to purchase gas cylinders from Hexagon Ragasco, the world's leading producer of composite LPG cylinders based in Norway (Eksfin, 2022). In a domestic supply chain, Ping An Property & Casualty Insurance provided insurance for bank loans obtained by downstream distributors to purchase food products from COFCO Group, China's largest food processor and manufacturer (Wang & Cai, 2023). Similar buyer credit insurance practices have been implemented by China Export & Credit Insurance and Pacific Property & Casualty Insurance.

Because these loans are based on supply chain transactions, borrowers usually receive support from their supply chain partners, which are often large and creditworthy companies. The involvement of insurance firms enhances borrowers' capabilities, benefiting all parties involved in the loan insurance process.

12.4.2 Bank Guarantee

A *bank guarantee* is a commitment by a bank to cover any losses when a debtor defaults on payments. The purpose of a bank guarantee could be to ensure required business performance, serve as collateral for transactions, warrant advance or deferred payment, and secure financial needs. Small businesses, compared to large corporations, are more likely to request bank guarantees to secure their transactions.

Bank guarantee comes in several ways:

- **Guarantee to a transaction with its own loan**: This type of bank guarantee often occurs by default when a bank provides traditional financing to a firm without other financing guarantees or third-party insurance. Because the bank takes responsibility for any borrower's default, it usually charges a higher interest rate as a risk premium. Most literature on bank financing implicitly assumes this type of bank guarantee due to its analytical simplicity (Jing et al., 2012).
- **Guarantee to a transaction without loan**: A bank may offer a guarantee to its partner firm in supply chain transactions, facilitating the transactions without directly lending money. This type of bank guarantee functions like third-party insurance. Both this and the above bank guarantee are also referred to as *direct guarantees*, in which the bank's security is issued directly to the beneficiary and does not depend on "the existence, validity, and enforceability of the main obligation" (Grant, 2018).
- **Guarantee to another bank who provides loan**: A bank provides a guarantee to a loan provided by another bank. For example, the roles of nominated banks and confirming banks in letters of credit represent this type of bank guarantee. In this case, bank guarantees serve as a double or even triple down on payment guarantees. This type of bank guarantee is also referred to as an *indirect guarantee* in international transactions when a foreign bank in the beneficiary's country must be involved in the transaction in cases where public entities or government agencies are the beneficiaries of the bank guarantee (Grant, 2018). This type of indirect bank guarantee has been seen in export finance, as illustrated in the following case study.

> **Case Study**
>
> *Export Finance with Indirect Bank Guarantee*
>
> To encourage exports to international markets, most developed countries have established Export Credit Agencies (ECAs) to facilitate trade and provide financial guarantees for global supply chain transactions (Trade Finance, 2022). However, to qualify for a loan guarantee, these ECAs typically require a significant percentage of domestically produced content, although the

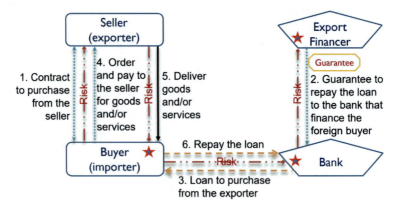

Fig. 12.2 Process flow of export finance with indirect guarantee

> requirement levels vary among countries (e.g., Export Development Canada requires 20%, while UK Export Finance requires 80%). Once granted, the ECA provides a loan repayment guarantee to the bank that offers a loan to the importer (buyer) who has signed a sales contract with the exporter (seller). The process flow of export finance is illustrated in Fig. 12.2.

- **Counter guarantee**: This is a unique case of the above guarantee provided to another bank in an exporting setting. A counter guarantee is typically offered by the exporter's instructing bank to cover payment from the importer's guarantor bank, especially when there are high economic and political risks in the importer's jurisdiction (e.g., a country at war). To better protect itself, the exporter may request a bank in its own jurisdiction to offer a guarantee to the importer's bank's guaranteed payment in an export transaction. Although the importer's guarantor bank may offer a demand guarantee to protect the importer, it might not be safe enough for the exporter. Therefore, while the counter guarantee may also protect the importer, it is designed primarily to safeguard the exporter against economic and political risks within the importer's jurisdiction.

The presence of a bank guarantee shifts the financial risk from the beneficiaries to the bank, making supply chain transactions viable. To compensate for the risk, the guaranteeing bank typically charges 0.5% to 1.5% of the guaranteed amount as its risk premium (Grant, 2018).

12.4.3 Credit Guarantee Scheme

Governments worldwide have also established or supported various credit guarantee schemes to further assist SMEs. For instance, in 2018, the Kenyan government collaborated with the International Fund for Agricultural Development and the Bill & Melinda Gates Foundation to provide a guarantee to the Equity Bank of Kenya for "$50 million in agricultural SME loans for farmers with little or no collateral," enabling farmers to "purchase quality seeds and other farm inputs" from their suppliers (Holle, 2017).

According to Aye Min Thein, managing director of Myanmar Insurance, "The banks are disbursing loans to SMEs at the designated amount. But owners who want more loans can buy credit guarantee insurance. For instance, one takes loans from the Small and Medium Industrial Development Bank with collateral worth Ks 10 million. But the bank disburses Ks 3–4 million in loans. The borrower can buy the credit guarantee insurance for the remaining Ks 6–7 million if he or she wants Ks 10 million in full" (Thiha, 2014).

Credit guarantee schemes are particularly useful during financial stresses. For example, in the first half of 2020, 41 countries launched 57 credit guarantee schemes for SMEs to cope with the negative impact of the COVID-19 pandemic (Dreyer & Nygaard, 2020). Governments also increased their initial guarantee coverage rates to better support SMEs in overcoming financial stress. Due to the budget-constrained nature of guaranteed borrowers and public policy initiatives (e.g., not profit maximization but social welfare improvement), the default rate of these credit guarantee schemes could be higher than that in bank loan insurance run by private insurance companies.

There are four major types of credit guarantee schemes: public guarantee, international guarantee, corporate guarantee, and mutual guarantee, in which governments might play a role (Green, 2003).

- *Public Guarantee Scheme*: Public guarantee schemes are sponsored by government public policy initiatives. They may be managed by a government administrative unit or a third party. This type of guarantee has higher credibility because the government would pay out in case of any loan default.
- *International Guarantee Scheme*: This scheme usually involves both local and international governments and/or organizations, such as the United Nations and the European Investment Fund. The previously mentioned example of credit guarantee support to farmers in Kenya exemplifies the international guarantee scheme.
- *Corporate Guarantee Scheme*: This scheme is generally supported by the private sector, such as chambers of commerce or banks. This scheme can benefit from supervision by experienced corporate leaders involved in the banking sector (OECD, 2009).

- **Mutual Guarantee Scheme**: Also called mutual guarantee associations or societies, this scheme is privately owned by a group of borrowers with limited access to bank loans (OECD, 2009). This scheme may receive support from their government and benefit from active member involvement.

According to a 2008 World Bank study of 76 guarantee schemes, credit guarantee fees are typically between 1 and 2% of the loan amount (OECD, 2009). A fee above 5% of the loan amount is considered too expensive. In general, some types of risk-sharing mechanisms exist. Among the 76 guarantee schemes, "56% of fees were paid by borrowers and 21% were paid by the financial institution receiving the guarantee" (OECD, 2009). The fee structures of these schemes vary significantly. Most guarantee schemes are not based on the risk level of applications; particularly, 57% of schemes charge fees based on the guaranteed amount, and 26% are based on the loan amount.

Related studies have demonstrated that guaranteed borrowers benefit from credit guarantee schemes, experiencing increased revenue and profits (OECD, 2009). However, it is important to note that a 100% guarantee coverage could lead to a *"strategic default"* moral hazard, making borrowers more likely to default because part of the collateral belongs to another party. As such, it is recommended that a coverage rate between 60 and 80% be maintained, which is sufficient to encourage lender participation while limiting moral hazard (Levitsky, 1997). In practice, the median coverage rate among the 76 schemes studied by the World Bank in 2008 was 80% (OECD, 2009).

12.4.4 Buyer Credit Guarantee for Export Contracts

Buyer credit guarantee provides a loan guarantee on a bank loan to an international buyer, based on a specific export order from a domestic seller (see Fig. 12.3). In Fig. 12.3, the insurer is typically an insurance company or financial institution sponsored by the exporter's government. For example, under a buyer credit guarantee, EKF (Export Kredit Fonden, Denmark's Export Credit Agency) guarantees payment to a bank that grants a loan to a foreign customer, enabling the customer to immediately pay a domestic exporter (EKF, 2022). The guarantee assures the bank that it will recover its money upon maturity, as EKF will compensate the bank if the foreign customer defaults for various reasons, such as currency control or war.

Buyer credit guarantee schemes have been employed by most countries to assist their domestic companies in exporting to other nations. For instance, in 2020, China, the largest export credit provider, authorized $18 billion in buyer credit guarantees to support its domestic companies in exporting (EXIM, 2021b). The second to fifth biggest providers are France ($12.1 billion), Germany ($8.6 billion), Italy ($8.4 billion), and Korea ($5 billion), respectively. The Export–Import Bank (EXIM) of the U.S. authorized $1.8 billion in 2020.

12.4 SCF-Based Insurance and Credit Guarantee

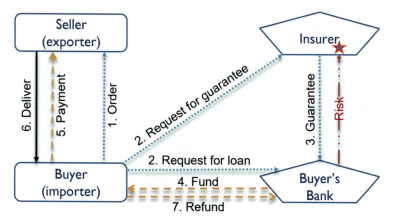

Fig. 12.3 Process flow of buyer credit guarantee

In its 2019 Competitiveness Report, the EXIM of the U.S. stated that its buyer credit guarantee insurance programs have benefitted the supply chains of those insured buyers (EXIM, 2021a). Indeed, the primary goal of a local insurer providing a buyer credit guarantee to an international buyer is to support the local supplier within the supply chain. Similar practices have thus demonstrated that bank loans and loan insurance can have an impact on the entire supply chain.

12.4.5 Trade Credit Insurance

Payment delays have become increasingly common in international trade due to factors such as extended shipment times, demand uncertainty, and retailer bargaining power. In domestic trade, buyers also demand a similar amount of time for payment delays, primarily because of their dominant position. This payment delay is also referred to as *trade credit*, which a supplier extends to its buyer.

Although the literature mainly describes trade credit as a financing offer from the supplier to its buyer, in practice, suppliers often have no choice but to accept payment delays under the guise of "*open accounts*" due to the buyer's dominance. Once trade credit is granted, the financial risk shifts from the buyer to the supplier, as the supplier bears the buyer's default risk arising from demand uncertainty, political intervention, and other factors.

Without trade credit or open accounts, buyers might face the following risks:

- Shipment does not arrive on time.
- Order is not fully fulfilled.
- Goods are damaged in-transit.
- Quality of goods does not meet the required standard.

Due to the above risks, buyers generally prefer open accounts, which also alleviate the financial burden of paying the supplier in advance or upon shipment. However, when trade credit is employed, suppliers may encounter the following risks:

- Financial burden of shipping goods without receiving payment.
- Buyer delaying payments for liquidity and interest reasons.
- Buyer refusing to accept shipments.
- Buyer's issuing bank going bankrupt.
- Buyer default, insolvency, or bankruptcy due to demand uncertainty, credit issues, political events, currency fluctuation, and other factors.
- Political intervention affecting the buyer's imports.
- War or social unrest disrupting the transaction.

These factors indicate that trade credit not only provides buyers with necessary financial flexibility but also transfers certain risks to suppliers, exposing them to potential financial and operational challenges. Understandably, suppliers would prefer cash-in-advance or early payments, or alternatively, letters of credit instead of trade credit to avoid the above risks. However, due to industry practices and buyer dominance, suppliers often have little choice but to accept open accounts in most supply chain transactions nowadays.

Under these circumstances, *trade credit insurance*, also known as business credit insurance, export credit insurance, or credit insurance, emerges as a solution to partially mitigate suppliers' financial risk by insuring against unpaid invoices or accounts receivable. With trade credit insurance, the insurance agency compensates the supplier or its funder for an agreed amount of unpaid invoice due to the buyer's default, insolvency, or bankruptcy.

Trade credit insurance is particularly useful when suppliers urgently need capital to continue production. This not only enables suppliers to secure additional loans from potential funders but also incentivizes them to sell more to their buyers. According to Allied Market Research, the global trade credit insurance market size was estimated at $9.39 billion in 2019 and is expected to reach $18.14 billion by 2027, with a compound annual growth rate of 8.6% (Aarti et al., 2021).

In practice, exporters often sign long-term (e.g., yearly) contracts with insurance companies to cover all transactions with a portfolio of buyers, although single-transaction contracts are also possible. If there are no disputes between the supplier and the buyers, the insurer usually pays a claim immediately. Depending on the involved parties' relationships, the insurer may still pay out and recover funds even if disputes arise, after they are resolved.

To minimize risk, insurers should focus more on buyers' risk profiles rather than suppliers', as the insurer's risk depends on whether buyers can repay their accounts receivable. Once a buyer is on board, with the help of the supplier, the insurer can assess the buyer's risk and set a credit limit. The insurer can also set a credit limit for the entire portfolio of buyers based on their profiles, meaning the supplier has a responsibility to verify buyers' creditworthiness. Insurance coverage can be tailored to specific risk factors and coverage levels. Due to the importance of trade credit insurance for a country's exports, such insurance programs often receive government support and offer more favorable rates.

While trade credit insurance is commonly used to insure suppliers directly against any default from buyers, it can also be used to insure the bank that owns accounts receivable via factoring or forfeiting. There are two major types of trade credit insurance for banks (Kurt, 2022):

- *Trade Credit Bank Insurance*: Protects the bank that purchases accounts receivable via factoring from the supplier (exporter).
- *Trade Credit Forfaiting Insurance*: Protects the bank that purchases accounts receivable via forfaiting from the supplier (exporter) on a non-recourse basis.

Although trade credit insurance primarily focuses on assisting exporters, similar support can be observed with Import Credit Insurance. Since the insurance mechanisms are similar, we will not discuss them in detail here.

Case Study

Trade Credit Insurance

Company XYZ, a growing SME, saw a surge in demand and received numerous new orders. However, buyers extended their payments up to 90 days, even though the agreed-upon payment period was 60 days. As XYZ continued producing products to meet orders, it faced a cash crunch for purchasing raw materials, which strained its working capital and hindered future growth opportunities.

Owing to XYZ's financial stress, banks were hesitant to provide large enough loans to cover all of XYZ's production costs. Consequently, XYZ opted to purchase a trade credit insurance policy to alleviate banks' risk when lending to the company. This allowed XYZ to use accounts receivable and even work-in-progress—before an invoice is generated—as collateral to fully support its production.

With the trade credit insurance, the partnering bank agreed to extend the eligibility time window for aged accounts receivable from 60 to 90 days. As a result, XYZ secured an additional $950,000 in working capital.

12.5 Guarantor Financing by Supply Chain Firms

In *guarantor financing*, the guarantor—a bank, insurer, or supply chain focal firm—assures a creditor that it will assume payment liability for a specific debtor in case the debtor defaults on a transaction. A 2020 study estimated that the global financial guarantee market would reach $34.47 billion in 2022 and $71.93 billion by 2030 (Valuates Reports, 2021).

Within the context of supply chain finance, guarantor financing can be seen as a unique type of insurance for payments stemming from supply chain transactions. For a focal firm in a supply chain, the guarantee can come from an upstream firm (i.e., the seller), a downstream firm (i.e., the buyer), or a third party (e.g., a third-party logistics provider, 3PL). Unlike the previous subsection discussing insurer or bank-provided guarantees, this section focuses on guarantor financing offered by a focal firm involved in the supply chain.

In guarantor financing provided by a supply chain focal firm, the capital-abundant firm (e.g., the manufacturer) offers a guarantee for the capital-constrained firm (e.g., the retailer), enabling the latter to borrow from a bank. The guarantor repays the firm's debt if it defaults on the agreed repayments. In developing countries where small firms have limited credit history and collateral, three major supply chain guarantor financing schemes are commonly used: seller guarantee, buyer guarantee, and 3PL guarantee.

12.5.1 Seller Guarantor Financing

Seller guarantor financing, also known as manufacturer guarantor financing when the seller is a manufacturer, involves the seller serving as the guarantor (Zhou et al., 2020). If the retailer defaults, the manufacturer covers the potential loss of the bank that lent to the retailer.

For example, the New Hope Group (NHG) is one of China's largest feed producers. Thousands of farmers purchase feed from NHG to raise dairy cows, chickens, and ducks. Most farmers operate on a small scale and face difficulties obtaining financing due to their lack of collateral. To address this financing challenge, NHG began offering guarantor financing to farmers in 2007, enabling them to secure loans from banks. By the end of 2014, NHG had facilitated loans of 18 billion yuan, supporting 90,000 farmers. Guarantor financing also boosted NHG's own sales; for instance, feed sales volume increased by 1,350,000 tons in 2014 (Zhou et al., 2020).

12.5.2 Buyer Guarantor Financing

In reality, many upstream firms, such as SME manufacturers and suppliers, are more likely to face capital constraints and require financial support from downstream firms. In this situation, more reliable retailers act as guarantors for their suppliers, enabling them to obtain loans from banks. These retailers may even introduce their suppliers to their financing network and provide the necessary guarantees based on their supply chain transactions. This type of supply chain guarantor financing is referred to as *buyer guarantor financing*. Large retailers, like Walmart, Amazon, and Jingdong, often offer buyer guarantor financing for their numerous smaller upstream sellers.

12.5.3 3PL Guarantor Financing

Another significant type of guarantor financing is *3PL guarantor financing*, in which 3PL firms (e.g., UPS Capital, AIMS Logistics, and Schneider Logistics) take on financing roles in supply chain procurement (Chen et al., 2019). The 3PL serves as the guarantor for the retailer to borrow from the bank. If the retailer defaults, the 3PL covers the potential loss of the bank for lending to the retailer.

In recent years, 3PL guarantor financing has rapidly gained popularity in developing countries like China. For example, Eternal Asia established a microcredit company in 2009 and further expanded investments in the company in 2013 to provide financial services for small businesses, particularly supply chain members, by assuming their default risks (Zhou et al., 2020). Since 2015, S.F. Express, China's leading 3PL company, has been offering similar guarantor financing services to customers using its logistics services.

12.5.4 Benefits and Risk Mitigation of Guarantor Financing

Guarantor financing benefits not only the beneficiaries but also the counterparties. The most evident advantage of guarantor financing is that it enables supply chain transactions to take place. A less apparent benefit is that the guarantee can boost demand for sellers and ultimately improve supply chain efficiency. In the case of seller guarantor financing, this happens because financial risks due to the buyer's default shift from the buyer to the guarantor, incentivizing the buyer to be more risk-seeking and order more from the seller. In the case of buyer guarantor financing, the guarantee enables the seller to offer a lower wholesale price, which leads to increased demand from the buyer.

As the guarantor takes on the liability at default, it must perform due diligence on the debtor applying for the guarantee. In bank guarantees, banks may rely on their historical relationship with the client (e.g., the bank is the debtor's bank) and examine the firm's financial statements and the characteristics of the supply chain transactions. The same applies to insurers in guarantee insurance. In supply chain guarantor financing, the guarantor may be in a better position to understand the market, supply chain performance of their counterparty, and creditworthiness in past transactions. In buyer guarantor financing, the buyer will hold the inventory of the final goods, enabling the guarantor to better mitigate financial risks. In all cases, it is also the guarantor's responsibility to prevent the debtor from diverting funds to other investments (i.e., moral hazard).

12.6 Financial Hedging

Hedging is an investment strategy used to counteract potential losses in other investments due to uncertainties. Hedging has been widely employed in financial markets, such as stocks, trade, and exchange markets. In supply chains, hedging can be utilized to offset risks in supply, demand, and price by applying various contractual and financial instruments. Since hedging requires more expertise, the following basic methods can be considered before implementing hedging techniques (Sodhi & Tang, 2012).

1. **Customer Surcharge**: A simple option is to establish contracts with buyers, allowing the supplier to pass on commodity price fluctuations to the buyers. However, many buyers, especially dominant ones like Walmart, may be reluctant to accept this kind of risk.
2. **Guarantee**:
   (a) *Supply or Demand Guarantee*: This can be achieved by purchasing insurance or a bank guarantee (as previously discussed) to ensure payments to the seller or cover damages to the buyer.
   (b) *Supplier Price Guarantee*: To avoid significant supply price increases, a buyer can seek price protection or price guarantees in the supply contract, provided that the supplier can manage the risk.

When the above options are not available or adequate, financial hedging instruments can be employed to hedge against risks, such as interest rate risk, foreign currency exchange risk, and commodity price risks. These hedging instruments can be traded over-the-counter or on exchanges.

An *over-the-counter (OTC) derivative* is a contract negotiated directly between two supply chain parties, without involving an intermediary (e.g., an exchange) (Rahman, 2015). Typically, OTC derivatives include swaps and forward rate agreements. The costs of OTC derivatives (e.g., a premium in exchange for a guaranteed future price) may be built into the price the buyer pays for a commodity or paid upfront. In either case, the buyer should determine whether the cost is worth mitigating the involved risks.

Similar derivatives can also be traded on exchanges, where the derivative contracts are standardized. Exchange-traded derivatives include options, currency futures, swaps, index futures, and so on. Compared to OTC derivatives, exchange-traded derivatives offer the advantages of standardization, liquidity, and elimination of default risk (Manning, 2022). A standardized derivative contains required transparent, essential information (e.g., value, lots, and security represented) and is generally smaller in size and more efficient, attracting more (small) investors. Since the exchange itself serves as the counterparty for every exchange-traded derivative transaction, default risk of the counterparty is minimized.

The International Swaps and Derivatives Association (ISDA) has established an industry standard for derivative products. According to ISDA.org, in 2021, the total trading volume for interest rate derivatives was $231 trillion, the total trade volume

12.6 Financial Hedging

for forward rate agreements was $53.4 trillion, overnight index swaps amounted to $55.2 trillion, and the total trade volume of credit derivatives reached $9.5 trillion (ISDA, 2021).

12.6.1 Swap

Swaps are widely used to exchange various financial instruments, such as fixed interest rates for variable rates, foreign currency exchange rates, stock indices, and commodity prices. For example, in a *fixed-to-floating interest rate swap* (IRS), one counterparty prefers a fixed interest rate, while the other counterparty opts for a floating interest rate. The maturity of a fixed-to-floating IRS typically ranges from 1 to 15 years. By convention, the fixed-rate payer is considered the buyer of the IRS, while the floating-rate payer is the IRS seller (Lowery, 2007). The involved counterparties must negotiate the swap period, settlement frequency, notional value on which the swap payments will be based, and the published reference rates to be used. In an IRS, the two counterparties do not actually exchange the principal amount; instead, they exchange interest payments based on a notional value (e.g., the principal or an amount agreed upon by both parties).

A swap may occur when two counterparties have different predictions about future rates, such as interest rates. One counterparty believes that the future rate will increase, whereas the other counterparty believes the opposite. Consequently, both counterparties ex-ante believe that they can benefit from the swap, although ex-post only one counterparty gains extra profit from the swap while the other one loses. Regardless of the outcome, one party's gain comes at the expense of the other. Therefore, having better predictive capabilities is crucial for successful swap investments.

> Regardless of the outcome, one party's gain comes at the cost of the other, emphasizing the importance of accurate forecasting in these transactions.

Case Study

An Interest Rate Swap

Company A has sold $1 million in 10-year corporate bonds with LIBOR + 100 basis points (i.e., 1.00%). The current 6-month U.S. Dollar LIBOR (London Interbank Offered Rate) is 3%. However, its analyst recently predicted that interest rates would increase in the near term. To capitalize on the potentially increasing interest rate, Company A decides to sell the corporate bonds to Investor D, who believes that future interest rates will decrease.

In the swap agreement, Company A agrees to pay Investor D a fixed interest rate of 4.00% on $1 million each year for 10 years. Investor D agrees to pay Company A $LIBOR + 100$ basis points (i.e., 1.00%) on $1 million each year for 10 years, which is equivalent to what Company A promised to its bondholders.

In this swap, Investor D is betting on a gain from a decrease in future interest rates (i.e., a difference of $4.00\% - LIBOR - 1.00\%$), while Company A is betting on cost savings (i.e., a difference of $LIBOR + 1.00\% - 4.00\%$). The outcome of whether Investor D or Company A achieves more gain depends on whether LIBOR rises or falls over the next 10 years, as shown below:

	LIBOR Rises	LIBOR Falls
Company A	+	−
Investor D	−	+

Note "+" indicates a "gain" for the associated party, while "−" indicates a "loss."

Counterparties may request to terminate the IRS contract if the swap becomes a significant financial burden; if so, termination fees will apply.

Given the impossibility of making 100% accurate predictions about future uncertainties, an institution cannot always win in swaps and other OTC derivatives. Assuming everyone performs equally well, in the long run, the chance of winning/losing in hedging will likely be 50%/50%. However, even if these institutions break even in hedging, they will have achieved the primary goal of financial hedging: reducing the volatility of uncertainties.

12.6.2 Overnight Index Swap

Overnight index swap (OIS) is an over-the-counter (OTC) derivative in which a party exchanges a fixed interest rate for the average cash rate over a specified period. OIS can be used for debt, equity, interest rate, and other price indexes. For interest rate swaps, OIS functions similarly to IRS, with two notable differences (RBA, 2002):

1. OIS is typically short-term (e.g., up to one year), compared to multiple years for IRS. The inherent reference rate is an overnight rate.
2. The floating rate of OIS is the overnight cash rate rather than a longer-term average for IRS (e.g., 90-day or 6-month LIBOR).

Case Study

Overnight Index Swaps

In this illustrative case, we assume that Company A and Investor D have decided to enter an OIS over the $1 million 10-year corporate bonds for only two months. The floating interest rate will be based on the overnight LIBOR rate, which is the average LIBOR rate for a specific day. During the two months, both institutions continue to pay their original interest rates without actually changing their investments or bonds. At the end of the contracted two months, both institutions calculate their total interest payments, and the party that pays less interest will pay the difference to the counterparty.

For example, suppose Investor D pays $66,666.66 based on the 4% fixed interest rate, while Company A pays $70,000.00 based on the 1% LIBOR floating rate. The difference is $70,000.00 - \$66,666.66 = \$3333.34$. According to their swap agreement, Investor D must pay $3,333.34 to Company A. On the other hand, if Company A pays only $60,000.00 total interest based on the 1% LIBOR floating rate, then Company A must pay $6,666.66 to Investor D according to their swap agreement.

In practice, the present value of the floating leg is computed either by compounding the overnight rate or using the geometric average of the rate over the swap term. The fixed interest rate in OIS is considered stable, while LIBOR is risky. The LIBOR–OIS spread has historically drifted around 10 basis points; however, the spread has been significantly higher during financial and economic crises in recent years (Wikipedia, 2023). From this perspective, the LIBOR–OIS spread provides insights into the general availability of funds for lending purposes and the health of the global credit markets.

12.6.3 Forward

Forward contracts are used by two independent parties to determine the rate of a specific asset (e.g., interest rate, currency exchange rate, or commodity price) on an agreed-upon date in the future.

12.6.3.1 Forward Price Agreement

For instance, a farmer and a buyer might agree to a total price of $300,000 for the farmer's crop planted in California, to be paid in 4 months when it is harvested. If the total market price of the crop drops below $300,000 when it is harvested, the farmer's income is secured at the predetermined price. However, if the price significantly increases above $300,000, the farmer will forfeit the extra profit.

12.6.3.2 Forward Rate Agreement

A *forward rate agreement* (FRA) is a linear interest rate derivative similar to interest rate swaps. The notation $n_1 \times n_2$ FRA represents a forward contract that starts n_1 months from now and lasts for $(n_2 - n_1)$ months, as illustrated below:

$n_1 \times n_2$	Effective Date (from now)	Termination Date (from now)	Underlying LIBOR
0×2	Today (SPOT)	2 months	2–0 = 2 months
2×6	2 months	6 months	6–2 = 4 months

A quote for an FRA [US$ 1 × 4 – 4.00/4.25% p.a.] means the FRA starts in 1 month, lasts for 3 months, has a deposit interest rate of 4.00% per annum, and a borrowing interest rate of 4.25% per annum. If it is a "receiver FRA," the receiver pays a 3-month floating LIBOR and receives a 4.00% fixed rate. If it is a "payer FRA," the payer pays the fixed rate of 4.25% and receives a floating 3-month LIBOR.

Based on the interest rates for time periods (t_1, t_2), corresponding to (n_1, n_2) respectively, we can estimate the *forward rate* or the future yield on the bond. Let r_1 and r_2 be the interest rates for periods $(0, t_1)$ and $(0, t_2)$, respectively, and $r_{1,2}$ denotes the forward rate between t_1 and t_2.

If the forward rate is calculated using the *simple rate* (Wikipedia, 2022b), we have:

$$(1 + r_1 t_1)(1 + r_{1,2}(t_2 - t_1)) = 1 + r_2 t_2$$

Thus,

$$r_{1,2} = \frac{1}{t_2 - t_1}\left(\frac{1 + r_2 t_2}{1 + r_1 t_1} - 1\right)$$

If the forward rate is calculated using a *continuously compound rate*, we have:

$$e^{r_1 t_1} \times e^{r_{1,2}(t_2 - t_1)} = e^{r_2 t_2}$$

Thus,

$$r_{1,2} = \frac{r_2 t_2 - r_1 t_1}{t_2 - t_1}$$

If the forward rate is calculated using a *yearly compounded rate* (Wikipedia, 2022b), we have:

$$(1 + r_1)^{t_1} \times (1 + r_{1,2})^{t_2 - t_1} = (1 + r_2)^{t_2}$$

12.6 Financial Hedging

Table 12.1 Calculation of different forward rates

	Simple Rate	Continuously Compounded Rate	Yearly Compounded Rate
n_1	30	30	30
n_2	120	120	120
t_1(Years, 1 Year = 360 Days)	0.0833	0.0833	0.0833
t_2(Years, 1 Year = 360 Days)	0.3333	0.3333	0.3333
Current t_1 LIBOR	4.00%	4.00%	4.00%
Current t_2 LIBOR	5.00%	5.00%	5.00%
t_1 Loan Rate	0.33%	0.33%	0.33%
t_2 Loan Rate	1.67%	1.67%	1.67%
Annualized Forward rate	5.32%	5.33%	5.34%

Thus,

$$r_{1,2} = \left(\frac{(1+r_2)^{t_2}}{(1+r_1)^{t_1}} \right)^{1/(t_2-t_1)} - 1$$

Assuming a 1 × 4 FRA with a current LIBOR at 4% for 30 days and 5% for 120 days, respectively, we can calculate the different forward rates as shown in Table 12.1.

12.6.4 Future

Futures are standardized contracts that allow parties to trade an underlying asset at an agreed-upon price on a specific date. Companies use futures contracts to hedge against unfavorable price movements by locking in a more favorable price for future transactions. This allows companies to reduce the negative impact of price uncertainties, particularly if they are risk-averse.

When a company plans to purchase a specific asset in the future, it can take a long position to protect against rising prices. Conversely, if the company plans to sell a specific asset in the future, it can take a short position instead.

> **Case Study**
>
> **Long and Short Positions**
>
> For example, Company A knows it needs 10,000 ounces of platinum to manufacture and fulfill an order in 6 months. The future price of platinum is $852 in 6 months. Company A can take a *long position* by buying a 6-month futures contract for 10,000 ounces of platinum at $852, anticipating a price

increase. If the price dramatically increases after 6 months, Company A's production plan will not be affected. However, if the price drops, Company A will forfeit the potential cost saving benefit.

On the other hand, if Company B plans to sell 10,000 ounces of platinum in 6 months, it can take a *short position* by selling a 6-month futures contract for 10,000 ounces of platinum at $852 to secure its revenue and avoid the risk of a price decrease. Similarly, Company B will lose extra profit if the platinum price rises above $852 in 6 months.

12.6.4.1 Currency Hedging

A popular application of futures is *currency hedging*, which involves simultaneously purchasing and selling currency contracts in two markets. This strategy anticipates that a loss on one contract can be offset by a gain on the other, effectively working like insurance to protect institutions from currency fluctuations, especially when they are risk-averse. A study on the MSCI EAFE Index (i.e., Morgan Stanley Capital International Europe, Australia, Far East Index) from January 1980 to June 1999 showed that currency hedging can indeed reduce earnings volatility, as illustrated below (Srinivasan & Youngren, 2001):

	Annualized Return (%)	Volatility (%)
Unhedged EAFE Return in US$	13.48	17.52
Hedged (US$) EAFE Return	13.51	15.29

Global supply chain firms selling products in foreign markets face currency volatility when exchanging foreign currency for domestic currency. Purchasing currency futures can help hedge against this currency volatility.

Case Study

Currency Hedging

On September 1, 2022, Chinese contract manufacturer Company A signed a contract to sell products worth $10,000,000 to a U.S. firm, with delivery scheduled for March 1, 2023. On September 1, 2022, the USD-CNH (US Dollar-Chinese Renminbi) exchange rate was 6.8650855, making the contract value 68,650,855 RMB. This value is subject to fluctuations in the Chinese RMB vs. USD exchange rate.

To lock in the contract value in RMB and mitigate exchange rate risk, Company A decided to "short" USD by purchasing CME Chinese Renminbi (CNH/USD) futures on September 1, 2022, and selling them on March 1, 2023. The Standard Futures contract size is $100,000, and the E-micro

12.6 Financial Hedging

Futures contract size is $10,000. The hedge ratio is calculated as follows:

$$\text{Hedge Ratio} = \frac{10,000,000}{100,000}$$
$$= 100 \text{ standard CME CNH\textbackslash USD futures}$$

To demonstrate how currency futures affect Company A's cash flow, we consider two scenarios (excluding transaction fees) as follows.

Scenario 12.1 CNH has fallen 5% vs. (appreciating) USD

	Spot CNH/ USD	USD/CNH Rate	CNH of $10 Million	CNH/USD Futures
September 1, 2022	0.14566461	6.8650855	¥68,650,855	Buy 100 Standard at 0.1457
March 1, 2023	0.13872820	7.2083398	¥72,083,398	Sell 100 Standard at 0.1387
Gain/Loss			¥3,432,543	−¥3,432,543

In Scenario 12.1, the CNH has fallen by 5%. The $10,000,000 payment is now worth ¥72,083,398, resulting in a ¥3,432,543 increase in profit. However, Company A loses the same amount (−¥3,432,543) in the futures transaction. Ultimately, Company A still gains ¥68,650,855 as expected when signing the contract with the U.S. firm.

Scenario 12.2 CNH has risen 5% vs. (declining) USD

	Spot CNH/ USD	USD/CNH Rate	CNH of $10 Million	CNH/USD Futures
September 1, 2022	0.14566461	6.8650855	¥68,650,855	Buy 100 Standard at 0.1457
March 1, 2023	0.15333117	6.5218312	¥65,218,312	Sell 100 Standard at 0.1387
Gain/Loss			−¥3,432,543	¥3,432,543

In Scenario 12.2, the CNH has appreciated by 5%, leading to a −¥3,432,543 profit loss. However, Company A gains the same amount (¥3,432,543) in the futures transaction. In the end, Company A still gains ¥68,650,855 as expected when signing the contract with the U.S. firm.

> Note that we have ignored all transaction costs and fees in these calculations. These two scenarios demonstrate that purchasing currency futures can help a company hedge against currency exchange rate fluctuations. While Company A does not gain extra profits from the futures contract, it avoids potential negative financial disruption (i.e., −¥3,432,543).

The above case study illustrates a *short* position in USD, as the exporter (Company A in China) will receive USD upon delivery. Conversely, if an importer expects to import from a U.S. company and pay in USD in the future, the importer can enter a USD futures contract in a *long* position to hedge against potential USD currency risks.

12.6.4.2 Freight Forward Agreement

Futures can also be applied to hedge against logistics price risks. For example, during the COVID-19 pandemic, container prices were extremely volatile. Given that freight costs can account for up to 20% of cargo value, managing container freight price risk has become critical. To mitigate container price risk, one can utilize CME Group's freight futures contracts for secure and efficient clearing of *freight forward agreement* transactions (CME, 2022).

12.6.4.3 Future vs. Forward

Both "future" and "forward" are financial terms used in trading that share similarities, yet possess distinct differences.

A *"future"* is a standardized contract between two parties to buy or sell a specific asset (such as a commodity, currency, or stock) at a predetermined price and date in the future. Futures contracts are traded on exchanges, with the buyer obligated to purchase the asset and the seller obligated to sell it at the agreed-upon price and date. These contracts are commonly used for hedging or speculation purposes.

Conversely, a *"forward"* is a private, customized contract between two parties to buy or sell an asset at a specified price and date in the future. Unlike futures contracts, forwards are traded over-the-counter (OTC), which means they are not traded on an exchange. As forwards are customized contracts, their terms and conditions can vary significantly. The buyer and seller must agree on all terms, including the asset, price, and delivery date.

In summary, while both futures and forwards involve agreements to buy or sell an asset at a predetermined future date and price, futures are standardized contracts traded on exchanges, whereas forwards are customized contracts traded over-the-counter.

12.6.5 Option

Options are contracts that allow an investor to buy or sell an underlying asset or instrument at a predetermined price on or before a specified date. A "European" option can only be exercised on the specified date, while an "American" option can be exercised at any time on or before the specified date.

Other variants, such as Asian, Barrier, Bermudan, Binary, and Exotic options, include special terms regarding exercise timing, pricing, settlement conditions, and more (Chen, 2022). In an Asian option, the payoff is calculated based on the average underlying price over a specified period. A Barrier option requires that the underlying security's price must pass a threshold level for the option to become active. A Bermudan option allows for the exercise on multiple specified dates. A Binary option must be exercised either fully or not at all, with no partial execution. Lastly, an Exotic option may encompass various other unique financial structures and conditions.

Both futures and options are derivative financial instruments used to hedge against future uncertainties. Unlike futures contracts, which must be exercised at maturity on the agreed-upon terms, options represent rights rather than obligations. This means that buyers can choose not to exercise their rights and let the contracts expire. As a trade-off, buyers must pay a premium for each contract to the sellers for the right not to execute their contracts.

Options can be categorized into "call" or "put" options depending on the type of right they represent. A *"call option"* gives the investor the right to buy the asset or instrument, while a *"put option"* grants the right to sell.

Options can be traded over-the-counter or on exchanges, and their underlying assets can vary, including interest rate options, bond options, stock options, index options, currency options, swap options, options for futures, and callable bull/bear contracts, which are listed on futures and options exchanges (Chen, 2022).

Case Study

Options for Fuels

The gas price has drastically risen and fluctuated during the COVID-19 pandemic and Ukraine War. To hedge against the risks of rising aviation fuel costs, airlines have been purchasing call options on aviation fuel. If the aviation fuel spot price rises above the exercise price, the airline will exercise the option; otherwise, it will buy the fuel from the spot market. However, such options are expensive, and airlines may hedge only a portion of their total demand portfolio (Rogers, 2022).

The usage of options has also become widespread in logistics and other supply chain areas. For example, the London-based Baltic Exchange provides option contracts on freight rates, allowing ship owners, charterers, and traders to hedge against the volatility of ocean freight costs (Alessi, 2010).

12.7 Operational Hedging

Operational hedging is a powerful tool for mitigating financial risks associated with currency, price, and other uncertainties, particularly for multinational companies. Often, operational hedging can be combined with financial hedging to manage risks effectively. Operational hedging can be applied in areas such as sourcing, inventory, and production.

12.7.1 Sourcing Hedging

Diversifying sourcing has been recognized as a useful strategy for reducing a company's reliance on too few upstream suppliers. A *multi-sourcing* approach can balance price fluctuations across various locations. When these locations are in different countries, multi-sourcing allows a firm to source more from a cheaper location to mitigate currency and price uncertainties. This approach is also referred to as *low-cost hopping*.

Nearshoring is a widely practiced strategy by large firms to save sourcing costs. It has been commonly adopted in industries such as automobiles (e.g., Detroit and Mexicofor the U.S. market) and IT (e.g., Silicon Valley). When suppliers and distributors are located nearby, production lead times can be significantly reduced, and logistics costs can substantially decrease. As supply chain firms are in the same region, they can also mitigate the impact of currency and political risks.

Offshoring manufacturing is a prevalent strategy for multinational firms seeking to take advantage of lower local labor costs. In fact, many large firms also offshore their procurement centers to counterbalance the negative impact of currency risk and benefit from lower local tax rates (see Table 12.2). By adjusting transfer prices, these multinational firms can partially control the portion of their profits subject to specific tax rates (Wu et al., 2024). This strategy might explain why large companies like Apple have kept substantial amounts of cash abroad.

The sourcing strategies mentioned above work differently but can complement each other. For example, nearshoring is often practiced within each location (inside an industry park, e.g., Shenzhen High-tech or Shanghai Industrial Parks) as part of offshoring and multi-sourcing strategies.

12.7.2 Inventory Hedging

Firms often aim to keep inventory levels low to save costs. However, building up inventory can occasionally serve as a useful hedging tool. For example, additional inventory can be used to hedge against environmental risks (e.g., hurricane season).

According to Anand et al. (2008), when there are sequentially repeated orders, strategically stockpiling extra inventory in earlier time periods can prevent the supplier from hiking the wholesale price in the future. Similar reasoning applies to farmers who can store some inventory when crop yields are high, preventing

12.7 Operational Hedging

Table 12.2 Multinational firms' offshoring tax rate difference

Multinational Companies	Headquarters Location (tax rate)	Procurement Relocation (tax rate)	Description
Barclays	UK (20%)	Singapore (17%)	Financial services firm Barclays shifts some "key roles" within its UK purchasing function to its offices in Singapore
Fuji Xerox	Japan (32.11%)	Singapore (17%)	Offshore finished products, parts, and assemblies to XC Trading Singapore Pte. Ltd., a local firm in Singapore
Grundfos	Denmark (22%)	Switzerland (17.92%)	Grundfos sets up a subsidiary, the Grundfos Corporate Purchase AG company
Gucci Group	Italy (27.5%)	Switzerland (17.92%)	Luxury Goods International SA maintains its logistics center in Switzerland
Samsung	South Korean (24.2%)	Singapore (17%)	Samsung S.E. Asia International Procurement Centre procures for Samsung worldwide
SABMiller	UK (20%)	Switzerland (17.92%)	SABMiller procures through Trinity Procurement, headquartered in Zug, Switzerland
Starbucks	US (35% + 0% − 12%)	Switzerland (17.92%)	Green beans are purchased from Starbucks Coffee Trading Company SARL in Switzerland
Unilever	Anglo-Dutch (20% − 25%)	Switzerland (17.92%)	Unilever Supply Chain Company AG operates a standalone entity in Schaffhausen, Switzerland
Walmart	US (35% + 0% − 12%)	Hong Kong/ Shenzhen (16.5%/15%)	The Walmart Global Procurement company manages the procurement business for all of China and its global purchasing network

significant price drops in good seasons. They can then sell the extra inventory when the yield is low to satisfy regular demand, assuming little spoilage occurs during the selling seasons.

> **Case Study**
>
> ***Inventory Burden or Inventory Hedging?***
>
> In the 1990s, car manufacturers Ford and General Motors (GM) faced challenges with palladium, a vital material for car manufacturing. Ford's procurement team, lacking coordination with R&D, secured palladium contracts

at record-high prices, only to have the required amount per car significantly reduced. This left Ford with an excess of overpriced palladium, leading to a $1 billion write off in 2002 (Tripathi & Wani, 2012). Conversely, GM strategically sold its palladium inventory (worth US$95 million in 2000) at a record high, simultaneously entering into forward contracts to repurchase it over the next six months for production. This sale lowered the palladium price, allowing GM to benefit from discounted prices in the following months.

12.7.3 Production Hedging

Manufacturers can utilize their multinational factories to hedge against currency risk by leveraging extra production capacity. For instance, OPEC countries have historically controlled their oil and gas production to influence prices and maintain a stable revenue stream.

Toyota provides another example of production hedging. The company mandates that each of its plants serves not only the local market but also at least one other global market. Through this manufacturing strategy, Toyota can shift production between plants to hedge against currency exchange rate fluctuations (Chopra & Sodhi, 2004).

12.8 Regulations, Ethics, and Sustainability

Supply chain finance plays a vital role in the global economy, but it must also address various risks and challenges that affect its sustainability and ethical practices. To tackle these issues, governments, regulatory bodies, and industry associations have established regulations and standards, such as the Basel Accords. Embracing ethical standards and best practices is crucial for fostering transparency, fairness, and social responsibility within supply chain finance. In this section, we will examine the regulations and ethical and sustainability concerns that influence supply chain finance and emphasize the significance of adopting ethical standards and best practices to encourage responsible and sustainable business practices.

12.8.1 Regulations

Supply chain finance is exposed to risks such as credit risk, liquidity risk, and market risk and can be susceptible to fraud and other financial crimes. To reduce these risks and ensure the safety and stability of supply chain financing activities, governments, regulatory bodies, and industry associations have devised various regulations and standards. These *regulations* encompass a wide array of issues, including capital adequacy, risk management, transparency, consumer protection, and anti-money laundering.

12.8.1.1 International Regulations

Several major international regulations and standards govern international banks and financial institutions, including the Basel Accords, Financial Action Task Force Recommendations, and International Financial Reporting Standards.

- *Basel Accords*: In 1988, the Basel Committee on Banking Supervision (BCBS) proposed a set of minimum capital requirements for banks, known as the 1988 Basel Accord, which was enforced by law in the Group of Ten (G-10) countries in 1992 (Wikipedia, 2022a). To protect a bank's solvency and overall economic stability, the Basel II Accord, initiated in 2004 and implemented in 2008, mandated that banks hold more capital when exposed to greater risks. The 2007–2009 Financial Crisis highlighted deficiencies in financial regulation, leading to the Basel III Accord's agreement by BCBS members in 2010. This strengthened bank capital requirements, increased bank liquidity, and reduced bank leverage. Basel III was implemented in 2018, but its full implementation has been postponed several times, with the current deadline set for January 2023 (Wikipedia, 2022a).
- *Financial Action Task Force Recommendations*: The Financial Action Task Force (FATF) is an intergovernmental organization that formulates policies to combat money laundering, terrorist financing, and other related threats to the international financial system's integrity (FATF, 2022). Its recommendations serve as the international standard for countries to implement effective anti-money laundering (AML) and counter-terrorism financing (CTF) measures.
- *International Financial Reporting Standards (IFRS)*: These are a set of accounting standards developed by the International Accounting Standards Board (IFRS, 2023). IFRS has implications for supply chain finance, particularly with regard to the accounting treatment of trade finance transactions and other forms of supply chain financing.

12.8.1.2 Regulations in the U.S.

Financial regulations in the U.S. play a crucial role in the nation's financial system, encompassing banking, securities, derivatives, insurance, and consumer protection. Various government agencies develop these regulations, including the Federal Reserve, the Securities and Exchange Commission (SEC), the Commodity Futures Trading Commission (CFTC), and the Consumer Financial Protection Bureau (CFPB).

- *Anti-Money Laundering (AML) and Know-Your-Customer (KYC) Regulations*: These regulations are designed to prevent money laundering and terrorist financing, and they require financial institutions to verify the identity of their customers and monitor their transactions (Sapers, 2023). AML/

KYC regulations have implications for supply chain finance, particularly with regard to trade finance and other forms of cross-border financing.
- **Dodd-Frank Wall Street Reform and Consumer Protection Act**: This is a U.S. law that includes provisions for regulating the financial industry and protecting consumers (CFTC, 2024). Dodd-Frank has implications for supply chain finance, particularly with regard to derivatives trading and other forms of financial risk management.
- **Uniform Commercial Code (UCC)**: This is a set of laws governing commercial transactions (ULC, 2023). The UCC has implications for supply chain finance, particularly with regard to the sale of goods and the security interests of lenders.

12.8.1.3 Regulations in Europe
Some financial regulations in the European Union (EU) include:

- **European Market Infrastructure Regulation (EMIR)**: This is a regulation that requires certain derivative contracts to be cleared through central counterparties (European Commission, 2023). EMIR has implications for supply chain finance, particularly with regard to the use of derivatives for hedging purposes.
- **General Data Protection Regulation (GDPR)**: This is a regulation that governs the collection, use, and processing of personal data (European Council, 2023). GDPR has implications for supply chain finance, particularly with regard to the use of electronic invoicing and other forms of digital documentation.
- **Markets in Financial Instruments Directive II (MiFID II)**: These directives aim to create a single, transparent market for investment services and activities (European Commission, 2022). MiFID II has implications for supply chain finance, particularly with regard to the reporting of trade transactions and the use of electronic platforms for trading.
- **Payment Services Directive 2 (PSD2)**: This is a directive that regulates payment services (European Central Bank, 2018). PSD2 has implications for supply chain finance, particularly with regard to the use of digital payment platforms and other forms of electronic payment.
- **Capital Requirements Regulation (CRR)**: This is a regulation that sets out the capital requirements for banks and other financial institutions (European Banking Authority, 2023). CRR has implications for supply chain finance, particularly with regard to the capital adequacy requirements for banks involved in supply chain financing activities.

12.8.1.4 Regulations in China
Some financial regulations in China include:

- **Regulations on Cross-Border RMB Business**: These regulations set out the rules for cross-border RMB transactions, which have implications for supply chain finance involving Chinese firms and their international trading partners (PNC, 2023).

12.8 Regulations, Ethics, and Sustainability

- ***The Customs Law***: This is a law that governs customs procedures in China and has implications for a wide range of financial activities, particularly with regard to the treatment of customs duties and taxes (GACC, 2014).
- ***The Banking Law***: This is a law that governs banking activities in China and has implications for a wide range of financial activities, particularly with regard to the capital adequacy and risk management requirements for banks (PBC, 2003).
- ***The Insurance Law***: This is a law that governs insurance activities in China and has implications for a wide range of financial activities, particularly with regard to the capital adequacy and risk management requirements for insurance companies (SPC, 2016).
- ***The Foreign Exchange Administration Regulations***: These regulations govern foreign exchange transactions in China and have implications for a wide range of financial activities involving foreign currencies and international trade (SAFE, 2023).
- ***The Securities Law***: This is a law that governs securities trading in China, and it has implications for supply chain finance, particularly with regard to the use of securities-based financing instruments (NPC, 2023).

In addition to the above regulations, there are many other country-specific regulations that impact supply chain finance globally. These regulations can vary widely from country to country and can have significant implications for supply chain financing activities. The purpose of these regulations is to ensure the safety, stability, and integrity of the financial system, as well as to protect consumers from financial fraud and abuse. Compliance with these regulations is essential for financial institutions and other stakeholders to succeed in the long term, by promoting the stability and efficiency of financial markets and protecting the interests of all parties involved. In this context, it is important for financial institutions and other stakeholders to understand and comply with relevant regulations to ensure safe and sustainable financial practices.

12.8.2 Ethics and Sustainability

Supply chain finance is a complex and dynamic area that can give rise to a wide range of ethical issues. These issues can occur when financial institutions or other stakeholders engage in practices that are deceptive, exploitative, or harmful to other parties in the supply chain. The scope of these issues is broad and can include bribery, corruption, labor abuses, and environmental violations, among others. Given the complexity of financial relationships between companies, which often span multiple countries and jurisdictions, ethical concerns can arise in a variety of areas, such as transparency, fair treatment of suppliers, and responsible lending practices.

One example of an ethical issue in supply chain finance is the use of factoring, which can result in suppliers receiving significantly less than the full amount owed for their goods or services. This can raise concerns around fair treatment and transparency in the supply chain. Additionally, some supply chain financing arrangements may involve lending to suppliers who have limited access to credit or face other financial challenges. In these cases, lenders must consider the ethical implications of their lending practices, such as the risk of pushing suppliers into unsustainable levels of debt.

Other ethical issues in supply chain finance include the use of child or forced labor, corruption, and the lack of environmental sustainability. For example, suppliers in developing countries may face poor working conditions or other forms of exploitation. Additionally, SCF transactions could potentially support environmentally harmful practices.

Here are some representative ethics and sustainability issues in supply chain finance:

- *Labor Rights*: Supply chain finance activities can support companies that may be engaged in labor practices that violate human rights and lead to poor working conditions. Ensuring that labor rights are respected and protected is a critical sustainability issue in supply chain finance.
- *Environmental Sustainability*: Supply chain finance activities can also support companies that may be engaged in practices that harm the environment, such as deforestation or pollution. Ensuring that companies adopt environmentally sustainable practices is another critical sustainability issue in supply chain finance.
- *Social Responsibility*: Ensuring that companies in the supply chain act in a socially responsible manner, including respecting the rights of local communities and promoting economic development, is another key sustainability issue.
- *Corruption and Bribery*: Supply chain finance can support suppliers that engage in corrupt practices, such as bribery and kickbacks, which can undermine the integrity of the supply chain and lead to negative economic, social, and environmental impacts.
- *Product Safety and Quality*: Supply chain finance can support suppliers that produce unsafe or low-quality products, which can have negative impacts on consumers, including health problems and loss of confidence in the supply chain.
- *Transparency*: Ensuring transparency and accountability in supply chain finance transactions is essential for promoting sustainability, as it allows stakeholders to identify and address issues related to labor rights, environmental sustainability, and social responsibility.
- *Fair Trade*: Ensuring that suppliers in the supply chain are paid fair prices for their goods and services is another important sustainability issue, as it promotes economic development and reduces poverty.
- *Animal Welfare*: Supply chain finance can support suppliers that engage in practices that harm animal welfare, such as factory farming, animal testing, and illegal wildlife trafficking.

- *Climate Change*: Climate change is an urgent sustainability issue that affects the entire planet. Ensuring that companies in the supply chain adopt environmentally sustainable practices and reduce their carbon footprint is essential for mitigating the impact of climate change.

To address these issues, financial institutions and stakeholders should adopt ethical standards and best practices that promote transparency, fairness, and social responsibility, focusing on responsible lending practices that foster sustainability and fair treatment for all parties. This may involve developing codes of conduct, implementing due diligence processes, and engaging in stakeholder engagement and reporting. By prioritizing ethical practices in supply chain finance, financial institutions and stakeholders can build trust among customers, suppliers, and other stakeholders while promoting sustainable and responsible business practices.

12.9 Summary

This chapter explores various aspects of risk mitigation, compliance, and sustainability in SCF. It discusses the foundational elements for SCF risk mitigation, traditional risk mitigation strategies, SCF-based insurance and credit guarantees, guarantor financing, financial hedging, operational hedging, and the impact of regulations, ethics, and sustainability on SCF.

Key Takeaways:

1. Foundation for SCF Risk Mitigation:
   - Introduce the Asymmetric Risk Theory.
   - Explore the risk-reward Pareto Frontier and the weakest link dilemma.
   - Develop and implement risk mitigation strategies.
2. Traditional Risk Mitigation Strategies:
   - Provide risk mitigation strategies for financial risks, supply chain risks, and non-commercial risks.
3. SCF-based Insurance and Credit Guarantee:
   - Utilize bank loan insurance, bank guarantee, and trade credit insurance to protect against non-payment risks.
   - Leverage credit guarantees to facilitate access to finance for sellers and buyers.
4. Guarantor Financing by Supply Chain Firms:
   - Leverage the creditworthiness of large sellers and buyers to support financing for buyers and sellers, respectively.
   - Utilize 3PL guarantees as risk mitigation tools.
5. Financial Hedging:
   - Use derivatives such as swaps, forwards, futures, and options to hedge against risks like currency fluctuations, interest rate changes, and commodity price volatility.

6. Operational Hedging:
   - Manage risks through operational strategies, including sourcing hedging, inventory hedging, and production hedging.
7. Regulations, Ethics, and Sustainability:
   - Understand and comply with international and regional regulations, such as Basel Accords and FATF Recommendations.
   - Address ethical concerns and promote sustainability in SCF by adopting transparent, fair, and socially responsible practices, as well as responsible lending practices.

12.10 Exercises

12.10.1 Practice Questions

1. What are the two primary benefits of using guarantor financing by supply chain firms?
2. Name two benefits of using supply chain finance-based insurance and credit guarantees.
3. In the context of supply chain finance, what is the difference between financial hedging and operational hedging?
4. Calculate the potential loss for a company that has a 50,000 GBP payable due in 60 days, given that the current GBP/USD exchange rate is 1.35 and the expected exchange rate in 60 days is 1.30.
5. What are key takeaways for ensuring ethics and sustainability in supply chain finance?
6. A company is using a foreign exchange forward contract to hedge a 100,000 EUR payable due in 90 days. The current EUR/USD exchange rate is 1.20, and the forward exchange rate for 90 days is 1.22. Calculate the amount the company will pay in USD after 90 days.
7. Name reasons why companies choose to use supply chain finance-based insurance products.
8. Calculate the potential gain for a company that has a 100,000 EUR receivable due in 90 days, given that the current EUR/USD exchange rate is 1.20 and the expected exchange rate in 90 days is 1.25.
9. What are key takeaways for managing operational risks in supply chain finance?
10. A company is considering a supply chain finance arrangement that involves borrowing $400,000 from a financial institution at an annual interest rate of 3.5%. Calculate the amount the company would have to repay to the financial institution after one year.

12.10.2 Case Studies

Case Study 1: OptimalTech—Navigating Supply Chain Financing Risks

Background

OptimalTech is a leading electronics company based in Taiwan that designs and manufactures a wide range of computer components. They have a well-established supply chain, with parts sourced globally and a significant portion of their products exported to the U.S. market. Their annual revenue is approximately $500 million, with 30% ($150 million) attributable to their exports.

While OptimalTech enjoys a robust reputation, the global electronics landscape is ever-evolving, characterized by rapidly changing technology, fierce competition, and a high degree of market volatility. Recent disruptions in global trade dynamics, coupled with unforeseen logistical challenges, have placed new strains on the company's financing.

Challenges

1. One of OptimalTech's main suppliers in Thailand is facing liquidity problems, endangering a supply worth $50 million annually.
2. Recent regulatory changes in the U.S. have tightened the credit guidelines for imported electronics, affecting OptimalTech's credit terms and raising the potential for increased costs.
3. Due to market volatilities, some of OptimalTech's retail partners in the U.S. are asking for extended credit terms, putting pressure on the company's cash flow.
4. OptimalTech's bank has revised its financing terms, reducing the available line of credit by 15% because of broader economic concerns.

Options for Risk Mitigation

1. **Supplier Credit Guarantee**: Collaborate with a financial institution to provide a credit guarantee to the liquidity-challenged supplier in Thailand, ensuring uninterrupted supplies.
2. **SCF-based Insurance**: Opt for a supply chain finance (SCF)-based insurance solution to safeguard against potential defaults from U.S. retailers asking for extended credit terms.
3. **Guarantor Financing**: To ease the credit pressure, OptimalTech can partner with a third-party logistics firm that can act as a guarantor, backing their financial obligations to their U.S. retail partners.
4. **Seek Alternative Financing**: Explore other regional and international banks or credit institutions for a more favorable line of credit.

Discussion Questions

1. How can a credit guarantee to a supplier ensure the stability of OptimalTech's supply chain?
2. Assess the potential risks and benefits of an SCF-based insurance solution in the context of U.S. retailers.
3. How does guarantor financing with a third-party logistics firm help in navigating the tightened U.S. credit guidelines?
4. Discuss the potential challenges OptimalTech might face when seeking alternative financing sources.

Case Study 2: PureFiber—Financial vs. Operational Hedging in Textile Production

Background

PureFiber is a leading textile manufacturer in Bangladesh with annual revenues of $10 million from its export-oriented operations. Over the past year, cotton prices surged from $70/kg to $95/kg, primarily attributed to unpredictable weather patterns impacting yields and heightened global demand. Moreover, historical data indicates that the local currency may depreciate by about 5% annually against the U.S. dollar, posing a significant challenge for PureFiber as 70% of its revenues are in USD.

Challenges

- The surge in cotton prices by $25/kg translates to a potential additional cost of $750,000, given the annual sourcing of 30 tons of cotton.
- Historical currency depreciation could result in a potential revenue loss of $500,000 annually due to exchange rate fluctuations.
- Dependence on a few significant local farms endangers the production of 2.4 million meters of fabric due to potential supply chain disruptions.
- A standing contract to deliver 1 million meters of fabric to an international brand at a pre-agreed price means fluctuating cotton prices could eat into margins.

Options for Risk Mitigation

- **Financial Hedging**: Procure futures contracts for cotton at $80/kg for the forthcoming season, effectively setting a ceiling on the price and potential loss. Similarly, secure forward contracts to fix the present exchange rate.
- **Operational Hedging**: Allocate $250,000 to engage five additional local farms and commence importing 20% of the necessary cotton at a consistent $75/kg instead of $95/kg. Dedicate $150,000 toward refining the inventory and order management system, which is anticipated to reduce holding costs by 10% (current holding costs represent 2.5% of total revenue).

Discussion Questions

1. How does securing a futures contract at $80/kg shield PureFiber from potential losses if cotton prices surge beyond $80/kg, given that the futures contract fees are negligible and there's a 40% likelihood of the price stabilizing at $70/kg and a 60% chance it will skyrocket to $100/kg?
2. Considering operational hedging, what are the potential savings from importing cotton at a fixed price of $75/kg compared to $95/kg? How does supplier diversification bolster PureFiber's operational resilience?
3. What are the financial implications of a 5% annual currency depreciation, and how can a forward contract safeguard against this?
4. Assess the ROI from the advanced inventory system in terms of trimmed holding costs.

Appendix: Academic Perspective

Guarantor Financing in a Four-party Supply Chain Game
Weihua Zhou, Tiantian Lin, and Gangshu (George) Cai[1]

Zhou et al. (2020)expand the classic selling-to-newsvendor model, which consists of a manufacturer selling through a retailer, to a four-party supply chain game involving a manufacturer, a 3PL firm, a capital-constrained retailer, and a bank. The game spans two time periods, with the first period involving the manufacturer setting the wholesale price, the 3PL firm deciding the logistics service rate, and the retailer determining its order quantity and obtaining a loan from the bank directly or under either manufacturer guarantor financing (MG) or 3PL guarantor financing (LG). The retailer then pays the manufacturer and 3PL for the order and delivery, respectively. The second period involves demand realization and the retailer repaying the bank.

The decision sequence between the manufacturer and the 3PL depends on the leadership type: either a Nash game or a manufacturer leadership Stackelberg game.

- Nash Game: The manufacturer and the 3PL sign contracts with the retailer separately, and neither firm knows the other's contract price with the retailer. Both firms determine their respective prices, anticipating the other's best response decision. This setting represents a situation where both firms have identical decision sequences and information states.

---

[1] This section reports some research findings from one of my publications, Zhou et al. (2020). Interested readers please refer to the full article: Zhou, W., Lin, T., & Cai, G. (2020). Guarantor financing in a four-party supply chain game with leadership influence. *Production and Operations Management*, 29(9), 2035–2056. For simplicity, we skip most references therein, so please refer to the paper for more details.

- Manufacturer Leadership Stackelberg Game: The manufacturer sets the wholesale price first, followed by the 3PL deciding its logistics service rate. This scenario often occurs when the 3PL can access product value information via insurance services or wholesale price information on B2B websites.

In the study, three financing schemes are analyzed: manufacturer guarantor financing (MG), 3PL guarantor financing (LG), and traditional bank financing (BF) with bank guarantee. If the retailer defaults in guarantor financing, the guarantor covers the remaining loan balance.

The research yields four main findings. Firstly, guarantor financing can surpass traditional bank financing for the entire supply chain, especially when upstream firm costs are relatively low and financial risk meets specific conditions in both game settings (see Fig. 12.4). The reason is that, although the retailer's total purchasing cost is higher in guarantor financing, its loan interest rate is lower, resulting in a larger order quantity than with BF. The interest rate advantage compensates for the purchasing cost drawback when upstream firms' costs are not excessively high.

Second, the willingness to act as a guarantor varies under different game leadership structures. In the Nash game, both the retailer and the supply chain are indifferent between the manufacturer or the 3PL acting as the guarantor. However, the manufacturer and the 3PL each prefer the other to be the guarantor, as being a free-rider in guarantor financing is more advantageous than being the guarantor itself.

This free-rider dilemma can be resolved if the manufacturer becomes the Stackelberg leader in the supply chain. In the manufacturer leadership Stackelberg game,

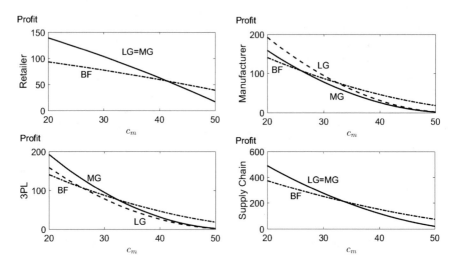

Fig. 12.4 Profits of different financing schemes under nash game with respect to the manufacturer's cost c_m

all firms prefer the follower to be the guarantor. The supply chain benefits from the follower-guarantor advantage because the leader constrains the follower from charging an excessively high risk premium. Meanwhile, the manufacturer, as the Stackelberg leader, does not charge an extremely high wholesale price for not bearing the guarantor's financial risk. This follower-guarantor advantage leads to a higher order quantity, benefiting all firms in the supply chain.

Third, a Stackelberg leader always prefers to free-ride on the other upstream firm's guarantor financing service. In contrast, the follower always prefers to be the guarantor due to the follower-guarantor advantage. However, from the guarantor's perspective, being the follower is not always advantageous. The Stackelberg leadership advantage can outweigh the follower-guarantor advantage when the financial risk level (i.e., the retailer's default risk) is sufficiently low. This outcome occurs because the Stackelberg leader can more easily transfer pricing pressure to the follower, demanding a larger profit margin for being the guarantor. Nonetheless, if the retailer is more likely to default, the guarantor benefits more from being a follower than being the leader.

Fourth, under LG, all firms and the supply chain perform better with a longer decision hierarchy (i.e., the Stackelberg game) than with a shorter decision hierarchy (i.e., the Nash game). This finding contradicts the conventional wisdom that a flatter decision hierarchy is more efficient, as confirmed under bank financing. This phenomenon occurs when financial risk is substantially high. In this situation, the manufacturer is more reluctant to increase its wholesale price in the Stackelberg game than in the Nash game, resulting in a lower wholesale price and a higher order quantity in the Stackelberg game.

References

Aarti, G., Pramod, B., & Vineet, K. (2021). *Trade credit insurance market size, share & growth.* https://www.alliedmarketresearch.com/trade-credit-insurance-market-A08305. Accessed July 22, 2022.

Alessi, C. (2010). *London shipping hedge fund's strategies pay off.* https://www.institutionalinvestor.com/article/b150qd0rbg65rc/london-shipping-hedge-funds-strategies-pay-off. Accessed May 11, 2023.

Anand, K., Anupindi, R., & Bassok, Y. (2008). Strategic inventories in vertical contracts. *Management Science, 54*(10), 1792–1804.

Caillaud, B., Dionne, G., & Jullien, B. (2000). Corporate insurance with optimal financial contracting. *Economic Theory, 16*(1), 77–105.

CFTC. (2024). Dodd-Frank Act. https://www.cftc.gov/LawRegulation/DoddFrankAct/index.htm. Accessed January 12, 2024.

Chen, J. (2022). Exotic option: Definition and comparison to traditional options. https://www.investopedia.com/terms/e/exoticoption.asp. Accessed July 2, 2023.

Chen, X., Cai, G., & Song, J. S. (2019). The cash flow advantages of 3PLs as supply chain orchestrators. *Manufacturing & Service Operations Management, 21*(2), 435–451.

Chopra, S., & Sodhi, M. S. (2004). Supply-chain breakdown. *MIT Sloan Management Review, 46*(1), 53–61.

CME. (2022). *Freight futures and options.* https://www.cmegroup.com/trading/energy/freight-futures-and-options.html. Accessed June 6, 2023.

Dong, L., & Tomlin, B. (2012). Managing disruption risk: The interplay between operations and insurance. *Management Science, 58*(10), 1898–1915.

Dreyer, M., & Nygaard, K. (2020). *Countries continue to adopt and update credit guarantee schemes for small business lending.* https://som.yale.edu/blog/countries-continue-to-adopt-and-update-credit-guarantee-schemes-for-small-business-lending. Accessed July 12, 2022.

EKF. (2022). *Buyer credit guarantee.* https://ekf.dk/en/ekf-s-guarantees/guarantees/buyer-credit-guarantee. Accessed December 2, 2022.

Eksfin. (2022). *Norwegian gas cylinders capture the Uruguayan domestic market.* https://www.eksfin.no/en/cases/uncategorized/norwegian-gas-cylinders-capture-the-uruguayan-domestic-market/. Accessed December 2, 2023.

European Banking Authority. (2023). *Capital Requirements Regulation (CRR).* https://www.eba.europa.eu/regulation-and-policy/single-rulebook/interactive-single-rulebook/12674. Assessed November 29, 2023.

European Central Bank. (2018). *The revised Payment Services Directive (PSD2) and the transition to stronger payments security.* https://www.ecb.europa.eu/paym/intro/mip-online/2018/html/1803_revisedpsd.en.html, assessed on September 9, 2023.

European Commission. (2023). *Derivatives/EMIR.* https://finance.ec.europa.eu/capital-markets-union-and-financial-markets/financial-markets/post-trade-services/derivatives-emir_en. Assessed September 19, 2023.

European Commission. (2022). *Implementing and delegated acts - MiFID II.* https://finance.ec.europa.eu/regulation-and-supervision/financial-services-legislation/implementing-and-delegated-acts/markets-financial-instruments-directive-ii_en. Assessed December 29, 2022.

European Council. (2023). *The general data protection regulation.* https://www.consilium.europa.eu/en/policies/data-protection/data-protection-regulation. Assessed October 9, 2023.

EXIM. (2021a, June). *2020 Report to the U.S. Congress on Global Export Credit Competition.* https://www.exim.gov/news/exim-releases-2020-competitiveness-report. Accessed December 2, 2021.

EXIM. (2021b). *EXIM Releases 2020 Competitiveness Report.* https://www.exim.gov/news/exim-releases-2020-competitiveness-report. Accessed December 2, 2021.

FATF. (2022), *FATF recommendations.* https://www.fatf-gafi.org/en/topics/fatf-recommendations.html. Accessed September 5, 2022.

GACC (General Administration of Customs of the People's Republic of China). (2014). *Customs Law of the People's Republic of China.* http://english.customs.gov.cn/statics/644dcaee-ca91-483a-86f4-bdc23695e3c3.html. Accessed November 19, 2023.

Grant, M. (2018). *Bank Guarantee.* https://www.investopedia.com/terms/b/bankguarantee.asp. Accessed December 13, 2021.

Green, A. (2003). *Credit guarantee schemes for small enterprises: An effective instrument to promote private sector-led growth?* UNIDO, Programme Development and Technical Cooperation Division.

Holle, N. (2017). *Credit Guarantee Schemes for Agricultural What Are Credit Guarantee Schemes and How.* Technical Summary by Agriculture Finance Support Facility and World Bank Group.

IFRS. (2023). *IFRS accounting standards navigator.* https://www.ifrs.org/issued-standards/list-of-standards/. Accessed May 25, 2023.

ISDA. (2021, February). SwapsInfo Full Year 2020 and the Fourth Quarter of 2020 Review. In *Isda*.

Kurt, D. (2022). *Trade credit insurance: Overview, advantages, alternatives.* https://www.investopedia.com/trade-credit-insurance-5190219. Accessed January 15, 2024.

Jing, B., Chen, X., & Cai, G. G. (2012). Equilibrium financing in a distribution channel with capital constraint. *Production and Operations Management, 21*(6), 1090–1101. https://doi.org/10.1111/j.1937-5956.2012.01328.x

Jorion, P. (2007). *Value at risk: The new benchmark for managing financial risk.* The McGraw-Hill Companies, Inc.

Levitsky, J. (1997). Best practice in credit guarantee schemes. *Financier-Burr Ridge, 4,* 86–94.

Lowery, D. (2007). Understanding interest rate swap math & pricing. *Business and Politics, 9*(2).

References

Manning, L. (2022). *Exchange-traded derivative definition*. Investopedia. https://www.investopedia.com/terms/e/exchange-traded-derivative.asp. Accessed January 5, 2023.

Marotta, D. (2022). *10 Supply Chain Risk Management Strategies*. Hitachi Solutions. https://global.hitachi-solutions.com/blog/supply-chain-risk-management/. Accessed January 15, 2023.

Mudge, D. T., & Wee, L.-S. (1993). Truer to type. *Risk, 6*(12), 16–19.

NPC (npc.gov.cn). (2023). *Securities Law of the People's Republic of China*. http://www.npc.gov.cn/zgrdw/englishnpc/Law/2007-12/11/content_1383569.htm. Accessed March 13, 2023.

OECD. (2009). Discussion Paper on Credit Guarantee Schemes. *OECD*, 1–19.

RBA. (2002). Overnight Indexed Swap Rates. In *Reserve Bank of Australia Bulletin* (Issue Graph 1).

PBC (The People's Bank of China). (2003). *Law of the People's Republic of China on Banking Regulation and Supervision*. http://www.pbc.gov.cn/english/130733/2830218/index.html. Accessed November 13, 2023.

PNC. (2023). *How to settle cross-border transactions in Renminbi*. https://www.pnc.com/insights/corporate-institutional/go-international/how-to-settle-cross-border-transactions-in-renminbi.html. Accessed November 11, 2023.

Rahman, A. (2015). Over-the-counter (OTC) derivatives, central clearing and financial stability. *Bank of england quarterly bulletin*, Q3.

Rogers, P. (2022). *Hedging*. https://www.scm-portal.net/glossary/hedging.shtml. Accessed December 7, 2022.

SAFE (State Administration of Foreign Exchange of China). (2023). *Rules and regulations*. https://www.safe.gov.cn/en/RulesandRegulations/index.html. Accessed March 23, 2023.

Sapers, R. (2023). AML & KYC: *What you need to know*. https://carta.com/blog/aml-kyc/. Accessed May 29, 2023.

Sodhi, M. S., & Tang, C. S. (2012). *Managing supply chain risk* (vol. 172). Springer Science & Business Media.

SPC (The Supreme People's Court of the People's Republic of China). (2016). *Insurance Law of the People's Republic of China*. https://english.court.gov.cn/2016-04/14/c_761424.htm. Accessed March 3, 2023.

Srinivasan, B. S., & Youngren, S. (2001). Using currency futures to hedge currency risk. In *Product Research & Development Chicago Mercantile Inc.* http://www.henley.ac.uk/web/FILES/REP/Currency_Futures.pdf

Thiha. (2014). *No buyers for credit guarantee insurance*. https://www.nationthailand.com/international/30249382. Accessed December 2, 2022.

Trade Finance. (2022). *What is export and agency finance?* https://tradefinanceanalytics.com/what-is-export-and-agency-finance. Accessed December 27, 2022.

Tripathi, A., & Wani, A. P. (2012). Hedging: A powerful tool in supply chain manager's arsenal. *Srrnkhala Supply Chain & Operations Club Magazine, 2*.

ULC (The Uniform Law Commission). (2023). *Uniform Commercial Code*. https://www.uniformlaws.org/acts/ucc. Accessed May 9, 2023.

Valuates Reports. (2021). *Financial guarantee market size to reach usd 71.93 billion by 2030 at cagr 9.6% - valuates reports*. https://www.prnewswire.com/in/news-releases/financial-guarantee-market-size-to-reach-usd-71-93-billion-by-2030-at-cagr-9-6-valuates-reports-844147736.html. Accessed December 15, 2022.

Wang, W., & Cai, G. G. (2023, June). Curtailing Bank Loan and Loan Insurance Under Risk Regulations in Supply Chain Finance. *Management Science*.https://doi.org/10.1287/mnsc.2023.4827

Witte, G. (2023). *5 core steps in the risk management process*. https://www.techtarget.com/searchcio/feature/Risk-management-process-What-are-the-5-steps. Accessed January 15, 2024.

Wikipedia. (2022a). *Basel III*. https://en.wikipedia.org/wiki/Basel_III. Accessed September 25, 2022.

Wikipedia. (2022b). *Forward rate*. https://en.wikipedia.org/wiki/Forward_rate. Accessed December 12, 2023.

Wikipedia. (2023). *Overnight indexed swap.* https://en.wikipedia.org/wiki/Overnight_indexed_swap. Accessed December 12, 2023.

Wu, Z., Zhen, X., Cai, G., & Tang, J. (2024). The internal decentralization effects in off-sourcing procurement. Working paper, Santa Clara University.

Zhou, W., Lin, T., & Cai, G. (2020). Guarantor financing in a four-party supply chain game with leadership influence. *Production and Operations Management., 29*(9), 2035–2056.

Part IV
Supply Chain Finance Technology

"Many catalysts—including digital delivery, fintech innovation, industry utilities, blockchain, and API technologies—could stimulate cheaper and more accessible SCF, but change has been slow. Now in 2020, the impact of COVID-19 has contributed to accelerating digital adoption and reconfiguration of trade and supply chains—for example, to improve resilience and diversify sourcing."
McKinsey (2020)

Digitalization and Technology   13

> **Learning Objectives:**
>
> 1. Grasp digitalization in supply chains, highlighting its role in boosting transparency and efficiency.
> 2. Assess the merits and challenges of supply chain finance (SCF) platforms in enhancing financial transactions and collaboration.
> 3. Dive into SCF technologies like the Internet of Things (IoT), Artificial Intelligence (AI), Machine Learning (ML), and Big Data, and understand their influence on risk management and operational prowess.
> 4. Understand the synergy of integrating various SCF technologies for improved capital management and stakeholder engagement in a digital ecosystem.

13.1 Introduction

With the advancement of information technology, including cloud computing, IoT, Big Data, AI, electronic invoicing and payments, application programming interfaces (APIs), and blockchain, the digitalization of supply chains and finance has become a prevailing trend for enterprises. Building on supply chain digitalization, supply chain firms and banks have established supply chain finance (SCF) platforms to facilitate their transactions and enhance their performance.

13.2 Supply Chain Digitalization

The digitalization era began around 2002, when the volume of digitized data overtook that of analog data. It's estimated that the volume of digitized data reached approximately 79.5 ZB (1 ZB equivalent to 1 billion TB) in 2022 and is projected to touch 175 ZB by 2025 (Coughlin, 2018). In the race to gain a competitive edge, firms are contending with each other to secure top-tier data-analytics capabilities in this age of digitalization.

Because supply chain management permeates all industries, a plethora of digital and intelligent technologies have been extensively applied across all facets of supply chain, spanning production, manufacturing, procurement and sourcing, logistics, marketing and channel management, supply chain finance, and risk management. For instance, at the heart of Industry 4.0 is the vision to establish smart factories, driven by online real-time data and advanced technologies like artificial intelligence and the Internet of Things.

Delving into the service and retail sectors, Alibaba employs Alipay to spearhead the digital metamorphosis of the service industry (Alipay, 2023). Meanwhile, Tencent champions the digital overhaul and elevation of the traditional retail industry through the rollout of smart retail initiatives (Tencent, 2023). Under Armour taps into its connected fitness data, predominantly from smart shoes and other sources, to devise algorithms aimed at offering customers superior products. Undeniably, the swift progression of digital technology has given rise to innovative retail formats, such as omnichannel supply chains (integrating online and offline experiences), social retail, live streaming, and platforms driven by short videos like TikTok and YouTube (Cai, 2019).

Within the logistics sphere, state-of-the-art solutions like drone deliveries, automated warehouses, autonomous stations, and distribution robots have been comprehensively employed across various dimensions, including intelligent warehousing and streamlined distribution. For instance, the Y division launched by JD.com in November 2016 is set on sculpting a smart supply chain fortified by big data, artificial intelligence, and unmanned tech products (Cai, 2019). This move empowers logistics through digitization, pares down logistics costs, and bolsters the enduring competitive stance of enterprises. In 2020, JD Logistics' R&D expenditure soared to an impressive 2.05 billion yuan, underlining the pivotal role of digital intelligence in shaping the future of supply chain management.

From the standpoint of supply chain finance and risk governance, the emergence of blockchain technology equips supply chain enterprises, banks, and other stakeholders with the tools to curtail financing risks and overheads. This is achieved through bespoke technologies, including distributed ledger information dissemination and smart contracts. Such advancements bolster the financing prospects for firms constrained by capital, consequently elevating the operational efficiency and profitability metrics of all entities integrated within supply chains.

13.2.1 5C Advantages and *TIGER* Challenges

The primary benefits of supply chain digitalization are evident and can be distilled into the following *5C advantages* (refer to Table 13.1):

13.2 Supply Chain Digitalization

Table 13.1 Five pros and five cons of supply chain digitalization

5C Advantages	TIGER Challenges
• **C**lear visibility	• **T**ime-consuming and costly efforts
• **C**ommunication and coordination	• **I**ntegration of systems, solutions and culture
• **C**ustomer-focused execution	• **G**lobal cybersecurity and confidentiality
• **C**lever ecosystem	• **E**xpertise and collaboration barriers
• **C**ompetitive positioning	• **R**egulations

1. **Clear Visibility**: While it may seem basic, achieving clear visibility can bring about transformative changes in how an organization perceives and harnesses data. This advantage promotes transparency among stakeholders, augments decision-making efficiency, and strengthens trust across supply chain entities. Given its undeniable benefits, achieving clear visibility is often the topmost priority for many firms.
2. **Communication and Coordination**: With the foundation of clear visibility, supply chain digitalization fosters seamless internal and external communication and enhances coordination among involved parties.
3. **Customer-Focused Execution**: Through digitalization, firms are better positioned to maintain a customer-centric approach in their analysis, forecasting, planning, and execution.
4. **Clever Ecosystem**: Armed with superior visualization and forecasting tools, companies can pursue more intelligent solutions to refine their ecosystems.
5. **Competitive Positioning**: At its core, supply chain digitalization aims to aid businesses in trimming operational expenses, boosting their profit margins, and enhancing their competitive edge.

The manifold advantages of supply chain digitalization, spanning from the holistic strategic level to the enterprise operational tier, have garnered the attention of political leaders and executives from major corporations. However, there are five primary obstacles—*TIGER challenges*—that companies might face on their journey towards successful supply chain digitalization:

1. **Time-Consuming and Costly Efforts**: While digitalization might sound straightforward, the process of data collection and storage is neither simple nor free. It can be time-consuming and costly. Companies may find themselves incurring high expenses with limited or no meaningful returns on their investments in digitalization.
2. **Integration of Systems, Solutions, and Culture**: Digitalizing supply chains often means supplanting legacy systems with modern IT infrastructures, substituting outdated procedures with contemporary methods, and transitioning from a conventional work culture to one that is digital-first. These shifts are immensely challenging and typically call for unwavering dedication from CEOs and other senior executives. Moreover, there's a potential

risk of resistance from existing staff, as digital transformation could necessitate replacing traditional employees with new hires proficient in IT and data analytics.
3. **Global Cybersecurity and Confidentiality**: With the ubiquity of internet access to digital data, security and confidentiality become paramount concerns for organizations and their patrons. More often than not, consumers fall prey to data breaches, leading businesses to grapple with both a diminishing customer base and reputational harm.
4. **Expertise and Collaboration Barriers**: The intricacies of digitalization frequently demand niche expertise in areas such as predictive analytics and artificial intelligence. While sourcing talent in these specialized domains can be arduous, fostering interdisciplinary collaboration can be even more formidable.
5. **Regulations**: Amid rising apprehensions about data security, privacy, and ethical considerations surrounding data analytics, governments worldwide have rolled out a plethora of regulations governing data and digitalization technologies, escalating the financial demands of compliance.

The strides made in supply chain digitalization have profoundly influenced the evolution of supply chain finance, notably in areas like online supply chain finance platforms and blockchain-backed supply chain finance. Once a firm effectively navigates the TIGER challenges intrinsic to supply chain digitalization, the 5C advantages can propel the organization towards a competitive ascendancy.

13.2.2 A Conceptual Framework

As projected by Gartner, a leading international supply chain consulting firm, by 2023, at least 50% of large global enterprises will incorporate information technologies such as IoT, big data, cloud computing, and AI into their supply chain management strategies (Hippold, 2021). In traditional supply chains, the flow of information is constrained, and the data format remains relatively rudimentary. However, in the digital intelligence era, the supply chain's information flow expands tremendously. The complexity of data formats escalates, and information sharing becomes technically more straightforward, paving the way for data-driven supply chain intelligence.

Perhaps the most immediate and pronounced effect of data visibility within supply chains manifests in logistics management. The movements of various products and services can be surveilled and traced in real time, enabling a comprehensive view of the supply chain, as illustrated in Fig. 13.1.

In a supply chain, the movement of goods is mirrored by the counter-movement of funds. Hence, augmenting logistics efficiency naturally accelerates the funds' circulation. A logistics system enhanced with greater visibility is inherently more secure, subsequently mitigating logistics-associated risks and curbing related financial losses for businesses. More crucially, heightened transparency in logistics and

13.2 Supply Chain Digitalization

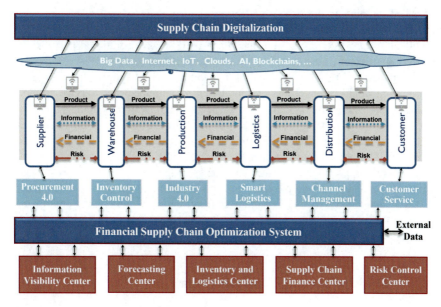

Fig. 13.1 Supply chain digitalization system

capital flows simplifies risk assessment for supply chain financing entities. This ensures that supply chain companies access more streamlined financing avenues, thus effectively amplifying the overarching supply chain profitability.

The full visibility offered by digitalized supply chains facilitates more encompassing risk assessments. These were formerly restricted to individual financing units within traditional supply chains. Now, risk flows evolve dynamically alongside logistics and financial flows, transforming into an entity that can be evaluated and even commoditized (e.g., in risk-based index option trading). This dynamic offers a solid analytical foundation for the sophisticated evolution of intelligent supply chain finance.

Throughout the digital and intelligent transformation of supply chains, enterprises must not only prioritize the development of their existing technology, talent, culture, and overarching strategy but also remain cognizant of the challenges faced by their upstream and downstream counterparts during this transformative phase. The isolated success of a single entity in its digitalization efforts cannot maximize the potential efficiencies and cost savings inherent to digital intelligence without the collaboration of other supply chain members. Particularly when subjected to uncontrollable externalities such as pandemics, natural disasters, or trade conflicts, the benefits of a singularly digitalized supply chain can be drastically curtailed if not holistically realized. Thus, to genuinely harness the potential of a digital supply chain, a thorough understanding of the operational structures and decision-making processes of all entities within the supply chain is essential.

Diverging from conventional supply chain management, the digital era allows supply chain enterprises to leverage technologies like the Internet, IoT, big data, and AI. This enables the timely collection of data, such as raw material sourcing, distribution patterns, and product demand. Such insights are invaluable for individual and collective decision-making, driving down operational costs while amplifying efficiency.

As depicted in Fig. 13.1, an ideal digital and intelligent supply chain management system ought to encompass an intelligent procurement and service system, an intelligent warehouse system, an Industry 4.0 production system, an intelligent logistics mechanism, a multi-channel retail framework, and an intelligent customer service setup. To realize this vision, a comprehensive analysis of the production, operations, logistics management, distribution, product retail, service management, supply chain finance, and risk management of core supply chain entities is mandatory. While pioneering digital technologies have been assimilated into the management processes of industry frontrunners, many smaller enterprises remain in the transition phase, working towards optimizing various aspects of their digital supply chain management.

13.2.3 Goals of Supply Chain Digitalization

After constructing *a supply chain digitalization platform*, firms can attain the subsequent goals, which consequently offer the associated benefits (refer to the *6-able goals* as shown in Fig. 13.2).

- *Information Flow Visible*: The clarity of products, services, capital, and all pertinent data is indispensable for digitalized platforms. This capability itself can shield firms from numerous decision-making missteps, enhancing supply chain efficiency and profitability. Predicated on data collection and information sharing, this function can be augmented using descriptive analytics tools and software. However, achieving such visibility can be challenging; data collection is both costly and time-consuming, and information sharing necessitates trust among supply chain participants.

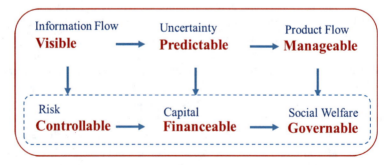

Fig. 13.2 6-able goals of supply chain digitalization

- *Uncertainty Predictable*: Uncertainty is often the principal impediment in realizing optimal outcomes across various supply chain processes. As such, predicting uncertainty often precedes decision-making. Once information visibility is secured, predictability advances the process further in digitalized supply chain platforms, paving the way for overall supply chain system enhancement. Through predictive analytics, firms can project demand, expenses, revenue, profitability, and other key metrics.
- *Product Flow Manageable*: After attaining both visibility and predictability, supply chain entities can govern ordering and inventory processes to curtail costs, refine logistics to minimize lead times, optimize production to elevate product quality, and manage customer relations to foster loyalty and satisfaction.
- *Risk Controllable*: Given the unpredictability of today's global landscape, risk management has surged in importance. The primary mechanism of supply chain finance is to alleviate and redistribute risks faced by associated supply chain entities. This, in turn, bolsters the working capital of more financially restricted firms, enhancing the efficiency of the entire supply chain.
- *Capital Financeable*: An effective digitalized supply chain platform should open up more financing opportunities for its partnered firms. This is due to the inherent features of visibility, predictability, manageability, and risk controllability within the supply chain finance platform. With enhanced clarity on risk profiles, financial institutions are more inclined to extend credit to firms.
- *Social Welfare Governable*: From a governmental standpoint, it's crucial to enforce relevant regulations and policies diligently. This not only refines the business environment for supply chain firms but also amplifies societal welfare.

> *The main mechanism of supply chain finance is to mitigate and shift risks.*

13.3 Supply Chain Finance Platforms

An SCF platform is appealing because it's open to a wide range of supply chain firms and financial institutions. These entities can conduct business transactions cohesively on the same platform. The platform's host could be a bank, a buyer, a seller, a 3PL, or even a third-party entity like an insurance firm.

Metcalfe's Law states that the value of a network is proportional to the square of the number of nodes in that network. By analogy, the value or impact of a platform might be closely tied to the number of firms participating in it, demonstrating a network effect. Once a platform manages to garner a critical mass of participants, it can nurture an organic ecosystem wherein all participants derive benefits from their involvement.

Not only does the SCF platform offer data visibility but it also furnishes predictive and prescriptive analytical tools that can further enhance the performance of the participating firms. Engaging with these platforms can significantly reduce transaction costs, thanks to the platform's efficiency in integrating diverse firms and organizations, including governmental entities, into one unified system. For instance, platforms can substantially slash transaction costs by speeding up communication processes and automating various business operations. Additionally, participants may find it less costly and more straightforward to identify potential partners and acquire the expertise needed to finalize transactions within the platform's environment.

13.3.1 Bank-Led Platform

Bank-led SCF platforms are a natural extension of the banking systems used for trade finance, albeit in digital form. Due to their relatively abundant capital, banks were among the first to support supply chain finance programs, offering them to numerous supply chain firms. Banks can also form consortiums to offer similar financial services to their joint customers.

A bank-led SCF platform may provide the following financial services, among others:

- Letter of credit
- Factoring
- Reverse factoring
- Guarantee financing
- Documentary collections
- Other SCF solutions (see Part II on SCF Mechanisms)

Since supply chain finance has substantially created new business opportunities for banks, most major banks have established a variety of supply chain finance programs/platforms on their websites. For instance, J.P. Morgan has launched programs such as early payment programs in partnership with major retailers (e.g., Taulia), supply chain finance (i.e., reverse factoring), and dynamic discounting for its customers worldwide (J.P. Morgan, 2022). Citi Group introduced the Supplier Finance portal and Sustainable Supply Chain Financing to offer financing solutions to various supply chain firms. As of 2022, Citi serves 225,000 suppliers and over 2,600 buyers in 96 countries (Citigroup, 2022).

In China, Shenzhen Development Bank was among the first banks to develop a supply chain finance program based on supply chain transactions. They introduced a unique "1+N" financing format. In this model, the bank relies on a focal company (referred to as the "1") to extend financing to this focal company's upstream and

13.3 Supply Chain Finance Platforms

downstream partners (referred to as the "N") based on their accounts payable and accounts receivable (Li, 2021). This focal company is typically a dominant and creditworthy leader in its supply chain, prompting the bank to be more willing to lend to its associated supply chain firms for two primary reasons:

1. Risks become more quantifiable based on the supply chain transaction data.
2. The bank's risks are mitigated through the focal company's endorsement and guarantee.

Subsequently, the "1+N" format evolved into "M+N" to encompass multiple focal companies (referred to as the "M"). On an SCF platform, the "1+N" and "M+N" formats can merge into a combination of several supply chain finance mechanisms, including factoring, reverse factoring, purchase order financing, and guarantor financing. Considering that banks are the primary capital sources in supply chain finance, they can be discerning in choosing the financing mechanisms (for instance, some of those involving banks, as discussed in Part II) based on profitability.

A bank-led SCF platform not only streamlines the financing process for the bank's established major clients but also unveils new avenues for SMEs, attributed to the lowered processing costs that arise from an enhanced visibility and predictability of these SMEs' risk profiles. An additional advantage of a bank-led platform is its direct access to the bank's capital resources and financing expertise. This allows the bank to leverage the focal firms' information and credibility and emphasizes the onboarding process for new borrowers to minimize financial risks.

13.3.2 Buyer-Led Platform

In a bid to assist their capital-constrained suppliers, dominant buyers, such as retailers, have collaborated with leading banks to extend financial support to these suppliers. Within a buyer-led platform, the dominant buyer may offer the following financial services to its suppliers:

- Partners with banks to allow them to offer direct loans to capital-constrained suppliers.
- Presents early payment programs for suppliers.
- Extends guarantees for its suppliers' loans.
- Facilitates and ensures reverse factoring for its suppliers.
- Supplies other financial services or assistance to its suppliers.

For instance, in 2019, Amazon joined forces with Bank of America, Merrill Lynch, Goldman Sachs, and ING to provide loans ranging from $1000 to $750,000 to handpicked suppliers through its SMB Lending program (CBinsights, 2022). In collaboration with Goldman Sachs' Marcus brand, Amazon provided a credit line of up to $1M to chosen merchants. Amazon also formed partnerships with other banks to roll out diverse financing programs, such as Amazon Community Lending, Early Payment, Capital Float (a platform in India designed to aid SMBs), and other initiatives for its global suppliers (CBinsights, 2022).

Other major retailers, including Costco, Home Depot, Macy's, Walgreens, and Walmart, have similarly financed their capital-constrained suppliers via their respective financing platforms (Chen et al., 2020). In China, JD Finance operates as the financial wing of JD.com, offering an array of financial products and services to its suppliers (JD, 2023). The Alipay enterprise platform has extended SCF services to Alibaba's online retail suppliers (i.e., Taobao and Tmall.com). Additionally, Alipay offers payment services to merchants utilizing its platform (Alipay, 2023).

13.3.3 Manufacturer-Led Platform

Prominent manufacturers might also establish an SCF platform for their buyers. Within a manufacturer-led platform, the dominant manufacturer can offer the following financial services to its buyers:

- Collaborates with banks to enable them to furnish direct loans to capital-constrained buyers.
- Enables factoring for its buyers.
- Offers guarantees for its buyers' loans.
- Supplies other financial services or assistance to its buyers.

For instance, beginning in 2016, Lenovo, one of the world's leading PC manufacturers, in association with banks such as the Bank of Shanghai and Ping An Bank, established the Lenovo JinFu platform (https://rz.lenovo.com/). This platform delivers a range of supply chain financial services to its distributors and retailers. By 2022, it had facilitated transactions amounting to 10 billion RMB over four years.

In another example, the ShaanGu Group formed partnerships with approximately 60 financial institutions to extend diverse financial services to its buyers.[1] As of September 2022, ShaanGu had secured credit lines amounting to 44 billion RMB from 37 financial institutions, benefiting over 200 companies (ShaanGu, 2023). The SCF platform of ShaanGu offers around 15 financial products, including Bank Guarantee, Buyer's Credit, Financial Leasing, Trust Loan, Accounts Receivable Factoring, and Industrial Fund. These are part of a comprehensive solution designed to assist its buyers and suppliers.

---

[1] ShaanGu Group, also known as Shaanxi Blower (Group) Co., Ltd., is a Chinese manufacturing company specializing in the creation of energy-efficient, clean, and environmentally friendly distributed energy system solutions.

13.3.4 3PL-Led Platform

Owing to its distinct role in supply chains, a 3PL firm possesses the logistics information of products and effectively "controls" the goods during transit. Since these in-transit items can be used as collateral for financing, major 3PL firms offer financial services to their clientele, capitalizing on the ownership of logistics data and collateral. Given that a 3PL firm typically engages with thousands of companies, it is well-positioned to introduce an SCF platform. This not only allows the 3PL firm to lure more clients seeking logistics services by providing related financial services but also, in turn, generates added financial returns for the 3PL firm, cultivating a beneficial cycle.

A 3PL-led SCF platform can offer the following services:

- Inventory in-transit financing
- 3PL guarantee for its customers' loans
- Trade credit insurance
- Other logistics-related financial services

UPS Capital was an early adopter that rendered SCF solutions to its clients (Chen & Cai, 2011). To draw more customers to its logistics offerings, UPS Capital provides services like cash on delivery, continuous custom bonds, trade credit insurance, and other merchant-related services.

Separately, China Material Storage and Transportation Group Co., Ltd. (CMST) has been offering logistics-centric supply chain financial services to its clientele since 1999 (CMST, 2023). To date, it has facilitated financing for over 5000 SMEs, totaling more than 600 billion RMB (equivalent to about $86 billion as of September 5, 2022).

13.3.5 Other Third-Party-Led Platforms

With the growth of SCF, a myriad of third-party institutions, including insurance companies and non-bank financial service providers, have ventured into establishing related platforms. For instance, taulia.com has dedicated itself to delivering supply chain finance solutions to a diverse clientele through its website, by forming partnerships with global banks.[2] These entities can also collaborate to establish consortium platforms.

The Export-Import Bank (EXIM) of the U.S. has devised a platform to offer analogous SCF solutions for businesses exporting to international destinations. Their solutions encompass trade credit insurance and credit guarantees (EXIM, 2022). Another noteworthy example is CALISTA, a trade orchestration platform conceived to provide a holistic range of services in compliance, logistics, and

---

[2] In 2022, Taulia.com was acquired by SAP, a software company.

financing. It aims to facilitate seamless information exchange among participants and ensure efficient managerial coordination across logistics, compliance, and financial domains. Linked to over 90 carriers and 50 ports, users on this platform have the capability to trade logistics services. Moreover, the system assists in fulfilling compliance requirements in over 180 countries (Bhattacharya & Appasamy, 2022).

13.4 Other Supply Chain Finance Technologies

In the evolving landscape of supply chain finance, the integration of cutting-edge technology has become paramount in enhancing efficiency, minimizing risk, and promoting collaboration among various stakeholders. This section delves into pivotal technologies that have reshaped supply chain finance. From IoT and AI to cloud computing and big data analytics, these groundbreaking solutions hold the promise of fundamentally transforming the way buyers, suppliers, and financial institutions manage their financial engagements. By tapping into the capabilities of these technologies, companies can optimize their working capital, simplify processes, and uncover new avenues for growth within supply chain finance. In the following, we will touch upon several relevant technologies briefly, and then delve more extensively into the subject of blockchain in the subsequent chapters.

13.4.1 Internet of Things

The *Internet of Things* (IoT) refers to the technology enabling objects to connect to the internet and communicate with other devices or systems. Within supply chain finance, IoT offers real-time insights into the movement of goods and the state of inventory, paving the way for reduced risk and optimized working capital. Here's how IoT has been integrated into supply chain finance:

- *Asset Tracking*: IoT sensors attached to products, vehicles, or other supply chain assets facilitate the monitoring of their location and condition. This real-time tracking minimizes risks associated with loss or theft and enhances supply chain planning, leading to swifter and more precise financing decisions.
- *Condition Monitoring*: By monitoring factors such as temperature, humidity, or vibration, IoT sensors ensure products are transported and stored under appropriate conditions. This minimizes risks related to damage or spoilage.
- *Predictive Maintenance*: IoT sensors observing the performance of machinery and equipment in the supply chain can preemptively identify potential malfunctions. This proactive approach minimizes downtime, boosts efficiency, and trims maintenance costs. Such detailed data can aid financing

13.4 Other Supply Chain Finance Technologies

methods like factoring or supply chain financing by presenting lenders with a comprehensive view of a borrower's inventory and transactional history.
- **Risk Mitigation**: Enhancing security and risk management within the supply chain, IoT tracks the movement and condition of goods, preventing theft, damage, and other potential disruptions. Such monitoring bolsters lender's confidence in a borrower's repayment capabilities, thereby lowering default risks.
- **Smart Contracts**: Enabled by IoT, smart contracts are self-executing contracts wherein the terms of an agreement between buyer and seller are encoded. The automatic execution of these contracts, triggered by IoT sensors upon meeting specific conditions (e.g., shipment delivery), negates the need for manual oversight and diminishes the potential for disputes or errors.

In essence, IoT's integration into supply chain finance offers enhanced visibility, transparency, and efficiency throughout the supply chain. This results in mitigated risks and improved working capital management, and opens avenues for further growth.

13.4.2 Artificial Intelligence and Machine Learning

Artificial intelligence (AI) and *machine learning* (ML) are revolutionizing the operations of supply chains. These technologies empower computers to learn from data, make predictions, and undertake actions based on that data. Here's how AI and ML can assist in supply chain finance:

- **Credit Risk Assessment**: Within supply chain finance, AI and ML enhance risk assessments and credit decision-making processes. Analyzing extensive data sets, these technologies identify patterns and trends that might elude human detection. For instance, they can assess historical transaction data, financial statements, and even social media activity to gauge the probability of a default or evaluate a borrower's creditworthiness. Such capabilities equip lenders with the insights required to make knowledgeable decisions, mitigate risk, and streamline lending operations.
- **Working Capital Improvement**: AI and ML are instrumental in refining supply chain operations and bolstering working capital management. By examining demand patterns, production schedules, and stock levels, these technologies assist businesses in more accurately forecasting demand, minimizing wastage, and optimizing inventory. The resultant liberation of working capital can then be channeled into financing or other essential business undertakings.
- **Fraud Detection and Cybersecurity**: Enhancing fraud detection measures and fortifying cybersecurity within the supply chain is another domain where AI and ML prove invaluable. By evaluating data from diverse sources, these

technologies can pinpoint unusual activities, subsequently alerting stakeholders about potential threats. This proactive approach mitigates fraudulent activities, bolsters supply chain security, and lessens financial risk exposures.
- *Payment Prediction*: AI and ML algorithms, when applied to transaction data, can predict the chances of defaults or payment delays. Such insights empower lenders with the necessary data to make decisions regarding credit extensions and minimize default risks. These algorithms can also highlight trends within transaction data, such as variations in demand or supplier behaviors, thereby informing financial strategies and enhancing operational efficiency.
- *Payment Automation*: Implementing AI and ML for tasks like invoice processing and payment reconciliation magnifies efficiency while reducing manual errors. Additionally, they can pinpoint opportunities to fine-tune payment conditions, thus decreasing the resources expended on invoice and payment processing.

In summary, AI and ML stand poised to redefine supply chain finance by offering businesses profound insights and tools to refine their operations and make educated financial decisions. Employing these technologies enables businesses to enhance financial results, diminish risks, and more effectively cater to their customers and stakeholders.

13.4.3 Robotic Process Automation

Robotic process automation (RPA) leverages software robots to automate routine, manual tasks. Within the realm of supply chain finance, RPA streamlines operations, minimizes errors, and enhances operational efficiency.

- *Financing Efficiency Improvement*: RPA is adept at automating repetitive and time-intensive tasks characteristic of supply chain finance processes, such as data entry, invoice processing, and payment reconciliation. By automating these processes, businesses can reallocate human resources to tasks that generate more value, such as in-depth analysis and informed decision-making.
- *Financing Task Automation*: RPA can be applied to automate numerous tasks in supply chain finance, encompassing data entry, invoice processing, and both accounts payable and receivable management. By streamlining these tasks, companies can decrease the resources devoted to manual data entry and processing, allowing staff to address more strategic responsibilities.
- *Data Accuracy Improvement*: Another significant benefit of RPA is its ability to bolster data accuracy and diminish errors in financial processes. Software robots execute tasks with impressive accuracy and consistency, minimizing potential mistakes and enhancing data quality. This precision

proves invaluable in areas like invoice processing, where errors can lead to payment delays and potentially strain supplier relationships. By mitigating human error and ensuring process uniformity, organizations can optimize their financial outcomes and diminish the potential for compliance breaches.

In conclusion, RPA holds the promise to elevate the efficiency and precision of supply chain finance processes, curtail costs, and uplift the overall quality of financial data. Embracing this technology empowers businesses to hone their operations, curtail errors, and channel efforts towards tasks of strategic importance.

13.4.4 Cloud Computing

Cloud computing entails the utilization of remote servers, accessible over the internet, for data storage, management, and processing. Within the sphere of supply chain finance, cloud computing offers enhanced collaboration, data access, and scalability.

- *Data Visibility*: Cloud-based supply chain finance platforms offer a unified hub for buyers, suppliers, and financial institutions to synergize and oversee their financial engagements. Such platforms deliver real-time insights into transactional data, empowering stakeholders to make educated determinations on credit and risk.
- *Collaboration Improvement*: Cloud computing enhances data access by granting stakeholders the convenience to retrieve information from any location, at any moment, via any device. This adaptability boosts collaboration and lessens the time and costs linked to manual data handling and processing.
- *Business Scalability*: The scalable nature of cloud computing offers firms an adaptable, cost-efficient IT framework. Through cloud solutions, businesses can effortlessly adjust their operations in alignment with their needs, avoiding hefty initial investments in IT infrastructure.
- *Data Security*: Cloud computing also bolsters data security, furnishing secure storage and backup options that safeguard against potential data compromises or theft. Furthermore, cloud systems typically exhibit higher resilience to disruptions, like power failures or natural calamities, as the data and applications are remotely stored and accessible from any location with internet connectivity.
- *Cost Reduction*: Cloud computing can diminish the expenses related to IT infrastructure, such as upkeep of hardware and software. By adopting cloud solutions, businesses can lower capital outlays, enhance scalability, and more effectively allocate their financial assets.

In summary, cloud computing possesses the capability to redefine the operations of supply chain finance by introducing potent tools that elevate collaboration, data accessibility, resilience, and adaptability. Through the adoption of cloud solutions, enterprises can elevate their financial outcomes, curtail risk, and offer superior services to their clientele and partners.

13.4.5 Big Data Analytics

Big data analytics involves the utilization of advanced analytical techniques and algorithms to interpret vast and intricate datasets. Using big data analytics, companies can discern patterns, trends, and insights that traditional methods might overlook. Within the realm of supply chain finance, big data analytics aids in refining financial decision-making, risk management, and operational efficiency.

- ***Pattern and Opportunity Identification***: Big data analytics can interpret transaction data to highlight trends and patterns that shape financial strategies and minimize risk. These analytical tools also spotlight opportunities to enhance working capital and operational efficiency, such as inventory cost reduction and supply chain visibility improvement.
- ***Risk Prevention***: Big data analytics can pinpoint risks in supply chain finance, such as potential supply chain disruptions from shipment delays or supplier insolvencies, and formulate contingency plans to counteract these risks.
- ***Better Financing Decision-Making***: Through the analysis of supplier data, big data analytics offers avenues to refine payment terms. It also sheds light on working capital optimization opportunities, like inventory cost reduction or cash flow enhancement. The assessment of large datasets from diverse sources delivers invaluable insights for supply chain finance, encompassing demand forecasting, supplier performance appraisal, and risk assessment. Consequently, organizations can make data-driven decisions and fine-tune their supply chain financing strategies.
- ***Financing Effectiveness Enhancement***: Big data analytics elevates the precision and efficacy of credit scoring and risk evaluation. By sifting through diverse data sources, including transaction records, credit histories, and social media information, big data analytics provides lenders with a holistic and accurate representation of a borrower's financial standing and associated risks.

In conclusion, big data analytics holds the transformative power over supply chain finance operations, equipping enterprises with robust insights and instruments to refine operations and make informed fiscal choices. Embracing big data analytics enables businesses to enhance financial outcomes, diminish risks, and deliver superior service to their clients and partners.

To encapsulate, the technologies—namely, these IoT, AI, and ML, RPA, cloud computing, and big data analytics—harbor the potential to reinvent interactions and financial dealings among buyers, suppliers, and financial institutions in supply chain finance. These avant-garde solutions present chances to optimize working capital, streamline operations, and bolster collaboration and decision-making across the supply chain. By harnessing these technologies, businesses can unveil new efficiencies and avenues for growth, simultaneously mitigating risks and boosting resilience.

13.5 Summary

This chapter delves into the pivotal role of digitalization and advanced technologies in transforming SCF. As businesses globally pivot towards automation and data-driven solutions, the realm of SCF is undergoing a similar revolution, driven by advancements like the IoT, AI and ML, RPA, cloud computing, and big data analytics. These technologies not only enhance efficiency and decision-making capabilities but also foster collaboration and reduce risks across the supply chain.

Key Takeaways:

1. Supply Chain Digitalization:
   - Digitalization in the supply chain realm facilitates seamless integration of various processes, enhancing transparency, and ensuring real-time visibility.
   - It optimizes operations, streamlines data management, and bolsters efficiency across the supply chain.
2. Supply Chain Finance Platforms:
   - These are centralized digital systems offering a collaborative hub for all stakeholders, from buyers and suppliers to financial institutions.
   - These platforms enable real-time transaction tracking, risk assessment, and data-driven financial decision-making, improving both efficiency and resilience.
3. Other Supply Chain Finance Technologies:
   - IoT provides real-time insights into product movements and conditions, facilitating asset tracking and risk mitigation.
   - AI and ML enhance predictive capabilities, credit risk assessment, and optimize working capital management.
   - RPA automates repetitive tasks, promoting efficiency and data accuracy.
   - Cloud Computing offers a centralized, scalable, and secure data management solution, fostering collaboration and reducing operational costs.
   - Big Data Analytics provides deep insights from vast datasets, aiding in pattern recognition, risk prevention, and decision-making processes.

13.6 Exercises

13.6.1 Practice Questions

1. What are the benefits and challenges of supply chain digitalization?

2. How can AI and ML be utilized to improve risk assessment in supply chain finance?
3. What advantages does cloud computing offer regarding data security in supply chain finance?
4. How can big data analytics optimize working capital in supply chain finance?
5. How do AI and ML contribute to fraud detection and cybersecurity in the supply chain?
6. How does cloud computing influence business scalability in supply chain finance?
7. In the context of supply chain finance, how can big data analytics assist in credit scoring and risk assessment?
8. What is the primary benefit of using RPA for invoice processing?
9. How can cloud computing reduce costs associated with IT infrastructure in supply chain finance?
10. Has your company been involved in any type of supply chain finance platform? If yes, can you detail the role of your company? What can you improve on the existing platform?

13.6.2 Case Study

Digital Transformation of GlobalTech's Supply Chain Finance

Background

GlobalTech, a leading electronics manufacturer, has a global presence with manufacturing units in Asia, Europe, and the Americas. The company has a vast supply chain network, collaborating with hundreds of suppliers to source components and materials. Traditional methods like paper invoices, manual data entry, and phone-based communication dominated their supply chain finance (SCF) operations.

Challenges

1. **Inefficiency**: Manual entry of invoice details led to frequent delays and errors in payment processing.
2. **Lack of Transparency**: Without a centralized system, tracking transactions and supplier credibility was tedious.
3. **Operational Costs**: Maintaining a large team for manual SCF processes was financially draining.
4. **Risk Management**: Without predictive analytics, potential risks related to credit, fraud, or supply chain disruptions were hard to foresee.

Options for Digital Transformation

1. **Introduce Artificial Intelligence (AI) and Machine Learning (ML)**: Implement AI and ML for predictive analytics to enhance risk assessment.
2. **Utilize Cloud Computing**: Shift data storage to the cloud for real-time data access and scalability.
3. **Implement Robotic Process Automation (RPA)**: Automate repetitive tasks like invoice processing.
4. **Integrate Big Data Analytics**: Enhance decision-making by analyzing vast transaction data.

Discussion Questions

1. Which digitalization options should GlobalTech prioritize and why?
2. How can RPA improve GlobalTech's relationship with its suppliers?
3. How can AI and ML help GlobalTech in fraud detection and cybersecurity?
4. What are the potential risks associated with shifting to cloud computing?
5. How would integrating big data analytics transform GlobalTech's financial decision-making?

References

Alipay. (2023). *Alipay product capabilities*. https://b.alipay.com/. Accessed 11 November 2023.

Bhattacharya, S., & Appasamy, L. (2022). *CALISTA: Enhancing digital trade infrastructure with value-added services*. Singapore Management University Product #: SMU052-PDF-ENG.

Cai, G. (2019). *Smart supply chain management*. A research proposal (in Chinese).

CBinsights. (2022). *What Amazon is doing in financial services as well as fintech*. https://www.cbinsights.com/research/report/amazon-across-financial-services-fintech/. Accessed 27 March 2023.

Chen, X., & Cai, G. G. (2011). Joint logistics and financial services by a 3PL firm. *European Journal of Operational Research, 214*(3), 579–587.

Chen, X., Lu, Q., & Cai, G. (2020). Buyer financing in pull supply chains: Zero-interest early payment or in-house factoring? *Production and Operations Management, 29*(10), 2307–2325. https://doi.org/10.1111/poms.13225

Citigroup. (2022). *Citi named world's best supply chain finance bank at global finance's trade finance awards*. https://www.citigroup.com/citi/news/2022/220110a.htm. Accessed 14 May 2023.

CMST. (2023). *Logistics financing in China Materials Storage & Transportation Group*. http://www.cmst.com.cn/zgwzcy/652620/652631/index.html (in Chinese). Accessed 14 March 2023.

Coughlin, T. (2018). *175 Zettabytes by 2025*. https://www.forbes.com/sites/tomcoughlin/2018/11/27/175-zettabytes-by-2025/?sh=5342cebd5459. Accessed 14 March 2023.

EXIM. (2022). *Supply chain finance*. https://www.exim.gov/solutions/working-capital/supply-chain-finance. Accessed 16 January 2023.

Hippold, S. (2021). *Emerging and maturing supply chain technology is a major source of competitive advantage*. https://www.gartner.com/en/articles/gartner-predicts-the-future-of-supply-chain-technology. Accessed 14 January 2024.

JD. (2023). *JD Finance*. https://jr.jd.com/. Accessed 23 October 2023.

J.P. Morgan. (2022). *Supply chain finance*. https://www.jpmorgan.com/payments/solutions/trade-and-working-capital/supply-chain-finance. Accessed 11 October 2022.

Li, Y. (2021). Research on the Shenzhen mode of China's state-owned enterprise reform serving industrial development in the new Era. *World Congress on Services* (pp. 83–97). Springer International Publishing.

ShaanGu. (2023). *Financial services in Shaangu Group*. http://www.shaangu-group.com/service/jin-rong-fu-wu.htm (in Chinese). Accessed 3 March 2023.

Tencent. (2023). *Smart retail*. https://www.tencent.com/en-us/business/smart-retail.html. Accessed 19 October 2023.

Blockchain Technology 14

> **Learning Objectives:**
>
> 1. Comprehend fundamental blockchain structures and mechanisms, distinguishing public, private, consortium, and hybrid blockchains.
> 2. Investigate the Bitcoin blockchain, its origin, functions, and traits, while assessing associated challenges and advantages.
> 3. Explore alternative public blockchain platforms beyond Bitcoin, focusing on distinct consensus methods, applications, and notable features.
> 4. Evaluate cryptocurrency risks and future prospects, emphasizing their impact on businesses, financial systems, and broader economies.

14.1 Introduction

Blockchain technology is based on a chain of blocks containing information. It is a decentralized database made up of a series of blocks stored across a distributed computer network worldwide. Each block's information, including a timestamp, is integrated into the header of the subsequent block. This structure ensures that any alteration to a block's contents disrupts the entire chain, emphasizing the technology's immutable nature. As a result, the blockchain assures data security, engendering trust among users without relying on any third party.

Originally introduced as the protocol for Bitcoin, a cryptocurrency, blockchain has since evolved into a versatile distributed ledger system (Haber & Stornetta, 1990). This system can record transactions and track assets in various businesses. Assets encompass everything from tangible items like cash, land, cars, and houses, to intangible assets such as copyrights, intellectual properties, and patents. In essence, almost any traceable and tradable item can be recorded on a blockchain network.

The inception of blockchain aimed to establish a system secured cryptographically where document timestamps couldn't be manipulated. As Sherman et al. (2019) highlighted, the rudimentary concept resembling blockchain was presented in cryptographer David Chaum's 1982 dissertation. Haber and Stornetta (1990) later expanded on this idea. They emphasized the ease with which digital documents could be altered and introduced a digital timestamping method focused on content's integrity rather than the storage medium itself. This approach prevented any changes to a document's timestamps, be it backdating or moving them forward, ensuring the document's complete privacy. Subsequently, Bayer et al. (1993) proposed using cryptographic hash functions to document events based on the content without disclosing the actual document. They advocated for the use of Merkle trees to make the storage and verification of timestamp certificates more manageable. Their method, which involved storing multiple certificates in a single block, was then publicized in *The New York Times* from 1995 onwards (Oberhaus, 2018).

The paradigm shift occurred in 2008 when an individual, or perhaps a group, using the pseudonym Satoshi Nakamoto published the Bitcoin white paper.[1] This paper elucidated the first decentralized ledger system, introducing the notions of blocks and chains—later amalgamated into the term "blockchain" (Nakamoto, 2008). The white paper laid out a cryptographic hashing method for timestamping blocks, eliminating the need for a central authority to validate timestamps. It also delineated how blocks would be added sequentially to the chain (Narayanan et al., 2016). Soon after, this design became integral to Bitcoin, serving as the decentralized cryptocurrency system's public ledger.

14.2 Blockchain Structures

Since the advent of the Bitcoin blockchain (detailed in the subsequent subsection), alternative blockchains have emerged to cater to diverse business requirements. One criterion to differentiate these blockchains is based on the need for permission to join the network.

- *Permissionless Blockchains*: These blockchains are open, allowing anyone to join without prior authorization. Users have the option of maintaining pseudo-anonymity, ensuring that while their actions are transparent, their identities remain concealed. There's no restriction on nodes joining this network (Wegrzyn & Wang, 2021).
- *Permissioned Blockchains*: Participation in these blockchains requires authorization from a governing entity. This central authority could be a government body, a predominant company, or a consortium of business partners.

---

[1] Satoshi Nakamoto is believed to be a pseudonym for an individual or group of individuals who began developing Bitcoin in 2007 (Lemieux, 2013).

14.2 Blockchain Structures

Users within these blockchains are privy to each other's identities. Certain nodes wield control over permissions and have elevated rights compared to others.

Permissionless blockchains, owing to their Proof of Work (PoW) and other consensus mechanisms, which necessitate verification by many nodes, are typically more secure than permissioned blockchains. The latter only require approval from a handful of authorities. Conversely, permissioned blockchains boast greater efficiency. This is attributed to the reduced transaction processing time, facilitated by the fewer nodes present. However, this limited node presence renders permissioned blockchains susceptible to security breaches. The potential for collusion is heightened, which can compromise the integrity of the network. As a consequence, administrators of permissioned blockchains often need to allocate substantial resources to ensure network security and to engender user trust (Table 14.1).

Elaborating on the permission levels, blockchains can be further segmented into four distinct categories (refer to Fig. 14.1):

- Public Blockchain
- Private Blockchain
- Consortium Blockchain
- Hybrid Blockchain

Public blockchains, like Bitcoin, tend to have slower transaction verification speeds, while private blockchains are notably more susceptible to fraud and other security breaches. Consortium and hybrid blockchains navigate a middle ground between these two extremes (i.e., public vs. private), aiming to mitigate the limitations of both public and private blockchains.

When evaluating against traditional databases in terms of decentralization levels, the relationship between various blockchains and databases becomes evident, as depicted in Fig. 14.2. In contrast to traditional databases that operate under centralization, all blockchains are—at a minimum—partially decentralized and possess an immutable data feature. Permissioned blockchains aim to marry the

Table 14.1 Permissionless vs. permissioned blockchains

	Permissionless	**Permissioned**
Transaction Efficiency	Lower	Higher
Trust Level	Higher	Lower
Users	Pseudo-anonymous	Known
Consensus Mechanism	Yes	Depends
Consensus Incentives	Native cryptocurrency	None
Application Scenario	Crypto economies	Enterprises leveraging distributed database technology

Permissionless
(no authority)
Permissioned
(authority)
Public
Hybrid
Private
Consortium

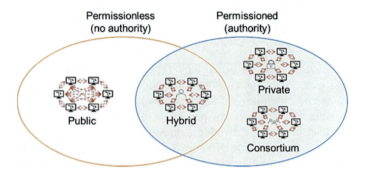

Fig. 14.1 Types of blockchain structures (*Source* Adapted from Wegrzyn & Wang, 2021)

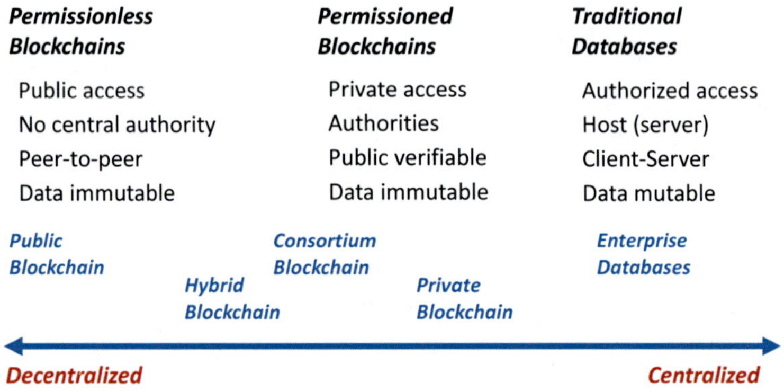

Permissionless Blockchains
Public access
No central authority
Peer-to-peer
Data immutable
Permissioned Blockchains
Private access
Authorities
Public verifiable
Data immutable
Traditional Databases
Authorized access
Host (server)
Client-Server
Data mutable
Public Blockchain
Hybrid Blockchain
Consortium Blockchain
Private Blockchain
Enterprise Databases
Decentralized
Centralized

Fig. 14.2 Comparison between blockchains and databases

security advantages of permissionless blockchains with the efficiency inherent in centralized systems.

14.3 The Bitcoin Blockchain

Bitcoin (₿) is a cryptocurrency utilized within the Bitcoin network. Although the economic status of Bitcoin as a potential bubble remains a topic of debate among economists, its foundational technology—the blockchain—has been recognized as a pivotal technological innovation since the 2010s (Sherman et al., 2019). Despite the evolution of blockchain technology beyond Bitcoin, the merits of the essential decentralized ledger mechanism persist in contemporary blockchain systems. This subsection offers an overview of the Bitcoin blockchain.

14.3.1 The Bitcoin Blockchain Structure

The *Bitcoin blockchain* embodies a digital, peer-to-peer, decentralized ledger system. Unlike traditional centralized banking systems that rely on a single server center, the data and core information system of the Bitcoin blockchain are distributed across numerous computers owned by individuals worldwide (refer to Fig. 14.3). In centralized systems (as shown in Fig. 14.3a), document verification hinges on the central server. Conversely, in a distributed (i.e., peer-to-peer) system, verification is shouldered by all computers (or nodes) in the network. While centralized systems pose risks associated with a single point of failure, decentralized systems might incur increased costs tied to node coordination and document verification.

Fundamentally, the Bitcoin blockchain's architecture leverages a hardware infrastructure comprising thousands of computers interconnected via the internet. This blockchain represents a conceptual chain of specially designed data blocks dispersed within the peer-to-peer computer network. Distinct from centralized databases, this decentralized database ensures every participating computer (node) retains a copy of the blockchain, eliminating the need for centralized authority trust. Each node operates the Bitcoin Core software, maintaining a comprehensive replica of the Bitcoin blockchain (Hartmann, 2021).

Data is housed within each block, interconnected to both its preceding and succeeding blocks via cryptographic hashes. Therefore, any alteration to the data within a block would modify its hash values, subsequently disrupting the chain's integrity. Viewed from a different angle, trust within the blockchain system paradoxically emerges from its inherent design predicated on mistrust: for instance, if one loses their private key, there's no recourse to recover the lost Bitcoins. In this sense, the blockchain is a "trustless" system. However, its trustworthiness is derived from its robust design that prevents any data tampering.

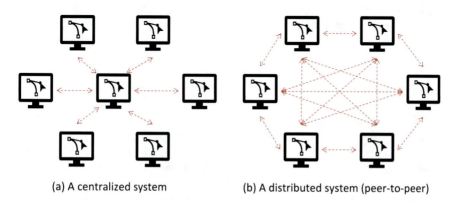

(a) A centralized system   (b) A distributed system (peer-to-peer)

Fig. 14.3 Centralized vs. distributed computer systems

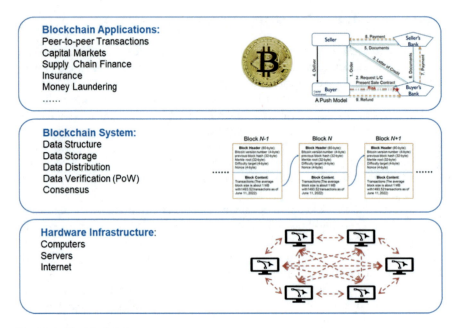

Fig. 14.4 The blockchain structure

> *The blockchain system is a "trustless" system that can be trusted, as its design inherently prevents any tampering with the data.*

Building upon the foundational blockchain systems, numerous applications have emerged, encompassing areas such as the cryptocurrency market, peer-to-peer transactions, and supply chain finance. For a visual representation of the blockchain's structure and further discussions on its varied applications, refer to Fig. 14.4.

14.3.2 Transactions, Cryptography, and Crypto Wallet

14.3.2.1 Transactions

Blockchain's primary function was to record financial transactions of Bitcoins, acting as a ledger. Each transaction specifies its inputs, which can come from one or multiple sources, and its outputs, which can be dispersed to several recipients. The cumulative sum of the inputs (i.e., the total number of coins) should be at least equal to the sum of the outputs. If the sum of inputs surpasses that of the outputs, an additional output is directed back to the payer. Any surplus input not utilized in the outputs is designated as the transaction fee (Wikipedia, 2023a). As blockchain has advanced, transactions have expanded beyond just cryptocurrency to include documents, contracts, and other information. While a transaction fee can be defined in these cases, it remains optional.

Upon initiation, a transaction is termed "pending" and is first integrated into a transaction pool, commonly known as "Mempool" (a term amalgamated from "memory" and "pool"). Transactions are chosen for block inclusion based on miner consensus. Thus, a transaction with a higher fee (measured in satoshis per byte, or sat/b, where one bitcoin equals 10^8 satoshis) relative to its storage size is more likely to be incorporated into a block. Conversely, a transaction without any fee could linger in the potential transaction pool indefinitely. For instance, in July 2022, tens of thousands of transactions remained stagnant in the transaction pool due to inadequate transaction fees. Hence, even if not mandatory, a higher transaction fee is often advised to expedite the inclusion of a transaction into the blockchain. As of June 12, 2022, the average cost per transaction in Bitcoin's history stood at 0.0042 BTC, and the mean transaction fee on that same day approximated $1.416 per transaction.

14.3.2.2 Public Key Cryptography

All transactions utilize public key cryptography. Each crypto/digital wallet (refer to Chapter 14.3.2.3 Crypto Wallet for further details) is secured with a secret private key belonging to the owner. This private key, a sequence of 32 bytes, is generated by the owner independently of the cryptocurrency protocol and can be created using the owner's wallet software. The private key establishes the ownership of the funds and authorizes the owner to spend the linked cryptocurrency. Consequently, if you misplace the private key, you also forfeit ownership of all related funds. Hence, safeguarding the private key against theft and accidental loss is of paramount importance.

> **Case Study**
>
> ***Bitcoin Scandals***
>
> Krause (2018) estimated that approximately 20% of all Bitcoins (equivalent to a market value of around $20 billion based on July 2018 prices) are unaccounted for. Leonard (2016) reported an instance from 2013 when a British IT consultant discarded an old computer hard drive that stored a digital wallet with 7500 Bitcoins mined back in 2009. Each Bitcoin was valued at over $1000 in 2013 and peaked at above $60,000 in 2022.
>
> As of January 5, 2023, the Mt. Gox debacle remains the most notorious Bitcoin scandal. Between 2011 and 2014, Bitcoins worth $450 million disappeared from the accounts of Mt. Gox, the leading Bitcoin Exchange in 2014. While Mt. Gox purportedly recovered these missing coins, relocating these coins from their current holders back to the original owners is impossible

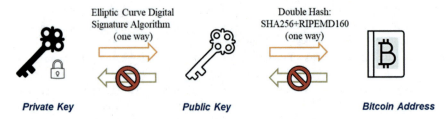

Fig. 14.5 Generation of public key and bitcoin address

> since the private addresses associated with them have been lost (Norman, 2017).

To keep the private key confidential while ensuring its functionality, a corresponding public key is generated based on the private key, following the relevant cryptographic algorithm (Wikipedia, 2023g). A single private key can be paired with multiple public keys, depending on the owner's preferences.

Public keys are shared with everyone in the network. Thus, in a Bitcoin transaction, the public key acts as the recipient's address and is utilized to create a Bitcoin address (i.e., public key hash) using a one-way cryptographic hash function, specifically the double hash functions SHA-256 and RIPEMD-160 (Antonopoulos, 2017). However, public keys can also be associated with other entities like documents, contracts, and various digital assets (Fig. 14.5).

While a private key can be used to generate a public key, the reverse is not possible. A public key cannot be used to deduce or generate the associated private key. This unidirectional process ensures the confidentiality of the private key even when the public key is public. Algorithms like the Elliptic Curve Digital Signature Algorithm, employed in the Bitcoin system, guarantee that the creation of the public key is a one-way procedure.

> *While a private key can be used to generate a public key, the reverse is not true; a public key cannot be used to deduce or generate its associated private key.*

There are several applications of public key cryptography:

1. ***Public Key Encryption (Asymmetric)***: Public key encryption uses the recipient's public key to encrypt transactions, which can then be decrypted using the recipient's private key (Wikipedia, 2023g).

    In the example illustrated by Figure 14.6, Jonas uses Lucas's public key to encrypt a confidential message intended for Lucas. Upon receiving the

14.3 The Bitcoin Blockchain

Fig. 14.6 Public key encryption

Fig. 14.7 Digital signature

encrypted message, Lucas uses his private key to decrypt it back into its original form. The confidentiality of the message is maintained because no other private key can decrypt the message, thanks to the secrecy of the private key and the uniqueness of the hashing mechanism.

2. **Digital Signature (Asymmetric)**: The digital signature is used to verify that a message originates from a specific sender (Wikipedia, 2023g).

   In the example portrayed in Fig. 14.7, Jonas encrypts the message using his own private key (i.e., Sign(Message, PrivateKey) = Signature). This allows anyone with Jonas's public key to decrypt the message (i.e., Verify(Message, Signature, PublicKey) = True/False). Thus, this encryption acts as a digital signature, demonstrating that the private key corresponds to the public key without revealing the actual private key information.

   For further confirmation of a public key's authenticity, one can consult a trusted third party (e.g., a public key infrastructure) or seek individual endorsements that verify a link between the sender and their public key. This ensures that both the public and private keys are authentically paired.

   In the Bitcoin system, participating miners autonomously validate the authenticity of transactions, ensuring the legitimacy of public and private key pairs.

3. **Combined Key Encryption (Asymmetric)**: This encryption method, also known as the Diffie-Hellman key exchange, combines public and private keys.[2]

   Illustrated in Figure 14.8, when Jonas wants to send a message and Bitcoin to Lucas, he employs Lucas's public key combined with his own private

---

[2] This encryption is named after Whitfield Diffie and Martin Hellman. Although the concept was first conceived by Ralph Merkle in 2002, Martin Hellman suggested renaming the encryption as the Diffie–Hellman–Merkle key exchange. For additional details, please refer to Wikipedia (2022b).

Fig. 14.8 Combined key encryption

key to encrypt the transaction. After Lucas receives the transaction, he uses his private key and Jonas's public key to finalize the transaction.

14.3.2.3 Crypto Wallet

Crypto wallets are essential for cryptocurrency transactions. Unlike traditional wallets that hold fiat currencies, a crypto wallet stores a user's private and public keys, which provide access to the user's cryptocurrencies. Most crypto wallets also offer an interface for users to manage their crypto balances and support the signing and encrypting of information through smart contracts (Wikipedia, 2023c).

Because the ownership of cryptocurrency belongs to the owner of the private key, possessing the crypto wallet is tantamount to owning the cryptocurrencies associated with that private key.

There are three types of crypto wallets:

- *Paper Wallets*: In this seemingly antiquated approach, the keys are written on paper and stored securely. Given that both public and private keys are lengthy (a series of 32 bytes each), using the keys can be inconvenient since all cryptocurrencies are documented in online blockchains. While paper wallets aren't vulnerable to online hackers, they can accidentally be destroyed or lost.
- *Online Wallets*: Online wallets have become increasingly popular due to their convenience and are accessible through applications and websites like Coinbase, SafePal, Ledger Nano S Plus, MetaMask, Trezor Model T, Mycelium, TrustWallet, Electrum, Blue Wallet, Exodus, and Crypto.com (Norman, 2017). Online crypto wallets function similarly to traditional digital wallets used for fiat currencies. The format of online wallets can vary, encompassing web-based, mobile, or desktop options. Although more convenient than paper wallets, online wallets are susceptible to cyberattacks.
- *Hardware Wallets*: With hardware wallets, the keys are stored in an external device, such as a USB drive or Bluetooth device, ensuring secure storage. The hardware wallet is connected to a computer when needed to manage cryptocurrencies. As it remains disconnected from the internet most of the time, a hardware wallet is less likely to be hacked. However, it's not immune to physical damage and is generally less convenient than an online wallet. There's also an associated cost for the external device.

14.3 The Bitcoin Blockchain   427

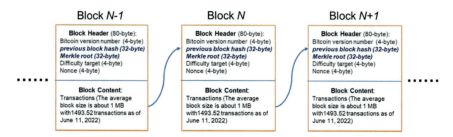

Fig. 14.9 Blocks in a blockchain

Hardware wallets strike a balance between paper and online wallets. Regardless of the type of wallet chosen, ensuring its safety is paramount to maintain ownership of the cryptocurrencies linked to it.

14.3.3 Blocks

Blocks serve as repositories for transactions and are the foundational units of the Bitcoin blockchain. While the primary purpose of the Bitcoin blockchain was to handle cryptocurrency transactions, blocks can encapsulate other relevant data.

Satoshi Nakamoto, upon initiating the Bitcoin blockchain, set a block size limit of one megabyte (1 MB). However, as time went on, there were proponents advocating for an increased block size to accommodate more data. This would facilitate quicker processing and verification of transactions on the Bitcoin network. In response to these considerations, the block size limit has been augmented to 4 megabytes (Bitcoin Magazine, 2020). As per data from cointelegraph.com on September 18, 2018, the average block size was 0.8 MB, encapsulating an average of 1609 transactions. Notably, on September 5, 2018, block #540,107, measuring 2.26 MB, was integrated into the Bitcoin blockchain (Thompson, 2018). Fast forward to June 11, 2022, the typical Bitcoin blocks expanded to 1.008 MB, with an average confirmation time of 14.67 minutes. On average, each block contained 1493.52 transactions.

Each block comprises a block header and the content of transactions. As depicted in Fig. 14.9, the block header is an 80-byte-long string. This string encompasses the Bitcoin version number (4-byte), the previous block hash (32-byte), the Merkle root (32-byte), the timestamp of the block (4-byte), the difficulty target set for the block's verification (4-byte), and the nonce, which miners utilize to successfully verify the block (4-byte).

Information pertaining to Block #500,000 is illustrated in Table 14.2, showcasing a block size of 1.049 MB.[3]

---

[3] The details of Bitcoin Block 500,000 are directly sourced from Blockchain.com (2017). The website provides the following description for Block 500,000: "This block was mined on December

Table 14.2 The block information of Block 500,000

Item	Content Details
Hash	00000000000000000024fb37364cbf81fd49cc2d5Ic09c75c35433c3al945d04
Confirmations	240,381
Timestamp	2017-12-18 10:35
Height	500,000
Miner	BTC.com
Number of Transactions	2701
Difficulty	1,873,105,475,221.61
Merkle Root	31951c69428a95a46b517ffb0de12fec1bd0b2392aec07b64573e03ded31621f
Version	$0 \times 20{,}000{,}000$
Bits	402,691,653
Weight	3,992,793 WU
Size	1,048,581 bytes
Nonce	1,560,058,197
Transaction Volume	14017.37618054 BTC
Base Reward	12.50000000 BTC
Fee Reward	3.39351625 BTC
Block Transactions	(2.70/*transaction details are skipped here*)

Source Blockchain.com (2017)

The majority of the header details for Block #500,000 can be observed in Table 14.2. It's important to note, however, that the specific hash value for Block #500,000 will be incorporated in the header of Block #500,001. In a similar manner, the block header of Block #500,000 contains the hash value of Block #499,999.

Some brief details regarding the first of the 2701 transactions in Block #500,000 are depicted in Table 14.3. The hashed value of this transaction begins with "21..." as indicated in the table. Given that the Bitcoin blockchain is a distributed ledger of Bitcoin transactions, Table 14.3 shows that 15.89351625 BTC were sent in this transaction from Block Reward to BTC.com 3, whose bitcoin address starts

---

18, 2017 at 10:35 AM PST by BTC.com. It currently has 240,382 confirmations on the Bitcoin blockchain. The miner(s) of this block earned a total [base] reward of 12.50000000 BTC ($355,998.50). The reward consisted of a base reward of 12.50000000 BTC ($355,998.50) with an additional 3.39351625 BTC ($96,646.94) reward paid as fees of the 2701 transactions which were included in the block. The Block rewards, also known as the Coinbase reward, were sent to this address. A total of 14,017.37618054 BTC ($399,213,191.54) were sent in the block with the average transaction being 5.18969870 BTC ($147,802.00)."

14.3 The Bitcoin Blockchain

Table 14.3 The first transaction information of Block 500,000

Item	Content Details
Hash ID	2157b554dcfda405233906e461ee593875ae4b1b97615872db6a25130ecc1dd6
Output Value (Amount)	15.89351625 BTC
Fee	0.00000000 BTC (0.000 sat/B - 0.000 sat/WU - 241 bytes) (0.000 sat/vByte - 214 virtual bytes)
Time	2017-12-18 10:35
From	Block Reward
To	2 outputs (BTC.com 3 15.89351625 BTC and Unknown 0.00000000 BTC)
BTC.com 3 Address	34qkc2iac6RsyxZVfyE2S5U5WcRsbg2dpK
COINBASE	Newly generated coins

Source Blockchain.com (2017)

with "34…," and another unidentified address. This transaction was timestamped at 10:35 on December 18, 2017. The format for the details of the remaining 2700 transactions is similar.

The *hash* in the block header is a cryptographic hash of the previous block. This ensures all blocks are interconnected, forming a chain based on their information. The timestamp records the moment the block was accepted into the blockchain. The Merkle root represents the hash for all transactions. The block header, which includes both the timestamp and the Merkle root, will be hashed and incorporated into the next block's header. Consequently, any alteration to data within a block necessitates changes to all subsequent blocks. This would likely invalidate the corresponding proof of work and demand the remaining of the affected blocks. As a result, once data is recorded in blockchains, it becomes nearly unmodifiable (i.e., immutable).

Data in blockchains is almost impossible to modify once recorded (i.e., immutable).

14.3.4 Hash

The *Merkle tree* structure is used to ensure that data stored in a block, as a whole, remains unaltered or undamaged. The structure of a conceptual Merkle root is illustrated in Fig. 14.10.

The transaction information, along with the timestamp of each terminal leaf of the Merkle tree, is hashed. Each pair of hashes is then further hashed into an upper-layer hash (i.e., branch) until only one final hash remains (i.e., the Merkle root).

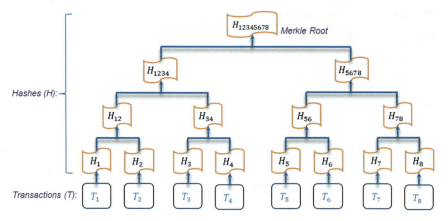

Fig. 14.10 Merkle root structure

Given that the upper-layer hashes depend on the lower-layer ones, the Merkle root encapsulates the hashes of all transactions.

The hash of each transaction or any message follows a specific cryptographic hash function. For instance, using the SHA-256 (Secure Hash Algorithm) for the message "supply chain finance" results in:

$$SHA256(\text{"supply chain finance"}) = aa2d34cc4229c12474730cf970d$$
$$10c27fe7420809d467dd4d86ae6eb2c675660$$

It's evident that the hash value contains not just numbers but also letters (A, B, C, D, E, and F). This format is called "Hexadecimal." Hexadecimal is utilized for its higher information density compared to binary (e.g., two digits can represent any number between 0 and 255). Additionally, it aligns with the binary system used by computers (a hexadecimal digit corresponds to 2^4, a multiple of 2, or 4 bits—half a byte).

For a hash to be reliable, unique, usable, and secure, a suitable hash function should have these characteristics:

- **Deterministic**: The same message will always result in an identical hash value.
- **Unique (i.e., collision resistance)**: Different messages will never produce the same hash value.
- **Computationally Efficient**: The hash value can be quickly computed using the algorithm.
- **Preimage Resistant**: Inferring the original message solely from its hash value should be impossible. This means the cryptographic function must be one-way (i.e., one-way function).
- **Standardized**: In the Bitcoin blockchain, irrespective of the message's content, its hash value is a consistent 64-digit hexadecimal number.

14.3 The Bitcoin Blockchain

Following the above requirements, a slightly different message typically results in a dramatically different hash value. This behavior is referred to as being pseudo-random; meaning that the hash value is always unpredictable, even if there's only a minor change in the message. For instance, the message "Supply chain finance" produces a hash value that looks drastically different from that of "supply chain finance," even though the only difference is the capitalization of the first letter "s."

SHA256("Supply chain finance") = d12964b0bd8558eeeec70c97e219b03a0dc9
dbdde936580c74f96b08c16c570e

The *SHA-256 algorithm* belongs to the SHA-2 family of algorithms and uses the Merkle–Damgård construction, derived from a one-way compression function, and the Davies–Meyer structure. The number 256 specifies the hash's length in bits (Wikipedia, 2022e).

After determining the hash value for each transaction, these hash values are used as data for further hierarchical hashing, as observed in the formation of the Merkle root (refer to Fig. 14.10). For instance, in Block #500,000, the hash value of the Merkle root is:

31951c69428a95a46b517ffb0de12fec1bd0b2392aec07b64573e03ded31621f.

The unique hash for this block is:

00000000000000000024fb37364cbf81fd49cc2d51c09c75c35433c3a1945d04,

and this value will be included in the next block's header. Owing to the interdependency of the hashes in the Merkle tree, any alteration or damage to any transaction data will change the Merkle root's hash value. Consequently, this block's hash value will be different. This means the entire block would disconnect from the chain and would necessitate the remaining of this and all subsequent blocks.

14.3.5 Why Mining?

"Mining" in the Bitcoin blockchain refers to the computational effort required to process and verify blocks for addition to the blockchain. Given that the Bitcoin blockchain is a decentralized database that stores digital information, this information can be copied, altered, and forged. Crucially, without adequate verification and preventive measures, cryptocurrencies circulating within the network can be "double-spent." Miners work to validate Bitcoin transactions, ensuring the integrity of the information stored in the blockchain.

The *double-spending problem* arises when a digital coin is used more than once without a preventative measure. Unlike a physical coin, which is spent once and then changes hands, a digital coin can be duplicated. To illustrate, a physical $10 bill can be used to buy a T-shirt, and once it's handed to the seller, it cannot be used again by the same buyer. Conversely, in the digital realm—akin to duplicating electronic documents—a digital coin could be dispatched to multiple sellers for distinct transactions, while still remaining in the original wallet, if no preventive measures are in place.

Mining serves as the mechanism that ensures the immutability of the recorded information in the blockchain and prevents double-spending. The system is designed such that becoming a miner is more lucrative than attempting to hack the blockchain. Miners are compensated for their work, while hacking the blockchain is highly challenging, if not impossible.

However, mining is labor-intensive and expensive. Costs arise from acquiring mining hardware, like graphics processing units (GPUs) or application-specific integrated circuits (ASICs),[4] and from the significant electricity consumption these devices entail.[5] Yet, the rewards from mining are sporadic and directly proportional to a miner's total computational power. To encourage miners to continually validate transactions, they are awarded cryptocurrency (e.g., Bitcoins) for their services. Early adopters of mining, driven by an entrepreneurial spirit, may have viewed cryptocurrency mining as a lucrative opportunity reminiscent of the gold rush era.

Moreover, mining is pivotal as it remains the primary method for introducing new Bitcoins into circulation. Satoshi Nakamoto's design limits the total supply of Bitcoins to 21 million, reserved as rewards for mining. In essence, miners receive Bitcoins as a reward for successfully adding blocks to the blockchain.

14.3.6 The Consensus Mechanism: Proof of Work

The genesis block (the very first block) was created by the Bitcoin founder, Satoshi Nakamoto. Every subsequent block must be verified before being added to the blockchain.

As depicted in Fig. 14.11, for a transaction to be "completed," the transaction's owner must offer a sufficiently large transaction fee (i.e., sign the transaction with their private key and specify the source of unspent Bitcoin to cover the fee). This ensures that at least one miner is incentivized to pick the transaction from the pool and add it to a block. Ideally, a transaction chosen from the Mempool to be included in a block should be verified at least six times to ensure a 99.99% probability of its validity (Hartmann, 2021). Subsequently, the related block must be verified by miners in the network and added to the blockchain.

To be added to the blockchain, a block must demonstrate PoW. In this process, miners must solve a cryptographic puzzle by finding a nonce (a number used only

---

[4] The cost of an application-specific integrated circuit (ASIC) ranged from $500 to $25,000 in July 2022. Miners acquire these machines exclusively for cryptocurrency mining.

[5] Given that the target for mining a block is 10 minutes, the difficulty of mining has rapidly increased as more miners have joined the network, each equipped with increasingly powerful mining devices. Since these devices consume a significant amount of electricity, the electricity consumption of the Bitcoin network has become a major environmental concern.

14.3 The Bitcoin Blockchain

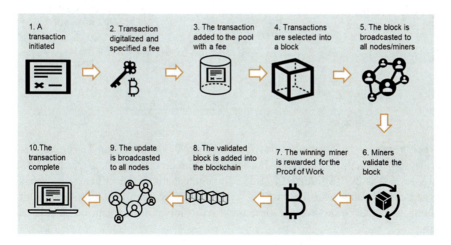

Fig. 14.11 Process of adding a block into the Bitcoin blockchain

once, representing a random string of numbers that miners must identify). This nonce, when combined with the hash of the block's contents, generates a new hash that is less than or equal to the target hash for that specific block. The size of a nonce is 32 bits, in contrast to the 256 bits of a block hash (e.g., the hash in Table 14.2) or a target hash.

The target hash in the Bitcoin blockchain is a verifiably random number produced using the SHA-256 hash algorithm. This design ensures that a predictable amount of mining power is required to find the hash (Hayes, 2021). While there is no minimum value for the target (it can even be zero), all targets must not exceed a specified upper limit:

00000000ffff0000000000000000000000000000000000000000000000000000.

Therefore, as dictated by the Bitcoin Protocol, all target hashes must begin with a sequence of leading zeros. The Bitcoin system is designed so that the average mining time for a new block is approximately 10 minutes. As mining power evolves (for instance, there are more advanced mining machines now than in previous years), the system adjusts the mining difficulty by altering the target hashes. Typically, the greater the number of leading zeros, the higher the mining difficulty.

The mining difficulty is recalibrated every 2016 blocks by comparing the time it took to mine the last 2016 blocks with the benchmark time of 20,160 minutes (i.e., $2016 \times 10 = 20{,}160$ minutes). To maintain an average block mining time of 10 minutes, the new difficulty level roughly equates to the previous difficulty level multiplied by the ratio of the standard 20,160 minutes to the actual time it took to mine the last 2016 blocks. However, to avert sudden shifts in mining difficulties, any adjustments to the difficulty cannot exceed or fall below four times the present difficulty level (that is, the range lies between −75% and +300%) (Sergeenkov, 2022).

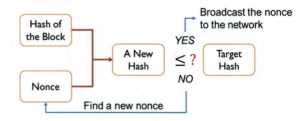

Fig. 14.12 Procedure of finding the right nonce

For instance, the difficulty level for Block #500,000 mined on December 18, 2017, was 1,873,105,475,221.61. For the block mined on July 18, 2022, the difficulty level was 29,152,798,808,271.88. This indicates that the difficulty level has surged considerably over the past five years, primarily due to the proliferation of mining machinery. The average time required to mine a block can be calculated using:

$$\text{Time} = \text{Difficulty} \times 2^{32}/\text{Hashrate}$$

Here, the *Hashrate* represents the number of hashes a miner can compute per second (Bitcoin Wiki, 2022).

Identifying the correct nonce, as depicted in Fig. 14.12, is computationally challenging. Given the intricacy of the hashing process and the uniqueness of each block hash, discovering a nonce that, when used, produces a hash value lower than or equal to the target hash is largely a matter of guesswork, necessitating significant computational resources.

The first miner who successfully finds a nonce that, when combined with the content hash, produces a new hash less than or equal to the target hash is rewarded for completing that block. As of July 2022, this reward stands at 6.25 Bitcoins plus all transaction fees included in the block.

The number of coins awarded for adding a block is halved every 210,000 blocks, approximately every four years. The reward was initially set at 50 coins when Bitcoin was first introduced in 2009. This halved to 25 coins in 2012 and then to 12.5 coins in 2016. The rate of 6.25 coins began on May 11, 2020. Given that each Bitcoin was valued at over $20,000 in 2022 (reaching highs of more than $73,000 in March 2024), this is a substantial incentive. It is projected that the reward will decrease to 3.125 coins by 2024 and will reach zero by 2140 when the last Bitcoin is mined. After this point, miners will only earn transaction fees from the blocks they add to the chain.

In addition to these rewards, miners also gain "voting" power in line with their hash power when it comes to Bitcoin network protocol proposals, such as the Bitcoin Improvement Protocol (BIP). This includes decisions related to forking.

The total number of potential solutions required for verifying each block is in the trillions, and this difficulty can only increase as more miners join the network. Therefore, miners need substantial computing power to earn the mining reward. For instance, high hash rates can now achieve gigahashes per second (GH/s) and even terahashes per second (TH/s).

In the early days of Bitcoin, it was feasible for an individual with a personal computer to mine Bitcoins. However, today, it is nearly impossible for a solitary PC to solve the hash puzzle. Modern professional miners often join mining pools and deploy thousands of specialized computers, accompanied by cooling systems, to guess the target hash. They aim to generate as many nonces as possible in the shortest time to succeed in this competitive environment.[6]

14.3.7 Blockchain Forks

When multiple blocks are added to a blockchain simultaneously, forks can occur, resulting in the creation of multiple chain branches. Forks can be classified based on the intention behind their creation: accidental fork, hard fork, and soft fork. Accidental forks arise without any change to the blockchain software, whereas hard forks and soft forks are the result of deliberate changes to the software and protocol.

14.3.7.1 Accidental Fork

With an estimated one million miners as of 2022, it's not uncommon for different miners to find solutions to the hash-guessing game for different blocks simultaneously. However, since only one solution can win, a simple majority rule (>50%) is used to decide the winner (Norman, 2017). In this context, the winning criterion is determined by who has completed the most work (i.e., verified the most transactions within a block). The block verified by the winner gets added to the blockchain, while the losing block is termed an "orphaned block" or a "stale block." In the Bitcoin system, miners receive no rewards for generating orphaned blocks.[7]

Even with this tie-breaking rule to select the winning block, forks—representing two or more potential block branches—can sometimes develop concurrently. This happens when the distributed system struggles to achieve consensus swiftly due to limited verification capabilities. When such a situation arises, the shorter fork gets abandoned, and the longer one becomes part of the blockchain.[8] As a result, accidental forks are typically short-lived.

---

[6] A mining pool is a collective of cryptocurrency miners who combine their computing power to share and proportionally distribute the rewards they earn. This arrangement allows miners to achieve a more consistent income stream.

[7] In other blockchains, such as Ethereum, there might be rewards for mining orphaned blocks. This is due to their Proof-of-Stake consensus mechanism which can offer smaller rewards for such blocks.

[8] Bitcoin and many other blockchains adhere to the longest-chain criterion. Alternatively, some blockchains use the heaviest-chain criterion, where the fork backed by the most computational effort prevails. This computational effort can be quantified by the cumulative difficulty level of the blocks.

14.3.7.2 Hard Fork

Both hard forks and soft forks arise because blockchains occasionally need to update their software to address security risks, enhance functionality, or manage disagreements among nodes. Installing a new software version for the blockchain is analogous to setting up an operating system update for a computer. These software changes lead to a fork in the blockchain because nodes equipped with the updated software verify blocks differently from nodes that retain the older software. As a result, new blocks may be deemed invalid by the old protocols, and conversely, old blocks may become invalid under the new protocols.

To reconcile the fork, all nodes must agree to a consistent set of rules, either the new or the old. For instance, on March 11, 2013, a temporary minor block fork emerged in the Bitcoin blockchain due to the transition to a newer software version (Wikipedia, 2023a). This fork was eventually resolved by reverting to the old rules.

A hard fork transpires when there's a fundamental alteration to the network's protocol and software, making the new protocols non-backward compatible with prior blocks. If certain nodes cling to the older protocols while others adopt the new ones, a permanent split in the blockchain—known as a hard fork—ensues.

Such a hard fork can also lead to cryptocurrency splits, serving as a mechanism to birth new cryptocurrencies. For instance, in 2017, Bitcoin Cash, a distinct cryptocurrency, emerged from a hard fork of Bitcoin because of differing transaction processing protocols (Reiff, 2023).

A hard fork can also introduce new features or address blockchain security issues. For example, to recover funds lost in a hack involving Ethereum's Decentralized Autonomous Organization (DAO), Ethereum executed a hard fork, leading to two separate chains: Ethereum (new) and Ethereum Classic (old). This allowed the original DAO owners to reclaim their funds (OpenSea, 2023).

14.3.7.3 Soft Fork

In the event of a soft fork, which results from minor software version modifications in the blockchain, the changes can be implemented in a backward-compatible manner with pre-fork blocks. If certain nodes opt not to adopt the new protocols, there's no need for them to update their software because all new blocks, even under the new rules, still comply with the old rules (backward compatibility) (OpenSea, 2023). However, for the blockchain's safety, the more nodes that adopt the new protocols, the better. Ideally, every node would embrace the new protocols, ensuring the continuation of a singular blockchain operating under the new set of rules.

14.3.7.4 Hard Fork vs. Soft Fork

Both hard forks and soft forks arise when a new software version is introduced to the blockchain and coexists alongside the older version. The primary distinction between a hard fork and a soft fork is that, with a hard fork, the original blockchain bifurcates into two parallel chains, both of which operate concurrently (OpenSea, 2023). In contrast, during a soft fork, a singular blockchain remains, even though new blocks and old blocks function on different software versions. While initiating a hard fork might require more computational effort, the potential gains in security and privacy often make it a more favored option compared to a soft fork.

14.3.8 Pros and Cons of Bitcoin Blockchain

As the inaugural public blockchain, Bitcoin captured global attention when its value soared to more than $67,600 in 2021. As of June 12, 2022, the total size of the Bitcoin blockchain stood at 410.89GB, having processed 740.52M transactions. The market capitalization of Bitcoin was $543.49B, with daily transaction fees totaling 11.28 BTC, or approximately $325,582.5.

Debates regarding the sustainability of Bitcoin's value have permeated major media outlets. To delve into this matter, we will examine the advantages that the Bitcoin blockchain offers. These strengths also explain why blockchain technology has expanded far beyond just Bitcoin, branching out into myriad other blockchains.

14.3.8.1 Benefits of Bitcoin Blockchain

- *Greater Security*: The consensus of thousands of participants combined with the PoW feature ensures that all data stored in the blockchain is, in principle, immutable. No individual or entity can alter or delete the data. This immutable nature helps authorities maintain evidence of any illicit activities or transactional malfeasance. The blockchain thus acts as a deterrent against data tampering by organizations.
- *Enhanced Trust*: The integration of public key cryptography allows users to manage access to their confidential data and discern who sends them messages. This cryptographic feature is pivotal in fostering trust among network participants.
- *Increased Transparency*: The robust security features—data immutability and inability to tamper—combined with the capacity to share information with trusted entities, enhance the credibility of businesses, especially those with limited credit history like SMEs.
- *Reduced Costs*: The know-your-customer (KYC) process, essential in business transactions, can be tedious and resource-intensive. Storing KYC data on the blockchain and sharing it with other entities can significantly diminish the associated transaction costs.
- *Higher Efficiency*: Since all data on the blockchain is identically distributed among participants, there's no need for time-consuming record reconciliations. Additionally, the advent of smart contracts—programs that execute automatically when predetermined conditions are met—has further expedited transaction processes.

Despite all the aforementioned benefits, every coin has two sides, and this holds true for the Bitcoin blockchain as well.

14.3.8.2 Limitations of Bitcoin Blockchain

- *Slow Transaction*: Due to the Bitcoin protocol, a block can be verified in about 10 minutes. Given that the average Bitcoin block size is around 1MB, containing roughly 2000 transactions on average, the transaction speed is unsatisfactory for real-world business transactions which might demand millions of transactions per second. This limitation could deter the Bitcoin blockchain from being adopted for most large-scale business transactions, prompting businesses to explore alternative blockchains.
- *Negative Environmental Impact*: Considering the enormous amount of electrical power required to verify every single Bitcoin, the environmental impact of Bitcoin mining has been a subject of debate since the 2010s. According to a 2022 estimate by Forbes, Bitcoin mining's annualized electricity consumption is 127 terawatt-hours (TWh), surpassing the entire annual electricity usage of Norway. The energy consumption per transaction is about 11 times that of the Ethereum Blockchain as of July 2022 (Schmidt & Powell, 2022). Krause and Tolaymat (2018) estimated that mining operations for Bitcoin, Ethereum, Litecoin, and Monero emitted between three to 15 million metric tons of carbon dioxide from January 1, 2016, to June 30, 2018.
- *Garbage in, Garbage out*: The lauded feature of immutability can only assure the authenticity of the content, not its quality. For instance, if an accounting error occurred in a prior transaction, that mistake cannot be retroactively corrected. The only solution is to record the error and rectify it in a subsequent transaction. This means the distributed ledger might be larger than ideally necessary. This feature carries further implications: Some firms may be reluctant to adopt blockchains, possibly due to a desire to manipulate their financial data. Conversely, blockchains can deter fraudulent accounting by permanently recording any discrepancies.
- *Legality of Bitcoin*: The high value attributed to Bitcoin arises from its designed scarcity (a total of 21 million coins will ever be mined). However, because Bitcoin ownership can remain anonymous, the cryptocurrency is often associated with illicit activities. Additionally, as Bitcoins are produced outside the realm of government-regulated fiat currencies, they potentially challenge financial markets and governmental authority. As a consequence, several countries—including Algeria, Bangladesh, Bolivia, China, Dominican Republic, Ecuador, Egypt, Morocco, Nepal, North Macedonia, Pakistan, Qatar, and Vietnam—have outlawed Bitcoin transactions and mining (Wikipedia, 2023b). Given these restrictions and the potential limitations on Bitcoin's utility, its future remains uncertain.

14.4 Other Public Blockchains and Cryptocurrencies

Public blockchains are open to the public, permissionless, and completely decentralized. They have been primary avenues for the cryptocurrency economy, represented by entities like Bitcoin, Ethereum, and Litecoin (Wikipedia, 2022a). In these public blockchains, much like in the Bitcoin blockchain, miners earn cryptocurrencies.

In recent years, cryptocurrencies have garnered significant attention from the media and consumers. When supply chain transactions are executed using smart contracts on blockchains, digital currencies are often favored for processing related payments. Although blockchains may seem more pivotal than cryptocurrencies, the value and role of cryptocurrencies—serving as payment mediums, assets, utilities, and more—continue to amplify.

There's been industry debate about the correct terminology: "crypto coin" or "crypto token." The terms are often used interchangeably. While some label Bitcoins and other cryptocurrencies (altcoins) as "digital tokens," others view tokens and coins synonymously. As the terminology evolves, this chapter aims to capture the "mainstream" definitions of these terms and their characteristics, albeit from my subjective viewpoint.

Cryptocurrency, colloquially known as "crypto," is a digital asset founded on blockchain technology. It branches into two primary categories: crypto coin and crypto token. Crypto coins, sometimes called native cryptocurrencies, primarily operate on their independent blockchains, like the Bitcoin and Ethereum blockchains. These coins are minted via PoW or PoS, as previously highlighted, and function as payment mechanisms for blockchain governance, transaction fees, and other purposes, similar to traditional fiat currencies.

In contrast, *crypto tokens*—often termed digital tokens—are crafted by platforms and applications for decentralized projects atop pre-existing blockchains. The creation of tokens doesn't necessitate mining. Tokens can represent assets, functionalities (such as security), governance, and utility. While each blockchain typically houses one type of crypto coin, a single blockchain can birth various crypto tokens. Presently, Ethereum stands as perhaps the most favored blockchain for crafting tokens for decentralized initiatives (Kriptomat, 2023). We will further discuss digital tokens in Chapter 15.3.

A *crypto coin* is a digital currency utilized in computer networks, especially blockchains, for payment. Bitcoin, the inaugural decentralized cryptocurrency, is arguably the most renowned. It was originally conceived as an alternative to conventional fiat currencies but faced challenges due to volatility, legal issues, and other constraints. While cryptocurrencies have found favor in countries like the U.S., they are prohibited in nations such as Bangladesh, China, Egypt, Pakistan, and Vietnam (Wikipedia, 2023b).

Despite the myriad concerns associated with cryptocurrencies, as previously examined with Bitcoin, the Bitcoin blockchain was initially devised to log distributed ledgers using Bitcoins. Consequently, crypto coins emerged as the intuitive payment method on blockchains and have since been broadly employed in smart contracts. Given that crypto coins are modeled after conventional fiat currencies, they embody several values, including:

- Payment for goods and services
- Equity
- Exchange for other currencies, like fiat currencies
- Additional functions, like voting rights

Subsequently, we will delve into a concise discussion about popular crypto coins beyond Bitcoin.

14.4.1 Altcoins

Cryptocurrencies other than Bitcoin are termed *altcoin*. The prominence of a specific altcoin often aligns with the popularity of its associated blockchain. For instance, Ethereum's cryptocurrency has emerged as the foremost altcoin, primarily because Ethereum's blockchain is extensively adopted across various industries. Another notable altcoin is Litecoin, which can process a block in just 2.5 minutes—much faster than Bitcoin's 10 minutes (Wikipedia, 2022b).

14.4.2 Ether (ETH) and Ethereum

Ether (ETH) is the native cryptocurrency of the Ethereum platform. As detailed by Ethereum.org, Ethereum is a community-driven platform that utilizes the cryptocurrency ether (ETH) to facilitate smart contracts, global payments, and a myriad of decentralized applications (Ethereum, 2022c). Ethereum's decentralized finance (DeFi) system delivers a financial infrastructure that allows for the global transmission, receipt, lending, investment, and streaming of funds. As of August 4, 2022, Ethereum supports 9672 nodes, the value of 1 ether stands at $1596, and the total value locked in DeFi reaches $57.14B (Coindesk, 2022; Ethereum, 2022b).

Ethereum can be employed to create non-fungible tokens (NFTs) which can tokenize various items, ranging from artwork and legal documents to tangible assets. This enables owners to accrue royalties or even use the token as security to secure a loan. Both Ethereum and its associated applications are open-source and have been developed in a variety of programming languages. For instance, Go Ethereum represents one rendition of the Ethereum protocol penned in Go. There are also versions available in JavaScript, C++, and Python (Wikipedia, 2022c).

14.4.2.1 The Proof of Stake Consensus Mechanism
The consensus mechanism for verifying transactions added to the Ethereum blockchain network is termed "staking." This began on December 1, 2020, with Beacon Chain, a fork of Ethereum, which is also known as Proof of Stake (PoS). Unlike Bitcoin's system, where anyone can mine, in Ethereum, one must deposit

14.4 Other Public Blockchains and Cryptocurrencies

32 ETH to become a validator. This deposit activates the validator software, empowering the validator to store data, process transactions, and add new blocks to the blockchain (Ethereum, 2022a). Validators receive rewards for consolidating transactions into new blocks and for verifying the work of other validators.

For enhanced network security, it's imperative to have more ETH staked. Echoing the dynamics of the Bitcoin blockchain, a validator might endanger the network if they control the majority of the ETH. It's considered best practice for a validator to operate independently on a single computer, known as solo home staking. This approach earns full participation rewards while supporting the system's decentralization. Alternatively, validators can entrust their staking tasks to service providers by sharing their signing keys and depositing the required 32 ETH—a process termed "staking as a service" (Ethereum, 2022a). For safety, the validator relying on this service should retain the keys for the deposited ETH. Another option includes joining pooled staking via third-party solutions or participating in centralized exchanges, which may introduce vulnerabilities since these centralized entities can become network threats or attack targets.

The time designated for validating a block is 12 seconds, referred to as a "slot." During this interval, a validator (or staker) is randomly selected to propose a block (Ethereum, 2023a). This chosen proposer is tasked with collating transactions into a new block, establishing a fresh "state" for that block, and then relaying this information to fellow validators. Once informed of the new block, other validators replicate the transactions, reach consensus, and incorporate the new block into their database.

Each block is targeted to contain 15 million gas, with a maximum limit of 30 million gas. Here, "gas" denotes the fee mandated for executing a transaction on Ethereum (Ethereum, 2023a). Intuitively, a more extensive block necessitates more computational power for execution. Fees are customarily quantified in "gwei," equivalent to 10^{-9} ETH. The precise cost of gas is influenced by factors like supply, demand, and network capability.

Let's estimate the price per unit of gas. Based on historical data, validators issue approximately 1,700 ETH per day. Assuming transactions are processed at the target speed, with 15 million gas being handled every 12 seconds, and these 1,700 ETH are evenly distributed across these gas units, the average price per gas unit can be calculated as follows:

$$\text{Price of a Gas} \cong 1700 \times \frac{12 \text{ seconds}}{24 \text{ hours} \times 60 \frac{\text{minutes}}{\text{hour}} \times 60 \frac{\text{seconds}}{\text{minute}}} / (15 \times 10^6) \text{ ETH}$$
$$= 1.574 \times 10^{-8} \text{ ETH} = 15.74 \text{ gwei}$$

Theoretically, Ethereum's target speed could accommodate 15,000,000/12 = 1.25 million transactions per second (TPS). However, as of January 29, 2023, the observed average transaction speed hovers around 28 TPS, as recorded by

Table 14.4 Bitcoin vs. Ethereum

	Bitcoin Blockchain	**Ethereum Blockchain**
Purpose	Decentralized platform for digital currency	Decentralized platform for decentralized applications (dApps) and smart contracts
Crypto Coin	Bitcoin	ETH
Consensus Mechanism	Proof of Work (PoW) using SHA-256 consensus algorithm	Initially PoW when launched in 2015, but transitioned to proof of stake (PoS) LMDGhost consensus algorithm after the Merge
Block Speed	Approximately every 10 minutes	Approximately every 12 seconds (Ethereum, 2023a)
Transaction Speed	Around 7 TPS	Potentially up to 100,000 TPS
Scalability	Low	High
Programmability	Limited	Allows creation of complex decentralized applications
Security	Higher	Lower
Coin Limit	Capped at 21 million coins	Unlimited
Energy Consumption	Extremely high; estimated at 161 TWh/year, surpassing Sweden, in 2022 (Pongratz & James, 2023)	Reduced post-Merge (estimated below 1 TWH/year)

ETHTPS.info. Therefore, the actual price per gas unit will be much higher than the estimated value above. In real-world scenarios, Barchat (2022) suggests that with PoS and sharding,[9] Ethereum's TPS might range between 20,000 and 100,000 in the future. This prediction signifies a substantial enhancement from the former 10–20 TPS prior to the "Merge" of the Mainnet and Beacon Chain in September 2022.

14.4.2.2 Ethereum Blockchain vs. Bitcoin Blockchain

To date, Bitcoin and Ethereum are the two most valuable blockchains based on their market capitalizations. While they share some similarities, they differ in numerous areas such as their objectives, consensus mechanisms, transaction speeds, and scalability. Their main differences are summarized in Table 14.4.

While Bitcoin is often referred to as "digital gold" due to its monetary focus, Ethereum serves as a foundational layer for many consortium and

---

[9] Sharding allows Ethereum to divide its entire database into 64 segments, each mirroring the entire Ethereum chain. According to Ethereum, the introduction of sharding, set for implementation in 2023, will not only boost Ethereum's scalability and capacity but also simplify node operations and reduce transaction fees (Ethereum, 2023b).

hybrid blockchains. Ethereum also boasts an enterprise version called Enterprise Ethereum, suitable for private, consortium, and hybrid blockchain platforms.

14.4.3 HBAR and Hedera

Hedera is an open-source decentralized public network designed for building decentralized applications (dApps) and services (Hedera, 2023b).[10] Positioned as the next generation of the web, Hedera aspires to power web3 ecosystems. The network offers its proprietary cryptocurrency, *Hedera Hashgraph* (HBAR), which operates as a medium of exchange and a unit of payment within the platform, much like cryptocurrencies on other blockchains.

Though Hedera presents itself as an alternative to blockchains, both Hedera and traditional blockchains are decentralized ledger systems (Hedera, 2023b). The primary distinction between Hedera and other blockchains is in their data structure and consensus mechanism. Unlike traditional blockchains that store data in a sequential chain of blocks, Hedera employs the *directed acyclic graph* (DAG) for data storage and processing. A DAG is a graph data structure composed of vertices and edges where each edge has a specific direction, and there are no closed loops in the graph (Wikipedia, 2023d). Within distributed ledger technology, a DAG-based consensus algorithm facilitates consensus among network nodes. This ensures transactions are validated and incorporated into the ledger securely and efficiently.

This DAG-based consensus algorithm is often termed the *Hedera Hashgraph* consensus, a distinct consensus mechanism tailored to offer quick, secure, and equitable transactions for businesses and individuals alike (Wikipedia, 2023e). The Hedera Hashgraph consensus employs a distributed ledger technique known as the "gossip about gossip" protocol (Hedera, 2023a). Herein, nodes relay information about the events they've encountered, establishing a consensus on event sequences. This consensus mechanism operates on virtual voting; nodes possess weight corresponding to their computational prowess, with consensus achieved via a mathematical algorithm.

Thanks to the Hashgraph mechanism, Hedera boasts superior speed, security, and fairness in its consensus processes. Specifically, Hedera can handle over 100 k transactions per second (Outlook, 2023). Regarding transaction volume, data from ycharts.com indicates that on January 31, 2023, Hedera executed 52 million transactions within 24 hours, dwarfing Ethereum's 1 million and Bitcoin's 0.31 million.

---

[10] Hedera was once exclusively owned and patented by Swirlds. However, on January 19, 2022, the consensus algorithm patent right was acquired by the Hedera Governing Council, which includes Swirlds, Google, IBM, Boeing, LG, among other companies. It was subsequently made open source under the Apache License (Wikipedia, 2023e).

Table 14.5 Comparison of cryptocurrencies on January 31, 2023[11]

	Bitcoin	**Ethereum**	**Hedera**
Crypto Coin	Bitcoin	ETH	HBAR
Market Cap	$445 billion	$192 billion	$1.6 billion
Transactions/Day	0.31 million	1 million	52 million
Transaction Speed	7 TPS	30 TPS	600 TPS
Unit Transaction Fee	$0.84	$0.65	$0.001
Energy/Transaction	1.173 kWh	0.03 kWh	0.00017 kWh

Nonetheless, HBAR's market cap stood at $1.6 billion, in stark contrast to Bitcoin's $445 billion and Ethereum's $192 billion. A more detailed comparison is provided in Table 14.5.

14.4.4 Litecoin

Litecoin, launched in October 2011, is often referred to as the "silver to Bitcoin's gold." It's a "lite" and slightly modified version of Bitcoin (Wikipedia, 2022d). It offers lower transaction fees and faster transaction confirmation times than Bitcoin. Litecoin has a supply limit of 84 million coins (which is four times the upper limit of 21 million Bitcoins). Its target block verification time is set at 2.5 minutes, which is one-fourth of Bitcoin's 10 minutes. Due to the shorter verification time, Litecoin's mining difficulty adjusts four times faster than Bitcoin's. As of August 2022, Litecoin ranks among the top 5 cryptocurrencies in terms of market capitalization (Coindesk, 2022).

14.4.5 Stablecoins

Cryptocurrencies have exhibited considerable volatility since their inception. To bring stability to the value of cryptocurrencies, certain coins can be backed by tangible assets. These are commonly referred to as reserve-backed stablecoins. However, even those stablecoins not backed by governmental entities can display notable volatility.

There are four primary types of reserve-backed stablecoins:

1. *Fiat-backed Stablecoins*: This is the most common type. These stablecoins peg their value to fiat currencies (e.g., the U.S. dollar) at a fixed ratio.

---

[11] Numbers are based on real data obtained from each blockchain's homepage and ycharts.com on January 31, 2023. The efficiency of Ethereum is expected to improve significantly following the final-stage implementation of the Merge plan, which began on September 15, 2022.

Consequently, the third-party-regulated financial entity is required to hold a corresponding amount of currency to back the stablecoin (Wikipedia, 2022f). Examples of fiat-backed stablecoins include TrueUSD (TUSD), USD Tether, and USD Coin. A primary reason for purchasing a fiat-backed stablecoin is to facilitate trading on cryptocurrency exchanges. Users can purchase stablecoins with fiat currencies and then trade them for other cryptocurrencies (e.g., Bitcoin). Investors might also buy stablecoins to use them for secured loans, thus earning interest.

2. *Commodity-backed Stablecoins*: These stablecoins are backed by tangible commodities. The amount of the commodity, whether it's gold or another valuable substance, must match the supply of the stablecoin. Owners of such stablecoins can redeem their coins for the underlying commodity.

3. *Cryptocurrency-backed Stablecoins*: Here, reserves of other cryptocurrencies act as collateral to issue new stablecoins. Unlike the first two types which use off-chain reserves, these are impacted by the volatility of the backing cryptocurrencies and potential bugs in the smart contracts that peg the stablecoins to them (Wikipedia, 2022f). To mitigate this volatility, the value of the collateral must far exceed the supply of the stablecoins.

4. *Algorithm-backed Stablecoins*: These rely on algorithms to automatically adjust the stablecoin supply in response to market dynamics, aiming to maintain its value (Wikipedia, 2022f). Specifically, if the price of the stablecoin rises, the algorithm introduces more coins to the market. If the price falls, the algorithm reduces the circulation, attempting to boost its value. As algorithmic stablecoins don't have tangible backing assets, they are considered the riskiest among the four types.

Case Study

Terra's UST Stablecoin Crash

Launched in September 2020, TerraUSD (UST) is an algorithmic stablecoin developed on the Terra blockchain, pegged to the U.S. Dollar (Terra, 2023). Leveraging its scalability and yield-bearing capabilities, UST boasts interest rate precision, interchain functionality, and superior scalability for its users. Inherent to its design, users can exchange 1 UST for $1 worth of LUNA, a non-stablecoin also developed by the parent entity, Terraform Labs.

Before the UST crash, its supporting coin, LUNA, had been experiencing a decline, moving from a peak of $119.51 on April 4, 2022, to roughly $17 on May 10, 2022 (Wikipedia, 2022f). On May 7, 2022, a significant $2 billion worth of Terra's UST stablecoin was sold, resulting in the stablecoin deviating from its peg to the U.S. Dollar and the value of UST plummeting to $0.91 (McGleenon, 2022). This precipitated a selling spree by UST holders. In response, the LUNA Foundation Guard mobilized $3.5 billion in an attempt to stabilize the UST's depreciating value. Nevertheless, these interventions were unable to prevent UST's value from sinking to a dismal $0.044 in May 2022 (Lim, 2022). Concurrently, LUNA's valuation plummeted to less than one cent. The crash resulted in a staggering $45 billion loss for investors within a week (Wikipedia, 2023b).

Question

1. What are the primary weaknesses of an algorithmic stablecoin?
2. How can we implement measures to avert a similar occurrence in the future?

Despite their aim to maintain stability, stablecoins elicit concerns. Firstly, even though stablecoins are pegged to other financial assets, their values can experience precipitous drops due to factors such as fraudulent activities in reserves, shifts in sentiment, and other external influences.

Moreover, auditing the reserves of stablecoins has proven to be a formidable challenge. For commodity reserves, an independent third-party auditor is required to verify both the quantity and quality of the commodity. When it comes to cryptocurrency reserves, the volatility of prices presents a challenge. Additionally, there are concerns about reserves being clandestinely removed or repurposed for other objectives.

Furthermore, stablecoins are also subject to various governmental regulations. As a case in point, the stablecoin project named Basis ceased operations despite securing $100 million in venture capital, largely due to regulatory challenges in the U.S. (Wikipedia, 2022d). As the cryptocurrency landscape continues to evolve, there is an anticipation of more stringent regulations being introduced, especially in areas like taxation, investment, user identity, and cryptocurrency security.

In the realm of supply chain transactions, for businesses that are risk-averse to cryptocurrency volatility, government-backed stablecoins (e.g., USD Coin) might assume a more prominent role in smart contracts. This is primarily because these businesses would lean towards a "more stable" stablecoin option to mitigate potential risks.

14.4.6 Other Coins and Top Performers

As of November 2, 2022, coinmarketcap.com listed 9286 distinct cryptocurrencies available in the market. Using transaction data sourced from coinmarketcap.com, we present the top 30 cryptocurrencies as of November 2, 2022, in Table 14.6.

14.4 Other Public Blockchains and Cryptocurrencies

Table 14.6 Top 30 cryptocurrencies as of November 2, 2022

#	Name	Price ($)	Market Cap	Volume (24 h)	Circulating Supply
1	Bitcoin	20,118.29	$ 387,047,557,492	$ 54,695,117,953.00	19,196,506 BTC
	BTC			2,712,729 BTC	
2	Ethereum	1510.1	$ 184,791,410,488	$ 22,603,117,786.00	122,373,863 ETH
	ETH			14,968,395 ETH	
3	Tether	1	$ 69,423,752,656	$ 74,605,143,542.00	69,419,933,938 USDT
	USDT			74,601,039,817 USDT	
4	BNB	317.86	$ 50,874,503,297	$ 1,382,803,001.00	159,977,789 BNB
	BNB			4,348,303 BNB	
5	USD Coin	1	$ 42,550,332,926	$ 6,486,375,137.00	42,549,484,164 USDC
	USDC			6,486,245,751 USDC	
6	XRP	0.4525	$ 22,630,091,749	$ 1,378,415,932.00	50,085,407,159 XRP
	XRP			3,050,739,872 XRP	
7	Binance USD	1	$ 21,663,085,312	$ 8,021,729,626.00	21,658,670,445 BUSD
	BUSD			8,020,094,823 BUSD	
8	Dogecoin	0.1262	$ 16,753,367,669	$ 4,726,220,063.00	132,670,764,300 DOGE
	DOGE			37,427,175,262 DOGE	
9	Cardano	0.3843	$ 13,213,484,720	$ 711,849,447.00	34,330,908,890 ADA
	ADA			1,849,507,457 ADA	
10	Solana	30.35	$ 10,905,374,233	$ 1,091,001,294.00	359,331,338 SOL
	SOL			35,948,418 SOL	
11	Polygon	0.8412	$ 7,360,942,993	$ 515,222,160.00	8,734,317,475 MATIC
	MATIC			611,350,192 MATIC	
12	Polkadot	6.22	$ 7,050,007,054	$ 356,238,855.00	1,132,728,287 DOT
	DOT			57,237,082 DOT	
13	Shiba Inu	0.00001175	$ 6,475,020,634	$ 687,440,011.00	549,063,278,876,302 SHIB
	SHIB			58,292,951,888,408 SHIB	
14	Dai	0.9991	$ 6,113,979,916	$ 283,529,884.00	6,120,324,104 DAI
	DAI			283,824,089 DAI	
15	TRON	0.06157	$ 5,681,708,214	$ 387,998,680.00	92,250,041,058 TRX
	TRX			6,299,671,299 TRX	
16	Uniswap	7.01	$ 5,339,137,742	$ 240,069,201.00	762,209,327 UNI
	UNI			34,272,010 UNI	
17	Avalanche	17.71	$ 5,292,859,075	$ 355,002,375.00	298,789,385 AVAX
	AVAX			20,040,386 AVAX	
18	Wrapped Bitcoin	20,139.03	$ 4,947,173,242	$ 164,679,014.00	245,480 WBTC
	WBTC			8,171 WBTC	
19	UNUS SED LEO	4.65	$ 4,435,690,929	$ 2,831,502.00	953,954,130 LEO
	LEO			608,952 LEO	
20	Litecoin	59.3	$ 4,243,234,209	$ 1,584,492,326.00	71,523,881 LTC
	LTC			26,708,175 LTC	

(continued)

Table 14.6 (continued)

#	Name	Price ($)	Market Cap	Volume (24 h)	Circulating Supply
21	Cosmos	13.12	$ 3,757,066,696	$ 307,238,751.00	286,370,297 ATOM
	ATOM			23,418,283 ATOM	
22	Chainlink	7.42	$ 3,648,876,073	$ 566,439,018.00	491,599,970 LINK
	LINK			76,314,295 LINK	
23	FTX Token	24.97	$ 3,327,213,112	$ 73,240,242.00	133,025,776 FTT
	FTT			2,928,228 FTT	
24	Ethereum Classic	22.83	$ 3,139,815,064	$ 507,318,311.00	137,726,058 ETC
	ETC			22,253,206 ETC	
25	Stellar	0.1074	$ 2,747,251,319	$ 106,783,545.00	25,622,447,071 XLM
	XLM			995,924,799 XLM	
26	Cronos	0.1075	$ 2,725,626,393	$ 41,046,837.00	25,263,013,692 CRO
	CRO			380,450,827 CRO	
27	Monero	145.14	$ 2,648,298,709	$ 94,068,563.00	18,195,520 XMR
	XMR			646,312 XMR	
28	Algorand	0.3537	$ 2,489,571,979	$ 189,781,101.00	7,074,692,330 ALGO
	ALGO			539,306,720 ALGO	
29	NEAR Protocol	2.87	$ 2,352,683,694	$ 215,753,292.00	818,119,979 NEAR
	NEAR			75,025,844 NEAR	
30	Bitcoin Cash	112.87	$ 2,171,295,569	$ 636,746,293.00	19,218,044 BCH
	BCH			5,635,814 BCH	

Source coinmarketcap.com

14.5 Risks and Future of Cryptocurrencies

The past decade has witnessed the ups and downs of Bitcoin and other cryptocurrencies due to security issues in blockchains, government regulations, and various other related social events (e.g., celebrity endorsements of NFTs). While the volatility of cryptocurrencies might continue to be high in the coming years, the future of cryptocurrencies is not crystal clear.

14.5.1 CeFi vs. DeFi

Centralized finance (CeFi) refers to the traditional financial system that operates on a centralized basis, with banks, financial institutions, and other intermediaries acting as gatekeepers and providers of financial services. In a centralized financial system, transactions are typically mediated by a trusted third party, such as a bank, which holds and manages customers' funds and facilitates transactions between parties. CeFi systems are often subject to regulation and are typically governed by central authorities, such as governments or central banks. Although CeFi has been the dominant form of finance for many years, the rise of decentralized finance

14.5 Risks and Future of Cryptocurrencies

(DeFi) has posed a challenge to the traditional centralized model, presenting an alternative vision of a more open, transparent, and accessible financial system that operates on a decentralized, peer-to-peer basis.

Decentralized finance (DeFi) refers to a financial system that operates on a decentralized, peer-to-peer network, using blockchain technology to facilitate secure and transparent financial transactions without the need for intermediaries like banks or financial institutions. DeFi aspires to craft an open, accessible, and transparent financial system available to anyone worldwide, without relying on traditional financial infrastructure. DeFi applications encompass decentralized exchanges, lending and borrowing platforms, stablecoins, and other financial tools and services that are constructed on decentralized protocols and are accessible to anyone with internet connectivity. DeFi is commonly tied to the cryptocurrency ecosystem, with many DeFi applications using cryptocurrencies as the foundational asset or medium of exchange.

Clearly, CeFi and DeFi represent two distinct approaches to finance, each with unique attributes in their structure, operations, and outcomes. Some key differences between CeFi and DeFi include:

- **Innovation**: While CeFi is a well-established domain often slower in embracing new technologies and methodologies, DeFi is a comparatively nascent and swiftly evolving sector marked by substantial innovation and exploration.
- **Structure**: CeFi relies on conventional financial institutions operating through centralized systems. In contrast, DeFi is constructed on decentralized blockchain networks like Ethereum, facilitating the development of decentralized applications (dApps) and smart contracts.
- **Control**: Control in CeFi is centralized, vested in financial institutions that deliver services and maintain custody of users' assets. Conversely, in DeFi, control is decentralized, giving users direct control over their assets and enabling them to engage in the network without intermediaries.
- **Transparency**: CeFi usually offers less transparency, with financial institutions largely governing information and transaction flows. DeFi is inherently transparent, with every transaction and data point recorded on the blockchain, and available to all participants.
- **Security**: Traditional security threats, such as hacks and thefts, can plague CeFi. DeFi leans on blockchain technology and cryptographic security measures to ensure heightened security for its users.
- **Accessibility**: While CeFi predominantly caters to conventional financial customers, DeFi aims to extend financial services to a broader audience, especially including those unbanked or underbanked.

In conclusion, both CeFi and DeFi have inherent strengths and limitations. The preference between the two hinges on various aspects, including individual inclinations, financial objectives, and risk appetite. It's pertinent to highlight that some entities are exploring hybrid frameworks, melding features from both CeFi and DeFi, to devise novel and innovative financial products and solutions.

14.5.2 Volatility of Cryptocurrencies

Bitcoin's value has displayed significant volatility since its inception, as demonstrated in Table 14.7 and Fig. 14.13. Bitcoin's value began at $0 in 2009 and climbed to $1 by February 2011. In 2013, when the Electronic Frontier Foundation (EFF) began accepting Bitcoin, there was a remarkable surge in Bitcoin's value, witnessing an increase of 6600% to reach $1100. Between 2014 and 2016, Bitcoin's price remained relatively stable but experienced another sharp rise in 2017, reaching $20,000. With the onset of COVID-19, Bitcoin's value saw an unexpected surge, achieving its highest ever at $68,789.63 per coin.

Bitcoin's volatility is not an isolated phenomenon. As illustrated in Fig. 14.14, the historical price of Ethereum (ETH) has also experienced rapid fluctuations. Comparing Fig. 14.14 with Fig. 14.13, it's evident that cryptocurrency prices share some correlation. This is likely because they are influenced by similar factors, including macroeconomic conditions, regulations surrounding cryptocurrencies, and public perceptions of digital currencies.

Table 14.7 Bitcoin's valuation from (2014 to 2022)

Year	2014	2015	2016	2017	2018	2019	2020	2021	2022
High	$457.09	$495.56	$979.40	$20,089.00	$17,712.40	$13,796.49	$29,244.88	$68,789.63	$48,086.84
Low	$289.30	$171.51	$354.91	$755.76	$3191.30	$3391.02	$4106.98	$28,722.76	$15,599.05

Source Yahoo Finance, https://finance.yahoo.com

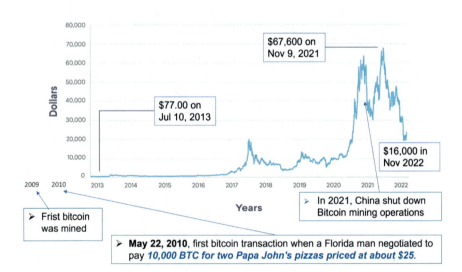

Fig. 14.13 Bitcoin's valuation over time (*Source* sofi.com)

14.5 Risks and Future of Cryptocurrencies

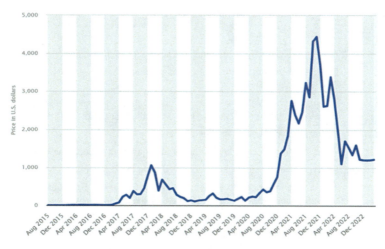

Fig. 14.14 The valuation of ETH over time (*Source* Statista, 2022)

14.5.3 Collapses of Crypto Marketplaces in 2022

While memories of the 2014 Mt. Gox incident still linger, 2022 saw a series of crypto marketplace crashes. The valuation of crypto markets reached its zenith at around $2.9 trillion in November 2021 but plummeted to about $800 billion by the end of 2022 (Bernstein & Kominers, 2022).

In early April 2022, the U.S. Securities and Exchange Commission (SEC) indicated an intention to tighten regulations on crypto agencies. On May 3, 2022, the Federal Reserve hiked the interest rate by 0.5%. These events catalyzed a widespread selloff of cryptocurrencies (Wikipedia, 2023b). By May 2022, Terra's UST stablecoin had decoupled from the U.S. Dollar, prompting a near-total devaluation of both UST and its supporting coin, LUNA. The downfall of Terra's UST initiated a domino effect, leading to the collapse of numerous stablecoins and crypto marketplaces, as outlined in Table 14.8.

These collapses underscore the volatile nature of the crypto markets and raise significant concerns about the future of cryptocurrencies. Importantly, these collapses don't signify a failure of blockchain technology but rather are consequences of government regulations, poor management in certain crypto companies, and financial crises. For instance, Terra's UST failure stemmed from its reliance on the inherently risky algorithmic stablecoin model without the backing of solid financial assets. In stark contrast, blockchain technology made notable advancements in 2022. For example, on September 15, 2022, the Ethereum (ETH-USD) blockchain underwent the "merge," transitioning from proof of work to proof of stake, marking a significant stride in reducing energy consumption by 99.95% (Ethereum, 2022b).

Table 14.8 Major crypto marketplace collapses in 2022

Date	Event
May 7	Terra's UST and LUNA plummeted, causing a $45 billion loss
June 1	Three Arrows Capital (3AC), the most significant holder of LUNA, filed for Chapter 15 bankruptcy
June 5	Voyager Digital (VYGVQ), a cryptocurrency brokerage and lender that had extended a $650 m unsecured loan to 3AC, filed for Chapter 11 bankruptcy
June 13	Celsius, a crypto-lender, declared bankruptcy
July 20	Vauld sought protection against creditors, equivalent to declaring bankruptcy
November 10	Tether, the largest stablecoin, decoupled from the U.S. Dollar
November 17	FTX.com, a major crypto exchange, filed for Chapter 11 bankruptcy, entangling approximately 130 affiliated companies in the process
November 28	BlockFi, an exchange and cryptocurrency custodial service provider, filed for Chapter 11 bankruptcy

Source McGleenon (2022) and Wikipedia (2023b)

14.5.4 Future of Cryptocurrencies

The significance of cryptocurrencies will persist into the future. While we anticipate similar volatility in cryptocurrency values in the coming years, it's probable that cryptocurrencies and crypto tokens will endure. The main reasons include:

- Blockchains have demonstrated their worth to both businesses and society at large. As the inherent tokens of blockchains, cryptocurrencies deliver valuable incentives to blockchain miners.
- Cryptocurrencies present a novel investment opportunity for both investors and speculators.
- Crypto coins and tokens have proven their utility in streamlining business transactions.
- Despite the sharp decline in the crypto market's value in 2022 from its peak, the private assets linked to the investments of millions of investors should be safeguarded under the constitution.

> *While we anticipate similar volatility in cryptocurrency values in the coming years, it's probable that cryptocurrencies and crypto tokens will endure.*

To temper the volatility of cryptocurrencies and tokens, we can expect heightened governmental regulations aimed at stabilizing the crypto market. Additionally, enhanced education on cryptocurrencies and crypto tokens might help in steadying investor sentiment.

14.6　Private Blockchains

Private blockchains, also known as managed blockchains, are permissioned blockchains controlled by a central authority (e.g., a company). Due to the presence of this central authority, private blockchains are distributed but not fully decentralized. Each computer node in the network might have varying rights. The distributed ledger still employs blockchain concepts, ensuring immutability and using cryptographic principles. Members of a private blockchain typically know each other's identities, which facilitates business interactions, a primary reason for joining the network.

Compared to public blockchains, private blockchains achieve faster transaction speeds and therefore higher transaction efficiencies, thanks to their increased centralization and fewer nodes. This efficiency also results in lower transaction costs. However, since a single authority can potentially alter some blocks in the blockchain, private blockchains forgo some degree of immutability. Nevertheless, altering blocks could irreparably harm the firm's reputation and reduce the likelihood of successfully launching another private blockchain in the future.

We further compare private blockchains to public blockchains in Table 14.9.

Major providers of private blockchains include Hyperledger Fabric, R3's Corda, Enterprise Ethereum, Ripple, and Quorum (some of which will be introduced in subsequent sections). While Hyperledger Fabric is versatile enough for any industry, both Corda and Ripple are tailored for the financial sector, though they are broadening their reach. In Ripple's case, it also offers a native token for its blockchain, facilitating transactions in mere seconds (Iredale, 2021).

Private blockchains appeal to many large companies because they combine the advantageous features of blockchains while enabling a company to retain control and ensure privacy. In recent years, private blockchains have been adopted across numerous industries, including financial services, supply chain management, retail, healthcare, government, real estate, and insurance. For instance, Walmart constructed a food traceability system utilizing IBM's Food Trust Hyperledger blockchain. Comcast, along with its partners, established Blockgraph to allow advertisers to target audiences while preserving viewer privacy. DHL employs its

Table 14.9 Private blockchain vs. public blockchain

	Private Blockchain	**Public Blockchain**
Consensus	Permissioned	Permissionless
Authority	A central authority	Anyone
Access	Authorized users	Anyone
Structure	Partially decentralized	Decentralized
Immutability	Partial	Full
Transaction Speed	Fast	Slow
Efficiency	High	Low
Transaction Cost	Low	High

Source This table is partially adapted from Iredale (2021)

private blockchain technology to digitally record shipments and secure its transactions. Financial institutions and insurance companies, such as JP Morgan and MetLife, leverage private blockchains to optimize and authenticate their contracts and transactions (Euromoney Learning, 2022).

Case Study

IBM Food Trust Blockchain for Food Safety

While the food systems in most countries are generally considered safe, occasional outbreaks of foodborne diseases and contaminants, like the *E. Coli* found in romaine lettuce and the poisoned milk scandal, do occur. When an outbreak arises, it becomes paramount to trace the source of the foodborne disease. However, identifying this source can sometimes take days or even weeks (Hyperledger, 2019). Before the exact source is pinpointed, the public is often advised to avoid a certain type of food or all foods from a specified area, leading to revenue losses for retailers and decreased consumer confidence in the implicated supply chain entities. Clearly, an enhanced traceability system can reduce these impacts by rapidly identifying the exact source.

To improve transparency and traceability of food products and foster a safer, more sustainable food ecosystem, IBM proposed the IBM Food Trust network concept in October 2016, formally introducing the system based on Hyperledger Fabric by August 2017 (CryptoMarketsWiki, 2021).

Hyperledger Fabric is open-source, boasting a modular architecture. This means that food retailers, along with their suppliers and even competitors, can join the project, optimizing food traceability (Hyperledger, 2019). The blockchain facilitates easy integration of components like consensus and membership services.[12] IBM has incorporated modules such as Trace, Fresh Insights, Certifications, and Data Entry and Access into the blockchain system, alongside fundamental blockchain components like APIs, Trust Anchors, Remote Deployment, and Smart Contracts (IBM Food Trust, 2019).

IBM Food Trust also exemplifies a food supply chain blockchain, creating an ecosystem for stakeholders like farmers, suppliers, manufacturers, distributors, retailers, and logistics firms. Per IBM's statement, the IBM Food Trust offers advantages like enhanced food safety, freshness, fraud prevention, waste reduction, brand trust, supply chain efficiency, and sustainability (IBM, 2023).

Walmart became the first company to collaborate with IBM Food Trust, seeking to employ a permissioned enterprise-grade blockchain technology to enhance traceability in the food supply chains. The permissioned system

---

[12] More information about Hyperledger Fabric can be found in Chapter 14.7 and Hyperledger (2023).

restricts access only to trusted transaction partners. As a senior director at Walmart highlighted, the blockchain is a suitable solution for this challenge due to its emphasis on "trust, immutability, and transparency" (Hyperledger, 2019). In October 2016, in collaboration with IBM, Walmart declared its intention to trace the origin of mangos sold in the U.S. and pork offered in its China-based stores. For U.S. mangos, the system now traces their origin in just 2.2 seconds, a significant reduction from the previous seven-day period. For pork in China, the system facilitates the upload of certificates of authenticity to the blockchain, assuring consumers of the product's legitimacy (Hyperledger, 2019).

On September 24, 2018, Walmart declared that "all suppliers of leafy green vegetables for Sam's and Walmart [must] upload their data to the blockchain by September 2019" (Miller, 2018). Since then, Walmart has broadened its tracing efforts to other products, including dairy, packaged salads, and baby foods (Hyperledger, 2019).

IBM Food Trust's successful collaboration with Walmart paved the way for partnerships with other food giants like Nestle, Unilever, Tyson Foods, Carrefour, Albertsons, Raw Seafoods, and CHO (Murphy, 2020).

Questions

1. What are the advantages of the IBM Food Trust System?
2. How would you envision implementing a private blockchain in your company or another enterprise?

14.7 Consortium Blockchains

Consortium blockchains, also known as federated blockchains, have emerged as an effective solution to address the vulnerability of a single authority in a permissioned network. Multiple authorities in such systems can offer greater resilience against external security attacks and mitigate the risk of internal monopolistic dominance. Consequently, consortium blockchains enjoy a higher level of security compared to private blockchains while maintaining more efficiency than public blockchains. According to research by Deloitte, approximately 74% of organizations prefer consortium blockchains (Banerjee, 2022).

14.7.1 Pros and Cons of Consortium Blockchains

Due to their distinct structure, consortium blockchains offer specific advantages and disadvantages, especially when compared to public blockchains such as Bitcoin.

Advantages of Consortium Blockchains

- *Security*: A consortium blockchain is restricted to a select group of participants, not the general public. This makes the validation process less susceptible to threats such as SQL injection,[13] distributed DOS (DDoS) attack,[14] man-in-the-middle attack (Wikipedia, 2023f).[15]
- *Efficiency*: With fewer members in the network compared to a public network, the verification process in consortium blockchains is much quicker than in systems like Bitcoin. Since a small, authenticated group of participants controls the network, they can more easily reach consensus on network protocols, modify transaction information, and even reverse incorrect transactions as per established protocols. This results in significantly higher operational efficiency and scalability compared to systems like Bitcoin.
- *Transaction Costs*: Consortium blockchains are often designed for specific purposes, leading to minimal or even nonexistent transaction fees. When compared to the mining costs associated with Bitcoin, the economic benefits of consortium blockchains become clear.
- *Environmental Impact*: Since consortium blockchains don't rely on energy-intensive mechanisms like the Proof of Work (PoW) used in Bitcoin, their energy requirements (often utilizing alternatives like Proof-of-Vote) are significantly lower.

Disadvantages of Consortium Blockchains

- *Threats*: With a limited number of authorities, the blockchain is susceptible to collusion among these authorities, potentially at the detriment of other participants.
- *Effectiveness*: The permission-only access to consortium blockchains may result in market segmentation if certain participants join one blockchain

---

[13] SQL injection is a prevalent web hacking technique wherein malicious code is inserted into SQL statements via web page input. Instead of inputting a standard username or user ID into a web form, a hacker using SQL injection might input a malicious SQL statement. For instance, they might enter something like "SELECT UserId, Name, Password FROM Users WHERE UserId = 8495 or 1 = 1." This could potentially return all the usernames and passwords stored in the database.

[14] In a DDoS attack, a server might become overwhelmingly busy, akin to an unexpected traffic jam, thereby exhausting web resources and preventing other users from accessing the service.

[15] The man-in-the-middle attack has various other names, including monster-in-the-middle, machine-in-the-middle, monkey-in-the-middle, meddler-in-the-middle, person-in-the-middle, and adversary-in-the-middle attack (Wikipedia, 2023f). This type of cyberattack occurs when an attacker secretly intercepts and possibly alters the communication between two parties without their knowledge. By doing this, the attacker can gain unauthorized access to the information being exchanged and even send deceptive messages of their own.

while others opt for a competing one. Given that consortium blockchains are still in their infancy, the evolution of markets intertwined with these blockchains remains uncertain.
- ***Coordination***: While the number of authorities in consortium blockchains is relatively small, significant effort is required from market leaders to initiate the consortium and achieve consensus on protocols and rules. Identifying the ideal authorities for the blockchain initiation can be intricate because each authority has its own priorities. This situation can become even more complex as additional participants join the network.

14.7.2 Consortium Blockchain Implementations

In the practical realm, major blockchain technology providers like R3's Corda, JP Morgan's Quorum, and Hyperledger offer templates for consortium blockchains. These consortium blockchains can be merged with a public blockchain to form a hybrid blockchain.

14.7.2.1 Corda

Corda, developed by R3, is an enterprise blockchain platform predominantly utilized in finance-related sectors. Corda is written in the Kotlin programming language and supports development in both Kotlin and Java. It is available in an open-source version as well as a paid enterprise edition. On Corda, each node represents an entity, which might be a company, a department within a company, or individuals. Adhering to the network protocol, nodes can interact and choose to exchange data either publicly or privately with specific members (Corda, 2022).

Applications on Corda are called CorDapps. These specify the transaction rules and the consensus mechanism (R3, 2023). Unlike the Bitcoin and Ethereum blockchains, where transactions are grouped into blocks and verified collectively, Corda verifies each transaction instantly on an individual basis, enhancing transaction throughput. The enterprise version of Corda boasts a greater transactional throughput compared to the open-source version (Phemex, 2021b).

While Corda, as a private blockchain, doesn't inherently require cryptocurrency, it does provide a Token SDK, a token standard specification for entities that want to incorporate tokens into their networks (R3, 2022). In March 2021, R3 collaborated with XinFin, a hybrid blockchain platform, to adopt XinFin's cryptocurrency, XDC—an Ethereum-compatible coin—as the primary settlement coin on Corda (Phemex, 2021b).

Corda is a leading blockchain entity in the finance and insurance sectors. It has secured investment and user interest from entities like Wells Fargo, UBS, MasterCard, Nasdaq, and major global banks (Phemex, 2021b). Companies leveraging Corda generally enhance their cooperative efficiency and diminish operational costs. For instance, within an insurance network based on Corda, stakeholders can optimize processes such as claims handling, documentation, data verification, payments, and other business operations (Morris, 2018).

14.7.2.2 Quorum

Quorum was developed as a modification of Go Ethereum in 2016 by JP Morgan Chase, targeting the finance, insurance, and banking sectors. Being an open-source project, Quorum retains many of Ethereum's primary functions, like smart contract capabilities using the Solidity language and tokenization. At the same time, it introduces features such as permissioned access, increased throughput, and transaction privacy (Phemex, 2021a).

- *Permissioned Access*: Quorum allows for enhanced security by permitting only certain nodes to participate in the network.
- *Efficient Throughput*: Based on the selected consensus mechanism, most Quorum users have been able to achieve faster transactions at a rate of several hundred transactions per second as of October 2022 (Github, 2023). Rather than using Bitcoin's proof of work or Ethereum's proof of stake, Quorum employs a raft-based consensus, grounded in the Practical Byzantine Fault Tolerance Algorithm (Consul, 2023).
- *Transaction Privacy*: With Quorum, users can control data accessibility, determining which network members can view specific data.

ConsenSys, the platform's proprietor since 2020, has created various enterprise applications on Quorum. Examples include the Tessera Private Transaction Manager, Codefi Payments, and Codefi Workflow, enabling users to seamlessly integrate blockchain technology into their operations (Consensys, 2023).

14.7.2.3 Hyperledger

Hyperledger is an umbrella initiative for open-source consortium blockchains, spearheaded by the Linux Foundation and backed by major tech companies like IBM, Intel, SAP, among others (Hyperledger, 2022). The primary goal of Hyperledger is to foster cross-industry cooperation, enhance the performance and reliability of blockchain systems, and bolster transactions in technology, finance, and supply chain sectors. By offering purpose-specific modules, Hyperledger aspires to unify various standalone open protocols and standards (Hyperledger, 2022).

The Hyperledger project offers a plethora of frameworks tailored to diverse user needs. For instance, Hyperledger Fabric stands out as a renowned modular framework, enabling businesses to craft their solutions and applications, encompassing functionalities like smart contracts and membership services (Hyperledger, 2019). Hyperledger Iroha is underpinned by PostgreSQL and C++, utilizing the Byzantine Fault Tolerant consensus algorithm. Meanwhile, Hyperledger Sawtooth Lake employs distributed ledger technologies within its modular platform (Hyperledger, 2022).

14.8 Hybrid Blockchains

A *hybrid blockchain* combines elements of both a private, permission-based system and a public, permissionless system. The hybrid network is managed by one or a few authorities; however, when required, transactions can be validated in the same manner as on a public blockchain, ensuring the transactions have a high level of immutability and security. Authorities can choose which transactions should remain private to only permissioned members and which should be accessible to the public.

A permissioned member, typically undergoing a KYC onboarding process, can access all data within the network. This member's data remains private unless involved in transactions with external parties (e.g., through smart contracts). Within the network, a member has limited anonymity, but their anonymity in public is largely preserved. However, only permissioned members can access the data, ensuring the data remains confidential within the network (i.e., privacy is maintained) (Geroni, 2021). As a result, a hybrid blockchain guarantees enhanced security by leveraging features from both public and private blockchains.

Hybrid blockchains offer additional advantages. For instance, they can mitigate the risk of a 51% attack since the network operates within a private, enclosed ecosystem.[16] Transaction fees on hybrid blockchains are notably lower than on public blockchains. This is because verifications can be conducted by a limited number of nodes, unlike the larger number of nodes involved in public blockchains. Similar to a private blockchain, the protocol of a hybrid blockchain can be revised if necessary, while still ensuring data remains immutable.

Hybrid blockchains are adaptable to a diverse array of applications, encompassing areas such as the Internet of Things (IoT), trade finance, supply chains, banking, governments, and enterprise services. Several illustrative examples include:

- **IoT**: For IoT, a hybrid blockchain can safeguard the privacy of devices within a private network while facilitating connectivity to a public network.
- **BaaS (Blockchain as a Service) Platforms**: Major companies are leveraging blockchain to enhance their offerings to clients. IBM, for instance, was an early provider of blockchain platforms catering to a broad spectrum of businesses. Amazon's blockchain offerings facilitate supply chain transactions, asset transfers, and trading.

---

[16] A 51% attack occurs when a group of miners gains control over more than half of the network's total mining hash rate or computational power, enabling them to manipulate a blockchain.

- **Digital Asset Creation**: Hybrid blockchains have significantly contributed to asset tokenization, paving the way for the digital embodiment of tangible assets such as intellectual property, debt, and art. For example, TOKO, a pioneering digital asset creation engine, aids asset proprietors in devising tokenized offerings, thus tapping into an expanded investor base (Tank et al., 2021).
- **Supply Chain Management**: Hybrid blockchains are inherently suitable for supply chain networks. This is because stakeholders within supply chains often desire to maintain transaction confidentiality internally while sustaining external global interactions.
- **Trade Finance**: In the realm of global trade finance, a hybrid blockchain can engender a secure, internal transactional environment for the parties involved, simultaneously granting access to external resources. Given their transactional efficiency and cost-effectiveness, consortium and hybrid blockchains are witnessing the most rapid growth in the supply chain sector (Wood, 2021).

Case Study

XinFin's XDC Network for Trade Finance

On August 18, 2021, the XDC Network became the inaugural blockchain entity to align with the global Trade Finance Distribution (TFD) Initiative, a consortium comprising trade originators, institutional financiers, and credit insurance providers (XinFin XDC Network, 2021). André Casterman, the Chair of the Fintech Committee at the International Trade and Forfaiting Association, remarked that the integration of XinFin's XDC would capacitate TFD "to bridge the US$19 trillion trade finance asset class with any type of funder through tokenization and digital assets."

XinFin (eXchange inFinite) is anchored in Singapore. It conceptualizes XDC as a paradigm of hybrid blockchains, employing Quorum for its private (consortium) aspect and Ethereum for its public facet, all propelled by the XinFin Delegated Proof of Stake Consensus network (XDPoS) (XinFin, 2023b). XinFin integrates seamlessly into banking ecosystems, ERP structures, SWIFT configurations, among other platforms. Relative to Bitcoin and Ethereum, XinFin boasts distinct advantages, as illustrated in Table 14.10 (XinFin, 2023a).

Table 14.10 Comparison among Bitcoin, Ethereum, and XinFin

	XinFin XDC	Ethereum ETH	Bitcoin BTC
Average Transaction Fee	$0.00001 USD	$10 USD	$15 USD
Transaction Confirmation Speed	2 Seconds	10–20 Seconds	10–60 Minutes
Smart Contract Support	YES	YES	NO
Energy Consumption	0.0000074 TWh	20.61 TWh	71.12 TWh

Source Adapted from Xinfin (2023c)

Evidently, a hybrid blockchain model like XinFin exhibits superior performance over Bitcoin and Ethereum, primarily because the authentication process in permissioned blockchains hinges on a select cluster of private nodes. Owing to its myriad benefits, XinFin has fostered collaborations with a spectrum of enterprises, including Copper, AiX, R3, and others (XinFin, 2023a). Its avant-garde blockchain technology has garnered endorsements from eminent financial institutions globally, such as AIG, ING Bank, Lloyds Bank, the Commonwealth Bank of Australia, and the International Chamber of Commerce (Finneseth, 2021).

Question

1. What catalyzed XinFin's XDC's recognition as the premier blockchain entity to be embraced by TFD?
2. What are the key differences between XinFin's XDC and Ethereum's ETH?

14.9 Summary

This chapter delves into the intricate world of blockchain technology, a decentralized ledger system pivotal in the digital transformation era. It outlines the underlying structures, the inception of Bitcoin as its vanguard, and the proliferation of diverse public and private blockchains and cryptocurrencies. The chapter also highlights the risks involved, potential future developments, and how enterprises are harnessing consortium and hybrid blockchains for optimized outcomes.

Key Takeaways:

1. Blockchain Structures:
    - Blockchains are decentralized digital ledgers where transactions are recorded in "blocks" and sequentially linked.
    - Consensus mechanisms, like Proof of Work and Proof of Stake, ensure data integrity across participants.
2. The Bitcoin Blockchain:
    - Bitcoin is the pioneer cryptocurrency enabled by blockchain technology.

- It operates on a decentralized, public ledger with a Proof of Work consensus mechanism and is known for its finite supply.
3. Other Public Blockchain and Cryptocurrencies:
    - Numerous cryptocurrencies, like Ethereum and Litecoin, emerged following Bitcoin's inception.
    - Each has its distinct features, such as Ethereum's smart contract functionality.
4. Risks and Future of Cryptocurrencies:
    - While cryptocurrencies promise financial freedom and decentralization, they're susceptible to market volatility, regulatory scrutiny, technological vulnerabilities, and scalability concerns.
    - Future trends may see more regulatory frameworks, increased adoption, and technological advancements addressing current challenges.
5. Private Blockchains:
    - Private blockchains restrict participation rights and are often used by businesses to maintain data privacy.
    - Platforms like Corda and Quorum exemplify how industries adopt private blockchains to streamline operations while preserving data security.
6. Consortium Blockchains:
    - Consortium blockchains operate under a group of organizations rather than a single entity, ensuring democratic control.
    - They balance between the openness of public blockchains and the privacy of private ones.
7. Hybrid Blockchains:
    - Hybrid blockchains amalgamate features from both public and private blockchains.
    - They offer flexibility, allowing certain data to be public while keeping other data private, which fuses benefits of both architectures for optimal utility.

14.10 Exercises

14.10.1 Practice Questions

1. What was the main reason to create Bitcoin?
2. What are the major differences between blockchains and traditional databases?
3. Can you describe the mining process and proof of work in the Bitcoin blockchain?
4. What are the pros and cons of the Bitcoin blockchain?
5. What are the major differences between a private blockchain and a public blockchain?
6. Why would consortium and hybrid blockchains become attractive to big enterprises? What is your suggestion to further improve them?

14.10 Exercises

7. Has your company involved in any blockchain project? If yes, how does that blockchain perform? If no, please imagine how your company would have done it. Please provide some details about the blockchain structure and main components inside the blockchain.
8. Has your company participated in any crypto investment or utilized crypto in business transactions? Could you share a specific example?
9. Have you heard of successful real-life cases of utilizing crypto coins and/or tokens in some companies that you are familiar with?
10. What are your suggestions to make stablecoins stable?

14.10.2 Case Studies

Case Study 1: Application of Blockchain Technology in Supply Chain Finance at Walmart

Background

Walmart, one of the largest retail chains globally, manages a vast supply chain with thousands of suppliers, handling products ranging from electronics to fresh produce. Supply chain finance (SCF) at such a magnitude aims to improve the financial efficiency by optimizing the use of working capital and reducing costs for both Walmart and its suppliers. Traditionally, the SCF process at Walmart, like many other companies, involves various intermediaries facilitating transactions and credit. This model, despite its advantages, has multiple challenges.

Challenges

1. **Lack of Transparency:** Given the sheer size of Walmart's operations, ensuring transparency with numerous suppliers is a considerable challenge.
2. **Delays in Payment:** The extended processing times in traditional SCF systems can cause liquidity issues for suppliers.
3. **High Costs:** Intermediary fees and reconciliation processes can inflate costs for all parties involved.
4. **Trust Issues:** Given Walmart's global operation, it deals with suppliers from various parts of the world, leading to trust issues, especially in cross-border transactions.

Options

Walmart, always at the forefront of technological adoption, considers blockchain to counter these challenges due to its inherent features:

1. **Public Blockchain:** An open, transparent network, but might be slower and more resource-intensive.

2. **Private Blockchain:** Faster and efficient but limited to Walmart's operations, potentially lacking the broad trust needed with international suppliers.
3. **Consortium Blockchain:** Involving multiple stakeholders, such as key suppliers or partner banks, offering a blend of efficiency and trust.

Discussion Questions

1. Which blockchain structure is most suitable for a retail giant like Walmart in optimizing its SCF?
2. How can Walmart's adoption of blockchain redefine trust in global supply chains?
3. Are there potential pitfalls Walmart should be aware of when integrating blockchain into its vast SCF ecosystem?

Case Study 2: Evaluating the Potential of Hybrid Blockchains in Supply Chain Management

Background

Supply chain management (SCM) is pivotal for businesses that want to maintain efficiency, ensure product quality, and sustain profitability. However, traditional SCM systems often suffer from issues like lack of transparency, inefficient tracking mechanisms, and fragmented data sources.

The International Supply Chain Organization (ISCO) is a multinational coalition of companies involved in manufacturing, distribution, and retail. With the rapid globalization of trade, ISCO members face challenges in ensuring real-time tracking of products, authenticating origin, and preventing counterfeits. They seek a modern solution to revamp their existing SCM systems.

Challenges

1. **Transparency and Trust:** Many ISCO members operate in jurisdictions where trust is a significant issue. There's a need for a system where participants can view but not alter the transaction history.
2. **Real-time Tracking:** With products being manufactured and shipped worldwide, real-time tracking is crucial.
3. **Interoperability:** Different members of ISCO use various SCM systems. Any new solution must be compatible or offer easy integration with these existing systems.
4. **Confidentiality:** While transparency is essential, not all supply chain data should be accessible to every participant, especially competitors.

Hybrid Blockchain as a Solution

A hybrid blockchain, which combines the features of both private and public blockchains, emerged as a potential solution. Such a system would:

- Ensure **transparency** by allowing all participants to view the transaction history.
- Utilize smart contracts to automate and streamline processes, enabling **real-time tracking**.
- Offer modular structures that allow easy integration with various existing SCM systems, ensuring **interoperability**.
- Ensure data **confidentiality** by allowing companies to keep certain transactions private, visible only to permissioned members, while others could be public.

Outcomes

ISCO initiated a pilot project, integrating a hybrid blockchain solution into the supply chains of ten member companies. The results were promising:

- Counterfeit incidents dropped by 70% within the first year.
- Real-time tracking reduced shipment delays and losses, improving efficiency by 50%.
- Enhanced transparency improved trust among members, leading to better collaborative projects and partnerships.
- The modular nature of the hybrid blockchain ensured smooth integration with existing systems, with 90% of the companies reporting easy adoption.

Discussion Questions

1. Why did the hybrid blockchain emerge as a superior solution for ISCO compared to purely private or public blockchains?
2. How do smart contracts play a role in improving the efficiency of supply chain management?
3. Considering the success of the pilot project, what challenges might ISCO face when scaling this solution to all its member companies?

Appendix: Consensus Mechanisms

In addition to the blockchain structure, the consensus mechanism is a crucial characteristic of a blockchain. It distinguishes one type of blockchain from another. Below, we provide a list of consensus mechanisms:

1. ***Proof of Work (PoW)***: In PoW, the first miner to solve the hashing puzzle and add a new block to the blockchain receives a cryptocurrency reward and transaction fees. Refer to Chapter 14.3.6 "The Consensus Mechanism: Proof of Work" for more details.
2. ***Proof of Stake (PoS)***: PoS is a consensus mechanism where validators are rewarded for creating the next block based on their stake (e.g., cryptocurrency holdings) in the network. For more on this, see Chapter 14.4.2 "Ether (ETH) and Ethereum."
3. ***Delegated Proof of Stake (DPoS)***: In DPoS, token holders vote to elect a limited number of "delegates" or "witnesses" responsible for adding the next block to the blockchain (Saad & Radzi, 2020). These delegates have an incentive to act honestly, as malicious behavior could result in their removal by token holder votes.
4. ***Practical Byzantine Fault Tolerance (PBFT)***: Within PBFT, a node known as the "primary" proposes and broadcasts a new block to the network (Castro & Liskov, 1999). "Replicas" or other nodes then independently verify this block and achieve consensus on its validity before inclusion. If 2/2 of the replicas concur, the block is added; otherwise, it's rejected. PBFT ensures blockchain integrity, even when malicious nodes are present, and is resilient to network failures.
5. ***Proof of Activity (PoA)***: PoA combines Proof of Work (PoW) and Proof of Stake (PoS) (Bentov et al., 2014). PoW miners initiate block creation, with PoS validators then confirming the transactions within. This method strikes a balance between PoS's energy efficiency and PoW's security.
6. ***Proof of Importance (PoI)***: In PoI-based platforms, nodes receive an "importance score" influenced by factors such as cryptocurrency holdings, transaction frequency, and transaction history (Bach et al., 2018). This score affects the probability of a node being chosen to validate transactions.
7. ***Proof of Burn (PoB)***: Validators prove their commitment by "burning" cryptocurrency, sending it to an unspendable address (Bybit, 2022). This act serves as proof of computational work and establishes their right to mine or validate. However, PoB isn't widespread due to potential supply constraints and centralization risks.
8. ***Proof of Capacity (PoC)***: Validators show their computational capacity by dedicating a segment of their hard drive for data storage and resolution (Investopedia, 2021). This data aids in validating transactions and block additions, relying on rapid data storage and retrieval.
9. ***Proof of Weight (PoW)***: Every miner is assigned a "weight." Miners with more weight have higher chances of getting chosen for validation. If cryptocurrency stake determines the "weight," it closely mirrors PoS. However, other criteria can define weight too (Compare, 2018).
10. ***Proof of Elapsed Time (PoET)***: In PoET, validators (also known as miners) wait for a random duration termed the "sleep time" before they can validate transactions and append blocks to the blockchain (Bowman et al.,

2021). The first validator to conclude its sleep time is chosen to authenticate transactions and incorporate blocks into the blockchain. PoET ensures fairness by giving every validator an equitable chance of being selected, simultaneously maintaining security by thwarting malevolent entities from dominating the validation process.

11. **Proof of Authority (PoA)**: In PoA, a select group of validators, termed "authorities," are designated to validate transactions and add blocks to the blockchain. PoA is commonly adopted in consortium or private blockchain setups where the emphasis is more on security and efficiency rather than complete decentralization.
12. **Hashgraph**: This consensus algorithm draws its foundation from the "gossip about gossip" principle and leverages virtual voting to achieve consensus regarding the sequence of transactions. For a detailed understanding, refer to Chapter 14.4.3 "HBAR and Hedera" for more information.

References

Antonopoulos, A. M. (2017). *Mastering Bitcoin: Programming the open blockchain*. O'Reilly Media.

Bach, L. M., Mihaljevic, B., & Zagar, M. (2018). Comparative analysis of blockchain consensus algorithms. In *2018 41st International convention on information and communication technology, electronics and microelectronics (MIPRO)* (pp. 1545–1550).

Banerjee, A. (2022). *Everything you need to know about consortium blockchain*. https://www.blockchain-council.org/blockchain/everything-you-need-to-know-about-consortium-blockchain/. Accessed June 21, 2022.

Barchat, C. (2022). *The Ethereum Merge (ETH 2.0) explained*. https://www.moonpay.com/blog/ethereum-merge-eth-2#frequently-asked-questions-faq. Accessed June 13, 2022.

Bayer, D., Haber, S., & Stornetta, W. S. (1993). Improving the efficiency and reliability of digital time-stamping. In *Sequences Ii* (pp. 329–334). Springer.

Bentov, I., Lee, C., Mizrahi, A., & Rosenfeld, M. (2014). Proof of activity: Extending bitcoin's proof of work via proof of stake [extended abstract] y. *ACM SIGMETRICS Performance Evaluation Review, 42*(3), 34–37.

Bernstein, S., & Kominers, S. D. (2022). Why decentralized crypto platforms are weathering the crash. *Harvard Business Review*. https://hbr.org/2022/12/why-decentralized-crypto-platforms-are-weathering-the-crash. Accessed June 19, 2022.

Bitcoin Wiki. (2022). *Difficulty*. https://en.bitcoin.it/wiki/Difficulty. Accessed June 21, 2022.

Blockchain.com. (2017). *Bitcoin block 500,000*. https://www.blockchain.com/btc/block/00000000000000000024fb37364cbf81fd49cc2d51c09c75c35433c3a1945d04?page=1. Accessed June 11, 2022.

Bowman, M., Das, D., Mandal, A., & Montgomery, H. (2021). On elapsed time consensus protocols. *Progress in Cryptology–INDOCRYPT 2021: 22nd International Conference on Cryptology in India, Jaipur, India, December 12–15, 2021, Proceedings 22*, 559–583.

Bybit. (2022). *Proof of Burn (PoB)*. https://learn.bybit.com/glossary/definition-proof-of-burn-pob/. Accessed June 22, 2022.

Castro, M., & Liskov, B. (1999). Practical byzantine fault tolerance. *Osdi, 99*(1999), 173–186.

Coindesk. (2022). *Cryptocurrency prices*. https://www.coindesk.com/price/ethereum/. Accessed July 11, 2022.

Compare, P. (2018). *What is proof of weight?* https://coincodex.com/article/2617/what-is-proof-of-weight/. Accessed June 1, 2022.

Consensys. (2023). *Everything you need to build the next generation of blockchain-based Enterprise solutions.* https://consensys.net/quorum/products/. Accessed October 11, 2023.

Consul. (2023). *Consensus protocol.* https://developer.hashicorp.com/consul/docs/architecture/consensus. Accessed June 5, 2023.

Corda. (2022). *The future of digital finance is built on trust.* https://corda.net/. Accessed June 21, 2022.

CryptoMarketsWiki. (2021). *IBM.* https://crypto.marketswiki.com/index.php?title=IBM. Accessed June 1, 2022.

Ethereum. (2022a). *Earn rewards while securing Ethereum.* https://ethereum.org/en/staking/. Accessed June 21, 2022.

Ethereum. (2022b). *The Merge.* Ethereum.Com. https://ethereum.org/en/upgrades/merge/. Accessed July 1, 2022.

Ethereum. (2022c). *Welcome to Ethereum.* https://ethereum.org/en/. Accessed July 11, 2022.

Ethereum. (2023a). *Blocks.* https://ethereum.org/en/developers/docs/blocks/. Accessed June 21, 2023.

Ethereum. (2023b). *Sharding.* https://ethereum.org/en/upgrades/sharding/. Accessed June 8, 2023.

Euromoney Learning. (2022). *The rise of private blockchains.* https://www.euromoney.com/learning/blockchain-explained/the-rise-of-private-blockchains. Accessed July 9, 2022.

Finneseth, J. (2021). *XinFin (XDC) hits a new ATH after fresh partnerships and exchange listings.* https://cointelegraph.com/news/xinfin-xdc-hits-a-new-ath-after-fresh-partnerships-and-exchange-listings. Accessed October 6, 2021.

Geroni, D. (2021). *Hybrid blockchain: The best of both worlds.* https://101blockchains.com/hybrid-blockchain/. Accessed September 21, 2021.

Github. (2023). *A permissioned implementation of Ethereum supporting data privacy.* https://github.com/ConsenSys/quorum. Accessed November 5, 2023.

Haber, S., & Stornetta, W. S. (1990). How to time-stamp a digital document. In *Conference on the theory and application of cryptography* (pp. 437–455).

Hartmann, T. (2021). *What is Bitcoin memory pool?* Captainaltcoin.Com. https://captainaltcoin.com/bitcoin-memory-pool-mempool/. Accessed December 11, 2021.

Hayes, A. (2021). *Target Hash.* https://www.investopedia.com/terms/t/target-hash.asp. Accessed June 18, 2022.

Hedera. (2023a). *How it works.* https://hedera.com/how-it-works. Accessed October 11, 2023.

Hedera. (2023b). *The open source public ledger.* https://hedera.com/. Accessed June 19, 2023.

Hyperledger. (2019). *Case study: How Walmart brought unprecedented transparency to the food supply chain with Hyperledger Fabric.* https://www.hyperledger.org/wp-content/uploads/2019/02/Hyperledger_CaseStudy_Walmart_Printable_V4.pdf. Accessed June 27, 2022.

Hyperledger. (2022). *Building better together.* https://www.hyperledger.org/. Accessed June 17, 2022.

Hyperledger. (2023). *Hyperledger fabric.* https://www.hyperledger.org/use/fabric. Accessed June 9, 2023.

IBM. (2023). *IBM supply chain intelligence suite: Food Trust.* Supply Chain Intelligence Suite. https://www.ibm.com/products/supply-chain-intelligence-suite/food-trust. Accessed June 16, 2023.

IBM Food Trust. (2019). *About IBM food trust.* www.ibm.com/food. Accessed June 13, 2022.

Investopedia. (2021). *Proof of capacity (Cryptocurrency).* https://www.investopedia.com/terms/p/proof-capacity-cryptocurrency.asp. Accessed June 16, 2022.

Iredale, G. (2021). *The rise of private blockchain technologies.* https://101blockchains.com/private-blockchain/. Accessed June 14, 2022.

Krause, E. (2018, July 5). A fifth of all Bitcoin is missing. These crypto hunters can help. *The Wall Street Journal.*

Krause, M. J., & Tolaymat, T. (2018). Quantification of energy and carbon costs for mining cryptocurrencies. *Nature Sustainability, 1*(11), 711–718.

Kriptomat. (2023). *The most popular blockchain networks.* https://kriptomat.io/blockchain/most-popular-blockchain-networks/. Accessed June 19, 2023.

References

Lemieux, P. (2013). Who is Satoshi Nakamoto? *Regulation, 36*(3), 14–16.

Leonard, C. (2016). Blocking the blockchain. *International Financial Law Review, 35*, 58.

Lim, S. (2022). *Market bottom: Can we trust it? Only if pro-risk momentum is sustained*. I3investor. https://klse.i3investor.com/web/blog/detail/MarketUpdatesataGlance/2022-05-27-story-h1623451612-Market_Bottom_can_we_trust_it_only_if_pro_risk_momentum_is_sustained. Accessed June 21, 2022.

Magazine, B. (2020). *What is the Bitcoin block size limit*. https://bitcoinmagazine.com/guides/what-is-the-bitcoin-block-size-limit. Accessed June 23, 2022.

McGleenon, B. (2022). *How crypto fell to earth in 2022: Eight charts that tell the story of a cruel crash*. https://news.yahoo.com/how-crypto-fell-2022-eight-charts-story-of-cruel-crash-060058350.html. Accessed November 21, 2022.

Miller, R. (2018). *Walmart is betting on the blockchain to improve food safety*. https://techcrunch.com/2018/09/24/walmart-is-betting-on-the-blockchain-to-improve-food-safety/. Accessed June 2, 2022.

Morris, N. (2018). *R3's Corda dominates insurance sector*. https://www.ledgerinsights.com/r3-corda-blockchain-insurance. Accessed June 6, 2022.

Murphy, M. (2020). *Who is buying into IBM's blockchain dreams?* https://www.protocol.com/ibm-blockchain-supply-produce-coffee. Accessed June 23, 2022.

Nakamoto, S. (2008). Re: Bitcoin P2P e-cash paper. *The Cryptography Mailing List*.

Narayanan, A., Bonneau, J., Felten, E., Miller, A., & Goldfeder, S. (2016). *Bitcoin and cryptocurrency technologies: A comprehensive introduction*. Princeton University Press.

Norman, A. T. (2017). *Blockchain technology explained: The ultimate beginner's guide about blockchain wallet, mining, Bitcoin, Ethereum, Litecoin, Zcash, Monero, Ripple, Dash*. CreateSpace Independent Publishing Platform.

Oberhaus, D. (2018). The world's oldest blockchain has been hiding in the New York Times since 1995. *Motherboard: Tech by Vice [Internet]*.

OpenSea. (2023). *What are blockchain forks?* https://opensea.io/learn/blockchain/what-are-blockchain-forks. Accessed January 16, 2024.

Outlook. (2023). *Can Hedera (HBAR), Tron (TRX), and Chronoly.io (CRNO) become market leading tokens?* https://www.outlookindia.com/business-spotlight/can-hedera-hbar-tron-trx-and-chronoly-io-crno-become-market-leading-tokens--news-219286. Accessed June 26, 2023.

Phemex. (2021a). *What is Quorum: A closer look at an enterprise blockchain giant*. https://phemex.com/academy/what-is-quorum-jp-morgan. Accessed July 21, 2022.

Phemex. (2021b). *What is R3 Corda: The finance world's leading enterprise blockchain*. https://phemex.com/academy/what-is-r3-corda. Accessed July 13, 2022.

Pongratz, N., & James, R. (2023). *Bitcoin mining used more electricity than sweden in 2022, says report*. https://beincrypto.com/btc-mining-used-more-electricity-than-sweden/. Accessed June 8, 2023.

R3. (2022). *Token SDK*. https://www.r3.com/wp-content/uploads/2022/09/TokenSDK_Factsheet__R3.July2019.pdf. Accessed June 21, 2022.

R3. (2023). *Digital finance is powered by Corda*. https://www.r3.com/products/corda. Accessed June 29, 2023.

Reiff, N. (2023). *Bitcoin vs. Bitcoin cash: What's the difference?* https://www.investopedia.com/tech/bitcoin-vs-bitcoin-cash-whats-difference. Accessed January 16, 2024.

Saad, S. M. S., & Radzi, R. Z. R. M. (2020). Comparative review of the blockchain consensus algorithm between proof of stake (pos) and delegated proof of stake (dpos). *International Journal of Innovative Computing, 10*(2).

Schmidt, J., & Powell, F. (2022). *Why does Bitcoin use so much energy?* https://www.forbes.com/advisor/investing/cryptocurrency/bitcoins-energy-usage-explained. Accessed June 21, 2023.

Sergeenkov, A. (2022). *Bitcoin mining difficulty: Everything you need to know*. https://www.coindesk.com/learn/bitcoin-mining-difficulty-everything-you-need-to-know/. Accessed June 2, 2023.

Sherman, A. T., Javani, F., Zhang, H., & Golaszewski, E. (2019). On the origins and variations of blockchain technologies. *IEEE Security & Privacy, 17*(1), 72–77.

Statista. (2022). *Ethereum (ETH) price per day from August, 2015 to December, 2022 (in U.S. dollars)*. A snapshot of ETH price history from Statista, https://www.statista.com/statistics/806453/price-of-ethereum/. Accessed December 23, 2022.

Tank, M., Radcliffe, M., & Caires, E. (2021). *Blockchain and digital assets news and trends*. https://www.dlapiper.com/en-us/insights/publications/blockchain-and-digital-assets-news-and-trends/2022/blockchain-and-digital-assets-news-and-trends-may-2021. Accessed June 2, 2022.

Terra. (2023). *About Terra*. https://www.terra.money/about-terra. Accessed June 21, 2023.

Thompson, P. (2018). *The current state of the Bitcoin network and its biggest block*. https://cointelegraph.com/news/the-current-state-of-the-bitcoin-network-and-its-biggest-block. Accessed June 2, 2022.

Wegrzyn, K. E., & Wang, E. (2021). *Types of blockchain: Public, private, or something in between*. https://www.foley.com/en/insights/publications/2021/08/types-of-blockchain-public-private-between. Accessed June 25, 2022.

Wikipedia. (2022a). *Cryptocurrency*. https://en.wikipedia.org/wiki/Cryptocurrency. Accessed June 21, 2022.

Wikipedia. (2022b). *Diffie–Hellman key exchange*. https://en.wikipedia.org/wiki/Diffie-Hellman_key_exchange. Accessed June 22, 2022.

Wikipedia. (2022c). *Ethereum*. https://en.wikipedia.org/wiki/Ethereum. Accessed June 23, 2022.

Wikipedia. (2022d). *Litecoin*. https://en.wikipedia.org/wiki/Litecoin. Accessed October 2, 2022.

Wikipedia. (2022e). *SHA-2*. https://en.wikipedia.org/wiki/SHA-2. Accessed November 21, 2022.

Wikipedia. (2022f). *Stablecoin*. https://en.wikipedia.org/wiki/Stablecoin. Accessed December 1, 2022.

Wikipedia. (2023a). *Bitcoin*. https://en.wikipedia.org/wiki/Bitcoin. Accessed May 2, 2023.

Wikipedia. (2023b). *Cryptocurrency bubble*. https://en.wikipedia.org/wiki/Cryptocurrency_bubble. Accessed March 7, 2023.

Wikipedia. (2023c). *Cryptocurrency wallet*. https://en.wikipedia.org/wiki/Cryptocurrency_wallet. Accessed July 2, 2023.

Wikipedia. (2023d). *Directed acyclic graph*. https://en.wikipedia.org/wiki/Directed_acyclic_graph. Accessed June 21, 2023.

Wikipedia. (2023e). *Hashgraph*. https://en.wikipedia.org/wiki/Hashgraph. Accessed July 6, 2023.

Wikipedia. (2023f). *Man-in-the-middle attack*. https://en.wikipedia.org/wiki/Man-in-the-middle_attack. Accessed August 2, 2023.

Wikipedia. (2023g). *Public-key cryptography*. https://en.wikipedia.org/wiki/Public-key_cryptography. Accessed May 8, 2023.

Wood, L. (2021). *The worldwide blockchain supply chain industry is expected to reach $3+ billion by 2026— ResearchAndMarkets.com*. Business Wire. https://www.businesswire.com/news/home/20210316005759/en/The-Worldwide-Blockchain-Supply-Chain-Industry-is-Expected-to-Reach-3-Billion-by-2026---ResearchAndMarkets.com. Accessed June 1, 2022.

XinFin. (2023a). *Enterprise ready hybrid blockchain for global trade and finance*. https://coinmarketcap.com/community/articles/656f897216787c05ab33051b/. Accessed June 13, 2023.

XinFin. (2023b). *XinFin XDPoS consensus*. https://www.xinfin.org/dpos_tech_brief. Accessed June 22, 2023.

Xinfin. (2023c). *Blockchain data*. https://xinfin.org. Accessed March 27, 2023.

XinFin XDC Network. (2021). *XinFin's XDC network selected as the first blockchain company to join the global trade finance distribution initiative*. CISION. https://www.prnewswire.com/news-releases/xinfins-xdc-network-selected-as-the-first-blockchain-company-to-join-the-global-trade-finance-distribution-initiative-301358050.html. Accessed July 1, 2022.

Blockchains for Supply Chain Finance   15

Learning Objectives:

1. Grasp blockchain's impact on transparency and efficiency in supply chain finance.
2. Discover types of digital tokens in supply chain transactions, like asset-backed tokens and non-fungible tokens (NFTs).
3. Evaluate the pros and cons of Initial Coin Offerings (ICOs) for startup funding and risk mitigation strategies.
4. Identify and understand the challenges associated with implementing blockchain in supply chains, ranging from technological hurdles to human errors.
5. Study successful blockchain applications in supply chain finance and their global trade impacts.

15.1 Introduction

According to a PwC study, the application of blockchains in business has the potential to add $1.76 trillion to global GDP over the next 10 years, representing about 1.4% of the projected global GDP in 2030 (Musharraf, 2020). Notably, in China and the U.S., the GDP increases attributed to blockchains are expected to be $440 billion and $407 billion, respectively (Musharraf, 2020).

Supplementary Information The online version contains supplementary material available at https://doi.org/10.1007/978-3-031-56125-2_15.

When a supply chain incorporates blockchain technology, it does more than just secure transaction data in a decentralized ledger system. The technology also offers the following benefits in terms of visibility, predictability, and controllability:

- *Visibility*: Participation in a blockchain system will digitalize all data within the chain. This facilitates firms to share data with trusted partners, thereby enhancing supply chain visibility for all involved parties.
- *Predictability*: Improved visibility paves the way for more accurate and timely demand forecasting, along with other crucial business metrics.
- *Controllability*: The use of smart contracts allows firms to manage their transactions more efficiently. As a result, they are better positioned to control and optimize their operations.

In this chapter, we will begin our exploration of utilizing blockchains in supply chain management and finance.

15.2 Blockchains in Supply Chain Management and Finance

Since the enactment of the Uniform Electronic Transactions Act (UETA) on June 30, 2000, electronic records and signatures have become increasingly recognized as legally valid in the U.S. (Norman-Eady, 2000). Parallel developments worldwide have laid a robust foundation for facilitating supply chain contracts on blockchains. Owing to the advantages of immutability, smart contracts, the adaptability of hybrid blockchains, and other related applications, many firms have begun to utilize blockchains to manage their supply chain transactions. In this context, a buyer must decide whether to establish a supply chain blockchain for its transactions and to what extent they should invite, or even mandate, their suppliers to join this blockchain. This integration might further be extended to even more upstream suppliers, and the same applies to a competent supplier.

Adopting blockchain in supply chains aims to bolster transparency, fortify the security of transactions, minimize intermediaries—thus reducing transaction costs—and consequently unveil new business opportunities. These positive effects can also escalate productivity, enhance supply chain efficiency, cut operational costs, and promote supply chain sustainability. Given these advantages, along with growing government initiatives, it has been projected that the market size for blockchain in supply chain management will soar from $253 million in 2020 to $3272 million in 2026, marking a compound annual growth rate (CAGR) of 53.2% (Wood, 2021).

Beyond the perks attributed to the Bitcoin blockchain—like security, transparency, efficiency, and cost-effectiveness—there are additional advantages to implementing blockchains in supply chain finance. This is especially the case when considering blockchains that might be more efficient than Bitcoin. Subsequently, we will delve into some of these benefits, including supply chain visibility, know-your-customer (KYC) protocols, accounting and auditing processes, and the implementation of smart contracts.

15.2.1 Supply Chain Visibility

Supply chain visibility is an essential precursor to achieving supply chain digitalization and establishing intelligent ecosystems. Presently, many supply chain and logistics networks are outdated, lacking in visibility, riddled with blind spots, and burdened by cumbersome processes—such as tedious manual documentation for supply chain transactions. Owing to budget constraints, numerous firms, especially small and medium-sized enterprises (SMEs), do not have adequate capital to digitalize their supply chains. This absence of supply chain visibility prevents firms from being agile, pinpointing issues, enhancing their individual performance, and optimizing the overall efficiency of the supply chain.

15.2.1.1 Impact of Blockchains on Supply Chain Visibility

With the evolving landscape of private, consortium, and hybrid blockchains, firms—particularly small businesses—have opportunities to integrate into private, consortium, or hybrid blockchain platforms. Heightened supply chain competition coupled with soaring costs in inventory and logistics render blockchain technology especially attractive. Engaging with a blockchain platform enables these businesses to gain comprehensive visibility into logistics systems, inventory, warehouses, distribution of goods, and invoicing processes.

One standout feature of blockchain technology is its immutability, which bestows a heightened level of trust and security upon the data stored within blockchains. Although blockchains cannot prevent the intake of erroneous documents, their immutable nature discourages firms from altering data or fabricating documents post-agreement. When affiliated firms opt to share specifics, like the whereabouts of shipments, they benefit from improved visibility and can track the real-time status of the entire supply chain. Concurrently, blockchain platforms can safeguard the confidentiality of any information earmarked as private by firms.

Enhanced supply chain visibility offers real-time insights into inventory levels, warehouse statuses, shipments, invoices, and demand trends. Such a visibility boost can result in more accurate demand forecasting and other critical business metrics, such as cost, revenue, and profit calculations. Additionally, it can promote better production planning, cost-effective inventory management, increased warehouse turnover rates, and overall, a more profitable supply chain.

Leveraging smart contracts, firms can substantially reduce manual processes and facilitate automated transactions and payments more swiftly, thereby benefiting the cash flow of all involved parties. For instance, it traditionally takes weeks for supply chain firms and their overseas banks to process bills of lading. However, with the aid of blockchain platforms, like the TradeLens platform co-developed by

Maersk and IBM, the processing time for the same bill of lading can be slashed to mere days, thanks to the increased visibility of the documentation process (Tradelens, 2023). It's worth noting that this expedited process can face delays if one or more stakeholders decline to integrate into a particular blockchain.

> **Case Study**
>
> ***Blockchain for Diamond***
>
> Brilliant Earth is a company that specializes in ethically sourced jewelry, including diamonds and other gemstones (Brilliant Earth, 2023). The company is committed to ensuring that each diamond's cut, color, clarity, and carat align with their specifications, and that every diamond they sell is ethically sourced. Cowen analyst Oliver Chen notes, "Consumer sentiment, particularly among younger generations, is rapidly gravitating towards jewelers that boast transparent and socially responsible supply chains" (Escobar, 2022). To fulfill this consumer demand, Brilliant Earth turned to blockchain technology to instill transparency into its diamond supply chain.
>
> In 2018, Brilliant Earth began a collaboration with Everledger to devise a blockchain tracking system for diamonds (Brilliant Earth, 2023). Starting from May 2019, diamonds have been traceable on the Everledger blockchain. This allows consumers to track a diamond's journey—right from the mine it originated from, through every phase of the supply chain, and finally to their homes.
>
>
>
> *Source* Images courtesy of BrilliantEarth.com

15.2.1.2 Blockchain Oracle for Data Visibility

Several significant obstacles in achieving supply chain visibility through blockchains include the restricted capacity of a decentralized blockchain and the diverse data structures utilized between decentralized blockchains and traditional centralized information systems. As both decentralized blockchains and centralized systems coexist, the need arises to bridge these two distinct systems. This can be achieved by establishing interfaces capable of decoding a wide range of

15.2 Blockchains in Supply Chain Management and Finance

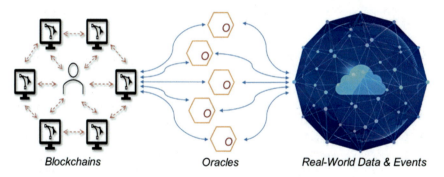

Fig. 15.1 Oracles bridging blockchains with real-world scenarios

data structures and seamlessly transferring information between these systems. The blockchain oracle has thus emerged as an instrumental tool in facilitating communication between decentralized blockchains and the external environment.

When integrating blockchains with external systems, a primary function of blockchain oracles is to empower the blockchain to execute smart contracts based on external inputs or to operationalize blockchain smart contracts in the real world (refer to Fig. 15.1). Consequently, blockchain oracles enable decentralized Web3 ecosystems to interface with prevailing legacy systems and diverse data sources (Chainlink, 2021). Blockchain oracles can either be on-chain (within the blockchain) or off-chain (external to the blockchain). These on-chain and off-chain infrastructures collaboratively underpin decentralized oracle networks (DONs) and decentralized applications (dApps). These platforms facilitate users in crafting hybrid smart contracts and in linking internal blockchain smart contracts with external real-world events (Chainlink, 2021).

Within blockchains, numerous smart contracts, like those in decentralized finance (DeFi) systems, necessitate data from the real world. Examples of such data include financial asset prices, users' credit histories, gaming randomness, ID information for verification, weather updates, insurance details, and IoT sensors for the supply chain, among others. This data, which comes in various formats, can be transmitted from off-chain oracles to on-chain oracles, and subsequently to the smart contracts within blockchains. This procedure permits blockchains to access external data while maintaining their inherent security features. Given the immutable nature of blockchains, it's vital for oracles to be decentralized as well, ensuring the precision of the data entered into blockchains.

Based on their distinct functionalities, blockchain oracles can be segmented into the following categories (Chainlink, 2021):

- *Input Oracles*: These oracles transmit data, like asset prices needed by smart contracts, from the real world to a blockchain.
- *Output Oracles*: These oracles empower smart contracts to initiate events in off-chain systems in the tangible world, examples being bank transactions or signaling an IoT system to switch off a garage light.
- *Cross-Chain Oracles*: These oracles retrieve data and activate smart contract events across different blockchains.
- *Compute-Enabled Oracles*: These oracles offer decentralized off-chain computational services, which may be unfeasible to perform on-chain due to technical, financial, or legal limitations.

Based on the interfaces of oracles, they can be further categorized into the following types (Mou, 2021):

- *Software Oracles*: These oracles convey information from software applications and online sources to blockchains.
- *Hardware Oracles*: These oracles assist smart contracts in gathering information from physical devices, including barcode scanners, Bluetooth devices, electronic sensors, and other data collection devices.
- *Human Oracles*: Knowledgeable human experts can act as oracles, relaying information directly to smart contracts.

15.2.2 Know-Your-Customer

Know-your-customer (KYC) procedures have long been laborious and time-intensive for financial institutions. When a new client opens an account, institutions are mandated to verify the client's identity. This is a regulatory requirement aimed at conducting due diligence, reducing investment risks, and preventing misuse of services by clients. However, the conventional KYC processes come with several challenges:

- *Duplication*: Much of the KYC information is repetitive across different institutions' systems.
- *Isolation*: While each institution might maintain its own transaction history with the same customer, this segregated view hampers a comprehensive understanding of the customer's risk profile.
- *Inefficiency*: The bulk of traditional KYC procedures are manual, making them protracted and cumbersome.

Implementing KYC procedures on blockchains can offer a solution to these issues. By doing so, the organizations and institutions involved can expedite the customer onboarding process. This not only ensures better compliance outcomes but also enhances supply chain efficiency and elevates the overall customer experience.

To ensure that the KYC profile on blockchains is beneficial and reusable across institutions, a comprehensive KYC standard procedure must be established and mutually agreed upon by all participating parties. KYC procedures can be categorized into different levels, as follows (Binance, 2021):

1. *Customer Identification Program (CIP)*: The CIP involves collecting and verifying a customer's data. This is typically necessary after a customer enrolls or registers for a service.
2. *Customer Due Diligence (CDD)*: This step may require a background check on the customer to further assess potential risks associated with them.
3. *Customer Ongoing Monitoring (COM)*: The COM entails updating any pertinent KYC information and closely monitoring ongoing transactions, with particular emphasis on suspicious activities (e.g., several large transactions in quick succession).

Every party can actively participate in and oversee the KYC process. Once an institution inputs a customer's KYC profile onto the blockchain, other institutions can request an information exchange transaction. Should there be any updates to the KYC profile, all institutions are alerted.

However, there are nuanced challenges to consider. As appealing as a decentralized, trusted KYC system might be, customers might be reticent to provide their comprehensive details to a system that is universally accessible. Furthermore, certain institutions, like banks, might still opt for their own due diligence. This could potentially diminish the overall efficacy of a blockchain-backed KYC system.

15.2.3 Accounting and Auditing

Blockchains function as distributed accounting systems. Given their unique attributes, blockchain technology has the potential to revolutionize all recordkeeping procedures, from the initiation and processing of transactions to their authorization, recording, and reporting. Since recordkeeping is simultaneous with transaction settlement, auditing can be performed in a real-time and more uniform manner.

However, apprehensions related to accounting fraud and auditing oversight come to the fore. As transactions and payments are documented on blockchains, they maintain all pertinent accounting data. Engaging with a blockchain can dissuade firms from manipulating accounting ledgers for tax evasion purposes. However, some companies might resist joining blockchains, especially in jurisdictions lacking robust auditing capabilities. They might only be inclined if the advantages offset potential taxes that could be avoided using a dual-accounting scheme.

The Dual-Accounting Dilemma:

a) If truthful, more tax; b) If untruthful, no loan.

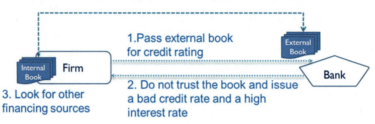

Fig. 15.2 The dual-accounting dilemma

15.2.3.1 The Dual-Accounting Dilemma

The immutability feature of blockchains can help address the *dual-accounting dilemma* faced in certain jurisdictions. This dilemma arises when companies maintain two distinct sets of accounting ledgers and financial records to evade taxes (refer to Fig. 15.2). Essentially, by having two ledgers, companies can conceal assets and cash flows to minimize their taxable income.

For supply chain finance to fully leverage the risk mitigation and sharing feature, a trustworthy culture and environment are indispensable. Employing dual-accounting ledgers for personal gain undermines trust in a firm.

Auditing plays a pivotal role in bolstering public confidence in an organization's disclosed accounting details. Given the unchangeable nature of data stored on blockchains, the technology can considerably diminish the role of auditors in validating this information. Moreover, since blockchains operate online and numerous tasks—like data gathering, reconciliation of accounting data, and data analysis—can be automated, many laborious and time-intensive manual processes associated with data extraction and audit preparation can be substantially reduced.

According to a 2016 survey of financial and IT auditors, 94% of respondents foresaw a significant impact of blockchains on their professions (Brender & Gauthier, 2018). As an increasing number of organizations adopt blockchain technology, the demand for auditors may decrease, and the auditing process can be streamlined and expedited.

15.2.3.2 Proof of Reserve

Given that business adoption of blockchains is still in its infancy and lacks a standardized approach, auditing blockchains becomes increasingly complex and necessitates specialized technology-based expertise.

An illustration of blockchain auditing is the *Proof of Reserve* (PoR) process, which verifies that a company or service provider holds the reserves it claims (Chainlink, 2022). Traditionally, this would require the intervention of a centralized auditor. However, with blockchain, the business's assets and reserves may already be meticulously recorded on the chain, allowing for automated audits via smart contracts and blockchain oracles.

> **Case Study**
>
> ***Chainlink Proof of Reserve (PoR)***
>
> Chainlink, a decentralized blockchain oracle network based on Ethereum, is designed to connect blockchains with off-chain real-world data sources. It ensures the provision of tamper-proof data from off-chain sources to on-chain smart contracts and vice versa (Chainlink, 2022). The proof of reserve is among Chainlink's services that employ smart contracts to assess on-chain assets backed by off-chain or cross-chain reserves.
>
> Using its decentralized oracles, Chainlink's PoR offers real-time autonomous audits of collateral to shield users' funds from fraudulent actions perpetrated by off-chain custodians. Instead of depending on paper guarantees from custodians, this automated, real-time on-chain audit presents a more robust assurance rooted in tangible assets and offers enhanced transparency for asset collateralization. Chainlink's PoR can be deployed to authenticate the minting and burning of wrapped tokens, as well as cross-chain assets like tokenized Bitcoin and fiat-backed stablecoins, and even assets in the conventional markets (Chainlink, 2022).

15.2.3.3 The Future of Auditing

Despite the advantages they offer in auditing, blockchains cannot completely replace auditors. An audit encompasses the collection of pertinent information and the evaluation of its relevance, accuracy, objectivity, reliability, and verifiability (Bible et al., 2017). While blockchains ensure the immutability of records, they cannot vouch for the accuracy of all transaction details. Therefore, additional scrutiny is essential to determine the legitimacy of a transaction, the involvement of multiple parties, and the possibility of off-chain payments.

Moreover, the advent of blockchains introduces new dimensions to the auditing process. For instance, the content of smart contracts may require auditing to ensure their alignment with business agreements and legal standards. Private and consortium blockchains need rigorous evaluation to uncover potential risks to users, understand the operational modalities of the blockchain, and prevent any misuse of authority by privileged entities within the blockchain system. Furthermore, given the confidentiality associated with cryptocurrencies and the pervasive nature of blockchains, the task of verifying "hidden" digital assets becomes increasingly intricate.

15.2.4 Smart Contract

Smart contracts play a pivotal role in supply chain transactions. Several blockchains, such as Ethereum, advocate the use of smart contracts as a decentralized financing solution. A smart contract is a transaction protocol that is computer-programmed, allowing transactions to be automatically executed once specific predetermined conditions are met (Szabo, 1997). Szabo, the originator of the term, likened a smart contract to a vending machine that fulfills the "contract" (i.e., dispenses the designated item) once the required condition (e.g., the correct amount of money) is satisfied.

The benefits of smart contracts encompass:

- Digitization of documentation.
- Ability to automatically complete transactions swiftly.
- Prevention of fraud through the smart contract, which enforces the pre-committed agreement upon detection of fraud (Gulker, 2017).
- Universal access for all parties within the blockchain.

The process for creating a smart contract typically follows these steps (Wang & Wegrzyn, 2022):

1. Define the objective of the smart contract.
2. Establish the conditions that trigger execution. A smart contract should unequivocally stipulate the terms and conditions that instigate an event.
3. Detail the resulting action when the predetermined conditions are met.
4. Encode the predetermined conditions and resultant actions into the blockchain.
5. Upon deployment of the smart contract, all resultant actions are recorded onto the blockchain.

Certain experts contend that a smart contract is not always a legally binding agreement but rather an accord between entities to ensure that payment obligations are met (Wikipedia, 2022d). Due to the close association of smart contracts with blockchains, they are often regarded as secure programmed procedures stored on blockchains, executable and overseen by the respective blockchain platforms. Notwithstanding, with the growing adoption of smart contracts, Belarus legally recognized smart contracts in its 2016 "Decree on the Development of the Digital Economy." Since 2018, an increasing number of U.S. states have enacted legislation endorsing the utilization of smart contracts (Wikipedia, 2022d).

15.2.4.1 Application of Smart Contracts
Within the realms of supply chain management and finance, smart contracts can facilitate the following:

- ***Documentation***
    - Recording shipment statuses.
    - Documenting delivery timings and product transfers.
    - Generating receipts for goods and services.
    - Crafting invoices.

- *Alerts*
  - Notifying about environmental fluctuations, such as changes in temperature or humidity inside containers and warehouses.
  - Alerting regarding market shifts, including price variations.
  - Signaling changes in inventory levels.
  - Prompting when specific transaction criteria are met.
- *Transaction Automation*
  - Executing a supply chain transaction upon the occurrence of predetermined events.
  - Initiating orders once inventory replenishment criteria are satisfied.
  - Processing financial transactions (e.g., bills of lading) sequentially in accordance with a pre-established procedure.
- *Payment Automation*
  - Facilitating automatic payment transfers between parties, such as from a buyer to a seller.

The execution of a smart contract can encompass all of the aforementioned aspects. For instance, a seller and a buyer (possibly alongside other third parties) might establish a smart contract. Through this contract, the buyer can facilitate payment to the seller using their digital wallets. After all participating parties consent to the terms of the smart contract, the seller proceeds to deliver the goods or services to the buyer. Upon inspection and acceptance of the delivery by the buyer, the smart contract automatically triggers, resulting in the designated payment amount transferring from the buyer's digital wallet to that of the seller. Throughout this process, IoT-enabled devices or sensors record various transactional statuses, such as shipment and delivery statuses, as well as ledger entries, onto the blockchain. The smart contract can also issue alerts to relevant stakeholders if unexpected events occur, like if the temperature deviates from a specified range. This allows for issues to be addressed autonomously without the immediate intervention of humans.

Moreover, smart contracts are versatile and have numerous other applications. They can be employed for inheritance disbursement upon the registration of a death certificate. Real estate transactions, as well as employment contracts—particularly those of a temporary nature—can be orchestrated and executed once their respective conditions are satisfied.

Case Study

Tracing the Journey of Your Cup of Tea

Unilever annually purchases approximately 10% of the global black tea supply from various countries, including China, Australia, and Kenya (Unilever, 2019). This translates to nearly 143 billion servings per year for consumers worldwide. Black and green tea combined account for 90% of Unilever's tea market, making the tracing of tea origins essential to ensure quality and safety for both Unilever and its consumers.

To authenticate the environmental and social credentials, as well as the authenticity of tea sources, Unilever collaborated with Provenance. Provenance has crafted a platform that utilizes smart contracts on the Ethereum blockchain to monitor the movement and origins of products throughout the supply chain. In May 2016, Provenance employed this blockchain technology to trace a tuna fish from its capture in Indonesia (the world's largest tuna producer) throughout its entire logistics journey, all the way to the consumer, ensuring the tuna was sustainably and ethically sourced (Provenance, 2016).

This system functions by bestowing unique digital identities upon products. These identities are then logged onto the blockchain at every stage of the supply chain. This method facilitates real-time tracking and authentication of a product's trajectory from its source to the end consumer. Through the use of smart contracts, the platform can instantly validate and carry out supply chain-related commitments, such as ownership transfers or goods payments. For instance, a smart contract can be designed to initiate a payment to a supplier once a shipment's receipt is verified by the purchasing company. This not only streamlines the payment procedure but also diminishes fraud risks, as payments are only executed once the stipulated conditions are satisfied.

Hence, smart contracts serve to automate supply chain management processes and enhance transparency and trust between businesses and consumers.

Questions

1. What capabilities do smart contracts offer?
2. How do smart contracts benefit supply chains and supply chain finance?

15.2.4.2 Issues of Using Smart Contracts

While smart contracts offer efficiency, they are not immune to bugs or other technical issues. Consequently, damages might occur before they are detected. Wang and Wegrzyn (2022) identified three common types of improperly coded smart contracts that can lead to serious problems:

- *Greedy Contract*: This is a smart contract that indefinitely locks funds. It typically arises when fund release instructions are not accurately coded.
- *Prodigal Contract*: This occurs when the parameters of a smart contract aren't correctly set, causing funds to be inadvertently leaked to random users.
- *Suicidal Contract*: Here, parameters of a smart contract are poorly coded, enabling the potential destruction of the contract itself.

Given that a smart contract must be precisely written, problems can surface if the original agreements between parties aren't accurately interpreted and subsequently coded into the smart contract. Moreover, due to the immutable nature of smart contracts once they're added to the blockchain, rectifying errors becomes a technical hurdle. Thus, the code should undergo thorough verification by all stakeholders to ensure that the smart contract consistently serves its intended purpose.

15.3 Digital Tokens

Digital tokens can also function as a payment medium in supply chain transactions. However, unlike traditional currencies, tokens typically do not possess inherent value and cannot be universally utilized in the same way as currencies. That said, tokens can be purchased and subsequently resold. This is because they may symbolize physical commodities or digital assets, acting as a digital representation of tangible assets. The realm of digital token economics has witnessed rapid expansion over recent years. As per the World Economic Forum's 2015 report, the total market volume of tokenized assets is anticipated to surge to $24 trillion by 2027, which would account for approximately 10% of global GDP (micobo GmbH, 2019).

There are four primary categories of tokens: native tokens, asset-backed tokens, non-fungible tokens, and utility tokens. Each of these is discussed in the sequence below.

15.3.1 Native Token

Native tokens, also known as intrinsic tokens, refer to those tokens that exist within a specific blockchain and are utilized to incentivize individuals to participate in the blockchain's transactions. Examples include Bitcoin in the Bitcoin blockchain and Ether (ETH) in the Ethereum blockchain. Both Bitcoin and ETH incentivize miners to validate transactions and construct blocks in the blockchain, as detailed in Chapter 14.

The value of these tokens emerges when the utility of the blockchains is acknowledged beyond their own networks. For instance, Bitcoins can be exchanged for tangible goods such as pizzas and cars. Presently, these native tokens function not only as payment instruments within their respective blockchains, similar to how fiat currencies operate in traditional markets, but they can also be traded for fiat currencies. As a result, these particular native tokens are often referred to as "cryptocurrencies," as previously mentioned, while tokens that aren't native continue to be termed simply as "tokens."

15.3.2 Asset-Backed Token

An *asset-backed token*, also known as an asset representation token, represents a stake, and thus ownership, in a physical asset such as corporate stocks, gold, oil, real estate, vehicles, or external enterprises (Schweifer, 2022). Therefore, the value of an asset-backed token is derived from an underlying physical asset that does not exist on the blockchain. This token can be viewed as a digital contract that represents a percentage of ownership in a valuable physical asset and can be stored on a blockchain.

Both companies and governments can issue these asset-based tokens, which serve purposes similar to securities like corporate stocks or bonds for investors. Being technically categorized as a security, an asset-backed token must comply with federal rules and regulations related to securities (micobo GmbH, 2019).

Leveraging blockchain technology, security tokens possess advantages like transparency, immutability, and transaction efficiency. The tokenization process is secure and compliant with predetermined rules. It also offers operational efficiency and cost-effectiveness (i.e., low transaction costs) (Milev, 2018).

In comparison to traditional contracts for physical assets, such as art or real estate, security tokens provide the added benefit of divisibility and fractional ownership. Here, a physical asset can be represented by numerous security tokens. For instance, a piece of commercial real estate (like an office space in San Francisco) valued at $50 million could be tokenized into 500 pieces and sold to investors for $100,000 per token. As illustrated in Fig. 15.3, the digitalized asset is first securitized into smaller pieces, then tokenized, and finally traded in the secondary market. This price point of $100,000 per token makes it more accessible and appealing to a broader range of investors, compared to purchasing the entire real estate outright. This fractional ownership feature enhances the liquidity of traditionally illiquid assets like real estate, thus unlocking vast amounts of capital that were previously tied up in such assets (micobo GmbH, 2019).

15.3.2.1 Types of Asset-Backed Tokens

The interpretation of asset-backed tokens isn't unanimous. In this book, we align with the prevailing interpretation found on websites, which equates asset-based tokens to security tokens. In the U.S., a "security is a tradable financial asset of

Fig. 15.3 Tokenized asset and fractional ownership

15.3 Digital Tokens

any kind" (Wikipedia, 2022c). On exchanges, securities can manifest as equity securities (e.g., corporate stocks), debt securities (e.g., bonds and banknotes), and derivatives. Given this, asset-backed tokens might actually encompass a broader scope than just security tokens. Generally speaking, security tokens can be associated with real estate, commodities, capital markets, equities, accounts payable and receivable, intellectual property, etc. (Hill, 2019). For clarity, we will define the assets in asset-backed tokens as tradable financial assets, implying that they're synonymous with security tokens. The two terms are used interchangeably in this context.

Below, we enumerate some illustrative subcategories of security tokens:

- *Equity Token*: These tokens mirror the value of shares issued by a company, akin to traditional corporate stocks.
- *Dividend Token*: Holders of these tokens are eligible for a share of the issuing company's profits.
- *Debt Token*: Debt tokens signify the debt owed by the holder, with accruing interest. Depending on whether the interest rate is fixed or variable, debt tokens can be further subdivided into stable debt tokens and variable debt tokens.
- *Commodity Token*: Tangible commodities such as gold, oil, wheat, and gas can be tokenized. However, thorough verification of these commodities is essential for transaction security. The custody of commodities might overlap with the subsequent depository receipt token.
- *Depository Receipt Token*: These tokens symbolize ownership of an underlying asset held in trust by a custodian (Lewis, 2018). For instance, a depository receipt token might represent a bank's receipt for gold stored in its vault. By presenting this token (i.e., a representation of the depository receipt), the holder can claim the gold from the bank.
- *Title Token*: Tokens of this kind serve as proofs of ownership (titles) for tangible assets like vehicles or real estate. An example is the commercial real estate (like an office space in San Francisco) valued at $60 million, tokenized into 600 units at $100,000 each. Each unit represents a partial title of the commercial real estate.
- *Contract Token*: Created upon mutual agreement between two parties concerning underlying assets. As an example, two entities might concur on an interest rate swap represented by a contract token.
- *Currency Token*: These tokens function as payment mediums akin to fiat currencies. They operate similarly to Bitcoin and other cryptocurrencies (Milev, 2018). Stablecoins can be perceived as a unique variant of stable asset-backed currency tokens.

15.3.2.2 Security Token Offerings

A *security token offering* (STO), sometimes referred to as a digital security offering (DSO), is a tokenized version of an initial public offering (IPO). Since asset-backed tokens are digital representations of physical assets, they inherently possess monetary value and symbolize ownership over said assets. These security tokens can be traded on cryptocurrency exchanges and are recorded on blockchain platforms. STOs are deemed more secure than initial coin offerings (ICOs, which are discussed in Chapter 15.4) because they adhere to regulations pertaining to securities (Wikipedia, 2023).

> **Case Study**
>
> ***Blockstream Bitcoin Mining STO***
>
> Blockstream is a blockchain technology company offering the Blockstream Mining Note (BMN) security token to investors keen on Bitcoin mining. This is achieved by simply acquiring BMN tokens, which correlate with a specific hash rate (Blockstream, 2023). As Partz (2021) elaborates, "Issued on the Liquid sidechain of Bitcoin, each BMN Series 1 entitles investors to up to 2000 terahashes per second of Bitcoin mined at Blockstream's enterprise-grade mining facilities." Over the course of six tranches of STO on Bitfinex Securities—a regulated STO platform in Kazakhstan (with the sixth tranche announced in July 2021)—Blockstream amassed €30.9 million (equivalent to $36 million) by vending its BMN security token. These BMN tokens are tradable, and upon maturity after a three-year term, the token holders receive the associated Bitcoin earnings (Partz, 2021).

STOs offer the following advantages (Cointelegraph, 2022b):

- **Cost Effectiveness**: STOs are more cost-effective compared to IPOs. Utilizing blockchain can eliminate the traditional paperwork associated with IPOs, and transactions can be significantly accelerated using smart contracts.
- **Security**: When compared to ICOs, STOs are perceived as more secure. This is because they adhere to regulations concerning securities, which are often bypassed in ICOs.
- **Investment Opportunity**: STOs offer investors greater investment opportunities, liquidity (such as crypto fractionalization), and convenience (like extended trading hours, available 24/7) compared to traditional financial markets.

STOs also have their own disadvantages (Cointelegraph, 2022b):

- **Regulation**: Regulatory adherence can be challenging for STO platforms. They are required to comply with securities laws as well as regulations governing blockchain technology—a nascent technology that is facing increasing scrutiny. Regulatory constraints might also limit the investor pool, both in numbers and in terms of residency.

- **Wallet Security**: It's imperative for investors to ensure the security of their wallet addresses. Failing to do so could result in a total loss of the investments stored in their wallets.

15.3.3 Non-Fungible Token

A *non-fungible token* (NFT) is a unique digital identifier that represents digital or non-digital assets, such as digital art (e.g., music, videos, digital pictures), real-world items (e.g., deeds of cars, invoices, e-tickets, legal documents), and many others. An NFT cannot be copied, substituted, or subdivided due to its uniqueness in identifying its corresponding assets. This is distinct from cryptocurrencies and some asset-backed tokens, which are fungible (Wikipedia, 2022b).

There is an overlap between asset-backed tokens and NFTs since both can represent assets. However, asset-backed tokens are not necessarily unique, while every NFT is. Each NFT has only one owner, and this ownership can be easily verified.

NFTs are minted through smart contracts on a blockchain network that manages ownership transfer. The ownership of an NFT must be unique and is managed through smart contracts, ensuring it cannot be duplicated (Hedera, 2022). When a person creates an NFT, they are the creator and can decide how to distribute it and how many replicas to sell. They can control its scarcity. Through smart contracts, they can choose to earn royalties every time the NFT is sold or transfer full ownership at a higher price without intermediaries.

Proponents claim NFTs empower content creators, giving them greater control over their work. However, disputes about NFT values persist. Supporters argue that NFTs offer proof of ownership or a certificate of authenticity, while detractors point out that copyright, intellectual property rights, or other legal rights are not inherently granted by NFTs (Wikipedia, 2022b). If an NFT owner also receives copyright, it must be explicitly stated.

The first NFT, "Quantum," was created in May 2014, and the first NFT project, "Etheria," was launched in October 2015 (TechGuy, 2021). The NFT market surged from 2020 to 2021, growing 210-fold from $82 million in 2020 to $17 billion in 2021 (Wikipedia, 2022b). Yet, by May 2022, daily NFT sales had plummeted by 92% compared to September 2021 (Vigna, 2022). This thus demonstrates that the future of NFTs remains uncertain.

Various blockchain networks have adopted different standards for NFTs. ERC-721, first introduced by Ethereum, is the most widely used standard. It is based on the Solidity smart contract and can track the owner of a unique identifier, facilitating a permitted transfer from one owner to another (Graves et al., 2022).

15.3.3.1 Application and Benefits of NFTs in Supply Chain

NFTs have potential applications in supply chains, notably for traceability, product authentication, and product certification (Wang & Wegrzyn, 2022).

Traceability: Visibility of the Product Flow

Given that NFTs can serve as digital representations of physical goods, they offer a unique way to trace product flow in supply chains, thereby creating a concurrent information flow about the product. For instance, in package tracking, NFTs can document ownership transfers and every phase of the delivery, helping prevent package losses. Similar traceability systems can be designed for packaged materials, luxury items, and high-value materials.

Product Authentication

NFTs present a robust authentication method to monitor the origin of products. By establishing a digital representation of items upon their creation and during ownership transfers, the origin and subsequent chain of custody become transparent. A notable example is the luxury watch brand Breitling, which introduced an NFT digital passport (essentially a digital twin) for each of its physical watches. This allows customers to use the digital passport to authenticate their watch when reselling it (Breitling, 2020). Furthermore, this digital passport can facilitate warranty and insurance programs (Girod, 2021).

Product Certification

Product certification, which helps classify product quality and characteristics (e.g., "organic" for food products), can greatly influence a product's marketability, potentially boosting sales. The immutable nature of blockchains can enhance consumer confidence by providing trustworthy product certificates. When a product earns a certification, the certifying authority (often a third-party entity) can mint an NFT corresponding to that product on a blockchain. This allows all stakeholders to verify the certification through the blockchain network at any time and from anywhere.

15.3.3.2 Other Applications of NFTs

The successful use of NFTs in digital art, games, music, films, and other areas is evident, even though the markets remain highly volatile. Given their potential link to supply chain finance, it's worth noting the emerging concepts of NFT-backed loans and fractional ownership.

NFT-Backed Loan

NFT can serve as collateral for borrowing from financial institutions. For instance, within the DeFi system, one could use some NFTs as collateral to borrow a specific amount (e.g., $10,000) in stablecoins or cryptocurrency.

Fractional Ownership

Unlike tangible items that can't be divided, NFT creators can segment their NFT into multiple "shares." This allows an investor to buy only a fraction of the asset the NFT represents, rather than the entire asset. For instance, an NFT creator might issue 100 shares for an NFT symbolizing a property in San Francisco, USA. This would enable an investor to purchase just 1/100th of that property.

15.3 Digital Tokens

Table 15.1 Top NFT marketplaces on January 3, 2023 (one-day snapshot)

#	Market	Avg. Price	Traders	Volume
1	**OpenSea**	$67.53	37,375	$12.76 M
	ETH, Polygon, Avalanche, …	9.92%	−12.11%	−16.06%
2	**Blur**	$717.28	5476	$7.22 M
	ETH	35.39%	−15.06%	−1.73%
3	**Magic Eden**	$92.98	17,948	$4.33 M
	Solana	15.49%	−11.85%	−7.44%
4	**X2Y2**	$807.75	2717	$3.29 M
	ETH	18.10%	20.05%	32.39%
5	**LooksRare**	$2.94 k	398	$1.08 M
	ETH	−39.86%	20.23%	−37.84%
6	**Immutable X Marketplace**	$27.32	3767	$429.04 k
	Immutable X	12.93%	12.11%	14.68%
7	**CryptoPunks**	$84.7 k	3	$169.41 k
	ETH	−15.78%	−78.56%	−83.16%
8	**Decentraland**	$22.58 k	49	$135.57 k
	ETH, Polygon	1369.80%	4.54%	1369.80%
9	**ThetaDrop**	$533.64	147	$104.06 k
	Theta	−13.57%	31.25%	28.66%
10	**NBA Top Shot**	$17.02	2823	$100.91 k
	Flow	34.10%	43.81%	115.72%

Source https://dappradar.com/nft/marketplaces

15.3.3.3 NFT Marketplaces

Tables 15.1 and 15.2 display the top NFT marketplaces on January 3, 2023, and the all-time leading NFT marketplaces up to that date, respectively.

15.3.3.4 Challenges of NFTs

Even though NFTs have grown in prominence in recent years, they face several challenges:

- *Compliance Challenge*: NFTs serve as digital representations of assets being transferred, but they don't contain the physical items or even the digital assets themselves.[1] Consequently, the terms and conditions for purchasing NFTs must be explicitly stated to avoid ambiguity and potential disputes concerning the assets. For example, if the NFT is linked to a physical good

---

[1] Due to the large sizes of digital assets, off-chain storage issues are common across all blockchains. Some techniques, like the InterPlanetary File System (IPFS), are used to address the storage of files referenced in NFTs.

Table 15.2 All-time leading NFT marketplaces as of January 3, 2023 (one-day snapshot)

#	Market	Avg. Price	Traders	Volume
1	**OpenSea**	$260.82	2,547,020	$33.88 B
	ETH, Polygon, Avalanche, …			
2	**Axie Marketplace**	$169.14	2,179,967	$4.26 B
	ETH, Ronin			
3	**CryptoPunks**	$131.44 k	7376	$3 B
	ETH			
4	**Magic Eden**	$121.13	1,400,567	$2 B
	Solana			
5	**LooksRare**	$5.91 k	125,050	$1.67 B
	ETH			
6	**X2Y2**	$600.66	180,956	$1 B
	ETH			
7	**NBA Top Shot**	$47.60	570,497	$978.28 M
	Flow			
8	**Mobox**	$509.75	88,195	$699.08 M
	BNB Chain			
9	**Solanart**	$893.17	245,260	$665.86 M
	Solana			
10	**BloctoBay**	$147.32	147,374	$462.02 M
	Flow			

Source https://dappradar.com/nft/marketplaces

that requires shipping to the new owner, there should be comprehensive agreements addressing warranties, delivery terms, return policies, rights, and responsibilities. Similarly, if the asset is intellectual property, the specific rights being transferred must be clearly articulated in the agreement.

- *Transaction Fees*: Conducting NFT transactions on blockchain platforms isn't free. Therefore, unless the NFT sells at a sufficiently high price, the seller's profit might be marginal after accounting for these fees.
- *Fraud and Plagiarism*: Given the complexities surrounding copyright and the temptation of easy profits, there have been instances where individuals have sold artworks and assets, which don't belong to them, in the form of NFTs.
- *Ponzi Schemes*: Some NFT buyers have been known to resell the same digital assets to others at higher prices, aiming for excessive profits.
- *Scams*: Some NFTs are listed at exorbitant prices without any justifiable reason, misleading potential buyers.
- *Security Concerns*: There's a risk that sellers might misuse buyers' IP addresses for purposes unrelated to the NFT transactions.

15.3.4 Utility Tokens

A *utility token* grants holder the right to use a specific product and/or service. The issuers bear the responsibility of providing the product/service to the token holder, who can redeem the product/service when available. Unlike asset-backed tokens, utility tokens are not tied to tradable assets in the same way asset-backed tokens are.

15.4 Initial Coin Offering

An *initial coin offering* (ICO) involves a company offering its new crypto tokens to investors in exchange for funding. These tokens may be tied to the company's assets and/or serve as a utility for certain products and services the company offers. If ICOs are classified as securities, they typically need to be registered or meet an exemption (SEC, 2022).

ICOs present a unique financing avenue for small businesses and startups that may not qualify for an initial public offering (IPO) to raise funds from the public. Between 2014 and 2021, the ICO boom resulted in the creation of about 16,000 cryptocurrencies. Of these, Filecoin and Tezos had the largest coin offerings, raising $257M and $232M, respectively (Handagama, 2021).

Both ICOs and IPOs aim to raise capital from the public. However, unlike IPOs, ICOs are not as heavily regulated, making them riskier for investors. For an IPO, a private company must undergo a rigorous process overseen by the government before going public. Typically, IPOs are underwritten by investment banks and then listed on stock exchanges. In contrast, ICOs function more like crowdfunding campaigns. Therefore, ICOs can be likened to angel funding or early-stage venture capital (VC) investments. In an ICO, without undergoing the same rigorous process as an IPO, a company can sell its cryptocurrency tokens (i.e., "coins") to investors in exchange for fiat currency or other established cryptocurrencies (e.g., Bitcoin) on the ICO's blockchain platform (Wikipedia, 2022a).

While the fewer regulations around ICOs enable firms to raise capital more quickly, this comes at a cost, making ICOs riskier for investors. Investors in ICOs are more susceptible to scams and fraudulent schemes. Though some ICOs have delivered notable returns for investors, many have underperformed, or worse, turned out to be scams. Due to the lack of oversight and the prevalence of scams, many ICOs have failed. Regulatory concerns and the risk of fraud have led some countries, including China and South Korea, to ban ICOs (Williams, 2020).

15.4.1 ICO Structures and White Paper

To launch an ICO, the issuing company must first determine which structure of the ICO will be employed. There are three major types (Frankenfield, 2022):

Fig. 15.4 A potential ICO white paper structure

- **Static Supply and Static Price**: The issuing company sets an upper limit on the number of tokens/coins to be sold, and the price of each token is fixed. Consequently, the total amount of capital raised from the ICO has a predetermined upper limit.
- **Static Supply and Dynamic Price**: The issuing company sets an upper limit on the number of coins to be offered and employs a dynamic pricing schedule for each token. Depending on the amount of funds raised, the price per token adjusts accordingly.
- **Dynamic Supply and Static Price**: The issuing company sets a fixed price, but the total supply of coins depends on overall demand. Thus, the issuing company can raise more capital if the demand is strong.

To launch an ICO, the issuing company typically publishes a whitepaper release. In this document, the company provides crucial information about the ICO, such as the purpose of the project, the target fundraising amount, the duration of the ICO, the ICO's structure, and so on. A whitepaper might encompass various components, considering perspectives like project goals, business model, market analysis, financial details, and team background (Cointelegraph, 2023). The potential structure of an ICO Whitepaper is illustrated in Fig. 15.4. It's worth noting that the content and organization of Fig. 15.4 might differ widely in actual implementations.[2]

---

[2] Some actual ICO whitepapers can be found at https://www.whitepaperdatabase.com.

15.4 Initial Coin Offering

For investors, setting up a digital wallet and an exchange account is necessary. Afterward, they can purchase the tokens that align with their investment objectives. If the ICO fails, the invested money will be returned. If the ICO succeeds, the funds raised will be allocated towards the project's development. Successful projects can yield profits for investors, but if a project fails, investors may lose their entire investment.

15.4.2 Pros and Cons of ICOs

When juxtaposed with IPOs and traditional funding methods, ICOs present distinct benefits (Finsmes, 2019).

- *Investment Opportunity*: ICOs furnish a broader spectrum of investment opportunities, catering to investors who seek alternatives beyond common stocks and venture capital.
- *Funding Opportunity*: ICOs offer a lifeline to startups that might not qualify for an IPO or obtain conventional funding. An ICO can accrue a substantial amount of capital for an embryonic company. Concurrently, the ICO event acts as a significant publicity boost for the company.
- *Online Accessibility*: The entirety of ICO transactions and accompanying information is readily accessible online. The whitepaper meticulously elaborates on the project, and comprehensive details about the founding team are also available for scrutiny. The underlying blockchain technology ensures continuous online updates regarding the project's progress.
- *Reduced Paperwork*: ICOs necessitate fewer regulatory submissions in comparison to traditional IPOs and other orthodox funding mechanisms.
- *High Liquidity*: Given that ICOs aren't tethered to the physical presence of assets, they inherently possess greater liquidity than some traditional assets.
- *Potential High Yield*: Investing in ICOs can potentially yield substantial returns. This is largely because nascent companies, being in their infancy, might be inclined to offer more favorable valuations to secure early-stage funding.

However, as with all endeavors, there are two sides to the coin. While ICOs have offered valuable funding avenues for numerous enterprises, they've also showcased significant pitfalls in recent years (Finsmes, 2019).

- *Broker Risk*: A reduction in regulations can lead to an uptick in fraudulent activities. Less oversight and regulatory scrutiny make it easier for novice ICO brokers to enter the scene. Consequently, compared to IPO professionals, ICO organizers might lack experience, exhibit a higher risk appetite, or even engage in speculative behavior, thereby escalating broker risks.
- *Accountability Risk*: Typically, ICO entities lack the capital to independently realize their proposed ventures, often starting with minimal initial funds.

This can amplify counterparty risks, as ICO organizers may be predisposed to defaults, having little at stake.
- *ICO Scams*: Stemming from the aforementioned accountability and other associated risks, ICOs can metamorphose into scams.

Case Study

ICO Scams

In April 2018, a Vietnamese firm initiated two ICO ventures: Ifan and Pincoin. After amassing over $660 million from 32,000 investors, the company's leaders vanished (Cunha & Murphy, 2019). In July 2017, Centra Tech, a crypto entity, executed an unauthorized ICO, deceptively touting partnerships with Master Card and Visa, thus accruing $25 million from backers (Akhtar, 2021). In 2021, Sohrab Sharma, Centra Tech's pioneer, received an eight-year prison sentence, while co-founder Robert Farkas was incarcerated for a year and a day for this illicit ICO. Notably, this ICO had received endorsements from celebrities such as Floyd Mayweather (Haig, 2021).

- *Valuation Volatility*: Although ICOs can yield lucrative returns, they come bundled with substantial risks due to elevated failure rates, scams, and other associated perils. Younger, untested startups are more susceptible to bankruptcy. Moreover, the valuation of an ICO might often be grounded in sheer speculation. As such, investors must brace themselves for the inherent uncertainties linked to nascent projects, which might merely be conceptual, devoid of a concrete execution blueprint.
- *Pump-and-Dump Scheme*: Scammers may resort to the "pump and dump" strategy, where they artificially inflate (or "pump") ICO prices, only to offload (or "dump") the tokens at a peak, securing profits in the process (Wikipedia, 2022a). Such manipulations can lead to erratic token valuations.
- *Project Transparency*: Paradoxically, despite the innate transparency of blockchain technology, ICO initiators might refrain from sharing intricate investment specifics with stakeholders once they've garnered the requisite funds.
- *Loss Recovery*: Since ICOs are orchestrated on blockchain frameworks, if investors lose their private coin keys, they might find it next to impossible to recuperate their investments.

15.4.3 Other Variants

The ICO boom reached its zenith in early 2018 but has since waned, primarily due to its inherent volatility and widespread fraudulent activities.[3] As the allure of ICOs dwindles for investors, several other offerings have surfaced as potential alternatives, aiming to address some of ICOs' challenges. Here are a few of these alternatives:

- **Initial Exchange Offering (IEO)**: An IEO bears a resemblance to an ICO in terms of its funding goal. The key distinction, however, lies in the platform of the offering: while ICOs are executed on the issuing company's platform, IEOs are facilitated by a third-party cryptocurrency exchange. This implies that established cryptocurrency exchanges will typically only feature projects that have made significant strides, making it imperative for developers to demonstrate substantial progress or have a minimum viable product (MVP) prepared prior to initiating an IEO. For instance, the crypto wallet service BRD already boasted a user base of a hundred million when it launched its IEO (Cointelegraph, 2022a).

  In comparison to ICOs, IEOs tend to garner greater trust from investors, primarily because they are hosted on a third-party exchange platform, which lends an added layer of legitimacy and credibility to the projects. Additionally, these third-party exchange platforms, equipped with specialized technical expertise, often offer a more seamless experience than the proprietary platforms of smaller enterprises. What's more, given that IEOs adhere to exchange-specific regulations, the chances of fraudulent activities are potentially diminished (Cointelegraph, 2022a).

  Nonetheless, IEOs are not without their shortcomings. The involvement of a third party frequently results in escalated transaction costs, including listing fees and commissions levied on the companies being listed. Moreover, the mere association with a third-party exchange doesn't necessarily immunize the process from "pump and dump" schemes. Investors should exercise discernment when evaluating the merit of exchange platforms, understanding that not all platforms maintain consistent standards in vetting listed enterprises or in adhering to regulatory mandates (Cointelegraph, 2022a).
- **Initial DEX Offering (IDO)**: Tokens in IDOs are launched via a decentralized liquidity exchange, which facilitates instant liquidity and trading. Investors in IDO don't acquire equity, but they can participate in certain facets of the project (Vasile & Prata, 2022). For instance, IDOs can serve as tools for community engagement, allowing for mechanisms like fan tokens which can be employed in sporting events.
- **Initial Stake Pool Offering (ISPO)**: An ISPO is a fusion of investment and staking. Investors participating in an ISPO receive the tokens of their

---

[3] According to Wikipedia (2022d), ICOs raised $7 billion from January to June 2018..

investment and then stake ADA, which is the native cryptocurrency of the Cardano blockchain, a Proof-of-Stake blockchain. They earn rewards for validating new blocks and maintaining the decentralized blockchain, and the ADA rewards are used to fund the project (Vasile & Prata, 2022). Unlike ICOs, ISPO participants maintain access to their funds and have the option to stake additional tokens for validating new blocks within the blockchain network.

> **Case Study**
>
> ***ISPO***
>
> A notable instance of an ISPO is Flickto, a media launchpad powered by Cardano. It commenced its ISPO on Nov. 1, 2021, culminating on Apr. 10, 2022. The primary objective of the Flickto project is to generate funds to support content creators in the production of new films, TV programs, and streaming content (Vasile & Prata, 2022).

15.5 Challenges in Blockchain Supply Chains

The rise of blockchain technology marks a notable shift in technological innovation. However, it brings with it a series of challenges that need attention.

15.5.1 Management Challenges

For businesses to integrate blockchain, they must be willing to modify their conventional operational procedures to align with blockchain protocols. For instance, buyers should initiate or modify their orders via the blockchain platform, while suppliers must adhere to procedures defined by relevant smart contracts within the blockchain.

In the realm of supply chain finance, smart contracts are typically used for payment transfers. Consequently, businesses need to establish digital wallets, create invoicing systems, and define delivery confirmation and acceptance protocols. This ensures the seamless execution of the entire transaction process. When IoT devices are employed for product tracking, appropriate care is required for the coding of smart contracts and oracles within the blockchain, as well as managing any associated process modifications.

Other operational aspects, like pricing strategies and inventory management, can also be integrated into the blockchain to amplify supply chain efficiency and profitability. For instance, inventory policies might be embedded in service-level

15.5 Challenges in Blockchain Supply Chains

agreements with suppliers. This way, inventory can be autonomously restocked as soon as certain replenishment thresholds are reached. Similarly, smart contracts can be designed for dynamic pricing, allowing prices to fluctuate based on prevailing demand and supply conditions. To supervise and coordinate the supply chain effectively, firms might consider embedding key performance indicators (KPIs) into the system to consistently evaluate supply chain performance.

15.5.2 Technology Challenges

With the rapid advancements in big data, cloud computing, and data digitalization, data storage has become a challenge for firms amassing vast amounts of data.

Furthermore, given the constraints on the size of each transaction record stored in blockchains—due to the need for swift transaction verification—it poses a technical challenge to securely and immutably link the transaction to the contents referred to within that transaction.

Businesses frequently opt for permissioned blockchains due to their various benefits. Nonetheless, these blockchains can exhibit lower security levels, primarily because of the fewer nodes participating in reaching a verification consensus.

15.5.3 Human Errors

While blockchains can enhance supply chain finance, they are not exempt from human errors, exemplified by the "Garbage-In-Garbage-Out" problem. Once mistakes are made, additional efforts are required to identify and rectify them. Some protocols have been designed to allow the blockchain owner to directly correct these errors. However, such protocols raise significant concerns about the immutability of the blockchain, potentially diminishing its trustworthiness.

To mitigate any significant adverse effects on stakeholders, companies should explicitly define the rights and responsibilities of all involved parties, as well as the conditions under which smart contracts or related supply chain agreements can be terminated. In case of disagreements, companies must detail the methods for resolving issues and errors in smart contracts. Given the automation provided by smart contracts, it's crucial to have a comprehensive force majeure clause in place to handle unforeseen contingencies.

15.5.4 Implementation Costs and Scaling

Replacing legacy systems with a blockchain system can be costly due to the purchase and installation of new equipment and software. Implementing a new blockchain system also necessitates training, education, and potential shifts in corporate culture. Moreover, hiring the right personnel can be challenging and expensive because of the specialized knowledge and expertise required.

While there have been considerable advancements in transaction speeds within permissioned blockchains over time, the scalability of permissionless blockchains still lags behind, particularly when compared to traditional databases. This persistent limitation in permissionless blockchains results in elevated marginal costs, which can adversely affect the profitability of firms that implement this technology.

15.5.5 Counterfeit Prevention

According to Incopro Research, 69% of UK consumers purchased between 1 and 3 counterfeit products over the past 12 months, while approximately 21% acquired 4–6 counterfeit items. The International Chamber of Commerce estimates that counterfeiting and piracy could reach a global value of $2.3 trillion in 2022 (Incopro, 2022). The ramifications of counterfeit products extend beyond financial losses for consumers; there are other detrimental effects, such as health-related issues. Incopro's research further highlighted that 32% of individuals who bought counterfeit goods experienced health problems as a result of these products.

Owing to its immutability feature, blockchain technology holds promise as a tool for counterfeit prevention. Blockchains can trace a product's lineage, confirming its point of origin from the consumer end of the supply chain all the way back to its inception. Such provenance, verified through blockchains, empowers legal enforcement agencies to detect and halt the spread of counterfeit products more effectively.

Enterprises can also embed the provenance data of their products onto blockchains using smart tags, which include QR codes, RFID tags, and signatures on metallic or ceramic surfaces (Wang & Wegrzyn, 2022). As these smart tags are applied to the products, the corresponding transaction data is recorded onto the blockchain. Should someone attempt to duplicate an authentic smart tag, scanning the counterfeit version would reveal inconsistent transaction details. For example, should a counterfeit product be sold under Company A's brand, scanning the smart tag would show that it originates from Company G.

Given that approximately 60–70% of counterfeit products target luxury brands, companies in the luxury sector are motivated to employ blockchain technology to safeguard their brand reputation (Wang & Wegrzyn, 2022). Case in point, the LVMH group (parent company of Louis Vuitton and Bvlgari), Prada, and Cartier founded the Aura Blockchain Consortium in 2021, with development by ConsenSys and Microsoft, to offer consumers transparent insights into their acquisitions. Implementing blockchain-backed authentication systems is projected to boost firms' revenue by an additional 2–5%.

15.5.6 Antitrust

Private, consortium, and hybrid blockchains offer an ideal platform for supply chain companies, encompassing both partners and competitors, to collaborate. However, entities not integrated into these blockchain platforms may find themselves at a significant business disadvantage compared to their peers who are on the blockchain. Such exclusivity can raise concerns of collusion (for example, sharing critical pricing information with competitors to artificially inflate market prices) and anti-competitive behavior (such as non-members of the blockchain platform being marginalized from future business prospects). The limited number of privileged hosts in consortium blockchains may exploit their control over transaction verification and validation to shut out competitors from specific business opportunities. Therefore, careful oversight is essential to ensure that the use of blockchain platforms aligns with antitrust laws, all the while preserving the advantages they offer to supply chain companies.

15.5.7 Regulation Compliance

Given the sensitivity, security, privacy, and significance of data, numerous regulations (like the EU's General Data Protection Regulation, GDPR) have emerged worldwide, focusing on data management and distribution. Creating a global blockchain that adheres to all these standards would be a formidable, if not unattainable, endeavor. For instance, blockchain's immutable nature poses potential data privacy challenges, especially considering GDPR stipulates that personal data must be deleted under specific conditions (such as when an individual revokes consent) (Wang & Wegrzyn, 2022). As such, meticulous attention must be directed towards adapting blockchains to conform to regional laws and regulations.

15.6 Applications of Blockchain in Supply Chain Finance

Blockchains have various applications in supply chain management and finance, such as:

- *Supply Chain Traceability*: One of the most notable and widely acknowledged applications of blockchain technology within supply chain management lies in its ability to trace the origin and journey of products across the supply chain. Leveraging blockchain-based smart contracts, each phase of the supply chain can be documented, yielding an immutable and transparent record of product movement. Such traceability is beneficial for inventory tracking, fraud prevention, counterfeit deterrence, and regulatory compliance.

Case Study

Implementing Blockchains in Supply Chain Traceability

Example 1: Monegraph blockchain enables creators to safeguard the usage and sharing rights of high-value digital assets within a digital media supply chain, extending from the original content creators to publishers, and eventually, distributors (Monegraph, 2023).

Example 2: Skuchain is dedicated to developing blockchain-based B2B trade and supply chain finance solutions. These solutions assist in facilitating finance (such as operational loans or short-term trade loans), payments (like letters of credit or wire transfers), and visibility (e.g., ERP systems) for various supply chain entities, including sellers, buyers, 3PLs, banks, customs, and other institutions (Skuchain, 2023).

Example 3: In 2018, Dianrong, an online lending enterprise in China, collaborated with R3 to establish their supply chain finance services on the Corda blockchain (Dianrong, 2018). As per Dianrong, this blockchain would support "comprehensive financing across the entire supply chain," promoting "transparency and fortifying trust amongst the involved parties."

- *Automated Compliance*: Blockchain-based smart contracts can automate compliance with regulations and industry standards in the supply chain. For instance, a smart contract might automatically verify that goods adhere to specific environmental or ethical standards prior to shipping.
- *Fraud Detection*: Blockchain-based smart contracts can help detect and prevent fraud in the supply chain by maintaining a tamper-proof record of all transactions and interactions.
- *Payment and Settlement*: Blockchain can streamline payments and settlements between supply chain partners. Using blockchain-based smart contracts, payments can be automated and triggered by specific milestones, like the successful delivery of goods.
- *Finance*: Blockchain technology offers diverse applications in finance, including the creation of digital assets, smart-contract-enabled loans, digital identity, and more. One notable application of blockchain in finance is cryptocurrency. Cryptocurrencies, such as Bitcoin and Ethereum, serve as decentralized and secure digital currencies, facilitating payments and money transfers.
- *Supply Chain Finance*: Blockchain can also revolutionize trade finance processes. Employing blockchain-based smart contracts, banks and other financial institutions can automate many manual processes involved in trade finance, including letters of credit, bills of lading, and invoice financing.

15.6 Applications of Blockchain in Supply Chain Finance

In conclusion, the integration of blockchain technology in these domains can enhance efficiency, cut costs, and bolster security and transparency throughout supply chains.

15.6.1 Case Studies: Application of Blockchain in Logistics

Case Study

TradeLens for Global Shipping

In 2016, Maersk partnered with IBM to launch the TradeLens platform. This blockchain-based ecosystem has since attracted over 170 organizations from the global shipping industry, including shippers, freight forwarders, ports and terminals, ocean carriers, intermodal operators, government authorities, customs brokers, and financial service providers (Belova, 2021). TradeLens comprises two main modules: Core for daily operations and management, and eBL for bills of lading.

TradeLens aims to boost efficiency, transparency, and the secure exchange of information, thereby fostering collaboration and trust throughout the global supply chain (TradeLens, 2022). Powered by Hyperledger Fabric blockchain technology and the IBM Cloud, TradeLens meticulously tracks and stores details about a shipment's journey. By August 2022, TradeLens had recorded 3.38 billion events encompassing over 63 million containers, averaging 13 million shipment events per week across more than 120 event types (e.g., gate-in, vessel departure, etc.).

The advantages of integrating blockchain into supply chain management and finance are evident. Before introducing TradeLens, a single Maersk shipment of frozen goods from East Africa to Europe would involve nearly 30 different organizations and individuals, resulting in over 200 interactions and communications (Vyas et al., 2019). Moreover, these processes were not just time-intensive but also susceptible to errors. Blockchain technology can heighten cost-efficiency by 30–40%. IBM highlighted that invoice payment disputes on any given date could tally up to roughly $100 million. Resolving these disputes pre-blockchain would require 21–40 days. However, blockchain reduced disputed payments to below $10 million, which took less than 5 days to settle (Machine Insider, 2020).

Nevertheless, on November 29, 2022, Maersk and IBM announced the discontinuation of the TradeLens platform by the close of the first quarter in 2023 (Maersk, 2022). Rotem Hershko, Head of Maersk Business Platforms at A.P. Moller, stated in the press release, "While we successfully developed a viable platform, the desired level of global industry collaboration remained elusive. Consequently, TradeLens did not achieve the commercial viability required to persist and meet our financial expectations as an independent entity" (Maersk, 2022).

Questions

1. What advantages does blockchain technology offer to global shipping companies?
2. What was the impact of the TradeLens platform on supply chain transactions up to the end of 2022?
3. Why was TradeLens terminated in 2023? In your perspective, what could have ensured TradeLens's longevity? Please consider external resources in your response.

Case Study

Blockchain in Transport Alliance (BiTA)

Founded in August 2017, BiTA is a commercial blockchain alliance advocating for blockchain applications in transportation and logistics. The BiTA Standards Council (BSC) is dedicated to establishing a standard blockchain framework for a commerce ecosystem, encompassing carriers, suppliers, shippers (e.g., UPS and FedEx), customers, and other stakeholders (BITA, 2022). As one of the largest commercial blockchain alliances globally, BiTA boasts approximately 500 members across over 25 countries, generating more than $1 trillion in annual revenue.

BSC has tackled issues such as location specification, tracking, party specification, shipment specification, bill of lading specification, smart contracts, equipment, and commodity specifications (Duffy, 2019). Duffy delineates the system as having seven layers: physical, data link, network, transport, session, presentation, and application. The incorporation of blockchains is anticipated to bolster areas including:

- Verification of chain of custody
- Shipment status tracking
- Data sharing among partners
- Customs and border management
- Shipment security management
- Empty container management
- Payment processing

15.6 Applications of Blockchain in Supply Chain Finance   503

Through blockchain, BiTA aspires for its members to achieve greater market transparency, liberate capital, diminish transportation costs, expedite processes, enhance operational efficiency, foster interoperability, and strengthen risk management capabilities.

Questions

1. How can blockchain technology benefit BiTA?
2. Can the blockchain system developed for BiTA be universally applied to other companies? Why or why not?

15.6.2 Machine-as-a-Service

Machine-as-a-Service (MaaS) is a leasing service that falls under the category of subscription-based services, similar to Software-as-a-Service, Infrastructure-as-a-Service, and Network-as-a-Service. MaaS offers a unique market for capital equipment that may be prohibitively expensive for many end consumers in supply chains. Unlike the traditional leasing model, a blockchain-based MaaS model isn't bound to a fixed monthly or weekly payment (Wang & Wegrzyn, 2022). Instead, MaaS contracts can hinge on the equipment's usage, especially when the equipment is integrated into an IoT network linked to the blockchain.

The blockchain network, bolstered by IoT, can monitor the equipment's location and usage (e.g., operational hours, units produced, efficiency, and other relevant statistics). Given the immutable nature of blockchain data, it assures accurate usage tracking and equitable pricing for leasing. Through smart contracts, both vendors and customers can coordinate timely payments for equipment usage and schedule automated maintenance. The meticulous documentation of equipment usage on the blockchain can also be invaluable when the equipment is subsequently leased or sold.

Since MaaS equipment is interconnected with the IoT network, the services offered can be tailored and configured based on end consumer demands. As such, both the pricing and functional aspects of usage can be dynamically adjusted. Smart contracts further streamline the service subscription, feature customization, and payment processes.

However, while MaaS presents a potential solution to amplify demand, it's not without its challenges. Firstly, given that smart contracts are unmodifiable once implemented on the blockchain (Dilmegani, 2023), customers might require services not originally included in the MaaS model. Thus, it's crucial to ensure that smart contracts are both comprehensive and adaptable to meet evolving customer requirements. Secondly, providing more flexible configurations tailored to end consumers might necessitate additional equipment design, which could either be cost-prohibitive or potentially compromise equipment reliability.

Case Study

Machine-as-a-Service (MaaS) in Blockchains

Cloud Computing: Blockchain-based platforms, such as iExec, permit users to lease out their idle computing power and storage to other users on an as-needed basis. Specifically, within iExec, users employ RLC, the platform's native token, to access computing resources on the iExec cloud platform (Apie, 2018).

Internet of Things (IoT): Platforms rooted in blockchain technology, like IOTA and IoT Chain, facilitate the rental of IoT devices tailored for specific roles, such as data acquisition and analysis. Notably, software can be embedded in a chip; inserting this chip into IoT devices seamlessly links them to the associated blockchain platform (Emre, 2018).

These instances underscore the versatility of Machine-as-a-Service (MaaS) in blockchains across diverse sectors. By harnessing blockchain technology, these rental services become more secure, transparent, and automated, paving the way for heightened efficiency and cost-effectiveness.

15.7 Summary

In this chapter, the pivotal role of blockchain in revolutionizing supply chain finance is explored in depth. Blockchain, a decentralized ledger, has emerged as a key technology offering transparency, immutability, and security, making it a potent tool for modern supply chain management and finance.

Key Takeaways:

1. Blockchains in Supply Chain Management and Finance:
    - Blockchains can track products throughout the entire supply chain, ensuring transparency and reducing fraud.
    - Collaboration becomes more robust, eliminating the need for intermediaries and fostering direct communication between parties.
    - Smart contracts enable automated, transparent, and irreversible transactions, further reducing inefficiencies and costs.
2. Digital Tokens:
    - A digital token is a digital representation of an asset, which can be traded, sold, or used within a particular blockchain environment.
    - These tokens can represent anything from physical goods to access rights, further simplifying the trading and transfer process in a supply chain.
3. Initial Coin Offering (ICO):
    - ICOs provide a means to raise funds for new projects or ventures using cryptocurrencies. It's analogous to an initial public offering (IPO) but in the digital space.

- It offers an avenue for supply chain businesses to obtain funding without traditional financial intermediaries, although it comes with its own set of risks and regulations.
4. Challenges in Blockchain Supply Chains:
   - While blockchain promises many benefits, challenges like scalability, energy consumption, interoperability, data privacy, and regulatory compliance pose significant hurdles.
   - Overcoming these challenges requires technological advancements and collaborations between industry stakeholders and regulatory bodies.
5. Application of Blockchains in Supply Chain Finance:
   - The chapter illustrates various applications, from ensuring traceability and fraud detection to automating compliance and simplifying payment processes.
   - Real-world case studies like TradeLens and BiTA highlight both the potential benefits and challenges in the real-world implementation of blockchain in the supply chain.
   - The introduction of concepts like Machine-as-a-Service (MaaS) underscores blockchain's transformative potential in redefining traditional business models.

15.8 Exercises

15.8.1 Practice Questions

1. Why can blockchains help supply chain visibility, onboarding, accounting, and auditing?
2. Are there challenges in implementing blockchains for supply chain management and finance?
3. What are the potential issues of using smart contracts in supply chain finance?
4. Can you name a case of blockchain in supply chain finance and provide some details?
5. What are major types of asset-backed tokens? How about NFTs?
6. What are the pros and cons of ICOs and how to address the cons?
7. How does the blockchain network, supported by IoT, benefit Machine-as-a-Service?
8. What is the fundamental difference between asset-backed tokens and NFTs?
9. What challenge is posed by smart contracts being immutable once they are deployed on the blockchain in the context of MaaS?
10. How is the use of blockchain technology expected to impact auditing processes?

15.8.2 Case Studies

Case Study 1: An ICO in the Supply Chain Industry

Background

In 2018, a startup named "SupplyChainY" emerged in the logistics and supply chain industry. They proposed a groundbreaking solution that aimed to streamline global logistics through the use of blockchain technology and their own digital token called "SCY Coin." The company's vision was to create an efficient, transparent, and decentralized global supply chain platform. They decided to conduct an ICO to fund their ambitious project.

Challenges

SupplyChainY faced several challenges when planning their ICO:

1. **Regulatory Compliance:** The team had to navigate complex and evolving regulations related to ICOs. They needed to ensure that their ICO complied with the legal requirements of different jurisdictions, which was a significant challenge due to the global nature of their project.
2. **Investor Trust:** Establishing trust among potential investors was vital. Many investors had previously fallen victim to fraudulent ICOs. SupplyChainY had to demonstrate their project's legitimacy and credibility to attract investment.
3. **Token Utility:** They needed to clearly define how the SCY Coin would be used within their ecosystem. This required a well-thought-out tokenomics model that ensured its utility and demand.

Options

To address these challenges, SupplyChainY considered several options:

1. **Legal Consultation:** They engaged legal experts specializing in blockchain and cryptocurrency regulations to ensure their ICO was compliant with various legal frameworks.
2. **Transparency and Credibility:** The team put an emphasis on transparency by publishing detailed project documentation, including a whitepaper, team information, and a roadmap. They also engaged with the community to build credibility.
3. **Utility Integration:** The team worked on partnerships with logistics companies to ensure that the SCY Coin would be utilized for various functions within the supply chain platform. This improved the token's utility and demand.

15.8 Exercises

Discussion Questions

1. What are the main challenges and risks associated with conducting an ICO in the supply chain industry?
2. How can a startup establish trust and credibility with potential ICO investors, especially in an environment with a history of fraudulent projects?
3. What are the key factors to consider when defining the utility of a digital token within a specific business ecosystem, such as the supply chain?
4. How can a blockchain-based supply chain platform like SupplyChainY add value to the industry? What potential benefits can be achieved?

Case Study 2: Transforming Supply Chain Finance with Blockchain

Background

In 2023, a multinational corporation, "BigTreeFin," operating in the logistics and supply chain industry, initiated a project to revolutionize its supply chain finance operations using blockchain technology. BigTreeFin aimed to enhance transparency, efficiency, and security in its supply chain financing, benefiting both suppliers and financial institutions.

Challenges

BigTreeFin faced several challenges during the implementation of blockchain in supply chain finance:

1. **Complex Supply Chain Ecosystem:** BigTreeFin operated in a complex global supply chain ecosystem with numerous suppliers, logistics partners, and financial institutions. Integrating them into a unified blockchain-based platform was a daunting task.
2. **Data Privacy and Security:** Ensuring the privacy of sensitive financial data while still benefiting from blockchain's transparency was a major challenge. The company needed to prevent unauthorized access to critical financial information.
3. **Regulatory Compliance:** As supply chain finance involves cross-border transactions, BigTreeFin had to navigate a web of international financial regulations to ensure compliance.
4. **Resistance to Change:** Encouraging various stakeholders, including suppliers and partner financial institutions, to adopt the new blockchain-based system was met with resistance due to the required changes in processes.

Options

To address these challenges, BigTreeFin considered several options:

1. **Blockchain Integration:** The company decided to adopt a consortium blockchain to ensure control and privacy over the network while maintaining transparency.
2. **Security Measures:** BigTreeFin implemented advanced encryption techniques and access controls to protect sensitive financial data.
3. **Legal Consultation:** The company sought legal advice to ensure compliance with various international financial regulations and worked closely with regulators to navigate the evolving landscape.
4. **Change Management:** BigTreeFin provided comprehensive training and support to suppliers and partner financial institutions to facilitate the transition to the new blockchain system.

Discussion Questions

1. What are the challenges and benefits of integrating a complex supply chain ecosystem into a blockchain-based platform for supply chain finance?
2. How can blockchain technology address the dual challenges of data privacy and regulatory compliance in the context of supply chain finance?
3. What strategies can a company like BigTreeFin employ to overcome resistance to change when implementing blockchain in supply chain finance?
4. How can blockchain technology transform traditional supply chain finance operations, and what are the key benefits it offers to various stakeholders?

References

Akhtar, T. (2021). *Centra Tech co-founder gets 8 years for crypto fraud*. https://www.coindesk.com/markets/2021/03/05/centra-tech-co-founder-gets-8-years-for-crypto-fraud/. Accessed 16 November 2022.

Apie. (2018). *iExec—The Golem Slayer*. https://steemit.com/cryptocurrency/@apie/iexe-the-golem-slayer. Accessed 8 November 2023.

Belova, K. (2021). How supply chain makes use of TradeLens—Maersk and IBM blockchain solution. *Pixelplex.Io*. https://pixelplex.io/blog/maersk-ibm-tradelens-blockchain-supply-management/. Accessed 8 August 2023.

Bible, W., Raphael, J., Riviello, M., Taylor, P., & Valiente, I. O. (2017). *Blockchain technology and its potential impact on the audit and assurance profession* (pp. 1–28). CPA Canada, AICPA. https://www.aicpa.org/content/dam/aicpa/interestareas/frc/assuranceadvisoryservices/downloadabledocuments/blockchain-technology-and-its-potential-impact-on-the-audit-and-assurance-profession.pdf. Accessed 5 May 2023.

Binance. (2021). *What Is KYC or identity verification, and how is it increasingly important for crypto?* https://www.binance.com/en/blog/ecosystem/what-is-kyc-or-identity-verification-and-how-is-it-increasingly-important-for-crypto-421499824684902130. Accessed 19 August 2022.

References

BITA. (2022). *BITA standards council.* https://bitastandardscouncil.org/. Accessed 29 November 2022.

Blockstream. (2023). *About blockstream.* https://blockstream.com/about/. Accessed 19 October 2023.

Breitling. (2020). *Breitling becomes the first luxury watchmaker to offer a digital passport based on blockchain for all of its new watches.* https://www.breitling.com/us-es/news/details/breitling-becomes-the-first-luxury-watchmaker-to-offer-a-digital-passport-based-on-blockchain-for-all-of-its-new-watches-33479. Accessed 16 November 2022.

Brender, N., & Gauthier, M. (2018). Impacts of blockchain on the auditing profession. *ISACA Journal, 5,* 27–32.

Brilliant Earth. (2023). *Brilliant Earth sustainable bridal & fine jewelry.* https://www.brilliantearth.com/. Accessed 13 November 2023.

Chainlink. (2021). *What is a blockchain oracle?* https://chain.link/education/blockchain-oracles. Accessed 29 December 2021.

Chainlink. (2022). *Understanding proof of reserves.* https://blog.chain.link/proof-of-reserves/. Accessed 23 November 2022.

Cointelegraph. (2022a). IEO 101: A beginner's guide to an exchange administered fundraising event. *Cointelegraph.Com.* https://cointelegraph.com/funding-for-beginners/ieo-101-a-beginners-guide-to-an-exchange-administered-fundraising-event. Accessed 6 October 2022.

Cointelegraph. (2022b). *STO 101: A beginner's guide on launching a security token offering.* https://cointelegraph.com/funding-for-beginners/sto-101-a-beginners-guide-on-launching-a-security-token-offering. Accessed 6 November 2022.

Cointelegraph. (2023). *What is a white paper and how to write it.* https://cointelegraph.com/ico-101/what-is-a-white-paper-and-how-to-write-it. Accessed 26 November 2023.

Cunha, J., & Murphy, C. (2019). Are cryptocurrencies a good investment? *The Journal of Investing, 28*(3), 45–56.

Dianrong. (2018). *Dianrong supply chain finance solution strategically added to r3's corda blockchain platform.* https://www.prnewswire.com/news-releases/dianrong-supply-chain-finance-solution-strategically-added-to-r3s-corda-blockchain-platform-300657142.html. Accessed 22 November 2022.

Dilmegani, C. (2023). *Smart contracts: What are they & why they matter in 2023.* https://research.aimultiple.com/smart-contracts/. Accessed 26 November 2023.

Duffy, P. (2019). *Blockchain for transportation alliance (BiTA) presentation.* https://www.hyperledger.org/learn/webinars/blockchain-for-transportation-alliance-bita-presentation. Accessed 18 November 2022.

Emre. (2018). *IoT chain (ITC) or IOTA.* https://medium.com/@k.emre/iot-chain-itc-or-iota-7bda065fc481. Accessed 7 July 2022.

Escobar, S. (2022). *How this company is using blockchain to buff up the image of diamonds.* https://www.barrons.com/articles/brilliant-earth-blockchain-diamonds-51647294829. Accessed 1 December 2022.

Finsmes. (2019). *ICO pros and cons: Is it worth the hype?* https://www.finsmes.com/2019/02/ico-pros-and-cons-is-it-worth-the-hype.html. Accessed 7 July 2023.

Frankenfield, J. (2022). *Initial coin offering (ICO): Coin launch defined, with examples.* https://www.investopedia.com/terms/i/initial-coin-offering-ico.asp. Accessed 18 June 2023.

Girod, J. S. (2021). Breitling shows other luxury brands how to future proof with agility. *Forbes.* https://www.forbes.com/sites/stephanegirod/2021/08/27/breitling-shows-other-luxury-brands-how-to-future-proof-with-agility/?sh=6a8a3ad762f6. Accessed 11 November 2022.

Graves, S., MoreReese, & Tran, K. C. (2022). What is ERC-721? The Ethereum NFT token standard. *Decrypt.* https://decrypt.co/resources/erc-721-ethereum-nft-token-standard. Accessed 19 March 2023.

Gulker, M. (2017). *Are smart contracts the future of fraud prevention?* AIER.

Haig, S. (2021). Co-founder of Floyd Mayweather-promoted ICO sentenced to 8 years. *Cointelegraph.Com.* https://cointelegraph.com/news/co-founder-of-floyd-mayweather-promoted-ico-sentenced-to-8-years. Accessed 9 November 2022.

Handagama, S. (2021). *Crypto coin listings exploded in 2021.* https://www.coindesk.com/markets/2021/08/09/crypto-coin-listings-exploded-in-2021/. Accessed 1 May 2023.

Hedera. (2022). *What Is an NFT smart contract?* https://hedera.com/learning/smart-contracts/nft-smart-contract. Accessed 3 December 2022.

Hill, E. (2019). *What is an asset-backed token? A complete guide to Security Token Assets.* https://thetokenizer.io/amp/2019/02/22/what-is-an-asset-backed-token-a-complete-guide-to-security-token-assets/. Accessed 6 June 2022.

Incopro. (2022). *The true cost of counterfeit goods.* https://www.incoproip.com/the-true-cost-of-counterfeit-goods/. Accessed 3 July 2023.

Lewis, A. (2018). *The basics of bitcoins and blockchains: an introduction to cryptocurrencies and the technology that powers them.* Mango Media Inc.

Machine Insider. (2020). *How blockchain can transform manufacturing.* https://www.machineinsider.com/how-blockchain-can-transform-manufacturing/. Accessed 29 November 2023.

Maersk. (2022). *A.P. Moller—Maersk and IBM to discontinue TradeLens, a blockchain-enabled global trade platform.* https://www.maersk.com/news/articles/2022/11/29/maersk-and-ibm-to-discontinue-tradelens. Accessed 28 November 2022.

micobo GmbH. (2019). *What is an asset-backed token?—Security tokens for beginners.* https://micobo.medium.com/what-is-an-asset-backed-token-security-tokens-for-beginners-b77adf3a9710. Accessed 16 August 2022.

Milev, A. (2018). *Dividend tokens, explained.* https://cointelegraph.com/explained/dividend-tokens-explained. Accessed 1 October 2022.

Monegraph. (2023). *About monegraph.* https://www.monegraph.com/. Accessed 1 November 2023.

Mou, V. (2021). *Blockchain oracles explained.* https://academy.binance.com/en/articles/blockchain-oracles-explained. Accessed 15 November 2021.

Musharraf, M. (2020). Blockchain can add $1.76 trillion to global GDP by 2030: PwC. *Cointelegraph.Com.* https://cointelegraph.com/news/blockchain-can-add-1-76-trillion-to-global-gdp-by-2030-says-report. Accessed 2 May 2022.

Norman-Eady, S. (2000). *Uniform electronic transaction act.* https://www.cga.ct.gov/2000/rpt/2000-R-1076.htm. Accessed 3 February 2023.

Partz, H. (2021). *Blockstream raises $16M for its Bitcoin mining STO in a matter of hours.* https://cointelegraph.com/news/blockstream-raises-16m-for-its-bitcoin-mining-sto-in-a-matter-of-hours. Accessed 5 May 2022.

Provenance. (2016). *From shore to plate: Tracking tuna on the blockchain.* https://www.provenance.org/tracking-tuna-on-the-blockchain. Accessed 5 November 2022.

Schweifer, J. (2022). *Asset-backed tokens.* https://coinmarketcap.com/alexandria/glossary/asset-backed-tokens. Accessed 6 October 2022.

SEC. (2022). *Spotlight on initial coin offerings (ICOs).* U.S. Securities and Exchange Commission. https://www.sec.gov/ICO. Accessed 26 November 2022.

Skuchain. (2023). *Skuchain: Here's how blockchain will save global trade a trillion dollars.* https://www.skuchain.com/skuchain-heres-how-blockchain-will-save-global-trade-a-trillion-dollars/. Accessed 13 November 2023.

Szabo, N. (1997). *The Idea of smart contracts.* https://www.fon.hum.uva.nl/rob/Courses/InformationInSpeech/CDROM/Literature/LOTwinterschool2006/szabo.best.vwh.net/idea.html. Accessed 6 October 2022.

TechGuy. (2021). *History of NFT.* https://techguysfdc.medium.com/history-of-nft-2ab748a3a9e9. Accessed 6 May 2023.

Tradelens. (2023). *Securely digitize your Bills of Lading with the click of a button.* https://www.tradelens.com/challenges/digital-bills-of-lading. Accessed 16 September 2023.

TradeLens. (2022). *A smarter way to engage in trade.* https://www.tradelens.com/technology. Accessed 16 August 2023.

Unilever. (2019). *Ever wondered where your favourite cup of tea comes from?* https://www.unilever.com/news/news-search/2019/ever-wondered-where-your-favourite-cup-of-tea-comes-from/. Accessed 6 August 2022.

References

Vasile, L., & Prata, L. (2022). Everything you need to know about initial stake pool offerings (ISPO). *Beincrypto.Com.* https://beincrypto.com/learn/initial-stake-pool-offerings/. Accessed 16 November 2023.

Vigna, P. (2022). *NFT sales are flatlining.* https://www.wsj.com/articles/nft-sales-are-flatlining-11651552616. Accessed 6 November 2022.

Vyas, N., Beije, A., & Krishnamachari, B. (2019). *Blockchain and the supply chain: Concepts, strategies and practical applications.* Kogan Page Publishers.

Wang, E., & Wegrzyn, K. (2022). *Blockchain in supply chain series.* https://www.foley.com/-/media/files/insights/publications/2022/06/foley-blockchain-in-supply-chain-ebook.pdf?la=en. Accessed 19 November 2022.

Wikipedia. (2022a). *Initial coin offering.* https://en.wikipedia.org/wiki/Initial_coin_offering. Accessed 11 November 2022.

Wikipedia. (2022b). *Non-fungible token.* https://en.wikipedia.org/wiki/Non-fungible_token. Accessed 14 November 2022.

Wikipedia. (2022c). *Security (finance).* https://en.wikipedia.org/wiki/Security_(finance). Accessed 11 November 2022.

Wikipedia. (2022d). *Smart contract.* https://en.wikipedia.org/wiki/Smart_contract. Accessed 13 November 2022.

Wikipedia. (2023). *Security token offering.* https://en.wikipedia.org/wiki/Security_token_offering. Accessed 6 November 2023.

Williams, R. (2020). *ICO regulations—Which are the countries with restrictions?* https://www.cryptonewsz.com/ico-regulations-which-are-the-countries-with-restrictions/. Accessed 6 October 2022.

Wood, L. (2021). The worldwide blockchain supply chain industry is expected to reach $3+ billion by 2026—ResearchAndMarkets.com. *Business Wire.* https://www.businesswire.com/news/home/20210316005759/en/The-Worldwide-Blockchain-Supply-Chain-Industry-is-Expected-to-Reach-3-Billion-by-2026---ResearchAndMarkets.com. Accessed 26 November 2022.

Index

0–9
3PL guarantor financing, 367
3PL-led SCF platform, 407
3PL-led in-transit inventory financing, 230
5C advantages, 398
5 Cs of credit, 292
6R model, 34, 37
6-able goals, 402

A
Absolute VaR, 311
Accidental fork, 435
Accounts payable (AP), 26, 79
Accounts receivable (AR), 26, 78
Accounts receivable financing, 140
Accounts receivable turnover ratio, 86
Advance LC, 114
Algorithm-backed stablecoin, 445
Altcoin, 440
Altman Z-score, 303
Artificial intelligence (AI), 409
Asset-backed securities (ABS), 166
Asset-backed token, 484
Asset-based bank financing, 231
Asset representation token, 484
Assets, 47
Asset securitization, 166
Asset-to-equity ratio, 96
Asset tracking, 408
Asset turnover ratio, 59
Asymmetric risk control, 338
Asymmetric risk mitigation capability, 338
Asymmetric risk theory, 338
Asymmetric risk value, 338
Average age of inventory, 83
Average working capital index, 98

B
Back-to-back LC, 116
Balance sheet, 46
Bank guarantee, 359
Bank-led SCF platforms, 404
Bank loan financing, 147
Bank loan insurance, 358
Bank payment obligation (BPO), 253
Bankruptcy risk, 283
Banks, 26
Barrel principle, 340
Benefits and risk mitigation of guarantor financing, 367
Big data analytics, 412
Bitcoin, 417, 420
Bitcoin blockchain, 421
Blockchain forks, 435
Blockchain oracle, 474
Blockchain technology, 417
Blocks, 427
Borrowing base facilities, 268
Business risk, 288
Business risk mitigation, 352
Buyer-backed PO finance (BPOF), 162
Buyer credit guarantee, 362
Buyer guarantor financing, 366
Buyer-led approved payables reverse securitization, 207
Buyer-led supply chain finance, 183

C
Capacity risk, 287
Capital availability and liquidity, 206
Capital employed, 54
Cash, 78
Cash conversion cycle (CCC), 88
Cash flow cycle, 78
Cash flow statement, 50
Cash-in-advance, 106, 107

514 Index

Cash index, 97
Centralized finance (CeFi), 448
Chain aggregated indexes (CAIs), 65
Chain equality indexes, 67
Cloud computing, 411
Coefficient of variation (CV), 302
Combined key encryption, 425
Commodity-backed stablecoins, 445
Commodity price risk, 283
Commodity token, 485
Competition risk, 288
Compute-enabled oracles, 476
Conditional VaR (CVaR), 319
Condition monitoring, 408
Confirmed LC, 113
Consignment, 107
Consortium blockchain, 455
Consumer focus principle, 39
Consumer preference risk, 286
Continuous risk assessment, 173
Contract token, 485
Contractual risk, 288
Conversion cycle, 28
Corda, 457
Corporate guarantee scheme, 361
Credibility enhancement, 148
Credit enhancement, 174
Credit guarantee scheme, 361
Credit risk, 24, 283
Credit risk mitigation, 345
Cross-chain oracles, 476
Crypto coin, 439
Cryptocurrency, 439
Cryptocurrency-backed stablecoins, 445
Crypto tokens, 439
Crypto wallets, 426
Currency hedging, 374
Currency token, 485
Current ratio, 93
Customer due diligence, 477
Customer identification program, 477
Customer onboarding, 477
Customer ongoing monitoring, 477

D

Days in inventory (DII), 83
Days inventory outstanding (DIO), 83
Days payable outstanding (DPO), 87
Days sales in accounts receivable, 84
Days sales of inventory (DSI), 83
Days sales outstanding (DSO), 84
Debt-to-assets ratio, 95
Debt-to-capital ratio, 96

Debt-to-EBITDA ratio, 96
Debt-to-equity ratio, 95
Debt token, 485
Decentralized finance (DeFi), 449
Default risk, 283
Deferred/usance payment, 112
Demand risk, 286
Demand risk mitigation, 349
Demand volatility, 286
Depository receipt token, 485
Design/innovation risk, 287
Differed/mixed payment LC, 115
Digital security offering (DSO), 485
Digital signature, 425
Digital tokens, 483
Disaster risk, 289
Disaster risk mitigation, 356
Discounting LC, 115
Distributor financing, 250
Dividend token, 485
Document against acceptance (D/A), 123
Document against payment (D/P), 123
Documentary collection (D/C), 123
Domino effect, 33
Downgrade risk, 283
Dual-accounting dilemma, 478
DuPont Analysis, 59
Dynamic advance rate adjustment, 173
Dynamic discounting, 184

E

Economic capital, 324
Economic value added (EVA), 58
Equity price risk, 282
Equity-to-asset ratio, 96
Equity token, 485
Ether (ETH), 440
Ethereum, 440
Ethics and sustainability, 383
Expected loss, 296, 324

F

Factoring, 140
Factoring cost, 144
Factor-push stress tests, 322
Fiat-backed stablecoins, 444
Financial flow, 23
Financial risk mitigation, 344
Financial risks, 282
Financial statements, 46
Financial supply chain (FSC), 6

Index

Financial supply chain management (FSCM), 5
First-in, first-out (FIFO), 82
Forecasting risk, 286
Foreign exchange risk, 283
Forfaiting, 153
Forward, 371
Forward rate agreement (FRA), 372
Fractional ownership, 488
Fraud risk, 285
Free cash flow (FCF), 81
Freight forward agreement, 376
Frequent, urgent, small, and short (FUSS), 13
Fully dynamic discounting, 184
Funding liquidity risk, 284
Future, 373

G
Garbage in, garbage out, 438
Global asset-based lending (GABL), 233
Greedy contract, 482
Green clause LC, 114
Gross profit margin, 52
Guarantor financing, 365

H
Halo effect, 34
Hard fork, 436
Hardware oracles, 476
Hardware wallets, 426
Hash, 429
Hedera, 443
Hedera Hashgraph, 443
Hedging, 368
Historical method, 313
Human factor risk, 285
Human oracles, 476
Hybrid blockchain, 459
Hyperledger, 458

I
ICO scams, 494
Income statement, 47
Incoterms®, 124
Information, cybersecurity, and coordination risk, 287
Information flow, 22
Initial coin offering (ICO), 491
Initial DEX offering (IDO), 495
Initial exchange offering (IEO), 495
Initial stake pool offering (ISPO), 495

Input oracles, 476
Integrating logistics and financial services (ILFS), 231
Interest rate risk, 283
Intermediaries, 27
International guarantee scheme, 361
Internet of Things (IoT), 408
In-transit inventory financing, 231
Inventory, 26
Inventory financing, 224
Inventory hedging, 378
Inventory line of credit, 224
Inventory loan, 224
Inventory risk, 287
Inventory turnover ratio, 82
Invested capital (IC), 55, 64
Invoice discounting, 158
Invoice issuance, 142
Irrevocable LC, 114

K
Know-your-customer (KYC), 206, 476

L
Labor risk, 287
Last-in, first-out (LIFO), 82
Legal and regulatory risks, 24
Legal framework assessment, 173
Legal risk, 288
Letter of credit (LC, L/C, or LOC), 109
Leverage ratios, 95
Liquidity risk, 24, 284
Liquidity risk mitigation, 346
Long position, 373
Low-cost hopping, 378

M
Machine-as-a-Service (MaaS), 503
Machine learning (ML), 409
Manufacturer-led platform, 406
Market risk, 24, 282
Market risk mitigation, 344
Measurement principle, 39
Merge, 442
Merkle tree, 429
Mining, 431
Miscommunication risk, 286
Model risk, 285
Monte Carlo simulation, 317
Monte Carlo stress tests, 322
Multi-sourcing, 378

Mutual guarantee scheme, 362

N
Native tokens, 483
Nearshoring, 378
Net-debt-to-EBITDA ratio, 96
Net operating profit after tax, 55
Net operating profit before tax, 55
Net operating profit less adjusted taxes (NOPLAT), 55
Net profit margin, 52
Net working capital, 79, 97
NFT-backed loan, 488
Non-commercial risk, 288
Non-commercial risk mitigation, 353
Non-fungible token (NFT), 440, 487
Non-notification factoring, 150
Non-recourse factoring, 151
Normalized working capital index, 98
Notification factoring, 150

O
Offshoring, 378
Online wallets, 426
Open account, 117
Operating cash flow ratio, 95
Operating cycle, 87
Operational hedging, 378
Operational risk, 24, 284
Operational risk mitigation, 347
Option, 377
Output oracles, 476
Overnight index swap, 370
Over-the-counter (OTC) derivative, 368

P
Paper wallets, 426
Pareto effect, 32
Payables period, 87
Payment at sight, 112
Permissioned blockchain, 418
Permissionless blockchain, 418
PIARA risk management, 342
Planning risk, 287
Political risk, 288
Political risk mitigation, 354
Post-shipment financing, 161
PPRR risk management, 341
Predictive maintenance, 408
Pre-export finance, 267
Pre-payment finance, 267

Pre-shipment financing, 161
Price sensitivity risk, 286
Private blockchain, 453
Probability distribution, 295
Process risk mitigation, 351
Process risks, 286
Procurement cycle, 28
Prodigal contract, 482
Product flow, 22
Production/manufacturing risk, 287
Production hedging, 380
Product lifecycle change risk, 286
Profit margin, 52
Proof of Reserve (PoR), 478
Proof of Stake (PoS), 440
Proof-of-work (PoW), 419, 432
Public blockchains, 419
Public guarantee scheme, 361
Public key encryption, 424
Pull supply chain, 107
Pump-and-dump scheme, 494
Purchase order (PO) financing, 161
Push supply chain, 106

Q
Qualitative analysis, 290
Quality control risk, 287
Quantitative analysis, 290
Quantitative risk analysis, 295
Quick ratio, 94
Quorum, 458

R
Receivable risk, 286
Receivable securitization, 174
Recourse factoring, 151
Red clause LC, 114
Regulations, 380
Regulatory and legal change risk, 286
Regulatory risk, 289
Regulatory risk mitigation, 354
Relationship effect, 32
Reliability and relationship, 36
Reputation risk, 289
Reputation risk mitigation, 355
Reserve-backed stablecoins, 444
Responsibility and reputation, 37
Responsiveness and R&D, 36
Return on assets (ROA), 55
Return on capital employed (ROCE), 54
Return on equity (ROE), 53
Return on invested capital (ROIC), 55

Index

Return on investment (ROI), 36
Return on net assets (RONA), 55
Return on risk-adjusted capital (RORAC), 326
Reverse factoring, 191, 204
Reverse securitization, 208
Revocable LC, 114
Revolving credit facility, 268
Revolving LC, 114
Ripple effect, 34
Risk-adjusted return on capital (RAROC), 324
Risk capital, 324
Risk flow, 21
Risk impact, 291
Risk isolation, 172
Risk mitigation, 36
Risk pooling, 173
Risk probability, 291
Risk-reward exchange, 339
Risk-reward pareto frontier, 339
Risk severity matrix, 291
Risk typology, 281
ROA DuPont model, 62
Robotic process automation (RPA), 410
ROE DuPont Model, 60
ROIC DuPont Model, 62

S

Sales/distribution cycle, 28
Security token offering (STO), 485
Seesaw effect, 32
Selection principles, 38
Seller guarantor financing, 366
Seller-led accounts receivable securitization, 166
Seller-led factoring, 141
Seller-led post-shipment financing, 259
Seller-led pre-shipment financing, 259
Seller-led supply chain finance, 140
Seller onboarding, 206
Semi-dynamic discounting, 184
Service risk, 287
Settlement risk, 283
SHA-256 algorithm, 431
Sharpe ratio, 327
Short position, 373
Small business, 10
Smart contracts, 409, 479
Social, environmental, and sustainability risk, 287
Soft fork, 436
Software oracles, 476
Sourcing and procurement risk, 285
Sourcing hedging, 378

Special purpose entity (SPE), 166
Special purpose vehicle (SPV), 166
Spot factoring, 153
Staking, 440
Standard deviation, 300
Standardization, 207
Standby LC, 114
Strategic capital, 324
Strategic risk, 288
Stress testing, 320
Structured commodity finance, 265
Suicidal contract, 482
Supplier risk, 285
Supplier risk mitigation, 348
Supply chain digitalization, 397
Supply chain digitalization platform, 402
Supply chain finance (SCF), 5, 7
Supply chain firms, 27
Supply chain risk mitigation, 348
Supply chain risks, 285
Supply chain self-financing, 27
Supply chain visibility, 473
Supply delivery risk, 286
Supply price risk, 286
Supply quality risk, 285
Supply quantity/shortage risk, 285
Supply risk, 285
Swap, 369
Synergy principle, 39
Systematic risk, 289
Systematic risk mitigation, 356

T

Technology risk, 285
Third-party logistics providers (3PLs), 230
TIGER challenges, 399
Title token, 485
Tolling finance, 268
Top-down principle, 39
Trade credit, 117, 119, 363
Trade credit bank insurance, 365
Trade credit forfaiting insurance, 365
Trade credit insurance, 364
Trade finance, 105
Trade services utility, 256
Trading liquidity risk, 284
Transaction, 422
Transferable LC, 114
Transportation and logistics risk, 287

U

Unrestricted LC, 114

Utility token, 491

V
Value-at-Risk, 310
Value chain, 24
Variance, 301
Variance-covariance method, 314, 316

W
Warehouse financing for commodity, 269
Weakest link dilemma, 340
Weighted average cost of capital, 58
Weighted average method, 82
Whole ledger factoring, 153
Working capital, 34, 79
Working capital index, 97

Printed in the United States
by Baker & Taylor Publisher Services